Emerging Market Bank Lending and Credit Risk Control

Statement

In writing this book, the author relied on his wealth of banking experience, research and consulting spanning nearly a quarter of a century. However, advice and instructions he proffered are strictly personal, subject to independent verification, and do not substitute for personal initiative and due diligence in entering into banking relationship and transactions or in making financial investments. There is always risk in following general advice without obtaining direct independent research with respect to financial investments, if anything. Thus the author and publisher are not liable for any loss, financial or otherwise, in applying advice, instructions and principles contained in this book.

Emerging Market Bank Lending and Credit Risk Control

Evolving Strategies to Mitigate Credit Risk, Optimize Lending Portfolios, and Check Delinquent Loans

Leo Onyiriuba

ELSEVIER

AMSTERDAM • BOSTON • HEIDELBERG • LONDON
NEW YORK • OXFORD • PARIS • SAN DIEGO
SAN FRANCISCO • SINGAPORE • SYDNEY • TOKYO

Academic Press is an imprint of Elsevier

Academic Press is an imprint of Elsevier
125 London Wall, London EC2Y 5AS, UK
525 B Street, Suite 1800, San Diego, CA 92101-4495, USA
225 Wyman Street, Waltham, MA 02451, USA
The Boulevard, Langford Lane, Kidlington, Oxford OX5 1GB, UK

Notices
Knowledge and best practice in this field are constantly changing. As new research and experience broaden our understanding, changes in research methods, professional practices, or medical treatment may become necessary.

Practitioners and researchers may always rely on their own experience and knowledge in evaluating and using any information, methods, compounds, or experiments described herein. In using such information or methods they should be mindful of their own safety and the safety of others, including parties for whom they have a professional responsibility.

To the fullest extent of the law, neither the Publisher nor the authors, contributors, or editors, assume any liability for any injury and/or damage to persons or property as a matter of products liability, negligence or otherwise, or from any use or operation of any methods, products, instructions, or ideas contained in the material herein.

Library of Congress Cataloging-in-Publication Data
A catalog record for this book is available from the Library of Congress

British Library Cataloguing-in-Publication Data
A catalogue record for this book is available from the British Library

ISBN: 978-0-12-803438-5

For information on all Academic Press publications
visit our website at http://store.elsevier.com/

Working together
to grow libraries in
developing countries

www.elsevier.com • www.bookaid.org

Publisher: Nikki Levy
Acquisition Editor: Scott Bentley
Editorial Project Manager: Susan Ikeda
Production Project Manager: Debbie Clark
Designer: Matthew Limbert

Typeset by TNQ Books and Journals
www.tnq.co.in

Dedication

To

My Mother and Children

— **With love**

Contents

Part II
Bank Credit Markets, Taxonomies and Risk Control
Sources of Lending Transactions and Credit Risk

Part III
Credit Risk Dynamics, Analysis, and Management
Approach to Credit Risk Management

Loan Documentation, Review and Compliance

Managing Non-Performing Credit Facilities

Part IV
Asset Portfolio Quality, Risk and Control
Basel Accords and Credit Portfolio Issues in Emerging Economies

About the Author

Leo Onyiriuba's books include "Analyzing and Managing Risks in Bank Lending" (2004), "Drive and Tasks in Bank Marketing" (2008), "Dictionary and Language of Banking" (2010), "Credit Risk: Taming a Hotbed of Reckless Banking" (2013), and "Banking Processing Risks and Control" (2014). Formerly a university lecturer, he runs a financial consultancy in Lagos, Nigeria, that helps clients succeed in their business, financial, and banking endeavors.

Preface

Motivation to write this book came from my experience as a banker from 1991 to 2003, during which I rose to the positions of divisional director (corporate banking) and member (executive management). I observed, studied, appreciated, and plugged loopholes in lending practices and decisions. I also saw firsthand the agony associated with bank failure, much of which could have been averted with sound credit policy, institutionalized lending culture, and responsible management of the risk assets portfolio. The problem was really overwhelming. I thought of writing a book that would chronicle the events leading to particular bank failures and the lessons they held for stakeholders in banking. Though that made sense, on second thought, I was loath to write a book with a heavy heart. Yet I had an overwhelming urge—which I could no longer resist—to write the book. The dearth of textbooks that solely documented the intricacies of this topic boosted my zeal for the book. The fact that seminars, workshops, conferences, and other such in-house and ad hoc training arrangements that banks use as fallbacks imparted only fleeting knowledge added to the boost. So I mustered confidence and started writing to fill the observed gap. Ironically, I tinkered with the original concept of the book when I eventually made up my mind to write. This book, which addresses thorny issues in bank lending and credit risk control, is the eventual outcome of the tinkering.

Two of my popular bestsellers made the precursors of this book. In 2004, I published the first of the two books entitled *Analyzing and Managing Risks of Bank Lending*. The success of this 17-chapter book was overwhelming. It was reprinted in 2005 and 2006 before its 30-chapter second edition was published in 2008 — with a reprint in 2009. The resounding market acceptance of the second edition was remarkable. Then I was convinced that the market needed more than a broadbrush book on the subject. So I decided to write a companion to it. The companion — *Credit Risk: Taming a Hotbed of Reckless Banking* — published concurrently with the third edition of the first book in 2013 was no less well received by the market.

However, there was a compelling need — soon after the companion was published — to merge the two books. That need was for an entirely new book that would combine the contents of the aforesaid precursors into one strong, unparalleled, revised volume — covering emerging markets in Africa, Asia, Eastern Europe, and Latin America. The idea came to fruition with the publishing of *Emerging Market Bank Lending and Credit Risk Control*. I imagine that bankers, practitioners, analysts, academics, and students around the world who have read and used the two books will sorely miss them. I advise them not to mourn the books' passing. The new book that supplants them, *Emerging Market Bank Lending and Credit Risk Control*, is superior and offers obvious gains as reflected in this preface.

OVERVIEW OF THE BOOK

Bank lending and credit risk control can be likened to the American-type presidential system of government, one powered by strong democratic values. In a presidential democracy, power is shared among three tiers of government and protected by clearly defined separation principles. The three tiers of government—executive, legislative, and judicial—function independently but under a checks-and-balances arrangement. Similarly, the crux of bank lending is usually three-pronged. This is depicted as the three Pillars of credit risk management—credit analysis (Pillar 1); credit policy and control—also referred to as credit administration or credit compliance (Pillar 2); and loan workout, remediation, and recovery (Pillar 3).

I summarize the purposes of the Pillars as follows:

Credit analysis institutionalizes processes for assessing lending risk and structuring a credit facility. This implies that credit risk must be properly identified, appraised, and effectively mitigated. This methodological framework, and the analytical functions it embodies, paves the way for efficient structuring of a credit facility.

Credit administration ensures that the lending portfolio is of high quality, profitable, and effectively managed. This Pillar subsumes issues involved in enforcing credit control and compliance. Regular portfolio review, loan loss provisions, and internal credit ratings are some of the critical assignments implied in credit administration functions.

Loan recovery seeks, regularizes, and adopts measures to ensure that a bank always has efficient processes for loan workouts, remediation of nonperforming loans, and the recovery of classified or lost risk assets. Each of these functions in Pillar 3 helps to improve the quality of and returns on the credit portfolio.

The approach to and methodology for dealing with issues implied in the Pillars have witnessed dramatic changes over time. Yet, the goal of credit risk control remains immutable. The goal in question is addressed and largely fulfilled in the content of and expatiation on Pillar 1.

An effective process in the pursuit of risk identification, risk analysis, and risk mitigation—all of which Pillar 1 subsumes—holds the key to successful lending. Striving to perfect these lending criteria has been, and will continue to be, the superstructure on which credit risk management hinges. One reason is that it defines a methodology that has become commonplace. Another reason is that it builds on the hallowed lending principles commonly referred to as the five Cs. The third reason is that the so-called five Cs of lending also underlie credit risk management in practical terms. A fourth reason is that Pillars 2 and 3 are simply postmortems on Pillar 1. Besides, Pillar 1 informs actions lending officers take in pursuit of Pillars 2 and 3. Yet in order to build a quality lending portfolio, the three Pillars should function in independent capacities within the dictates of checks-and-balances rules.

However, working relationships among the Pillars are scarcely well ordered in banks in emerging economies, thus leaving room for avoidable lapses. In drawing the analogy between a presidential democracy and credit risk control in banking, I make a case for the institutionalization of oversight of lending as a means of attaining quality portfolios in emerging economies.

DEFINING THE PROBLEM

It is bad enough that regulators try—but all to no avail—to tame the excessive risk appetites of banks. It is worse that reckless lending persists in banks and keeps the financial system on the edge of a precipice. Sadly, global financial crises in recent history originated in inefficient lending and failed risk management. More worrying yet is that this quirk has become a recurring phenomenon. Most disturbing is that the problem is unlikely to give way without a serious overhaul of the methodology for risk management. Ironically, the pursuit of this goal—a foolproof credit risk management methodology—has been an absolute nightmare for bank management and regulators. Today, many see credit risk as a hotbed of reckless banking. More than ever before, the attention of banking and finance experts around the world is now focused on credit risk. The Basel Committee has led this cause with Basel I (1988), Basel II (2004), and Basel III (2010). While Basel I dealt exclusively with credit risk—to underscore its importance—Basel II and Basel III advanced the cause even as they also focused on market, operational, and liquidity risks. Regrettably, crises in the global financial system have never been well ordered.

The financial crises of the 1970s and 1980s were not anticipated, as was also the case for those of the 1990s. They caught regulators and bank management completely unawares. Some of the emerging markets and regions that experienced crises included Latin America (1980s), Mexico (1994−1995), and Asia (1997−1998). In each case, the crisis left bitter lessons of experience for government, economists, and financial experts, especially bank managements. The banking systems in the emerging markets of Africa, Europe, and the Middle East have suffered similar fates at one time or the other. In most cases, the crises became a contagion and had practical and compelling lessons. But for the large stock of nonperforming risk assets within these banking system portfolios, the tempo of the crises and magnitude of national economic losses incurred by the countries would have been manageable. Unfortunately, an unmanageable volume of nonperforming risk assets tends to cause liquidity pressure for banks and make them vulnerable to such systemic crises. The financial crisis of 2007−2009 was the most embarrassing and lingered on for too long. The main culprit whenever financial crisis rocked the industry, especially in the 2007−2009 case, was usually credit risk. On each occasion of crisis, regulators found ways to rationalize a flawed supervisory framework in the wake of a crisis, while bank management prevaricated reckless lending.

The public tends to distrust regulators and bank managements when authorities make hollow excuses for avoidable crisis. Besides, failure to anticipate crises impinges on the soundness of the financial system. Often, as would be expected under the circumstances, a postmortem on each crisis triggered some regulatory response. Basel I addressed findings from the postmortem of the 1970s and 1980s crises. The postmortem of the 1990s crises informed enactment of Basel II. In the manner of its predecessors, Basel III originated in the 2007 to 2009 financial crisis. Now, hopes are high that Basel Accords would address observed loopholes in the supervision of global banks. Yet we should not accept this optimism uncritically or as a given. Success of the Accords depends on the ingenuity that regulators bring to banking supervision. What is needed for the future is a more and continuing proactive approach to credit risk. With such a disposition, the authorities and bank management would catch on to credit risk and be able to forestall global financial crises. It would also help to temper financial crises when they cannot be avoided.

REINVENTING CREDIT RISK CONTROL

The need to reinvent credit risk control in emerging economies derives from observed flaws, highlighted throughout this book, that negate international best practices. But it is also founded on the need to strengthen the credit process, institutionalize the risk control culture, and improve the conduct of bank lending in emerging economies. These require complete overhaul of the current methodology for credit risk control. A critical issue is how best to devolve credit authority and responsibility to lending officers and to enforce accountability for reckless lending. Implicit in this issue is the fact that the internal credit process remains a melting pot. Throughout the book, I develop an analytical framework that explains the foundation of the problem and how to reinvent the credit process. I relate the problem to flawed risk control and highlight lessons and findings that impinge on the lending function.

STRUCTURE OF THE BOOK

This book is a practical text for managing bank lending and credit risk in emerging economies. It is enriched with case studies and analyses, as well as empirical examples and illustrations. It equips bankers, deposit insurers, analysts, academics, and students with an understanding of the workings and outcomes of risk management in bank lending. The book profiles contemporary credit risk crises. These define the problem that takes center stage in the book. Diagnosing credit risk as the canker of financial crisis in the banking system, it challenges management of credit risk in banks in emerging economies. Using the framework of volatile markets, it discusses theoretical and practical foundations of the problem with implications for bank management.

Then it introduces the ways that risk affects credit analysis and decisions. In doing so, it discusses how credit risk should be correctly anticipated, and its impact mitigated, within a framework of sound credit culture and processes in line with the Basel Accords. The book is divided into four parts, comprising 10 sections and 38 chapters. Each chapter features an overview that introduces the subject of the chapter, its learning focus, and its outcomes. Chapters include review questions.

TARGET AUDIENCE

The book targets bankers, deposit insurers, analysts, academics, and students in—or interested in—banking in emerging economies. It solves five critical problems for the target audience. The problems relate to:

- How to attain desired asset and portfolio quality through efficient lending and credit risk management in high-risk-prone emerging economies
- A craving for a simple structure, devoid of complex models, for creating, assessing, and managing credit and portfolio risks in emerging economies
- The dearth of practical books that specifically guide bankers through the analysis and management of the peculiar credit risks of counterparties in emerging economies
- Confusing credit risk incidence, dynamics, and management requirements that impact and determine portfolio quality and returns in emerging economies
- Technicality of Basel Accords and the rigors of their practical applications in risk-based supervision of deposit money banks (DMBs) in emerging economies.

CRITICAL FUNCTIONS

This book fulfills numerous needs for its target audience. Its main functions can be summarized in understanding that it:

- Furnishes a structure for creating, assessing, and managing bank lending and credit portfolio risks, with a view to optimizing risk assets quality and portfolio returns in emerging economies
- Distills the Basel Accords into a nontechnical guide to managing credit risk and building risk assets quality, and in doing so discusses the implications and applicability of the Accords to the risk-based supervision of deposit money banks (DMBs) in emerging economies
- Provides bankers, deposit insurers, analysts, academics, and students with a practical understanding of credit risk incidence, dynamics, and management requirements tuned in to the need for optimum asset portfolios and returns in emerging economies.

Leo Onyiriuba
Lagos

Acknowledgments

I was encouraged in writing this book by banker endorsements. Praise for my books keeps pouring in from West Africa and beyond. Indeed I am humbled by kind words of encouragement I receive from bankers too numerous to acknowledge individually here. Many of these bankers are among over 2000 connections I have on the LinkedIn network. Some are my friends on Facebook, while others are following me on Twitter. I love them and treasure their interest in me and my writing. I will certainly continue to do them proud.

I owe a special debt of gratitude to my marketing partners in Nigeria, Ghana, Sierra Leone, and other parts of West Africa. My special thanks go to Chris Obikara (Nigeria), Benedict Frimpong (Ghana), Godfred Kofi Ofori (Ghana), and Beatrice Anderson (Sierra Leone) for their invaluable support. The same goes for customers in America, Europe, and elsewhere who patronize Amazon.com for my books. Their approval was one of the factors that spurred me to write this book. I must say how unreservedly grateful I am to CreateSpace, an Amazon company. It's a good launchpad from which I benefited immensely.

I have come across incredibly kind professionals in the course of promoting my works in Nigeria. I cannot list all of them in these acknowledgments. However, it is difficult for me not to mention a few of them whose rare kindness touched me in a special way:

- Abiola Babajide, PhD (Mrs.)—HOD, Banking and Finance, Covenant University, Nigeria
- Adigun—University Librarian, Crawford University, Igbesa, Nigeria
- Christopher Nkiko, PhD—Librarian, Covenant University, Ota, Nigeria
- Clement Omagbemi—Librarian, Bells University of Technology, Ota, Nigeria
- Emeka Ezike (Professor)—Department of Finance, University of Lagos
- Emmanuel Adebayo, PhD—University Librarian, Redeemer's University, Nigeria
- Evans Woherem, PhD—Former ED, Banking Operations, Unity Bank, Nigeria
- Grace Okoro, Professor (Mrs.)—Librarian, Babcock University, Ilishan-Remo, Nigeria
- Imo Akpan—Acquisitions Section, University Library, University of Lagos

- Ochei Ikpefan, PhD—Senior Lecturer, Banking and Finance, Covenant University, Nigeria
- Olukemi Fadehan, PhD (Mrs.)—University Librarian, University of Lagos
- Kuburat Oluwakemi Towolawi (Mrs.)—Resources Development Librarian, The Bells University of Technology, Nigeria
- Promise Ilo (Mrs.)—Acquisitions Librarian, Covenant University, Ota, Nigeria
- Sam Oyovbaire, Emeritus Professor—Former Nigeria Minister of Information
- Stella Anasi, PhD (Mrs.)—Acquisitions Librarian, University of Lagos, Akoka-Yaba, Lagos
- 'Uju Ogubunka, PhD—Former Registrar, Chartered Institute of Bankers of Nigeria

I am infinitely grateful to my dear friends: Yinka Sanni—Managing Director & Chief Executive Officer, Stanbic IBTC Bank Limited, Nigeria; Sam Osuala—Chief Investment Officer, Aong Capital Limited; Matthew Uponi—Procurement Manager at Shell Canada Energy; Chika Okoli—Chief Executive Officer, WABECO (Nigeria) Limited; and Hon G C Ogenyi—Commissioner for Human Capital Development and Poverty Reduction, Enugu State, Nigeria. They are trustworthy, real gems, and true friends in need.

I owe the greatest debt of gratitude to Scott J. Bentley (PhD), Senior Acquisitions Editor at Elsevier Inc, for showing interest in my book project, for believing in my writing, and for proposing and offering me the Elsevier contract. He painstakingly guided me through writing a good prospectus for the project. Scott was yet kind enough to help me to put peer reviewers' opinions through, and with the follow-through. It was he still who guided me through the processes leading to the contract itself. I really cannot thank him enough. He's awesome!

I am equally indebted to Susan Ikeda, Editorial Project Manager at Elsevier, who worked tirelessly with me on the chapter manuscripts and related documents toward production of this book. Susan was ever enthusiastic about the project. She is a really good motivator. Her subtle encouragement boosted my morale to finish writing the book earlier than originally scheduled.

My heartfelt thanks go to Debbie Clark, the book's Project Production Manager at Elsevier, to whom I remain grateful and immeasurably indebted. Debbie demonstrated rare care in coordinating the book's copyediting, typesetting, proofreading, and sundry production work. Her great attention to detail is unparalleled. Besides, she is exceptionally considerate. She always asked for how to fit work she had for me into my busy schedule.

I express my unreserved appreciation for all of Cindy Minor's hard work, in much the same vein. Cindy handles the marketing aspects of book projects. Needless to say, the success of a book has a lot to do with marketing, beyond the quality of writing and contents. In this sense, the buck stops with her.

I acknowledge the immeasurable support of my mother and children. My heart leaps knowing they stand by me always. They are my beloved ever. I dedicate this book to them. Ultimately, I say "glory to God." Needless to say, He is a merciful God, the Almighty, who makes the impossible possible in His infinite mercies.

Part I

Background, the Setting and Perspective

Overview of the Subject Matter

Chapter 1

Questions in the Making of Emerging Economies and Markets

Chapter Outline

LEARNING FOCUS AND OUTCOMES

The post—World War II era witnessed a long-running debate over the meaning and connotation of economic development. The debate continued into the 1970s and remained unsettled at the turn of the century. The contending issues were underlain by the development crisis of that epoch, ostensibly reflecting a lack of consensus on an approach to economic development analysis. Writers on the subject, most of whom were renowned economists, did not take sides—thus fostering the debate.

The contentious issues bordered on seeming anger at the frustrating life that was the lot of ordinary people in the so-called "Third World" countries. Economists evolved constructs, some of which had conflicting connotations, to picture and depict this situation. They did so in largely contrasting ways, apparently in search of appropriate characterization of the development phenomenon. Unfortunately, the quest for consensus remained elusive. Thus the debate raged on.

Emerging Market Bank Lending and Credit Risk Control. http://dx.doi.org/10.1016/B978-0-12-803438-5.00001-5

In this chapter I review the historical context of the debate. Then I demonstrate how the debate informed current thinking on the meaning and inner workings of development. I take a stand on the question of economic development, one that clarifies the context of this book. I define emerging economies within the broader context of social change. The objective in doing so is to appreciate the intricacies of doing business in emerging economies.

I explore the term "market" as applied in economic analysis to establish whether and how it informs the concept of emerging markets. In doing so, I investigate whether emerging markets and emerging economies are synonymous—and if they are not, how they are different. I draw conclusions based on the industrializing experiences of the BRICS, Asian Tiger, and Tiger economies. The reader will learn about:

- Concepts used by economists to denote levels of development attained by different countries and regions of the world
- Issues in the historical context of the debate over the meaning and applications of economic development constructs
- How the debate has influenced current thinking on, and understanding of, the concept and inner workings of economic development
- What constitutes "development" in practical terms based on evidence of the plight of ordinary people in emerging economies
- The definitions and meanings of, as well as differences and relationships between, emerging economies and emerging markets
- How emerging economies, emerging markets, and emerging-market economies are strictly defined in the context of this book

SETTING THE SCENE

Service Bank Limited had 170 branches nationwide, of which the Lagos region boasted more than half.[1] With its headquarters in Victoria Island, Lagos, the bank held a regular monthly performance review (MPR) meeting on the last workday of each month. All of the bank's branch managers reported promptly for the meeting. The EDs and heads of the business and operations divisions also attended the meeting. Usually the bank's MD presided over each MPR meeting, ostensibly to underscore its importance. In most cases, the fate that befell branch managers who were fired originated in the fallout of MPR meetings. That's the reason the MPR often panicked branch managers who were unprepared for the demands it made on them.

Besides financial performance, one of the thorny issues that always topped the agenda for the MPR meeting was the quality of the risk-assets portfolio.

---

1. Although this story is set in Lagos, Nigeria, the name of the bank and those of the individuals in the story are purely imaginary and for illustration purposes only. They do not relate to any known or unknown bank or persons in Nigeria or elsewhere.

Often a review of criticized risk assets became the subject of heated debate during the meeting. On occasion, tempers flared during the meetings. The bearing of some branch managers betrayed their character and emotions. This was usually evident in their frantic efforts to free themselves from charges of wriggling out of their responsibilities.

One particular incident during an MPR meeting aptly captured the mood of the participants. It would seem that the MD was in a foul mood that day. He shouted at branch managers who either reported losses or made huge provisions on their lending portfolios. He confronted the managers about the poor performance and warned that he would not hesitate to fire them if their branches failed to improve. For a moment, the managers were completely taken aback by his unkind remarks. A deafening silence ensued.

One of the managers, Steve, summoned courage and found his voice—trying to explain his peculiar situation.

"Sir, I agree with your observations." His voice trembled. "I will do my best for the bank. I shall endeavor to meet performance targets assigned to me," he promised. "But I face a peculiar situation in the Island Estate branch, which I took over from the former manager three weeks ago. A lot of things—especially lending decisions—were wrong with the branch from its past. Let us look back at where this branch is coming from. Here is a branch that has had four managers before me in less than one year…"

"Stop, Steve!" the MD cut in on him. "We know that history too well," he ridiculed. "It is rash of you to want to distract us by dwelling on the past," he lashed out at him. "Don't ever look back!" he warned sternly, staring at him. "If you look back, you turn into salt," he intimidated.

He paused for a moment, glanced at his watch, and leaned over to whisper something to the ED in charge of the Lagos branches. All eyes were riveted on him.

Then he resumed his deeply offensive remarks—not minding, apparently, whether the managers thought badly of him. "Our bank will be in dire straits if we have many managers like you, Steve. You and others in the same boat had better settle down to serious work and stop passing the buck. Make sure you are better prepared—with facts and figures of the performance of your branches—for the next MPR meeting."

At the root of the poor performance of some branches was credit risk crisis. Many branches had large holdings of nonperforming loans in their portfolios. Thus, these branches reported losses even as their managers did their utmost to make handsome profits. The losses mainly resulted from the application of specific and general loan loss provisions to the earnings of the branches. This internal financial reporting procedure—one that mainly served MPR purposes—had demoralizing effects on otherwise hard-working managers.

Like Steve, the most frustrated managers—and there were quite a number of them—were those who inherited a large number of criticized risk assets and whose branches were made to bear the brunt of their associated loan loss provisions. The fear and effects of bad loans were so overwhelming that some branch managers started tinkering with their game plans. In most cases, they realigned their balance sheets with a view to optimizing and retaining earnings. In doing so, many opted to play it safe—focusing on the liabilities rather than assets side of the balance sheet.

Playing their budgets this way, the managers were assured of low to moderate, but quality, earnings—devoid of loan loss provisions. But not all branch managers were cowed into tinkering with their business strategies. Rather than do that, they set about honing their skills.

Meanwhile, Steve met and discussed the fate that befell him at the MPR meeting with some of his counterparts from other banks the following day. They were surprised at the MD's verbal attacks on Steve despite his commitment to turning around his badly performing branch.

"We are all doomed to failure," one of the managers said in anger. "Can't you understand?" he queried, gazing into space. "We operate in a developing economy," he continued, becoming more forceful. "I'm sorry, but that is our bane and the truth," he said bluntly. Then he posed the big question, "How on earth can an employer so humiliate someone of a manager's standing? That can't be what happens in the developed world," he concluded sadly.

The foregoing views mirror the conflicting conceptions, misconceptions, and enduring debate on the content and inner workings of development. The question is when would a country be said to be developed, underdeveloped, less developed, developing, poor, backward, or in the Third World? Under what circumstances is it appropriate to describe a nation as an emerging economy or emerging market? These are real questions. This chapter explores the questions in a way that sets the stage for the entire book. First, a review of the country risk of the developing economies to which a manager in the story above alluded is pertinent. Following that is a case study of credit card lending in its still rudimentary form in emerging economies.

RISK IN COUNTRIES EVOLVING INTO EMERGING ECONOMIES

Usually the notion of country risk is that investors stand the chance of diminution or outright loss of wealth in a risky country. Risk in this sense refers to a myriad of factors that may ravage the value of assets an investor has in a country directly, or through a stock exchange or other regulated market. Besides the diminution of asset value, losses resulting from country risk often reflect an erosion of operating profit. Investors are scared to commit funds to projects in countries that have high risk ratings, ostensibly in strict display of economic rationality. Of course, no one wants to be exposed to the potential loss of hard-earned wealth. What factors condition the perception of risk in countries evolving into emerging economies? I provide the answer to this question using the African region as the setting.

Four main factors have historically contributed significantly to enduring country risk in the African region. Ethnicity fueled by alien political models is the foremost factor. Then there is the issue of militant and terrorist activities. Military incursion into politics is also a contributory factor, while politicization of the civil service caps the factors. These factors precipitate sundry instabilities in the system, which adversely affect foreign investment, local business, and industry. The same factors hold sway whether the problems at issue are analyzed from the perspectives of sovereign risk or economic and transfer risks. For example, it could be argued that the vexatious issue of corruption in emerging African economies is rooted in military incursion into politics and the politicization of civil service, among other factors.

Ethnicity Fueled by Alien Political Models

Democratization of politics in Africa has proven to be an arduous task as the countries have bungled its practice. Western democratic norms were alien to Africa's political culture. The historical claim to political power by certain ethnic groups in some of the countries still lingers in contradiction to modern democratic values. In many states, it has not been easy to substitute modern democracy for the traditional hereditary practice for leadership changes. In principle, the countries accepted the new democratic constitutions on which the exits of colonial rulers were predicated. But in practice, the leaders of these countries were strongly inclined to uphold their various ethnic traditions. The resultant strife, internal disorder, and civil wars soon engulfed one country after another.

This situation continues to take a heavy toll on banking in Africa's emerging markets, especially in the lending sphere. The case of African Development Bank (AfDB) clearly illustrates how political instability adversely affects banking operations. The Bank had to relocate from its statutory headquarters in Abidjan to Tunis following the civil war in Cote d'Ivoire. It operated from Tunis for 10 years before returning its headquarters operations back to Abidjan in 2014 after peace and order were restored. Of course, the crisis affected the Bank's funding of projects in that and countries similarly affected by either civil war or other political strife.

Militant and Terrorist Activities

A typical example of an unfavorable condition for bank lending in Africa's emerging economies is the prevalence of political upheaval. Let me illustrate this—and therefore the impact of militancy and activities of terrorists on lending decisions—with reference to happenings in Nigeria's Niger Delta and North-Eastern regions, and in some Northern African and Middle Eastern countries, in the recent past. Disturbances that started as street protests demanding political reforms and democratic governance in some Northern

African countries soon snowballed into grave political upheaval. Between January and September 2011, wild protests by aggrieved citizens crippled economic activity and toppled the governments in Tunisia, Egypt, and Libya, in that order. In Iran, government forces ruthlessly crushed similar protests, while protests in Syria claimed thousands of lives.

In the case of Nigeria, a mutiny of militant youths in the Niger Delta region took to arms to press for reforms in the country's oil sector and the development of the oil-rich Niger Delta, and a voice in the distribution of oil revenue. While all of this was happening, economic activity became paralyzed. For instance, some oil exploration and mining companies in the troubled region closed or relocated their major operations in the wake of the crisis. A more serious unfavorable condition for bank lending was the emergence of terrorism in Nigeria's North-Eastern region. Terrorist activities in the region, and the federal government's response to the attendant security crisis, came to the fore in 2012. With mounting insecurity of lives and property, businesses in states that had become hotbeds of terrorism could no longer function effectively. Some even relocated their operations just to save their investments from wanton destruction.

It seems inconceivable that a bank would want to lend money to individuals or companies doing businesses in these turbulent zones. Rather than lend, banks would demand the paying down or outright repayment of existing credit facilities. This is one of the realities of bank lending and credit risk management in Africa's emerging economies.

Military Incursion into Politics

Political instability was accentuated by military intervention into the politics and governance of the countries. Like a wild bushfire, the trapping of political power by military officers swept Africa. In 1963, the military struck and took over power in Togo. In 1967, history repeated itself in that country when a junta overthrew the government. In 1965, Algeria, Dahomey, and Congo (Kinshasa), in like manner, experienced the shock of military coups that sacked their democratically elected civilian regimes. It was the turn of Upper Volta, Central African Republic, Nigeria, and Ghana in 1966 when the ill wind of military coup d'état blew through them and swept their elected civilian governments out of office. Even while most of these countries experienced several fresh coups, counter-coups, and abortive coups d'état, additional countries became infested with the disease.

Authoritarian government lacking in accountability engendered military rule. This situation is not propitious for economic development. It is both wasteful and irresponsible. The economic misery to which African states have been subjected in the postcolonial period can largely be explained in terms of failed democratic processes. The reasons for and objectives of military rule in Africa are indeed diverse. Thus it would be futile to start differentiating them here on the basis of a country by country analysis—that is beyond the scope of this book. However, it must be emphasized that military interventions into politics in Africa exacerbated political instability in the region and adversely affected long-term state, business, and financial sector development.

Politicization of Civil Service

The Nigerian case best exemplifies politicization of civil service. Under President Babangida's regime during the late 1980s and early 1990s, political director generals were appointed to oversee federal ministries. Career permanent secretaries were displaced as chief executives of the ministries. Thus, and in other African countries with the same experience, the bureaucracy lost its hallmark—the capacity to maintain the neutrality of civil servants irrespective of which party was in power. Although suppression of the opposition and hijacking of the bureaucracy were usually resisted by some pressure groups, the affected political leaders maintained an uncompromising posture. Thus, one of the enduring colonial legacies—the civil service—became a plaything of politicians. As the public services are being manipulated to suit the whims and caprices of political leaders, mediocrity tends to replace quality performance. This happens to the detriment of political and economic progress.

Case Study 1.1

Grappling with credit card lending in emerging economies Ola Musa's secretary ushered a smartly dressed lady into the office of his boss, whom the lady had come to see. Ola was the owner-manager of Youth Future (Nigeria) Limited[2]—a business initiative to empower the youth with entrepreneurial skills in various indigenous vocations.

"Good morning, Sir," she greeted Ola, fixing him with a warm smile.

"Welcome, and please have a seat," responded Ola, smiling. "How may I help you? he enquired.

"My name is Clara. I work in marketing for Blue Bank (Nigeria) Limited. I'm here to introduce our bank's unique Naira[3] credit card (NCC) to you. It functions like a traditional MasterCard or Visa card. The only difference is that the NCC is our bank's initiative to offer its discerning customers—a select group of high net worth individuals like you—a local alternative. The NCC is available in three variants—standard, gold, and platinum brands. The beauty of the card is that it provides you with an unsecured line-of-credit facility with a term of five years—can you beat that? I would propose a limit of ₦10 million in the platinum category for you. To someone of your standing, lending even ₦20 million unsecured isn't a big deal—what do you think?" she joked.

"How can I use the card? Can I get money with it to run my business—in the same way that I use my ATM card?" Ola asked excitedly.

"Yes, you can. You may—if you so wish—even get cash over the counter. In that case, you simply fill out a cash withdrawal slip and submit it across the counter to a teller—and the cash you need is all yours! It's that simple. Also, you can shop in supermarkets and pay bills with the card. You simply swipe your card at a POS machine where you shop, and your bill is instantly paid online. You can do all this without a hitch provided that transactions are denominated in naira and conducted in Nigeria. You can pay money into your NCC account and withdraw money from it at any time without notice to the bank. This means that you can always pay back and redraw the money you use on your card at any time. In this way, the card operates as an overdraft facility," Clara explained.

"What of charges on the facility? You've not talked about the interest rate the bank charges on the NCC—or is it interest-free?" Ola asked inquisitively, laughing.

"Like an overdraft, interest is charged on the outstanding balance at the pre-vailing money market rate plus a one-off fee payable at the point of initial drawdown on the credit facility," answered Clara.

"Is there any other pertinent information about the NCC that I should know?" asked Ola.

"The information I have given you is all that you need to know about the workings of the NCC facility," said Clara.

"I must confess that the features of the NCC interest me. How may I obtain the card?" Ola asked enthusiastically.

Clara told him to apply for the card so that she could formally process, recommend, and present it for approval by the credit committee. Thereafter the bank would issue the card to him.

Ola applied for ₦10 million NCC in the platinum brand category a couple of days after Clara introduced the product to him. Clara was happy that her mar-keting yielded fruition in the new NCC account she was about to open for Ola Musa. She processed Ola's application and secured approval for his request. Armed with the approval, she took personal guarantee and statement of personal net worth documents to Ola. He was to execute and return the documents to the bank as the only condition precedent to drawdown on the NCC facility.

Once Ola fulfilled the condition, he started utilizing the NCC facility. He did not bother to shop with the card. Neither did he consider the ATM option. His preferred drawing option was cash withdrawal over-the-counter in banking halls—perhaps because he usually withdrew a large sum of money every time he used the card. On one occasion, he went to cash ₦500,000 on his NCC facility. The cashier told him that the balance in his account was insufficient to pay the amount he wanted to withdraw. The available balance in the account was ₦36,000. This implied that there was an outstanding balance of ₦9.9 million. He instantly disputed the balance—but without making headway.

When he returned to his office, he asked his accountant to reconcile the balance in the bank's records with his drawings on the NCC facility. The accountant found that a total debit of ₦3.5 million from the account was not accounted for by Ola's drawings. The total of his various drawings on the NCC facility was ₦6.5 million.

The following day Ola returned to the bank—this time to the branch where his NCC account was domiciled. He wanted an explanation for the ₦3.5 million in unaccounted-for debits from his NCC account. Again he did not make headway.

He had gone to see Clara first. Clara, who had stood up to welcome him, was hardly done with greetings to him when he cut in on her.

"Your bank has messed me up! What in the world is going on? My NCC account is in a mess!" he stated angrily.

"What's the problem, Sir?" Clara asked, bewildered.

"I was at Blue Bank's Victoria Island branch yesterday to draw cash, only to be informed that my NCC account was in debit to the tune of more than 9.9 million naira. All I have withdrawn on the NCC to date is 6.5 million naira. I don't know where the huge difference of 3.5 million naira came from. I'm here to find that out from you."

"May I apologize to you for all the troubles your complaint has caused you. The difference you talked about relates to interest and other charges to the account…"

She was still talking when Ola cut in on her.

"What interest?—3.5 million naira my foot! What rate of interest and charges would amount to so much money in so short a period? As you know, I have used the NCC for less than 10 months," he said. "And by the way, why haven't I been getting bank statements on my NCC account? What rate of interest are we really talking about? Tell me, what are the charges—and for what purposes were they debited from my account?" he asked in quick succession.

"The interest rate applicable to the NCC facility is 35% per annum. There are other charges—including penalty charges to which the NCC facility is subject—apart from a 3% flat fee charged at drawdown. I remember I mentioned that to you at the time I was selling the product to you," Clara explained.

"Outrageous! This is incredible, ludicrous, and insulting to customers' intelligence," Ola shouted, and then paused momentarily. "Call up the account now and show me figures, facts, and full details of all the charges and interest debited from my account right from the inception," he ordered, fuming.

"I'm sorry Sir, but I can't do all that now. It's not as simple as you think. The NCC facility has a complex structure and configuration. It's not straightforward. For instance, you are supposed to pay money into the account at least once a month. And that payment must be made on or before the 17th day of the month. Failing to do so results in a 2% flat fee on the outstanding balance. There are sundry other charges that I can't easily explain to you now," Clara explained.

"Look, I've had enough of this nonsense from you. All that you've said has made no sense to me. I won't take the debits—period!" Ola said as he stormed out of Clara's office.

He went to see the branch manager, who had been oblivious of his preceding rancorous meeting with Clara. Without wasting time, he confronted the manager with his complaint. The manager calmed him down.

"The charges and interest burden on you would have been substantially reduced if you had occasionally lodged money in the account. I advise that you pay down on the outstanding balance lest it becomes sticky and classified as a collections account," he counseled.

"It doesn't seem that you understood my concern," retorted Ola. "I want a printout of statements on the account from its inception. Clara has told me the interest rate, initial drawdown fee, and penalty rate for nondeposit activity that are applied to the account. My accountant will cross-check those figures when I get back to the office. Can you expatiate on the so-called sundry other charges?" Ola queried.

"I'm sorry, there's nothing I can do to help at this time. It's difficult for me, and the reason is simple. All over the world, the credit card is a complex financial product—it embodies unusual credit risk and is priced accordingly. What do I mean? Credit cards are usually very expensive—and those who use them are aware of this fact. So please don't see the NCC facility as the normal overdraft or advance—it's not. Even so, it is sometimes difficult to appreciate that fact. If you like, you can meet my colleagues in e-banking at our head office—they are the ones who created the product. They should be in a better position to answer all your questions," the manager explained.

Ola simply nodded and thanked the branch manager for his time. He left the branch, dejected.

Hints for analyzing this case study Clara convinced Ola Musa to open an NCC account by deception that was rooted in the veiled structure of the product. The actual features of the NCC were at variance with its marketing claims! With the NCC, Blue Bank exploited a price-insensitive market—high net worth individuals (HNI). Though that served the earnings needs of the bank, as a credit product the NCC was not customer-friendly. Curiously, Blue Bank staff, with the exception of some product development staff in the head office, didn't know much about the NCC's features. Perhaps this was deliberate, in order to assure market acceptance of the deceptive product. By doing so, the bank would have hoped to attain its NCC budget goal. Blue Bank pursued this crazy goal at the expense of unsuspecting customers. That goal also informed the deceptive marketing style that Clara employed in opening Ola Musa's NCC account. The greatest victims of the ploy were HNI, especially those who didn't keep meticulous account records—those who did would soon discover the ploy and resist the painful exploitation.

Questions on the case study

1. **(a)** In what sense does pursuit of budget goals inform the contemporary approach of banks to the marketing of financial services?
   (b) What factors underscore the view that banks tend to drive lending along the lines of overambitious budget goals?
   (c) Are the factors you identified in (b) above evident in Clara's marketing of Blue Bank's Naira credit card (NCC) to Ola Musa as presented in this chapter's case study?
2. **(a)** How could competition for market leadership based on standing in bogus earnings, and balance sheet growth and size, be inimical to the quality of asset portfolios of banks? Justify your answer with reference to the fate of any two named failed banks in Nigeria.
   (b) Critique the accusation leveled by some HNI against banks, that misleading claims and deception are used in the structuring, developing, and marketing of credit cards.
3. **(a)** Evaluate Blue Bank's Naira credit card as presented in this chapter's case study against a backdrop of suspicion that the bank designed the product to exploit unsuspecting customers.

(b) Identify and discuss the ploys that the marketing staff of Blue Bank adopted to win customers for the bank's Naira credit card.

(c) What options are open to victims of such ploys to seek and obtain redress without necessarily hurting their banking relationship with the bank?

4. **(a)** What would you say informed the buildup Clara gave to the NCC in order to get Ola Musa to open an NCC account?

(b) How did the buildup contribute to the possible loss of the account in the end?

2. The use of Nigeria as the setting for this case study is for illustration purposes only, in order to demonstrate how the case study plays itself out in a typical emerging economy. The names used for the company, bank, and individuals in the illustration are imaginary and do not relate to any known or unknown company, bank, or persons in Nigeria or elsewhere.

3. Naira is the name of Nigeria's national currency and represented by the symbol ₦.

BACKGROUND—A HISTORICAL PERSPECTIVE

What then—drawing on the foregoing experience of the African countries— are the contending issues in economic development? In order to answer this question, we should appreciate the historical background of contemporary thinking on economic development. Countries are classified as developed, less developed, developing, underdeveloped, backward, poor, and so on based on some imaginary economic scale.

During the course of the 1950s–1970s, development was predominantly gauged by gains in per capita GNP growth. It was expected that increases in GNP would translate into jobs, economic opportunities, and a wider distribution of socioeconomic benefits. Ironically, writers and analysts did not share a common view on the crux of development. Divergent views were derived from misconstruction of the adverse economic conditions of developing countries during that period. It was thought that development eluded countries that had low income per capita. Underdevelopment was measured by the ratio of capital to population. A country was considered to be underdeveloped or not developing if it recorded a consistently declining or low GNP per capita, especially in comparison with its historical standards or performance.

Development in the 1960s and 1970s was thought to reflect in the ability of a country to increase and sustain its annual gross GNP. The UN, in 1961 and 1970, dubbed the 1960s and 1970s the "Development Decades." It specified a six percent growth rate for GNP and used per capita real incomes of the United States, Canada, Australia, and Western Europe as benchmarks of development. This view assumed that an increase in per capita real income was a proxy for a rise in the standard of living resulting from a high ratio of income to population, reduction in the poverty level, and high propensity to save. The measures were shown to be flawed when most developing countries achieved appreciable GDP and per capita income growth rates without improving quality of life. Then the emphasis shifted to industrialization funded largely with the proceeds from agricultural production. The attendant rapid urbanization was achieved at the expense of rural development—a situation that exacerbated poverty. Thus the development paradigm shifted once again, to an import substitution strategy aimed at protecting infant industries. This approach could not stand the test of time. It would seem that foregoing policies failed because it is difficult in practice to accurately predict what will happen to consumption vis-à-vis savings and poverty levels as a result of an increase in per capita real income. Thus, the policies were faulted on grounds of failure to address the inner meaning and content of development.

Developing countries soon became disenchanted with the measurement of national progress in absolute GNP terms. The disenchantment reached its crescendo in the 1970s, forcing the jettisoning of the GNP approach. In the 1980s and beyond, the evolving paradigms of development were pitched at a radical social change level. Development economists started considering the content and quality of development more seriously. Meanwhile, most developing countries had plunged into serious economic straits as their economic problems had festered. Difficulties in grappling with macroeconomic instability topped the major concerns. The problems demanded solution through the adoption of SAP under the auspices of the IMF and World Bank. Many developing countries adopted SAP in pursuit of the new development drive—and, above all, as a panacea for their economic woes. The idea of SAP, which swept developing countries in the 1980s and 1990s, stemmed from the economic imbalances that the countries experienced as a result of prolonged structural distortions in key economic sectors, including:

- Declining agricultural production in the face of rapidly growing population
- Balance of payments disequilibria caused mainly by persistently worsening terms of trade
- Huge and rising external debt, the servicing of which could not be sustained with dwindling export receipts and foreign reserves
- Inefficient public sector investment reflected in the proliferation of nonregenerative projects

During the SAP era, some writers started to include noneconomic factors in their analyses of the problems of economic development. Though casual, references to social indicators such as gains in education, health, and housing were typical. SAP was a strong and popular strategy. Yet it failed due to poor coordination, halfhearted implementation, bureaucratic bottlenecks, and excessive government intervention.

DEVELOPED, DEVELOPING, AND EMERGING ECONOMIES

Emerging economies are not backward countries—far from it. They are, rather, developing at a fast and commendable rate. Nor are they underdeveloped in the sense of lacking in modern industry or in the ability to fully exploit their economic potential. They are not poor either—in most cases, they are endowed with some natural or other productive resources. Yet equating emerging economies to "less developed" or "developing" economies begs the question—if an economy is not developed, it must be less developed or developing. Ideally, backward, underdeveloped, poor, and suchlike depict economies in which the pace of development does not match up with the tempo of emerging economies—which are considered faster, often spectacular, and more successful too. In view of their fast pace of growth, emerging economies command attention within the world economic sphere.

Developing economies are at the lower rung, struggling to meet basic development demands—for which, in most cases, they expect and often receive aid from international donors and trade partners. Features of developing economies include low income per capita and the preponderance of ignorance, disease, and squalor. In most cases, developing economies also feature environmental degradation, political instability, threats to individual liberty, and disconnected sociocultural values. Nowadays the Human Development Index (HDI), which takes many factors into account, is used as a metric to measure a country's level of development.

Developed economies are seen as nations with high rates of GDP and real income per capita that complement an enviable quality of life for their citizens. Thus development is an economic process of improving the quality of life. It is achieved when the march of progress leads to advances in education, health, and nutrition, as well as increased employment, reduced poverty, more equity in the system, and a healthier environment. Development permeates every aspect of human and national life—the values, attitudes, institutions, and material well-being of the people. Most European countries make the list of developed economies, as do the United States, Canada, New Zealand, Australia, and Japan. The Asian Tigers are also numbered among developed nations.

Countries tagged as emerging economies have high levels of development powered by rapid industrialization and exceptional rates of growth in three key economic sectors—energy, information technology, and telecommunications. In most cases, agriculture is not the mainstay of their economies. They are seen as industrializing nations that have moved on, the aforementioned features setting them apart from developing economies. However, in order to test if a country is an emerging economy, we must ask the right questions. Is the march of progress in the country significantly improving the quality of life of ordinary people? Is it building confidence in the economy? Is it creating possibilities for doing business well? Is it attracting local and foreign investment? Does it have social change possibilities?

The foregoing questions must be answered in the affirmative in the first place for an economy to be tagged "emerging." If it is, sustained GNP growth and appreciable real income per capita, as well as progressive institutional change, would be evident. These factors set the stage for sustained progress. But they also energize the drive to catch up with developed nations. In most cases, blueprints and transformation frameworks inform the catching-up strategy that is well-ordered in many countries. Thus emerging economies are moving on. Their quest for economic and structural transformation is ongoing and unmistakable. The economy is performing well overall—at its own level and relative to international standards. Usually the end result—social change—is in sight.

LESSONS OF THE ASIAN TIGER, BRICS, AND TIGER ECONOMIES

It was not until the most recent decade that poverty alleviation programs of developing countries—through economic reforms—started yielding modest fruit. In Nigeria, citizens had demanded a "better life" from political leaders and economic administrators, beginning in the mid-1980s, in sheer repugnance of their poor living conditions and as a measure of good governance. From then on, until 1993, the Nigerian government supported a program of "Better Life for Rural Dwellers," instituted by the country's First Lady, ostensibly to effect radical positive change in the deplorable living conditions of the rural population. It was a laudable attempt, no doubt about it. However, the emphasis on rural dwellers skewed a wider perspective of the problem. Rural dwellers are not the only ones afflicted by the disease of poverty—the problem of the urban poor has been equally worrying to government and social workers in developing countries.

Now the question is, how did industrialized nations accomplish their long journey to economic development? Why and how did the process of development work for the pioneers of industrial revolution—the United Kingdom, the United States, and Japan—but not for most developing countries? Are there significant differences in the initial conditions that made the process flourish in the pioneer industrialized nations? Why has it been particularly difficult for developing countries to achieve a feat considered ordinary, judging by analysis of the process? Why did the Asian Tigers—countries that ultimately caught up with the industrial revolution—find it relatively much easier to achieve the feat? The *answers* to these questions are beyond the scope of this book. But the *questions themselves* are pertinent in tuning our minds to the critical issues that define the vital targets at which developing countries should aim in their urge to develop. The questions establish a basis for investigating the march of progress in emerging economies.

The Asian Tiger—comprising South Korea, Hong Kong, Taiwan, and Singapore—achieved consistent spectacular economic performance, progress, and development beginning in the 1960s, thus making it relatively easy for them to catch up with the pioneers of industrial revolution. Their progress was anchored in robust export earnings, rapid industrialization, resilient economies, vibrant financial markets, and strong manufacturing industries. The Asian Tiger did so well that some of their counterparts in the "Tiger" economy family—namely Indonesia, Malaysia, Thailand, and China—followed suit. These countries achieved and sustained significant economic progress in the 1980s and 1990s even as the Asian financial crisis of 1997—1998 put them marginally into reverse. While large inflows of foreign investment fueled economic growth, the reverse resulted from huge debt service obligations and socioeconomic inequities.

Countries in the BRIC fold—Brazil, Russia, India, and China—epitomize the enterprising spirit that characterizes the radical transformation of one-time developing economies into the ranks of developed or emerging economies. Today, BRIC countries are widely acknowledged as models of highly successful emerging economies. Some analysts include South Africa among models of emerging economies. Thus the acronym BRICS reflects the expanded model economies (BRIC plus South Africa). Like the Asian Tiger and Tiger countries, the BRICS countries boast strong economies fostered by sustained growth, diversified financial markets, appreciable returns on investment, and moderate to low investment and business risks. What confounds analysts is that the lessons of their experience, nay that of the Asian Tiger and Tiger economies, have scarcely been properly learned and applied by developing countries.

STRICTLY DEFINING EMERGING ECONOMIES

The rate at which the pioneers of advanced nations emerged from under-development spanned a longer period than it took for Brazil and the Asian Tiger. It would seem that developing countries have not properly learned and applied the lessons of experience of the pioneers of development and the BRIC, Asian Tiger and Tiger economies—all of which achieved spectacular economic performance, progress, and development. This is especially the case with countries constituting sub-Saharan Africa. Thus it became necessary to isolate countries that are striving to develop—leading to the coinage of "emerging economies" and "emerging markets."

Analysts tend to use the two terms as interchangeable constructs. On occasion, the two terms are used as a combined construct, named "emerging market economies." Unfortunately, the terms convey a loose meaning—whether used in isolation from each other or in the combined form—leading to considerable confusion. The confusion is evident in bundling together countries that have markedly different development standing and then christening them emerging economies. In some cases, the same countries bundled together were unbundled to satisfy some tenuous viewpoint on emerging economies. Thus the confusion persists.

The confusion originated in the criteria for classifying countries as emerging economies. Usually the primary criteria lay emphasis on a country's shift from a closed- to open-market economy, economic development reforms, and economic progress. Thus a country is regarded as an emerging economy if it has embarked on sweeping economic and structural reforms that open it up to market forces and discipline. Ostensibly, the reforms and restructuring would strengthen the economy and make it more competitive in international markets. Often the visible outcomes of the reforms reflect a fast-growing economy evidenced in increases in the rate of GDP growth, level of per capita income, and investment. These results make the economy attractive to both local and foreign investors and lead to increases in both portfolio and direct investments. Investor confidence is perhaps the most significant payback of reforms, one that boosts capacity for economic regeneration.

On occasion, a reform program may target a particular sector of the economy considered crucial to the success of other reforms that may ensue. Nigerian banking reform is a typical emerging economy scene. In 2004, the Central Bank of Nigeria (CBN), under Governor Charles Soludo, started implementing far-reaching reform of the country's banking sector. The governor had announced a 14-point agenda, widely acclaimed as the first serious blueprint for solving systemic issues in the industry since the 1990s, following its deregulation in 1986. The most intriguing fallout of the reform resulted from the dramatic increase in the required capital base of licensed banks to ₦25 billon, from barely ₦2 billion, with the 18-month deadline for compliance expiring December 31, 2005. Major shareholders, directors, and chief executives of banks scampered to meet the deadline, but painfully not all of them were successful. After the deadline, the ax fell on 14 banks that failed to forge mergers or lend themselves to acquisition.

In a speech announcing the appointment of Soludo as the new CBN governor in 2004, Nigerian President Olusegun Obasanjo set the tone for the drastic reform to follow. While sacking incumbent CBN Governor Joseph Sanusi, Obasanjo had hinted that it was time the role of the CBN shifted from rudimentary regulatory and monetary management functions. The time had come, according to him, for emphasis to be laid on macroeconomic management so as to meet the country's daunting developmental needs. In the end, the number of banks in the country shrank from 84 to 25 following hurriedly packaged mergers and acquisitions, and the withdrawal of operating licenses of banks that could not meet the deadline. The reform buoyed up confidence in Nigeria's banking system after all was said and done. Its positive effect rubbed-off on the entire economy as foreign direct investment surged in the aftermath of the reform. Soludo was honored at home and abroad for the feat. While presenting him with an award, London-based *The Banker* magazine praised his achievement. The reform, its attendant intrigues, and the frosty dispositions of major stakeholders and operators were typical of an emerging economy scene.

Apparently, emerging economies are in transition. Thus economic giants such as China and Russia are classified as emerging economies—just as minor economies like Thailand and Vietnam are. Ironically, reforms in the countries are aimed at not only improving market efficiency, but building and institutionalizing transparency, strict accountability, and standards in the public and private spheres. Yet it is suspect to lump all transitional economies together and christen them emerging economies when, in fact, they are worlds apart. This book adopts this view and proposes an alternative perspective that fits with current thinking in bank lending and credit risk control circles.

A typical emerging economy, in the context of this book, is characterized by weak and inefficient institutions, systems, and bureaucracies that are being reformed. The reforms are opening up the economy and promoting its reliance on market and economic forces. Quality of life—evidenced by an increasing rate of GDP growth and level of per capita income, as well as other economic indicators—especially HDI—is improving. The march of progress notwithstanding, the system may often not be fully transparent. There may not be strict standards for accountability, regulation, and supervision of public and private sector institutions. Doing business could be quite profitable but is often fraught with intricate risks that the authorities are trying to ease. In most cases, poor infrastructure, a volatile exchange rate, political instability, a dearth of critical statistical data, and sundry inequities—all of which exacerbate risk—are in the reform agenda. Economies associated with foregoing conditions are essentially in an emerging state. Table 1.1 shows the countries widely regarded as emerging market economies, and the regions to which they belong.

TABLE 1.1 Countries Classified as Emerging Economies and Their Related Regions

Africa	Eastern Europe	Latin America	Asia	Southeast Asia
Egypt	Bulgaria	Argentina	Bangladesh	Indonesia[c]
Morocco	Czech Rep	Brazil[a]	China[a,c]	Malaysia[c]
Nigeria	Estonia	Chile	Hong Kong[b]	Philippines
South Africa[a]	Greece	Colombia	India[a]	Singapore[b,c]
	Hungary	Mexico	Iran	Thailand[c]
	Latvia	Peru	Israel	Vietnam
	Lithuania	Venezuela	Oman	
	Poland		Pakistan	
	Romania		Qatar	

Continued

TABLE 1.1 Countries Classified as Emerging Economies and Their Related Regions—cont'd

Africa	Eastern Europe	Latin America	Asia	Southeast Asia
	Slovenia		Russia	
	Ukraine		South Korea[b,c]	
			Taiwan[b]	
			Turkey	
			UAE	

[a]Indicates emerging economies represented by the acronym BRICS.
[b]Indicates so-called "Asian Tiger."
[c]Indicates so-called "Tiger" economies.

COMPARING EMERGING ECONOMIES WITH EMERGING MARKETS

There are many shades of opinion about the meaning and implications of emerging markets (also often referred to as emerging market economies). But how emerging markets differ from or relate to emerging economies has scarcely been fully explored. Though seemingly related, "emerging economy" is a broader concept than "emerging market" in a strict economic sense. Thus the scope and depth of meaning of the two economic constructs define the subtle differences between them.[4]

Economists tend to have differing views on the terms "economy" and "market" depending on the object of analysis. In one usage, an "economy" can be simply equated with a country—just as a "market" could also imply a country—in a loose, largely business sense. When the two terms are used as synonyms to refer to a country, as in the foregoing, emphasis is usually on their understanding as:

- An area of land and the people living in it that a particular government controls,
- A territory in the mold of the first definition where companies trade in goods and services, including the financial exchanges that underlie the transactions.

---

4. In this book, emerging economies, emerging markets, and emerging market economies are used in different but related contexts depending on the subject matter—and not necessarily as synonyms.

Thus we can talk of the market for a particular product in a given country. The gold market in Ghana, Nigeria's huge market for crude petroleum, and China's main overseas markets spanning Europe and America are typical examples. In this sense, it would be right to use "emerging economy" and "emerging market" as interchangeable constructs depicting transforming countries. As countries undergoing economic and structural reforms, BRICS and suchlike should be rightly categorized as emerging economies or emerging markets.

However, in a strict economic sense, "economy" contrasts subtly with "market"—the former being a broader concept. This book conceptualizes an economy from the perspective of organized patterns of productive activities by which a country seeks to attain social change or to improve its standing as a developed nation. This definition subsumes a whole gamut of activities and issues in producing, managing, and using a country's wealth for the benefit of its citizens. Thus we talk of a mixed economy, a capitalist economy, a socialist economy, and so on, or the decline, growth, and stagnation of a country's economy.

In the context of this book, a "market" has a rather deeper connotation than simply a territory where companies buy and sell goods and services. It depicts opportunities and structures for transactions and financial exchanges that a country offers companies to encourage them to do business within its territories, including the threats to which the companies might be exposed in so doing. It is common, consistent with this meaning, to hear people talk of a difficult market, faltering market, market failure, market dynamics, and so on. There is nothing "emerging" about economies that fit with the foregoing meaning.

It follows therefore that emerging markets, as used in this book, implies evolving structures and opportunities in emerging economies for local and international transactions and financial exchanges, including risks and threats to business and investment. This is also the context in which this book uses the term, "emerging market economies."

QUESTIONS FOR DISCUSSION AND REVIEW

1. In what ways did the historical debate on economic development concepts inform or not inform current and evolving thinking on the meaning and inner workings of development?
2. What are the contemporary and contentious issues in the making of emerging economies and markets? Your answer should reflect emerging economies within the broader context of social change.
3. To what extent does this chapter define the perspective of this book on emerging economies and shed light on the possible risks and intricacies of doing business in any named emerging market in Southeast Asia?

4. Why would you agree or disagree with the view that emerging economies differ significantly from developed and developing countries? Use any named developed nation in Europe, and developing country in Latin America, to illustrate your answer.
5. How does the term "market" as applied in economic analysis inform or not inform the concept of emerging markets? Your answer should show how emerging markets and emerging economies compare.

Chapter 2

Conceptual Survey of Risk and Its Applications in Banking

LEARNING FOCUS AND OUTCOMES

Concern and discussions in banking circles in emerging economies are often dominated by the personal experiences of staff and customers, as well as the corporate strategies of banks for dealing with uncertainty and risk management. In most cases, a myriad of tricky matters are at issue. While efficient operations and the profitability of transactions remain critical, the pursuit of risk mitigation holds sway. Ostensibly, the most critical issue borders on how banks and their customers can anticipate risk correctly and therefore manage counterparty credit risk effectively. In practice, however, banks and customers should strive to deal with uncertainty and risk on all fronts. This is necessary for those wanting to survive and make a success of their endeavors in the long run.

Emerging Market Bank Lending and Credit Risk Control. http://dx.doi.org/10.1016/B978-0-12-803438-5.00002-7

Besides risk, lending officers will have to deal with uncertainty—a construct that exists in the futuristic realm. Uncertainty is expressed in human incapability to correctly foresee events that belong in the future. Unfortunately, while bank management can check risk to a large extent, it lacks the capacity to control uncertainty. One reason is that dealing with uncertainty defies the use of a methodical framework or approach. Another reason is that the mitigation of uncertainty does not lend itself to quantitative analysis—unlike risk management. Yet, a bank should devise an effective strategy to deal with uncertainty. In doing so, the bank can better anticipate and manage the risk that uncertainty often occasions. Formulation and implementation of contingency plans have been some of the effective responses to uncertainty in contemporary banking practice. But a bank must first determine its strategic intent, marshal its operations and resources well, and then look to the future. Contingency plans help banks to anticipate uncertainty. They enable them to look to the future with confidence—in a way that inspires investment in earning assets and the overall growth of the banks.

The foregoing informs the constant need to sensitize bankers and regulators to uncertainty and risk. It underscores risk management as the focus of interest in this book—in a way that readers can appreciate. It also tasks bankers and regulators to cleanse the banking industry of reckless lending. In addition to an understanding of the nature, incidence, and dimensions of credit risk, I highlight evolving thinking on bank credit best practices in this chapter. The reader will learn about:

- The general meanings of risk and uncertainty as defined in the context of this book, and their influence on bank lending
- Key issues that underscore risk and uncertainty as critical factors in bank lending functions
- Issues with which bankers and banking regulators contend regarding uncertainty and credit risk
- Evolving thinking on, and concerns about, effective management of bank credit risk in emerging economies
- Methodological issues and frameworks for bank credit risk management in emerging markets
- How bank management can correctly anticipate uncertainty and its concomitant credit risk

CREATION OF RISK—A GENERAL OVERVIEW

We all are exposed to various hazards in the conduct of our daily activities. Someone could be involved in a road accident. Some other person's possession could be stolen. Or, a student might fail an examination. There's even risk in the possibility of sudden death. These are examples of circumstances that we sometimes think about but the occurrence of which, unfortunately, cannot be exactly predicted. Consider the investment decisions you make. Are you convinced that you will realize your expected returns? Do you think that possible returns will justify your investments? You may answer these questions in the affirmative, especially when you have painstakingly analyzed opportunities and threats applicable to particular investments. But such an answer would be true only to the same extent as the possibility that your expectations would fall through. As a result, people talk of risk as a variable that permeates all activities of humankind. There is risk in business and in everyday living. Risk is pervasive, almost always a part of everyday life. Every human endeavor has its peculiar inherent risks. Risk, indeed, is endemic to nature—manifesting in every conceivable human activity, including marriage, eating, investment in equity stocks, and gambling.

We often try to interpret most human attitudes as behavior toward risk. Even while many people appear indifferent to risk, most would pay a price to avoid it. A few others, however, surprisingly display risk preference behavior. In each case, the outcome of risk-taking is an influencing consideration. Yet risk-taking is justified as a rational behavior. The import of this advice is that risk-taking should be thought through properly and therefore be a carefully considered decision. Dealing with risk in banking equally requires an appreciation of and appropriate response to uncertainty. It is possibly for these reasons that banking reforms in recent times in various emerging economies were intended to address uncertainty, tame the risk-taking appetite of banks, and institutionalize a sound financial system. Banking can be rightly described as a high-risk business after all. For this reason, much attention is directed at risk management in banking. The need for emphasis on risk management becomes even more urgent as banks grapple with large and increasing volumes of nonperforming risk assets.

The emphasis on risk and uncertainty informs two pertinent conceptual questions that I now ask. What do financial experts exactly mean by the terms risk and uncertainty? In what respects are risk and uncertainty comparable, and how do they differ—and how do they impact bank lending processes? The answers to these questions form a basis for the implications of risk and uncertainty for bank lending and management that I highlight throughout this book.

Case Study 2.1

The monster of bank credit risk in emerging economies

Dele Smith—the high-flying manager of the Istanbul metropolis branch of New Trust Bank Limited (NTB)[1]—had been on a winning streak for six consecutive months. During this period, his branch consistently surpassed its monthly budget targets for financial performance and risk asset quality. The branch earned substantial income from lending to large corporate borrowers. Dele never considered playing with a liabilities-driven balance sheet, even as his branch made a strong showing in deposits mobilization.

Evidently he towered over all other branch managers. In the first place, notwithstanding his regular promotions, he was still retained as the manager of the Istanbul metropolis branch. He remained in this position even after he was promoted to assistant general manager—other branch managers were of either manager rank or below. Secondly, his branch was designated a prime and strategic profit center. Thirdly, Dele was the only branch manager who reported directly to an executive director. The rest had their respective regional managers as their bosses.

Soon Dele became the toast of NTB's management and his colleagues alike. He did his utmost to retain this top billing and never rested on his oars. Often the desire to ever be the top star got him constantly thinking of—and searching for—big ticket banking deals. Usually foreign currency—denominated transactions and lending satisfied his craving for substantial earnings to meet budget goals. In this and several other goal-directed ambitious ways, he took responsibility for the smooth running of his branch.

But the crunch was bound to come—and when it did, it caught him off guard! That happened when his branch experienced a hiccup as a result of a fraudulent drawing on a credit facility for KunChem Limited. The company was a large-borrowing corporate customer of the branch. The incident demystified Dele's world of branch banking and management. How he was so easily and roundly beaten this time, at his own game, was the puzzle that investigators of the credit fraud tried to unravel.

Dele was aware that Sanjay, his point man and the CEO of KunChem, traveled out of Istanbul on frequent business trips abroad. A major feature of the account was its high level of transactions activity—even when Sanjay traveled out of the country. The branch earned more than a quarter of its monthly COT income from turnover of transactions in the account. On that fateful day, Dele got a call from Sanjay.

"Hello Dele, this is Sanjay speaking. How are you doing?"

"I'm doing well, Sir, thank you," answered Dele.

"I called to inform you that we urgently need to remit $1.25 million dollars to a major manufacturer of one of our leading products. The company is based here in the US. I just concluded meeting with its export and finance directors. I will e-mail details of the company's account to you so that your bank can wire the money tomorrow. I hope to be back in Istanbul in a week's time."

"Ok, Sir," Dele responded. "Let me see what I can do about your request. But the timing is too urgent considering that your request requires not only executive approval but due diligence," he explained.

"I know you're equal to the task. You've done it for us in the past and I believe you can do it again this time," said Sanjay.

"No problem, Sir. I will do my best," Dele promised. About 30 min later he went to see his line boss—an ED. He discussed the transaction with him but his boss was not convinced.

"Hasn't KunChem fully drawn down on its credit facility?" he asked Dele, who was apparently surprised at the question.

"You're right, Sir. The company has fully utilized the existing facility," answered Dele.

"So what do you want me to do now?" wondered his boss.

"I plan to propose an increase to accommodate the additional borrowing," Dele explained.

"How do you intend to secure the proposed additional lending?" queried his boss.

"We will advise our legal office to up the bank's registered charge on the property securing the existing facility to accommodate the incremental lending. That way, we won't need to treat this request as a new credit facility. After all, its purpose tallies with that of the existing facility," Dele explained to the satisfaction of his boss.

"I think we should bounce our ideas off the MD before we proceed," suggested Dele's boss.

The MD was not comfortable with the idea of conducting a credit transaction over the phone.

"Are you sure that the person who spoke to you on the telephone was Sanjay?" he queried Dele.

"I'm sure he was the one, Sir. I can't mistake his voice," he answered.

"Do you have the telephone number that he used to call you?" the MD asked further.

"Yes I do, Sir," Dele answered.

"In that case, come over here so that you can call and speak to him on the telephone in our presence. Use the speakerphone—and don't forget to ask him to e-mail us a formal request for the loan," the MD instructed.

Dele was obliged to honor the MD's instruction. At the end of the telephone discussion, the MD and ED were convinced.

Back in his office, Dele telephoned KunChem's finance manager to confirm the transaction further.

"Your MD spoke to me on the telephone about an hour ago concerning an urgent incremental borrowing to pay for product supplied from the US. Did he discuss the intended borrowing with you before he traveled?" Dele asked.

"He discussed the underlying transaction with me yesterday. He hinted that he might be requesting funds to execute the transaction from your bank," he explained.

Dele thanked him for his time and hung up.

As agreed, Sanjay sent Dele an e-mail later that day in which he formally applied for the additional $1.25-million credit facility from New Trust Bank. He also promised to e-mail the supplier's account details to Dele the following day when he had concluded the remaining aspects of the deal.

Dele packaged the credit request and adopted the fast track to obtain approval for it. The next day, he received the e-mail that Sanjay promised to send, with details of the account to which the $1.25 million should be transferred. With supporting documents—the credit analysis summary (CAS), MD's approval, collateral analysis report, and e-mail copies of Sanjay's request and disbursement instructions—he sent a memo through his line boss to the treasury office to wire the money.

The treasurer of the bank promptly acted on the memo. Toward the close of work that day, Dele received yet another e-mail from Sanjay giving details of the supplier's account. The account differed from the one he received earlier and to which the bank had already wired the $1.25 million. It was a startling discovery. He called Sanjay immediately on the telephone to clarify the difference.

"Sir, I just read the second e-mail you sent to me about the supplier's account. I notice differences in the two account details. I think there's a mistake somewhere," he guessed.

Sanjay quickly countered him.

"I didn't send two e-mails about the supplier's account details to you. I've sent only one e-mail to you about the account—and that's the one I sent about fifteen minutes ago," Sanjay clarified.

Dele was already sweating profusely in his highly air-conditioned office as he listened to an incredible refutation of their documented communication.

"But Sir, the two e-mails emanated from your e-mail address. I didn't have cause to doubt you at all. As I speak to you, the bank has wired the money with details of the account I received earlier from your e-mail address," he bemoaned.

"What you're telling me is unbelievable, Dele. I never sent the e-mail in question. Why didn't you call me to confirm the mystery e-mail when you received it—just the way you did now?" Sanjay queried in utter disappointment.

That's the big question—and, of course, Dele didn't have an answer to it. He took a deep breath, thanked Sanjay, and hung up. He stormed out of his office and made for the treasurer's office—ostensibly to see if it was possible to cancel and recall the remittance. But, alas, Dele had been caught napping and the fraud had beaten the system.

Hints for Answering This Case Study

Dele Smith ordinarily did a good job of authenticating the credit request—its origin, purpose, collateral, and so on. It could be argued—rightly or wrongly—to this extent that he exercised due diligence. Those who may hold this view might argue that it would be unfair to expect Dele to play God in the failed lending. But this view begs the question. The stark reality is that the bank has lost $1.25 million. That was as curious as it exposed a flawed credit process. It is intriguing that the MD, ED, and Dele—all high-ranking officials of the bank—failed to correctly anticipate the risk embedded in this credit request. The real question is what really skewed their sense of judgment in this lending? Were they hypnotized? Of course, they weren't. Strangely, they flouted the bank's credit policy. Now they cannot but go back to the drawing board and reinvent the bank-wide credit process. I think relationship pressure mired in overzealous disposition was the culprit for the failings in the lending. Ideally, standard credit policy prescribes the mode of disbursement of a credit facility. The usual mode is to permit utilization of a credit through the loan account. But Dele and his bosses bungled it. In my opinion, had Dele adopted proven credit process, outlined below, the fraud could have been averted—or the bank would not have been liable for the loss of the funds:

- Disbursed the credit directly to KunChem's loan account with the bank
- Dele advises Sanjay to send his mandate to wire the funds through his company in Istanbul

- KunChem's accredited official formally presents Sanjay's e-mail mandate, printed on the company's letterhead, to the bank
- Dele compares the e-mail mandate with the one Sanjay had sent to him
- Other authorized signatories to KunChem's account countersign the e-mail mandate
- The e-mail mandate clearly provides details of the US supplier's bank account to which the funds should be wired
- Dele compares account details of KunChem's US supplier with the ones in the e-mail he received from Sanjay
- Checks prove the request to be in order
- NTB debits the funds from KunChem's account and wires same to the supplier as instructed

Questions on the Case Study

1. In what ways can one rightly or wrongly describe the lending in this case study as curious and flawed?
2. In your opinion, how did the mode adopted by Dele in disbursing the loan violate NTB's credit process?
3. **(a)** Why would you agree or disagree that Dele and his bosses failed to correctly anticipate the risk of the credit?
   (b) What do you think really skewed their sense of judgment in the lending?
4. **(a)** Do you think that NTB has a credible credit culture and policy?
   (b) What do you think went awry with the lending—if you answered (a) in the affirmative?
   (c) Which aspects of a standard credit policy were not observed in the lending—if you answered (a) in the negative?
5. Critically defend or oppose the author's opinion that "relationship pressure mired in overzealous disposition was the culprit for the fraud?"
6. **(a)** Who do you suspect of being the mastermind behind the fraud? Your answer should show a clear understanding of the dynamics of the fraud.
   (b) To what cause would you trace the making of the fraud and its success?

1. The setting of this illustration in Istanbul, Turkey and the United States is strictly for learning purposes and does not imply that the two countries were in fact involved in any way in the underlying transaction. In much the same vein, the names used for the company, bank, and individuals in the illustration are imaginary and do not relate to any known or unknown company, bank or persons in Turkey or elsewhere.

DEFINING RISK AND ITS RELATIONSHIP TO UNCERTAINTY

There are numerous definitions of risk in the finance literature. The definitions differ as much as their authors, ostensibly corroborating the lack of a widely accepted view. A common belief is that risk exists when an action has variable outcomes (i.e., its actual and expected outcomes differ). Besides credit risk, banks in emerging economies face a myriad of risks including operational, market, and liquidity risks, among others.

The term *risk*, at first glance, may appear easily understood; yet it is far from straightforward. How can I define risk in such a way that it adequately represents everyone's opinion or understanding of the concept—considering the diversity of life's endeavors and their peculiar risks? Depending on the standpoint from which it is viewed and someone's orientation, the term risk may be defined in various ways. Much in the same vein, some authors hasten to point out that there is no universally accepted definition of risk. This is not as strange as it is justified, as in the foregoing, on the grounds of its diverse applications.

The World Bank (2013) defines *risk* as simply "the possibility of loss" (p. 5) that "can be imposed from outside or taken on voluntarily in the pursuit of opportunities." (p. 61) It categorizes risk into two broad types—systemic and idiosyncratic. While the former "is common to most members of an entire system," the latter "is specific to some members of a system." (World Bank, 2013) The Bank notes that "risk is not all bad, however, because taking risks is necessary to pursue opportunity." Defined as "the possibility of gain," the Bank sees opportunity as "the upside of risk." (p. 11) It notes that "confronting risk, as the possibility of loss, is a burden—but it is also necessary to the pursuit of opportunity." This is because "risk and opportunity go hand in hand in most decisions and actions taken by countries, enterprises, and families as they seek to improve their fate" (p. 5).

Risk is a function of uncertainty, the inability to foresee the future correctly. Uncertainty is more intractable than risk. Unlike risk, there is no proven methodological framework that banks can use to manage it due to its subjective nature. Yet, a bank has to deal with uncertainty, and its adverse effects, in a pragmatic way. Uncertainty is defined as "the situation of not knowing what the outcome will be." (World Bank, 2013, p. 61) This ordinary meaning contrasts with "deep uncertainty," defined as "a situation in which parties to a decision do not know or cannot agree on the key forces that shape the future, the probability distributions of the main variables and parameters in their models, or the value of alternative outcomes." (p. 81) The Bank talked about "the repercussions of extreme instances of lack of information and knowledge—so-called 'deep' uncertainty." (p. 16) People would as well be at risk in investing in a corporate bond as when they buy cars or other assets. The company issuing the bond, on the one hand, may default on its obligation to pay interest and redeem the bond. A newly bought car, on the other, could be stolen or lost to a road accident. These two possible events cannot be foreseen with any degree of exactitude, such as one could have when predicting hunger or sleep. Theft or accidental destruction of the car is a risky event, shrouded in uncertainty. Yet such situations define the order of life in which humankind is entangled as though in a web of misfortune. As a result, there is widespread interest among academics, professionals, and indeed everyone from all walks of life in the making and nature of risk.

In finance parlance, *risk* is usually explained in terms of variability of expected returns. Rational investment decisions are based on expectation of commensurate returns, or cash inflows. However, at the time of commitment of funds, it will not be certain if the expectation will be realized. One reason is that future events on which the expectation depends are uncertain, and can alter forecasts about future outcomes. Thus, risk results from the inability of investors to make forecasts of future cash flows or returns with certainty. An investment will be more or less risky depending on the degree of variability of its expected returns. For two investments, the one with greater variability of expected returns relative to expectation would be riskier than the other.

A generalized functional definition of risk should highlight its key attributes and incorporate the foregoing views. In order to fulfill this need, I proffer a three-pronged definition of the concept of risk. I propound below, and have reflected in Figure 2.1, the three qualifying attributes of risk. I do so believing that the definition that follows will meet a broad spectrum of interests. An event or occurrence should be considered a *risk* or to be *risky* if it:

- creates doubt because possible outcomes of an action may not fulfill expectation;
- threatens the interest of someone, a business, or an organization through exposure to harm, because it is a peril, or because it potentially leads to a loss; and
- can be anticipated, observed, and assessed objectively

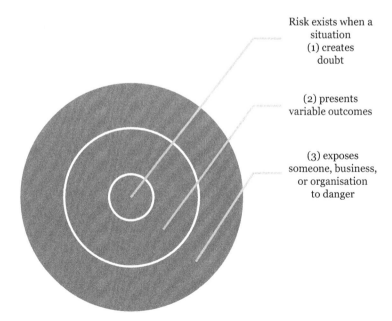

Risk exists when a
situation
(1) creates
doubt

(2) presents
variable outcomes

(3) exposes
someone, business,
or organisation
to danger

FIGURE 2.1 Pictorial depiction of the functional definition of risk.

This definition clarifies the concept of risk for many purposes. It accommodates most of the diverse views of risk commonly found in the literature. It sees risk simply in terms of any situation where there is imperfect knowledge (uncertainty) concerning possible outcomes of an event. Such an event (risk) must be a cause of some loss (if it occurs) to someone, a business, or an organization. But unlike uncertainty, every risk must lend itself to objective analysis and measurement. The high point of this definition is the association between risk and uncertainty that it very clearly brings out. This is significant for the fact that most risks would be easily anticipated and therefore could be prevented in the absence of uncertainty.

Options for risk management include prevention, assumption, and insurance. Unfortunately, while banks assume credit risk and strive to mitigate its adverse effect, they scarcely can fully prevent or insure against it. As a bank cannot do without lending, it must devise effective means to manage credit risk. Effective management of credit risk is imperative for the long-term survival and success of a bank. Risk should be anticipated, measured, and planned for. The three basic approaches to credit risk management are risk identification, risk analysis, and risk mitigation.

The World Bank (2013) emphasizes the need to stay on top of risk and uncertainty. The Bank notes that "the world is constantly changing, and with change comes uncertainty. Amid this uncertainty, people must consider different options for how to prepare for risks they may face." (p. 60) The significance of uncertainty consists primarily in its association with risk. Owing to uncertainty, individuals are incapable of seeing beyond the realm of the present when they make critical decisions that can lead to a loss. This fact underlies the risk and bane of business—an endeavor shrouded in uncertainty. Uncertainty in bank lending is associated with occasional—sometimes untimely—negative influences that, though not quantifiable, affect outcomes for banks and the industry. Such negative influences are usually subjective in nature, and in practice they cause risk and loss. Uncertainty thrives in some form of rational conjecture of events with which a bank must contend. A prognosis of future business upset drives it. This is desirable so long as it encourages positive or proactive action to shield a bank from the adverse effects of a conjectured event if it turns out to be a reality.

COMMON BANKING RISKS IN EMERGING ECONOMIES

This book is all about how to manage bank credit risk well in emerging economies. However, besides credit risk, banks in emerging economies contend with market risk, operational risk, and liquidity risk—all of which the Basel Accords identify as critical—and a host of other risks that are outside the scope of this book. There are a myriad of risks with which bankers in emerging economies tend to be preoccupied. The main risks to which the banks are prone are presented below—showing, where necessary, how they relate to credit risk and possible implications for bank management.

The Basel II Accord clarifies procedures for the calculation of Minimum Capital Requirements under its Pillar 1. Input into the calculation of regulatory capital, under the Pillar 1 framework, comes from the assessments of credit risk, operational risk, and market risk. Pillar 1 seeks to determine regulatory capital that cushions the impact of these three risks. With respect to the three risks, Pillar 1 fulfills the need to assess these particular risks, as indicated in the following summaries.

Credit risk

Pillar 1 of Basel II clarifies how to risk-weight, rate, and provide for risk inherent in bank assets, mainly risk assets (i.e., loans and advances). The credit risk aspect of Pillar 1 encompasses three methodologies that underlie risk weighting, and rating of riskiness, of bank assets to determine regulatory capital: the standardized approach, the internal ratings-based approach, and the securitization framework. These innovative approaches redress the criticisms of the methodology Basel I had adopted for the assessment and rating of the riskiness of bank assets.

Operational risk

Basel II, Pillar 1, devises means to manage operational risk in banking. In order to manage its operational risk, a bank should be able to hedge against the risk of abuse, infringement, or failure of its internal operating system. Issues involved in any discussion of operational risk border more on requirements for effective bank management than in analyzing and managing bank credit risk—and are therefore beyond the scope of this book.

Market risk

Pillar 1 of Basel II advises how to reflect losses that a bank suffers as a result of fluctuations in asset prices. A bank should do this in order to manage market risk. Unmitigated market risk impinges on a bank's financial performance. Thus it has an indirect effect on a bank's lending portfolio. The nature of that effect falls outside the scope of this book.

Liquidity risk

The Basel Committee accords high priority to liquidity risk, a fact that is evident in the manner by which it devoted the whole of Basel III to detailing regulations bordering on liquidity risk management. Often used synonymously with funding risk—liquidity risk could be defined in two different ways as:

1. the danger that a bank may not have sufficient cash or cash inflows, or may not be able to quickly convert assets to cash with little or no resultant loss of value
2. the chances that a bank's operations may be adversely affected by its inability to generate sufficient cash or cash inflows, or to quickly convert assets to cash.

Due to the their great influence over bank lending decisions in emerging markets, liquidity and funding risks are usually taken into account in bank lending calculations.

Default risk

Default risk relates to operational aspects of bank lending and treasury funding. In bank lending—in relation to approving, disbursing, and repaying credit facility—it refers to:

1. the danger that a borrower would be unable to pay back a loan made by a bank, when the loan matures
2. the chance that a borrower may not fulfill one, some or all of the terms and conditions of a loan that a bank has granted it
3. the probability that a borrower will not be able to generate sufficient cash inflows to service and repay a bank loan on its due date.

However, in treasury funding—in relation to deposit transactions, inter-bank dealing and payments—default risk implies the probability that a bank may not be able to pay back a deposit it takes from another bank on its due date or on the agreed terms and conditions.

Repayment risk

This risk relates to operational aspects of bank lending and treasury funding. In bank lending—in relation to credit analysis, administration, and risk management—it refers to:

1. the danger that a borrower may default on a loan (i.e., fail to pay back the loan on the due date) or on the agreed terms and conditions for a loan
2. the chance that a borrower may not generate adequate cash inflows to pay back the loan (i.e., principal plus accrued interest and charges) to a bank on its due date
3. the chance that defaults on one, some, or all of the terms and conditions of a loan may endanger a borrower's ability to pay back a loan (i.e., principal plus accrued interest and charges).

In treasury funding—in relation to paying back deposits, interbank takings, and funds management—it means:

1. the likelihood that a taker (i.e., the bank that has taken a deposit as a placement from another) may default on the taking (i.e., fail to pay it back on its due date or on agreed terms);
2. the chance that a bank that has taken a deposit from a person, company, or organization may default on the deposit (i.e., fail to pay it back on the due date or on agreed terms).

Settlement risk

Usually banks face settlement risk mainly in treasury operations. For example, treasury dealings in the money market involve interbank takings and placements. The funds taken must be paid back on the due date. Thus the activities of money market dealers give rise to settlement risk in terms of the obligation to pay back takings. In much the same vein, depositors' funds must be paid back at maturity. Settlement risk is therefore defined in three different but related senses as:

1. the probability that banks engaged in interbank trading may not fulfill their financial obligations to one another
2. the chance of default on interbank trading obligation of one bank to another or a counterparty
3. the failure of one bank to perform on a mutual agreement that involves the transfer of funds to the other or a counterparty

Banks that don't manage settlement risk well tend to lose goodwill in the money market. The same fate awaits banks that are seen as interbank "net takers." Such banks tend to use takings to settle matured placements with them, thus awkwardly mitigating settlement risk to which it is exposed through the use of new takings rather than by using internal funds. It is dangerous for a bank to be seen in such a bad light.

Counterparty risk

Counterparty risk refers to the possibility of loss resulting from the failure of someone, or an organization, with whom a bank has conducted a transaction, to fulfill its obligation to the bank. In bank lending, the obligor to the bank is the counterparty. Usually the obligor is the borrower to whom the bank has granted a particular credit facility. Thus, counterparty credit risk reflects the chance that the borrower would default on its loan repayment.

Foreign exchange risk

Foreign exchange risk refers to the danger that a bank might lose money on a lending or foreign currency transaction due to unanticipated adverse changes in exchange rates. Due to weak currencies, banks in emerging economies deal with exchange rate issues on a daily basis. In fact, foreign exchange gains or losses occasioned by volatile exchange rates determine, to a large extent, the financial performance of banks in emerging markets. Thus most banks in emerging economies are very active in both official and autonomous foreign exchange markets. Unfortunately, the majority of the issues regulatory authorities have with banks in emerging economies result from sharp practice in foreign exchange markets.

Interest rate risk

There are three possible aspects to the meaning of interest rate risk. In terms of banking in emerging economies, two simplified definitions that shed light on interest rate risk can be proffered as follows:

1. the danger that a bank may lose money on a loan or interbank placement as a result of unexpected adverse changes in the money market interest rate
2. the chance that someone or an organization may lose income on its nonfixed deposit as a result of unexpected adverse changes in interest rates in the money market.

Whether to a bank or its customers, interest rate risk should be anticipated to avoid financial loss on assets. Usually, trend analysis and follow-through come in handy. Diminution of earnings on account of unmitigated money market interest rate risk can be avoided.

Reputational risk

Banks in emerging economies perhaps face the worst and most mind-boggling risk in the form of threats to their reputation as custodians of wealth for both private and public sector investors. Reputational risk takes a great toll on banks in emerging economies. This sad situation is born from the insensitivity of the banks to customer care and breaches of the trust the public reposes in the banks. The banks are especially prone to reputational risk on account of sharp practice. They struggle with mean success to build goodwill on the one hand, but maneuver transactions and regulations, and cook the books, on the other. These acts—often intended to satisfy budget goals—deal a blow to the corporate reputations of the banks. However, while reputational risk has implications for bank management, it does not significantly impact bank lending. Perhaps its greatest negative impact is on deposit mobilization and the liabilities portfolio—both of which are critical for sustaining a bank's liquidity.

Financial risk

Banks in emerging markets have a penchant for applying purchased funds, usually from depositors, as the main plank of finances for their operations.

With barely minimum regulatory capital, the banks hardly trade on equity. This situation defines financial risk for the banks—using more debt than equity to run business operations. Thus financial risk may be defined as the chance that a bank may default on its obligations to its depositors and other creditors, especially in the interbank money market, due to a dearth of funds for operations. With a paucity of cash flow, a bank faced with financial risk may not be able to fulfill its financial obligations—a situation that a flawed financial structure exacerbates. In most cases, the flaw originates in over-dependence on short-term depositors' funds and interbank takings to meet the day-to-day financial obligations of running a bank.

Business risk

In banking, business risk refers to the chance that a bank might not be able to generate sufficient cash flow relative to its operating expenses. This implies that the bank faces the danger that it will find itself in a situation where it is unable to continue to render normal banking services to its customers. In practical terms, a run on a bank evidences the typical outcome from business risk that has snowballed into a treasury crisis. Usually, in nonbanking situations, business risk is understood from two main perspectives as:

1. an adverse occurrence that has a chance of causing damage to commercial operations in which someone, a company, or an organization is engaged
2. the probability that a company may encounter operational setback resulting from the length of its asset-conversion cycle.

In the foregoing contexts, business risk is always a key credit issue in appraising bank loan requests from corporate borrowers. This fact is reflected in the relevant topics in the chapters of this book. In Chapter 9, for example, the asset conversion cycle is discussed and diagrammatically presented to highlight the causes of business risk for a typical small-sized manufacturing company in an emerging economy.

Industry risk

The two distinct but related ways in which industry risk could be defined refer essentially to:

1. the likelihood that an industry may suffer or experience an adverse or harmful incident
2. the danger that an industry may suffer a business or other setback that could adversely affect financial performance of companies or organizations in its sphere

In emerging economies, industry risks that banks face emanate mainly from macroeconomic issues and the actions of banking regulatory authorities.

Bank customers respond to these sources of risk, and in time the whole industry is put into a terrible mess. This happens when a bank fails to put a contingency plan in place to deal with the unintended side effects of regulatory interventions and macroeconomic policies.

Country risk

Country risk is a major cause of concern for bankers in emerging economies. It affects the quality of the risk assets portfolios of banks and the banking system. For this reason, Chapter 1 of this book discusses aspects of country risk issues. Country risk could be defined in four distinct ways as:

1. the adverse conditions in a country that can cause the loss of a credit facility, treasury income, or profit for a bank or business
2. the danger that a bank would lose a credit facility, income, or profit as a result of adverse conditions in a country
3. the possibility that a country where a borrower does business would be a cause of the borrower's default on a loan
4. the chance that a bank may lose principal and interest on a loan as a result of adverse conditions in a country where the borrower operates.

BANK CREDIT RISK MANAGEMENT PROCESS—AN OVERVIEW

Risk management is imperative for the success of a bank. Risk must be anticipated, measured, and planned for at any point in time. Thus, statistical probability is used to measure the likelihood that an event will occur. On the strategy of risk transfer, it's obvious that not all risks are transferable by means of insurance. In fact, most credit risks would not satisfy the characteristics of insurable risks.

Risk management, according to the World Bank (2013) "is the process of confronting risks, preparing for them," (ex-ante risk management) "and coping with their effects" (ex-post risk management). (pp. 12, 61) In its opinion, "the goal of risk management is to both decrease the losses and increase the benefits that people experience when they face and take on risk." It sheds light on how effective risk management may be achieved as it suggests that "risk management needs to combine the capacity to prepare for risk with the ability to cope afterward—taking into account how the up-front cost of preparation compares with its probable benefit." The Bank argues that for risk management to be strong, it should include "knowledge, protection, insurance, and coping." These components of risk management, according to the Bank, "interact with each other, potentially improving each other's quality" (p. 12).

A bank must continually anticipate risk. For practical purposes, it should be able to identify, analyze, and mitigate risk in the course of its operations.

In order to succeed, it should work out and adopt an efficient strategy for risk management. The credit literature, fortunately, is replete with workable lending principles and theories. Regrettably, controversy over appropriate risk management methodology lingers.

Risk varies with credit requests or proposals. It is difficult, if not impossible—for practical purposes—to meaningfully discuss all the risks that credit officers should analyze in all lending situations. What appears practicable is to treat each credit request on its own merits. In fact, most basic credit courses are structured around the need to adopt this lending approach—and, accordingly, trainees are orientated toward it. It would be even more arduous to contemplate any specific pattern of analysis for all risks inherent in all conceivable credit proposals—especially in a book like this that is written for students and practitioners alike.

It is however feasible (as I have demonstrated in this book) to give a generalized taxonomy of the common risks analyzed in most lending situations. Most credit analysts sense risks largely within the five Cs of lending. Yet risks are subsumed in such issues as the borrower's business, market, or industry; finances or operations (liquidity, profitability, asset quality, leverage, and so on); and management, among others.

The three basic processes of or issues in bank lending risk management for credit officers are to identify risk, analyze risk, and mitigate risk as survival, growth, and business strategies, as illustrated in Figure 2.2. I discuss the requirements and implications of each of these risk management tasks in the following sections.

FIGURE 2.2 Pictorial depiction of the basic credit risk management process.

Risk identification

The risks of lending can be innumerable, and sometimes intractable. But there are also riskless loans—in the sense that such loans are more than 100% cash collateralized. In any case, the number, type, and characteristics of risk can only be analyzed meaningfully in the context of specific loans. For this reason, clearing lending doubts begins with risk identification—discovering and knowing the risk, including its structure and incidence.

A particular loan request can be associated with certain risks that the credit analyst must identify in a credit analysis memorandum (CAM). A credit analyst should list as many of the risks as can be conceivably identified, and give an indication of their nature and characteristics. Even when a loan is fully cash collateralized, credit analysis is still necessary. This may sound unusual to nonbankers. But it's defensible on a rational basis. Its import is that every credit request embodies some risk. Thus, credit analysis establishes the risk, and therefore gives meaning to or justifies the cash collateral taken to secure a loan.

In direct lending to finance *working capital* needs, for instance, the analyst should identify such risks as the probability of liquidity stress, cash flow deficiency, income or business volatility, collateral inadequacy, and outright default. If the lending is of the asset-based type, the focus of the analyst should shift to risks subsumed in the *transaction dynamics*, such as possible diversion of funds (that is, the proceeds of the loan) by the borrower, lack of control over the items financed by the bank, the inability of the borrower to secure specific confirmed sales orders, and so on.

In the same vein, there are peculiar risks in lending that finances export transactions, term loans, agricultural production, and indeed any other imaginable type of credit facility.

Risk analysis

The completion of risk identification sets the credit analyst's mind on the real task of lending—risk analysis—seen as an extension of the former. The traditional approach to risk analysis is often geared to identifying and mitigating risks inherent in the so-called five Cs of lending—character, capacity, capital, collateral, and conditions. These factors still remain the superstructure on which banks build risk analysis for lending purposes.

There may be no bank that does not require definite and conclusive statements reflecting a credit analyst's opinion on each of the five Cs in a CAM or other credit report. The analyst's opinions on the five Cs are often embedded in so-called key credit issues in a credit report. Of course, the analyst's judgment is a critical factor for consideration in making the final lending decision.

In risk analysis, the lending officer describes the pattern of incidence of each of the identified risks. For instance, the export finance risk of nonperformance can be analyzed to recognize the fact that the transaction places the responsibility for securing the export contract, obtaining the letter of credit, and arranging for shipment on the borrower. Thus, the main risk of the credit is that the borrower may not be able to or may fail to carry out these duties. However, the lending officer should emphasize the specific risks that can cause nonperformance, such as diversion of disbursed funds, unfavorable spot market prices, sourcing of products that do not meet buyer specifications, and so on.

The lending officer should articulate and precisely analyze all identifiable risks in every loan request. But it's pertinent to go a step further to *evaluate* and, if possible, *quantify* the risks. This involves determination of the magnitude, or estimation of value, of the risks by means of some logical procedure. In project financing, for instance, credit analysts tend to rely on income, balance sheet, and cash flow forecasts to evaluate the risks of a venture. In doing so, they employ the discounted cash flow technique to ascertain the *net present value* (NPV) of the project. This is often complemented with calculation of the project's profitability index, return on investment, and payback period. Each of the calculated values should be related to the bank's standard appraisal criteria to know whether the project should be accepted, rejected, or modified. In each case, the value of risk is represented by the difference between a particular risk acceptance criterion and the applicable calculated value.

However, in conventional lending to formal organizations—companies and institutions that have proper accounting records—the aim of risk analysis is usually to determine long-term solvency and stability of the borrower; the borrower's short-term solvency and liquidity; and profitability and earnings ability of the borrower. Lending officers largely rely on historical financial statements to analyze the risks of this category of borrowers. The values so derived are relative ratios of the variables of the financial statements for at least the immediate past three years. The ratios are considered satisfactory when they compare favorably with industry standards or if they satisfy internal requirements of a bank. I assume that the reader is familiar with financial ratios and do not intend to discuss them any more here other than to mention that banks rely a great deal on them in making lending decisions.

Risk mitigation

Lending officers must suggest at least one way of alleviating any identified credit risk. This is a risk management approach aimed at minimizing the incidence or impact of risk through the adoption of specific measures. In purchase order (PO) financing, for instance, risk can be mitigated as follows:

- Disbursement of loan for direct payment to the supplier of goods
- Domiciliation of proceeds of the PO to the bank

- Requiring the borrower to make a certain minimum equity contribution for the transaction
- Establishing the bank's lien over shipping documents for the goods (in the case of a PO executed on an import arrangement), and so on

Generally, risk is ultimately mitigated when a bank properly structures credit, takes adequate collateral to secure the loan, ensures that perfected security is in place, and effectively monitors the loan and its transaction path.

QUESTIONS FOR DISCUSSION AND REVIEW

1. Do you agree with the view that it is difficult to have a generally accepted definition of risk? In what respects, in your own opinion, are risk and uncertainty comparable, and how do they differ?
2. How do risk and uncertainty influence bank lending in any named emerging economy in Africa or elsewhere?
3. In what ways should lending officers anticipate and mitigate bank credit risk in a typical volatile emerging market?
4. How should risk be identified, analyzed, and mitigated within the framework of a sound bank lending process?
5. Do you think that credit risk can be realistically modeled using some mathematical functions?

REFERENCE

World Bank, 2013. World Development Report 2014: Risk and Opportunity—Managing Risk for Development. World Bank, Washington, DC. http://dx.doi.org/10.1596/978-0-8213-9903-3. License: Creative Commons Attribution CC BY 3.0.

FURTHER READING

Basel Committee on Banking Supervision, 2005. 'International Convergence of Capital Measurement and Capital Standards: A Revised Framework'. Amendment to the Capital Accord to Incorporate Market Risks. Bank for International Settlements, Basel.

Basel Committee on Banking Supervision, 2006. International Convergence of Capital Measurement and Capital Standards: A Revised Framework, as Amended. Bank for International Settlements, Basel.

Basel Committee on Banking Supervision, 2010. Basel III: International Framework for Liquidity Risk Measurement, Standards and Monitoring. Bank for International Settlements, Basel.

Chapter 3

Insights into Bank Credit Risk Issues in Emerging Economies

LEARNING FOCUS AND OUTCOMES

Managing bank lending and credit risk can be likened to the American-type presidential system of government, one that is powered by strong democratic values. In a presidential democracy, power is shared among three tiers of government and protected by clearly defined separation principles. The three tiers—executive, legislative, and judicial—function independently, but under a checks and balances arrangement.

Similarly, the crux of the lending function is usually three-pronged—depicted as the three pillars of credit risk management: credit analysis (pillar 1); credit policy and control—also referred to as credit administration or credit compliance (pillar 2); and loan workout, remediation, and recovery (pillar 3). As in a presidential democracy, these three pillars should function in independent capacities within the dictates of checks and balances rules.

In drawing an analogy between a presidential democracy and credit risk management, a case is made for the institutionalization of oversight of lending in banks in emerging economies. Unfortunately, relationships between the three-pillar functions of credit risk management are scarcely well ordered in

Emerging Market Bank Lending and Credit Risk Control. http://dx.doi.org/10.1016/B978-0-12-803438-5.00003-9

banks in emerging economies—leaving room for avoidable lapses. In some emerging economies, the lapses snowball and cause major credit risk crises.

In this chapter, I profile the nature of the crisis, assess its buildup, and pinpoint the culprits for it. In doing so, I identify the ignominious role of bank management in the festering crisis of credit risk. I introduce how risk impacts credit analysis and decisions, and discuss how credit risk should be anticipated and its impact mitigated within the framework of the credit process. The objective in doing so is to contribute knowledge that would help in the long run to stabilize the banking system and stem future financial crises in emerging economies. The reader will learn about:

- The contemporary profile of credit risk, one that sheds light on the crisis of risk management in bank lending in emerging economies
- How turbulent times contribute significantly to the making of the credit risk crisis in the banks of emerging markets
- How pursuit of bogus earnings, balance sheet growth, and size is inimical to the quality of the asset portfolio of banks in emerging economies
- How reckless lending is intricately mired in excessive risk-taking, both of which render credit risk crisis in banks in emerging economies intractable
- Ways in which bank management and lending officers perpetrate insider abuse in the lending function—and why those acts constitute credit fraud

DEFINING BANK CREDIT RISK CRISIS IN EMERGING ECONOMIES

As a business, banking has its own inherent risks. But it is sometimes bedeviled by excessive risk-taking. Risks in banking originate in the use of depositors' funds to trade in the financial market. Since a bank cannot avoid risk in the conduct of its operations, it must formulate appropriate risk acceptance criteria. Striking the right balance between risks it takes and returns it expects enhances success. One of the ways a bank can strike the right balance is to take moderate risk and tame its budget goals concurrently.

Credit risk arises when banks create earning assets (i.e., loans and advances) through lending to borrowers. They do so in pursuit of their budget goals—especially to achieve their earnings targets. While a bank cannot do without lending, it must devise effective means to manage credit risk well. Effective management of credit risk is imperative for the long-term survival and success of the bank.

It is incredible, though hardly surprising, that the credit risk crisis is snowballing. Like a raging forest fire, this canker of bank distress and failure has remained wild—apparently defying solution. The problem has confounded financial system regulations and the internal control systems of banks. It has especially humbled bank management and regulators. In this way, credit risk holds industry stakeholders for ransom. The financial system continues to struggle with the monster of credit risk crisis in what appears to be a losing battle. This situation sheds light on the foundation of the topic of this chapter, in which I introduce the creation of and forces behind credit risk crisis in banks of emerging markets.

I discern the plight of ordinary people whose life savings are trapped each time a bank fails. I am challenged, in doing so, to think of a concrete contribution that I could make toward solving the problem. What problem? What solution? And for what and whose benefit? The problem relates to inefficient bank lending. My thoughts on a solution border on how to improve the quality of lending decisions in banks in emerging economies. If the quality of lending decisions is improved, loan losses will be reduced, liquidity crises would be stemmed, and bank failures would be checked. People and businesses will regain confidence in the industry, and society at large will be set on the path of progress.

The problems of the banking industry became exacerbated and peaked in the aftermath of the global financial meltdown of 2007−2009. The monster—credit risk—continues to ravage and take its toll on banks and the financial system. In this book, I discuss issues in credit risk crisis and management in emerging economies. Unfortunately, the state of the industry shows that some of the operators have not learned from past mistakes. Neither does the situation give hope that they are willing to turn over a new leaf. As usual, they are obsessed with meeting budget goals. Like the infamous banks, they do so in a reckless manner that is evident in excessive risk-taking. This has been the greatest undoing of the industry, one that defines its perennial crisis. Notwithstanding the seeming hopelessness of the situation, I build this book on a positive outlook for the future.

Case Study 3.1

Trust v. Character of Borrower—Which Would You Cast Your Lot with?

Jamiu Yusuf runs a firm of general contractors in a lively ASEAN city.[1] His company, YanGaun Contractors Limited (YGC), is popular and wins a chunk of the juicy contracts awarded by government ministries, parastatals, and agencies. It operates ultra-active current accounts with a number of banks in the city. Banks covet its account mainly because of its strong ability to generate float deposit. It's easy for the company to achieve this feat because the name "YanGaun" opens doors in high places—especially among politicians. However, Social Change Bank Limited (SCB) controls over 60% of YGC's current account transactions. It has accounts in two of the bank's branches in the city.

YGC started chasing a major contract worth $500 million with one of the ministries. Jamiu intimated to Aisha, who managed the regional office of SCB in the city, of the contract. He did so when she visited him in his office. She regularly made routine calls to the company. On this occasion, Jamiu was overly happy as he discussed with Aisha the prospect of winning the contract.

"I expect that the purchase order (PO) for the contract would be ready this week," he told Aisha, laughing loudly.

"That would be great," she responded, smiling.

"I can't wait to see yet another huge inflow into YanGaun's account," she said.

"It's as good as done, I assure you," Jamiu boasted. "I will give you details of the contract when I receive the PO—hopefully this week."

"But while I wait for the details, may I ask what the contract is all about—so that I can tune my mind to it ahead of the PO," Aisha requested.

"Oh, cool! No problem at all. I will tell you right away," Jamiu said and paused. "I'm sorry, Aisha," he apologized. "I think, on second thought, that I shouldn't let the cat out of the bag at this time," he said. "Just exercise patience. You will know everything about the contract—and actually take our proposal for its funding to your bank next week," he assured her.

"It's alright, Sir," said Aisha. "As you know, I always have confidence in you. I don't think that this transaction will be an exception. Just keep me duly informed about the transaction," she requested.

YGC eventually won the contract. It was a project for the computerization of the Ministry. It involves supply, installation, and maintenance of various IT hardware and software. Jamiu personally collected the PO from the permanent secretary's office. He did not waste any time in inviting Aisha to his office to break the good news to her. He gave her a letter of application for the $250 million that YGC urgently needed in order to procure the hardware and software components.

"I hope that your bank will be fast in approving our request?" he asked as he handed a copy of the PO to her.

"Yes, of course. We don't waste time on this sort of self-liquidating lending," she answered.

Aisha was excited as she thanked Jamiu and left his office. When she returned to her office, she quickly wrote her call memo:

"...My marketing today," she informed, "yielded fruit. It's possible that we will get a huge cash inflow in a lump sum from a contract that one of our valued customers, YGC, has been chasing in the Ministry. From my discussions with the customer, we should receive the inflow next week," she concluded.

She sent the call memo to her boss and a copy to their line executive director. Thereafter she started writing a credit analysis memorandum (CAM) for the proposed PO financing facility. She packaged the credit request accordingly for approval. Public sector credit proposals like this do not necessarily have to go through the credit committee. They normally follow a fast-track credit process that bypasses the rigor of credit presentation, debate, and defense at credit committee meetings.

The bank's offer letter was ready and delivered to YGC three days after Jamiu gave Aisha the company's application for the loan.

"Congrats Jamiu," Aisha said warmly. "Here you go." She handed him a letter containing the bank's offer of the contract finance facility to YGC.

"Thank you very much, Aisha," responded Jamiu as he stretched out his hand to collect the offer letter from her. "I'm happy at this outcome. It shows how committed you are to our banking transactions and requests. I assure you that we will not disappoint you and your bank," he promised.

"Jamiu, as I've always told you, SCB will do everything possible to satisfy your banking needs—for as long as you remain one of the bank's loyal and trusted customers," responded Aisha. "You will notice when you read the offer letter that collateral for the loan is domiciliation of payment on the contract in YGC's account with the bank, and your personal guarantee. Please ensure that you accept the offer letter and fulfill all the conditions of the loan," she requested.

As Aisha requested, the company accepted the offer letter and returned a copy of it to the bank the following day. Jamiu personally returned the accepted offer letter to the bank.

"Here you are, a copy of your bank's offer letter duly accepted by us," he said to Aisha as he handed her the letter.

It fulfilled all the conditions precedent to drawdown, including security documentation. The bank disbursed the loan according to the dynamics of the transaction. Aisha tenaciously monitored the procurement and delivery of the items to the Ministry to ensure proper utilization of the loan. She was only relaxed when the delivery and installation of the hardware and software were completed.

The Ministry would pay for the PO not later than 60 days from the date of its certification of completion of the contract. Aisha kept a close tab on YGC so as to know when the Ministry would pay for the PO. On occasion, she went to the Ministry to nose around for the same purpose. But her contact in the Ministry was a middle-level staff member who mightn't have been privy to payment arrangements for such a big contract.

Eventually the Ministry issued a certified check for $500 million in favor of SCB for the account of YGC, as full payment on the PO. Jamiu collected the check. However, he lodged it in YGC's account in a branch of the bank different from the regional office that processed, secured approval, and obtained financing for the contract—whose manager was Aisha.

As instructed by Jamiu, SCB transferred the money to YGC's account at another bank when the check cleared. His intention in doing so was to turn the funds over in YGC's business for one month, at the end of which the PO finance facility would be due for repayment. He could do this because he was able to muscle the Ministry to pay the PO in a record 30 days from the date of certification of contract execution.

Hints for Analyzing This Case Study

The characterization of Jamiu Yusuf as an influential customer vis-à-vis his diversion of the loan proceeds in the foregoing case study is quite instructive. The case demonstrates what often occurs when managing credit relationships with influential but dishonest borrowers. Unfortunately, Aisha was uncritical of Jamiu's character, as she took it for granted. In doing so, to my mind, she laid herself open to charges of negligence. But the root of the problem of the loan was her failure to know when Jamiu collected the check. She shouldn't have "relaxed when the delivery and installation of the hardware and software were completed." Aisha did a good job of tenaciously monitoring "the procurement and delivery of the items to the Ministry to ensure proper utilization of the loan." But failing in her commitment to keep "a close tab on YGC so as to know when the Ministry would pay for the PO" was her undoing. The domiciliation of payment agreement was vulnerable to manipulation—and Jamiu promptly exploited it. In the final analysis, it's the character of the borrower that's at issue in most lending situations and loan default cases. For this reason, lending officers should not take the character of any borrower for granted. Good character must be consistent—not occasional or one-off—if anything.

Questions on the Case Study

1. Would you say that Jamiu really defaulted considering that he wanted to "turn the funds over in YGC's business for one month, at the end of which the PO finance facility would be due for repayment?"

   In what ways did the identified actions of SCB, YGC, and the Ministry contribute to the fate of the contract finance facility?

2. In your opinion, should SCB indict and punish Aisha on account of the following?

   (a) Poor investigation of Jamiu Yusuf's character

   (b) Failure to know when the Ministry issued the check for the contract

3. What do you think was the main reason Aisha failed to know when the Ministry issued the check?

4. Do you think that the Ministry acted in good faith when it released the check for payment on the contract to Jamiu Yusuf rather than to the bank? Your answer should take cognizance of the following facts:

   (a) A tripartite domiciliation of payment agreement to which the Ministry was a signatory was in place.

   (b) The Ministry issued and crossed the check in favor of the YGC account with Social Change Bank Limited.

---

1. The use of ASEAN in this case study serves an illustration purpose only—to bring out the lessons more clearly and in a natural, real world setting. While the case study typifies some real world credit risk issues which banks in emerging economies have to deal with, it does not imply that it actually took place in the ASEAN region or any of the countries in its fold. Also, the names used for the company, bank, and individuals in the illustration are imaginary and do not relate to any known or unknown company, bank, or persons in ASEAN countries or elsewhere.

THE STATE OF BANKS LENDING AND CREDIT RISK CRISIS IN EMERGING ECONOMIES

The financial crisis of 2007—2009—more commonly referred to as the global financial meltdown—shook the foundations of financial centers around the world. But it originated in failings in credit risk management. While the crisis ravaged the global economy, its key lesson was a pointer to the weakness of risk management in global banks in emerging economies. It proved that the banks needed to sharpen their risk management techniques in forthcoming years. Above all, it challenged banking practitioners and regulators to brace themselves for the daunting task of continually keeping an eye on risk—holding it in check. Even as they do so, it is nonetheless difficult to completely keep risk at bay.

The reality is that banking can never be devoid of risk. Bankers must be conscious of this fact and carefully formulate their risk acceptance criteria accordingly. The era of deliberately chasing transactions with so-called *bankable* risks is over. Inadvertently, that risk-taking disposition elevated moneymaking lending to the top of management priorities at the expense of building quality assets. But it turned out to be an error of judgment, and banks in emerging economies paid dearly for it. Growing portfolios of nonperforming assets plunged many banks into liquidity crisis and distress. Some banks—those that could not withstand the pressure—even failed. Thus, the way banks in emerging economies manage risk determines whether they will succeed or fail in the long run.

A bank that seeks to manage risk well—and therefore hopes to succeed in the long run—should strike a balance between its appetite for risk and the earnings goal it is pursuing. While the bank should not be risk averse, it shouldn't adopt a risk preference disposition, either. This point becomes more meaningful in appreciating the inverse relationship between *risk* and *return*. There is always a trade-off between these two possible business outcomes: a higher risk tends to result in more profit and vice versa. In banking, strictly speaking, I extend this relationship to imply that the more a bank achieves and retains liquidity (less risk), the less it gains in profitability (less returns) and vice versa. A bank would strike the right balance and be likely to succeed in the long run when it takes moderate risk and tames its budget goals. The risk—return principle is instructive, and failing to observe it, or the inability to balance it, could be a recipe for financial disaster.

The World Bank (2013) states the foregoing point more succinctly. The Bank argues that "when risks are taken on voluntarily in pursuit of opportunity, another trade-off emerges: expected returns must be weighed against the potential losses of a course of action." This risk-taking behavior has a fundamental basis on which the Bank sheds light. The trade-off in risk-taking, according to the Bank, "is intensified when a higher return is possible only if more risk is accepted." This is not surprising as it "is often the case with financial investments, where a lower yield is characteristic of a more secure position, and higher yields with riskier positions" (p. 10).

A bank takes credit risk when it grants a loan with the expectation that the borrower should utilize the loan according to agreed terms and conditions—and ultimately repay the loan on its due date. Usually, repayment of the loan is expected from some cash flow projection that may or may not be realized. Uncertainty of cash flows notwithstanding, the bank must pay back customers' deposits that fund its loan portfolio—on demand, at short notice, or on due dates. Risk, in this case, is the chance that borrowers may default whereas depositors must be paid their deposits on or before due dates. This situation often arises where assets and liabilities are mismatched, and as a result a bank may fund only some of its deposit maturities payments from loan repayments. But it happens more frequently when there is a deficiency in deposit inflows, an unsustainable default in loan repayment, or a situation where unusually large cash withdrawals exist or persist for a long time.

A bank should always be cautious about the risks it takes—it should anticipate, measure, and plan for them. Banking reforms in recent times in many emerging economies were intended to tame the risk-taking appetite of banks and institutionalize a sound financial system. Unfortunately, uncertainty—another variable that also affects banking outcomes—is more intractable than risk. Unlike risk, there is no proven methodological framework that banks can use to identify, quantify, analyze, or mitigate uncertainty. For this reason, it is widely believed that uncertainty is a necessary evil, ostensibly defying solution.

Yet, a bank has to deal with uncertainty and its adverse effects one way or the other. This is because uncertainty plays a decisive role in banking business and outcomes. The regulatory authorities require every bank to formulate, adopt, and implement specific contingency master plans to deal with uncertainties that affect the industry. It is understandable that regulators lay emphasis on contingency management. They do so to underscore the need for effective response to uncertainty, and to complement the survival strategies of banks.

BANK CREDIT RISK PECULIARITIES
OF EMERGING MARKETS

Often the trend and process of the buildup of credit risk crisis differ from one bank to another. The underlying factor in the observed differences—one that determines the momentum of the crisis and its remedy—is usually the character of bank management. Is bank management disposed to build and sustain a quality lending portfolio? Does it pay lip service to oversight of lending? Will it want to commit itself to shunning reckless lending? These are some questions to ask in order to feel the force and effects of the criticized character of bank management in the making of credit risk crises in emerging markets.

It is possible in some cases for bank management to detect, acknowledge, and strive to address the buildup of a credit risk crisis. In doing so, it can respond to the crisis with appropriate internal risk management contingency measures. Unfortunately, rarely does bank management in emerging markets take the initiative and act in this manner. In most cases, credit risk crises in recent history have caught bank managements off guard, if anything. In Nigeria, for example, the situation worsened with the heady atmosphere of the nineties, which lingered into the twenty-first century, following the deregulation of banking business during the mid-eighties. Certainly, the architects of the government's economic reforms in the eighties would never have imagined that a liberalized banking industry would breed an intractable crisis—especially in the lending function.

Due to lack of diligence, bank management in several emerging economies was oblivious to the buildup of crisis. This underscores the need for bank management to always stay on top of things. Often the road to credit risk crisis builds on breaches of internal credit policy over time. The process of remedying the crisis is always painfully harsh and usually demands some urgency. One of the painful measures that regulators enforce to arrest credit risk crisis is to compel bank management to clean up its act. Besides, the regulatory authorities could—and indeed do—fire bank managements, revoke banking licenses, and prosecute indicted bank officials. They perform these actions in the exercise of their oversight powers.

The rank-and-file employees of banks feel the pinch when they lose their jobs, their allowances are stopped, or their salaries are cut—in a desperate bid to regain liquidity and cash flows by banks in distress. Usually customers have had more than their fair share of fallout of credit risk crisis. Often this happened where the authorities forced banks to charge off terminally bad loans from their risk assets portfolios. In Nigeria, for example, those banks that survived the onslaught of regulatory intervention in 2009 to return sanity to the industry reported huge operating losses, or sharp reductions in earnings, that year. Some of the banks posted similar figures in 2010 and 2011 as well.

Now the question is what manner of factors would result in such a buildup to the observed crisis? It is on this question that I now focus—isolating the factors that underlie bank credit risk crisis in emerging markets.

Overambitious budget goals

Many critics scorn reported earnings of banks in emerging markets. They hold that the earnings are mere paper profits, ostensibly to underscore the inconsistency between earnings and the perennial liquidity pressure that characterizes the operations of the banks. How in the world, were the reported earnings to be real, would banks—in pursuit of liquidity—be desperate about having customers beat a path to their door? In doing so, unfortunately, they unwittingly—presumably—expose their marketing officers to untold abuses. Inordinate pursuit of budget goals, implied in the foregoing, also has adverse side effects on the lending function. This is largely seen, for example, in reckless lending and excessive risk-taking to meet profit targets. But it is also a major factor in accounting for illegal lending and—to some extent—abuse of insider credit facilities.

The massive sacking, retrenching, and retiring of employees across banks in Nigeria between 2009 and 2012—the largest in recent history—betray the fact that reported earnings of the banks were unfounded, dubious, or highly suspect. In most cases such actions render the reported earnings hollow, if anything. But bank management remains adamant—committed to defending bogus financial performance and reports. It could do anything, under the circumstances, but relent in prodding credit and marketing staff into doing everything possible to meet earnings and deposit targets. At the root of this carefree banking attitude is the monster of overambitious budget goals. Perhaps the wanton pursuit of budget goals by bank management to the detriment of quality assets reached its crescendo in 2009 as the global financial meltdown was underway.

Regular bank examination by officials of Central Bank of Nigeria and the NDIC showed that reported earnings of some banks could not be defended in terms of their asset size and quality. The situation prompted the CBN governor to issue a stern warning in 2009 to CEOs of banks. The governor had advised that it was better for banks to report losses than to cook the books and mislead the public. He warned that while it was not illegal to post real losses, it was a criminal offense to doctor the books in order to post unfounded earnings. Now bankers in Nigeria are left in no doubt about the determination of the CBN to criminalize falsification of financial reports.

Unfortunately, bank managements have reduced competition for market leadership to a bank's standing in terms of bogus earnings, balance sheet growth, and size. Scarcely do they pay equal attention to the quality of risk assets—the lending portfolio—and the earnings that those assets generate. Banks eagerly pursue the false driving forces behind rankings on financial performance. In doing so, they are often pressured to engage in unprofessional conduct. The ignominious act is usually observed in cases where books of accounts—financial statements and annual reports of banks—are just window dressing. It also obtains in situations where banks cook the books and compel their auditors to fall into line.

It remains incredible to the purists that Intercontinental Bank, Oceanic Bank, Bank PHB, Afribank, and Spring Bank—to mention but a few—were distressed even as they were reporting strong financial performance! That was before the CBN sacked the boards of the banks in 2009. Interim management boards, which the CBN constituted for the banks, supplanted the sacked boards. Ironically, the stocks of the banks were also doing well on the Nigerian Stock Exchange up to the time the CBN declared them terminally distressed.

The public had been led through this deceptive banking for too long before the CBN clamped down on erring bank management. In supporting the CBN's action, the purists posit that no amount of price paid to sanitize the banking industry should be considered too much—no matter whose ox is gored. Banks should learn to operate by the rules. In doing so, they should keep their craze for profit under control in submission to the professional conduct that their calling demands.

In pursuit of budget goals in the era of universal banking, for example, banks were a bit incautious in investing in their subsidiaries. They compromised on their lending principles. The case of pre-2009 Union Bank of Nigeria PLC, which lent money to some of its subsidiaries to buy its shares so as to meet recapitalization requirements, was both instructive and typical. This aberration in the credit process happened under different guises in other banks. How else can one explain why nationalized Afribank (Nigeria) PLC invested depositors' funds toward acquiring controlling equity interest in African Petroleum PLC?

Turbulent times

Economic volatility impacts credit risk crises. Borrowers occasionally contend with harsh economic realities that weaken their cash flows and loan repayment ability. In time, the borrowers start to default on their loans. In most cases, the workings of economic cycles ensure that instability of business operations marks certain stages of those cycles. Thus, individuals and corporate borrowers are often exposed to recurrent upheavals that constrain their loan repayment abilities. This is particularly evident in emerging market economies.

The fate of borrowers in volatile business environments—mainly those in emerging economies—informs the credit risk crises that might befall banks. In turbulent times, business transactions become unusually risky, while the bases of financial projections are flawed—rendering outlook for the future bleak. Even when loans are adequately secured with tangible collateral, it would be difficult to dispose of the underlying assets. In the case of unsecured loans, a hoped-for loan repayment or recovery hangs in the balance. This situation, one that bank managements in emerging economies occasionally face, compounds the liquidity pressure inherent in the nature of the banking business.

In some cases, even so-called transaction-based credit facilities—the hallmark of which is their self-liquidating feature—may not be spared. One reason is that such credits thrive on robust transaction dynamics founded on predictable outcomes. Unfortunately, such outcomes are a far cry from what occurs in turbulent times. Another reason relates to the size of the portfolio of self-liquidating loans. In most cases, this category of loans accounts for a negligible proportion of a bank's lending portfolio. In fact, the bulk of a bank's lending portfolio carries varying levels of credit risk that are alien to the principle of self-liquidating loans. With the increasing sophistication of business activities as well as credit fraud, risk management in bank lending in emerging economies will continue to take center stage for a long time. Poor management of credit risk portends dire consequences for a bank. It is now common knowledge that credit risk is linked with liquidity risk after all. The fact of this view is evident in recent cases of failed banks in Nigeria and elsewhere.

Banks typically faced turbulent times in the aftermath of the 2007–2009 global financial meltdown. Many businesses went under. Even in leading advanced countries like the United States and UK, corporate survivors requested bailouts. The US government responded with a bailout for some companies in strategic industries—including banks. In the UK, the government also intervened with a financial bailout of key banks. The situation fanned out the credit risk crisis beyond the banks, as the meltdown rubbed off on borrowers in varying degrees. Incidentally, it is generally believed that reckless lending by banks in the United States triggered the global financial meltdown that threatened the foundation of financial markets across the globe.

The authorities and analysts pointed accusing fingers to unguarded transactions in financial derivatives. Derivatives—the conversion of credit facilities into financial instruments (i.e., paper assets) in which the public could and does invest—served short-term liquidity and balance sheet needs of banks. But the practice snowballed into crisis when the assets backing the instruments turned out to be suspect and of poor quality. This informed the credit risk crisis that the banks faced at the time. Regulators turned their attention more than ever before to derivatives and loan securitization in the aftermath of the financial meltdown. The problem at issue—how to tame the engineering of exotic financial products—has unusually taxed the ingenuity of regulators.

CULPRITS FOR BANK CREDIT RISK CRISIS IN EMERGING MARKETS

Light can be shed on four main factors—reckless lending, excessive risk-taking, credit fraud, and insider abuse—as culprits for bank credit risk crises in emerging markets. In the following discussion, I highlight the features of these factors and how they constrain the effectiveness of bank management.

Reckless bank lending

On occasion reckless lending has plunged a bank into a credit risk crisis. In extreme situations, the crisis has overwhelmed bank management and incapacitated banking operations. One symptom of the crisis manifests itself in the form of liquidity pressure. Often poor-quality asset portfolios inform and exacerbate the crisis. Reckless lending is usually deliberate! It is perpetrated in the pursuit of some goal without bothering about the possible adverse consequences to the bank.

This is ironic—considering that the goal in question could be positive and meant to advance the cause of the bank. The puzzle of how an action taken in the interest of a bank could be adjudged to be inimical to the bank defines the irony. The flip side of reckless lending is that it may serve the personal or selfish interests of directors or other executives to the detriment of the bank. It is in this context that one may appreciate why the act of reckless lending persists.

Diligent and committed bank management will not want to indulge in reckless lending. This work behavior disposes it toward lending decisions that serve the interests of the bank. In time the bank would build a quality risk assets portfolio. On the other hand, self-serving bank management would rather institutionalize a culture of arbitrary lending. Doing so inadvertently compounds the crisis of credit risk.

Credit officers perpetrate reckless lending in various ways, but a few of these are especially instructive. A typical example is when a bank grants loans to its subsidiaries in pursuit of some nonbanking interests. In this case, lending officers would be compelled to compromise themselves and their principles. One reason is that such lending is usually packaged, offered, accepted, and disbursed in disregard of lending policy and the credit process. Another reason is that loans in this category are usually unsecured. Where there is collateral at all, it is often imaginary—just to make believe that the loan is secured and satisfies legal documentation. A third reason is that the bank, as a holding company to the borrower, is really indirectly the obligor for the loan.

In Nigeria, this implies that the bank lent money to itself in order to conduct a nonbanking transaction in contravention of Banks and Other Financial Institutions Act No. 25 of 1991 (as amended). Were bank examiners and regulators to uncover and confront lending officers about the credit, those officers would most likely claim that they were boxed in. But it would be extremely difficult for them to make such an excuse. So they must find an alternative explanation, one that absolves them of blame. Interestingly, bank management would want to lay the act at the door of the board of directors. Again, like the lending officers, it wouldn't want to incur the wrath of the directors.

Experienced bank examiners and regulators would want to get to the root of the matter—and do so discreetly. Of course, they realize that they should do anything but trump up charges against bank management or the lending officers. Usually, as would be expected under the circumstances, horse-trading ensues from the conflicting needs of the regulators and bank. But there is always a uniting cause for bank management and lending officers. They would put up a common front—sinking their differences so as to explain and defend the lending transaction before the examiners and regulators.

Bank management, on the one hand, may see criticized lending to its subsidiary simply as a sharp practice, but regulators would on the other hand regard it as a breach of professional duty. Where bank examiners have teeth, they will not bow to possible pressure from bank management. Ideally they should also not be cowed into compromising themselves. Based on the reports of examiners, regulators may impose a particular sanction on the erring bank. The sanction should be severe enough to serve as a deterrent to other banks in addition to the offender.

Excessive risk-taking in bank lending

Often in bank lending, recklessness is intricately mired in excessive risk-taking. These two criticized attributes of the contemporary lending function combine to render credit risk crisis in banks intractable. It would seem that excessive risk-taking is more problematic than reckless lending. But there shouldn't be a choice of one in preference to the other. In truth, the two negative lending attributes should be avoided like the plague. Doing otherwise would be tantamount to choosing between the devil and the deep blue sea.

Concentration of credit in particular sectors of the economy is one of the fallible lending practices in which excessive risk-taking manifests itself.

Another criticized practice is deliberate disregard for the principle of single-obligor limit. Disregard for single-obligor limit has been the bane of bank management of late. Several other flawed lending practices—besides credit concentration and flouting of single-obligor limit—accentuate the credit risk crisis for banks in emerging economies.

Bank management often portrays credit concentration—especially in key industries such as the energy (oil and gas) sector—as strategic, but nothing could be further from the truth. A bank should strive to spread its credit exposure, with painstaking attention to risk mitigation. It can do so by planning its lending in a way that enables it to grant and secure risk-mitigated loans to borrowers in different target markets. The purpose of this credit risk management strategy is that a bank should be able to avoid portfolio concentration risk.

Three possible lending situations can give rise to concentration risk. A bank is exposed to concentration risk if it holds its risk assets portfolio in particular economic sectors, when a few large borrowers make up its loan portfolio, and when its risk assets portfolio comprises few types of credit facilities. The risk in question is the probability that the bank's operations might be impaired by a liquidity crunch or plunged into crisis. In the foregoing sense, concentration risk is completely antithetical to risk diversification. In bank lending, the latter is both the alternative and solution to the former—and always desirable. A bank will diversify its credit portfolio risk when it grants different types and amounts of loans to various borrowers in different target markets, industries, or economic sectors.

One gets the impression that bank management and lending officers often feel boxed in. Lending officers' tendency to justify excessive risk-taking on the grounds of this excuse has become commonplace. At face value, critics may feel that nothing could be further from the truth. But there is some truth in the excuse. I think that such a complaint should be judged on its merits. Of course we can't just wish away the undue interference of vested interests in the credit process.

I don't think that a situation where bank management or lending officers feel or actually are boxed in will ever do any good. The regulatory authorities should devise a means to check for incapacitation of the credit process in this or other ways. It is no good hoping to achieve a sound banking system in the midst of frustration with banking regulation. My take on this issue is rather simple and straightforward. Banking regulators in emerging markets should empower bank management and lending officers to boldly tell vested interests that their hands are tied. And bank management and lending officers should do so rather than complain that they feel boxed in.

This might sound a bit difficult considering that the vested interests usually hold most of the aces in influencing lending decisions that border on excessive risk-taking. In most cases, they are employers of bank management—and, of course, the lending officers. I think that legal protection for victimized members of bank management and lending officers will go a long way toward checking the influence of the vested interests in the credit process.

Taking Nigeria as an example, there is a further cause for optimism. Some of the recent banking reforms in the country will hopefully address the problem of vested interests in bank lending. The notable reforms include the following:

- Increased capitalization requirement
  This policy forced all but the foreign banks in Nigeria to go public. The weak banks were acquired while others either merged or went solo to meet the required capitalization. In order to go public, the indigenous banks sought and obtained quotation on the Nigerian Stock Exchange.
- Tenure of office for bank CEOs
  Fixing the tenure of office for chief executive officers of banks to a maximum term of 10 years will help to check overbearing CEOs who see the office they occupy as their birthright—perhaps because of their majority shareholdings in the banks, either directly or through cronies.
- Constitution of the boards of banks
  The proposal to professionalize the constitution of boards of directors of banks in Nigeria is a welcome development. In line with this proposal, board members should not necessarily be major shareholders or their nominees. On the contrary, they should be individuals with professional banking backgrounds.
- Prosecution of indicted bank executives
  The indictment and prosecution of executives of seven banks,[2] to all intents and purposes, is serving as a deterrent to current and future members of bank management

With committed implementation of the foregoing reforms, the public has at last started to see the light at the end of the tunnel.

ILLEGAL LENDING AND CREDIT FRAUD

There are basically two aspects to the question of illegal lending and credit fraud. The first relates to the manner in which lending officers package, propose, and endorse otherwise weak credit proposals for approval. The second concerns bank management that willfully creates fictitious assets in the bank's loan book in order to satisfy some regulatory or other internal purpose. Chapter 28 of this book deals extensively with the first aspect. The second aspect presents a more difficult problem of analysis by reason of its criminalization in the banking laws. It is largely for this reason that efforts by the

---

2. The banks were Afribank, Bank PHB, FinBank, Intercontinental, Oceanic Bank, Spring Bank and Union Bank.

regulatory authorities to detect it often fall through. Usually bank management perpetrates the fraud surreptitiously. Often it covers its tracks by falsifying and carefully handling documents relating to the assets. This curious finding—common to most failed banks in emerging economies—is established through the investigation of banks.

Insider abuse

The problem of insider abuse features under various topics in this book largely because of its profound link to credit risk crisis in emerging economies. It is discussed, in each case, to underscore the relevant problem at issue. It is a condemnable act, one that bankers must shun. On grounds of moral rectitude, bank management should not only distance itself from insider abuse but strictly uphold the spirit of best lending practices. This implies that it should defend, rather than abuse, the internal lending policy and credit process. In doing so, it acquires the moral strength to enforce professional conduct down the cadres of employees in the lending function. On the other hand, if bank management is bereft of scruples, it will lack the moral standing to discipline morally bankrupt lending officers. In such a situation, it becomes the exception rather than the rule to observe lending policy, let alone fulfill the credit process.

QUESTIONS FOR DISCUSSION AND REVIEW

1. How do CEOs of banks contribute to the crisis of credit risk? Your answer should bear reference to decided court cases on allegations of professional misconduct that the CBN leveled against executives of some failed banks in Nigeria in 2009.
2. **(a)** Critically appraise the role of lending officers in the creation of credit risk crises in banks of emerging economies.
   (b) In what ways can account officers and relationship managers help bank management to stem the crisis of credit risk?
3. **(a)** In what sense does pursuit of budget goals inform the contemporary approach of banks to the marketing of credit products?
   (b) What factors underscore the view that banks tend to drive lending along the lines of overambitious budget goals?
4. How could competition for market leadership based on bogus earnings, balance sheet growth, and size be inimical to the quality of the asset portfolios of banks? Justify your answer with reference to the fate of any two named failed banks in Nigeria.
5. **(a)** Why would you agree or disagree with the view that reckless lending is usually deliberate?
   (b) How does the fact that reckless lending is intricately mired in excessive risk-taking render credit risk crisis in banks intractable?

6. Are there situations in which credit concentration would realistically be considered strategic to a bank's business?
7. **(a)** Are financial analysts justified in pointing accusing fingers at regulators in accounting for the crisis of credit risk in banks?
   (b) How, notwithstanding supervision, would the condition of a bank deteriorate to a level where failure becomes imminent?
8. **(a)** Do you think that recent banking reforms in Nigeria will address the problem of vested interests in bank lending?
   (b) In what sense can you argue that the reforms truly give cause for optimism about the possibility of seeing the light at the end of the tunnel?

REFERENCE

World Bank, 2013. World Development Report 2014: Risk and Opportunity—Managing Risk for Development. World Bank, Washington, DC. License: Creative Commons Attribution CC BY 3.0. http://dx.doi.org/10.1596/978-0-8213-9903−3.

Chapter 4

Putting the Bank Lending Process in Emerging Markets into Perspective

LEARNING FOCUS AND OUTCOMES

Bank lending can be conducted well or poorly depending on the methodology adopted. An effective methodology builds on a clearly defined credit policy. It is informed by rigorously enforced credit control and administration. In this way, lending officers are impelled to observe and rely on an institutionalized procedure in fulfilling the lending function. A criticized methodology is often contrived and usually flawed. In most cases, inefficient lending is its outcome. This is because it lends itself to functional maneuvering.

For the credit process to be effective, it must build on the same fundamental principles on which good lending decisions are based—this blend makes good credits after all. Bankers should do anything but conduct the credit process arbitrarily. Otherwise, the process will lack credibility. It must be transparent and follow some ordered approach, if anything. Credit risk may be daunting—and uncertainty, harrowing—but a bank can forge on. It can conduct lending well in its target markets. This is possible once a proven credit process is in place.

Emerging Market Bank Lending and Credit Risk Control. http://dx.doi.org/10.1016/B978-0-12-803438-5.00004-0

The credit process should be tailored to the needs of banks and their target markets. This ensures that it concurrently satisfies the credit risk management and funding needs of both banks and borrowers respectively. In Chapters 7 and 8 of this book, I characterize the credit risk of some industries that banks define as their target markets. In doing so, I consider risk acceptance criteria (RAC) for the target markets.

In this chapter, I examine lending methodology and assess its impact on the credit processes of banks. I do so against a backdrop of the enduring crisis of credit risk in banks in emerging markets. The reader will learn about:

- The methodology and procedures that banks in emerging markets should adopt for effective conduct of the lending function
- Why and how a quality lending portfolio should be built on sound and institutionalized credit policy and culture
- Challenges that banks in emerging markets face in conducting interbank credit checks and inquiries on prospective borrowers

CHARACTERIZING THE CREDIT PROCESS

Lending remains a basic function of a bank. The traditional role of banks is to lend money to economic units that have deficits in their funding or cash flow. The funds so lent to them are usually obtained, or mobilized, from economic units that have surpluses of funds and want or are willing to invest the funds in some treasury or other products that banks offer. In this process of financial intermediation, banks create, build up, and maintain deposit liabilities and risk asset portfolios.

Thus, in its simplest form and definition, a bank is commonly seen as an institution that mobilizes and lends money. There may be several other nonbank—sometimes informal—institutions that fulfill these or similar roles. But, unlike banks, this category of institutions is not necessarily required by law to maintain certain levels of risk assets, deposit liabilities, and cash reserves within its capital structure. In some cases, as in traditional societies, nonbank institutions operate in the informal economy. In other words, such institutions are usually not—if at all—strictly regulated, as is the case with banks.

However, the size of a bank influences the types and volumes of credit facilities it may want to grant to its borrowing customers. Unlike big banks, small banks may not want to be involved in complicated, large-volume lending activities—perhaps because of limited capital funds or a low risk appetite. The big banks, on the other hand, may want to shun small-volume borrowing accounts. Yet they can scarcely afford to adopt such a blanket credit posture. This is because the demand for credit facilities reflects the composition of a bank's customer base. In each case, there is always a trade-off between lending risk and the target market preferences of the banks.

Overall, successful banking in each target market should be based on a clear understanding of pertinent variables, such as:

- appropriate financial services and products that may be offered to customers
- volumes of available and potential banking transactions from customers
- how a bank should lend money and ensure that the loans are performing
- types of probable collateral that a bank could take to secure loans

---

Case Study 4.1

Excesses in Bank Lending and Borrowing

Al Heed Industries Limited is a medium-sized company that was incorporated on April 31, 1974 to engage in the manufacture and sale of textile products in Ukraine.[1] It has an asset base of $350 million, made up largely of plants, machinery, and floating assets. At the peak of its business during most months of 2001, it achieved average monthly sales turnover of over $50 million. Spurred by the need to meet growing demand and thus expand its scope of operations, the company leased more machines for operations and three heavy-duty electricity-generating plants from three banks—Tent, Silver, and Golden.

Of the total factory machines, 20 were leased from Tent Bank, and four from Silver Bank. The electricity-generating plants were leased from Silver and Golden Banks. From Tent, Silver, and two other banks—Super and Boost—Al Heed obtained overdraft and import finance facilities. It also borrowed from two more banks—Cruise and Bounty. Cruise Bank granted an import finance facility (IFF), while Bounty Bank provided an asset refinancing facility.

In the specific case of Silver Bank, the company opened its account in January 2000. Between March and May 2000, Silver granted it credit facilities totaling $55 million. The loans—comprising facilities of $30 million for import finance, $10 million for leasing, and $15 million for overdrafts—were fully disbursed. The IFF was applied to financing importation of raw materials, while the lease facility financed the local purchase of a 500 kva electricity-generating plant. The overdraft augmented working capital needs.

The equipment lease facility was originally secured as follows:

- Legal ownership of the electricity power generator pledged to the bank and covered by a lease agreement that gave the bank right of repossession
- Comprehensive insurance of the leased asset, with Silver Bank noted as the first loss payee beneficiary
- Upfront payment of the first lease rental and security deposit installment

The collateral for the import finance facility (IFF) was structured as follows:

- Lien over shipping documents
- Execution of deed of hypothecation over the stock of raw materials financed by the bank
- Provision of 10% counterpart funding by the customer at the point of establishment of a letter of credit and 90% funding at the point of release of shipping documents
- Full and unconditional personal guarantee of Al Heed Ali, the company's managing director and chief executive officer

The overdraft was secured with a pari passu share in a debenture over the company's assets. The debenture covered all fixed and floating assets of the company, and was valued at $350 million as of December 10, 1999.

Due to a lack of serious commitment by the customer to repay the loans, Silver Bank collapsed all outstanding accrued interest and principal into the current account. This was done in line with the bank's automated process of linking every customer's loan account to its current account to enable account officers to adequately monitor the entire bank's exposure vis-à-vis the security in place. In April 2000, the account started showing signs of delinquency with the bank's total exposure standing at $68.6 million. Interest was not being serviced, and principal repayments had stopped. Compounding balances on the loan further worsened prospects for full repayment. At this time, the company's machinery and raw materials at the seaport could not be cleared due to cash flow problems.

Considering that the credit facilities had been expired since August 2000, a meeting was held between the officials of the company and the bank. At the meeting it was agreed that the loans should be renewed and restructured to encourage the company to properly operate the facilities. It was also agreed that the company should make efforts to reduce the overdraft balance to $20 million, while satisfying the IFF and lease facilities repayments. Thus, the loans were renewed and restructured to a new limit of $75 million: an import finance facility of $25 million; lease finance facility of $20 million; and overdraft facility of $30 million. The renewal and restructuring of the loans did not involve fresh disbursement of funds. The overall objective was to harmonize the outstanding balances in the loan accounts for convenience of management, reporting, and repayment.

The consignments of raw materials and two Milacron Cincinnati molding machines were cleared and warehoused by the bank's warehousing agent as part of the collateral for the facilities. The agent cleared the goods but could not warehouse all of them. Owing to space constraints, the warehouse could only accommodate the two Milacron Cincinnati machines. The agent obtained the bank's consent to warehouse the stock of raw materials in the customer's factory, provided that the agent's staff would be put on guard to protect the bank's interest in the raw materials stock.

In its bid to attain full production capacity, the company requested that the bank release 50 tons (out of 100 tons) of propylene copolymer raw materials as well as the two Milacron Cincinnati machines. The customer supported the request with a $5 million lodgment into its current account. It had posited that instead of using the meager funds available to it to purchase raw materials from outside vendors, it would be more economical to use the available stock. After painstakingly analyzing the request, the bank granted approval to release the machines and 50 tons of raw materials. Further releases were to be secured by additional lodgments equal to the full naira market value of the goods.

The company proposed several repayment plans that it never kept. Rather, Al Heed Ali threatened the staff of the warehousing agent posted to guard the stock in the company's factory when he was observed pilfering the stock of raw materials from the warehouse in the agent's custody. When this was brought to the bank's notice, it confronted Ali with the facts. He admitted to the pilfering, but blamed the act on production pressure for raw materials that he could not meet. In order to pacify the bank, he pledged postdated checks to replace the $10 million worth of raw materials that he had illegally removed from the warehouse.

Of the checks pledged, only about $4 million cleared when presented for deposit, with the rest returned unpaid. The account officer had to intensify close monitoring of the company before unpaid checks were replaced and successfully cleared. Problems with the account persisted, while the bank continued to respond as appropriate until it was agreed in May 2001 that a weekly lodgment of $1 million should be made to the account. This was to enable the company to liquidate the entire loan. This arrangement notwithstanding, the loan account remained dormant.

In late August 2001, Ali met with officials of Silver Bank and asked for a reconciliation of his account with the bank's records, with a view to determining the actual indebtedness of Al Heed to the bank and liquidating the debt. The need for reconciliation arose from his suspicion that the account had been charged excessive interest, fees, and penalties due to its poor performance. The reconciliation was being worked on when on January 10, 2002, the warehousing agent reported to the bank that Al Heed's premises had been sealed off and the workers locked out.

With two of the bank's security men, the account officer went to the company for an on-the-spot assessment and confirmation of the information. Not only was the information found to be true, but the entire management team of the company had absconded. They had left Ukraine for undisclosed countries, perhaps outside of Europe. It was also found that Bounty Bank had locked up the main entrances to the factory after removing some of the factory machines leased to Al Heed by Tent and Silver Banks.

Further investigations revealed that before he absconded from the country, Ali had intimated his impending departure to the management of Bounty Bank because of his closeness to its chairman. With the information from and cooperation of Ali, Bounty Bank was able to remove machines, finished products, and raw materials to cover its lending exposure of more than $50 million to the company. In order to protect the remaining assets of the company, Silver Bank counterlocked the factory and stationed two of its security operatives on the premises.

One week after absconding, Ali sent letters to all of the lenders, asking them to liquidate the assets of the company and settle each party's indebtedness, as the company could no longer cope with the harsh business environment that had caused its liabilities to exceed its assets. The plan to lock up the factory was hatched, perfected, and executed between January 2 and 3, 2002. For this reason, Silver Bank had indicted the warehousing agent for negligence and dereliction of duty.

The agent was held liable for damages the bank might have incurred as a result of the incident. The bank had reasoned that if the agent meant to open and close the factory each day was regular at his duty post, he would have informed the bank that Ali had absconded and Bounty Bank had carried away some of the company's assets. The agent, however, refuted the charge and claimed that he was regularly at the factory, but still was not privy to Ali's plan. He tried to absolve himself from the charges of incompetence, negligence, and dereliction of duty leveled by Silver Bank.

With the situation at hand, Silver Bank quickly increased its charge on the assets of the company from $20 million to $80 million to adequately cover its exposure. Subsequently, it appointed a receiver-manager, since it had first registered the charge over the company's assets through an all-assets debenture. It also sent out letters to other lenders requesting a meeting to agree on a possible common front for the realization of company assets. When the lenders met, they quickly discovered that Al Heed had similarly defaulted on all of the banks. The company's indebtedness to the banks exceeded $400 million, most of it unsecured.

Hints for analyzing this case study

Al Heed Ali exploited a loophole in the failure of the banks to conduct interbank credit checks on existing and prospective borrowers. His company was able to contract new credit facilities from unsuspecting banks even as it had defaulted on others. Ali's character could be called into question as well. He led lending officers at the banks to believe that his company was genuinely committed to fulfilling its obligations to them. It is also curious that Silver Bank didn't correctly interpret Ali's intentions even when he pilfered raw materials from the stock in his warehouse. The manner in which the banks selfishly pursued their loan recovery agendas left a lot to be desired.

Questions on the Case Study

1. Critically assess Ali's reasons for absconding from Ukraine in the wake of Al Heed Industries' default on its credit facilities.
2. Do you think Al Heed Industries' default could have been averted? Why or why not?
   Your answer should reflect the shortcomings of the lending made to the company.
3. Identify and discuss the key credit issues that the banks downplayed in lending to Al Heed Industries Limited.
4. The main credit issue in the Al Heed Industries case study can be summarized, with emphasis, as *excesses in lending to a borrower*. How does this contention shed light on the outcome of the banks' lending to the company?
5. (a) Taking a critical hard look at the problems at issue in the case study, how would you account for the role of the banks in the loan defaults?
   (b) What do you think the banks could have done differently to avert default on the loans?
   (c) Using the basic principles of lending as a basis, at whose door would you lay blame for Al Heed's default?

1. This case study is set in Ukraine strictly for learning and illustration purposes. It does not imply that the lending transactions actually took place in Ukraine or any other countries and regions mentioned in the case study. Similarly, the names used for the company, banks, and individuals in the case study are imaginary and do not relate to any known or unknown company, banks, or persons in Ukraine or elsewhere.

ATTRACTING APPROPRIATE CREDITS

Demand for bank credit underscores the interesting divergence in the business pursuits and activities of individuals, companies, and organizations. These economic units seek bank loans for all sorts of purposes. Some borrowing causes may not satisfy a bank's lending criteria. Only a few qualify for bank financing, and may be funded accordingly. Thus, banks receive more credit requests from customers and prospects than they can accommodate at any point in time.

There should therefore be a filter system that a bank can adopt to sift through credit requests. In this case, the purpose of sifting is to make an informed credit decision—one that builds on an appreciation of a borrower's credibility and creditworthiness. This approach is often served by credit analysis and authorization processes. In practice, the processes may be rigorous. Sometimes they can involve long customer-waiting periods. Waiting periods could be up to one week and more than one month for minor and major credit requests respectively. These are estimated periods during which a decision to grant or decline a loan application may be communicated to the applicant. But this happens more frequently in banks where credit requests are adjudged the initiative of borrowers. Such banks simply wait for borrowers to apply for credit facilities. Once they receive loan requests, they process and approve or decline them.

In adopting such a credit posture, a bank may unwittingly be opening the floodgates for trivial, questionable, and—sometimes—fraudulent loan applications. Of course, a few credible applications may be sifted out from the lot. But time and effort would have been spent—indeed, wasted—in appraising all, especially unsuccessful, loan requests. Banks tend to rationalize this waste of labor resources, believing it's a sacrifice for customer service. Yet in reality, borrowers are made worse off by declining their loan applications after prolonged periods of appraisal. A pragmatic approach would be to decline a request that lacks the merit of a good credit facility without delay. This should be done as soon as a preliminary review of the request is completed. It is always good to communicate a decline of a credit request in a way that does not hurt the banking relationship that underlies it. As experienced bankers would politely explain, the decline could be due to a portfolio constraint. Good loan proposals, from credible and creditworthy borrowers, should always be treated with honor within the framework of a due credit process. Otherwise, the relationship could be lost to competition.

The alternative to waiting for good credit applications is for a bank to anticipate and directly source credits in which it is interested. This requires that the bank define its target markets and risk acceptance criteria. Once this is done, it becomes the responsibility of the bank's marketing officers to attract quality credits from preferred markets. This approach succeeds most in banks that have effective marketing and relationship management teams. With this practice, a bank knows—right from the outset—the types of credit transactions to which it is predisposed. Thus, it can easily shun frivolous credit requests. This practice saves the effort that would otherwise be dissipated in appraising such loan requests.

LETTER OF APPLICATION FOR LOAN

A borrower that wants to obtain a loan from a bank should send a formal letter of application or request for the loan to the bank. This is usually a necessary, though not sufficient, step to obtaining a bank loan. The letter should clearly state the cause of the intended borrowing. It should be written on the borrower's letterhead (in the case of a company or organization). With respect to the loan, the letter should provide pertinent information, including:

- Type, amount, and purpose of the requested loan. The purpose establishes the borrowing cause.
- Tenor of the proposed credit (i.e., period during which the loan will be disbursed by the bank, utilized, and fully repaid by the borrower).
- Mode of utilization and source of repayment for the loan. Banks demand a clear statement of a borrower's envisaged pattern of drawing on a credit facility, as well as how the loan will be repaid.
- Dynamics of the underlying borrowing cause or transaction to be funded with the loan. This is required for appraising the life cycle of the transaction, the anticipated flows and uses of funds within the stages of the cycle, and the efficacy of the transaction path in ensuring that the loan is fully repaid on or prior to maturity.
- Brief reports on the shareholders, directors, and management of the company. The required information should include names, ages, qualifications, and positions of members of management of the company. It is also pertinent to ascertain the experience and official responsibilities of members of the management team.
- A brief description of the business in which the company is engaged, including analysis of its industry, market share, major suppliers, customers, and so on.
- Identification of property or other assets that the borrower is offering the bank as collateral to secure the loan.

Information other than the foregoing, which loan applicants consider necessary—especially if it would strengthen the loan request—may be included in the letter of application.

In sending a loan request to a bank, the borrower should also enclose photocopies of the following documents:

- Certificate of incorporation
  Credit analysts ascertain how long ago a company legally came into existence from the certificate of incorporation. Often, the date of incorporation differs from the actual date of commencement of operation.
- Memorandum and articles of association
  These documents specify the types of businesses in which a company engages. The powers of directors to borrow money on behalf of the company should also be explicitly stated in the memorandum and articles of association.
- Financial statement and annual reports
  Banks usually require audited financial statements and annual reports for the immediate past five years. A bank may accept a period of three years if a company does not meet the five-year standard.

- Management reports and accounts
  A company that has been in business for less than one year—or one whose financial statements are not ready at the time it applies for loan—should submit management accounts for the current period.
- Business plan
  When a borrower is a start-up, it should furnish the bank with its business plan. The plan should contain and be informed by a statement of the firm's financial affairs.
- Cash flow projections
  There should be cash flow projections covering the tenor of the proposed loan. Cash flow projections are needed in evaluating the borrower's capacity to repay the loan from its normal business operations. The cash flow projections should also indicate income that is expected from extraordinary sources.

Credit documentation is incomplete without a formal letter of application for the loan. Indeed, the letter establishes the basis of a credit relationship in the first place. It also evidences the origin of a credit facility that a bank grants to a particular borrower. Similarly, the letter of application would be incomplete without the aforementioned supporting documents.

ACKNOWLEDGMENT OF LOAN APPLICATION

A bank should always acknowledge receipt of letters of application for loans. Banks can acknowledge loan request letters in either of two ways. Acknowledgment may be effected at the point of delivery of a letter of application for loan or afterward. At the point of its receipt, a copy of the letter retained by the loan applicant may be stamped or initialed. Otherwise, a formal letter of acknowledgment should be sent to the loan applicant afterward.

It is usually better to acknowledge a loan request by means of a formal letter. A letter of acknowledgment serves certain purposes, including the following:

- It gives the applicant a sense of value placed on the loan request by the bank. This is in line with the dictates of quality and professional service.
- The loan officer may request specific clarifications, additional documents, and/or information about the proposed credit.
- It is a reference document for both the bank and customer on matters of originality, need, and initiating the credit facility. Indeed, it is part of the general documentation of a credit relationship.
- The bank may need to buy time while the loan officer is conducting an exploratory investigation of the borrower's creditworthiness. In such a circumstance, the acknowledgment letter provides a holding action on the loan request.
- The customer may be thanked for the application, informed that its preliminary review is being conducted, and advised that the bank will respond soon.

Acknowledgment of the loan application provides an internal means to check tardiness in appraising loan requests. Since the acknowledgment shows the date the loan request was received, applicants can easily draw attention to unjustifiable delays in processing their requests.

Loan request interview

Loan applicants should be interviewed on any important aspects of their requests. The essence of the interview is to better understand the borrowing cause and appreciate the applicant's financing circumstances. It also affords lending officers an opportunity to assess firsthand the viability of the transaction for which the loan application is made. During the interview, the loan applicant is offered advice on the appropriate amount, tenor, structure, and security for the loan.

Also, a common understanding of the basis and terms of the intended credit relationship is established, including agreement on the pricing of the credit facility (if granted). Other purposes of a pre−credit analysis interview with loan applicants are as follows:

- Some key loan appraisal information, such as ownership structure and business activities of the prospective borrower (in the case of a company) can be easily obtained.
- It permits lending officers to assess the seriousness and practicality of the borrowing cause at first hand.
- Loan applicants are most willing, at this stage of the intended credit relationship, to cooperate with the lending officers in obtaining all loan-support materials and documents.

It is obvious from the foregoing that the loan interview can take place prior to or after receipt of a formal application from the prospective borrower. It can also be achieved either in the course of marketing for quality credits or while acknowledging receipt of the loan request. In this case, the subjects of the interview would form part of the clarifications required.

CREDIT CHECKS AND INQUIRIES

It is necessary to always conduct interbank credit checks on customers, especially new or prospective borrowing accounts, prior to granting credit facilities to them. Credit checks help to ascertain the creditworthiness and track record of loan applicants in repaying bank loans. The checks are normally conducted with existing and former banks with which loan applicants have had banking relationships.

A particular credit check may be designed to fulfill specific objectives. In general, however, credit checks seek to ascertain information such as:

- total outstanding credit facilities that particular loan applicants may have with other banks

- whether credits that other banks have granted to the loan applicants were, have been, or are being effectively serviced
- type and value (if obtainable) of collateral securing credit facilities that the loan applicants have with other banks
- character of the loan applicants—usually confidential information that, unfortunately, competing banks scarcely furnish outright

Other sources of information on prospective borrowers include trade checks, professional checks, market associations, government offices, and employers (in the case of individual borrowers).

Observed setbacks

Credit inquiries, unfortunately, have been neither effective nor popular among banks in emerging economies. There has been lack of cooperation among the banks largely because of the dictates of competition. It could also be explained in terms of the reprehensible attitude of sheer indifference of some people to the plight of others. Banks have been falling victim to this omission one after another. This is reflected in observations of huge and increasing annual loan loss provisions. It is more worrying that a borrower that defaults on one or some banks could yet get fresh credit facilities from other unsuspecting banks. This frequently happens as a result of neglect of credit checks or the levity with which they are treated. Credit inquiries help a bank to reconfirm the appropriateness of a decision to lend money to a particular prospective borrower after all.

Consider an unusual situation where the outcome of a bank's credit check on a prospective borrower is unfavorable. Assume in this case that the bank could not easily decline the credit request for some reason. On occasion this happens, especially in situations where a bank is looking beyond current lending in chasing an up-and-coming banking relationship. In this situation, information obtained through credit checks and inquiries comes in handy. It will guide the bank in devising an appropriate relationship management response to forestall loan default. But it's risky to ignore negative findings from credit checks—for any reason!

External assistance

A bank may seek external assistance for its credit check efforts. Banks should do so if it would facilitate feedback in difficult situations. However, the approach of agents or functionaries that banks engage for this purpose should be discreet. Besides, there is a need for regulation of the external assistance that banks may wish to seek for credit checks. Regulation will ensure that the process of credit checks is not abused. Above all, it will defend confidentiality of customer information while permitting fair credit inquiries.

Central Bank of Nigeria (CBN) initiative

Like the private-sector banks operating in the country, the Central Bank of Nigeria (CBN) appreciates the relevance of pre-lending checks on prospective borrowers. The CBN took the initiative in 1992 to evolve a means of assisting banks with credit checks and inquiries. In that year, it established a credit risk management system (CRMS), known as the Credit Bureau, in its banking supervision department to further the cause of credit checks on prospective borrowers. The Credit Bureau performs specific credit risk management functions for the banks. It collates and builds up the database from which banks obtain information about all past and current borrowing accounts in Nigeria.

In addition to interbank credit checks and inquiries, banks should obtain useful information through the CRMS. For instance, the CBN makes it mandatory for banks in Nigeria to refer to the CRMS for all borrowing requests in excess of ₦1,000,000 (one million naira). This rule is applicable to existing and prospective borrowers. It does not matter that a bank observes the rule with or without knowledge of borrowers. What really matters is the integrity of the report and the process that produces it.

The usefulness of the CRMS derives essentially from the provisions of the Central Bank of Nigeria Act No. 24 of 1991 (sections 28 and 52), as amended, which empower the Bank "to compile and circulate the list of classified debtors." In addition, section 2 (c) of the Act provides that:

> The Central Bank of Nigeria shall have power to compile and circulate to all banks in Nigeria, a list of debtors whose outstanding debts to any bank had been classified by bank examiners under the bad debt category, the objective being to promote monetary stability in Nigeria.

The CBN is empowered under the Act "to obtain from all banks, returns on all credits with a minimum outstanding balance of ₦1,000,000 and above of principal and interest, for compilation and dissemination by way of status report to any interested party (i.e., operators or regulators)."

Yet, the use of the facility of the CRMS has not been altogether foolproof in satisfying the needs of banks for an efficient credit inquiry mechanism. Thus, the banking system remains riddled with largely avoidable swindles that account for huge annual financial losses to the banks. The CRMS has major shortcomings, including the following—all of which border on its failings:

- The CBN has not been able to enforce strict compliance of banks with the CRMS guidelines for its workings
- On occasion CRMS reports may be suspect due to the system's inability to authenticate data supplied to it by banks
- Though it is Web enabled, the CRMS does not currently offer online, real-time credit risk management information to banks

In view of the foregoing shortcomings, there is a need for the CBN to commit itself to constantly improving the workings of the Bureau. Sustained improvement will enable the CRMS to fulfill its lofty goal of helping to rid the industry of "predatory debtors in the banking system whose modus operandi involved the abandonment of their debt obligations in some banks only to contract new debts in other banks,"[2] which combined with reckless lending compounds the credit risk crisis in banks.

Formation of CRIMA

In 2000, a group of loan officers of banks in Nigeria formed the Credit Risk Managers Association (CRIMA). The immediate aim of CRIMA was to advance the cause of credit checks and inquiries to which its members were committed. By doing so, the Association hoped to contribute to mitigation of the rising incidence of bad debts at banks. The primary objectives for which the Association was formed were specified in section 5 of its constitution and designed to:

- Establish and maintain an Association of licensed financial institutions engaged in lending operations
- Promote and protect the interest of members of the Association in their conduct of lending business
- Formulate and maintain standards of conduct for members and to encourage professional lending practices
- Present the views of members on any matter that may affect lending business
- Provide facilities for the flow of information among members engaged in research into lending operations and related problems and to disseminate the results in such manner as may be thought fit
- Increase awareness of members through seminars, lectures, and other forms of information
- Collaborate with government and other regulatory bodies in formulating policies pertaining to lending business
- Establish a general fund through subscription and any other fundraising activities for the maintenance and promotion of research into lending operations and related matters, and in financing any of the objects of the Association

The formation of CRIMA was timely. Concerns about the failings of interbank credit checks and inquiries had peaked at the time the Association was formed. Particularly worrisome at the time were mounting criticisms of the Nigerian banking system. Critiques focused on the nonchalance of bank

---

2. See Central Bank of Nigeria. Credit Risk Management System. Banking Supervision Department. http://www.cenbank.org/Supervision/crms.asp.

management toward the establishment of an effective mechanism for interbank credit checks and inquiries.

It was not certain that CRIMA would attain all its objectives. It did not seem that it enjoyed the recognition of most banks. It was seen as an Association of independently minded loan officers, if anything. Bank employees at the middle management cadre formed the Association and are in the forefront of the execution of its cause. Their concern about the worsening poor quality of risk assets portfolios in the banking system was proven, and informed their determination to form the Association and their desire to see the project through.

At the inaugural meeting of the Association, members expressed dissatisfaction with unhealthy competitive lending tendencies among banks in the country. The criticized lending practices, according to them, left no bank better off than the other. If anything, the banks and their industry were worse off as they continued to contend with the unabated credit risk crisis. CRIMA is now part of an umbrella body of risk managers of banks in Nigeria known as the Risk Managers Association of Nigeria (RIMAN).

CREDIT ANALYSIS

Let me now introduce the aspects of credit analysis as essential inputs to the credit process. Later in Chapters 27 and 28, I discuss the preparation and relevance of the CAM and CAF to the credit process. Credit analysis is usually presented as a detailed report on a particular borrowing request. But it is often christened "credit analysis memorandum" (CAM). Approval or decline of a loan request is based largely on information contained in the CAM. However, actual approval of a credit is effected in a "credit approval form" (CAF).

Credit analysis is the cornerstone of the bank lending function. It is easily the most worthwhile exercise in lending activities. Those who hold this view would argue that a poorly analyzed credit is as good as lost in the first place. In practical terms, this view makes a lot of sense. One reason is that the postmortem function of credit administration draws relevance from information that credit analysis furnishes. Another reason is that credit analysis informs agreement on the mode of disbursement, source of repayment, collateral securing the loan, and so on. The same goes for other issues that impact transaction dynamics of a credit facility. Also, the guts of credit risk management are built on the rigor of credit analysis.

A good credit analysis bears the hallmark of well-ordered lending methodology. It furnishes useful hints about possible uncertainties and risks of a credit—and how to mitigate them. For this reason, a typical credit package is made up of the CAM and CAF. These two important credit documents serve specific purposes and have unique distinguishing features that the reader should appreciate better after reading Chapters 27 and 28 of this book.

CREDIT APPROVAL

Credit analysts recommend approval or decline of a loan request in the course of preparing the loan's CAM. The import of this rule is that bank management often looks to credit analysts to make credit decisions. In most cases, an analyst's recommendation of a credit's approval or decline is preceded by well-articulated key credit issues. Yet lending authorities are not bound by opinions of the analyst. If anything, credit recommendations are advisory in nature. While credit analysts may forcefully make cases for approval or decline of loan requests, the credit committee or responsible lending officers still reserve the right to approve or decline the credit.

A credit request must be formally approved by particular or designated lending officers, secured, and properly documented before it can be disbursed. The factors that determine the mode and process of credit approval include the loan amount, workings of the credit committee, and credit authorization limits of lending officers. These factors often dictate whether a loan request and its CAM or credit report should be sent to either executive management or particular lending officers for approval. Of course, the board of directors remains the highest authority for approving credits. Recourse to the board of directors is usually necessitated when a particular loan request involves consideration for lending beyond the powers of executive management and the credit committee.

I shed more light on intrigues that impact the credit process and decisions in Chapter 28 of this book. Sometimes the ultimate influence on credit approval decisions could seem irrational. In such situations, the integrity of the credit process may be called into question. A major problem faced by banking regulators in emerging markets is how to forestall irrational tendencies in credit approvals. Not infrequently, bank examiners make startling findings about abuse of the credit process. Often insider abuse is the culprit.

QUESTIONS FOR DISCUSSION AND REVIEW

1. Assess the effectiveness of any identified bank procedure for conducting lending, and suggest possible improvements to enhance its efficacy.
2. Critically assess the effectiveness of the methodological framework used by banks in emerging markets for analyzing credit proposals.
3. Lending is about the riskiest of all normal functions of a bank. In what ways does the credit process reflect how a bank should conduct lending to minimize loan losses?
4. In view of the crippling effects of credit risk on bank management, why and how do banks continue to invest heavily in credit products?

Chapter 5

Bank Credit versus Equity and Economic Performance of Emerging Markets

Chapter Outline

LEARNING FOCUS AND OUTCOMES

The promoters of Target Trusts Limited (TTL) were committed to forming a diversified investment company in Nigeria that would transmute to a full-fledged bank by obtaining a new banking license, acquiring an existing bank, or securing core/strategic investor status (i.e., holding at least a 51% equity

Emerging Market Bank Lending and Credit Risk Control. http://dx.doi.org/10.1016/B978-0-12-803438-5.00005-2
Copyright © 2016 Elsevier Inc. All rights reserved.

stake) in a bank, on or before December 31, 2006. There were precedents that favored the actualization of their mission. That investment path was a familiar terrain for operators and stakeholders in Nigeria's financial system.

In 1996, Banc Garanti Limited (now known as BGL)—purely an investment company—acquired a controlling equity stake in the failed Merchant Bank of Commerce (MBCOM) and later renamed it Continental Trust Bank Limited. In 1997, under a similar arrangement and the auspices of the Central Bank of Nigeria (CBN), BGL/MBCOM also acquired Crystal Bank of Africa Limited, which it renamed Standard Trust Bank. A couple years later, another investment company—Finacorp Building Society Limited—acquired the failed Nationwide Merchant Bank Limited, and as in the foregoing examples, renamed it Platinum Bank Limited. The policy direction of the CBN regarding rescue measures for failing banks was clearly propitious to negotiated takeovers/acquisitions of ailing banks by more enterprising core/strategic investors. Examples of CBN-supported acquisitions of formerly failing banks at the time included the takeover of Assurance Bank, Access Bank, New World Merchant Bank (renamed Trust Bank of Africa), New Nigerian Bank, Orient Bank (renamed Afex Bank), Gamji Bank (renamed International Trust Bank), African Continental Bank, Liberty Bank, National Bank, Pacific Bank, and so on.

In its avowed pursuit of regulatory measures aimed at sanitizing and enthroning a sound financial system, it was unlikely that the CBN would change its rescue policy on failing banks at the time. Considering the usually unintended side effects of bank closure, it was obvious then more than ever before that the CBN was not altogether interested in or keen on liquidating banks. Instead, the CBN's policy outlook pointed to possible continuation of support for and encouragement of strategic alliances, mergers, and acquisitions. That policy outlook was in tune with the TTL promoters' idea for proposing the formation of an investment company as a means of acquiring a bank or obtaining a new banking license. They set out on their venture project—ostensibly to accomplish a feat in Nigeria's finance and banking landscape. The reader will learn about:

- How bank credit and equity financing compare, such that both entrepreneurs and investors find appropriate opportunities in the two external financing options
- The ways in which the disposition of banks toward risk-taking in and lending to some borrowing causes can affect entrepreneurial endeavors
- Why and how entrepreneurs should painstakingly explore alternative sources of external financing for their proposed ventures
- Implications of patterns of bank financing for economic performance, growth, and development of emerging markets

Case Study 5.1

Granting and disbursing a temporary overdraft

Franca, the manager of the Singapore Downtown branch of Online Bank Limited,[1] was about to enter her office to start work for the day when her mobile phone rang.

"Hello! Speak on—I can hear you," she answered unsuccessfully three times before she established contact with the caller.

Singh, the MD of Trade Link Limited, was on the phone to discuss an important banking request with her.

"We have issued a check for $7.8 million in favor of Technology Group Limited. Please make sure that the check is honored when it's presented for payment," he requested.

"Sir, Trade Link's account has a credit balance of $2.8 million and cannot accommodate the check it has issued," Franca informed him.

"I am aware that the available balance in our account is insufficient to pay the check. That's why I called you, so that you can put a temporary overdraft (TOD) in place for us," suggested Singh.

"How much TOD are you requesting, and how soon will Trade Link repay it?" Franca asked. "Please bear in mind that accounts with TOD balances must be regularized on or before the last day of the month," she added.

"We need a TOD of $5 million urgently in Trade Link's current account to fund the check. The credit will help us to complete an important business transaction," he explained.

"Are you sure that Trade Link will repay the TOD within the next 12 days before month-end?" Franca asked. "It's already the 18th today, you know."

"Don't worry about our ability to repay the loan. Check out the turnover in our account. Our average monthly turnover is over $25 million," Singh informed her.

"I know, but this is the first time Trade Link has requested a TOD, and I need to acquaint you with its workings. My job will be on the line if Trade Link's account is not regularized by the end of the month," Franca clarified.

"What do you mean? How is that possible?" Singh queried.

"It's the new credit policy on TOD facilities. I will be placed on an indefinite suspension and my salary account debited with $5 million—the amount of the TOD—if Trade Link defaults. The suspension will be in force until the TOD is fully liquidated, including accrued interest and charges," she further clarified.

"I didn't know about what you're telling me; nevertheless, the issue of default shouldn't arise in the first place. We have the capacity to regularize our account within a week," Singh promised.

He thanked the manager for her time and consideration and hung up.

While waiting for approval of Trade Link's TOD request, he stepped up the company's marketing and sales effort. He did so because he wanted to generate sufficient revenue to fund the $7.8 million check in case the bank declined his TOD request.

The manager obtained approval for Trade Link's $5 million TOD request. The company's current account was subsequently credited for that amount. Meanwhile, some of Trade Link's debtors paid down their debts following the pressure that Singh had put on them. That was one of the actions he took to ensure that the $7.8 million check would be honored at Clearing. Sales staff also gave a good account of themselves. They raked it in—realizing over $3 million in new sales during the week that the check was presented for clearing.

In the end, the check was paid—ending a week of financial anxiety for Singh, who roundly commended Trade Link's sales staff for their performance and dedication to duty. He did so after he found that the company's account had a credit balance of $6.1 million after the $7.8 million check had been debited from it. He drew $6 million from the available balance to settle outstanding supply bills. He planned to call Online Bank's bluff for declining his TOD request. He would give the manager a piece of his mind when next he called her on the phone or visited her in her office.

To his utter dismay, Trade Link's account statement showed a debit balance of $4.4 million at the end of the month. Unknown to him, the $5 million TOD had dropped into the company's current account and put it in the red. Singh could not control his anger. He went straight to see the manager.

"Our account is in the red after we funded it to pay the $7.8 million check and a cash withdrawal of $6 million. How is that possible?" Singh asked Franca as his face twisted in a grimace of anger.

"Yes, I'm aware that Trade Link's account has a debit of about $4.4 million after the $5 million TOD dropped at month-end. As a matter of fact, I wanted to draw your attention to it today," she explained.

"Which TOD are you talking about?" Singh asked, showing unmistaken surprise at what the manager had just told him.

"It's the $5 million TOD you requested, of course. It was approved and credited to your account accordingly. Didn't you see a credit of $4.8 million to Trade Link's account on the 17th of March? That amount was disbursement of the $5 million TOD net of the 3.5% flat processing fee," Franca explained.

"Please, I don't understand what you're saying! Do you mean that our request for $5 million TOD was granted, and you didn't tell me about the approval and that it was posted to our account?" Singh wondered.

"As I said earlier," reiterated Franca, "you should have seen the credit in Trade Link's account. That's why I didn't bother to talk to you about it at the time."

"That's where you made a mistake," countered Singh. "Our account is very active. I see a lot of inflows into the account from our customers all over the country. I wouldn't know which inflow is from which particular customer or source except when we're notified," he explained. "What do we do now?" Singh asked as Franca stared at him in utter disbelief.

Her fear about the TOD had been realized!

"You have to quickly regularize the account. Please, you should do so with a sense of responsibility—and without delay, too. Else, I'm finished," she begged.

Singh was not moved by what Franca's fate would be. He felt that he was not to blame for the unauthorized overdraft that Trade Link's account was now enjoying at the risk of the manager's job.

"Let me see if there's anything that I can do to help at this time. We'll endeavor to start reducing the outstanding balance. But it's really difficult for us. We can't ground our business because of this mix-up in our account," he clarified.

While Trade Link's account remained overdrawn, the bank placed Franca on an indefinite suspension. Her salary was also suspended pending her regularizing of the company's account. Unfortunately, her appeal to management of the bank for leniency was ignored.

"While I sincerely regret this sad outcome, it's unfair to lay a clear case of conversion of loan proceeds by the borrower at my door," she protested.

Hints for analyzing this case study

The lending officers, and especially the branch manager, left avoidable major loopholes in the TOD facility. It appears, unfortunately, that Singh saw the loopholes and exploited them. But this view is not incontrovertible. At least one reason is obvious. In view of the loopholes, it's difficult to charge him with conversion of the loan proceeds as Franca did in her protest memo. The loopholes in the lending observed in this case study could have been avoided had loan officers followed an ordered credit process. Overall, any or all of the following three possible reasons underscore the default: in the first place, it could be that the lending officers—including the branch manager—were lax in ensuring diligent follow-through. The second reason could be that perhaps the officers did not strictly adhere to the bank's credit policy. A third reason could be that the bank's credit policy and controls are flawed.

Questions on the case study

1. **(a)** What specific lending loopholes do you identify in the Trade Link Limited case study?
    (b) How did the loopholes facilitate default on the loan? Your answer should demonstrate understanding of the standard credit process.
2. **(a)** Using the loopholes you identified in 1(a) as a basis, at whose door would you lay blame for the loan default? Support your answer with practical illustrations that bear on the loopholes.
    (b) Did the bank act rightly or wrongly in suspending Franca indefinitely from work and withholding her salary?

1. This case study, set in Singapore, is strictly for illustration and learning purposes and does not in actual fact imply that the country was involved in any way in the underlying transaction. In much the same vein, the names used for the company, bank and individuals in the illustration are imaginary and do not relate to any known or unknown company, bank or persons in Singapore or elsewhere.

ISSUES IN RAISING FINANCING FOR A BUSINESS VENTURE

Five ex-banker entrepreneurs in Nigeria dreamed of owning a bank. They were convinced that their ambition was realistic given their professional backgrounds and deep knowledge of the banking business and industry. But how to actualize their dream in the face of huge regulatory capital requirement baffled them. Though the rigor and cost of raising the required capital base were scary, they were persuaded by their business sense, and some calculation, to forge ahead with their plan to found a bank. However, they did not want to plunge headlong into it. They decided to float an investment company, Target Trusts Limited (TTL), that would transmute into a full-fledged commercial bank. The question of capital bothered them still. Thus they decided, after painstaking deliberation, to explore all available options to raise the required start-up capital. It is widely believed that bank credit is a popular and primary means of external financing for businesses in emerging economies. This thinking builds on the assumption that capital markets in emerging economies are scarcely developed. While this observation is largely true, its negative impact is usually more on small and medium enterprises (SMEs) than on the large corporates. In the case of TTL, the options fell into two broad categories of financing alternatives—they would either obtain bank credit or sell equity shares to raise the required capital for the venture.

The first option, funding with bank credit and the promoters' equity, was a hard choice. It entailed asking the founding promoters to take up and pay for equity shares in the proposed business. Equity shares bestow ownership rights to investors while limiting their liability to the amount of their investment in the event of failure of the business. Investors in equity shares receive a dividend that is paid—if declared—on profits after tax. This implies that there is no return on the equity investment if a dividend is not paid in any accounting year. Of course, funds committed to equity shares have opportunity costs that investors bear. The promoters of TTL appreciated the fact that the equity option demanded 100 percent funding from them. In reality, the promoters had sufficient ideas and the expertise to run the business—but not the amount of hard cash required. It was unlikely that they could contribute more than 10 percent of the required equity capital—which would entitle them to barely one board seat. Nevertheless, each of them mustered confidence and contributed ₦10 million from personal funds to demonstrate their commitment to the venture. In that way, they raised ₦50 million, which they deposited in an escrow account while exploring other options for securing the balance of ₦450 million.

With the option of borrowing the risk capital, the promoters could raise the required capital funds in the local money market from a bank or nonbank lending institution. Bank credit is usually a credible alternative to raising money in equity capital markets. While the borrowing process may not be straightforward, good credit proposals usually come in handy. Unlike capital markets funds that have high fixed costs, borrowers can negotiate interest rates and charges with their banks—depending on the risks of their borrowing causes. Bank credit also tends to be more attractive than and preferred to equity raised in the capital markets because it is amenable to the different financing needs of borrowers. Yet a further advantage of bank credit over equity relates to flexibility in meeting mutually preferred tenor and repayment arrangements for the bank and borrower. In view of the foregoing advantages, borrowing from a bank or other financial institution was a strong option for the TTL promoters, no doubt about it. Unfortunately, none of the banks and lending institutions would want to lend money to a start-up venture—especially in the highly volatile financial services industry. As ex-bankers, they appreciated this fact very well and were not surprised that lending institutions were not interested in their project. Besides, their ₦50 million contribution works out to a debt/equity ratio of 9 for the ₦450 million loan they needed. The banks and nonbank lending institutions they approached considered the gearing high, on the one hand, and their level of equity too low, on the other, for the venture. Most importantly, the promoters didn't have tangible collateral in the form of land or buildings to secure the loan. Accordingly, the banks and nonbank lenders declined their loan request. Of course, the lending institutions would have analyzed other key credit issues to which the promoters wouldn't have been privy in arriving at the decision to decline their application for the loan.

The promoters' third option was recourse to the capital markets to seek quotation on the Nigerian Stock Exchange (NSE) under the second-tier securities scheme for SME businesses. The stock exchange—the leading institution of the capital markets—plays vital roles in fulfilling external financing needs for businesses around the world. Investors patronize the stock exchanges for shares of quoted companies. Upon doing so, they expect income from the profits of buying and selling shares on the one hand, and capital gains on the shares they hold for sale in the future, speculating that share prices will appreciate, on the other. Investors who painstakingly follow and understand stock market trends make handsome earnings from these two investment targets and approaches. Unfortunately, the foregoing benefits are fully realized mostly in economies with highly developed capital markets. Businesses and investors in emerging economies make do with very basic and inefficient capital markets. It would seem that the capital markets option would solve the risk capital raising problem of the TTL promoters. Yet it wasn't going to fly. One reason is that it entailed fulfilling rigorous formalities and applying for an initial public offering (IPO) of shares of the venture. An existing company with a proven track record is more likely to succeed with an IPO issue than a start-up. Another reason is that legal, documentation, and other costs associated with an IPO could be substantial and discouraging. A dearth of funds to bankroll the IPO became a decisive factor in this case. A third reason bordered on the difficulty that start-ups experience in fulfilling stringent Securities and Exchange Commission (SEC) rules. Thus the TTL promoters discarded this option.

Arranging and marketing a private placement of shares of the proposed business venture to select high net worth individuals (HNIs) was the last option. This option does not have regulatory, interest, or other fixed or flexible financing costs as in the cases of bank credit and equities sourced in the capital markets. Ultimately, the promoters settled for the private placement option in mid-2004. On doing so, they decided to personally market the private placement. The promoters and investors who bought into the private placement idea would now be owners of the proposed business—to the extent of their equity. The founding promoters welcomed this implied diminution of their intended stake in the business as the price for getting their dream off the ground.

They prepared a meticulous business plan to back a private placement offer to raise ₦500 million (inclusive of their ₦50 million) in equity capital for the business. They also produced an information memorandum (not presented in this discussion and illustration) that was a companion to the business plan. Potential investors needed the two documents to make informed decisions.

PLAN AND PRIVATE PLACEMENT FOR A BUSINESS VENTURE

The idea behind the private placement option became popular when the first three options fell through. The TTL promoters tried to accomplish it in a pragmatic manner. The outcome was intriguing, to say the least. Let me now present an abridged version of the business plan with which the promoters sought to raise an additional ₦450 million in equity for the proposed business venture. The highlights of the plan that follow mirror the commitment of the promoters to the project.

Background

The financial system remains easily the most vibrant sector of the Nigerian economy. It is also one of the most profitable economic sectors in terms of return on investment. This explains the boom in business that the sector has experienced since the mid-1980s following its deregulation in 1986. Besides the traditional household names, the explosion in business is evident in the remarkable success of some new-generation financial institutions. The occasional hiccups in the sector, sometimes characterized as distress syndrome, were often triggered by management failings in a few institutions. With good corporate governance and a sound regulatory environment, investment in the financial system remains a worthwhile venture. It is perhaps in the highly capital-intensive energy (oil & gas) and telecommunications sectors that return on investment compares with that obtained in the financial sector. For this reason, high net worth investors long to invest in these preferred sectors. It is in this context that the thought of forming the proposed diversified financial services company, which will later convert to a full-fledged bank, was conceived. Were it possible to raise the required minimum paid-up capital of ₦2 billion now, we would have opted for a banking license without going through the route of an investment company.

Incorporation and Ownership

The CBN will first license the proposed company before it would be incorporated at the Corporate Affairs Commission. The incorporation will reflect private ownership of the company and limited liability of its shareholders. Its authorized share capital will comprise 1,000,000,000 ordinary shares with a total value of ₦500 million at 50 kobo per share. The present and future subscribers to the share capital shall own the company in proportion to their shareholding at any point in time.

Organizational Structure

The organizational structure of the proposed company will derive from six key financial services areas in which it will transact businesses—leasing, advisory services, trade finance, funds management, capital markets, and insurance brokerage. The need for efficient management of human and material resources will also be recognized. The activities of the proposed company would be organized in three functional divisions—marketing, risk management, and administration. The company will recruit experienced and competent staff.

Board Composition

The board will have persons who can add value to the company's vision and business. The chairperson may not have equity in the company. The overriding considerations shall include competence, goodwill, network, and willingness to identify with the cause of the company. The CEO will be free to subscribe to the shares of the company once offered and to pay for their shareholding. A board seat shall be automatically reserved for any shareholder who subscribes to and fully pays for at least 20% of the called-up capital. This level of stake is considered reasonable to ensure their commitment as a board member.

Management Profile

The management team will draw from experienced and practicing bankers, chartered accountants, economists, financial analysts, and insurance and stock brokers. In view of this, and for reasons of confidentiality, the identity of the key management staff is being reserved and would be disclosed to confirmed prospective investors on request. Yet, the board of directors shall confirm the appointment of the managing director, who shall be the chief executive officer as well.

Business Strategy

Our strategy for business will emphasize deployment of marketing intelligence and the building of deposit mobilization capacity. Our overall objective is take only bankable risks, especially on foreign exchange transactions and borrowing accounts. Implicit in this goal is our desire to achieve earnings growth and broaden the customer base through efficient transactions processing and relationship management.

Market Analysis

Market Definition

The financial services market in Nigeria subsumes all individuals, public sector institutions, nongovernmental organizations, and local corporates engaged in diverse trading, manufacturing, and service businesses.

Target Markets

Our main target markets shall be the energy sector, the public sector, commerce, high net worth individuals, and money and capital markets. For the chosen target markets, we will concentrate efforts in attracting and retaining business relationships with individuals and enterprises operating vibrant economic enterprises.

Competition

There is a keen competition among operators of the financial system. Intensity of competition is nowadays amplified by the insatiable thirsts of competitors for increasing deposit liabilities as a means of enhancing liquidity. Since financial products are largely generic, the main competitive tools become essentially liquidity strength, level of capitalization, and marketing capabilities, as well as the quality of human resources.

Anticipated Business Segments

The company will focus on securing business relationships and satisfying the major needs of customers. We have carefully defined anticipated key areas of business, which we shall seek to exploit from the market segments. The flagship products are credit facilities, especially leasing, foreign exchange transactions, and portfolio management.

Risk Acceptance Criteria

We characterize risks in the target markets, and in doing so (1) consider appropriate product(s) for the selected customers in each of the markets; (2) assess the volumes of available and potential business in each of the markets; (3) determine how we should lend money to selected customers in each market; and, (4) identify types of collateral we could take to secure loans.

Resource Requirements

The proposed company will require the following operating facilities, equipment, and human resources, which are reflected in Tables 5.1 and 5.2.

Staffing: The total staff employee requirement is estimated at 24 persons as shown in Table 5.1.

TABLE 5.1 Projected Staff Costs for an Investment Company

First Full Year of Operation		Per Month (₦)	Per Annum (₦)
MD & CEO (Negotiable)	1	—	—
Mgr., Marketing	1	2,55,050.14	30,60,613.68
Mgr., Risk Management	1	2,55,050.14	30,60,613.68
AM, Corporate Finance	1	1,85,550.30	22,26,615.60
AM, Treasury	1	1,85,550.30	22,26,615.60
Sr. Officer, Fincon	1	1,55,204.28	18,62,463.36
Corp Sec/Legal Adviser	1	1,55,204.28	18,62,463.36
Sr. Officer, T. Services	1	1,55,204.28	18,62,463.36
Officer (Credit Analyst)	1	1,25,110.56	15,01,338.72
EA2 (Treasury Dealer)	1	1,05,110.56	12,61,338.72
EA2 (Opscon)	1	1,05,110.56	12,61,338.72
EA3 (Marketing Officers)	4	3,80,438.80	45,65,313.60
EA3 (TS Officer)	1	95,109.70	11,41,328.40
Admin Officer	1	50,040.10	6,00,493.20
Office Assistants	2	80,018.44	9,60,245.28
Drivers	4	1,00,080.20	12,01,010.40
Dispatch Rider	1	15,007.22	1,80,098.64
	24	24,02,839.86	2,88,34,354.32

Security: There will be a need for adequate security against armed robbery within the company's premises. In view of this, the company would require four security guards to patrol the office on a day/night rotational basis. In addition, there would be a need for two permanent police officers to guard the company.

Equipment: The various items of equipment required for the takeoff of the company are shown in Table 5.2.

Vehicles: There would be a need for five cars at the start-up stage—one for the MD and Chief Executive Officer; one each for the marketing and risk managers; and two for marketing assignments, otherwise designated for "pool" use. There will be one motorbike to be procured for the dispatch rider.

TABLE 5.2 Projected Fixed Assets and Costs for an Investment Company

	Item	Qty	Unit Cost (₦)	Total Value (₦)
1	Validating machine	1	60,000	60,000
2	Note counter (big)	1	2,80,000	2,80,000
3	Note counter (small)	1	1,25,000	1,25,000
4	Counterfeit note detector	1	1,55,000	1,55,000
5	Photocopier	1	2,30,000	2,30,000
6	Burglar alarm system	1	3,50,000	3,50,000
7	Regiscope machine	1	2,62,000	2,62,000
8	Facsimile machine	1	48,000	48,000
9	Power voltage stabilizers	6	6200	37,200
10	Cash till boxes	2	6000	12,000
11	Adding machines	3	20,000	60,000
12	Desk calculators	5	5000	25,000
13	Fire extinguishers	5	6000	30,000
14	Fireproof cabinet	3	90,000	2,70,000
15	Office cabinets	6	8000	48,000
16	Tables	15	35,000	5,25,000
17	Chairs	15	20,000	3,00,000
18	Customer seats (sets)	2	45,000	90,000
19	Computers	10	1,50,000	15,00,000
20	Telephone lines	5	40,000	2,00,000
21	Official cars	3	27,50,000	82,50,000
22	Pool cars	2	25,00,000	50,00,000
23	Motorcycle	1	1,20,000	1,20,000
24	Embossing machine	1	1,55,000	1,55,000
25	Microfilming machine	1	5,30,000	5,30,000
26	Laminating machine	1	12,000	12,000
27	Generator	1	13,00,000	13,00,000
28	Vault safe	2	2,80,000	5,60,000
29	Note binder	1	2,65,000	2,65,000
30	Vault door	1	9,45,000	9,45,000
31	IT system	1	50,00,000	50,00,000
32	Leasehold	1	1,10,10,250	1,10,10,250
				3,77,54,450

Assumptions Underlying Business Plan Projections

In making financial projections for the proposed company, we made assumptions as follows:

1. *Fixed assets/depreciation*: The items that make up the fixed assets during the projected first year of operations are shown in Table 5.2. The total value of the fixed assets is depreciated over a five-year period using the straight-line depreciation method.
2. Loans and advances, and leases, account for 10% and 30%, respectively, of the total deposit liability portfolio and deposit for shares in the first year of operation. Other assets represent 10% of customers' deposits. Risk assets (loans & advances, and leases) are priced at 36% per annum.
3. Cash and short-term funds are estimated at 55% of total deposit liabilities, and marketable securities would account for 55% of customers' deposits. Of the total portfolio of cash and short-term funds, 95% would be invested in the money market at the rate of 18.5% per annum.
4. The liability portfolio arising from customers' deposits will comprise "call placements" (15%), "time deposits" (55%), "current account float" (20%), and "product related deposits" (10%). The applicable interest rates on the deposit liability products would be as follows: time deposits (18%), call placements (10%), product deposits (15%), and current account (0%).
5. It is expected that "debit turnover" would be triple the "current account float" and be charged commission on turnover (COT) at the rate of ₦3.00 per mille.
6. The volume of forex deals is assumed at 55% of loans and advances, on which income is projected at the rate of 1% flat. L/C is assumed at 20% of loans and advances. Commission on L/Cs is calculated at 1% flat on projected outstanding total volumes of import finance facilities (IFF).
7. Transactions that would be subject to commissions and fees are estimated at 25% of the sum of the outstanding balances in leases, loans, and advances. The applicable fee for these would be 1% flat.
8. The projections for operating expenses represent 60% of total staff costs.

FINANCIAL APPRAISAL OF THE BUSINESS PLAN

The promoters constructed projected financial statements of the proposed business for the first three years. Their report started with an executive summary to apprise potential investors of key financial variables that hold the keys to the financial performance and success of the proposed business venture.

Executive Summary

The proposed company has prospects of good earnings and profits, even in its first year of operation. It is envisaged that it would achieve a balance sheet size of ₦1.09 billion, with an average footing of ₦801.94 million, at the end of its first year of operation. The main earning assets of the company will comprise short-term funds, marketable securities, and credit facilities, including equipment leasing. The sources of deposit liabilities would be current, call, and fixed deposit accounts. From the projected income statement, the company is expected to achieve total gross earnings of ₦204.38 million in its first year of operation. With forecast interest, operating, and administration expenses at ₦127.69 million, the enterprise would make a profit before tax of ₦76.69 million at the end of its first year of operation. Most of the expected earnings would come from interest, commissions, and fees. The main items of expenditure would include interest expense, staff costs, and other overhead.

It would seem unusual that a start-up company could make profit in the first month of operation, and as much as ₦76.69 million at the end of first full year of operation. The normal trend is to record a streak of losses for up to six months before the break-even point is attained. However, in the case of the proposed company, it is easy to make the projected profits because of the level of capitalization and the profitability of the envisaged transactions. Highlights of the financial projections are provided in Table 5.3. Details of the financial projections (balance sheets and income statements for the first three years of operation) are presented later in this chapter. The highlights of the financial projections[a] are analyzed in the table, with implications for our proposed investment to obtain operating license.

All indices of analyses show prospects of a prosperous enterprise. The high loan-to-deposit ratio in the second and third years of operation is intended to boost earning capacity toward the company's ultimate investment objective. In doing so, the company would maintain a very high but calculated level of risk aversion or risk mitigation behavior. The promoters intend to sustain increasing levels of profit margin through a deliberate expense reduction program as reflected in the decreasing expense/revenue ratio.

Sources of Investment Finance

Our ultimate objective in this venture is accumulate funds with which to obtain a full-fledged banking license after a maximum three years of operations. In the worst-case scenario, we should be able to secure core/strategic investor status in a bank by acquiring an equity stake of at least 51 percent. In order to achieve this goal, we need to invest up to ₦2 billion, considering there are indications that the paid-up capital for banks is likely to be increased in the near future. This is in anticipation of the implementation of the Basel Accord in 2007 when the share capital of banks is expected to hit a record ₦5 billion. This is instructive in causing a sustained desire to obtain the banking license ahead of the envisioned change in the paid-up capital requirement. The breakdown of the sum of funds from operations of the

TABLE 5.3 Highlights of Financial Projections[a]

	No. of Years of Operation		
	1	2	3
	₦ million		
Total assets	1,092.29	1,289.96	1,517.52
Shareholders' funds[b]	72.15	645.70	759.72
Total liabilities[c]	1,020.14	624.46	757.80
Loans and advances	376.08	420.08	480.77
Short-term funds	374.32	472.60	540.86
Marketable securities	253.11	302.62	386.06
Deposit liabilities	460.19	550.21	701.92
Profit before tax	76.69	137.57	167.68
Float for investment[d]	552.15	625.70	1500.00
Loan/deposit ratio	40%	76%	68%
Return on equity	14%	21%	22%
Expense/revenue	48%	35%	30%
Profit margin	38%	44%	47%

[a]Details of the financial projections (balance sheets and income statements for the first three years of operation) are provided in Tables 5.5–5.10.
[b]The figure of shareholders' funds should indeed be higher considering that we have assumed a corporate tax rate of 32 per cent, which can really be significantly reduced in practice.
[c]Total liabilities decreased to ₦624.46 million at the end of the second year of operation because of the capitalization of ₦480.0 million deposits for shares after the first full year of operation. The retention of the "deposit for shares" throughout the first year of operation is to allow the company to stabilize before incurring the huge bill for registration of all the shares with the Corporate Affairs Commission.
[d]This represents realistic estimation of funds that should be available for investment to acquire a banking license or secure core/strategic investor status in a bank, which implies holding a minimum equity stake of 51 per cent. This is our overriding objective in the decision to form the proposed investment company in the first place.

proposed company, with which we intend to secure the banking license, is shown in Table 5.4.

It is possible to take more funds from the proposed company to make up ₦2 billion (instead of recourse to equity), but we will not do that because we intend to continue the company's business after divesting much of the shareholders' funds to invest in the planned bank. Indeed, we will be mindful, as reflected in this analysis, to sustain the liquidity of the investment company after the partial divestment from it. This arrangement also ensures that

TABLE 5.4 Projected Sources of Investment Finance

	₦ m
Shareholders' funds[a]	739.72
Liquidation of marketable securities	386.06
Float from short-term funds[b]	319.71
Reversal of 80% tax provision	100.00
Rights issue/sale of shares	455.51
	2000.00

[a]Of the projected shareholders' funds of ₦759.72 at the end of the third year of operation, we deducted the required statutory minimum paid-up capital of ₦20.0 million to arrive at the available float of ₦739.72 toward the banking license project.
[b]The figure of the float is calculated as the sum of short-term funds, loans, and leases at the end of the third year of operation less the total deposit liabilities of the company for the comparable period.

depositors' funds are not put at risk. For instance, this analysis makes provision for adequate liquidity to cater to depositors' withdrawal requests and transactional needs after the planned equity divestment. This is indicated in the equalizing of total deposit liabilities (₦701.92 million) at the end of the third year of operation to the sum of residual short-term funds (₦221.15 million) and investment in loans and leases (₦480.77 million), while maintaining paid-up capital of ₦20 million. The figure for residual short-term funds is arrived at after deducting that of float from short-term funds (₦319.71 million) as shown in Table 5.4 above.

Financial Projections

Presented in the appendix, Tables 5.5–5.10 show detailed financial projections (balance sheets and income statements) for the first three years of operation.

Sensitivity Analysis

The key variable that holds sway for the success of the proposed business is the ability to raise the full required equity capital of ₦500 million on or before December 31, 2006. Insofar as we are able to raise the required capital funds, most of the financial projections will be actualized. However, in the unlikely event that the full capital requirement is not met, there would be extra effort on the part of the shareholders, board, and management to attain the goal of obtaining a banking license through operations of the investment company.

The proposed investment company would remain profitable, and certainly pay a good dividend to shareholders, at less than ₦500 million in equity investments. However, at a reduced level of equity, it will not have enough financial muscle to realize our objective of leveraging on its financial standing to obtain a banking license. This implies that we must raise the minimum paid-up capital of ₦500 million so as to achieve our objective. Indeed, rather than thinking of a reduced goal, we could stretch our goal by reaching out to even more high net worth individuals with a view to raising up to ₦2 billion, which satisfies the requirement to acquire a bank or obtain a license to start a new bank.

Conclusion

The mission and strategy of the proposed investment company are realistic in practical terms. The promoters have all it takes to actualize the mission of the company (i.e., obtaining a new banking license, taking over an existing bank, or acquiring controlling equity interest as a core or strategic investor in a bank) once the required equity capital is in place. The projected financials of the proposed company indicate a high capacity to realize the set goals. The shareholders will still have a liquid and solvent going concern after the intended partial equity divestment to invest in the banking license or bank acquisition project. We envisage a situation where, as a result of enormous interest to invest in the proposed company by prospective subscribers to its shares, we would be encouraged to go for the option of either bidding to acquire controlling equity interest in, or working out a plan to take over, an existing bank. In that case, the idea of forming an investment company first will become superfluous.

FRUSTRATION OF A NOBLE BUSINESS PLAN

The promoters of the venture were making steady progress toward marketing of the private placement. They were aggressive—holding a series of meetings with HNIs, some of whom had pledged handsome amounts of money ranging from ₦5 million to ₦25 million. This outcome excited them and boosted their morale. But that was the climax of their success story—sadly. The promoters, alas, met a stumbling block to their business plan along the way. The CBN Governor, Charles Soludo, had in mid-2004 announced a 14-point agenda for banking reform in Nigeria. Topmost on the reform agenda was an increase in the regulatory capital of banks from ₦2 billion to a whopping ₦25 billion. While announcing far-reaching measures in the agenda to the Bankers Committee, the Governor allowed 18 months—ending December 31, 2005—for compliance.

Leading stakeholders in the banking industry protested what they saw as draconian measures. They were quite upset and complained bitterly about the arrogance of the Governor. How on earth the Governor made the damning capital increase decision without consulting them through the Bankers Committee was quite unsettling. With the new policy, many of them feared—and justifiably so—that they stood a chance of losing controlling equity or ownership of their banks. The fear was realistic. Paradoxically, the policy only prepared the way for mergers, acquisitions, or failure of the weak banks. To stakeholders in banks on the one hand, it was a bitter pill to swallow, but to TTL promoters on the other, it was a strange twist of fate. Ironically, people in societies that are in dire need of social change—and who are struggling to make it—tend to define their situation in terms of fate. The majority of emerging and developing economies are typical examples of such societies. However, "fate" is a misnomer, since the societies in question are powered by inherently dysfunctional economies. Unfortunately, dysfunctional economies frustrate enterprise—even in avoidable circumstances. Thus, thwarted ambitions are a common emerging economy scene and really have nothing to do with fate.

Yet, on occasion, fate plays cruel tricks. The reality in this case is certain: the policy had roundly thwarted the well-thought-out dream, ambition, and vision of TTL promoters for their venture project. They were downcast and utterly frustrated by this unexpected event. It was unimaginable that they should contemplate working toward the new regulatory capital base of ₦25 billion, when in fact raising ₦2 billion was proving to be an uphill task. They were rudely shocked, looking back at how they had surmounted the long odds against their ambition—only to be stopped by regulatory fiat. Nevertheless, the TTL promoters decided to take their medicine. Now the question is what is the import of this reality for TTL promoters and several other budding entrepreneurial talents that abound in emerging economies who may be in the same boat as them? Certainly frustrating business and financing situations have implications for economic performance in emerging markets.

ECONOMIC PERFORMANCE OF EMERGING MARKETS

Bank credit and a vibrant capital market are essential for sustained economic growth and development in emerging markets. The two sources of external finance for business and other endeavors complement each other in well-functioning financial markets. Entrepreneurial ideas could then be translated into realistic economic goals fostered by easy and affordable access to funding. This reflects the spirit of economic transformation that emerging economies need to advance to the next level. Banks in emerging economies are not doing enough on this count. Undue emphasis on earnings skews their lending policies.

The Business Correspondent Model of YES Bank Limited in India shows how bank credit could be applied to facilitate economic growth and development in emerging markets. YES Bank adopts the Model to finance low-income female borrowers and small-scale farmers in rural India. In order to access the financing, female borrowers form self-help groups through which the bank disburses the loans to them. Smallholder farmers benefit directly from the lending arrangement. The financing fulfills three major business needs for them. It enhances their output by affording them investment finance, positioning them to benefit from value chains in agriculture, and improving their access to markets. It also promotes rural financial inclusion as it builds the income earning capacity of borrowers. It is the main plank of YES Bank's long-term goal of building robust portfolios of credits it grants for agricultural production and to self-help groups.

The financing program certainly has a positive impact on India's economic performance. Consider that over two-thirds of the population of India operates in the agriculture sector. The myriad risks in agriculture that I discuss extensively in Chapter 8 are evident in India and threaten the incomes and food security of a majority of the country's population. The financing mitigates the risks, ameliorates rural poverty, and bolsters growth of the agriculture sector. In recognition of its potency, the Asian Development Bank (ADB) partners with YES Bank to strengthen the lending program, considered to be strategic for poverty alleviation in India. In 2014, the ADB granted YES Bank a loan of $200 million to boost the strategic lending model. The ADB loan is to be utilized as working capital and investment loans to organized women's self-help groups and smallholder farmers. The ADB loan package includes $1 million for capacity-building technical assistance. The technical assistance focuses on improving financial literacy and devising financial service products to link smallholder farmers to markets.

Meanwhile, there are concerns in many quarters of late about perceived deterioration of bank lending conditions in emerging markets. There are two possible interpretations of this perception. It is seen as a sign of deceleration of economic growth in emerging markets. Some think that it marks the vulnerability of emerging markets to the possible pullout of the US Federal Reserve from the so-called "easy money policies" of the US Central Bank. Many believe that lending conditions in Asia, Latin America, Africa, the Middle East, and Europe are in dire straits. Tightening credit terms in these regions are reflected in decreasing demand for and supply of loans, while the increasing number of portfolios of nonperforming risk assets evidences an impending industry crisis. The falling supply of loans is less worrisome than the falling demand for loans. The latter fuels concerns about declining investment—the implication of which is slow economic growth. The volatile currency, bond, and stock markets that characterize emerging economies exacerbate the concerns.

Nonetheless, banks typically follow their lending instincts—analyze and mitigate risk in pursuit of earnings. As Table 5.11 shows regarding credit distribution by industry in Singapore, banks crave lending to highly profitable and less risky sectors such as building and construction, general commerce, financial institutions, and housing. When doing so, they analyze and target prospects for diverse, profitable transactions—especially in the commercial and middle-tier markets. In most cases, the prospects look good in emerging economies. However, banks gear their marketing drives to attract only established good accounts and deals. Their focus is usually on firms engaged in high volume—especially international—business. Medium to large-scale merchandising firms that are found in general commerce also make the target for coveted customers. There is a constraint in the pursuit of this marketing objective though. Most of the emerging economies have not succeeded in evolving a realistic import-substitution trade strategy. Neither have they aggressively pursued the goal of export promotion. These trade policy goals are of critical importance to the countries. Their import can be explained from three main perspectives. In the first place, they strengthen supply-side economics, and by doing so they protect so-called infant industries. Secondly, a large volume of exports boosts foreign exchange earnings. Thirdly, import substitution leads to savings in foreign exchange. Thus, if properly formulated and implemented, the policies can enhance foreign exchange earnings and reserves for the countries—conditions that are propitious to economic growth.

Credit portfolio distribution by sectors in India, presented in Table 5.12, also shows where the interest of banks in lending lies. As is the case in Singapore, trade, housing, and financial institutions are prime targets—even as agriculture had a good showing and large corporates got the lion's share. That the commercial sector in emerging economies booms with bank lending owes to abnormal profits the banks make at less than average risk compared with the other economic sectors. Exploiting a price-insensitive market segment is really appealing to the banks. A further boost to the sector is the interest of entrepreneurs. Most of the small business owner-managers in emerging economies are found in the commercial sector. Thus there is potential for continued growth of the sector, particularly distributive trade and related endeavors. Indeed, an unusual explosion in the volume of consumption imports marks the growth of merchandising in emerging economies. Even as the tempo of economic activity fluctuates, consumption of certain household products has continued to boom owing to their importance as indispensable items. Regulatory changes have also been geared to reforming the activities and businesses of large-scale importers. This will ultimately strengthen the enterprises of marginal traders who constitute the bulk of secondary players in the import chain. The local corporates engaged in medium-scale manufacturing and service-oriented businesses will also benefit from the reforms.

However, banks in emerging markets should increase and sustain lending to noncommercial sectors as a means of support for economic performance of the countries. They should reinvent lending to take care of all sectors and borrowing causes without taking undue credit risk. This holds the key to sustained economic growth and development in emerging markets. However, there is yet a snag in the erratic electricity power supply to industries in some of the emerging economies. This setback tends to reverse any positive impact of reform policies and agenda of the government. It is disheartening that after decades of their existence as sovereign countries, some emerging economies cannot afford regular electricity supply to power their economies to greater heights. Worse still, it does not seem that a workable solution for this energy crisis could be achieved in the foreseeable future. This scenario presents a gloomy outlook for economic units. It does not encourage optimal business performance. Yet, it has become a reality with which the people and business community have had to live! Government must have the right vision, capacity, and will in order to solve the problem. It is only then that businesses and the people will have realistic hope for an end to the crisis and enhanced access to external financing for their endeavors.

QUESTIONS FOR REVIEW AND DISCUSSION

1. Compare bank credit with equity financing in the context of a small-scale venture in the manufacturing sector
2. In what ways does the disposition of banks toward risk-taking in and lending to some borrowing causes affect entrepreneurial endeavors in a named emerging market in Africa or elsewhere?
3. Why and how should entrepreneurs painstakingly explore alternative sources of external financing for their proposed ventures?
4. Assess how observed patterns of bank financing affect economic performance, growth, and development of a named emerging market?
5. What recommendations can you proffer to reinvent entrepreneurial spirit in an investor whose business plan is declined by a bank?

APPENDIX

TABLE 5.5 Projected Profit and Loss Account—First Full Year of Operation

	Month of Operation												Total
	1	2	3	4	5	6	7	8	9	10	11	12	
Interest Income													
Funds placements	39,53,491.55	41,24,615.65	46,17,273.62	46,85,933.52	48,06,326.16	51,30,990.39	52,06,858.15	53,40,396.49	54,29,641.05	54,57,380.51	55,20,636.61	55,87,328.72	5,98,60,872.42
Marketable securities	1,89,397.59	7,88,793.75	8,96,395.83	10,16,298.96	11,60,745.59	13,40,167.79	15,56,717.10	18,28,265.80	21,41,958.15	25,09,581.79	29,33,899.60	34,30,063.17	1,97,92,285.10
Full payout leases	46,23,262.16	53,58,884.72	54,90,941.83	56,38,095.67	58,15,371.08	60,35,571.05	63,01,336.11	66,34,600.42	70,19,586.49	74,70,760.95	79,91,514.64	86,00,442.66	7,69,80,367.79
Loans & advances	15,41,087.39	16,71,050.08	18,30,313.94	18,18,740.54	19,38,457.03	22,71,451.47	21,00,445.37	22,11,533.47	22,64,382.74	24,90,253.65	25,77,907.95	28,66,814.22	2,55,82,437.84
	1,03,07,238.69	1,19,43,344.20	1,28,34,925.22	1,31,59,068.68	1,37,20,899.85	1,47,78,180.70	1,51,65,356.73	1,60,14,796.18	1,68,55,568.42	1,79,27,976.90	1,90,23,958.80	2,04,84,648.77	18,22,15,963.16
Interest Expense													
Call deposits	32,283.68	1,34,453.48	1,52,794.74	1,73,232.78	1,97,854.36	2,28,437.69	2,65,349.51	3,11,636.22	3,65,106.50	4,27,769.62	5,00,096.52	5,84,669.86	33,73,684.96
Time deposits	2,13,072.28	8,30,141.81	10,08,445.31	11,06,454.51	13,05,838.79	14,59,053.64	17,51,306.74	20,56,799.02	23,31,970.56	28,23,279.51	31,94,164.89	38,58,821.07	2,19,39,348.13
Other	32,283.68	1,25,779.06	1,52,794.74	1,67,644.62	1,97,854.36	2,21,068.73	2,65,349.51	3,11,636.22	3,53,328.87	4,27,769.62	4,83,964.38	5,84,669.86	33,24,143.66
	2,77,639.64	10,90,374.35	13,14,034.80	14,47,331.91	17,01,547.51	19,08,560.07	22,82,005.75	26,80,071.45	30,50,405.94	36,78,818.75	41,78,225.79	50,26,160.79	2,86,37,176.75

													Total
Net Interest Margin	1,00,29,599.05	1,08,52,969.85	1,15,20,890.42	1,17,11,736.77	1,20,19,352.34	1,28,69,620.64	1,28,83,350.98	1,33,34,724.73	1,38,05,162.49	1,42,49,158.15	1,48,45,733.01	1,54,56,487.98	15,35,78,786.41
Commissions on turnover	45,738.68	1,90,490.22	2,16,475.65	2,45,431.73	2,80,314.95	3,23,644.63	3,75,940.33	4,41,518.15	5,17,273.47	6,06,052.96	7,08,523.85	8,28,345.17	47,79,749.79
Exchange income	2,77,975.71	3,22,205.35	3,30,145.34	3,38,993.03	3,49,651.79	3,62,891.41	3,78,870.66	3,98,908.32	4,22,055.78	4,49,182.85	4,80,493.40	5,17,105.47	46,28,479.10
L/C commissions	1,01,082.08	1,17,165.58	1,20,052.85	1,23,270.19	1,27,146.11	1,31,960.51	1,37,771.15	1,45,057.57	1,53,474.83	1,63,339.22	1,74,724.87	1,88,038.35	16,83,083.31
Commissions and fees	5,05,410.38	5,85,827.90	6,00,264.25	6,16,350.96	6,35,730.53	6,59,802.57	6,88,855.74	7,25,287.86	7,67,374.15	8,16,696.09	8,73,624.36	9,40,191.76	84,15,416.55
Other income	25,410.38	1,05,827.90	1,20,264.25	1,36,350.96	1,55,730.53	1,79,802.57	2,08,855.74	2,45,287.86	2,87,374.15	3,36,696.09	3,93,624.36	4,60,191.76	26,55,416.55
Total Revenue	1,09,85,216.27	1,21,74,486.79	1,29,08,092.76	1,31,72,133.64	1,35,67,926.25	1,45,27,722.33	1,46,73,644.60	1,52,90,784.49	1,59,52,714.87	1,66,21,125.36	1,74,76,723.85	1,83,90,360.49	17,57,40,931.71
Staff costs	30,50,020.10	30,50,020.10	30,50,020.10	30,50,020.10	30,50,020.10	30,50,020.10	30,50,020.10	30,50,020.10	30,50,020.10	30,50,020.10	30,50,020.10	30,50,020.10	3,66,00,241.20
Operating expenses	45,75,030.15	45,75,030.15	45,75,030.15	45,75,030.15	45,75,030.15	45,75,030.15	45,75,030.15	45,75,030.15	45,75,030.15	45,75,030.15	45,75,030.15	45,75,030.15	5,49,00,361.80
Depreciation	6,29,240.83	6,29,240.83	6,29,240.83	6,29,240.83	6,29,240.83	6,29,240.83	6,29,240.83	6,29,240.83	6,29,240.83	6,29,240.83	6,29,240.83	6,29,240.83	75,50,890.00
Total Expenses	82,54,291.08	82,54,291.08	82,54,291.08	82,54,291.08	82,54,291.08	82,54,291.08	82,54,291.08	82,54,291.08	82,54,291.08	82,54,291.08	82,54,291.08	82,54,291.08	9,90,51,493.00
Profit before tax	27,30,925.19	39,20,195.71	46,53,801.68	49,17,842.55	53,13,635.17	62,73,431.25	64,19,353.52	70,36,493.41	76,98,423.79	83,66,834.28	92,22,432.77	1,01,36,069.40	7,66,89,438.71
Corporate tax (32%)	8,73,896.06	12,54,462.63	14,89,216.54	15,73,709.62	17,00,363.25	20,07,498.00	20,54,193.13	22,51,677.89	24,63,495.61	26,77,386.97	29,51,178.49	32,43,542.21	2,45,40,620.39
Profit after tax	18,57,029.13	26,65,733.08	31,64,585.14	33,44,132.94	36,13,271.92	42,65,933.25	43,65,160.39	47,84,815.52	52,34,928.43	56,89,447.31	62,71,254.28	68,92,527.19	5,21,48,818.32

TABLE 5.6 Projected Balance Sheet—First Full Year of Operation

	Month of Operation												
	1	2	3	4	5	6	7	8	9	10	11	12	Avg
							₦'000						
Assets													
Cash & short-term funds	2,64,860.17	2,76,324.46	3,09,329.58	3,13,929.38	3,21,994.96	3,43,745.51	3,48,828.20	3,57,774.46	3,63,753.31	3,65,611.69	3,69,849.47	3,74,317.44	3,34,193.22
Marketable securities	13,975.71	58,205.35	66,145.34	74,993.03	85,651.79	98,891.41	1,14,870.66	1,34,908.32	1,58,055.78	1,85,182.85	2,16,493.40	2,53,105.47	1,21,706.59
Loans and advances	50,541.04	58,582.79	60,026.43	61,635.10	63,573.05	65,980.26	68,885.57	72,528.79	76,737.42	81,669.61	87,362.44	94,019.18	70,128.47
Advance under finance lease	1,51,623.11	1,75,748.37	1,80,079.28	1,84,905.29	1,90,719.16	1,97,940.77	2,06,656.72	2,17,586.36	2,30,212.25	2,45,008.83	2,62,087.31	2,82,057.53	2,10,385.41
Other assets	10,010.48	10,582.79	12,026.43	13,635.10	15,573.05	17,980.26	20,885.57	24,528.79	28,737.42	33,669.61	39,362.44	46,019.18	22,750.92
Preoperational expenses	5020.10	5020.10	5020.10	5020.10	5020.10	5020.10	5020.10	5020.10	5020.10	5020.10	5020.10	5020.10	5020.10
Fixed assets	37,754.45	37,754.45	37,754.45	37,754.45	37,754.45	37,754.45	37,754.45	37,754.45	37,754.45	37,754.45	37,754.45	37,754.45	37,754.45
Total assets	5,33,785.06	6,22,218.30	6,70,381.59	6,91,872.44	7,20,286.57	7,67,312.76	8,02,901.27	8,50,101.27	9,00,270.72	9,53,917.13	10,17,929.60	10,92,293.34	8,01,939.17
Liabilities													
Deposit liabilities	25,410.38	1,05,827.90	1,20,264.25	1,36,350.96	1,55,730.53	1,79,802.57	2,08,855.74	2,45,287.86	2,87,374.15	3,36,696.09	3,93,624.36	4,60,191.76	2,21,284.71
Deposit for shares	4,80,000.00	4,80,000.00	4,80,000.00	4,80,000.00	4,80,000.00	4,80,000.00	4,80,000.00	4,80,000.00	4,80,000.00	4,80,000.00	4,80,000.00	4,80,000.00	4,80,000.00
Other liabilities	6517.65	11,867.64	42,429.99	44,490.00	49,911.29	68,599.51	70,769.69	76,752.74	79,600.98	78,236.01	79,048.94	79,952.76	57,348.10
Total liabilities	5,11,928.03	5,97,695.54	6,42,694.24	6,60,840.96	6,85,641.82	7,28,402.08	7,59,625.43	8,02,040.60	8,46,975.13	8,94,932.10	9,52,673.30	10,20,144.52	7,58,632.81
Net assets	21,857.03	24,522.76	27,687.35	31,031.48	34,644.75	38,910.68	43,275.84	48,060.67	53,295.59	58,985.03	65,256.30	72,148.82	43,306.36
Capital & Reserves													
Called-up capital	20,000.00	20,000.00	20,000.00	20,000.00	20,000.00	20,000.00	20,000.00	20,000.00	20,000.00	20,000.00	20,000.00	20,000.00	20,000.00
Retained earnings	1857.03	4522.76	7687.35	11,031.48	14,644.75	18,910.69	23,275.85	28,060.66	33,295.59	38,985.04	45,256.29	52,148.82	23,306.36
Shareholders' Funds	21,857.03	24,522.76	27,687.35	31,031.48	34,644.75	38,910.69	43,275.85	48,060.66	53,295.59	58,985.04	65,256.29	72,148.82	43,306.36

TABLE 5.7 Projected Profit and Loss Account—Second Full Year of Operation

						Month of Operation							
	1	2	3	4	5	6	7	8	9	10	11	12	Total
Interest Income													
Funds placements	64,95,994.54	65,43,056.81	65,90,825.01	66,39,309.73	66,88,521.72	67,38,471.89	67,89,171.32	68,40,631.23	68,92,863.05	69,45,878.34	69,99,688.86	70,54,306.54	8,12,18,719.02
Marketable securities	34,81,514.12	35,33,736.83	35,86,742.88	36,40,544.03	36,95,152.19	37,50,579.47	38,06,838.16	38,63,940.74	39,21,859.85	39,80,728.34	40,40,439.27	41,01,045.86	4,54,03,161.74
Full payout leases	88,46,537.82	89,10,629.33	89,75,682.21	90,41,710.89	91,08,730.00	91,76,754.39	92,45,799.15	93,15,879.58	93,87,011.21	94,59,209.82	95,32,491.41	96,06,872.23	11,06,07,308.04
Loans & advances	29,48,845.94	27,78,583.34	29,91,894.07	29,16,680.93	30,36,243.33	34,53,617.24	30,81,933.05	31,05,293.19	30,28,068.13	31,53,069.94	30,74,997.23	32,02,290.74	3,67,71,517.15
	2,17,72,892.43	2,17,66,006.31	2,21,45,144.18	2,22,38,245.58	2,25,28,647.24	2,31,19,422.99	2,29,23,741.67	2,31,25,744.74	2,32,29,842.24	2,35,38,886.45	2,36,47,616.77	2,39,64,515.37	27,40,00,705.95
Interest Expense													
Call deposits	5,93,439.91	6,02,341.51	6,11,376.63	6,20,547.28	6,29,855.49	6,39,303.32	6,48,892.87	6,58,626.26	6,68,505.66	6,78,533.24	6,88,711.24	6,99,041.91	77,39,175.30
Time deposits	39,16,703.39	37,18,973.04	40,35,085.75	39,63,495.51	41,57,046.21	40,83,292.17	42,82,692.93	43,46,933.33	42,69,810.32	44,78,319.39	43,98,865.33	46,13,676.59	5,02,64,893.95
Other	5,93,439.91	5,63,480.76	6,11,376.63	6,00,529.62	6,29,855.49	6,18,680.63	6,48,892.87	6,58,626.26	6,46,940.96	6,78,533.24	6,66,494.75	6,99,041.91	76,15,893.02
	51,03,583.20	48,84,795.31	52,57,839.00	51,84,572.42	54,16,757.19	53,41,276.12	55,80,478.67	56,64,185.85	55,85,256.93	58,35,385.87	57,54,071.32	60,11,760.41	6,56,19,962.27
Net Interest Margin	1,66,69,309.23	1,68,81,211.01	1,68,87,305.18	1,70,53,673.16	1,71,11,890.05	1,77,78,146.88	1,73,43,263.00	1,74,61,558.88	1,76,44,585.31	1,77,03,500.58	1,78,93,545.45	1,79,52,754.96	20,83,80,743.68
Commissions on turnover	8,40,770.35	8,53,381.90	8,66,182.63	8,79,175.37	8,92,363.00	9,05,748.44	9,19,334.67	9,33,124.69	9,47,121.56	9,61,328.38	9,75,748.31	9,90,384.54	1,09,64,663.84
Exchange income	5,31,902.05	5,35,755.58	5,39,666.91	5,43,636.92	5,47,666.47	5,51,756.47	5,55,907.82	5,60,121.43	5,64,398.25	5,68,739.23	5,73,145.32	5,77,617.50	66,50,313.95

Continued

TABLE 5.7 Projected Profit and Loss Account—Second Full Year of Operation—cont'd

	Month of Operation												Total
	1	2	3	4	5	6	7	8	9	10	11	12	
U/C commissions	1,93,418.93	1,94,820.21	1,96,242.51	1,97,686.15	1,99,151.44	2,00,638.72	2,02,148.30	2,03,680.52	2,05,235.73	2,06,814.26	2,08,416.48	2,10,042.73	24,18,295.98
Commissions and fees	9,67,094.64	9,74,101.06	9,81,212.57	9,88,430.76	9,95,757.22	10,03,193.58	10,10,741.48	10,18,402.61	10,26,178.65	10,34,071.32	10,42,082.39	10,50,213.63	1,20,91,479.91
Other income	4,67,094.64	4,74,101.06	4,81,212.57	4,88,430.76	4,95,757.22	5,03,193.58	5,10,741.48	5,18,402.61	5,26,178.65	5,34,071.32	5,42,082.39	5,50,213.63	60,91,479.91
Total Revenue	1,96,69,589.82	1,99,13,370.81	1,99,51,822.38	2,01,51,033.12	2,02,42,585.41	2,09,42,677.67	2,05,42,136.75	2,06,95,290.74	2,09,13,698.14	2,10,08,525.11	2,12,35,020.35	2,13,31,226.98	24,65,96,977.28
Staff costs	32,02,521.11	32,02,521.11	32,02,521.11	32,02,521.11	32,02,521.11	32,02,521.11	32,02,521.11	32,02,521.11	32,02,521.11	32,02,521.11	32,02,521.11	32,02,521.11	3,84,30,253.26
Operating expenses	48,03,781.67	48,03,781.67	48,03,781.67	48,03,781.67	48,03,781.67	48,03,781.67	48,03,781.67	48,03,781.67	48,03,781.67	48,03,781.67	48,03,781.67	48,03,781.67	5,76,45,380.04
Preoperational expenses	4,18,341.67	4,18,341.67	4,18,341.67	4,18,341.67	4,18,341.67	4,18,341.67	4,18,341.67	4,18,341.67	4,18,341.67	4,18,341.67	4,18,341.67	4,18,341.67	50,20,100.00
Depreciation	6,60,702.88	6,60,702.88	6,60,702.88	6,60,702.88	6,60,702.88	6,60,702.88	6,60,702.88	6,60,702.88	6,60,702.88	6,60,702.88	6,60,702.88	6,60,702.88	79,28,434.50
Total Expenses	90,85,347.32	90,85,347.32	90,85,347.32	90,85,347.32	90,85,347.32	90,85,347.32	90,85,347.32	90,85,347.32	90,85,347.32	90,85,347.32	90,85,347.32	90,85,347.32	10,90,24,167.80
Profit before tax	1,05,84,242.51	1,08,28,023.49	1,08,66,475.06	1,10,65,685.81	1,11,57,238.09	1,18,57,330.35	1,14,56,789.44	1,16,09,943.43	1,18,28,350.83	1,19,23,177.79	1,21,49,673.03	1,22,45,879.66	13,75,72,809.48
Corporate tax (32%)	33,86,957.60	34,64,967.52	34,77,272.02	35,41,019.46	35,70,316.19	37,94,345.71	36,66,172.62	37,15,181.90	37,85,072.26	38,15,416.89	38,87,895.37	39,18,681.49	4,40,23,299.03
Profit after tax	71,97,284.90	73,63,055.98	73,89,203.04	75,24,666.35	75,86,921.90	80,62,984.64	77,90,616.82	78,94,761.53	80,43,278.56	81,07,760.90	82,61,777.66	83,27,198.17	9,35,49,510.45

TABLE 5.8 Projected Balance Sheet—Second Full Year of Operation

							Month of Operation						
	1	2	3	4	5	6	7	8	9	10	11	12	Avg
							₦'000						
Assets													
Cash & short-term funds	4,35,192.59	4,38,345.48	4,41,545.66	4,44,793.84	4,48,090.75	4,51,437.11	4,54,833.67	4,58,281.17	4,61,780.39	4,65,332.10	4,68,937.08	4,72,596.13	4,53,430.50
Marketable securities	2,56,902.05	2,60,755.58	2,64,666.91	2,68,636.92	2,72,666.47	2,76,756.47	2,80,907.82	2,85,121.43	2,89,398.25	2,93,739.23	2,98,145.32	3,02,617.50	2,79,192.83
Loans and advances	96,709.46	97,410.11	98,121.26	98,843.08	99,575.72	1,00,319.36	1,01,074.15	1,01,840.26	1,02,617.86	1,03,407.13	1,04,208.24	1,05,021.36	1,00,762.33
Advance under finance lease	2,90,128.39	2,92,230.32	2,94,363.77	2,96,529.23	2,98,727.17	3,00,958.07	3,03,222.45	3,05,520.78	3,07,853.59	3,10,221.40	3,12,624.72	3,15,064.09	3,02,287.00
Other assets	46,709.46	47,410.11	48,121.26	48,843.08	49,575.72	50,319.36	51,074.15	51,840.26	52,617.86	53,407.13	54,208.24	55,021.36	50,762.33
Fixed assets	39,642.17	39,642.17	39,642.17	39,642.17	39,642.17	39,642.17	39,642.17	39,642.17	39,542.17	39,642.17	39,642.17	39,642.17	39,642.17
Total assets	11,65,284.13	11,75,793.76	11,86,461.03	11,97,288.31	12,08,278.01	12,19,432.54	12,30,754.40	12,42,246.08	12,53,910.14	12,65,749.16	12,77,765.76	12,89,962.62	12,26,077.16
Liabilities													
Deposit liabilities	4,67,094.64	4,74,101.06	4,81,212.57	4,88,430.76	4,95,757.22	5,03,193.58	5,10,741.48	5,18,402.61	5,26,178.65	5,34,071.32	5,42,082.39	5,50,213.63	5,07,623.33
Other liabilities	1,38,843.39	1,34,983.54	1,31,150.09	1,27,234.52	1,23,310.83	1,18,966.02	1,14,949.37	1,10,885.17	1,06,729.90	1,02,568.48	98,312.24	94,050.66	1,16,832.02
Total liabilities	6,05,938.03	6,09,084.60	6,12,362.66	6,15,665.28	6,19,068.05	6,22,159.60	6,25,690.85	6,29,287.77	6,32,908.55	6,36,639.81	6,40,394.63	6,44,264.29	6,24,455.34
Net assets	5,59,346.10	5,66,709.16	5,74,098.37	5,81,623.03	5,89,209.95	5,97,272.94	6,05,063.55	6,12,958.31	6,21,031.59	6,29,109.35	6,37,371.13	6,45,698.33	6,01,621.82
Capital & Reserves													
Called-up capital	5,00,000.00	5,00,000.00	5,00,000.00	5,00,000.00	5,00,000.00	5,00,000.00	5,00,000.00	5,00,000.00	5,00,000.00	5,00,000.00	5,00,000.00	5,00,000.00	5,00,000.00
Retained earnings	59,346.10	66,709.16	74,098.36	81,623.03	89,209.95	97,272.94	1,05,063.55	1,12,958.31	1,21,001.59	1,29,109.35	1,37,371.13	1,45,698.33	1,01,621.82
Shareholders' Funds	5,59,346.10	5,66,709.16	5,74,098.36	5,81,623.03	5,89,209.95	5,97,272.94	6,05,063.55	6,12,958.31	6,21,001.59	6,29,109.35	6,37,371.13	6,45,698.33	6,01,621.82

TABLE 5.9 Projected Profit and Loss Account—Third Full Year of Operation

	Month of Operation												Total
	1	2	3	4	5	6	7	8	9	10	11	12	
Interest income													
Funds placements	71,30,070.36	72,07,387.34	72,86,289.32	73,66,808.79	74,48,978.91	75,32,833.51	76,18,407.14	77,05,735.03	77,94,853.13	78,85,798.16	79,78,607.56	80,73,319.56	9,10,29,088.80
Marketable securities	41,85,117.29	42,70,912.20	43,58,465.90	44,47,814.45	45,38,994.65	46,32,044.04	47,27,000.94	48,23,904.46	49,22,794.50	50,23,711.79	51,26,697.88	52,31,795.18	5,62,89,253.27
Full payout leases	97,10,050.81	98,15,344.55	99,22,796.82	1,00,32,451.86	1,01,44,354.83	1,02,58,551.81	1,03,75,089.83	1,04,94,016.87	1,06,15,381.92	1,07,39,234.96	1,08,65,626.98	1,09,94,610.04	12,39,67,511.28
Loans & advances	32,36,683.60	30,60,698.84	33,07,598.94	32,36,274.79	33,81,451.61	38,60,745.30	34,58,363.28	34,98,005.62	34,24,316.75	35,79,744.99	35,05,040.96	36,64,870.01	4,12,13,794.70
	2,42,61,922.06	2,43,54,342.93	2,48,75,150.98	2,50,83,349.89	2,55,13,779.99	2,62,84,174.66	2,61,78,861.18	2,65,21,661.98	2,67,57,346.31	2,72,28,489.89	2,74,75,973.38	2,79,64,594.79	31,24,99,648.05
Interest expense													
Call deposits	7,13,372.27	7,27,996.40	7,42,920.32	7,58,150.19	7,73,692.27	7,89,552.96	8,05,738.80	8,22,256.44	8,39,112.70	8,56,314.51	8,73,868.96	8,91,783.27	95,94,759.08
Time deposits	47,08,256.96	44,94,790.66	49,03,274.14	48,42,378.63	51,06,368.98	50,42,951.17	53,17,876.06	54,26,892.52	53,59,494.01	56,51,675.76	55,81,485.59	58,85,769.58	6,23,21,214.05
Other	7,13,372.27	6,81,028.89	7,42,920.32	7,33,693.73	7,73,692.27	7,64,083.51	8,05,738.80	8,22,256.44	8,12,044.55	8,56,314.51	8,45,679.64	8,91,783.27	94,42,608.19
	61,35,001.49	59,03,815.95	63,89,114.78	63,34,222.56	66,53,753.52	65,96,587.64	69,29,353.65	70,71,405.40	70,10,651.26	73,64,304.78	73,01,034.19	76,69,336.12	8,13,58,581.32
Net interest margin	1,81,26,920.57	1,84,50,526.98	1,84,86,036.20	1,87,49,127.34	1,88,60,026.48	1,96,87,587.02	1,92,49,507.53	1,94,50,256.58	1,97,46,695.05	1,98,64,185.11	2,01,74,939.20	2,02,95,258.67	23,11,41,066.73

Commissions on turnover	10,10,687.42	10,31,406.51	10,52,550.34	10,74,127.62	10,96,147.24	11,18,618.26	11,41,549.93	11,64,951.71	11,88,833.22	12,13,204.30	12,38,074.99	12,63,455.52	1,35,93,607.06
Exchange income	5,83,821.16	5,90,151.99	5,96,612.60	6,03,205.66	6,09,933.88	6,16,800.02	6,23,806.92	6,30,957.47	6,38,254.59	6,45,701.31	6,53,300.69	6,61,055.85	74,53,602.16
L/C commissions	2,12,298.60	2,14,600.72	2,16,950.04	2,19,347.51	2,21,794.14	2,24,290.92	2,26,838.88	2,29,439.08	2,32,092.58	2,34,800.48	2,37,563.89	2,40,383.95	27,10,400.78
Commissions and fees	10,61,493.01	10,73,003.62	10,84,750.19	10,96,737.57	11,08,970.69	11,21,454.59	11,34,194.41	11,47,195.39	11,66,462.90	11,74,002.39	11,87,819.44	12,01,919.74	1,35,52,003.92
Other income	5,61,493.01	5,73,003.62	5,84,750.19	5,96,737.57	6,08,970.69	6,21,454.59	6,34,194.41	6,47,195.39	6,60,462.90	6,74,002.39	6,87,819.44	7,01,919.74	75,52,003.92
Total Revenue	2,15,56,713.76	2,19,32,693.44	2,20,21,649.56	2,23,39,283.28	2,25,05,843.11	2,33,90,205.40	2,30,10,092.09	2,32,69,995.62	2,36,26,801.24	2,38,05,895.98	2,41,79,517.63	2,43,63,993.46	27,60,02,684.57
	48,43,813.18												
Staff costs	35,22,773.22	35,22,773.22	35,22,773.22	35,22,773.22	35,22,773.22	35,22,773.22	35,22,773.22	35,22,773.22	35,22,773.22	35,22,773.22	35,22,773.22	35,22,773.22	4,22,73,278.65
Operating expenses	48,43,813.18	48,43,813.18	48,43,813.18	48,43,813.18	48,43,813.18	48,43,813.18	48,43,813.18	48,43,813.18	48,43,813.18	48,43,813.18	48,43,813.18	48,43,813.18	5,81,25,758.16
Depreciation	6,60,702.88	6,60,702.88	6,60,702.88	6,60,702.88	6,60,702.88	6,60,702.88	6,60,702.88	6,60,702.88	6,60,702.88	6,60,702.88	6,60,702.88	6,60,702.88	79,28,434.50
Total Expenses	90,27,289.28	90,27,289.28	90,27,289.28	90,27,289.28	90,27,289.28	90,27,289.28	90,27,289.28	90,27,289.28	90,27,289.28	90,27,289.28	90,27,289.28	90,27,289.28	10,83,27,471.31
Profit before tax	1,25,29,424.49	1,29,05,404.16	1,29,94,360.29	1,33,11,994.00	1,34,78,553.84	1,43,62,916.13	1,39,82,802.81	1,42,42,706.34	1,45,99,511.96	1,47,78,606.70	1,51,52,228.36	1,53,36,704.19	16,76,75,213.26
Corporate tax (32%)	40,09,415.84	41,29,729.33	41,58,195.29	42,59,838.08	43,13,137.23	45,96,133.16	44,74,496.90	45,57,666.03	46,71,843.83	47,29,154.14	48,48,713.07	49,07,745.34	5,36,56,068.24
Profit after tax	85,20,008.65	87,75,674.83	88,36,164.99	90,52,155.92	91,65,416.61	97,66,782.97	95,08,305.91	96,85,040.31	99,27,668.13	1,00,49,452.56	1,03,03,515.28	1,04,28,958.85	11,40,19,145.02

TABLE 5.10 Projected Balance Sheet—Third Full Year of Operation

	Month of operation												Avg
	1	2	3	4	5	6	7	8	9	10	11	12	
	₦'000												
Assets													
Cash & short-term funds	4,77,671.85	4,82,851.63	4,88,137.59	4,93,531.91	4,99,036.81	5,04,654.56	5,10,387.48	5,16,237.93	5,22,208.30	5,28,301.07	5,34,518.75	5,40,863.88	5,08,200.15
Marketable securities	3,08,821.16	3,15,151.99	3,21,612.60	3,28,205.66	3,34,933.88	3,41,800.02	3,48,806.92	3,55,957.47	3,63,254.59	3,70,701.31	3,78,300.69	3,86,055.85	3,46,133.51
Loans and advances	1,06,149.30	1,07,300.36	1,08,475.02	1,09,673.76	1,10,897.07	1,12,145.46	1,13,419.44	1,14,719.54	1,16,046.29	1,17,400.24	1,18,781.94	1,20,191.97	1,12,933.37
Advance under finance lease	3,18,447.90	3,21,901.08	3,25,425.06	3,29,021.27	3,32,691.21	3,36,436.38	3,40,258.32	3,44,158.62	3,48,138.87	3,52,200.72	3,56,345.83	3,60,575.92	3,38,800.10
Other assets	56,149.30	57,300.36	58,475.02	59,673.76	60,897.07	62,145.46	63,419.44	64,719.54	66,046.29	67,400.24	68,781.94	70,191.97	62,933.37
Fixed assets	39,642.17	39,642.17	39,642.17	39,642.17	39,642.17	39,642.17	39,642.17	39,642.17	39,642.17	39,642.17	39,642.17	39,642.17	39,642.17
Total assets	13,06,881.69	13,24,147.60	13,41,767.46	13,59,748.53	13,78,098.21	13,96,824.06	14,15,933.78	14,35,435.26	14,55,336.52	14,75,645.75	14,96,371.33	15,17,521.78	14,08,642.66
Liabilities													
Deposit liabilities	5,61,493.01	5,73,003.62	5,84,750.19	5,96,737.57	6,08,970.69	6,21,454.59	6,34,194.41	6,47,195.39	6,60,462.90	6,74,002.39	6,87,819.44	7,01,919.74	6,29,333.66
Other liabilities	91,170.34	88,149.96	85,187.09	82,128.62	79,079.77	75,554.94	72,416.54	69,231.99	65,938.08	62,658.37	59,263.37	55,884.57	73,888.64
Total liabilities	6,52,663.35	6,61,153.58	6,69,937.28	6,78,866.19	6,88,050.46	6,97,009.52	7,06,610.95	7,16,427.38	7,26,400.98	7,36,660.76	7,47,082.81	7,57,804.30	7,03,222.30
Net assets	6,54,218.34	6,62,994.02	6,71,830.17	6,80,882.34	6,90,047.75	6,99,814.53	7,09,322.84	7,19,007.88	7,28,935.54	7,38,985.00	7,49,288.52	7,59,717.48	7,05,420.37
Capital & Reserves													
Called-up capital	5,00,000.00	5,00,000.00	5,00,000.00	5,00,000.00	5,00,000.00	5,00,000.00	5,00,000.00	5,00,000.00	5,00,000.00	5,00,000.00	5,00,000.00	5,00,000.00	5,00,000.00
Retained earnings	1,54,218.34	1,62,994.01	1,71,830.18	1,80,882.33	1,90,047.75	1,99,814.53	2,09,322.84	2,19,007.88	2,28,935.55	2,38,985.00	2,49,288.51	2,59,717.47	2,05,420.37
Shareholders' Funds	6,54,218.34	6,62,994.01	6,71,830.18	6,80,882.33	6,90,047.75	6,99,814.53	7,09,322.84	7,19,007.88	7,28,935.55	7,38,985.00	7,49,288.51	7,59,717.47	7,05,420.37

TABLE 5.11 Singapore—Loans and Advances of Domestic Banking Units (DBUs) to Nonbank Customers by Industry

	S$ million	% (a, b)	% (a + b)
Total loans to business (a)	371,520.2		
Agriculture, mining, and quarrying	6245.6	1.68	1.03
Manufacturing	29,618.8	7.97	4.87
Building and construction	103,712.4	27.92	17.06
General commerce	78,084.2	21.02	12.84
Transport, storage, and communication	21,128.5	5.69	3.48
Business services	8586.9	2.31	1.41
Financial institutions	80,895.0	21.77	13.31
Professional and private individuals—business purposes	9746.0	2.62	1.60
Other	34,502.8	9.29	5.68
Total consumer loans (b)	236,439.9		
Housing and bridge loans	177,434.6	75.04	29.19
Car loans	8641.5	3.65	1.42
Credit cards	10,422.4	4.41	1.71
Share financing	989.6	0.42	0.16
Other	38,961.8	16.48	6.41
Total loan portfolio (a + b)	607,960.0		
Key financial ratios			
Business loans to total loans			61.11
Consumer loans to total loans			38.89

Extracted from Monetary Authority of Singapore, *Loans and advances of DBUs to non-bank customers by industry*. All ratios were computed based on data extracted from this source.

TABLE 5.12 India—Deployment of Gross Bank Credit by Major Sectors as of December 26, 2014

Economic Sector	Amount (Rs. billion)	% of Sector Total
Gross bank credit	59,330.00	
Food credit	1065.00	1.80
Agriculture and allied activities	7512.00	12.66
Industry (micro and small, medium, and large)	25,752.00	43.40
Micro and small	3684.00	14.31
Medium	1268.00	4.92
Large	20,800.00	80.77
Services	13,502.00	22.76
Transport operators	883	6.54
Computer software	171	1.27
Tourism, hotels, and restaurants	360	2.67
Shipping	96	0.71
Professional services	717	5.31
Trade	3313.00	24.54
Wholesale trade (other than food procurement)	1649.00	
Retail trade	1664.00	
Commercial real estate	1643.00	12.17
Nonbanking financial companies	3000.00	22.22
Other services	3320.00	24.59
Personal loans	11,499.00	19.38
Consumer durables	147	1.28
Housing (including priority sector housing)	6015.00	52.31
Advances against fixed deposits	600	5.22
Advances to individuals against shares, bonds, etc.	41	0.36
Cards outstanding	303	2.64
Education	630	5.48
Vehicle loans	1457.00	12.67
Other personal loans	2307.00	20.06

Reserve Bank of India, *Deployment of gross bank credit by major sectors.* Ratios were computed based on data extracted from this source.

Part II

Bank Credit Markets, Taxonomies and Risk Control

Sources of Lending Transactions and Credit Risk

Chapter 6

Market Analysis for Credit Risk Control in Emerging Economies

Chapter Outline

LEARNING FOCUS AND OUTCOMES

In this chapter, I focus on target markets definition (TMD) and credit risk acceptance criteria (RAC) for banks in emerging markets. I define and discuss aspects of the key sectors in which banks in emerging markets play. I do so focusing on the banking potential, appeal, and credit risk of operators in these markets. Specifically, I explore risk-mitigating measures in lending to retail, consumer, commercial, corporate, and public sector customers of banks in emerging markets.

From the perspective of the regulatory retail portfolio enunciated by the Basel Committee, I examine the retail banking sector. In doing so, I highlight the credit risk and management implications of lending to retail banking customers. Then I take a critical look at consumer and private banking as a single business unit. I analyze the commercial banking and middle-tier markets, shedding light on the import of "middle-tier" and "extended middle-tier" that Citigroup popularized in the 1990s and considered strategic to its emerging markets business.

Grouping conglomerates and multinationals together as blue-chip companies—for convenience of analysis—I underscore their similarities.

Emerging Market Bank Lending and Credit Risk Control. http://dx.doi.org/10.1016/B978-0-12-803438-5.00006-4
115

I evaluate ordinary corporates—that is, local corporates excluding conglomerates—and assess their relevance to the corporate banking strategy of banks in emerging markets. I characterize the public sector and discuss its appeal to banks in emerging markets. The reader will learn about:

- How banks in emerging markets determine the TMD and RAC for lending and credit risk control purposes
- Key banking sectors in emerging markets and the banking potential, appeal, and credit risk of operators in those sectors
- Risk-mitigating measures in lending to retail, consumer, commercial, corporate, and public sector customers of banks in emerging markets

MARKET SEGMENTATION AND ANALYSIS

Most banks pursue growth through business development in their chosen economic sectors. Within the targeted sectors, marketing emphasis may be placed on corporate, commercial, retail, or consumer banking—based on the business orientation of the operators. In some instances, the target markets could be further defined in terms of the size, legal status, and organization of the business activities of the coveted customers. With this approach, a bank's target markets could be small businesses, public sector, blue chips, multinationals, conglomerates, and so on. It is also not unusual to find banks that define their target markets simply in terms of top-, middle-, and lower-tier market segments—with definitions of the qualifying attributes for the chosen market categories.

Perhaps, the most unwieldy approach to defining and analyzing banking target markets adopts a strict focus on the exact activities in which economic units are engaged. This implies that a bank should, for instance, define its target markets to reflect its interest in doing business with firms and other enterprises in, say, food and beverages, pharmaceuticals, energy (oil and gas), trading, commercial services, and agricultural sectors. Within each of these economic sectors, operators that constitute the target markets could be manufacturers, wholesalers, distributors, importers, exporters, retailers, service providers, and so on. Notwithstanding the unwieldiness of this approach, bankers still find it more expedient in guiding their marketing activities. For this reason, it is the approach that I adopt in this book for analyzing the risks of the various economic sectors in which banks in emerging economies define their target markets.

In all cases of analysis, it is pertinent to recognize the notion of target marketing as part of strategic business focus. Thus, in evolving plans to drive business in specific economic sectors, it is necessary—first and foremost—to:

- Define the bank's preferred market segments, businesses, and transactions (i.e., the TMD)
- Analyze the banking habits and attributes of the customers, i.e., transactions processing needs, costs, pricing, and so on

- Characterize risks associated with banking transactions, relationships, and lending in the chosen sectors or target markets (i.e., the RAC)
- Examine probable or alternative collateral available to banks to secure credit exposure to the borrowing accounts
- Assess customer relationship management expectations, tasks, and strategies, as well as success requirements, appropriate for each target market

In doing so, the overall objective is to be able to take only bankable risk, especially on foreign exchange transactions and borrowing accounts. Implicit in this goal would be a desire to increase earnings growth and broaden the profitable customer base through efficient transactions processing and relationship management.

The corporate, commercial, retail, and consumer banking markets subsume businesses, entrepreneurs, and individuals engaged in diverse economic activities such as manufacturing, trading and service enterprises. Most of these economic units—in the cases of entrepreneurs and individuals as well as commercial and retail banking customers—do not have formal organizational structures. But a more strict definition would restrict the scope of meaning of mass banking markets to *upper-*, *middle-*, and *lower-tier* local enterprises. There could be variations of this classification, such as *lower-upper*, *upper-lower*, and so on. These market segmentation categories exist in most economic sectors in emerging markets. Examples of preferred target markets for a typical small bank in Nigeria are provided in Table 6.1.

RETAIL BANKING SECTOR

Consumer, private, and retail banking were not considered distinct functions in the recent past. In some banks, the three banking units were bundled together under common supervisory responsibility. Merging them facilitated the evolution of *strategic* retail banks. As a result, banks fulfilled the needs of consumer banking customers in strictly retail transactions. While private banking formed a part of consumer banking, the latter was subsumed in retail banking. However, it became necessary to separate the units over the course of time. In doing so, banks wanted to serve particular banking needs well or better.

I unbundle the retail bank in this book and discuss consumer (and private) banking separately. I do so for the reader to understand critical aspects of consumer banking. I focus on consumer behavior—how it influences and is influenced by the dynamics of modern banking. Thus, the scope of contemporary retail banking is narrower than it was in the past. Essentially, it nowadays covers the provision of financial services to the following small business and socioeconomic units:

- Owner-managed services

Schools, hospitals, professional firms (e.g., legal, accounting, advertising, and stock broking), estate firms, and so on.

TABLE 6.1 Preferred Economic Sectors, Lines of Business, and Target Markets for a Typical Small Bank in Nigeria

Preferred Sector	Probable Business Focus	Target Customers
Food & beverages	Distilled, rectified, and blended spirits	Nigeria Distillers Limited, International Distillers Limited, distributors
	Bottled & canned soft drinks, carbonated waters	Distributors of Guinness Nigeria PLC, Nigerian Breweries PLC, Seven-Up Bottling Company PLC, Nigerian Bottling Company PLC, and so on
	Macaroni, spaghetti, vermicelli, general food products	Distributors for Dangote Flour Mills PLC, Honeywell Flour Mills PLC, Flour Mills of Nigeria PLC, and so on; importers, wholesalers of the products
	Tobacco products	Distributors for British-American Tobacco Limited; importers and wholesalers; distributors of the major brands
Energy (oil & gas)	Petroleum importation, marketing, and distribution	Ibeto Petrochemical Industries Limited, WABECO, Sahara Oil, Marca, Zenon, and so on; independent petroleum marketers; and so on
	Petroleum refining; oil and gas sector	Contractors of Nigerian National Petroleum Corporation (NNPC), Pipelines and Products Marketing Company (PPMC), Petroleum Products Pricing and Regulatory Commission (PPPRC), NPRC, and so on
	Oil & gas services firms	StatOil, Remm, Oil Test, BJ Services, and so on
	Oil exploration and drilling	Contractors of Shell, Mobil, Chevron, ConOil, and so on
Communications	Telecommunications (GSM, fixed and fixed wireless)	Dealers and distributors for MTN, Airtel, Globacom, Etisalat, Starcomms, and so on
	Print and electronic media	Radio stations; newspapers and news magazines, TV stations
Commerce	Commodities, chemicals and allied products; leather and leather products; general durable goods	Nosak (Nigeria) Limited; Distributors for Dangote; Importers and distributors of fast-selling commodities, and so on

- Small family businesses

May or may not be incorporated, and usually have informal organizational structures.

- Associations

Clubs, town unions, professional bodies, religious organizations, trade unions, and so on.

- Small enterprises

Petty traders, sole proprietors, technicians, craftspersons, artisans, peasants, beauty salons, bookshops, tailors, and so on.

- Local government

Made up of the various bureaus in the three arms of government (i.e., executive, legislative, and judicial)

This list is by no means exhaustive. Yet, it captures the essence and most of the elements that constitute the retail banking sector. Banks in emerging markets should devise appropriate strategies for this market in order to attain optimal results.

CONSUMER AND PRIVATE BANKING SECTORS

It is doubtful that students and practitioners are availed sufficient literature on the behavioral aspects of the consumer and private banking markets. Also, it is not certain that existing literature provides adequate knowledge of influences on consumer banking behavior. The literature in question should clarify lending to and managing borrowing relationships with these markets in practical ways. Unfortunately, these markets haven't received the attention they deserve at some banks.

Yet, it is imperative that the practitioners understand the intricacies of applying such knowledge in accomplishing their marketing, lending, and relationship management assignments. Such knowledge is altogether different from that gained through carrying on with banking maneuvers in a pragmatic sense. In order to bridge the observed knowledge gap, it is necessary to have a general working knowledge of consumer behavior and its implications for marketing, developing, lending, and managing consumer banking relationships.

I have used the phrase *consumer banking* in this chapter to comprise *private* and *consumer* banking segments of the mass market. However, the emphasis is on understanding, appreciating, predicting, and maneuvering the borrowing needs and behavior of customers in order to attain specific lending goals of the bank. In doing so, the bank must not compromise the interests of its customers. It should instead consciously offer value-added credit products that satisfy the perceived needs of customers.

The most critical issue from the foregoing is for students and practitioners to understand the behavior that influences the borrowing habits of individuals. How is that behavior formed, influenced, and sustained? On their part, banks should understand and anticipate that behavior in order to attain their consumer lending goals.

Perhaps, the most critical issue in consumer lending is how and with what approaches to appropriately understand behavior that influences the borrowing attitudes and habits of individuals. In *consumer banking*, the focus of study is on understanding contemporary issues in marketing, managing relationships, and offering solutions to the banking needs of individual customers—and of course, how to perform these functions for a reasonable cost. Some banks carve out private banking groups from the consumer banking department. In so doing, the banks strive to satisfy the financial services needs of high net worth and middle-income individuals.

Private banking is an integral part of consumer banking. Therefore a definition of *consumer banking* should subsume attributes normally associated with *private banking*. Consumer banking may be defined as a financial services structure designed to satisfy the banking needs of high net worth, middle-income, and low-income individuals. It embodies the facility to market and manage relationships with existing and potential individual customers of a bank. The goal of consumer banking is to ascertain and offer value-added solutions to meet the banking needs of individuals.

COMMERCIAL BANKING AND MIDDLE-TIER MARKETS

The use of the term "commercial" in describing a particular segment of the mass banking market seems inappropriate. It would ordinarily be wrong to ascribe the term to any particular market segment when in fact all market segments are engaged in commercial activities. Perhaps the only exceptions—entities that are not driven by commercial orientation and considerations—are the public sector, NGOs, and other such not-for-profit organizations. Thus, all economic units that have banking needs engage in one form of commercial activity or another. This fact notwithstanding, we must acknowledge that the phrase "commercial banking" enjoys popular and more specific application in the banking industry. In most cases, this category of bank customers experiences volatile business situations that impart risk to their transactions and operations. In particular, companies that make up the commercial banking target market for banks in emerging economies tend to be vulnerable to adverse economic changes.

One reason for this is that the market for trading and commercial services in emerging economies is very dynamic—ever in flux. Another reason is that local and international trade policies reflect the state of flux in which the market tends to be. The operators—especially traders—are barely able to respond to the dynamics of the market and the policies that inform them. Often, doing so becomes laden with pressure that encourages maneuvering of aspects of policies by operators. Such maneuvering portends credit risk that lending and marketing officers must appreciate in dealing with operators.

However, this market segment remains attractive to bankers in emerging economies despite its risk. Its operators continue to sustain business growth and appreciable financial performance. In fact, operators are instrumental in generating the banking boom of the sector. The boom has been evidenced by the increasing attention that banks pay to the sector. In addition, commercial banking has of late been institutionalized as a global business unit in most banks. In furtherance of their exploits in this market segment, banks in emerging markets now talk of middle-tier and extended middle-tier markets—both of which are offshoots of the commercial banking sector.

Commercial banking customers constitute an intermediate market sector. They represent a segment of the mass market in which operators or businesses engage in medium-scale trading, manufacturing, or similar economic activities. Trading dominates activity in this market. Perhaps this explains the use of "commercial" in describing it. Banks are becoming increasingly interested in commercial banking transactions of late. It is not surprising that they are disposed to commerce, considering the boom in the sector.

Commercial banking refers to structures, activities, and resources that banks deploy in satisfying the financial services needs of medium-sized, largely unstructured companies. I should qualify this definition and put it in perspective. Businesses engaged in commerce are often the focus of interest in commercial banking. Commercial services also typically belong in this market. However, commerce dominates the market, accounting for the bulk of customers that banks in emerging economies chase. The banks strive to provide their customers with appropriate service facilities. However, they must bear in mind the risk characteristics of the market. Of course they must—and at all times. It is understandable that banks have risk management concerns in this market segment. The sector is not only volatile but also still in a state of flux. In such a situation, a risk-averse orientation would not be out of place. A risk-conscious attitude is necessary—and should be especially evident—in lending to commercial borrowers. This approach is informed by the disposition of many customers to take avoidable—sometimes speculative—risks. It is disheartening to know that they take such risks—often with reckless abandon.

Commercial banking customers ever cherish a bid to satisfy their financial service needs. But they are often at sea when it comes to the excessive orientation of banks toward risk aversion. This state of inner conflict is at the root of the challenges in commercial banking. It is the single most important factor that frustrates customers—and weakens their banking relationships. The learning outcomes of this chapter reflect an unmistakable focus on this and other developments in the sector. Based on analysis of the underlying issues, I characterize the market and suggest appropriate lending criteria that meet its needs. My overriding objective is to develop a framework for risk analysis and control in lending to the commercial banking sector and middle-tier market.

Categories of commercial banking customers

Certain categories of economic units make commercial banking customers of banks. Such customers are found at a level above the retail banking market segment. However, the attribute characterizing commercial banking customers, from a banker's point of view, is often defined in terms of annual sales or income turnover that a business achieves. For instance, an account may be classified as a commercial banking customer, on the one hand, if it achieves annual sales or income turnover of at least $2 million but not more than $5 million. The accounts that achieve annual sales or income turnover of more than $5 million but less than $20 million, on the other hand, would be classified as *middle-tier* market customers.

There could be nomenclatural variation in the way and purposes for which banks use the phrase middle-tier market—ostensibly to serve particular lending needs. In the mid-1990s, for instance, Citibank Nigeria adopted the phrase *extended* middle-tier market as part of its overall marketing coverage and lending strategy. Thus, all private sector firms and nonbusiness organizations that achieve annual gross sales or income turnover in excess of $5 million but less than $20 million could be grouped as extended middle-tier market accounts. Though largely incorporated like other, larger commercial banking customers, middle-tier companies are often owner-dominated. They may be somewhat structured, but there's usually no clear-cut separation of the personal and official responsibilities of the owners. Managing such firms requires an unusually high level of personal attention for success. In general, companies that constitute target customers—commercial, middle-tier, and extended middle-tier—are drawn mainly from four categories by type of economic unit, namely:

- Relatively large trading companies, including major wholesalers, suppliers, and distributors of consumer and industrial products
- Firms and institutions that render particular economic services, such as educational institutions, advertising agencies, and accounting and legal firms
- Medium-scale manufacturing enterprises in various sectors of the economy
- Some relatively big NGOs and other private sector not-for-profit organizations

Some banks classify accounts of state governments under commercial banking customers. However, such accounts are more appropriately classified under the public sector as I have done in this book.

In principle and in legal terms, all companies registered in Nigeria under the Companies and Allied Matters Act, 1990, are corporate personalities. For purposes of lending and managing their banking relationships, however, not all of them are so classified. In discussing the following topics, I highlight elements that characterize commercial banking, middle-tier, and extended middle-tier customers. In doing so, I emphasize their attributes, banking habits, and risks.

Market features and practices

The depth of commercial banking and the middle-tier markets is extensive. But it is enhanced by the variety, volumes, and frequency of customer account transactions. Major customer transactions are processed mainly through current accounts. The transactions include letters of credit, funds transfers, overdrafts, and import finance facilities. Unlike retail banking, *pay-and-receive* transactions are not significant in this market segment. On the other hand, current account deposits are often regular and significant.

The foregoing banking activities determine the turnover that customers achieve in their accounts. Accounts of firms in this market are scarcely good candidates for tenor deposits. Yet most of them usually generate high transaction flows and sales turnover. Thus, income earned from commission on turnover (COT) and miscellaneous charges often account for a substantial proportion of total earnings for banks serving these customers. But the main appeal of these accounts is their ability to generate sustained net positive demand deposit float.

In the middle-tier market, banks look for specific attributes in the companies with which they want to establish banking relationships. Consider the case of a medium-sized manufacturing company. Suppose that a bank intends to win its account and start a banking relationship with it. The bank would first assess the risk and banking potential of the company. Thereafter it would investigate the company's product lines. Its findings will help it to determine whether the company's products are well diversified. These are some of the key issues for lending and credit risk management purposes.

Banks tend to shun, at least for lending purposes, companies that have mono product lines, as lending to such companies is often fraught with risk. The market risk of such companies impacts credit risk. Credit risk is exacerbated when there is deficiency in demand for the mono product. A similar effect would be experienced if an unfavorable market condition, such as adverse competitive forces, affected demand for the mono product line. On the other hand, banks covet companies that manufacture multiple lines of consumer, industrial, or intermediate products. With a diversified products strategy, such companies are better positioned to absorb market shocks.

Let me give further illustration with firms engaged in the export business. For the purpose of this illustration, I classify major exporters of manufactured, semiprocessed, and agricultural produce as middle-tier market firms. In practice—though not in general—they are so classified. The main products of these agricultural firms include rubber, cashew nuts, cocoa, ginger, gum arabic, sesame seeds, palm oil, and palm kernel. The credit risk of these companies is mitigated when the following situations exist:

- There are established or proven export markets for products of the firms
- There are reliable local sources of supply of the export produce—in the case of agriculture
- The companies have good management and proven track records in exports

CORPORATE BANKING SECTOR AND CUSTOMERS

Corporate banking is a very important sector of a bank's target markets. As a business unit, it provides financial services to large corporations, organizations, and institutions. Often the services bear the hallmark of world class transactions. Banks deploy exceptional professional skills in order to meet this service criterion. This orientation to excellence is apparent in how banks market and manage corporate banking relationships.

Not only is corporate banking a coveted banking sector, it is also the hub and centerpiece of relationship management in banking. In terms of transactions, corporate customers consummate large-volume transactions and generate product linkages. Professional financial reporting, disciplined management, and management succession plans are some other key features of corporate banking customers and accounts. These attributes are evident in blue-chip companies, such as multinationals and some local corporates in the conglomerates class.

Account officers, relationship managers, and indeed bank management are ever tasked to ensure that this category of customers has a cutting edge. Perhaps it's in serving the banking needs of the corporates that application of the 80/20 business rule—the Pareto optimality principle—is best enunciated and amplified. For banks, diligently fulfilling the banking needs of corporate customers has a payoff. This payoff has three implications for nurturing the banking relationships between banks and corporate customers. Firstly, it helps to sustain the appeal of corporate accounts to bankers. Secondly, banks sometimes—and in fact are willing to—go the extra mile for service. Doing so keeps banks in contention for corporate banking transactions. Thirdly, banks feel the honor of having good corporate accounts as customers—and in their lending portfolios.

There are two broad categories of accounts that make up the corporate banking sector—local corporates and multinationals. The former are of two main types, namely ordinary corporates and conglomerates. Ordinary corporates encompass all incorporated private sector firms that are a step above commercial banking customers. They have fairly formal organization structures, maintain the required books of accounts, and document business transactions. In general, they are seen as accounts that achieve annual sales or income turnover of more than $20 million but less than $150 million.

To some extent, ordinary corporates share some features characterizing conglomerates and multinationals. However, there are basic differences between them. Multinationals, and to a lesser extent conglomerates, tend to adhere strictly to standard business principles and best practices. In the case of ordinary corporates, this practice is often lacking. For instance, they may be amenable to compromises under difficult business situations. On occasion business pressure and expediency dictate the road to compromise for ordinary corporates. Stricter adherence to business principles and best practices tends to confer a perception of stronger integrity on the business and financial performance of multinationals and conglomerates.

Conglomerates are usually large corporations, having subsidiaries or related companies, and operating in multiple sectors of the economy. In most cases, they are private sector corporations and have formal organizational structures. They achieve average annual sales or income turnover of not less than $150 million. Multinationals are generally regarded as blue-chip companies. Though they are incorporated in the countries where they are based, they are usually affiliated with their parent companies in foreign countries. Yet, there is a subtle difference between a blue-chip company and a multinational corporation. For example, some local corporates (especially conglomerates) satisfy the criteria of being a blue-chip company and are so designated. This implies that the term blue chip is not exclusively reserved for multinational corporations. Perhaps the adoption of blue-chip in expressing class for some category of companies evolved with the craving of banks for a unique way of identifying such high-profile corporate banking customers or accounts.

I have in this chapter regarded conglomerates and multinationals as blue-chip companies for the convenience of discussion and analysis. This approach underlines a basic fact in analyzing their potential for mutually beneficial banking relationships—they share common advantages as corporate banking customers. The advantages relate to their large sizes and transaction volumes. In most cases, they also require similar lending, marketing, and account and relationship management strategies. My primary objective is to assess the borrowing causes and attributes of companies that constitute the corporate banking market. The companies are drawn from ordinary corporates, conglomerates, and multinationals. This entails a critical analysis of their business strengths and weaknesses, as well as the framework for their credit risk management.

Vicissitudes of conglomerates

A radical transformation in the character of the banking business became apparent in the early 1990s. The observed trend was a marked decline in the relevance of conglomerates relative to other target markets. The contribution of conglomerates to annual earnings and profitability at many banks declined progressively for several years. The sector continued to decline in importance over time. Competition among banks was historically targeted at getting a hold on conglomerates—in addition to blue chips and multinationals. Ironically, the conglomerate sector represented not more than 5% of the banking market in terms of size. Yet, the sector helped banks make their marks in profitability. At that time, blue chips, multinationals, and conglomerates accounted for over 70% of gross annual earnings of banks. In time banks started to relegate conglomerates. The vicissitudes of business were at issue, taking a heavy toll on their financial performance. As expected no bank was willing to take credit risk on the declining sector.

The case of United Trading Company (Nigeria) Limited (UTC) serves as an example to illustrate the vicissitudes of conglomerates. Once a large trading corporation, UTC offered high-quality personal care, and consumer and industrial products and services. Every bank struggled to win its accounts. Opening an account for UTC, let alone having a banking relationship with it—even if only for peripheral transactions—was a big deal for banks. That a bank had UTC as a customer was all that mattered. However, UTC suffered a fate similar to that of the railroad in Theodore Levitt's *marketing myopia* thesis. The company experienced a gradual loss of market share. The decline culminated in huge financial losses beginning in the late 1980s, with the company entering a downward spiral. The downward trend continued until this one-time industry giant went into receivership with massive debts. In the late 1990s, a consortium of banks to which UTC was indebted invoked default clauses against the company and foreclosed on its assets. The company was ultimately sold to some investors who aimed at a complete turnaround. The new UTC downsized operations, sold unproductive assets, and started the progressive liquidation of its indebtedness.

A similar fate befell several other conglomerates like UAC of Nigeria PLC, Lever Brothers PLC (now Unilever Nigeria PLC), and PZ Industries PLC. Like UTC, they suffered severe business declines in the wake of deregulation of the Nigerian economy in the mid-1980s. The problems of these companies were largely the consequence of trade liberalization. This policy opened up the economy as a means of promoting reliance on market forces. Nigeria's structural adjustment program and implementation of the WTO agenda exacerbated the crisis of these companies. Thus the unfettered grip of the companies on the country's economy was broken. In time the middle-tier market—made up mainly of large importers and wholesalers of competing products and services—became a check on their cartel power. Today conglomerates are fringe players in some of the markets that were their traditional strongholds. Nonetheless, they retain their appeal as an important target market for banks.

The financial performance of banks that have a predominantly conglomerate customer base was also adversely affected. However, the banks responded strongly to the problem of the diminishing relevance of the conglomerate market. They repositioned marketing and business development strategies targeted at operators in other segments of the mass market. Nowadays banks pay unusual attention to consumer banking, small businesses, the public sector, and the middle-tier market. This was one of the strategic moves of Citibank Nigeria at the turn of the millennium. The bank defined and opted for a new target market that it christened the extended middle-tier market. Its target customers in this market included medium-scale trading companies. The central premise of this move was that the loss in business from conglomerates would be offset by gains in this new but riskier market. Thus, the bank started building specific risk management competencies appropriate for the market. It also reviewed its general business strategy along the lines of the foregoing move. It changed its former business orientation, which had favored setting up of branches on high streets in big cities. Now it is common to find Citibank branches in locations near its new target markets. Examples of other elitist banks that followed suit include GTBank, Standard Chartered Bank, Ecobank, and Stanbic IBTC Bank. These and several other banks took a cue from Citibank Nigeria. The common denominator of all of these banks is how they responded appropriately to the vicissitudes of conglomerates.

There are still other obvious reasons for the declining fortunes of companies in the conglomerate market. In most cases, the reasons are informed by economic distortions, especially in developing countries. The conglomerates—usually large manufacturing corporations—must contend with a myriad of systemic economic problems. This poses business challenges to the companies. Structural rigidities render some of the economies dysfunctional. The major problems include the following:

- Dumping of imported goods at cheaper prices than locally made goods, just to satisfy a craving for such products in the local market
- Fierce competition from companies engaged in general commerce. This is a consequence of the flourishing market for consumption expenditure on *cheap* products.
- Paucity of local raw materials supplies in the face of high and rising costs for imported raw materials
- Rising costs for borrowed funds and general banking transactions. Money market instability worsens the problem
- A downward spiral of depreciating value of local currencies. Volatile foreign exchange markets make it difficult for companies to realize business and financial projections.
- Market insensitivity, reflecting the popular disease of *marketing myopia*, from which most of the early businesses such as the railroads suffered

These problems negatively affected the performance of the conglomerate sector.

The problems have continued to painfully pose critical challenges to the operations of the conglomerates. It is common knowledge, for instance, that dumping is a major problem of industrial growth in developing countries. In some cases, this and similar setbacks impelled banks to switch favor from conglomerates to other target markets, such as the middle-tier market, the public sector, small businesses, and consumers.

GOVERNMENT AND THE PUBLIC SECTOR

Government, its agencies, and parastatals—known collectively as the *public sector*—constitute a major target market for banks in every country.[1] Perhaps the significance of the public sector for banking relationships is more evident in less developed countries. This is because the private sector trails in driving developmental programs and economic activities in those countries. Government is the largest, most homogenous, and predictable single economic unit among all target markets that banks chase for banking relationships. As the almighty sector of the economy, it takes precedence over other economic entities in terms of volumes of banking transactions both within and outside a country. No wonder banks pay a lot of attention to the sector.

It would be unusual to find a sector of the economy that does more business than the public sector. This view is based on counts of aggregate annual expenditure and gross realizable revenues. The significance of government is best appreciated when we realize that it operates in every sector of the economy, either directly or indirectly. This ubiquity trait defines its appeal for banking relationships. Banks chase one or more public sector accounts because of expectations of huge current account transactions, deposit floats from various taxes, profitable lending opportunities, and fixed deposits from unapplied capital funds or budget surpluses.

QUESTIONS FOR DISCUSSION AND REVIEW

1. Identify and discuss any five named categories of retail banking customers and discuss their main features.
2. Discuss a framework that bank management can formulate and apply to anticipate, analyze, and manage the risks of lending to individuals.
3. Using trading companies as a basis, how would you characterize commercial banking customers to help bankers appreciate their traits and financing needs?
4. Discuss a practical risk analysis and control framework that banks can adopt in lending to the commercial banking and middle-tier markets.
5. **(a)** What are the criteria for designating particular bank customers as corporate?
   (b) Discuss the view that two broad categories of accounts make up the corporate banking sector.
6. Why and how may it be dicey to lend money to the public sector? Your answer should elucidate tasks in analyzing and managing lending to the sector and its credit risk.

---

1. I have throughout this book used the terms *government* and *public sector* interchangeably to refer to all non-private sector economic units, institutions and establishments, whether or not engaged in business, which particularly provide social services and security of lives and property to the citizens.

Chapter 7

SME Credit Risk, Analysis, and Control in Emerging Economies

Chapter Outline

LEARNING FOCUS AND OUTCOMES

Often how to assess the creditworthiness of potential small and medium-sized enterprise (SME) borrowers bothers lending officers in emerging markets. In most cases, issues underlying the concerns border on how to correctly evaluate the commercial viability of SMEs, the feasibility of their projects, their business sustainability, and the ability of their management to meet set goals and business plans. Much in the same vein, a dearth of skills and abilities to anticipate SMEs' future challenges and performance can be quite frustrating.

Skill gaps are particularly evident in quantitative assessment of SME credit risk. On occasion, lending officers find it difficult to devise and apply a simple cash flow forecasting model to sensitize and evaluate assumptions that shed light on the risks of lending to SMEs and ability of the SMEs to service and repay their debts. Yet such risk analytics are useful to appreciate and assess alternative funding needs, sources, and the risks applicable to particular SME borrowers and to the SME sector in general. With a strong analytical footing, lending officers can also monitor SME loans and enforce appropriate SME covenants that protect the bank against loan loss.

In view of the foregoing, I explore the informal nature of SME businesses and operations. The knowledge that this furnishes is reckoned to be a critical success factor in lending to SMEs. One reason is that the informal business organization impinges on SME financial prudence. Another reason is that it exacerbates the risk of lending to SMEs. I examine how banks could handle the external financing needs of SMEs so as to mitigate the attendant lending risks. This is essential, as SMEs constitute the bulk of retail and commercial banking customers and contribute over 70% of gross domestic product (GDP) in emerging economies.

I examine the role and implications of the collaboration of the International Finance Corporation (IFC) and central banks to strengthen the ability of SMEs to secure bank loans for business operations in emerging economies. A typical collaboration for building SME capacity for external financing is "collateral registration for movable assets" under the auspices of the IFC's Secured Transactions and Collateral Registries program. I need mention here that the institution that regulates banking business is known by various names in different countries. In Nigeria, it is named the Central Bank.

Other examples include the State Bank of Pakistan, Peoples Bank of China, and Reserve Bank of India. In order to have a common understanding of the name of these institutions, irrespective of countries in question, I adopt "Central Bank" as a uniform designation. The reader will learn about:

- Key issues that underscore risk and uncertainty in bank lending to SME borrowers in emerging economies
- How to correctly identify, assess, and mitigate risks inherent in SME proposals for bank loans
- How to evaluate SME management in terms of the vision, competence, and integrity implied in the feasibility studies of their project finance proposals.
- Tasks involved in appropriately structuring, analyzing, and packaging SME credit facilities
- How to determine and obtain appropriate information for assessing the creditworthiness of SME borrowers
- Critical ways to analyze SME loan proposals with emphasis on mitigating fundamental SME credit risks

DEFINING SMALL AND MEDIUM-SIZED ENTERPRISES

Ideally, the term *small and medium-sized enterprises* should convey the same meaning as *small-scale enterprises, small-scale industries*, and such other related terms. Yet it has not been easy to exactly define what these concepts collectively mean in practical terms. The problem is evident in UNIDO's identification of 50 different definitions of small-scale industries in 75 countries (Evborokhai, 1989). Every emerging economy—indeed, every country— tends to define SMEs to suit its economic or development needs. Thus while the basic criteria used to define SMEs tend to be the same among countries, quantitative measures of the criteria often vary from one country to another. The basic criteria on the one hand relate to sales turnover, balance sheet size, paid-up capital, and number of employees, while the quantitative measures on the other specify levels for each of the defining criteria. So there is no universally accepted definition of SMEs—one that is applicable in all countries and for all purposes of economic analysis.

In defining the basic criteria of SMEs, the European Union (EU) relates number of employees with sales turnover and/or balance sheet size. It defines SMEs as enterprises that employ not more than 250 persons and whose annual turnover is less than €50 million, and/or a maximum annual balance sheet footing of €43 million. It unbundles SMEs into three distinct economic units—medium-sized, small, and micro enterprises—that are subsumed in its definition.

The Taiwanese authorities adopt largely similar SME-defining criteria. However, their approach differs from that of the EU. While using the basic criteria of sales turnover and number of employees, paid-up capital is substituted for balance sheet size. In a revised definition of SMEs issued in 2009, the Taiwanese economy is divided into two broad categories—manufacturing, construction, mining and quarrying industries (category 1); and agriculture, services, and other sectors (category 2). While SMEs are defined for the first category in terms of paid-up capital and number of employees, it is sales revenue and number of employees that are the basic criteria for SMEs in the second category. In order to qualify as an SME in the first category, an enterprise should have paid-up capital of not more than NT$80 million (about US$2.42 million) and have less than 200 employees. SMEs in the second category are expected to have achieved not more than NT$100 million (US$3.03 million) in sales revenue in the last year and have less than 100 employees.

Singapore has a straightforward definition. Starting April 2011, it adopted a new definition for SMEs that emphasizes either sales turnover or employee size. Thus there are two routes to defining SMEs in the case of Singapore. An enterprise would be designated as an SME if either its annual sales turnover is not more than S$100 million or its employment size is not more than 200 workers.

In Malaysia, SMEs are defined in terms of either sales turnover or full-time employment of workers. As in the case of Singapore, the economy is categorized into two—manufacturing (category 1), and services and other sectors (category 2). For category 1, an enterprise is designated as an SME if it either achieves annual sales turnover of RM50 million or employs not more than 200 workers. In category 2 are enterprises whose annual sales turnover is not more than RM20 million, or whose number of full-time employees is not more than 75 workers.

SMEs are characterized by diverse business orientations. They are found in every economic sector. Unfortunately, their banking needs and financing problems reflect similar diversity. The firms exist in various forms. While most operate as owner-managed, many are owned and managed as family enterprises. Few have formal organizational structures. For these reasons, it would be futile to attempt any discussion of their various activities. In most cases, ownership is not clearly separated from management. The fusion of management and control presents the most difficult challenge in managing their banking relationships. Banks scarcely take credit risk on entrepreneurs whose businesses are unstructured—neither would they be comfortable with those in which owner-managers interfere with day-to-day operations. I expatiate on these SME attributes later in this chapter. Presently I concern myself with investigating SME definitions in emerging economies.

MOTIVATIONS OF SME ENTREPRENEURS

In developed economies, governments recognize the importance of SMEs and ensure that they have unrestricted access to external business finance.

In emerging economies, one sees a totally different situation—one in which the financing needs of SMEs are downplayed in public policy formulation. This sheds light on the need to provide a favorable business link between banks and SME entrepreneurs in emerging economies. However, certain critical banking relationship issues affecting both parties must be analyzed, understood, and borne in mind before any attempt at resolving the problem of inadequate financing of SMEs can yield fruition. These issues are implied in the following questions:

- What are the motivational determinants of performance among small business owner-managers?
- How readily do small-scale enterprises attract external financing to support business operations?
- Are banks being discouraged from financing small-scale businesses because of peculiar risks inherent in their nature and mode of operation?
- What should be done to enhance the flow of credit to the SME subsector?

Studies of small businesses in emerging economies, unfortunately, have focused mostly on the general characteristics, including finance and administration, of SME entrepreneurs. The nature of the SME financing need and problem, and the effects of these on self-employment efforts of prospective entrepreneurs, have largely been neglected. This chapter is set to bridge this missing link in the hope that it would generate further investigation of the problem.

An individual may establish a small-scale business to satisfy a drive for self-employment. The person often provides necessary risk capital through personally raised funds, assumes control of the business, and employs some category of labor. The owner-manager, who nevertheless also bears the burden of business risk, enjoys pride of ownership.

Sometimes the efforts of individuals to set up and run their own small businesses fail because of the lack of or inability to raise sufficient funds. Often such persons are compelled to suppress their desire for self-employment. In silence, but often dissatisfied, they remain employees rather than becoming self-employed. Thus I distinguish three groups of SME entrepreneurs with respect to self-employment motivation:

- Individuals who, having the urge for self-employment, are able to set up SME businesses to actualize their self-employment drive
- Individuals who, for want of finance, have been unable to set up and run their own SMEs and thus cannot actualize their desire for self-employment
- Individuals on whom the realities of unemployment foist the self-employment drive—compelling them to set up some SME business one way or the other

The three groups, however, face a common problem—each needs financing that may not be available in the quantum they need. The capital may also not be available as and when required. Often entrepreneurs face problems in trying to raise capital in the financial market (see Chapter 5).

In spite of these constraints, the government continues to prod the unemployed to set up small-scale businesses as a means to ease the unemployment crunch. Failing this, most of them will be impoverished. But the threat of unemployment is not the only factor that can trigger entrepreneurial efforts. Some SME entrepreneurs are motivated by profit, the desire for recognition, or a desire to render service to their communities (Evborokhai, 1989).

SIGNIFICANCE OF SMES FOR EMERGING MARKET ECONOMIES

One of the reasons economic growth in emerging economies falters is neglect of the financing needs of small-scale industries. In industrialized economies, on the contrary, the role of small businesses in economic growth is appreciated. Sound macroeconomic policies bolster the SME role in the economy. Even in advanced nations, small businesses have proven to be a key factor for sustaining economic growth. Banks target SME credits at the budding populations of existing and potential entrepreneurs, ostensibly to ease their external financing difficulties. That underscores the significance of small businesses. They make positive contributions toward the overall growth and development of a country. This role stands SMEs in good stead to impact the economic life of a country. One reason is that small-scale enterprises contribute significantly to national output and employment growth. Another is that their activities impart resilience to the economy.

One notices tenuous efforts that Central Banks in emerging economies make to enforce specific credit control measures in support of SMEs. The Banks do so through regular monetary and credit policy circulars or other media, depending on the regulatory requirements of the country. On occasion the Central Banks set a minimum quantum of aggregate banking system credits that banks must disburse to the SME sector. Were banks to comply fully with these guidelines, such enterprises—especially the indigenous SMEs—would have had guaranteed access to bank credit. Such an outcome should encourage and sustain the involvement of SMEs in economic growth and development. But this approach has not been effective for the same reasons that most banks in emerging economies shun agricultural financing. The reasons border on scary risks.

For this reason, save for SMEs engaged in activities related to commerce, there is a wide financing gap for SMEs in emerging economies. SMEs do need and long for medium- to long-term loans to finance real growth. The usual 90-day credits that banks offer them at best are inappropriate to their funding needs. While banks in emerging economies appear committed to implementing the sectoral credit guidelines that the Central Banks issue, they rarely meet set targets. Occasionally operators of SMEs protest that banks are indifferent to their financing needs. The protest marks the disenchantment of the sector with half-hearted compliance by banks, even with credit regulation in its favor. This situation is not peculiar to SMEs. Some organized private-sector groups also protest that a bank credit freeze stifles their operations.

Ideally, banks in emerging economies should worry about the unfavorable perception of their lending to SMEs. But it would seem the situation does not perturb banks in the least. Bank management seems adamant that it will stick with so-called strategic lending to its target markets, if anything. Banks respond nonchalantly to criticism of their negative attitude toward lending to SMEs. They stoutly defend their stance. But SME entrepreneurs are skeptical of their claims, ostensibly taking issue with them. Unfortunately, while this stance benefits bank, it frustrates the goal of economic growth and development. Government intervention could solve the problem of the paucity of financing for SMEs.

There is no doubt that the government is concerned about the fate of SMEs. In Nigeria, the government set up Peoples Bank of Nigeria (PBN) in the late 1980s. In the 1990s and during the decade that followed, it introduced community and microfinance banking, respectively. There is also National Economic Reconstruction Fund (NERF), which is yet another source of financing for SMEs. Ordinarily, the establishment of these development and people-oriented banks and institutions would suffice. However, the institutions seem overwhelmed by the task at hand. They were either inadequately capitalized or saddled with large stocks of nonperforming assets in the course of their operations or both. There could also have been a problem of political interference in the operations and management of PBN and NERF.

These and similar financing programs are found in other emerging economies. There could be nomenclatural differences, but the institutions exist in one form or another. The private sector takes the initiative in filling the financing gap for SMEs in emerging economies where the government's role is found wanting. It is either that the government failed to or does not effectively tackle the need for the institutions. In Bangladesh, Yunus Mohammad set up Grameen Bank in 1983 so that the poor-especially women entrepreneurs— could avail themselves of the opportunity to access micro credit. Grameen Bank became a success story soon after its founding—prompting the Nobel Committee to award the 2006 Nobel Peace Prize to Yunus. This way the role of SMEs in the economy is better appreciated.

It is strongly advised that bank management should connect with entrepreneurs, ostensibly to boost national economic growth and development. In the course of this chapter, I affirm the importance of SMEs to both banks and the public. In doing so, I review their main features; assess their banking needs; examine their depth, prospects, and potential; and, analyze bank–customer relationship issues that impact their operations.

SME ATTRIBUTES, BUSINESS PRACTICES, AND CREDIT RISKS

Besides overdrafts, SMEs often need asset-based credit, advances, project financing, performance bonds, and bank guarantees. A bank may grant a proven loan request, one that a rigorous credit analysis corroborates. In all cases, credit risk must be effectively mitigated. I will not elaborate on canons and contemporary methodology of bank lending implied in this statement since I specifically discuss them extensively in Chapters 20 to 22—and, indeed, as the need arises elsewhere in this book. I focus here on defining SME credit risk vis-à-vis bank expectations.

The risk of lending to SMEs could be quite high. Often the probability of occurrence of the risk is also high. Thus banks are scared to take on the credit risk of SME entrepreneurs—especially those whose businesses are unstructured and show signs of the owner-manager's informal interference in operations. However, banks would lend money to SMEs once they are satisfied that the amount being requested, purpose of the borrowing, and character of the borrower pass their credit test and rating. Loan officers will also normally want to analyze the borrower's financial commitment to the business (capital invested in relation to debt), its capacity to succeed in the particular line of business, and the prevailing macroeconomic conditions that may affect the ability of the SME to repay its loan according to the terms and conditions agreed to with the bank. If the risks associated with these key credit issues are mitigated, a loan request may be granted—but not until the bank has taken adequate collateral on which it can fall back in the event of default.

SMEs tend to engage in highly speculative ventures and deals. They do so perhaps with the expectation of a huge profit or return on investment. Unfortunately, such ventures do not interest banks. Uncertainty of expected returns is usually at issue. Thus, it is usually risky for banks to lend money to such ventures. As start-ups, banks at best subject such lending proposals to rigorous credit analysis. The loan losses attendant on financing transactions in this category could be colossal and unavoidable, even at that. In the highly volatile business environment characteristic of emerging economies, banks cannot afford to take a gamble on lending to ventures. With good calculations, venture capitalists may earn their projected income. Yet banks will be critical of the assumptions underlying the income forecast.

Where a bank is in doubt about the quality of SME management—and this is often the case—it may decline its credit request. It is only in few cases that SME entrepreneurs in emerging economies possess requisite managerial skills appropriate for the businesses in which they are engaged. Banks also investigate this risk factor before making a lending decision. This risk relates to the capacity of SME entrepreneurs to effectively carry out their business tasks. A bank must be satisfied with the technical competence—the entrepreneurial abilities—of small business owner-managers. Otherwise, it would be difficult for the bank to lend money on their projects or other capital investments.

SMEs suffer yet another crucial setback to the flow of bank credit to their operations. Often SME entrepreneurs fail or are unable to back up their loan requests with an acceptable feasibility study and report. This setback is seen mainly in applications for the funding of capital expenditure projects. But it is also common in requests for venture capital. Banks find it difficult to appraise and grant such credit requests, ostensibly to underlie their risk. SME entrepreneurs who hope to obtain long-term loans should furnish their banks with a comprehensive, accurate, and current feasibility study for the project in which they are interested. As I demonstrate in this chapter, a feasibility study always proves helpful in bank lending to start-ups. It shows that a project or venture for which the SME entrepreneur requires a bank loan is technically feasible and commercially viable. There is a real difficulty here, though. A lack of reliable statistical data could frustrate a feasibility study. In emerging economies, this has become commonplace. Often statistical data contained in feasibility studies are either outdated or mere guesstimates.

If an SME has a keyman management, it may find it difficult to obtain credit facility from a bank. This is especially the case where an SME does not have the potential to survive in the event of the unexpected demise of the owner-manager. Yet this is a common feature of most SMEs in emerging economies. This situation poses a credit risk from which banks shy away. But it is avoidable in the sense that SME entrepreneurs can take either of two steps to mitigate this risk. Firstly, the management of the business can be broadened, with clear evidence of a mastery of its operations by at least the line officers. Secondly, if keyman management is inevitable, the life of the owner-manager should be insured. These devices could provide acceptable security for a loan as they somewhat mitigate the credit risk.

SMEs are also often characterized by the fusion of the family and personal responsibilities of owner-managers with those of the enterprises. This problem is common in the management of SME financial resources. In the absence of a total separation of the business and personal funds of the entrepreneur, financial prudence would not be achieved, and the flow of bank credit would remain hampered. A situation of this sort sends out a risk-warning signal to loan officers that if a loan is granted, its proceeds could be diverted or misused.

The capacity of SMEs to obtain credit facilities through the banking system is also limited by their unstructured or irregular mode of operations. The future business activities of most SME entrepreneurs cannot in most cases be accurately predicted on the basis of past patterns of operations. In view of the inconsistent business goals, pursuits, and practices of most SMEs, banks feel restrained in granting them credit facilities, especially for purposes of meeting working capital needs.

Banks also demand the granting of and indeed could grant credit facilities on the strength of the borrower's financial records, especially the balance sheet and income statement. But this is yet another important requirement for bank credit that SMEs do not always satisfy. Their business and accounting data, if any, are marked by incomplete records. Of course, banks place a lot of emphasis on documentation of business transactions, especially accounting records. Accounting information furnishes evidence of SME financial performance and health. Banks have not been in a position to meet the credit needs of SMEs on the grounds of their accounting failings.

SME EXTERNAL FINANCING NEEDS

Business ventures are run on the buffer of equity and debt. Thus the mix of funding sources determines the financial risk of a business. A high debt-to-equity ratio imparts capital structure risk to a business. This is a volatile condition that might adversely affect the long-term viability of the enterprise. In order to mitigate financial risk, and thus be able to attract external financing, SMEs must achieve an optimum mix of debt and equity in their capital structures. How have SME entrepreneurs in emerging markets coped with this task? In a nutshell, how do we state or define the SME external financing problem?

Lack of adequate capital is one of the significant problems of SMEs in emerging economies. Inadequate funding constrains the operations of SMEs in emerging markets. However, it would be unfair to hold banks wholly responsible for the insufficient flow of credit to the sector. The risk-aversion orientation of banks is always the culprit, if anything. This is usually the case when banks fail to meet their target credits for the sector. Banks are custodians of depositors' funds and have a responsibility to manage the funds well and ensure that they are safe at all times. Yet banks take the lead among the sources of funds available to SMEs in emerging economies—no matter how one tries to analyze the problem of the poor financing of the sector.

Governments in emerging economies are not indifferent to SME financing needs either. That governments and Central Banks in emerging economies classify SMEs as a priority sector tells of their interest in SME operations. One of the ways that governments in emerging economies have shown strong interest in SMEs is seen in the institutional and policy frameworks they put in place to manage the sector's financing needs. In Nigeria, the establishment and funding of the National Economic Reconstruction Fund (NERF), Small and Medium-Scale Enterprises (SME) Apex Unit, Bank of Industry (BoI), Nigerian Export-Import Bank (NEXIM), and Nigerian Agricultural Insurance Company (NAIC) are some government initiatives to support the SME sector. These institutions also exist but are either similarly or differently christened in other emerging economies.

Small-scale enterprises on the lower rung of SMEs—those found mainly in the informal economy—also benefit from policy interventions of governments. The disbanded Peoples Bank of Nigeria (PBN) is typical of such intervention.

The same goes for the rescinded community banking policy. In place of these institutions, the Central Bank of Nigeria introduced microfinance banking. These policies show that the government has always been interested in SME affairs and how to promote them. Unfortunately, the financing problem of the sector tends to defy such institutional antidotes.

It may be difficult to pinpoint issues that underlie the fate of SMEs. One reason is that their financing and management have become a hydra. But there is a three-pronged way forward. Firstly, banks should increase lending to the sector. Secondly, policy intervention must be constructive. Thirdly, entrepreneurs must build capacity and tame their risk-taking appetites.

APPRAISING AN SME PROJECT FOR BANK LENDING

One of the key issues in bank lending to SMEs is how to critically appraise the feasibility of their proposed projects. In most cases, the business plan that informs a project is hazy—if not lacking altogether. The feasibility study and report that should provide a roadmap to the project often lacks a critical sensitivity analysis. I discussed issues relating to the business plan and how to sensitize financial projections in Chapter 5. Presently I focus on how SME entrepreneurs can prepare credible feasibility studies and reports on their own. That is necessary if a bank may consider and grant their loan requests. In doing so, I guide lending officers through the analysis and interpretation of the feasibility study and report. This involves teaching how to construct, analyze, and interpret financial statements from the assumptions underlying a feasibility study.

Let us assume a hypothetical situation in which some potential SME entrepreneurs decide to establish a newsmagazine in Lagos, Nigeria, and need bank financing for the project. Conducting a feasibility study of the project before approaching a bank with their loan request is pertinent. The essence of the study is to determine whether the project is technically feasible and commercially viable. The promoters can do this by themselves if they are knowledgeable about the publishing business—and therefore their proposed project. If they lack knowledge for the project, they should engage professional consultants in that field to conduct the study on their behalf. Of course, the consultants would charge a professional fee that would add to the project's cost. In this hypothetical example, the promoters conducted the feasibility study, prepared the report on the study, and approached a bank to finance the project.

ABRIDGED FEASIBILITY STUDY OF SME BUSINESS VENTURE

Background

Nigeria's financial system is still at the rudimentary stage of development. But its growth potential is enormous. It remains the engine house for powering the largest single country economy in Africa. Yet it has not been properly positioned to perform this role. The sector has retrogressed due to several years of neglect and mismanagement by successive governments. Private enterprise initiatives to harness the vast business opportunities opened up to it by the sector have been grossly discouraged as a result of public policy inconsistency, misconceptions, and faulty or half-hearted implementation.

The long period of a strict government interventionist stance in managing the sector, up to 1986, only produced deep-seated structural rigidities and systemic distortions. The partial liberalization introduced with the country's structural adjustment program in 1986 did radically transform the business character of the system. However, its real effects were felt in the sudden increase in the number of ill-equipped operators and the relatively easy access to the limited infrastructure of the system, especially the money and capital markets.

The task remains to attain the model of one of the most efficient financial systems in the world. This requires unfettered government commitment as well as private sector involvement. But it also demands a liberal operating environment, empowerment of regulatory institutions, and encouragement of private enterprise initiatives. Above all, there is a need for transparency, efficiency, and continuous investment in the system by the operators and the government.

Perhaps the greatest challenge for Nigeria's financial system at the moment is the building of structures that will perfectly align with the lightning speed of globalization of the world economy. With the help of information technology and telecommunications, the world is now seen as a global village—where information is freely transmitted and business easily conducted through such high-tech facilities as the Internet, e-mail, satellite cable, and so on. It is in this context that the idea of a newsmagazine was conceptualized, and later settled, for aiding the development of the financial system through the provision of the researched current and historical technical information required by operators and other stakeholders in the economy.

The project

The project is the publication of a monthly newsmagazine that would provide researched current and historical information and outlooks on wide-ranging issues of general economic interest including finance, business, politics, and the environment. Its mission is to contribute literature and knowledge capable of transforming Nigeria to a respectable member of the international financial system. The project is being sponsored by private entrepreneurs engaged in aiding Nigeria's economic development through the provision of research and consulting services to the stakeholders and operators of the economy.

Ownership structure

The Company is fully owned by Nigerians. It has authorized share capital of ₦100,000 (one hundred thousand naira only), divided into 100,000 ordinary shares of ₦1.00 each. The shares are fully paid up. The present ownership structure is shown in Table 7.1:

TABLE 7.1 Current Shareholdings in the Company	
Shareholder	(%)
Frank Adamu	95
Ismaila Jacob	5
	100

However, the project will necessitate external financing by way of a bank loan of ₦10,000,000 (ten million naira only).

Cost estimates

The total cost of the project is estimated at ₦15,625,000 (fifteen million, six hundred and twenty five thousand naira only) and would be financed with a mix of equity and a bank loan. The project would be self-liquidating and generate adequate cash flows on a daily basis to fund its operations and service and repay the bank loan.

Market analysis

There are various print magazines on sale in Nigeria at the moment. Their variety is dictated by the diversity of interests of their publishers. While some are soft sell in nature, others are simply classified as newsmagazines. There are also research-oriented journals that focus on clearly defined issues in given fields of study and are usually published by academic and research institutions. Some organizations yet publish in-house newsletters that deal with their activities over a given period of time. Of course, there are several national and local newspapers that sell daily and weekly across the country.

The orientations of the magazines are different, with most of them adopting a purely commercial posture. Some are intended to enrich the body of knowledge in their chosen fields of coverage (academic journals). Others are designed to constantly update their audiences with current and anticipated events (in-house newsletters). The overly commercial magazines (newsmagazines and the soft sell) report news, events, and activities of celebrities, as well as personality profiles. Most of the magazines, especially the commercial ones, are published weekly. The academic journals and in-house newsletters are often published quarterly.

Product identification

The proposed magazine, *Financial System Review* (FSR), would be published monthly. It would be essentially a financial-cum-economics magazine, covering wide-ranging topics about Nigeria's economics, finance, business, politics, and environment. It would provide information that keep readers one step ahead in the stated areas. It would therefore be the only magazine-cum-journal in the country at the moment that deals with such broad national issues in a single periodical. From the light or soft sell to the weekly newsmagazines, FSR would be differentiated in terms of focus, as well as incisiveness, originality, quality, and professionalism. These attributes, together with a commitment to focus, will be its unique selling points.

Estimate of supply

There are basically two main sources of supply of print commercial magazines to the Nigerian readership market. While a few are imported, most are produced locally. The proposed magazine does not really have close substitutes at the moment. It is neither news oriented nor soft sell in nature. Thus, though there are several commercial magazines on sale in the marketplace, none would compete with FSR in terms of focus. The supply of noncompeting magazines is presented in Table 7.2 below. The table excludes the soft sell magazines, which are completely outside the category of serious-minded magazines to which FSR belongs.

TABLE 7.2 Existing (Known) Local Weekly Newsmagazines

Name of News Magazine/Company[a]	Annual Supply (Copies)[b]
Newswatch	6,240,000
The News	5,200,000
Business Times	7,800,000
Tell	5,980,000
Policy	2,600,000
Total	27,820,000

[a]*Although these newsmagazines represent real publications in print currently or sometime in the past, the use of them here is for illustration purposes only.*
[b]*Figures are hypothetical.*

TABLE 7.3 Existing Local Quarterly/Biannual Academic Journals

Name of Journal	Annual Supply (Copies)[a]
Management in Nigeria	600,000
The Journal of Banking and Finance	100,000
UBA Economic Review	20,000
First Bank Economic Review	20,000
BGL Economic Review	8,000
Others	1,020,000
Total	1,768,000

[a]*Figures are hypothetical.*

As shown in Tables 7.2−7.4, the annual number of known, non−soft sell magazines and journals supplied to the market sum to 32,890,000. All located in Lagos State, the market leaders are *Newswatch, Business Times,* and *Tell.* Their annual supply represents 61% of the total number of known, non−soft sell magazines and journals supplied to the market. Our market investigations revealed that the 32,890,000 figure represents about 82% of the total supply of magazines and journals to the market, which equals 40,109,756.

The numerous soft sell and other unidentified magazines that occasionally cover business and economic news account for the remaining 18%. During the five years from 2016 to 2020, we project an annual growth rate of 3.5% on the supply figure of 40,109,756, due mainly to the expectation of new entrants into the business and the reflection of unknown existing production. The outcome is shown in Table 7.5.

TABLE 7.4 Existing (Known) Foreign Weekly Newsmagazines in Nigeria

Name of News Magazine	Annual Supply (Copies)[a]
The Economist	1,560,000
Time	1,300,000
African Business	260,000
Africa Today	182,000
Total	3,302,000

[a]*Figures are hypothetical.*

TABLE 7.5 Projected Supply of Newsmagazines and Journals

Year	Projected Supply
2016	41,513,597
2017	42,966,572
2018	44,470,402
2019	46,026,866
2020	47,637,806

Source: Computed from Table 7.2 and results of market survey.

Table 7.5 shows that the supply of the various magazines and journals in the country would increase from 41,513,597 copies in 2016 to 47,637,806 copies in 2020.

Forecast for Financial System Review

The possible supply of FSR to the market, shown in Table 7.6, would be influenced by the following considerations:

- Nigeria's population is estimated at 110,000,000 people.
- Of this figure, the literacy rate is about 65%, which implies a total readership market of about 71,500,000 people.
- About 5% of the readership market can afford the purchase of a magazine of some sort at any point in time—implying an effective annual market demand of 3,575,000 copies.

TABLE 7.6 Five-Year Sales Forecast for *Financial System Review*

Year	Projected Demand
1	120,656
2	150,820
3	188,525
4	235,656
5	294,570

Source: Computed based on forecast for the proposed newsmagazine above.

- Demand by corporate bodies, institutions, and public agencies would approximate 35% of effective annual market demand, which would be 1,251,250 copies.
- The estimated annual size of the market for FSR is 4,826,250 copies.

Considering the elitist posture of the proposed magazine, we have adopted a conservative stance by basing our first-year production forecast on about 2.5% of estimated market potential. This gives initial annual sales of 120,656 copies. Assuming an average annual increase of 25%, the projected total sales for the first five years of production are shown in Table 7.6.

Market prospects

The proposed magazine will enjoy extensive market coverage and the widest acceptability by the readership market in view of its orientation and appeal to troubleshooting societal issues, writing with the highest level of incisiveness, originality, and professionalism, and simple, easily comprehensible language. It appeals to corporate establishments, the organized private sector, the government (including its parastatals and agencies), nongovernmental organizations, foreign missions and embassies, academic and research institutions, libraries, and international organizations. It would particularly appeal to adult minds—executives, managers, administrators, workers, and entrepreneurs. It is indeed a magazine for those who have responsibility to advance the cause of society—those who seek to attain the peak in their industry and who aspire to obtain technical information regarding practices in key sectors of the economy.

Competitive strategy

Financial System Review would be sold at strategic traffic jam spots. We would employ our own vendors who would market only it. They would earn a fixed salary and commission based on their sales volumes and targets. Salary would take cognizance of what a newspaper vendor earns on the average in a day. The marketing locations would cover every part of Nigeria.

Technical analysis

Project description

The project involves the acquisition of modern computer and information technology systems used mainly in various editorial preparations, typesetting, artwork, and general prepress lithographic works. The actual printing work requires a modern press with state-of-the-art facilities to achieve the highest possible quality output. While the company would do most prepress work in-house, the high-tech aspects and actual printing of the magazine shall be contracted out to a commercial press. This approach is cheaper and would yet be more effective for the company during the initial five years of operation.

Production process

The process and technology of magazine production is simple. The items of plant, machinery, and equipment required include printing machines and lithographic equipment. There are three main production processes as highlighted below.

Editorial

This involves the research, writing, editing, and approval of articles for publication. It includes decisions regarding the content and context of the various discourses and editorials. This section manages relationships with contributing analysts and editors. But its main assignment is preparation of the magazine manuscript for publication.

Lithographic

This section is usually equipped with computers, color separation equipment, film, and platemaking machines.

Printing

In the printing section, the plates are fitted to the appropriate printing machines to produce the magazine. Printing is followed by cutting, stitching, and packaging for delivery to vendors.

Human resources

The entire staff of the company shall remain the most important resource for the attainment of the set goals of the project. Yet the promoters shall personally ensure the success of the project through selfless services and devotion to the cause of the investors. The arrangement for effective management of the project is as stated below.

Management

The Company shall be divided into four functional groups—the Chief Responsibility Officer's Office, Operations, Business Development, and Finance. The Company's day-to-day management shall be entrusted to an executive management team comprising the Chief Responsibility Officer, Chief Operations Officer (*Managing Editor*), and Chief Business Officer. This team shall be responsible for the interpretation, execution, and implementation of Board policies and decisions. It shall also report to the Board through the Chief Responsibility Officer.

Capital cost of project

The estimated total cost of the project is ₦15,625,000 (fifteen million, six hundred and twenty five thousand naira only), broken down as follows (Table 7.7):

TABLE 7.7 Total Capital Cost of Project

Item of Expenditure	(₦'000)		
	Existing Assets	New Assets	Total Assets
Office space, renovation, and furnishing		1,250,000	1,250,000
Telephone, facsimile, PMB, e-mail, and Web site		200,000	200,000
Computers, UPS, stabilizers, and printer		350,000	350,000
Photocopier, scanning machine, and accessories		375,000	375,000
Generator (50 kva)		450,000	450,000
Vehicles		1,850,000	1,850,000
Furniture, fixtures, fittings, and equipment		500,000	500,000
Preoperational expenses and capitalized consulting		5,625,000	5,625,000
Working capital		5,025,000	5,025,000
Total cost	5,625,000	10,000,000	15,625,000

Office space, renovation, and furnishing

The provision of ₦1.25 million would be utilized to rent befitting office accommodations in Lagos, Abuja, and Port Harcourt. The offices should have modern facilities suitable for the provision of a challenging work environment. The Lagos office would serve as the head office, while the offices in Abuja and Port Harcourt would function as regional offices for correspondence purposes.

Technology and communications

The company shall be provided with all modern communications facilities, such as telephones, facsimile, Internet, and a Web site. These facilities should be in place before the end of March 2016. There would be adequate systems facilities to provide an excellent information technology network. Computers, UPS, stabilizers, copiers, laser jet printer, and a scanning machine would be acquired.

Power-generating set

The power requirement for sustaining a good work-quality environment shall be supplied by Eko Electricity Company Limited. However, there is the need to ensure a continuous power supply during periods of failure of the public power system, which necessitates procurement of a standby generating set with a capacity of 50 kva. Diesel and lubricant shall be required for running the generating set and shall be procured from local fuel stations.

Vehicles

The sum of ₦1,850,000 (one million, eight hundred and fifty thousand naira only) has been earmarked for the purchase of three used cars for the initial takeoff of the company. More cars will be purchased in due course as the need arises.

Furniture, fittings, and equipment

The budget for furniture, fittings, and equipment is ₦500,000 (five hundred thousand naira only). This is considered adequate for the initial five years of operation.

Preoperation and consulting service

The sum of ₦5,625,000 (five million, six hundred and twenty five thousand naira only) in the total cost of the project represents preoperational expenses (company incorporation, feasibility study, and so on) and the capitalized cost of consulting service (in editorial, *shadow* executive management, and so on) during the first five years of operation.

Working capital

The estimated total working capital requirement of ₦5,025,000 (five million, and twenty five thousand naira only) for the company is based on the assumptions shown in Table 7.8:

TABLE 7.8 Estimation of Working Capital for the Project

Cash at Hand	1 week	₦1,256,250
Raw materials	3 months	2,763,750
Goods-in-progress	5 days	402,500
Finished goods	1 month	502,500
Debtors	Nil	—
Creditors	1 month	100,000
		5,025,000

Assumptions underlying financial projections and analysis

Revenue

The following assumptions underlie projected revenues for the company:

- Average annual increase of 25% in sales is anticipated based on our estimation of goodwill and early market acceptance that the magazine would enjoy
- Ex-warehouse average price used for the projections is ₦250 (two hundred and fifty naira only) per magazine
- First year turnover is estimated at 2.5% of the estimated market potential
- Operating schedule of one shift per day of 8 h, and 300 workdays per annum
- Printing costs are estimated at ₦75 per copy, increasing by 20% every year. Sales price remains constant at ₦250 per copy throughout the forecast period.
- Cost of management and labor increases by 25% per annum
- Advertising sales are assumed at ₦17.74 million each year, determined as shown in Table 7.9.
- Paper cost is estimated at ₦1.68 million in the first year of operation, with expectation of an annual 5% increase.
- Fuel, diesel, and electricity costs sum to 10% of labor costs
- The bank loan required is ₦10 million, with an interest rate assumed at 35% per annum. Other bank charges are estimated at 5% of interest cost.

Pricing considers that a new edition of the magazine would be offered to the market only once a month, as opposed to the popular weekly magazines sold in the country at the moment. Thus, the proposed higher price for the magazine, on relative analysis, is reasonable and affordable. The price is considered fixed for the first five years of operation. In the event that the cover price is increased during the period, the company would enjoy even healthier cash flow and profitability.

Operating costs

Raw materials

The main raw materials for the production of the magazine are paper, printing consumables, and articles for publication. Paper and most of the printing consumables are imported, although a local source of supply (for newsprint) is available in Akwa Ibom State. However, like most publishing houses in the country, the company would depend on imported brands of paper because of considerations of quality and the reliability of supply. The raw materials would be purchased from importers or on the open market.

TABLE 7.9 Projected Advertising Space Sales

	Color		Black & White	
Outside back cover	₦200,000 × 12	₦2,400,000	Full page	80,000 × 4 × 12	₦3,840,000
Inside back cover	150,000 × 12	1,800,000	Half page	50,000 × 2 × 12	1,200,000
Inside front cover	175,000 × 12	2,100,000	Quarter	30,000 × 1 × 12	360,000
Center spread	250,000 × 12	3,000,000	Advertorial	100,000 × 1 × 4	400,000
Roll-over page	120,000 × 12	1,440,000		
Flash on cover	100,000 × 12	1,200,000		
Total		11,940,000			5,800,000

Depreciation

Depreciation allowances are based on the straight-line method with the applicable rates shown in Table 7.10:

TABLE 7.10 Specification of Depreciation Rates

Equipment	20%
Furniture & fittings	20%
Generator	20%
Vehicles	25%

Amortization

Preoperational expenses are capitalized and amortized over the first five years of operation.

Overhead

Administrative overhead comprising rent and rates, insurance on assets, welfare, medical costs, and so on is estimated at ₦750,000 (seven hundred and fifty thousand naira only) for the first year of operation as shown in Table 7.11.

TABLE 7.11 Estimate of Depreciation Allowance

Items	Value at Cost ₦'000	Nominal Rate %	Allowance ₦'000
Direct			
Standby generator	450	20	90
Computers, UPS, stabilizers, printer, scanner, copier, and so on	925	20	185
Indirect			
Vehicles	1850	25	463
Furniture, fixtures, fittings, and equipment	500	20	100
			838

Salaries and wages

Total remuneration in the first year of operation is estimated at ₦8,846,000 (eight million, eight hundred and forty six thousand naira only), details of which are shown in Table 7.12.

TABLE 7.12 Cost of Management and Labor (Direct and Indirect)—First Year of Operation

Designation	Scale/Annum (₦)	Number	Total (₦)
Direct			
Managing Editor	520,000	1	520,000
Chief Economist	480,000	1	480,000
Editor	450,000	1	450,000
Analysts	300,000	2	600,000
Researchers	240,000	3	720,000
Computer Operators	96,000	2	192,000
		10	2,962,000
Indirect			
Chief Responsibility Officer	600,000	1	600,000
Chief Business Officer	520,000	1	520,000
Futurist	480,000	1	480,000
Chief Financial Officer	450,000	1	450,000
Company Secretary	450,000	1	450,000
Advertising Executives	180,000 + commission	3	540,000
Administrative Officer	180,000	1	180,000
Accounts Officer	180,000	1	180,000
Executive Assistants	140,000	2	280,000
Sales Agents	60,000 + commission	30	1,800,000
Advertising/Subscription Brokers	—	35	—
Drivers	130,000	2	260,000
Unskilled labor	36,000	4	144,000
		86	5,884,000
Grand total		**96**	**8,846,000**

CONSTRUCTING AND ANALYZING FINANCIALS FOR AN SME FEASIBILITY STUDY

There are seven basic steps a credit analyst should follow to analyze the financial aspects of a project's feasibility study. The steps involve constructing particular financial statements and accounts, as well as the analytical tools applicable to them. The steps summarized below apply irrespective of the type or nature of the project.

Step 1—estimation of bank loan, interest expense, and other financing costs

It is important to know how much external financing is needed for the project. In most cases, that financing represents the amount of bank loan to apply for, and to be granted, for execution of the project. The lending officer should project or corroborate the loan amount based on assumptions extracted from the feasibility study. Of course, this should be done in collaboration with the promoters of the project. In this hypothetical example, the amount of bank loan required for the project is ₦10 million (see Table 7.7). Using the interest and other financing rates stated in the assumptions for the financial analysis, the estimated financing costs for the project may be constructed and presented as shown in Table 7.13.

TABLE 7.13 Estimation of Bank Loan, Interest Expense, and Other Charges (₦'000)

	Initial Value (₦'000)	End Year 1	End Year 2	End Year 3	End Year 4	End Year 5
Loan granted	10,000	–	–	–	–	–
Repayment of loan	–	2000	2000	2000	2000	2000
Balance on loan	–	8000	6000	4000	2000	–
Interest on loan	–	3500	2800	2100	1400	700
Other charges	–	175	140	105	70	35
Total financing cost	–	**3675**	**2940**	**2205**	**1470**	**735**

Step 2—projection of profit and loss account for the project

The main test of a proposed project's commercial viability lies in its profitability. No SME entrepreneur will want to invest in an unprofitable venture. Neither will a bank want to lend money to such a project. So lending officers should establish that the projects for which bank loans are sought for execution are profitable. In order to do so, officers should forecast the profit and loss account for each project. The constructed profit and loss account for the hypothetical newsmagazine project is presented in Table 7.14.

TABLE 7.14 Projected Profit and Loss Account for Five Years (₦'000)

Year of operation	Year 1	Year 2	Year 3	Year 4	Year 5
Total production	241,312	251,367	269,321	294,570	327,300
Total number sold	120,656	150,820	188,525	235,656	294,570
Sales Revenue					
Net sales revenue	30,164.00	37,705.00	47,131.25	58,914.00	73,642.50
Advertising sales	17,740.00	17,740.00	17,740.00	17,740.00	17,740.00
Total net sales	**47,904.00**	**55,445.00**	**64,871.25**	**76,654.00**	**91,382.50**
Cost of Production					
Direct Costs					
Printing costs	18,098.40	18,852.50	20,199.11	22,092.75	24,547.50
Raw materials (paper)	1680.00	1764.00	1852.20	1944.81	2042.05
Management and labor	2962.00	3702.50	4628.13	5785.16	7231.45
Fuel, electricity, & diesel	834.60	1043.25	1304.06	1630.08	2037.60
Depreciation	757.50	846.63	865.27	1153.19	1020.79
Total direct costs	**24,332.50**	**26,208.88**	**28,848.76**	**32,605.98**	**36,879.38**
Indirect Costs					
Management and labor	5384.00	6730.00	8412.50	10,515.63	13,144.53
G&A	1197.60	1386.13	1621.78	1916.35	2284.56
Advertising and selling	7185.60	8316.75	9730.69	11,498.10	13,707.38
Amortization of preoperational expenses	1125.00	1125.00	1125.00	1125.00	1125.00

TABLE 7.14 Projected Profit and Loss Account for Five Years (₦'000)—cont'd

Year of operation	Year 1	Year 2	Year 3	Year 4	Year 5
Total indirect costs	14,892.20	17,557.88	20,889.97	25,055.08	30,261.47
Total production costs	39,224.70	43,766.76	49,738.73	57,661.06	67,140.85
Profit (loss) before tax & financing	8679.30	11,678.25	15,132.52	18,992.94	24,241.65
Less financing costs	3675.00	2940.00	2205.00	1470.00	735.00
Profit (loss) before tax	5004.30	8738.25	12,927.52	17,522.94	23,506.65
Les company tax @ 32%	1601.38	2796.24	4136.81	5607.34	7522.13
Profit (loss) after tax	3402.92	5942.01	8790.71	11,915.60	15,984.52
% Net profit margin	0.09	0.14	0.18	0.21	0.24
% Return on net sales	0.10	0.16	0.20	0.23	0.26
% Return on shareholders' funds	0.27	0.35	0.35	0.33	0.32

The lending officer should then compute relevant financial ratios to gain insight into possible future financial performance of the company. The three main ratios shown in Table 7.14 may be calculated to determine the profitability of the project. While positive ratios are good, net profit margin and return on net sales seem low compared with return on shareholders' funds. This finding may be explained by leverage and financing cost levels characteristic of the newsmagazine business.

Step 3—projection of balance sheet for the project

The third step is to construct a forecast balance sheet statement for the project based on the assumptions for its feasibility study. I present a five-year projected balance sheet in Table 7.15 to highlight the expected financial leverage of the

TABLE 7.15 Projected Balance Sheet for Five Years (₦'000)

Year of Operation	Year 1	Year 2	Year 3	Year 4	Year 5
Fixed Assets					
Vehicles	1750.00	1962.50	2121.88	3141.41	2906.05
Generator	450.00	360.00	288.00	230.40	184.32
Equipment	650.00	1020.00	816.00	1152.80	922.24
Furniture & fittings	500.00	400.00	570.00	456.00	364.80
Depreciation	−757.50	−846.63	−865.27	−1153.19	−1020.79
Net fixed assets	**2592.50**	**2895.88**	**2930.61**	**3827.41**	**3356.63**
Current Assets					
Stocks	10,859.04	11,311.50	12,119.46	13,255.65	14,728.50
Cash and bank balance	−239.58	6224.06	14,305.04	26,148.83	42,479.14
Less: Current liabilities	−834.04	−3236.51	−4494.47	−7580.65	−10,053.51
Net current assets	**9785.42**	**14,299.05**	**21,930.04**	**31,823.83**	**47,154.13**
Total net assets	**12,377.92**	**17,194.93**	**24,860.64**	**35,651.25**	**50,510.76**
Financed by					
Paid-up capital	100.00	100.00	100.00	100.00	100.00
Bank credit	10,000.00	10,000.00	10,000.00	10,000.00	10,000.00
Retained earnings	3402.92	9344.93	18,135.64	30,051.24	46,035.76
Less: Preoperation	−1125.00	−2250.00	−3375.00	−4500.00	−5625.00
Shareholders' funds	**12,377.92**	**17,194.93**	**24,860.64**	**35,651.24**	**50,510.76**
Current ratio	12.73	5.42	5.88	5.20	5.69
Quick ratio	−0.29	1.92	3.18	3.45	4.23
Leverage ratio	2.85	1.06	0.55	0.33	0.22

project. With the projected highest balance sheet footing of ₦50.5 million in the project's fifth year of operation, its expected maximum leverage would be 2.85 in the first year.

As shown in Table 7.15, these ratios are good considering that increases in balance sheet size and decreases in the leverage ratio will be sustained from Year 1. Current ratios are especially good throughout the five-year projected period. However, the expected quick ratio of −0.29 in the first year of operation is not good even though the ratios improve consistently in subsequent years—peaking at 4.23 in Year 5.

Step 4—projection of cash flow statement for the project

The cash flow projection can be approached from two perspectives. The lending officer might want to build the bank loan, interest on the loan, and bank charges into the projected cash flow statement. The objective in doing so might be to assess net operating cash flow after financing costs and charges. Alternatively, the analyst might apply only the bank loan, to see how it impacts the project prior to financing charges. That way, the credit analyst would be arguing that net operating cash flows were adequate or inadequate to service and repay the requested loan. As Table 7.16 shows, the approach I adopted for the project being analyzed is to build both bank loan and financing costs into the cash flow projection. That enables a more critical look at the behavior of the project with the financing arrangement applicable to it. Yet you can adopt either of the two approaches, and you cannot go wrong.

Now compare Table 7.16 with the cash flow analysis I discussed in Chapters 23 and 24 of this book. What differences do you notice? You will appreciate that the projected cash flows for a start-up company are a lot simpler to analyze than those of well-established corporates like the ones analyzed in Chapters 23 and 24. Yet the analysis presented in Table 7.16 suffices to illustrate how to construct and analyze cash flows based on feasibility study projections. It shows that the project promises strong cash flows that a bank may use as the basis for granting the ₦10.0 million loan request. This is despite the forecast negative net cumulative cash flows in the first two years of operations.

Step 5—computation of the project's break-even point

It is important to know the break-even point for the project. Applying net sales revenue and fixed and variable costs, the lending officer can determine the break-even point for the project. As Table 7.17 shows, the projected sales break-even point for Year 3 is ₦38.26 million.

TABLE 7.16 Projected Cash Flow Statement (₦'000)

Year of Operation	Year 0	Year 1	Year 2	Year 3	Year 4	Year 5
Sources of Funds						
Share capital	100.00	0.00	0.00	0.00	0.00	0.00
Bank loan	10,000.00	0.00	0.00	0.00	0.00	0.00
Profit before tax		8679.30	11,678.25	15,132.52	18,992.94	24,241.65
Depreciation		757.50	846.63	865.27	1153.19	1020.79
Amortization		1125.00	1125.00	1125.00	1125.00	1125.00
Total sources	**10,100.00**	**10,561.80**	**13,649.88**	**17,122.79**	**21,271.13**	**26,387.44**
Uses of Funds						
Movable assets	3725.00	0.00	650.00	650.00	1550.00	550.00
Preoperational expenses	5625.00	0.00	0.00	0.00	0.00	0.00
Office space	1250.00	0.00	0.00	1250.00	0.00	1250.00
Financing costs	0.00	3675.00	2940.00	2205.00	1470.00	735.00
Taxation	0.00	1601.38	2796.24	4136.81	5607.34	7522.13
Working capital change	0.00	5025.00	800.00	800.00	800.00	0.00
Total uses	**10,600.00**	**10,301.38**	**7186.24**	**9041.81**	**9427.34**	**10,057.13**
Cash balance	−500.00	260.42	6463.64	8080.98	11,843.79	16,330.31
Balance C/F	0.00	−500.00	−239.58	6224.06	14,305.04	26,148.83
Cumulative balance	−500.00	−239.58	6224.06	14,305.04	26,148.83	42,479.14

TABLE 7.17 Computation and Analysis of Break-Even Point for Year 3

	Fixed Cost (₦'000)	Variable Cost (₦'000)
Raw materials	–	1852.20
Printing costs	–	20,199.11
Advertising and selling expenses	9730.69	–
Amortization of preoperational expenses	1125.00	–
Depreciation	865.27	–
Admin and general expenses	1621.78	–
Fuel, electricity, and diesel		1304.06
Management and labor	8412.50	4628.13
	21,755.24	27,983.49

Using information from Table 7.17, and projected sales revenue of ₦64,871.25 for Year 3, the break-even point is calculated as follows:

$$\text{Breakeven point(sales)} = \text{Fixed Cost}/[1 - [\text{Variable Cost}/\text{Sales}]]$$
$$= 21,755.24/[1 - [27,983.49/64,871.25]]$$
$$= 21,755.24/[1 - 0.4314]$$
$$= 21,755.25/0.5686$$
$$= ₦38,261.06$$

Step 6—computation of the project's payback period

The payback period for the project would be two years and three months. Table 7.18 shows how lending officers can compute the payback period for a start-up project. The need for doing so is to be assured that projected net operating cash flows for the project would be adequate to repay the bank loan financing it in good time. The forecast payback period for this project is satisfactory considering the high intensity of competition in the newsmagazine industry.

Step 7—sensitivity analyses of financial statements

The last of the steps, sensitivity analysis, furnishes further lending comfort. It helps lending officers and a bank's loan approving authorities gauge the ability

TABLE 7.18 Computation and Analysis of Payback Period (₦'000)

Year	Project Cost	PAT	Depreciation	Amortization	Net Cash Flow	Cumulative
0	−15,625.00	0.00	0.00	0.00	0.00	−15,625.00
1	0.00	3402.92	757.50	1125.00	5285.42	−10,339.58
2	0.00	5942.01	846.63	1125.00	7913.64	−2425.94
3	0.00	8790.71	865.27	1125.00	10,780.98	8355.04
4	0.00	11,915.60	1153.19	1125.00	14,193.79	22,548.83
5	0.00	15,984.52	1020.79	1125.00	18,130.31	40,679.14

$$\text{Payback period} = 2 \text{ years} + \frac{2425.94}{10,780.98} \times 12$$

$$= 2 \text{ years}, 3 \text{ months}$$

of the project to continue to operate profitably in the face of exogenous shocks. In sensitivity analysis, the lending officer subjects one or more variables that affect financial performance of the project to imagined systemic changes. The objective in doing so is to see how changes in the variables might affect the project's liquidity and earnings—and therefore its ability to repay the bank loan.

Lending officers should decide the variables to sensitize depending on the particular lending and risk control expectations of the bank. In most cases, lending officers sensitize the forecast price, sales revenue, and operating cost of the project to some adverse events. A common adverse change used for sensitivity analysis of start-up projects is the probability of a decrease in price—and therefore in sales revenue. Supposing that operating costs would increase is equally common.

In the case of this project, I applied two scenarios in sensitizing the financial projections. In the first place, I reassessed the commercial viability of the project if sales revenue were to decrease by 15 percent. The project would make a loss before taxes of ₦2,991,010 in Year 1 and a marginal profit of ₦151,760 in Year 2. Similarly, there would be negative shareholders' funds at ₦3,058,890 in Year 1. A combination of the foregoing findings would result in a negative quick ratio of (0.06) in Year 1, and less than 1.00 in Years 2, 3, and 4, at 0.19, 0.53, and 0.95, respectively. In addition, both the net and cumulative cash flow balances would be negative in Year 1 at (₦5,176,390) and (₦51,390), respectively.

Then I checked how an increase in the printing cost of up to 35 percent would affect the financial performance of the project. The results are similar to those for a 15% decrease in sales revenue. The findings suggest that this project is highly sensitive to adverse changes in revenue and operating cost. It embodies moderate risk that the bank should mitigate one way or the other. In view of the foregoing, the bank should place limited reliance on the projected cash flows for repayment of the loan. It should seek additional comfort—perhaps by taking some tangible collateral or a charge on movable assets.

SECURING SME CREDIT FACILITIES

Considering the foregoing issues, one cannot help but ask—what should be done to cater to SME financing needs in more practical terms? It has for two reasons become necessary to ask this question. Firstly, the importance of SMEs in economic development is not in doubt. In some emerging economies, the government has demonstrated a desire to provide the necessary public support to enhance SME sector development and performance. Yet the sector has remained largely incapable of fulfilling its expected role. Secondly, there is a tendency to associate the failure of SMEs with the banking system credit squeeze that does not appear to be ebbing over the years. How could the flow of scarce bank credit be directed to the sector to enhance its performance? Or perhaps, what should SME entrepreneurs on their own do to minimize their external financing difficulties?

Any attempt to answer these questions takes us back to my earlier discussion of SME attributes, practices, and credit risks. SME entrepreneurs should first put their own houses in order before pointing accusing fingers at banks. By doing so, they would be in a position to transfer their financing pressure to banks. The financing crisis faced by SMEs could be minimized if entrepreneurs could organize and form themselves into a strong and viable business pressure group. Although this suggestion may sound like the much-talked-about cooperative society, it is a much larger engagement. In cooperative societies, emphasis is usually on small businesses in the informal economy as I discussed in Chapter 18 of this book. If the cooperators were serious-minded entrepreneurs, they would be able to pool and manage financial resources to satisfy their business demands. A business pressure group can more forcefully press authorities for their causes and get results.

It would be futile to think that government would be involved in solving the SME financing problem beyond putting in place the necessary policy and institutional framework for assisting the development of the sector. The IFC—in collaboration with Central Banks in emerging economies—furnishes a reliable institutional framework to solve the SME financing problem.

Collateral registration for movable assets

The IFC and the Central Banks in some emerging economies collaborate to strengthen the ability of SMEs to secure bank loans for business operations. This IFC's initiative, tagged "Collateral Registration for Movable Assets," has been implemented successfully in China and Ghana. As of mid-2014, the IFC was working on the project in Nigeria and Vietnam. Many emerging economies will surely embrace the project due to its efficacy. I should now ask, what is the import and basis of this project? The answer to this question, which I provide right away, informs the cause of the project.

The project derives from the IFC's Secured Transactions and Collateral Registries Program, borne out of the institution's goal of increasing the access to credit for firms, especially SMEs, in developing countries. Secured transactions should be understood within the context I use in discussing asset-based lending in Chapter 11 of this book. There is an obvious difference, though. While Chapter 11 deals with the collateral question from a bank's internal risk control perspective, the IFC program involves state-backed legal frameworks, collateral registries, and capacity building for banks and other lenders. Nonetheless, the two approaches share a common objective. Their intent is to boost the confidence of banks and other lenders in financing SME businesses, projects, and operations. There are two beneficial aspects to this confidence boosting—the flow of credit to SMEs increases while the cost of credit for the sector decreases. This is the overriding contribution of movable collateral to SME development in emerging economies.

These benefits have a strong positive impact on economic development. One reason is that SMEs operate mainly in rural economies in dire need of economic progress. Of course, rural economies are bedeviled by mass unemployment. Employing large workforces from rural populations and the urban poor, which SMEs do, eases the problem of lack of progress. Thus SMEs contribute to economic development. Another reason is that movable collateral helps to strengthen the financial system. This will happen when banks and other lenders are able to:

- Diversify collateral assets used to secure SME loans beyond the traditional emphasis on land and buildings
- Spread portfolio credit risk to the SME sector, thus reducing credit concentration in traditional sectors
- Facilitate the liquidity of trading assets, such as inventory and accounts receivables, as collateral for SME loans

The effect of incorporating nonbank lenders gives a further boost to the financial system development potential of the program. Besides, it will enhance competition for credit products in the financial sector and improve the regulation of credit risk in line with the Basel I and Basel II Accords. The foregoing are certainly tenable goals.

The IFC cites the examples of China and Ghana to illustrate the typical successful implementation and beneficial impact of the Collateral Registration for Movable Assets project. The IFC gives specific accounts of the China and Ghana success stories to underscore how SMEs could leverage their trading assets to boost capital for their businesses and operations. As Nigeria and Vietnam follow suit, this empirical success evidence serves as a wake-up call to governments in other emerging economies. The relevant authorities should institutionalize appropriate legal frameworks that permit collateralization of bank loans with SME movable assets. The China and Ghana success stories can surely be replicated in other emerging economies once the countries institutionalize appropriate legal frameworks and collateral registries as basic instruments of bank lending to the SME sector.

QUESTIONS FOR DISCUSSION AND REVIEW

1. How would you define an SME from the perspective of business in emerging economies? Your answer should demonstrate an understanding of SME attributes, business practices, and risk profiles.
2. Why do governments in emerging economies tend to emphasize so-called priority sectors in their economic policies?
3. Identify one SME-dominated priority sector and explain how it contributes to economic development in a named emerging economy.

4. What factors tend to constrain the access of SMEs to external financing in emerging economies?
5. Critically assess the risk control measures and expectations of banks in lending to SMEs in emerging economies.
6. Assess the ways in which the characteristics of SMEs in emerging economies affect bank lending to the sector.
7. Discuss one state-backed institutional framework that enhances the flow of bank credit to SMEs in emerging economies.
8. Outline and discuss the basic steps that a lending officer is likely to follow in appraising the feasibility study of an SME soapmaking plant.

REFERENCE

Evborokhai, J., 1989. Survival strategy of small business enterprises in an ailing economy. In: Unpublished Master of Business Administration Research Project. School of Postgraduate Studies, ESUT, Nigeria.

FURTHER READING

Central Bank of Nigeria, 1996. Monetary, Credit, Foreign Trade and Exchange Policy Guidelines for 1996 Fiscal Year.
European Union, 2015. Enterprise and Industry Publications: The New SME Definition − User Guide and Model Declaration. Commission Recommendation 2003/361/EC.
SME Corp. Malaysia Secretariat to the National SME Development Council, 2013. Guideline for New SME Definition.

Chapter 8

Sectoral and Industry Credit Risk and Control in Emerging Economies

Emerging Market Bank Lending and Credit Risk Control. http://dx.doi.org/10.1016/B978-0-12-803438-5.00008-8

LEARNING FOCUS AND OUTCOMES

On occasion regulatory authorities may allow banks some flexibility in choosing methods they consider expedient for risk assets portfolio reporting. However, the common approaches to classifying risk assets in the lending portfolios of banks in emerging economies are as follows:

- Market segmentation (as in consumer loans, corporate lending, public sector finance, small and medium-sized enterprise [SME] credits, and so on)
- Activities in which borrowers are engaged (exemplified in contract finance, trade finance, and so on)
- Maturity profile of the loans (as in short-, medium-, and long-term credit facilities); overdraft credit facilities may also be grouped in this category.
- Sectors and industries in which borrowers operate (as in manufacturing, agriculture, energy (oil and gas), telecommunications, trading, and so on)
- Consortium lending arrangements (when the amount lent to a borrower is large and therefore requires syndication)
- Purpose of the loans (such as working capital credits, project finance, invoice discounting facility [IDF], and so on)

Classification based on the maturity profile of the risk assets in the lending portfolio tends to be popular among banks in emerging markets. The reasons for this are not far-fetched. It has appeal to a bank's expectations on when borrowers are likely to repay their loans. It also helps banks in portfolio planning to meet their liquidity needs. This approach is yet useful because the other methods could easily be expressed in terms of maturity profile of the related risk assets. For example, loans classified on the bases of market segmentation, activities in which borrowers are engaged, the purpose of borrowing, and so on must have been granted for some definite tenors. The reader will learn about:

- Bank credit products that are appropriate to particular sectors and industries in emerging economies
- Risk-determined characteristics of the major economic sectors in emerging economies
- How banks in emerging economies should identify and control risks associated with lending to the sectors
- Critical ways banks in emerging economies can structure credit facilities to the major industries
- Appropriate lending criteria that banks in emerging economies could adopt to mitigate loan losses

TRADING AND COMMERCIAL SERVICES

This market segment offers the hub of commercial banking activities. It is one of the highly profitable—but arguably, the riskiest of all—banking target markets. In most cases, transactions are unstructured and sometimes speculative. This is quite instructive. Many traders and some commercial service providers tend to be impulsive in their conduct of business transactions. This attitude is often driven by profit considerations. Banks have to grapple with this behavioral tendency. On occasion it is difficult to do so—largely because it could be really problematic. Thus banks face unusual difficulty when they want to grant credit facilities to borrowers in this sector. The challenge borders on the strict definition of the credit risk that banks are disposed to take on borrowers.

Traders and firms that provide commercial services typically need funds transfer services—for both local and international purposes. Banks should market this product with a particularly modern service facility. Contemporary technologies that facilitate funds transfer build on the power and functioning of the Internet. Nowadays electronic banking services powered by the Internet have become commonplace. The beauty of the Internet is its online facility. Thus, electronic and traditional banking transactions are now conducted online in real-time.

In order to tap the benefits of advancing technologies in the provision of financial services, banks must have strong branch networks and loops. This is especially necessary in building an effective financial services delivery system. Customers should be able to initiate funds transfer transactions in any branch of their bank near to them. They could also use ATMs or applicable electronic gadgets that have similar service facility to conduct some self-service banking transactions at any bank of their choice. These modern banking facilities have significantly eased commercial banking transactions. It would seem that traders are the greater beneficiaries of the emergent technologies. Hitherto traders carried large sums of money in cash from one place to another to buy goods for resale or to pay their creditors. This mode of payment has inherent risks—especially in the conduct of interstate transactions and payments.

Few traders may want to open confirmed letters of credit. Ideally, letters of credit help them to utilize foreign exchange for their import finance facilities (IFFs). Thus, the market has potential for increasing foreign exchange transactions and earnings for banks. Some traders do free funds transactions. This implies that they obtain foreign exchange from autonomous sources. In reference here is foreign exchange procured outside of sales by central banks in countries that have administered foreign exchange policies. Banks should adhere strictly to prevailing foreign exchange regulations. They should endeavor to operate within regulatory requirements at all times. Critical issues often border on disclosure or reporting of foreign exchange sources and transactions.

Banks tend to drive transaction velocity or activity with recoverable pricing incentives. Typical incentives that meet either criterion include concessions on commission on turnover (applicable in Nigeria). This incentive is applicable when a bank wants to boost turnover on an account. A bank may also offer same- or next-day value for confirmed bank drafts or certified checks.

Lending criteria

Bank lending to traders is predominantly in the form of IFFs. Ideally, such loans should be structured as 90-day banker's acceptance facilities for the importation of stock-in-trade—inventory that forms the main products in a borrower's established lines of business. Banks should not grant loans to fund open account import transactions. Traders who import goods on open account terms will want to source foreign exchange in the parallel market. Thereafter they remit the foreign exchange to their foreign suppliers.

Payment of import bills in this way should, as much as possible, be discouraged. It is expensive and increases the cost of import finance. It is also a very risky mode of international trade finance. Dishonest suppliers may not acknowledge receipt of funds remitted to them. Besides, unscrupulous suppliers may ship substandard goods after receiving payment for the goods from the importers. This rule—not to grant an IFF for open account transactions—may not apply to customers that have an overdraft facility. A bank tends to lose oversight of utilization of the overdraft once it is duly approved and secured with tangible collateral. Yet this is the main setback of the overdraft, one that often crystallizes its credit risk.

In Nigeria, free funds transactions are illegal. However, the Central Bank of Nigeria (CBN) may allow them in exceptional cases. For example, a bank can back up the use of free funds to fund open account transaction with necessary documents. The bank may not be penalized once it fulfills specified documentation requirements. But it should also report the transaction officially to regulatory authorities. It should be noted that modern electronic banking, powered by the Internet, has changed the outlook for foreign exchange regulation in countries around the world. Individuals, companies, and organizations now easily engage in one form of e-business or another. They can buy and remit foreign exchange online to pay bills, make purchases, and so on—outside the official foreign exchange market. Banks make more money on the import accounts of commercial banking customers under these circumstances. They tap into options that importers have to source and utilize foreign exchange in the autonomous market.

Banks can increase earnings on commercial banking transactions if they are not averse to a temporary overdraft (TOD) and drawing against uncleared effects (DAUE). However, banks should grant TODs and DAUEs in exceptional circumstances. For example, a bank may grant a TOD to a customer that has maintained a very active nonborrowing current account for a consecutive period of not less than six months. The bank may yet grant a TOD to enable a trader to clear a consignment of imported goods from the seaport. In all cases, the TOD amount may not exceed 25% of the average credit turnover in the account during the minimum six-month period of review of its credit turnover.

Possible risks

Banks must contend with the risks of financial services and transactions in the commercial banking sector. In particular, dealing with traders is fraught with risks. The possible risks are as follows:

Maneuvering of transactions

It is perhaps in the commercial banking sector that operators most ruthlessly manifest this risk. A major factor in the making of the risk is often the inclination of operators toward moneymaking schemes. Profit is always in their psyches. Thus, they are usually given to sharp practices. Banks can mitigate this risk in two main ways. Sticking to business policies and operations manuals is always helpful. Banks should ever be critical of requests for waivers, deferrals, and so on. Due process should be followed if it is unavoidable to grant particular waivers or deferrals.

Diversion of proceeds of loan

This is a common risk among borrowers who run unstructured businesses. Owner-managers of SMEs and traders are often the chief culprits. These categories of borrowers are a test case of the danger of the fusion of ownership, management, and control in a business. Borrowers may take advantage of this abnormal organizational structure to divert loans to personal uses. In most cases, effective monitoring of credit facilities mitigates the risk of diversion of loans. Account officers should work closely with relationship managers to monitor loans in their portfolios.

Falsification of financial records

Borrowers could—and in fact sometimes do—doctor their financial records in order to obtain credit facilities. This is a reality with which bankers should come to grips—if they have not already. It may sound incredible, but it has gradually gained ground among borrowers—especially in the commercial banking sector. There is one major way that this risk can be mitigated. Banks should—and they do—reject unaudited accounts as source documents for financial statement analysis. They should insist on financial statements and annual reports for at least the immediate past three years—audited by reputable chartered accounting firms. It is important that bank management takes this measure a step further. It should liaise with Institutes of Chartered Accountants and similar bodies to bring erring practitioners to book.

Compromising of bank staff

This risk is predominant among junior employees, especially those who have marketing, credit, and account management responsibilities. It is also perhaps the most excruciating challenge of bank management in the commercial banking sector. Typical acceptable standards of behavior for bankers are clearly stated in *Code of Ethics and Professionalism in the Banking and Financial Industry* published by the Nigeria Bankers' Committee.

AGRICULTURAL PRODUCTION AND RISK CONTROL

It is perhaps in most emerging markets' agricultural sectors that businesses are predominantly small-scale in nature. Unfortunately, banking features of small businesses cannot be generalized for agribusinesses. The reason is that in general, banks are scared to take credit risk on agricultural production. In the following discussion, I review features of agriculture that inform the scare. I conclude that the authorities and operators must address the underlying factors. This is one way to mitigate concerns about investment and exposure of banks in agricultural production.

Nature of risks in agriculture

Ray (1981) painstakingly articulates the risks in agriculture in developing countries. A number of agricultural entrepreneurs and experts also shed light on the making of agricultural risks in the same setting (Adepetu; Adesimi & Alli; Omodu; and Oputa—each of whom presented a paper at a 1987 agricultural national symposium held in Ilorin, Nigeria). A review of these and similar works shows that agriculture is certainly a high-risk industry. The sector faces peculiar risks due to the havoc that Nature wreaks on agribusiness. Farm enterprises suffer losses from natural causes such as drought, windstorm, and flood. There is also the risk of plant or animal disease. Insects and other pests that attack farm crops cause further risk. Price fluctuations and the structural rigidity of agribusiness contribute to its risks. In the case of crops, the effect of natural hazards cuts across all stages of activity—from planting, through growth and harvesting, to the marketing of produce. At the planting and growth stages, crops may be washed away by flood, scorched by drought, and felled or torn apart by windstorm.

Drought is easily the most devastating agricultural risk in many emerging economies like Nigeria. This view takes cognizance of three main factors: geographical area affected; extent of damage to farm investment; and therefore, losses incurred by farmers. It is also the risk likely to be the least amenable to control by the farmer. Three major factors—delayed onset of rains, sporadic or uneven distribution of rains, and lack of rains during most periods of the farming season—underlie the incidence of drought. Pests and diseases occur after seed germination and crop harvest. Thus, they are a potential cause of risk during output storage and marketing. Other storage hazards such as moldiness and spoilage are common occurrences. Distribution and marketing risks are rarely avoidable—price fluctuations, supply gluts, and logistical hitches. Farmers also face risks of theft and accidents—both of which are encountered in the course of distribution of farm produce.

Due to its nature, agribusiness does not depend for good performance on the quality of planning, organization, and management of resources. The influence of erratic natural forces dictates the performance levels that farmers attain. For example, the vagaries of weather often render business forecasts as nullities. The biological nature of crops and livestock is yet another important cause of risk. It renders crops and livestock susceptible to adverse environmental conditions. The foregoing are typical risks over which farmers have little or no control.

Often the risk of agribusiness stems from inflexible operations, irregular responses, or even unresponsiveness of operations to market forces. The demand for and supply of agricultural products are subject to some structural rigidity. For example, agricultural production would require longer periods of time to adjust to market conditions than in other industries. Many crops require a year for their production. The expansion of agricultural production, such as into livestock farming, requires several years. Thus, there is a fixed gestation period for agricultural supplies to adjust to changes in demand. Farm enterprises are exposed to the risk of price fluctuations on the one hand, while farmers are unable to easily adjust their organizations and outputs on the other.

Crops and livestock have gestation periods during which production must not be expected. For several years in some cases, farmers will have to anxiously wait for crop fruition and harvesting. It is only after these precarious stages that they may begin to recover their investment, let alone make a profit. During the gestation period, prices might be favorable but farmers would not be in a position to bring supply to market. On occasion farmers who produce seasonal crops experience a glut that depresses earnings due to low market prices. They face a similar challenge when crops with long gestation periods bear fruit in the midst of a lull in business. Farmers incur losses when this happens. Notwithstanding the lull, they must harvest and sell the produce—even at a loss. Otherwise the produce will spoil and cause more loss.

In agriculture, it is not easy to adjust production to sudden or unexpected market changes. Output may not be easily increased to satisfy surging demand. There may be a bumper harvest while demand is declining. The previous year's harvest may not be relied upon for the current year's projections. This is one of the harsh realities of agricultural production. Erratic natural hazards are at the root of the problem. These and similar hazards occur without warning and cause huge losses to farmers. Agricultural analysts are agreed that the risks of agricultural production are beyond the control of farmers.

Common problems of agriculture in developing and emerging economies are structural in nature. Problems exist in the following areas: use of outmoded tools; low technical skill; lack of processing, storage, and transportation facilities; weak agricultural extension and research services; lack of infrastructure including rural electrification, pipe-borne water, and access roads; inadequate loans to farmers; and poor agricultural practices.

Financing of agriculture

Of all the productive sectors in many emerging economies, agriculture attracts the least volume of credits from banks. This negates the role expected of banks in the growth process of these economies. It is expected that banks should pool and channel funds to the productive sectors of economies. Over the years, banks have maintained target markets and risk acceptance criteria that have almost precluded lending to agriculture. This widely criticized practice persists despite regulatory intervention. On occasion the regulatory authorities issue sectoral credit guidelines. Often the guidelines stipulate minimum credits that banks should grant for agricultural production. However, banks remain unwilling to lend to agriculture, let alone aspire to meet the targets. They prefer paying penalties to complying with regulatory policy on lending to agriculture. Perhaps the banking expediency of lending to less risky, or even riskless, but profitable accounts undermines the efficacy of the policy. If this is true, it explains why banks flout the regulations. Thus, it is an imperative that impels banks in emerging economies to lend more to commerce, lend less to manufacturing, and resist loans to agriculture.

However, economic development indicators point to the need to develop the agricultural sector. Unfortunately, government analyzes risk in a different way. It considers the probability of good management of funds disbursed to farmers. But it also analyzes the opportunity cost of additional investment in agriculture. On the contrary, banks always suspect that farmers will default. Their reason for this is not far-fetched and builds on some rational analysis. It is either that farmers may not earn expected returns, or that losses caused by natural disasters are unavoidable in agriculture. This thinking constrains banks from granting loans for agricultural production. It is a deep-seated aversion to risk. That agricultural risks crystallize in huge losses has been the rule rather than the exception. This is the reality of agricultural production that hinders its financing and private sector investment in it.

Foreign agricultural loans to emerging economies have not kept pace with the development needs of the sector. Foreign investment in agriculture might be large. In real terms, there has been a stagnation or decline in some emerging economies. Surprisingly, domestic investment in agriculture is unable to fill the gap. In real terms, there may actually have been a consistent downward trend—if anything. Banks, governments, and international lending agencies appear either overwhelmed or scared by risks and losses associated with agricultural production. For most banks in emerging economies, to invest in agriculture is to deliberately incur avoidable losses. It would seem that risks in agriculture have not been kept in check. Banks have maintained the rebuff on the credit needs of the sector. Foreign agricultural loans are received in trickles and for purposes that cannot altogether revolutionize existing practices, rigidities, and bottlenecks in the sector. Intervention by government is anything but realistic. In most cases, government makes feeble excuses for the failure of its agricultural policies.

Agricultural risk control measures

Many agribusiness risks defy all known control devices because they are "acts of God." Farmers should try to minimize risks rather than hope to eliminate them—because they can't. What are the common risk management techniques at farmers' disposal in emerging economies? Which of the risk management techniques are effective? Farmers in emerging economies adopt several cultural devices to manage risk. In the case of Nigeria, the following risk control devices are applicable:

- Regular clearing of farm borders to scare animal pests
- Setting of traps to kill animal pests
- Fencing the farm to prevent animals from breaking into it
- Making bounds to check erosion and planting cover crops to check flooding
- Using vigilante groups as security in farms
- Using dummies and scarecrows to keep away birds
- Planting windbreakers
- Ensuring that crops are planted on terraces to avoid their being washed away by flood
- Adjusting planting periods with changes in weather (Oni, 1988; NICON, 1988)

These measures could be effective for small farm enterprises in a subsistence economy.

However, the breakthrough needed in agricultural production in emerging economies demands more effective risk management techniques. The aforementioned practices will not satisfy this need. The risks in agriculture are a macroeconomic problem. Therefore its solution must be conceived and geared to reverse the macroeconomic and social consequences of the risks. In order to achieve this goal, the status of agriculture must advance from subsistence to commercial production. Advancing of agriculture should be oriented toward the export market and satisfying domestic food demand. The focus should be on few but committed farmers. Specific risk management and public support programs should be targeted at them. This fits with the drive for increased food and export production. In this way the burden of managing risk at numerous individual small-scale farm levels will be reduced.

Unfortunately, ignorance, illiteracy, and lack of public support, or the enabling environment constrains farmers from making progress. Yet farmers must move forward. In doing so, it is imperative for them to adopt modern agricultural practices. They should do all of the following:

- Procure and use better and improved varieties of hybrid seeds
- Use an irrigation system to ensure a regular and constant supply of water to the farm
- Purchase insecticides required for spraying crops against pests
- Adopt crop rotational practices
- Secure the adequate supply and use of fertilizers
- Implement recommended vaccination of animals against pests and diseases
- Procure and use improved breeds of stock and feed for livestock (Oni, 1988; NICON, 1988)

These are some of the areas that require urgent public support in managing the risks in agriculture.

Farmers should adopt agricultural diversification as a means of distributing risks that may be encountered in the process of production. Diversification is achieved through multiple farm locations, intercropping, and the planting of the same crop at different times. A variant of diversification is mixed farming, which combines crop and animal production. Farmers can manage economic risks by making projections into the future about the prices and yields of crops. The projections help to forecast expected revenues and cash flows. With good cash flow forecasts, farmers will know the amount of cash they may need and when they will need it. It will also help them to guide against financial problems. The risk of an uncertain market could be mitigated through futures contracts. Farmers can negotiate sales of produce to buyers at some preagreed future prices. Keeping a good record of yields and prices of produce should guide them in making decisions for the future.

Role of agricultural insurance

Insurance is one of the avenues for risk management in agriculture. In fact, agricultural insurance is the most potent of the various risk management techniques. The flow of credit to the agricultural sector would increase once a good number of insurance firms begin to provide cover against agricultural risks. With insurance cover for crops, farmers who suffer losses as a result of natural hazards could be indemnified. Indemnity should be up to, but perhaps not more than, amounts sufficient to keep farmers in business after losses. This, in fact, is the essence of agricultural insurance. In the absence of an insurance scheme, government may be compelled to compensate farmers who suffer losses as a result of natural disasters, from some natural disaster relief fund. But this would be an ad hoc approach, and thus would not be dependable.

Most of the risks of agricultural production cannot be prevented, because of the unpredictable nature of their incidence. The risks are largely due to uncertainties of weather, and as such cannot be avoided. Loss prevention is possible where the risk can be anticipated so that steps could be taken to prevent it from happening. The magnitude of losses incurred by farmers on account of natural calamities alone makes any idea of risk assumption unacceptable for practical purposes. Yet farmers in some emerging economies have continued to helplessly bear the burden of huge agricultural losses, for lack of an insurance scheme.

The agricultural insurance scheme adopted by Nigeria, according to *Federal Might* (1988) newsletter, seeks to promote agricultural production, provide financial support to farmers in the event of losses arising from natural disasters, increase the flow of agricultural credit from lending institutions to farmers, and minimize or eliminate the need for emergency assistance provided by the government during periods of natural disaster. In evolving the scheme, the government took the following into consideration:

- Unpredictable and risky nature of agricultural production
- Importance of the agricultural sector to the national economy
- The urge to provide additional incentives to further enhance the development of agriculture
- Increasing demand by lending institutions and farmers for an appropriate risk-aversion measure (NICON, 1988)

It is expected that the scheme would offer protection to farmers from the effects of natural disasters. It would also ensure payment of appropriate compensation sufficient to keep farmers in business after suffering losses.

MANUFACTURING INDUSTRY CREDIT RISK AND CONTROL

Banks do not usually covet accounts in the manufacturing sector. The reason is simple—manufacturers in emerging economies tend to contend with a myriad of problems. In some emerging economies, operational hitches in manufacturing are systemic. For instance, there could be a dearth of essential raw materials on the one hand, and a paucity of electricity to power industries on the other. It becomes difficult to achieve good financial performance under these circumstances. It would seem that no segment of the sector is immune to these problems. Yet, a few continue to give a good account of their operations. A typical example would be food and beverage manufacturers. Market demand for most of their products is and will remain appreciable for the foreseeable future. The main reason is that food and beverages (except tobacco, distilled spirits, bottled soft drinks, and carbonated waters) are essential for life. Yet, nonessential food and beverages have traditionally enjoyed good market patronage.

Credit products

Banks that are averse to risk should offer IFFs to companies in their target markets within the sector. This implies the opening of both confirmed and unconfirmed letters of credit, as well as facilitating bills for collection transactions, on behalf of customers. Banks should explore the possibility of getting the cash collection business of market leaders, as well as their foreign exchange transactions. However, it is always pertinent for banks to be wary of foreign exchange demand for nonimport or other official transactions. Other products that banks could target include funds transfer transactions. They can render this service to the major distributors of market leaders.

Good branch networks and loops come in handy. Banks should also be well disposed toward guarantees to the suppliers of major distributors. Besides regular guarantees, contractors and major distributors of leading manufacturers often need other forms of off-balance sheet credit products. They might request bid or performance bonds. On occasion a contractor may need an advance payment guarantee.

Lending criteria

Banks should structure IFFs they grant to manufacturers as 90-day banker's acceptances. The purpose of the facility would be to finance importation of raw materials or stock-in-trade. Distillers, for example, need to import and have a stock of ethanol. This is the main raw material for their products. In addition to any regular structured credit facilities, banks may offer a TOD, including DAUE, to major distributors of the products of market leaders.

The risk aversion disposition of banks demands that they grant TODs only in exceptional circumstances. There is a general criterion—a rule of thumb—that banks favor and often adopt. It is a rule with which banks tend to feel at home when they grant TODs to borrowers. The rule is that an account that needs a TOD must have been very active and run on a nonborrowing basis for a consecutive period of not less than six months. While this formula may be a useful guide, it should be applied with caution. For example, a bank should not grant a TOD request for more than 25% of the average credit turnover in the account during a given review period, say six months.

Ironically, banks sometimes grant TODs to already borrowing accounts. They do so for several reasons, most of which border on fulfilling some relationship demands. Banks scarcely decline TOD requests from their prime customers. Similarly, they easily grant such requests when the underlying banking relationship is mutually beneficial. Notwithstanding relationships, a borrower in this category might have a compelling financing need—one that its existing loans cannot accommodate. It could also be that there isn't a fit between the structure and need for the TOD, and its existing loans.

Collateral and loan repayment

A common practice in emerging economies is for banks to target lending to the upper-tier and financially strong borrowing customers. In order to mitigate credit risk, collateral securing the IFF should be carefully worked out. Ideally it is built into and reflected in the structure and transaction dynamics of the credits. A typical structure—one that underlies the threshold of risk in import financing—would be as follows:

- The borrower, usually a corporate customer, makes an initial equity contribution—say, 25% of the local currency equivalent of the letter of credit (L/C) amount. The contribution serves as its counterpart funding for the transaction. The bank applies the equity contribution toward the foreign exchange bid for the L/C. Thus, the bank lends 75% of the total local currency amount required to bid for the foreign exchange for the L/C. In doing so, it assumes credit risk—right from the time it provides local currency cover for the foreign exchange bid for the L/C on behalf of the borrower.
- At the time of—or toward—L/C confirmation, the borrower pays back 30% of the import bill (i.e., the L/C value). With this payment, the bank's secured exposure to the borrower drops to 45% of the L/C value.
- When the bank receives shipping documents for the import transaction, it asks the borrower to pay back 25% of the L/C value. This payment is mandatory for the bank to release the shipping documents to the borrower.
- Now the bank becomes unsecured once it releases the shipping documents to the borrower. Its unsecured exposure at this point is 20% of the L/C value. In this illustration, the 20% unsecured amount is typical of credit risk that banks in emerging economies take on their prime or other creditworthy customers.
- Often banks require borrowers to pay the outstanding 20% value of the L/C within 30 days after the release of shipping documents to them. Usually some understanding underlies the 30-day grace period to liquidate the loan. It is often based on an understanding that the IFF should be fully liquidated at or prior to the expiration of its tenor—usually 90 days.

The foregoing is not a universal arrangement for securing and repaying IFFs. It is applicable in countries where Central Banks or other regulatory authorities administer the demand and utilization of foreign exchange. But the illustration depicts the Dutch auction system of foreign exchange bidding and implies that the actual exposure of a bank on the IFF is only 45% of the related L/C value. There is yet another risk-mitigating measure built into the transaction dynamics—the 45% exposure is for a period of not more than 60 days.

That the IFF has an inbuilt risk control mechanism does not imply that it is risk-free. Sometimes it goes awry and becomes delinquent. Often problems arise from its structure, especially when its dynamics are suspect. For example, the borrower may not meet the repayment timelines. Usually this happens when timelines are ambitious or born out of unfounded optimism. Banks should, as a matter of risk control policy, avoid IFF structuring that could and does sometimes culminate in inventory warehousing arrangements.

Collateral to secure a TOD should be mainly a charge on a fixed deposit, quoted stocks, or a guarantee of the borrower. A guarantee counts when the borrower is adjudged to be creditworthy based on a proven track record. Some collateral types are not suitable for TOD facilities. Such collateral includes legal charges on land, buildings, factories, and so on. To all intents and purposes, the amount and tenor of a TOD do not usually warrant the rigor of having collateral in such tangible assets. Banks may consider stock-in-trade sparingly. They may also consider an equitable mortgage based on the execution of a memorandum of deposit of title deeds.

Mitigation of possible risks

Credit risk arises when local production is heavily import-dependent. Frequently, this happens in situations where essential raw materials cannot be satisfied or sourced in local markets. In those cases, the fortunes of manufacturers are intricately tied to the vagaries of foreign exchange markets and maneuverings.

Banks should realistically mitigate credit risk that a paucity of raw materials poses. For example, lending may be tied to specific local and foreign transactions that have short tenors and especially are self-liquidating. This could be achieved, for instance, when a bank decides to transact business with local distributors of market leaders.

It is pertinent that banks devise a way to mitigate the risk of the unsecured part of IFF transaction dynamics. That borrowers sometimes fail to meet IFF repayment timelines informs the need for some comfort. On occasion, trust receipts fill this gap. They offer some measure of feeble comfort to banks. But banks should not rely on them for security. Unscrupulous borrowers abuse the arrangement with reckless abandon.

ENERGY (OIL AND GAS) SECTOR CREDIT RISK AND CONTROL

The energy sector is the most strategic, lucrative, and perhaps volatile market for bank lending in Nigeria of late. The situation is the same in other emerging economies that are endowed with abundant mineral resources. Since the 1970s in the case of Nigeria, the sector has accounted for over 80% of the country's foreign exchange earnings. It also has the largest concentration of direct foreign private investment in the country. Unfortunately, violence has threatened the production and marketing of petroleum products—and other essential activities in the country's energy sector—in recent years. Militant youth activists have protested environmental degradation among other socio-economic demands. Nowadays banks are averse to funding major operations in the sector. That is how oil and gas, a one-time most coveted banking market, became a mixed blessing.

Credit products

With good risk management policy, banks can offer premium financial products and services to the oil and gas target market. The usual products—credit facilities, foreign exchange deals, funds transfer, cash collection, bonds, and guarantees—come in handy. An invoice and receivables discounting facility is a popular credit product in the energy sector. Banks offer it to contractors of major oil and gas companies in this target market.

Funds transfer service is a generic product for all industry operators. On the other hand, the main targets for foreign exchange transactions should be the major oil and gas companies—Shell, Mobil, Chevron, and so on. Incidentally, most of the oil and gas giants are major supply sources of foreign exchange for banks. The companies earn large amounts of foreign exchange that they regularly sell in the money market. They generate much of the foreign exchange from their operations in offshore oil fields and onshore oil production. Ideally, banks should tap into opportunities in foreign exchange trading with these industry giants.

In the case of cash collection service, downstream operators may be the main target market. The target market comprises mainly the major oil and strong independent petroleum marketers. Banks must ensure that their cash collection service is tailored to the cashless policy of the Central Bank. The use of a technology-driven collection arrangement would be appropriate. It will also help banks to closely monitor customers' sales—especially if they set up collection centers or offices within the premises of the major operators.

Lending criteria

The focus of the lending strategy of small banks should be on major contractors that provide various services to such industry leaders as Shell, Chevron, Mobil, and so on. In the case of banks in Nigeria, the focus should include the contractors of the energy sector parastatals—NNPC, PPMC, NPRC, and PPPRC. Banks should offer short-term credit facilities to the contractors. Small banks should avoid contract financing and other forms of direct lending that result in direct disbursement of funds on capital projects.

The big banks may want to grant some forms of venture capital or project finance to the upstream operators—companies engaged in oil exploration, drilling, and so on. In doing so, they should put foolproof risk-mitigating measures in place. In general, a bank that seeks to play it safe in the energy sector will probably only offer an IDF, and only to major contractors of industry leaders. Such a loan is often structured as a receivables finance facility. The bank would perhaps advance not more than 80% of the value of confirmed invoices for executed jobs or contracts.

Most banks will want to offer performance bond and bank guarantee facilities to strong independent marketers of petroleum products. The credit facilities enable the borrowers to obtain stock of products from local and international suppliers. In this case, banks take only off-balance sheet risk on the borrowers. Usually banks chase off-balance sheet credits because exposure on them seems remote. The risk attendant on such credits is contingent upon some future occurrence, if anything. Banks should not countenance this flawed thinking. One reason is that it places credit risk management on the wrong lines. It also creates the illusion that off-balance sheet credits are risk-free—or that they would not incur the concomitant contingent liability.

This illusion informs the appeal of off-balance sheet lending to banks. However, as I demonstrate in Chapter 16 of this book, credit risk is real in both on- and off-balance sheet lending. This implies that the rigor of risk analysis and mitigation in on-balance sheet lending equally applies in off-balance sheet lending. In some cases for operators in Nigeria, banks could lend the money to finance payments for petroleum products that PPMC allocates to marketers. Such credits may be structured as short-term banker's acceptance facilities with a maximum tenor of 120 days.

In order to be eligible for an IDF, a bond, and a guarantee, the respective borrower must have a proven track record of consistent good performance. This should be evident in records of its performance on such credit facilities that other banks have granted it for similar borrowing causes.

Collateral, loan repayment, and risk

Energy sector credit facilities must be well structured. There is no uniform structure for all energy sector credits. Each credit request should be appraised and structured on its merit. For example, the two main types of credit facilities that banks offer to operators in the energy (oil and gas) sector—IDFs and bonds/guarantees—are self-liquidating. In general, self-liquidating loans are less problematic. Usually banks hold most of the aces in structuring them. In the case of an IDF, the loan structure and dynamics offer security for the credit facility as follows:

- The borrower—a corporate customer—should have, or open, a current account with the bank that will provide IDF credit to it.
- It nominates the account to a named industry leader in the energy (oil and gas) sector—say, Shell. This illustration presupposes that the borrower has executed or hopes to execute some contract for Shell.

- The leading energy sector company—in this case, Shell—notes the bank and account that the borrower nominates to receive proceeds of the contract it awards to the borrower.
- This arrangement operates effectively as domiciliation of payment to the bank. Once it is in place, a bank may confidently grant the loan to an energy sector contractor.
- The bank must confirm that the borrower has an invoice certified for payment in its favor for already executed jobs.

Lending to finance procurement of petroleum products from PPMC (for operators in Nigeria) or other local suppliers requires different transaction dynamics. The borrower must have its own depot, marketing network, and good sales outlets or a good base of clientele. A tripartite collateral monitoring agreement between the bank, the borrower, and a warehousing agent would secure the lending. This arrangement assures that lodgment of funds in the borrower's account with the bank offsets release of products from its tanks for sale. The lodgments would be applied toward repayment of the loan.

Mitigation of possible risks

The usual direct risk—return correlation, or trade-off, applies in the energy (oil and gas) sector. This implies that as the sector promises high investment returns, it also presents a high-risk profile for investors. The magnitude of risk varies depending on whether investment is in the upstream or downstream subsector. Operators in the upstream own oil blocks, engage in oil exploration, and produce crude oil for export and local refining. Players in the downstream subsector market finished petroleum products.

Oil services firms—considered to be marginal industry players—facilitate the work of operators in the upstream and downstream subsectors. Thus, they operate at both ends of the industry. In doing so, they add value to the work of major players, especially industry leaders. There is less risk in downstream operations compared with operations in the upstream. This implies that upstream operators assume more risk than downstream operators and oil services firms.

There are particular key credit issues that inform the risk of lending in the energy (oil and gas) sector. The major factors include the following:

- The industry—encompassing exploration, drilling, refining, and marketing of petroleum products—is capital intensive
- Investment outcomes (especially for operators in the upstream subsector) are largely uncertain
- Major financing needs are often for long terms—largely because of the long gestation periods of many energy sector projects
- Politicization of oil in both local and international markets often influences the financial performance of operators.

Huge capital outlays, high risk profiles, and the uncertainty of returns are some of the defining problems at issue. Small banks may have to restrict credit exposures to a few operators and service firms in the downstream subsector. Such banks should tie control of credit risk to their choice of—and the structure of the credit facilities they grant to—operators in the industry.

TELECOMMUNICATIONS SECTOR CREDIT RISK AND CONTROL

Telecommunications is easily the most vibrant industry in emerging economies. The advent of the global system for mobile communications (GSM) revolutionized the sector. Soon the new telecommunications system became a cash cow for its operators. Not only did it jump-start the industry, it also opened up a lot of business opportunities. The boom in the sector is evident in the performance of such industry giants as MTN, Airtel, and Globacom (in Nigeria). As expected, the abnormal profits engendered stiff competition among the operators.

Characterized as capital intensive for investments and projects, the sector serves the telecommunications needs of governments, individuals, companies, and organizations. Thus, like health and education, telecommunications is a big industry—serving various extensive markets. The GSM revolution impacted positively on the business activities of telecom operators, including banking transactions. The industry is not only booming but also growth-oriented.

Lending criteria

Banks that are risk averse should adopt an indirect lending strategy in the telecommunications industry. They should grant short-term credit facilities to selected major distributors of handsets and recharge cards for the major operators. In some cases, a bank may consider granting IFFs to major operators to fund the importation of handsets and equipment. The success of this lending strategy would depend on a number of key credit issues, including the following:

- Liquidity of banks and their dispositions toward self-liquidating credits vis-à-vis the industry demand for loans
- Performance and market acceptance of the operators, their networks, and their customer service
- Track records of operators on their past and existing credit facilities with banks

A bank may grant an IFF if prevailing conditions are favorable. The loan may be structured as 90-day banker's acceptance facility for the importation of handsets and equipment, and production of recharge cards. The structure and repayment of the IFF should be as in the case of the manufacturing industry discussed earlier in this chapter.

Collateral and loan repayment

The structure of loans to the distributors of major operators should be simple. It should inform clear transaction dynamics. Both the structure and transaction dynamics must be tuned to the self-liquidating credit principle. Banks should lend money to finance procurement of stocks of handsets for major distributors. The financing and collateral arrangement would be as follows:

- Distributor—typically a corporate borrower or customer—contributes at least 30% counterpart funding. This amount represents its equity toward payment of the total cost of the handsets to be imported with the proceeds of the loan.
- Bank contributes the 70% balance of the cost of the transaction and takes custody of the handsets. Ideally the bank would do this under a tripartite collateral monitoring agreement with the borrower and a reputable warehousing agent.
- Bank releases stock worth up to 20% of the total value of the handset consignment to the borrower.
- Borrower pays proceeds of sales of the stock released to it into its account with the bank to enable further releases of stock.
- The actual quantity of stock released is a function of the amount of money the borrower has paid into its account toward repayment of the loan. More stock is released as the outstanding balance on the loan decreases.

Mitigation of possible risks

Observed abnormal earnings in Nigeria's telecommunications industry or elsewhere would certainly be checked. Profits will decline in the face of stiff competition. Price wars among operators will underlie the intensity of the competition. Regulation of the industry is also likely to become stringent to curb the excesses of operators. The interplay of forces in these issues defines the immediate source of risk of the industry. As in the energy sector, the small banks should deliberately seek to mitigate risks in the telecommunications sector. For example, they may restrict credit transactions to the major distributors and wholesalers of handsets. Lending emphasis should be on financing transactions engendered by unfulfilled market needs within wholesale distribution chains.

SOCIAL PROJECTS CREDIT RISK AND CONTROL

The government—including its ministries, parastatals, and agencies—embarks on various social and economic projects. The national assembly and its counterparts in the states appropriate budgetary funds for the execution of projects. Sometimes, the funds would be inadequate, necessitating deficit financing of some of the projects. In most cases, the government finances the deficits by borrowing from the local financial market. This provides an opportunity for the local banks to package and extend appropriate credit facilities to the government to enable it meet its various funding needs.

The government borrows from banks on various terms. It does a large part of the borrowing through the sale of government papers or financial instruments, such as treasury bills, treasury certificates, development stocks, and so on. The government could also borrow directly from banks. However, such loans are usually granted to finance specific government contracts or capital projects, or to meet recurrent expenditure needs such as the payment of salaries of workers and other overhead. Loans in this category are often structured as self-liquidating credit facilities. The transaction dynamics of such credit facilities ensure that sources for repayment of the loans are tied to monthly deductions from the government's statutory allocations from the Federation Account (in the case of Nigeria).

However, few banks in emerging economies would think that lending to the public sector should be pursued as a deliberate strategy of asset expansion, whether in the short or long run. Such banks might have reasons for their reluctance to lend to the public sector. In general, lending to the public sector tends to be unattractive to many banks for several reasons, including the following:

- Inability of banks to accurately foresee and plan for possible changes in government actions and programs
- The tendency of incoming governments to disregard projects started by their predecessors, largely for political reasons
- Complexity of most public sector financing needs, for which some banks do not have the requisite in-house risk analysis capabilities
- Most public sector projects are financed on the basis of their sociopolitical value, as opposed to the strict economic consideration of return on investment to which banks are oriented
- In most cases, expected revenue allocations or projections—which might not be realized—take precedence over the more practical reliance on cash flow analysis for loan repayment

In Nigeria, the Central Bank emphasizes and often warns banks about risks inherent in lending to the public sector. The demoralizing effect of its circular that directs banks to make a 50% provision on all loans to the public sector is a strong disincentive for bank. Notwithstanding risk warnings—and especially the CBN directive—lending to the public sector has remained an attractive business for the leading banks in Nigeria.

QUESTIONS FOR DISCUSSION AND REVIEW

1. What are the probable risks of bank lending to traders in emerging economies? How can banks mitigate the risks?

2. With reference to a named emerging economy in Asia, discuss the risks of agricultural production. In what ways do the risks affect bank lending to the sector?

3. In your opinion, how should banks in emerging economies structure loans to the manufacturing sector to mitigate the probability of default?

4. Identify the major causes of bank credit risk in the energy (oil and gas) sector of a named emerging economy in Africa or Eastern Europe.

5. Assess the chances of bank loan loss in the telecommunications industry in a named emerging economy in Southeast Asia or Latin America.

REFERENCES

Adepetu, J.A., 1987. Risk of crop production and the need for crop insurance in Nigeria. In: National Symposium on the Place of Risks and Insurance in Agricultural Production in Nigeria. A.R.M.T.I., Ilorin.

Adesimi, A.A., Alli, K.M., 1987. Crop yield insurance program: a suggested policy approach to stabilize farm income in Old Western Nigeria. In Adepetu, J.A., Op. Cit.

National Insurance Corporation of Nigeria, 1988. Federal Might, 2 (9).

Omodu, G.A.O., 1987. The problems and prospects of crop insurance. In: National Symposium on the Place of Risks and Insurance in Agricultural Production in Nigeria. A.R.M.T.I., Ilorin.

Oni, O., February 27, 1988. Risk Management in Agriculture. Business Times, Lagos, Nigeria.

Oputa, C.O., 1987. The risks of crop production in Nigeria and the need for crop insurance. In: National Symposium on the Place of Risks and Insurance in Agricultural Production in Nigeria. A.R.M.T.I., Ilorin.

Ray, P.K., 1981. Agricultural Insurance: Theory and Practice and Application to Developing Countries, second ed. Pergamon Press, Oxford.

The Bankers' Committee, Code of Ethics and Professionalism in the Banking and Financial Industry. The Chartered Institute of Bankers of Nigeria, Lagos.

Short-term Lending and
Recurrent Credits

Chapter 9

Advance, Overdraft, and Current Line Risks and Control

LEARNING FOCUS AND OUTCOMES

Banks lend money to individuals mainly on a short-term basis. The exceptions are mortgages, leases, and the financing of capital projects. These categories of credit demand a more rigorous credit analysis. Long tenors and dependence on uncertain future cash flows for repayment of such credits inform the rigor. Thus, banks structure nontransactional loans to individuals as either an advance or an overdraft. In addition, banks grant several transactions-based and specialized credit facilities to individuals. The loans, such as credit cards, mortgages, leases, and other asset acquisition credits, are usually packaged under various consumer lending arrangements. On the contrary, banks grant various loans to companies and organizations on both short- and long-term bases. But rarely do they grant an advance to corporate bodies, mainly because corporates are never consumer borrowers. Besides, due to its nature, an advance is not suitable for corporate financing needs.

Unlike an advance, an overdraft does not have a restricted target market. It is useful to individuals, companies, and organizations. While the advance may be the oldest credit product, the overdraft is the most popular. The attributes of the overdraft fit the practical needs of most borrowers. It comes in

Emerging Market Bank Lending and Credit Risk Control. http://dx.doi.org/10.1016/B978-0-12-803438-5.00009-X
189

handy where companies need short-term funding to augment working capital. Thus, it fulfills urgent cash needs considered essential to sustaining liquidity. Its greatest appeal is in filling financing gaps that cash flow timing differences occasion. The asset conversion cycle clarifies this important cause of an overdraft or other short-term financing in business.

Banks started tinkering with the overdraft over time. Their aim was to strengthen it and sustain its relevance to corporate borrowers. A current line—a logical alternative to an overdraft—evolved out of the tinkering. It needs to be emphasized that a current line is a substitute, not a companion, to an overdraft. It is an extension of an overdraft to accommodate broader financing needs. Bankers sometimes ignore this subtle difference and structure the one as though it is the other. A credit in this case is better granted as a current line than as an overdraft. The preference for the former is due to its wider utilization scope than the latter.

In this chapter I will discuss critical aspects of the traditional short-term credits, using the following learning outcomes as the framework of analysis. The reader will learn about:

- Differences between an overdraft and an advance on the one hand, and an overdraft and a current line on the other
- The features of an overdraft—noting, in so doing, why they might be considered unique to the overdraft
- Risks of an overdraft and measures that banks should adopt to mitigate them
- Business risk and how the asset conversion cycle sheds light on its main cause

CONTRASTS AND SIMILARITIES

The short-term credit facility is the most common classification or constituent of a bank's risk assets portfolio. It depicts all loans that banks grant to their customers for a *tenor* of not more than 12 months per *transaction cycle*. Often its purpose is to meet or augment working capital requirements. Typically, loans that are normally grouped under short-term credits are the *overdraft* and the *advance*. However, there are several other forms of loans that are more appropriately classified as short-term credits or that can be utilized under a *current line* facility. Such loans include—but are not limited to—*PO finance*, *asset-based finance*, and so on.

A *current line* facility is a typical example of a short-term credit facility. It operates like an overdraft facility, although it may have a wider scope for utilization. It is usually granted for a maximum utilization period of one calendar year to meet various short-term borrowing needs of customers. But its utilization could cover a lot more areas of financing needs. Such needs include establishment of letters of credit, local trade financing, advances, guarantees, and so on. Its appeal to borrowers is that it can be utilized to meet any of their numerous short-term borrowing needs. Instead of applying for a credit facility each time it has different short-term borrowing needs, a borrower could ask for a current line facility. I have in this chapter treated *overdraft* and *current line* facilities as synonymous. Yet, it is pertinent to note that the latter fulfills a wider scope of short-term financing needs for borrowers.

Banks that lend short do so because of the term structure of their deposit liability portfolio. Such banks largely get short-term deposits from their customers—and therefore cannot afford to lend for long terms. Banks might also wish to remain liquid even when they experience unanticipated adverse changes in the money market. Let me briefly explain the dynamics and risks of each of the usual short-term credit facilities. I also examine credit risk management tasks associated with such lending. Specifically, I review the nature and mitigation of risks of the direct advance, overdraft, and current line as follows.

Case Study 9.1

Flaws in Structuring an Overdraft Facility

Clem Wood went to see Alan Jack—the Rio de Janeiro[1] regional manager of Beach Island Bank Limited—with an important loan request. After an exchange of pleasantries, he introduced his objective of visiting Alan that early Monday morning.

"I need bank financing for a very crucial project in which I am interested through my company—Line Industries Limited," he intimated.

"What's the project about?" Alan asked curiously.

"I have during the past 18 months been working on a feasibility study for the establishment of a cement factory here in Rio de Janeiro. I can now tell you in confidence that everything looks great for the project. It is commercially viable and technically feasible. Above all, the project is highly profitable—based on the feasibility report," Clem said with entrepreneurial optimism as he handed Alan a copy of the project's feasibility report.

Alan looked it over and kept it on his table.

"I will review the feasibility report and get back to you during the week," promised Alan.

Two days later, he invited Clem back for a meeting on the cement factory project—having perused the feasibility report.

"I think your credit request for the project is going to fly. I have already asked one of the branch managers in my region to start work on it immediately," hinted Alan.

"The manager—Constance Forster—will contact you for more information on the project to enable her to structure and package the credit expeditiously."

"Thank you very much," Clem said appreciatively. "I sincerely hope that the management of Beach Island Bank will approve the credit with the urgency that it demands."

"I don't think that the credit will have a problem at Credit Committee," responded Alan.

At last, Beach Island Bank granted a R$500 million overdraft facility to Line Industries Limited to establish and operate a cement factory in Rio de Janeiro, Brazil. The company fulfilled all the conditions precedent to drawdown, including legal and security documentation, and started drawing on the facility.

The owner of the company, Clem Wood, operated the loan account as a sole signatory. He utilized the overdraft through cash withdrawals and the issuing of clearing checks. He made cash drawings at the branch where the overdraft account was domiciled. The manager of the branch, who was also the account's relationship manager, authorized each drawing on the account. He honored clearing checks issued by Clem as well as his requests for cash withdrawals.

Soon the overdraft was fully utilized while the project was yet at the construction stage. The company applied to the bank for an increase of R$150 million on the overdraft. The increase would enable it to complete and operationalize the cement factory. The bank declined the request on the grounds that it fixed the overdraft limit at R$500 million based on its review of the project's forecast cost and sensitivity analysis. Besides, Clem could not establish that there was a cost overrun that would require additional funding.

It became a dilemma for the bank—whether to stick to its decision at the risk of the R$500 million it had already disbursed, or to concede the increase of R$150 million to the company. Meanwhile, it directed its Credit Policy and Control office to review the loan account. Investigation of the account showed that some drawings were not related to the project. Clem occasionally drew money from the account to meet personal and other financial needs. The control staff demonstrated that the approved overdraft limit of R$500 million would have been adequate were it to have been applied strictly to the project.

Based on their findings, the investigators concluded that Clem willfully diverted some of the proceeds of the loan. They did not exonerate the branch manager and account officer from blame.

"The manager," according to the investigators, "was aware of the diversion and allowed it—clearly aiding and abetting it—largely because he authorized all of Clem's drawings that didn't contribute to execution of the project."

They also insisted that the branch manager and account officer did not monitor the project so as to reconcile the drawings with the progress of its execution. In view of the foregoing, investigators from the control office issued a query to the manager of the branch asking him to account for the observed lapses in operation of the loan account. He was also to explain why disciplinary action should not be taken against him for his role in the diversion of some of the proceeds of the loan.

"Although the loan was structured as an overdraft," insisted the investigators, "it nevertheless had an implied caveat that its utilization should be tied to the funding of the underlying project."

In his response, the branch manager absolved herself from blame.

"I don't have control over how a borrower utilizes a secured overdraft facility," she argued.

"On what basis should I scrutinize the purpose of each and every drawing on the loan account?" she queried.

In their report to the bank's management, the investigators described her response as "hollow, puerile, and diversionary." Management accepted the report of investigators as presented. It therefore placed her on an indefinite suspension pending a progress report on efforts to regularize the loan account. Ultimately, she was fired following her indictment in the investigator's report. Thus, the fallout of the investigation's indictment was that it cost Constance her job.

Meanwhile, Clem had threatened to abandon the project and sue the bank if his request for an increase on the overdraft was not granted. Amid pressure from him, the bank approved an additional R$100 million to fill the gap in the project's funding.

Hints for Answering This Case Study

It is the responsibility of lending officers to structure and analyze every credit request prior to packaging and presenting it to senior management for approval. On the other hand, senior management—often represented by a credit strategy committee—should always be critical of every credit proposal presented to it for approval. A critical disposition makes for a painstaking review of credit proposals to ensure that all loopholes are fixed. On occasion, unfortunately, lending officers unwittingly abdicate this responsibility to borrowers. Often they do so to satisfy some banking relationship demands, perhaps. Flawed credit structure, dictated by the interests of borrowers, has become commonplace. Credit risk under these circumstances is exacerbated. Faulty structure makes monitoring of loan utilization difficult. One reason is that structure both determines and is influenced by transaction dynamics. Once the structure is flawed, the credit is doomed from the start. In the Line Industries case, lending officers did a really poor job of structuring the credit. This flaw aided the diversion of part of the loan, and the eventual default.

Questions on the Case Study

1. Critically examine the investigators' charge that Constance aided and abetted diversion of some drawings on the loan in this case study.
2. In your opinion, what are the strengths and weaknesses of Constance's defense that she didn't have control over how a borrower utilizes a secured overdraft facility?

1. Setting this case study in Rio de Janeiro, Brazil, is strictly for learning and illustration purposes. It does not in actual fact imply that the lending transaction took place in Brazil. Also, the names used for the borrowing company, bank, and individuals in the case study are imaginary and do not relate to any known or unknown company, banks, or persons in Brazil or elsewhere.

DIRECT ADVANCE

An advance is a short-term credit facility that banks grant mainly to individuals to meet personal financial needs or obligations. An advance is a popular type of credit facility, especially in the consumer banking sector. Many banks maintain a sizable portfolio of consumer loans to cater to the borrowing needs of low-income individuals. Banks also grant direct advance facilities to high net worth individuals (HNIs)—and on occasion to small- and medium-scale enterprises. It is also popular among professionals such as lawyers, doctors, advertisers, estate agents, and so on. Other good candidates for an advance include NGOs, churches, schools, clubs, associations, and so on.

Banks grant direct advances to the aforementioned categories of customers for various purposes. In most cases, the borrowers need an advance to:

- carry on normal business activities that, in the case of low-income consumers, are often located in the informal economy
- purchase or refinance household equipment such as a deep freezer, air conditioner, furniture, and so on
- procure personal assets such as a utility car or other vehicle to enhance self-concept and personal self-worth
- furnish their business offices with such items as computers, fax machines, telephones, and so on
- make one-off payment on personal mortgages that enables them to own houses or other landed property

Banks nowadays advance credits to their customers to meet these financing purposes under terms of asset acquisition lending programs. The loans are usually of small amounts compared with other types of credit facilities. But on aggregate, they make up a substantial portion of a bank's lending portfolio. In Brazil, for instance—following the government's directive in mid-2003 that banks should lend at least two percent of their sight deposits to low-income consumers at a fixed monthly interest rate of two percent per annum—the portfolio of such risk assets was R$1.5 billion.

In the case of HNIs and professionals, loan amounts are determined based on ability of borrowers to provide collateral. They must also justify borrowing causes for the advance. Unfortunately, lack of collateral limits the availability of loans to low-income earners and small companies. Yet, the growth of these market segments is essential for economic growth and development. From its operations and business activities, the state benefits from reductions in unemployment and social unrest. This was the basis of the economic empowerment initiative of President Luiz Inacio Lula da Silva of Brazil. In 2003 he announced some measures aimed at making banking services more accessible to low-income consumers and small enterprises. In Brazil, as is the case in many other emerging markets, small- and medium-scale enterprises employ over 50% of the official workforce. The main risks of direct advance facilities arise from the *character* of the borrower.

OVERDRAFT FACILITY

An overdraft is a credit facility that banks usually grant to corporate borrowers. On occasion individuals may obtain overdrafts from banks. An overdraft facility allows borrowers to draw amounts of money in excess of the credit balance in their current accounts. Typically the overdraft has a specified tenor, usually not exceeding 12 months. A borrower may draw and utilize money from the overdraft during its tenor. This implies that an overdraft account must always be in debit—unless the facility has been paid off or liquidated. Obligors must provide tangible collateral to secure their overdraft. Banks prefer legal charges on land, buildings, factories, premises, or such other real assets as collateral for overdraft facilities.

An overdraft facility is usually permitted only for current account holders to meet occasional short-term business needs. Short-term financing needs of a business are often reflected in working capital shortfalls. An overdraft augments working capital; it fills the shortfall in a company's finances. The company must fill the funding gap in order to sustain its operations. An overdraft facility is repayable on demand. Although an overdraft would usually have tenor, a bank's offer letter normally carries a caveat that the loan is repayable on demand. Customers are not usually worried by this requirement because they realize that an overdraft serves only a transient funding need. In practice, however, it is rarely repaid on demand. The obligor might need it for as long as the business has a short-term funding gap. But the obligor, as in other borrowing situations, should maintain a good and credible banking relationship with the bank. In most cases, obligors utilize the overdraft for its full tenor. They ask and may get rollover on an annual basis upon satisfactory utilization, if anything.

With ATMs, powered by the Internet, it's now possible for individuals to run their overdraft accounts by means of credit cards. However, individuals to whom a bank grants an overdraft or credit card must have current accounts with the bank. In this case, current accounts function as loan accounts and make it possible and easy to operationalize the overdraft. On the other hand, an advance does not require a current account to be operationalized. But it requires a loan account to document the lending transaction.

From a bank's point of view, an overdraft account is regarded as performing when it generates satisfactory turnover or activity. It should also maintain satisfactory swings within its approved limit. The swings reflect the obligor's ability to repay the overdraft at reasonable notice. A common feature of an overdraft is the insertion by a bank in its offer of the credit to a borrower that repayment of the loan would be on demand. In practice, some borrowers would require a reasonable period of notice to fully liquidate the loan. It would seem that the *on demand* clause is intended to provide a constant reminder to the borrower that the bank could call in the loan at any time. In other words, an overdraft facility should not necessarily be fully utilized; it can indeed sometimes have credit balances. This is the essence of swings in overdraft accounts. The customer pays interest on the daily debit balances on the account. A bank should gain insight into the ability of an obligor to easily repay an overdraft. Analyses of historical audited financial statements and annual reports, or projected accounts and cash flows, are always helpful.

Features of an overdraft

An overdraft facility has unique features that distinguish it from other types of loan accounts. From the foregoing discussion, I summarize important distinguishing features of the overdraft facility as follows:

- The tenor of an overdraft facility will usually not exceed 12 calendar months from the date of its offer, acceptance, or disbursement—whichever comes first.
- The borrower—sometimes referred to as the obligor—is permitted to *overdraw* its *current accounts* up to, but not exceeding, the approved amount (or limit) of the overdraft facility.
- The bank earns income from the overdraft facility by charging interest to the account. Interest is calculated at the rate agreed upon with the borrower based on the average daily debit balances in the account.
- Banks usually seek to adequately secure the overdraft with tangible collateral. They do so because they rely in most cases on the observed good performance of a current account to grant the loan in the first place.
- An overdraft account has an inbuilt mechanism by which it achieves occasional *swings* with regard to its daily closing balances. The transaction velocity of the account dictates the swings.
- An overdraft facility is typically utilized for a wide range of purposes encapsulated in so-called working capital requirements. A bank may not effectively control utilization of an overdraft.
- Utilization and performance of an overdraft require unusually close monitoring by account officers and relationship managers. Unfortunately, monitoring the utilization of an overdraft often proves difficult. The main reason is that overdrafts do not lend themselves to clear-cut transaction paths or dynamics.
- Banks tend to grant overdrafts only to customers that open, operate, and achieve a particular transaction volume (turnover or activity) in their current accounts with bank.
- In principle, an overdraft is *repayable on demand.* This implies that a bank does not have to give formal notice to the obligor of its intention to call in the loan. Thus, the borrower is obliged to repay the loan on demand—*unconditionally.*
- Appraisal of an overdraft request often requires a rigorous analysis of the borrower's financial statements and annual reports. Usually the required documents are mainly audited accounts (in the case of corporate borrowers). For other categories of borrowers—especially individuals—banks make do with bank statements.

Risks of an overdraft

An overdraft is associated with certain credit risks that should be mitigated to avoid loss of the asset. Some common risks are inherent in the loan structure.

The main issues usually border on the mode of disbursement and utilization, as well as the source of repayment. There may also be a problem with the integrity of the borrower. Close monitoring of an overdraft tends to be ineffectual where obligors lack integrity. Banks take particular credit risks—especially the following—when they grant an overdraft to borrowers.

Veracity of cash flows

The veracity of financial statements, cash flows, and other sources of repayment of the overdraft might be in doubt. Ironically, banks hinge their expectations of timely liquidation of the loan on these documents. Yet, banks must rely—to a large extent—on critical analyses of historical and projected accounts, and loan repayment sources, in making lending decisions. In order to mitigate this risk, banks should insist on and work with financial statements and annual reports audited by reputable chartered accounting firms. Besides financial statement analysis, lending officers would not go wrong if they were to take peeks at sales records, bank statements, and so on.

Possible misuse of loan

In view of the wide scope of uses that banks allow for an overdraft, the facility could be subject to abuses. Possible abuses include willful diversion of proceeds of the loan by the borrower. This risk largely has to do with the character or integrity of the borrower. Banks should rely on the know-your-customer, or KYC, process to deal with this risk. Good knowledge of borrowers must stem from an all-embracing credit risk analysis. Such analysis should encompass the borrower's track record and its current standings for credit history and rating.

Monitoring difficulty

Often monitoring of the disbursement and utilization of an overdraft could be difficult. In most cases, once a bank approves an overdraft facility and sets its limit, the obligor simply draws cash from or issues checks on the loan account. Most of the drawings might be payments to third parties. It becomes rather clumsy, under the circumstances, to monitor the loan. Trying to ascertain every detail—including appropriateness—of every payment, let alone its underlying transaction dynamics becomes impracticable. Yet account officers must do their utmost to be on top of the utilization of the overdraft. That remains the most effective way to mitigate the risk of loan diversion. Unfortunately, lending officers have a laid-back attitude toward the monitoring of overdrafts. There tends to be a sense of security in the tangible collateral for the overdraft.

Loan recovery difficulty

Recovery of an overdraft in the event of default often proves to be an unusually difficult task. On occasion the usual fallback on the collateral is the culprit.

Tangible collateral might be attractive to banks but it may also not be easily realizable in the event of default. Good collateral has particular attributes. Lending officers should pay attention to critical qualities in deciding the appropriate security for an overdraft. I have in Chapter 27 of this book discussed some of the important attributes. Collateral that fulfills these qualities mitigates credit risk.

Tendency to evergreen

Frequently an overdraft facility becomes *evergreen*. This unwholesome situation happens as a result of multiple renewals, rollovers, or reschedulings of repayment. An evergreen overdraft tends to cover up the weak repayment ability of a borrower. It often takes a long time, under the circumstances, before eventual default on the loan is established. In order to mitigate this risk, lending officers must make sure that the expired overdraft is fully repaid before it might be renewed. Furthermore, one-off liquidation of an overdraft at expiration of the loan does not indicate strong loan repayment ability. An obligor could make an ad hoc arrangement to liquidate an overdraft if it's certain that the bank would renew the facility. So banks should look to swings that result in occasional cleanup during the tenor of the overdraft. In this way banks can effectively mitigate the risk of an evergreen overdraft.

BUSINESS (ASSET CONVERSION) RISK

In the case of corporate borrowers—the most critical beneficiaries of overdrafts—a bank should focus more on the analysis of business risk. If corporate business risk is adequately mitigated, chances are that an overdraft would be timely repaid. In order to mitigate business risk, lending officers should analyze the company's *asset conversion cycle* as discussed below. For complete appraisal of the loan repayment ability of the borrower, two major forms of risk *must* be analyzed—*business* and *financial* risk. It is not uncommon to find a different classification that recognizes business, financial, and performance risks separately. I separate financial and business risks in this book. Incidentally, both deal with the ability of a company to achieve optimum financial resources and employ them efficiently in its production process. Good standing in business and financial risks is reflected in the company's liquidity, gearing (leverage), and profitability (see Chapter 24 of this book).

For a borrowing company, business risk is almost always associated with the length of its asset conversion cycle—a measure of the time taken to convert raw materials through production, inventory, and accounts receivable to cash. Generally, risk increases with the length of the asset conversion cycle and vice versa. This is because a company with a short asset conversion cycle would not

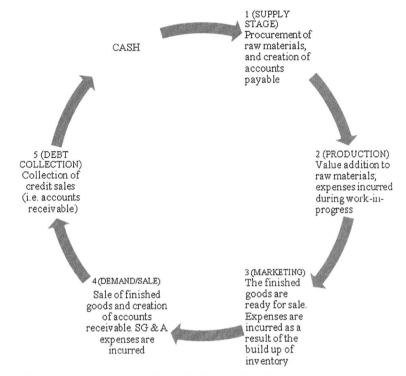

FIGURE 9.1   Typical asset conversion cycle of a manufacturing company.

normally tie down cash for long periods in the process of marketing, production, and sales, as opposed to one that has a long asset conversion cycle. Of course, cash flow (or liquidity) is the lifeblood of a business; it is in fact a major determinant of a company's ability to meet financial obligations. Most trading companies on the one hand, and certain categories of technical machinery manufacturers on the other, are examples of companies with short and long asset conversion cycles, respectively.

The causes and nature of specific risks inherent in the asset conversion cycle are discussed below (bearing in mind that expenses are incurred at each stage of the cycle), and the typical asset conversion cycle of a manufacturing company is depicted in Figure 9.1.

Raw materials

A bank should worry that a corporate borrower depends heavily on imported raw materials to manufacture its products. Such a borrower would be exposed to systematic risk. Regulatory controls—especially on foreign exchange—and import restrictions may constrain its ability to source raw materials on favorable terms. In such circumstances, the company will not effectively match competition from those that have access to local raw materials sources. In order to minimize risk, an import-dependent company should have or develop alternative sources of raw materials. It should also bargain for liberal credit terms—and by doing so, generate accounts payable—with its raw materials suppliers. The company should then seek to exercise some influence over supplier prices. Otherwise, a loan that a bank may grant to it would have a high probability of poor performance or loss.

Production (work-in-progress)

Lending officers should critically examine the production process that a borrower utilizes. This will help them to determine the efficiency and reliability of the production process to always yield quality products. Risk occasionally manifests itself at the *work-in-progress* stage of the asset conversion cycle—a stage during which *value* is added to raw materials. There could be a general breakdown of machinery; workers may go on strike or embark on a work-to-rule action, the regular supply of energy (e.g., electricity power) may not be guaranteed; the performance of machines and equipment may be affected by obsolescence; a major disaster necessitating plant shutdown may occur; staff may have poor skills, values, and competencies to meet work requirements, and so on. These and similar key credit issues define the magnitude of the risk of lending.

Sales (finished goods)

With finished goods (perhaps in the warehouse or with distributors), the company is exposed to yet another type of risk that the credit analyst must recognize. Common product risks, for lending purposes, relate largely to quality, price, demand, competition, promotion, and the physical distribution network. It is also important to consider the type of credit terms, if any, that the company gives to its customers, as well as the possibility of the risk of spoilage. Good ratings on these factors would favorably affect the chance of extending a credit facility to the company.

Accounts receivable

Perhaps this is the most important stage of the asset conversion cycle—when the company builds up accounts receivable through credit sales. It would have, in the process, incurred selling and general administrative expenses without getting cash proceeds. As this situation is bound to stress its cash flows, the company may default on its financial obligations to its creditors. For this reason, there is a need to determine the company's *average accounts receivable days on hand* ratio. This ratio gives an insight into the company's debt collection ability, which the bank needs in projecting its future cash flow sequence. It also enables the credit analyst to make projections on possible *bad debt*, loss *provision*, and outright *write-off* levels on accounts.

QUESTIONS FOR DISCUSSION AND REVIEW

1. Distinguish between an advance and an overdraft. How does an overdraft differ from a current line?
2. Why is the character of the borrower a critical risk factor in granting advance, overdraft, and current line facilities?
3. Discuss the features of overdrafts. Why would or wouldn't you consider the features of an overdraft unique?
4. Identify and assess the risks of overdrafts in emerging markets. As a credit analyst, how would you mitigate the identified risks?
5. How should a lending officer analyze business risk in any named emerging market? In what ways does the asset conversion cycle contribute to business risk in that market?
6. What factors favor or discourage the use of ATMs to operate an overdraft account?

Chapter 10

Margin Lending, Credit Risk, and Stock Markets in Emerging Economies

LEARNING FOCUS AND OUTCOMES

Nonbank lending institutions—such as a stockbrokerage firm—might and often do grant margin loans to their customers. They do so in just the same way and for the same purpose that banks grant margin loans to stockbrokers. The difference is that customers of stockbrokers are mainly retail dealers and investors in stocks, while those of banks deal in stocks as wholesalers. Ideally, margin lending comes within the purview of the stock market and depicts stockbrokers' lending to their clients. On occasion, quite incidentally, banks dabble in this highly risky business to which they are not oriented or the risk for which they are ill-equipped to handle, if anything. Unfortunately, even daring banks have gotten their fingers badly burned as a result. For this reason, I focus on banks—the mechanics, risks, and control of their margin lending to stockbrokers and other corporate wholesale dealers in quoted stocks.

Emerging Market Bank Lending and Credit Risk Control. http://dx.doi.org/10.1016/B978-0-12-803438-5.00010-6

Margin lending is a unique financing arrangement by which banks grant loans to borrowers who trade in quoted stocks. Naturally, stockbrokers are the main margin borrowers in emerging economies. Lending follows particular technical rules and adopts a methodology that is largely unconventional. The famous risk—return trade-off paradigm in finance plays itself out here. Returns tend to be high from stock trading when the market booms and capitalization is rising. In this scenario, market makers and stockbrokers are bullish and take more risk in committing huge funds to investment in the stocks they fancy. The bulls take control of the market as they try to sustain the rising tempo of market activity, transaction volume, and the capitalization index. The flip side of the stock market is that returns from stock trading tend to be low when the market experiences a lull and capitalization is falling. With this scenario, market makers and stockbrokers become bearish and take less risk by cutting down on investment in stocks. As the bears assume control of the market, they try to reduce the tempo of market activity, which ultimately forces down the volume of trading and market capitalization.

In general, stock market behavior and risk are informed by information fluidity and speculation. Market players and analysts continually search for, obtain, and analyze all sorts of information in order to make informed purchase or sale decisions. Smallholder and individual investors are not left out in this practice, as they are equally concerned about the fate of the stocks they crave and to which they have committed funds. However, insider information is outlawed in this business practice. Overall, dealers in stocks are driven to make money on the stock exchange. On occasion, in doing so they take uncalculated risks and get their fingers badly burned. As would be expected under the circumstances, banks that grant them credit facilities in terms of margin lending suffer the same fate. The reader will learn about:

- The meaning and applications of margin lending in banking in emerging economies
- The influence of margin lending and regulatory intervention on the boom to bust in the stock market
- Margin lending methodology and the transaction dynamics that underlie its conduct
- The nature, incidence, and causes of risks in margin lending in emerging markets
- How margin loans should be structured to mitigate the credit risks attendant on them

---

Case Study 10.1

Illustration of Abuse of Banking and Capital Market Regulation
In keeping with its program of privatization of public enterprises and utilities, the Nigerian government decided early in the twenty-first century to divest its investment in a certain energy sector company in which it held a majority equity

share. The Privatizing Office appointed Wood Bank as the registrar for privatization of the company. As the registrar, the proceeds of the company's privatization were domiciled with Wood Bank pending the allotment of related shares to members of the public who subscribed to the public offer of the shares. At the end of the exercise, the offer was oversubscribed. This necessitated rationing of shares among the subscribers and the return of monies corresponding to unsuccessful subscriptions. Wood Bank remitted funds to the Privatizing Office for all shares allotted to subscribers, but held back return monies for the subscribers who got partial or no share allotments. In doing so, Wood Bank had intended to temporarily use the return monies to cushion liquidity pressure it was experiencing at the time, as well as meet other operational financial needs. It had reasoned that the process of returning money to unsuccessful subscribers in such a public offer often lingered for several weeks, or in some cases months. This is because the arrangement for sending return monies involves:

- Printing of payment warrants for each of the beneficiaries
- Sending the warrants to their beneficiaries through the postal system
- Receipt and presentation of the warrants by beneficiaries to their banks for payment
- Presentation of the warrants by the beneficiaries' banks to Wood Bank for payment through the clearing house

During the envisaged delay, the bank thought it would have sorted out its liquidity pressure and satisfied other short-term operational financial needs. Thus, it used a chunk of the return monies to fund the disbursement of outstanding loan commitments. However, no sooner had the bank utilized the funds than the Privatizing Office made a demand for an immediate release of the return monies directly to beneficiaries. The bank objected to this directive, contending that it contravened the Check Payment Act and the aforesaid procedure for sending return monies to beneficiaries. Besides, the bank pointed out, it would be difficult for it to ascertain the true identities of the beneficiaries of return monies, since the only information about them at its disposal were names and postal addresses.

The opinion of the Privatizing Office on the matter emboldened the agents of the owners of more than 95% of the return monies, who had subscribed for the shares using surrogate names. Thus, notwithstanding the contentions of Wood Bank, they insisted on direct payment of the related return monies to them on behalf of their principals. The bank refused to oblige the request and maintained its position. This upset the Privatizing Office, which gave the bank an ultimatum to pay the money within four days or face severe punishment. The Privatizing Office followed its ultimatum with formal reporting of the case to the regulatory authority for appropriate sanction. As the problem lingered, the press fed on the news and it made it to members of the banking public, which created adverse publicity for the bank. It started experiencing unusual customer demands for deposit withdrawals. Most of the bank's depositors thought that the bank was unable to pay the return monies because it was broke. Perhaps their suspicion was correct. In the heat of the problem, the bank had tried, but to no avail, to obtain funds to meet the return monies obligation. It realized that even though it might have made a good case to the authorities, its decision to book more loans with the return monies was erroneous. It would have been possible for it to pay the return monies had it rather invested the funds in money market instruments, which are less risky than loans.

Meanwhile, the regulatory authority investigated the complaint of the Privatizing Office. On the basis of its findings, it suspended the bank's capital market operating license for six months, in the first stance, pending its full compliance with the directive of the Privatizing Office on the return monies. So, the bank had no choice but to borrow a whopping sum at very exorbitant rates from interbank sources to satisfy the directive of the Privatizing Office in order to remain in business. The problem, unfortunately, rubbed off on the banks that gave the interbank placements as Wood Bank defaulted on the due dates.

THE STOCK MARKET: GOING FROM BOOM TO BUST

On occasion the stock market booms with increasing and sustained volumes of daily transactions. Investors make brisk incomes from stock trading while the boom lasts. Of course, the bulls channel more energy and financial resources to maintain the tempo of transactions. A mark of success is reflected in a rising market capitalization index. Yet, the stock market frequently experiences shocks that adversely affect trading in stocks and the financial performance of stockbrokers. Often the shocks cause a liquidity crunch that enthrones a bearish stock market. The capitalization index tends to plunge sharply when the stock market is bearish. A dramatic plunge in the capitalization index evidences a period of consistently falling prices of quoted shares on the stock exchange. In most cases, investors suffer huge financial losses where the bears are able to sustain the plunge in share prices.

A capitalization index is a measure of the total monetary value of all stocks quoted and traded on a particular stock exchange as of a given date. It mirrors the level of confidence of direct and portfolio investors in an economy. The index rises when investment in the economy through the stock exchange increases, and falls when there is a decline in investment. This is termed boom to bust—a characteristic feature in the nature of the stock market. Certain factors contribute to stock markets going from boom to bust in emerging economies. For instance, an economy that is opening up, so as to rely more on market forces than controls, is likely to witness an upsurge in local and international direct and portfolio investments. Increasing investment in this way boosts the stock market. As would be expected, the stock market booms with the boost. However, there has to be an efficient, transparent, and vibrant stock exchange before the economy could benefit from the boost. There will also be the need for a diversified financial market. A conducive business environment, political stability, and an efficient reward system in emerging economies are also essential and inevitable.

Let me illustrate the boom to bust mechanism with the state of Nigeria's stock market from 2004 to 2010. The Central Bank of Nigeria (CBN) announced an increase in the regulatory capital of banks in Nigeria from a mere ₦2 billion to ₦25 billion in mid-2004—with an 18-month grace period for compliance. There were jitters in banking circles about an imminent crisis that was bound to lead to forced mergers, acquisitions, and closures. Chief executives, directors, and major shareholders who attended the Bankers Committee meeting where the CBN Governor made the announcement stormed out in anger. Some scampered off, in the confusion that ensued in the aftermath of the meeting, got into their cars and headed to their offices. Concerned stakeholders in banking lobbied for a change of the policy, ostensibly to ward off the threat to their investments in banks, but all was to no avail. Apparently, the policy was immutable.

In the end only 24 banks—out of a total of about 84 commercial banks in the country—made it! Fourteen banks failed to meet the deadline and had their banking licenses withdrawn by the CBN, while the rest—with the exception of Citibank, First Bank, Guaranty Trust Bank, Standard Chartered Bank, and Zenith Bank—either merged or were acquired, resulting in the surviving 24 at the end of the deadline on December 31, 2005. All but two banks—Citibank and Standard Chartered Bank—raised the required funds from the capital market. There were initial public offerings (IPOs) of the shares of the unquoted banks. Quoted banks issued more shares to the public and sold rights issues to existing shareholders. In doing so, banks invariably converted to public limited companies after selling equity shares to individual and corporate investors in the foregoing ways. These actions engendered unprecedented high volumes of transactions in the shares of banks. There was a boom as investors scrambled for bank shares on offer in the market.

The boom festered in the cutthroat world of banking. The big banks flexed their competitive muscles. Claims and counterclaims of market leadership took center stage in the ensuing intense rivalry among the leading banks. Soon the rivalry was taken to the margin lending arena. Banks granted margin loans in a reckless manner to boost trading in their own shares on the Nigerian Stock Exchange. Most of the borrowers were cronies of directors or affiliates of the banks. There was the case of a bank granting over ₦80 billion in margin loans to a nobody given to carrying a briefcase around and within the Stock Exchange as though he were a serious stockbroker. The case of Union Bank of Nigeria was not only embarrassing but an insult to the sensibilities of regulatory authorities. The bank had raised funds from its subsidiaries to invest in its own shares as a means of fulfilling the ₦25 billion regulatory capital requirement.

The banking sector became the toast of stockbrokers on the floor of the Nigerian Stock Exchange. Shares of banks yielded incredibly excellent returns on investment from handsome dividends and price appreciation. Banks consistently paid interim and final dividends, complemented by enviable bonuses, scripts, and rights issues. Individuals, companies, and organizations scraped up more funds that they invested in shares of banks. Professional investors and amateurs alike borrowed money from friends, relations, and financial institutions to acquire equity stakes in the banking industry. Interestingly, investors in property and realtors, who traditionally consider investment in stocks very risky, jumped on the bandwagon. Curiously, many of them divested from property as they switched to stocks. Their actions crashed the otherwise naturally stable property market. Values of residential and commercial properties, and the rents on them, nose-dived to the lowest ebb. In all this, the driving force behind the investment trend was easy access to margin loans fueled by windfall gains. Thus while the stock market was booming under the auspices of margin lending, investors in property were counting the cost. Ironically, the boom was a bubble in disguise building up in the stock market.

Then the bubble burst. The boom had lasted for four years—from 2004 to 2008. Signs of cracks in the stock market came to the fore in late 2007 while the global financial meltdown was underway. The authorities dismissed the signs as inconsequential, ostensibly suggesting that Nigeria's financial system was immune to the meltdown. The chief executive of one of the banks argued that the crisis was limited to the highly developed financial markets—and would not affect countries like Nigeria and other developing economies because they did not deal in exotic financial products, unlike their counterparts in developed nations. The stock market remained in the doldrums until 2012, when it recorded a marginal recovery.

REGULATORY INTERVENTION TO STEM THE TIDE OF A HAMMER BLOW

Nigeria's stock market crisis had far-reaching implications for the country's banking sector and economy. Many banks started depending on the Central Bank's overnight liquidity window to fund day-to-day transactions and operating costs. Technically, the banks had become distressed and were failing. The CBN linked the fate of the banks to the acute liquidity crunch occasioned by unprecedented reckless deployment of bank capital and deposits in the funding of margin lending. The banks had huge exposures to margin loans that had gone bad as a result of decreases in share prices, the stock market crisis, and the decline. Share prices had fallen drastically to the lowest ebb ever.

When reality dawned in 2008, it was obvious that Nigeria's banking sector and stock market were in a serious trouble. Beyond the burst bubble, systemic financial crisis was brewing. Fear of imminent bank failures loomed large in stakeholders' minds. The CBN Governor responded forcefully to the fear. In an unprecedented move to save the banks, he sacked, and prevailed on the Economic and Financial Crimes Commission (EFCC) to arrest and prosecute, the chief executives and directors of 8 of the 24 banks in the country. The immediate effect of this action was a run on banks and the stock market. Regulatory authorities of the two financial sectors tried, but to no avail, to douse investors' anxiety. Their efforts fell through as nerves had started to fray. Quickly the CBN rallied funds and injected ₦620 billion of taxpayer money into the banking sector to save investments in the eight troubled banks. The Federal Government took over ownership and control of three banks and christened them bridge banks. The remaining five troubled banks were acquired by banks that remained strong in the aftermath of the crisis.

While the nerves of investors in the banking sector were successfully calmed, it would seem that investors in stocks were left to their fate. The stock market crash lingered painfully for more than three years, starting in 2008. The bears took over control of transactions on the floor of the Nigerian Stock Exchange. Unfortunately this adverse situation affected stocks and sectors across the board, as it was not limited to shares of banks and the banking sector. Investors in the stock market were at a loss. Their dilemma was how to recover their funds locked up in shares. They dreaded holding the shares in the hope that the stock market would bounce back, just as much as they were loath to sell the shares at very huge losses.

As bank debtors—borrowers—remained loath to sell off parts of their share portfolios, their margin loans deteriorated further. The banks could not invoke relevant terms of the loans in order to sell the shares and apply the sale proceeds to recover the loans. Ordinarily, that was a certain and sure fallback for them under the circumstances. But they were constrained to hold off recovery action for the same reason that borrowers were loath to sell shares. There seemed not to be a way out under the circumstances—a situation that exacerbated the liquidity problem of the banks. This was the situation of things when the CBN intervened in a rare move to salvage the distressed banks and industry.

While briefing the press on April 16, 2010, Sanusi Lamido Sanusi—then CBN Governor—outlined drastic measures to check the "wild beast" of margin loans. The briefing came hard on the heels of resolutions of the 69th special session of the Monetary Policy Committee and those of the Board of the Central Bank. The Governor attributed the crisis that was rocking Nigeria's banking industry to sharp and unprecedented diminution in value of shares securing margin loans banks granted to stockbrokers and other investors in the capital markets. As stockbrokers incurred huge losses as a result of sustained declines in share prices, they defaulted on their margin loans. A liquidity crisis set in with weakened cash flows and a large stock of delinquent and classified assets in margin loans. A particularly startling finding was that more than 60% of total banking system capital had been lost in 2009 alone—due to reckless lending, especially loans granted for purchase of shares of banks in the capital markets.

Ultimately, the CBN and the Securities and Exchange Commission (SEC) intervened in the mess, and by doing so halted the malaise within the financial system. Input from the CBN was informed by advice from its Financial Services Regulation Coordinating Committee (FSRCC). The CBN–SEC measures in the main targeted how banks and stockbrokers should conduct margin lending in the future. The measures came as guidelines, the chief provision of which was a limit on exposure based on a required minimum margin. Other rules included certification of banks and stockbrokers, and share qualification, for margin lending. The guidelines also set criteria for assessing eligibility of all capital markets operators.

DEFINING MARGIN LENDING

The question, with foregoing background, is what is margin lending? How can it be appropriately defined? I characterized margin lending as a unique financing arrangement for trading in quoted stocks in the Learning Focus and Outcomes of this chapter. The uniqueness borders on its reliance on a technical process that departs from the regular framework for bank lending and credit risk control. Now I should explain the meaning and methodology of margin lending in a more detailed and direct way. Don't be confused when you see other terms used in the same context as margin lending. It is normal for authors to adopt the term they fancy in preference to another. On occasion the credit literature features margin lending as synonymous with gearing or borrowing to invest. In order to be consistent, I adopted margin lending throughout this chapter.

Take a look at the table of contents for this book. You will see that I grouped margin lending under short-term lending and recurrent credits. This classification is apt given the fact that margin lending is a current line facility. It is more strictly defined as simply a line of credit facility. While there are other types of lines of credit, its distinguishing feature—one that marks its uniqueness—is that it is usually secured with the borrower's portfolios of cash, managed funds, and quoted stocks. Cash is the most liquid asset of all time and therefore furnishes inviolable collateral to secure bank loans. Conversely, stocks are illiquid and highly volatile as collateral for bank loans. The volatility of stocks stems from the price fluctuation that is inherent in the capricious nature of the stock market. However, the fate of managed funds depends largely on the level of care the funds' managers exhibit in their capital market transactions. Thus managed funds could boost collateral when viewed from the perspective of how they strengthen the borrower's balance sheet. Using the three collateral assets in combination strengthens margin lending and borrowing. Without the collateral as a fallback, a bank would not have the confidence to grant margin loans in the first place.

Perhaps the best way to appreciate the import of the foregoing meaning is for me to define margin lending from another, self-explanatory perspective—without changing its meaning. I do so now. Margin lending is a secured financing arrangement that a bank has with its customer that allows the customer to use bank funds as a loan for investment in stocks and/or other financial assets—usually in the capital markets. A secured arrangement in this sense implies that the customer must pledge particular collateral as a condition precedent to utilization of bank funds. In this case, the collateral is intangible but acceptable as offering good security for funds the bank advances to the borrower as a margin loan. Usually the collateral is cash and the financial assets acquired with the margin loan. However, the main financial asset against which a bank grants a margin loan is quoted stocks. Often the customer who is the borrower and obligor for the loan is a stockbroker or dealer in other capital markets products.

Let me now offer a synthesized definition from the foregoing meanings. Margin lending is an arrangement into which a borrower enters with a bank to invest funds the bank advances to it in financial assets traded in the capital markets, and to pledge the same assets acquired with the funds as collateral for the advance. Funds advanced by the bank are termed a margin loan, while financial assets pledged to secure it could be stocks or other eligible capital markets products. Usually eligibility implies quotation on the stock exchange. The borrower may be a stockbroker or other dealer in the capital markets. What is unique about the arrangement is the use of the same assets acquired with the margin loan as the collateral to secure the loan. The mode of utilization and its monitoring are also unique. The amount of the margin loan is a function of the value of collateral assets pledged as security for it. A borrower can obtain a larger amount of margin loan when, in addition to assets acquired with the loan, they boost their collateral value by pledging more eligible assets in their portfolio. This is what borrowers tend to do in bullish markets—to increase investment at current or higher risk levels in pursuit of profit, capital gains, or a windfall. But it could lead to overtrading and its concomitant liquidity stress and risk.

BENEFITS OF A MARGIN LOAN TO THE BORROWER

A margin loan benefits stockbrokers and other operators in the capital markets in various ways. Beyond augmenting working capital, it boosts cash flows, increases investment portfolios, and unlocks equity for business. It also enhances flexibility in stock trading—and above all, it is tax deductible. I discuss aspects of these benefits below.

Boost to borrower's cash flow

Stockbrokers apply margin loans to beef up their investment opportunities. This is achieved when they have a strong capital base and can increase and sustain their portfolios of investments in the capital markets. That way, a margin loan complements the capital funds available to the borrower. It encourages stockbrokers and other capital market operators who are not risk-averse to speculate and deal confidently in stocks and other financial assets. Besides, it boosts cash flows for stock trading. This has liquidity implications for stockbrokers.

Investment in stocks could be of short duration for investors looking to make a quick profit. Such investors buy and sell shares based on the availability of profitable investment opportunities. Investors interested in capital appreciation invest for longer terms. The fluidity of the stock market enhances the liquidity of financial assets. For instance, a stockbroker can buy a large volume of shares of a particular company and offload the same shares onto another stockbroker or other willing buyer in one day. This is unlike what obtains in the real property sector, such as the housing market, where investment is typically long-term oriented.

On occasion, with a strong cash flow position, margin loan can help stockbrokers to build long-term investment outlooks. Under the auspices of stock exchanges, and being cognizant of applicable risks, it affords them greater access to markets.

Increase in investment portfolios

Stockbrokers should normally have portfolios of cash, managed funds, and quoted shares of their own before they approach a bank with margin loan requests. Ideally, stockbrokers regularly invest a portion of cash available to them in new financial assets. With more cash from margin loans at their disposal, they could continue to build up investment portfolios in the capital markets. In doing so, they create more wealth. This process multiplies wealth over time as stockbrokers seize investment opportunities in markets. The drive to achieve and sustain increasing portfolios of investments as a wealth creation strategy is the main borrowing cause for the margin loan. This benefit is more apparent in a bullish than bearish market. While the former portends the possibility of profit-making for stockbrokers, the latter is prone to risk of loss.

Unlocking of equity for business

The use of stocks and other assets in an investor's portfolios as collateral for margin loans frees the investor's equity capital that is otherwise tied up in those financial assets. The freed equity can then be reinvested in new assets. In this way, the investor is able to raise funds for other or more investments without diminution of its asset portfolios. This benefits the investor in two main ways. Firstly, it increases the volume and monetary value of its asset portfolios. Secondly, the investor could effectively and profitably diversify its portfolios of financial assets. Portfolio diversification is made possible by the availability of more investible funds from margin loans. With more funds, a stockbroker could target and invest in different securities in different sectors of the economy as a risk control strategy. In this way, margin loans facilitate the diversification of the asset portfolios of stockbrokers in emerging markets.

Flexibility in stock trading

Margin loans enhance flexibility in stock trading. Stockbrokers can trade in stocks within their secured margin loan limits. They could quickly make or change investment decisions based on the realities of the markets. They decide how much margin loan they need or with which they are comfortable to trade. This implies that stockbrokers have control over their gearing—a situation that contrasts with capital budgeting, where projects dictate the level of required financing and therefore the gearing ratio. There is also flexibility in the choice that stockbrokers have to liquidate portions of their asset portfolios at any time without recourse to the bank. This is possible as long as the margin loan remains secured at the current level of the stockbroker's financial asset portfolios.

Tax deductible interest costs

Astute stockbrokers could easily make enough money with margin loans to be able to repay the loan by utilizing the earnings the loan generates. In most cases, this is the wish of every stockbroker and other investors in capital markets products. A borrower that liquidates its margin loan from earnings in this way would then be trading on equity. This benefit is enhanced in emerging markets, where interest borrowers pay on margin loans is tax deductible. These benefits tend to be more realistic when borrowers take only calculated risks that are also effectively mitigated within the framework of regulatory rules.

MARGIN LENDING RISKS, ANALYSIS, AND CONTROL

Banks engaged in margin lending tend to contend with unusual types of credit risk. Risk exposures of banks differ in incidence and dynamics from those of regular forms of lending. A near semblance may be what obtains in asset-based lending, or lending against collateral in movable assets, if anything. The main source of risk in margin lending is the predominant use of stocks as collateral to secure the loan. As a floating asset, stocks do not offer effective security for a bank loan. Of course, banks should place limited—not absolute—reliance on floating assets for loan repayment. Let me now discuss how flouting of this rule in margin lending could precipitate credit risk.

Changing loan-to-value ratio

The stock market is not only volatile but highly unpredictable. These features impart risks to the investment and lending against security in stocks. As the market and value of stocks go from boom to bust, investors gain or lose on their capital. It follows that a bank should specify its required loan-to-value ratio (LVR) right at the outset. The LVR is a measure of the amount of loan that a bank grants a borrower against the agreed value of the borrower's portfolio of collateral assets securing the loan. Ideally, the LVR must fit with the bank's risk acceptance criteria for the capital markets sector. This is important because the portfolio value of stocks falls or rises as the stock market declines or increases, as its capitalization index reflects.

In emerging and volatile stock markets, banks may require up to 100% collateral cover on a margin loan. This works out to a ratio of 1:2—in which case the bank lends not more than 50% of the collateral value. However, the LVR should not be seen as immutable. It is subject to change without prior notice to the borrower depending on prevailing market conditions. The change could be an increase or a reduction to any rate within a zero and 100% ratio band. Nonetheless, changes are tied to the bank's target markets definition and risk acceptance criteria. The import of this is that borrowers should be careful with their utilization of margin loans. Good utilization dictates that they should target only premium stocks that have a proven track record in returning high value on investment.

On its part, banks should be looking to lend only to borrowers with a good track record of investing in a regulated capital market. This demands that borrowers should be more on top of their stock trading to avoid careless mistakes and the loss of income or capital. They should be well versed in stock trading and markets. In addition, they should be able to analyze and predict market dynamics and trends. These are some of the measures that mitigate the risk of possible breach of loan-to-value ratio rules.

Volatile money and stock markets

Margin loans tend to be volatile—because their risks and those of stock market transactions are intricately intertwined. This common feature implies that falling or rising stock market prices and capitalization impact margin loans negatively or positively, due mainly to the structure and dynamics of margin lending. The market capitalization index evidences booms or slumps in stock trading that result in gains or losses to the bank and borrower. However, banks are affected by stock market behavior more or less than borrowers depending on how the borrower manages the risk attendant on market volatility. Close monitoring of the stockbroker's investment portfolios and trading account will help lending officers to detect adverse trends in the changing value of investments within their portfolios.

Usually, market decline goes with diminution of security portfolio value. Sustained market decline may erode collateral cover for margin loans and exacerbate credit risk for the bank. The net effect is that borrowing limits are reduced or exceeded—leading to an unintended rise in gearing. This is an inevitable outcome: while collateral value falls with a market decline, outstanding loan balances increase with compounding interest and charges. The usual lending clause that ties interest rates on loans to prevailing money market conditions does not help matters. Variability of interest costs imparts further risk, and to make matters worse, dividend timing differences complicate loan servicing. Unless interest and dividend payment times or dates coincide, the borrower might default due to timing differences. Also, in a typical declining market, interest expense on loans tends to exceed the dividends earned on equity stock investments.

Banks can mitigate credit risk in volatile markets by structuring interest and charges on margin loans on fixed—not variable—terms. In this way, borrowers can better anticipate financing costs and apply earnings to offset them on due dates. On their part, borrowers should have a fallback on other sources of income for loan servicing and repayment. Otherwise, they would be exposed to the risk of a margin call when their loan balance exceeds their borrowing limit. In the absence of this fallback position, the borrower should have a buffer against a funding shortfall and its concomitant risk of a margin call. The borrower could do this by not exhausting the borrowing limits that banks approve for it. That helps to keep its gearing ratio in check and to forestall a margin call.

Probability of a margin call

A margin call is one term that features regularly in any discussion of margin lending. In view of its importance, I should now define it briefly in the context of how banks should manage risks in margin lending. As a concept, a margin call refers to a demand that a bank makes on a stockbroker or other capital markets operator to whom it grants a margin loan, to regularize its account with the bank so that it operates within the approved borrowing limit. In stock market parlance, the limit in question is known as the minimum maintenance margin—a level below which the bank cannot allow further drawing on the loan account. This is a risk-mitigating measure, since the collateral value would no longer cover the bank's exposure on the margin loan. In order to regularize the account, the borrower should deposit more cash into the account or pledge additional securities to beef up the margin loan collateral. These actions will restore the LVR to the approved benchmark.

Once a bank sets the LVR benchmark—i.e., the maximum amount to lend against collateral value—it must ensure that borrowers stick to it. Borrowers should beef up their collateral portfolio value to meet the benchmark whenever the market experiences a decline. Failure to do so has two main risk implications bordering on the probability of a margin call and how that affects the bank and borrower. There will be a mismatch between the required LVR and the outstanding balance on the margin loan. Usually the mismatch reflects in an amount owing on the loan that exceeds the collateral value of the assets portfolio securing the loan. The resultant collateral gap evidences the risk faced by the bank. The risk manifests itself in the loss attendant on a forced sale, when a bank must of necessity liquidate collateral assets to recover the outstanding loan.

In the event of the foregoing, the LVR will exceed the set benchmark—a situation that might lead to a margin call. Usually, a margin call is the main risk that borrowers face when the collateral value of their assets portfolio falls short of the outstanding balance in their margin loan account. A strong probability of a margin call evidences risk that the borrower might have been overtrading or misusing its margin loan. Borrowers in this situation could sell some of the profitable stocks and use the sale proceeds to reduce the outstanding balance of their margin loan account. They could also buy and add more eligible stocks, whose prices have crashed, to their collateral assets portfolio. These and similar measures will restore good collateral standing and mitigate the risk of a margin call.

Variable returns on investment

A bank can mitigate the risk of a breach of LVR rules by the borrower, and avoid margin calls on the account, with the support of the borrower. It can do this in two main ways. Firstly, credit officers should effectively monitor and regularly review the utilization of margin loans. They could do so by requesting, obtaining, and scrutinizing daily closing stock market reports that the stock exchange furnishes at the close of business every day. Often analysis of the borrower's daily stock trading report comes in handy. Ideally, the reports should reflect some trend that might be useful in managing the credit risk in margin lending.

Secondly, there should not be a fresh disbursement on a margin loan without obtaining independently verifiable status of collateral value. Lending officers should regularly review technical and fundamental analyses of leading stocks traded on the stock exchange and the companies that issued them. Stockbrokers rely heavily on the two analytical reports to make investment decisions in the capital markets. So credit analysts should demand the reports from potential margin borrowers. Analyzing and using the reports, they should be in a position to make informed lending decisions.

In a bearish market, stockbrokers hardly make a profit from stock trading. The implication is that they might be spending more money to service their loans than they are earning from dividends, bonuses, and such like that make returns on investment. One of the ways stockbrokers can mitigate the risk of variable stock and portfolio returns is to constantly look to their investment pattern and the strategy underlying it. Long-term investments in well-researched stocks tend to be effective in building stock-trading capacity. A program of reinvestment of dividends and earnings complements this investment strategy. Its risk-mitigating benefit is that it allows investments to stabilize, with the potential for capital gains and a boosted buffer for funding transactions in the future.

It is widely believed, especially in financial management parlance, that portfolio diversification effectively mitigates the risk occasioned by the variability of expected returns on investments. This is the main thrust of Markowitz's (1952) famous portfolio theory that many believe was ground-breaking. Stockbrokers and other capital market investors should avail themselves of this theory to diversify their investments as a means of mitigating the risk associated with variable returns. In doing so, they should invest in stocks across a range of sectors and industries. A large pool of stocks in a portfolio spread in this way tends to yield a higher return on investment than concentrated portfolios do. Diversified portfolios also tend to withstand market shocks better than portfolios concentrated in particular or a few sectors and industries.

QUESTIONS FOR DISCUSSION AND REVIEW

1. What is margin lending? In what ways does a margin loan compare with asset-based credit, overdrafts, and current line facilities?

2. Under what circumstances can margin lending cause stock markets to go from boom to bust in a typical emerging economy?

3. What roles do a country's Central Bank and Securities and Exchange Commission play in stemming the tide of a hammer blow for the stock market?

4. Why, in your opinion, is investment in stocks ever prone to risk? How should banks and stockbrokers anticipate risks associated with margin loans?

5. What verifiable benefits derive from margin lending to stockbrokers and other investors in capital markets products?

6. What options are open to banks and stockbrokers in emerging economies to effectively mitigate margin loan risks?

REFERENCE

Markowitz, H.M., 1952. Portfolio selection. J. Finance 7 (1), 77–91.

Chapter 11

Asset-Based Transactions, Lending and Credit Risk Control

LEARNING FOCUS AND OUTCOMES

Loans granted to manufacturing and trading companies as asset-based credits account for a substantial portion of the loan portfolio in many banks. This is not surprising considering that borrowers in this category create chains of business activities, especially in the wholesale and distributive trade. Besides manufacturers, wholesalers, and distributors, asset-based lending finds critical uses in service organizations. Most of the relevant service providers operate in the middle-tier market. These businesses often borrow money against security furnished by specific trading assets. Meanwhile, since importers and contractors engaged in local supply of goods have unique financing attributes, they are given special consideration and are not usually lumped with general trading. The main eligible trading assets are accounts receivable and stocks-in-trade or inventories.

Emerging Market Bank Lending and Credit Risk Control. http://dx.doi.org/10.1016/B978-0-12-803438-5.00011-8

Asset-based credit evolved with increasing pressure on the finances of companies engaged in commerce and manufacturing. Businesses in these sectors sometimes find that their working capital is tied up in inventory and accounts receivable. Slow-moving stock and delinquent receivables compound their cash flow stress. Even with fast-selling inventory and current invoices for confirmed receivables, funds committed to the transactions are not available for business. Thus, the role of asset-based credit is to free such funds by substituting a loan for the tied-up trading assets. This is achieved when a bank refinances stockpiled inventory or discounts invoices for confirmed receivables. Asset-based credit is the vehicle through which a bank fulfills these roles.

A unique feature of asset-based credits is the reliance of banks on the assets financed for security of the loans. This fact holds two basic implications for the bank and borrower. Firstly, asset-based credit must necessarily be transaction based. This means that the loan must be tied to particular stock-in-trade, usually in a warehouse, or receivables that could be discounted based on confirmed sale or job invoices. This arrangement defines the transaction path, one that assures security of the loan. In essence, specific trading assets—stocks and receivables—collateralize the loan. Secondly, the trading assets on which the bank relies for security of the lending must be of exceptional quality. This required collateral attribute is critical for an obvious reason: Slow-selling stocks or aging receivables may serve some collateral comfort—but definitely not full risk-mitigation need. It would be difficult for the bank to ignore this key credit issue.

The budding interest of banks in asset-based lending is changing the way manufacturers and traders do business, renewing confidence in their operations. Following this development, there are prospects for sustained growth of the sector. My focus in this chapter is on measures to strengthen risk analysis and control in asset-based lending. The reader will learn about:

- Emerging trends and challenges in lending against security of trading assets
- Contemporary issues and future requirements for effective asset-based lending
- Measures to strengthen risk analysis and control in asset-based lending
- Approaches that banks should adopt to mitigate risk and loan losses in purchase order financing

OVERVIEW OF ASSET-BASED LENDING

The borrowing cause for some of the borrowers that require asset-based credit is to meet specific *stockpiling* need based on anticipated demand or confirmed sale order. Bank lending to meet the borrowing needs of this category of customers may be granted under terms of seasonal line of credit facility. However, this type of lending is not common among banks in emerging markets. Besides building up inventories, asset-based credit may be utilized to solve temporary cash flow problems. A company may experience cash flow deficiency as a result of unsustainable buildup of accounts receivable. In order to avoid cash flow stress, the company can seek to refinance its receivables as a means of regaining liquidity and easing the pressure. Thus, receivables discounting and inventory refinancing facilities are the main components of asset-based credit facilities granted by banks. Overall, asset-based loans are attractive to borrowers because they impart funding flexibility to their operations. Borrowers apply for, obtain, and utilize the loans to meet some funding flexibility. This is possible because asset-based loans could be utilized to meet various short-term business financing needs.

Banks, on the other hand, favor asset-based lending because of its self-liquidating feature. Besides, asset-based loans have clear transaction paths and tend to be well secured. The offer letter (sometimes referred to as financing agreement) often stipulates that collateral for the loan should include future trading assets acquired by the borrower. Once secured with receivables or inventories, the loans assume the flexibility of revolving credit facilities. At any point in time, the amount of loan outstanding varies with changes in the collateral value as new inventories are acquired or as more accounts receivable are created.

As in the case of overdraft facility, interest on the loan is calculated and charged on the average daily debit balances in the account. Also, the bank has an option to ask for full or partial repayment of the loan *on demand*. This loan repayment clause is intended to protect the bank against unanticipated, or the borrower's willful, depletion of the value of the collateral asset. However, as shown below in the discussion of the two main examples of asset-based loans, banks adopt certain measures to mitigate risk in asset-based lending. In this chapter, I assess emerging trends and challenges in lending against security of trading assets. In doing so, I highlight contemporary issues and future requirements for effective asset-based lending.

Case Study 11.1

Good versus Bad Lending Precepts—How They Often Play Themselves Out in Emerging Markets

Nana was a diligent staff and manager of City Center branch of Great Future Bank Limited (GFB) based in Slovenia.[1] His branch was at a difficult location for banking transactions. He worked very hard to meet the branch's budget— pursuing a liability-driven balance sheet and profitability. With monthly increases in budget targets, he realized that he needed to support the liability game with risk assets. His major problem though was the lack of big commercial enterprises in the area. He was not comfortable with lending to small business owner-managers. So he shunned their credit requests.

In order to find and start banking relationships with large creditworthy companies, he extended his marketing beyond City Center's environs. His efforts to woo executives of companies proved abortive. To some of the executives, he was importunate. On occasion, he could not get past the executives' secretary. He reinvented his marketing strategy, and not long after doing so, his determination paid off. He attracted a major oil exploration and marketing company, Trans

Coastal Petroleum Limited (TCP), based in City Center's environs. The company was one of the oil companies that leading banks in Slovenia coveted because it has the largest petroleum depot in the country. In fact, it is a cash cow for the banks that were lucky to have its account. Its finance director, Donald, was disposed to domicile the company's account in Nana's branch. The managing director (MD) of the company especially gave exceptional approval to open the account at City Center due to Nana's persistence.

Nana nurtured the banking relationship between the company and bank. Soon the company became the most profitable account in the branch. It elevated the branch's performance ranking in terms of earnings. Within three months of featuring the account in his monthly performance review (MPR) meeting presentations, the bank's management started taking interest in the company.

One Tuesday morning, Nana went to see Donald on a routine marketing call.

"Welcome, please have a seat. I'm glad to see you," said Donald as Nana entered his office.

"Thank you, sir," responded Nana, a little anxious about what could be amiss.

"I hope there's no problem," he sought to clarify from Donald after exchange of pleasantries.

"There's no problem," he said. "Instead, we have a juicy business transaction for you. It's a credit proposal, one that I think your bank will be glad to handle," he intimated.

"Oh, that's good. I'm happy at the prospect that GFB would soon start lending money to TCP," Nana said, smiling.

"Let's go over to the MD's office. He will give details of the transaction and borrowing to you firsthand," informed Donald.

Once his secretary informed him that Nana was around with Donald, the MD permitted that they come in to see him. He explained details of the transaction and its funding implications. Nana thanked him and promised to expedite processing and approval of the loan.

"It's alright, sir," responded Nana. "We shall revert to you with an appropriate credit package for Trans Coastal Petroleum—one that will satisfy its need for flexibility and competitive pricing," he promised.

"I hope to package the credit and obtain approval for it within two weeks from the date we receive TCP's formal application for the loan. Thereafter, we will make an offer of the credit to the company," he added.

"FD, what do you think?" the MD asked Donald.

"I'm fine with his promise. I know he will deliver as usual," he answered.

"I think we should work on our proposal and expect feedback from the bank in the coming weeks," the MD said.

When he returned to his branch, Nana wrote a call memo on the outcome of the meeting. The memo received favorable comments from his boss and the MD to whom he also sent a copy of it. Following this outcome, he packaged the credit—highlighting, in doing so, its dynamics.

"The defining issue in the proposed credit," he noted, "is its transaction dynamics—the mode of disbursement, utilization, and repayment of the credit facility, including fallback for the bank in the event of default."

"The loan could be utilized through letters of credit, purchase orders, or bank guarantee—each of which is distinguished by its dynamics," he informed.

In the credit analysis memorandum (CAM) for the credit, Nana presented the dynamics of each of the options for utilization of the credit facility. The bank approved the credit the way Nana packaged, presented, and defended it.

Nana handed the offer letter to Donald who looked it over, acknowledged receipt, and promised to give Nana feedback on it as soon as possible. When Nana left his office, the FD painstakingly read the offer letter—highlighting significant points, including the requirement for personal guarantee of the MD of Trans Coastal Petroleum Limited. Afterward, he went to see the MD with the offer letter. He waited while the MD glanced through it and gave a directive on the offer before returning with it to his office. As the MD looked it over, he stopped abruptly and looked at Donald.

"Didn't you tell Nana that I don't sign personal guarantees for any bank?" He asked the FD, fuming.

"I did, Sir," answered Donald.

"Yet they want my personal guarantee as one of the conditions of the loan. Why would they?" He queried the FD further.

"We can do anything but give my personal guarantee to secure their loan to us," he added.

"Let me talk to Nana so that he can get that condition waived for Trans Coastal," suggested Donald.

"You have to do that immediately," advised the MD. "Let them know that we run transparent operations. That's why none of the banks that lend money to us ask for stringent conditions or collateral. Our integrity is our guarantee and greatest asset for the loan. GFB should appreciate this fact," he directed.

The FD called Nana on the phone and told him that GFB should forget about the personal guarantee of the MD because he never guaranteed any of the company's credit facilities.

"Otherwise, every other thing about the offer of the credit facility is satisfactory and acceptable to us," he told Nana.

Nana was not happy at this outcome. He knew that GFB would not grant or disburse a loan to a company whose directors withhold their personal and collective guarantee.

"I will be right in your office soon—to see you on the issue you've just raised," he responded for want of something better to say.

Donald advised him to prevail on GFB to expunge the clause requiring the MD's personal guarantee and reissue the offer letter. Nana tried, but all to no avail, to persuade the MD to accept the offer letter. He made it clear to the MD that GFB was unlikely to amend the offer letter because the clause in question was a standard condition in the bank's credit offer letters.

"That means we won't borrow from your bank," said the MD to him point-blank.

"Let me go back and see what I can do about this issue," said Nana as he begged to leave the MD's office with Donald.

Back in his branch, Nana wrote a carefully worded memo through the fast-track credit channel to the MD of GFB, with support from his line boss. The MD redirected the memo to the secretary of the credit committee with an instruction to present it for discussion at the next meeting of the committee.

After much deliberation, the committee decided that the requirement for the personal guarantee of the MD of TCP should be retained in the offer letter.

The committee advised Nana and his boss to let go of their interest in the account if the company's MD did not want to accept the bank's lending conditions.

Nana was devastated by the decision of the credit committee. He did not know how best to inform Donald and the MD of TCP of this outcome. One reason was that he was sure that they would not budge on the issue. Another reason was that he would certainly lose the account, and once that happened, his branch would slip into loss-making operations. That meant more headaches for him at MPR meetings. He summoned courage and went to see Donald and the MD of TCP with the bad news. It was a difficult meeting. In the end, Nana took his medicine like a man.

A week later, he went to see Donald with a request that GFB would want to continue to offer nonlending banking services to TCP. He was stunned when he found, on getting to the company's office, that Bounty Bank Limited (BB) had granted the same credit facility on the same terms and conditions that GFB declined. BB had positioned a transit cabin office near TCP's depot and was collecting daily cash sales of the company's products—mainly PMS, AGO, and DPK—on behalf of TCP. Donald told him that BB was doing everything TCP wanted and in return was entitled to most of TCP's banking transactions.

The MD of BB, Ken, had paid an unscheduled visit to TCP. The company's MD made the same credit proposal that GFB declined to him. Ken gave verbal approval with a promise that formal offer and documentation would follow afterward.

Hints for Analyzing This Case Study

The management of Great Future Bank was strong willed. Obviously, this disposition permeated the rank-and-file employees of the bank. This was evident in the decision of the bank's credit strategy committee on Trans Coastal Petroleum's request for the bank to waive its CEO's personal guarantee. In order to defend the credit process, members of the credit strategy committee demonstrated strong wills—forcing branch managers and lending officers to toe the line. That the bank strictly adhered to good lending precepts was a logical conclusion. On the other hand, the action of the MD of Bounty Bank was a typical example of bad lending precept. He threw caution to the winds and committed his bank to unmitigated huge credit risk. That was indeed reckless! But it was also typical of the heady atmosphere of the era of voodoo banking when the so-called cowboy bankers held sway. It is no surprise that the bank that BB represented in the case study became distressed less than five years later. A combination of credit risk crisis and management problems made distress of the bank inevitable.

Questions on the Case Study

1. **(a)** In your opinion, does the verdict implied in foregoing hints roundly condemn sharp practices in bank lending?
   (b) What would you rather have as the verdict?
2. **(a)** How does playing out "one man's meat is another man's poison" in this case study underscore the making of either reckless lending or excessive risk-taking in lending?

(b) Is there anything that Nana or the management of Great Future Bank should have done to satisfy the financing needs of Trans Coastal Petroleum?

(c) As a lending officer, what fundamental credit issues did the MD of Bounty Bank disregard in granting TCP's borrowing request?

---

1. The use of Slovenia as the setting for this case study is for illustration purposes only to demonstrate how the case study plays itself out in a typical emerging market. The names used for the company, banks, and individuals in the illustration are imaginary and do not relate to any known or unknown company, banks, or persons in Slovenia or elsewhere.

RECEIVABLES DISCOUNTING FACILITY

In analyzing a company's balance sheet to determine its short-term solvency and liquidity for lending purposes, it is sometimes necessary to ascertain receivables days on hand, i.e., the average collection period for sales or debts. Such analysis sometimes reveals that a lot of funds are tied up in this *trading asset*, with adverse implications for liquidity and cash flow ability of the company. A similar case is observed when contractors execute particular local purchase orders with their own funds but would wait for a certain period (perhaps up to one year) before they would receive payment for the items or materials supplied. During the *waiting* period, the contractors tie up capital in receivables on the purchase order.

Faced with such a situation, the company can approach a bank to refinance or discount properly documented and acknowledged accounts receivable, or supply invoices certified for payment. This type of credit facility is sometimes referred to as "invoice discounting facility." This description is more appropriately used when the receivables or invoices are expected from executed jobs, such as energy sector contracts. However, prior to and in order to grant the company's request, the bank should do all of the following:

- Confirm the *genuineness* of the accounts receivable. This entails inspection of the borrower's books of accounts, as well as credit transactions records.
- Analyze the *creditworthiness* of the debtors on whom the accounts receivable are created. Taking collateral on debtors with poor credit ratings would be an ineffectual approach to securing the loan.
- Get the debtors to agree to assignment of their debts to the bank. This implies that payments on their debts would be formally *domiciled* directly in the bank.
- Check if there is *encumbrance* on the accounts receivable. This is a critical requirement to ensure that the same debts have not been previously assigned to another lender.
- Obtain a *charge* or *lien* over the accounts receivable. The borrower should formally *assign* the accounts receivable to the bank as collateral to secure the loan.

It would be feasible for the bank to implement the foregoing checks and conditions only when the sum of the accounts receivable, or supply invoices, which is to be refinanced or rediscounted, is represented by few large debts. Otherwise, it would be useless to embark on such a cumbersome exercise that might turn futile. Similarly, the suggested credit process will be unnecessary if the borrower provides alternative collateral, such as an *all-assets debenture*, to secure the loan. In that case, the emphasis on the quality of, charge on, and assessment of the pledged receivables or invoices should be minimized.

The bank charges a premium on such credit facility. The premium is often a reflection of the risk associated with the loan. This is in addition to securing the loan with adequate tangible collateral. Banks adopt these security measures because the target borrowers lack the capacity to attract balance sheet lending. In this context, the pricing of the loan often takes cognizance of the risks that might reflect in high gearing, operating losses, weak management, and so on. For the same considerations of risk, the bank *discounts* expected proceeds of the receivables in determining the appropriate amount of loan to grant. But this is applicable where accounts receivable are used to secure the loan. The discount operates to ensure that the borrower does not receive more than, perhaps, 80% of the proceeds of the receivables as loan.

However, banks sometimes vary the discount ratio depending on their assessment of the lending risks. This is instructive to the extent that the quality of the receivables could be diluted as a result of bad debts, rejections, and so on. Thus, risk would be minimized if the bank painstakingly isolates the ineligible accounts. The term *ineligible accounts* is used here to denote invoices or accounts receivable, which, though pledged by the borrower to secure the loan, are not acceptable to the bank for certain reasons. Some examples of typical ineligible receivables would usually include invoices on *progress billing* accounts, invoices *past due* of up to 90 days or more, extraordinary or claim-type receivables (as in warranty, or insurance), and so on.

INVENTORY REFINANCING FACILITY

This is yet another important type of asset-based lending. Also known as inventory finance facility, it is sometimes supported with stock hypothecation and warehousing arrangement. In this case, borrowers approach banks to obtain a loan equivalent to an agreed proportion of in-store stock-in-trade on which critical working capital for their businesses is tied. As a rule, the banks would probably not lend more than 60–70% of the total cost or market value (whichever is lower) of the eligible inventories. The term *eligible inventory* as used in this context refers to stock items that satisfy the bank's selection criteria for asset-based lending. The lending risks would be mitigated to a large extent if the banks make accurate judgments in selecting the eligible inventories.

For example, the risk level will be high if the inventories are composed of mainly work-in-progress, obsolete and perishable goods. Such goods would clearly be ineligible for use as a lending base by the banks. There are other possible ineligible inventories, including the following:

- Dated products—those that will lose value and perhaps be destroyed after their expiration dates
- Fashionable products—those that are subject to frequent changes in styles, sizes, and colors
- Agricultural produce, especially livestock and crops that are subject to the vagaries of natural perils
- New products that will face established competition and are yet to gain full market acceptance

The best example of an inventory component that banks may easily accept as eligible for use as a lending base is finished goods. Similarly, banks tend to choose industrial raw materials (especially those required for the manufacturing of essential commodities) as eligible inventory.

Risk control measures

In inventory lending, banks seek to ascertain the aging profile of the pledged stocks. This could be achieved through the calculation of the average inventory days on hand for each item of the eligible stocks. From such analysis, it would be easy to isolate the slow-moving or obsolete products. This is one of the effective measures to mitigate risk—one that banks may adopt in inventory refinancing. However, there are other risk control measures that banks can take. Proof of ownership of inventories, inspection of the stocks, survey of products markets, investigation of encumbrance, and stock hypothecation are some of the effective measures. I discuss these elements of credit risk control process in inventory refinancing as follows.

Ownership of inventories

It is necessary to verify ownership of the pledged (eligible) inventories. The bank should certify that the stocks-in-trade being pledged to it actually belong to the prospective borrower. This could be achieved through inspection of the customer's import documents (mainly, the bill of lading, in the case of imported goods), purchase receipts (for goods procured in the local market), and so on.

Physical inspection of the stocks

There should be physical inspection of the pledged stocks-in-trade, including its location (perhaps in the customer's warehouse) and assessment of its security or safety (often assured with an insurance policy that covers the risks of fire, burglary, and so on). Such a site visit enables lending officers to see and possibly ask any questions about the stocks firsthand.

Survey of the market

Loan officers should carry out market surveys as part of credit risk control in inventory refinancing. They should thoroughly investigate aspects of markets for the inventories to be refinanced. In doing so, emphasis should be on detecting factors that are likely to affect sale of the inventories. Survey of the markets should be carried out with a view to determining the following:

- Competitive strength of the inventories (in the case of finished products)
- The market's knowledge and acceptance of, or demand for, the inventories
- Value of the eligible stocks that would be used as the lending base to the borrower

Investigation of encumbrance

The loan officer should check to ascertain if there is *encumbrance* on the pledged stocks-in-trade. As in receivables (invoices) discounting facility, this remains a critical requirement to ensure that the same inventories have not been previously assigned to another lender. The Central Bank of Nigeria offers assistance in this regard through its Credit Risk Management System (CRMS). But the information could sometimes be obtained through interbank credit checks and enquiries.

Stock hypothecation

The bank should take collateral in *stock hypothecation*, complemented with *bill of sale*, to secure the loan. The stock hypothecation essentially confers the bank with legal *charge* or *lien* over the pledged stocks-in-trade. In other words, the borrower should formally *assign* the pledged inventories to the bank. The bill of sale establishes the bank's right to dispose of the inventories in the event of default by the borrower.

Although stock hypothecation and bill of sale documents are often attached with schedules of the pledged inventories, there is no assurance that the particular (i.e., original) stocks would be available at the time of default. This is because the quantities of the stocks-in-trade fluctuate with changes in market demand or sales and replenishments.

Therefore, in order to forestall possible abuses of the stock hypothecation agreement by the borrower, the bank might want to structure the loan to incorporate a *warehousing* arrangement of sorts. Indeed, some of such loans are even booked as warehousing facilities, in which goods are released to the customer against agreed payments to the account. From experience, bankers realize that only goods that are *finished* for consumption, industrial use, or in the intermediate state for industrial processing are best suited for the warehouse finance arrangement.

PURCHASE ORDER FINANCE

The use of *purchase order* (PO) in describing a particular type of bank credit facility evolved with increasing demand from customers to raise funds to meet specific local materials supply obligations. Thus, the phrase *PO finance facility* depicts a loan made available to a borrower to finance the supply of materials or execution of a specific *supply* contract. Such POs that meet the financing requirements of the banks are usually awarded by reputable organizations, such as large corporations, nongovernmental organizations or NGOs, multinationals, government agencies, and so on. The loan may not appeal to a bank if the PO is not from such strong industry names as the major oil companies (e.g., Shell, Chevron, Mobil, and so on) or other blue chips. Yet a bank should be assured that the underlying transaction is self-liquidating by its ability to generate sufficient cash flow to repay the loan in the shortest possible time.

A typical PO finance in which a bank would be interested collateralizes itself for up to the time the assets to be supplied are delivered to the third party that issued the purchase order. Most POs are issued for delivery or supply periods of not more than 12 calendar months. This is why PO finance is classified as a short-term credit facility. It would only be in a rare situation that a company would issue a PO for a supply period or date of more than one year. In most cases, the materials or items to be supplied would be procured from the local markets or sources.

RISKS OF PURCHASE ORDER FINANCE

The loan officer must understand the dynamics of PO finance to avoid loss of the credit. Most PO transactions are fraught with risks that loan officers must identify, analyse, and reasonably mitigate in their recommendations to senior management. The key considerations or risks are as follows:

Genuineness of the PO

Once a PO is presented to a bank for financing, lending officers must first and foremost confirm the genuineness of the PO from its issuer. This can be achieved in different ways. The issuer of the PO could formally endorse it in the presence of the loan officer. Key officers of the company that issued the PO, especially the sole or a signatory on the contract, could endorse it.

Availability of materials or items

If the material to be supplied is not available in the local market, the loan (if granted) will have a high probability of default because of the chance of inability to secure a foreign supply source on favorable terms. This risk will, however, be mitigated if borrowers factor cost overrun in their calculations and are aware of locations from where the materials could be purchased in overseas markets. The loan officer should also show appreciation for a related consideration, which is the *capacity* of available local supply sources to perform as envisaged by the bank and borrower.

Quality specifications

It is of utmost importance that the quality of the materials to be supplied meets the PO specifications. If variations are observed in specifications between materials ordered and supplied, the issuer of the PO may reject and refuse to pay for the materials. Thus, the borrower will be unable to liquidate the loan. In order to mitigate this risk, the loan officer must ensure that specifications in the pro forma invoice submitted by the customer agree with those in the PO.

Diversion of funds

The customer may, even if inadvertently, divert the loan to some personal uses. When this happens, the transaction becomes frustrated and aborted, leading to outright loss of funds disbursed by the bank. In order to forestall this risk, the bank should make payment directly to the supplier of the materials financed. The loan officer may consider arranging for haulage (if materials are sourced locally) or arrange for clearing (in the case of imported materials) and delivery of the materials to the premises of the PO issuer.

Obligor's commitment

It is normal for a bank to require the customer to contribute a substantial part of the cost of executing the PO. Such equity or counterpart funding establishes the borrower's commitment to the transaction. The risks identified with a particular PO will determine how much equity contribution the borrower may be expected to make toward its execution. However, a bank is unlikely to require less than 25% of the total funding cost of the PO from the borrower.

Domiciliation of payment

The bank is further secured when the issuer of the PO executes a *domiciliation* of payment undertaken in favor of the bank. This establishes a tripartite agreement involving the bank, borrower, and issuer of the PO. The agreement should expressly state that all payments due on the PO shall be made in favor of the bank for the account of the contractor. In the alternative, the PO issuer should honor irrevocable payment instructions that it agreed to with the contractor. In order to honor such an agreement, the bank must provide the required funds, while the contractor shall execute the order as specified by the issuer of the PO.

Secondary market

One of the *ways out* for a bank on PO finance is the existence of a secondary market for the materials financed. In the event that the issuer of the PO refuses to accept the items for any reason, such as late delivery or disagreement on price variation, the bank could recover the loan by immediately disposing of the materials. In such a situation, the bank may yet incur some loss, as the items would attract only *forced* sale values. But this is all the better for the bank rather than outright loss of the credit.

Lead or delivery time

A PO must be executed within the specified time frame. Otherwise, the issuer of the PO may repudiate it and thus render it unenforceable. The borrower must therefore ensure that delivery of the items on order at the premises of the issuer or agreed site is concluded within the time specified on the PO.

Profit margin

There should be a reasonable buffer, offered by the margin on the PO, for the bank to finance it. This implies that the differential between the PO value and cost of its execution should be sufficient to offset bank charges and other incidental expenses that the borrower might incur. This protects the bank's loan against cost overrun, which may arise from unforeseen expenditure on the transaction. For most banks, a margin of at least 25% is acceptable.

Credibility of PO issuer

The loan officer should not have doubts regarding the creditworthiness of the issuer of the PO. Risk is minimized when a company that has a proven track record of payment capability is the issuer of the PO. If such a company is willing to sign a domiciliation agreement on the proceeds of the PO or comply with an irrevocable payment instruction on the order, then risk will be almost completely mitigated.

QUESTIONS FOR DISCUSSION AND REVIEW

1. What risk-mitigating measures can banks in emerging markets adopt to check loan losses in asset-based lending?
2. How do business trends and challenges impact the disposition of bank management to asset-based lending in emerging markets?

3. What are trading assets? Assess the efficacy of trading assets as security for asset-based credits.
4. In what ways can banks in emerging markets strengthen risk analysis and control in asset-based lending?
5. Do you think that banks in emerging markets can effectively mitigate risks inherent in purchase order financing? Identify the risks and discuss practical ways the banks can mitigate them.

Chapter 12

International Trade Financing, Payments and Credit Risk Control

Chapter Outline

LEARNING FOCUS AND OUTCOMES

With the growth of international trade, and expanding local markets, banks are nowadays becoming increasingly involved in granting trade finance facilities. They grant such credit facilities to their commercial banking customers, mainly those engaged in various large trading, manufacturing, and service-oriented business activities. As would be expected, the highest bank patronage for trade finance comes from customers in the middle-tier market—wholesalers, distributors, importers, exporters, manufacturers' representatives, and so on. The exact volume of cumulative annual transactions that pass through the banking system from these businesses is not certain. But the thinking is that trade finance offers the biggest aggregate annual volume of transactions to banks ahead of long-term and other short-term credit facilities. Perhaps, trade finance is also about the riskiest and most profitable of all normal types of bank lending transactions in developing countries.

Besides advances in international trade, technological revolutions have imparted significant impetus to the import and export financing roles of banks. Internet technology has dramatically changed the conduct of business, rendering the world a global village. The intermediary and financing roles of banks in international trade have been eased in the wake of globalization of the financial system. Even before the advent of the Internet, it would not have been easy to conduct across-border trade without the involvement of banks to facilitate payments and receipts between importers and exporters. A combination of marked differences in national currencies, and several methods of payments for goods and services, makes trade finance both risky and profitable. This is a lending reality in trade finance—one that fits well with the risk-return trade-off logic.

Lending officers should appreciate how these dramatic changes have affected trust between importers and exporters, on the one hand, and issuing and advising banks, on the other hand, in international trade. Such knowledge is of the essence to mitigate credit risk. Appropriate letters of credit should be used to pay for goods and services. In doing so, banks would be helping to instill mutual trust between parties to a trade finance transaction.

Trade finance lending and payments could sometimes be tricky. Movement of foreign exchange to fund international trade complicates credit risk. Thus, lending officers should take care to ensure proper conduct of transactions, a requirement that informs the focus and outcomes of this chapter. The reader will learn about:

- General principles of international trade payments and documentation
- Common types and features of trade finance credit facilities
- Critical financing requirements for specific trade finance transactions
- How banks should structure and mitigate risks associated with trade finance credits

Case Study 12.1

Complication to International Trade Finance

An expatriate, Ibrahim Dada, lived and owned a trading business in Mexico.[1] He had a cordial banking relationship with Frontier Bank Limited where his company's account was domiciled. He especially related very well with the ED, corporate banking, who was the bank's point man on marketing and relationship management. The ED wielded immense influence that made it possible for Ibrahim to have easy access to the bank's management.

Ibrahim's company, Stride and Company Limited, had a $500 million overdraft facility, secured with all-assets debenture, with Frontier Bank. On occasion, the ED gauged how satisfied Ibrahim was with the bank's services through his account officer.

"Ben, how's Stride's facility performing?" he would typically ask the account officer.

"The account is doing well, Sir," Ben would normally answer.

"Make sure you're diligent at all times with your account management responsibilities—especially, with that account," he occasionally advised Ben.

"Don't worry, Sir; I'm always on top of things," Ben would simply assure him.

"In fact, I make sure that Ibrahim gets daily a report and update on activities in Stride's account. I promptly confirm inward clearing checks with him and ensure that the overdraft operates within its approved limit. I have had cause to put TOD and EOL facilities in place for the account to take care of unanticipated funding pressure. Besides, I make regular calls to his offices, especially the sales outlets, to observe activities of the company firsthand," Ben once explained to the ED.

He never left the ED in doubt about his commitment to ensuring that Stride's overdraft facility operated very well.

One Monday morning, Ibrahim came to the bank with a trade finance proposal. Prior to going to see the ED he had bounced the proposal off his account officer. Ben was not enthusiastic about it even as he was sure that his boss would give him positive response.

"We have reached an agreement with some foreign suppliers to ship goods to Stride on the basis of an unconfirmed letter of credit issued by Frontier Bank," he told Ben in confidence.

"Just think it through," he added, "while I go upstairs to discuss details of the transaction. I will be right back when I'm done."

In about 30 min the ED invited the account officer to his office.

"Please join me in a meeting with your customer, the MD of Stride," he said as Ben entered his office.

Ibrahim, your request is for Frontier Bank to open unconfirmed L/C for $5 million in favor of your supplier in the Middle East—right?" asked the ED gazing into space.

Ben marvelled at the huge exposure to which the ED was about to commit Frontier Bank. He was quiet and still in his chair. His eyes were riveted on the ED in obvious disbelief.

"You're right," responded Ibrahim. "It's a straightforward transaction. Frontier Bank will neither fund the L/C nor disburse any money for the transaction. Stride will fund its account to pay for the goods shipped by the suppliers and any commitment on the L/C. But time is of the essence here. The L/C should be opened quickly to enable the supplier to ship the goods to us without delay. That way, we should be able to clear and sell the consignment in the forthcoming season. Let me mention at once that it's from the sale proceeds that Stride plans to liquidate the overdraft and fund negotiation of the L/C," he explained.

The look on Ben's face while he listened to Ibrahim betrayed his discomfort with what he felt was a bogus transaction.

"What goods are we talking about now?" he managed to ask.

"You know that our traditional lines are our strength in business. We can't afford to deviate from our focus at this time," answered Ibrahim smiling mischievously.

"But your traditional suppliers are based in Europe, not the Middle East," wondered Ben.

"You're right, but we just found better supply sources in the Middle East. They have quality and pricing advantages over our existing suppliers," responded Ibrahim.

Ben was not convinced, but nevertheless he kept his cool.

"Do you need further clarification, or have any other questions to ask him about the transaction?" the ED asked Ben with a stern look.

"No, Sir," he answered and paused to listen to his directive.

"Go and package the proposal for presentation at the next meeting of the credit strategy committee," he instructed Ben.

Frontier Bank opened the L/C, but its correspondent bank complained later that it was unable to contact the beneficiary. It made several attempts to advise the L/C but all to no avail. Thus, the fate of the L/C hung in the balance for about 180 days before Stride asked Frontier Bank to transfer it to Offshore Bank Limited where it also had an account relationship. Frontier bank obliged the request. In doing so, it endorsed the underlying Form "M" for the L/C to Offshore Bank.

Ibrahim later told Ben why Stride asked for transfer of the L/C.

"Offshore Bank is a stronger bank and has a better network than Frontier Bank in the international financial market. I believe it will identify and use a suitable correspondent bank to trace and advise the L/C to the beneficiary. We can't continue to waste time on your bank," he said.

No sooner had Frontier Bank transferred the L/C to Offshore Bank than Stride started experiencing cash flow pressure. Turnover in its overdraft account declined miserably, while accrued interest remained unpaid for more than three months, forcing the facility to exceed its approved limit. Ibrahim was upset at Frontier Bank.

"You guys caused the problem Stride's account is now facing," he told Ben point-blank.

"Frontier Bank was unable to get the L/C advised to its beneficiary for too long," he argued.

Ben countered him. "It would seem you'd intended to default on the overdraft from the outset. How come you didn't pay proceeds of the L/C into Stride's account to liquidate the overdraft when Offshore Bank's correspondent bank successfully advised the L/C to its beneficiary? My investigation shows that you have since cleared and sold the goods," Ben said angrily.

Meanwhile, the board of Frontier Bank had retired the ED unceremoniously. His exit from the bank worsened the banking relationship between Stride and Frontier Bank. Things came to a head for the company when bank examiners from the regulatory authorities classified its overdraft facility as nonperforming and placed it in the "doubtful" category. With the classification, the bank started making provisions for its gradual write-off according to prudential guidelines for provisioning on classified risk assets. While making the mandatory loan loss provision, Frontier Bank transferred the account to its loan recovery office.

The loan recovery staff swung into action. In their preliminary investigation of the account, they contacted Stride's account officer at Offshore Bank. They wanted to corroborate Ben's report that the company had cleared and sold the goods on which liquidation of its overdraft with Frontier Bank depended. They had at this time realized that the all-assets debenture held by Frontier Bank was ineffectual as Stride had no physical assets other than stock-in-trade, most of which were subsumed in the $5 million unconfirmed L/C consignment.

At Offshore Bank, the investigators made startling findings. Offshore Bank had relied on trust receipts to endorse and release shipping documents for the consignment funded with the unconfirmed L/C to Stride. The company cleared and sold the consignment without funding its account with all of the sale proceeds. Thus, Offshore Bank was unable to remit the $5 million to the advising bank to enable it to negotiate the L/C.

On due date of the L/C, the beneficiary presented relevant documents for the negotiation of the L/C to the advising bank. The advising bank had no option than to debit Offshore Bank's account with $5 million so as to negotiate the L/C. In turn, Offshore Bank debited Stride's account with the local currency equivalent of $5 million at the prevailing exchange rate to the dollar.

Meanwhile, the outstanding balance in the company's O/D account with Frontier Bank at the time was $586,428,921.98 and had been classified as doubtful by the Bank Examiners. The most worrisome issue for Offshore Bank was that there was no realistic source for Stride to liquidate the huge contingent liability that had crystallized. The Company had sold the whole consignment secured with the trust receipts and was doing only marginal transactions to sustain its dwindling operations.

Hints for Analyzing This Case Study
The ED, corporate banking, at Frontier Bank had a vested interest in Stride's transactions. This flaw disposed him to irrational commitment to lending to the company—irrespective of the risks involved! This is the foundation of the problems that culminated in Stride's default. It is a given that reckless lending feeds on vested interests. For this reason, lending officers—especially members of bank management—should do anything but be involved or get caught up in unprofessional conduct. It would seem that Offshore Bank was also swayed by some vested interest to accept transfer of the problematic L/C to it. The manner in which it endorsed the L/C betrayed this thinking. Though the bank ultimately got the L/C advised to the beneficiary, it made a shoddy credit decision. Like Frontier Bank, it did not do a rigorous credit analysis, focusing on contingent liability—i.e., credit risk—attendant on approving the off-balance sheet transaction. In both cases,

lending officers compromised themselves. They also compromised on the credit process—time-honored principles on which quality lending decisions depend!

Questions on the Case Study

1. (a) Expatiate on the verdict implied in foregoing hints on this case study.
   (b) Can the hints be realistically generalized in accounting for credit risk crisis in banks in emerging economies? Why or why not?
2. (a) What do you consider to be the main flaws of the off-balance sheet exposure taken by Frontier and Offshore banks on Stride and Company Limited?
   (b) Identify and discuss specific key credit issues that lending officers of the two banks ignored in acceding to the company's credit requests.
3. (a) Critically appraise the role of lending officers in the making of crisis of credit risk in banks in emerging economies.
   (b) In what ways can account officers and relationship managers help bank management to ameliorate crisis of credit risk?
   (c) How would you characterize Ben, the account officer of Stride and Company Limited?

1. While this case study is set in Mexico, it does not in fact imply that the lending transactions took place in Mexico or any other countries and regions mentioned in the case study. The case study is purely for learning and illustration purposes. In much the same vein, the names used for the borrowing company, banks, and individuals in the case study are imaginary and do not relate to any known or unknown companies, banks, or persons in Mexico or elsewhere.

OVERVIEW OF TRADE FINANCE

The appeal of trade finance facilities to both banks and customers derives from the unique modern requirements for transactions processing and payments, especially in international trade. For example, in order to conduct international trade businesses successfully, the customer—whether importer or exporter—needs to fulfill certain transactions documentation processes. The nature and types of the required documentation vary from one country to another. But a common feature of international trade is that its documentation is facilitated by the banking system. Also, the processing of transactions is conducted in banks where the traders have accounts. In the same vein, the impact of banks in local trade finance is equally worthy of note, should be appreciated, and complementary to that of international trade.

The growth of international trade has bestowed a significant impetus to the import and export financing roles of banks, especially as an intermediary between various businesses. It would not have been easy to conduct across-border trade without the involvement of banks to facilitate payments and receipts between the importers and exporters of various goods and services—notwithstanding the marked differences in national currencies. There are several methods of payments for goods and services in international trade through the banking system. Let me first give an overview of some of the more common, nondocumentary credit, modes of payment. Thereafter, I consider documentary credit as a means of international trade payment by which banks take lending risks.

I place emphasis in this chapter on aspects of foreign trade-related credit risk—how to identify, analyze, and mitigate it. My focus was mainly on documentary credit. I provide a critical analysis of letters of credit as a means of international trade payment by which banks take credit risk. In doing so, I provide answers to the following and other questions that the topics of this chapter necessitate: What are the common types and features of trade finance facilities? What are the main financing requirements and accounting treatment of trade finance transactions? How do banks structure and mitigate risks associated with such credit facilities? What are the general principles of international trade documentation and payments?

NONDOCUMENTARY PAYMENT

In the conduct of international trade, there exist different methods of payment for visible imports. Each method is associated with peculiar risks. However, the level of trust between the trading parties directly influences the choice of payment method. In some cases, either the supplier or the importer dictates the mode of payment. It is also possible for the parties to adopt a mutually agreed upon mode of payment based on some arrangement that satisfies their particular needs. Some of the more common methods of payment in international trade include the following.

Open account

An open account transaction commences when the seller dispatches goods to the buyer (without payment) with an agreement that the buyer makes payment either immediately after taking delivery of the goods or within a specified period. The seller delivers the underlying documents relating to the goods *directly* to the buyer without entrusting them to its bankers. The greater risk is borne by the seller while trust is a basic prerequisite for this method of transaction and payment.

Bills for collection

A bill for collection transaction commences when the seller dispatches goods to the buyer (without payment) with an agreement that the buyer makes payment either immediately after taking delivery of the goods or within a specified period. The seller delivers the underlying documents relating to the goods to its banker, technically referred to as the remitting bank, with instructions to collect the proceeds for the seller.

There are basically two types of collections: clean collection and documentary collection. When clean collection is adopted, the bank collects the value of financial documents on behalf of a customer. Common examples of financial documents are checks, promissory notes, bills of exchange, and other similar instruments used for obtaining payment. In documentary collection, the bank collects financial documents accompanied by commercial documents or collects the value of only commercial documents not accompanied by financial documents. The examples of commercial documents include transport documents, documents of title, commercial invoices, and any other documents whatsoever, not being financial documents.

As in open account, the risk of bill for collection transaction is also borne by the seller who parts with value (the goods) first before receiving payment. There is risk of nonpayment by the buyer after receiving the goods. Trust between the parties is also necessary to facilitate this mode of payment.

Advance payment

With this mode of payment, the buyer pays the seller before goods are exchanged. The buyer therefore bears the risk of nonperformance by the seller. Specifically, the buyer is exposed to the risk of the seller's probable forwarding of goods that do not meet the buyer's original specifications. The arrangement presupposes the existence of a high level of trust between the buyer and seller.

DOCUMENTARY (LETTER OF CREDIT) PAYMENT

In acting as the go-between in the flow of international trade, banks inevitably get involved in granting credit facilities to support their customers' transactions. The main functions of the banks—i.e., the importer's and exporter's banks—in the conduct of international trade finance are generally expressed in terms of *opening*, *advising*, *negotiation*, and *payment* of letters of credit on behalf of their customers. These roles represent the activities or transactions that create the risks of financial intermediation for the banks.

Meaning and features of letter of credit

Before I examine aspects of the trade finance roles and risks of banks, it is imperative that we understand the meaning of the phrase *letter of credit*. In banking parlance, the term *letter of credit* (L/C) is often used to refer to a debt instrument, which a bank issues on behalf of its customers engaged in international trade for the purpose of facilitating their importation of goods or services from some overseas suppliers. It is an arrangement in which a bank, acting on the instructions of its customer, is to make payment to a third party against certain stipulated financial or commercial documents—or both.

In effect, the bank's role in a letter of credit transaction can be likened to that of a guarantor. It could be inferred, from this meaning, that for the seller to request for a letter of credit from the buyer before parting with goods, the level of trust between them is low. However, the letter of credit mitigates the risks not only for the seller but also for the buyer. The sellers, on the one hand, part with the goods only after receiving assurance of payment (i.e., the letter of credit instrument) from their bankers while the buyers, on the other hand, part with their money only after having evidence that the sellers have dispatched the goods. Another effect of the letter of credit is the substitution of the credit worthiness of the bank for that of the buyer. It is therefore imperative that the issuing (opening) bank carries out proper analysis of the creditworthiness of the customer before establishment of a letter of credit. This is to ensure that importers have the capacity to pay for their letters of credit if and when they are called upon to do so (i.e., in all cases of unconfirmed letters of credit as discussed below).

Once understood in the foregoing context, the seller of the imported goods or services (i.e., the foreign supplier) is recognized as the beneficiary of the letter of credit instrument. In general, however, for letter of credit processes to be effective, the following parties must exist:

Parties to a letter of credit transaction

Applicant: This is usually the buyer (importer) who is a customer of the bank issuing the letter of credit.

Issuing bank: The issuing bank is usually the buyer's bank resident in the country of the buyer

Advising bank: Usually a foreign bank located in the country of the seller (beneficiary)

Beneficiary: Usually the foreign supplier or seller of the goods that requires the letter of credit

Thus, the need for a letter of credit is triggered when the purchaser (importer) and supplier (exporter) agree to adopt this mode of settling international trade obligations between them. In this case, the purchasers would approach their local banks with requests to issue or forward letters of credit to particular overseas suppliers through the local bank's correspondent banks.

In more general terms, the International Chamber of Commerce defines a letter of credit in its 1984 edition of *Uniform Customs and Practices for Documentary Credits* (UCP) as "an arrangement, however named or described, whereby a bank (the issuing bank) acting at the request and on the instructions of a customer (the applicant for the credit):

- is to make payment to or to the order of a third party (the beneficiary) or is to pay or accept bills of exchange (drafts) drawn by the beneficiary, or
- authorizes another bank to effect such payment or to pay, accept or negotiate such bills of exchange (drafts), against stipulated documents, provided that the terms and conditions of the credit are complied with."

From this definition, it is obvious that a letter of credit must have certain terms and conditions that are binding on the parties. For instance, a letter of credit must have a fixed amount (denominated in a given convertible currency agreed by the parties) and an expiry date (after which the L/C would lose its validity unless it is renewed—usually with mutual agreement of the parties). Perhaps the most significant of the UCP's prescriptions is the stipulation that all parties to letters of credit do not deal in goods, services, or other performances to which the documents may relate; rather they deal strictly in documents. Therefore, a letter of credit exposes the issuing bank to a primary financial obligation to the beneficiary based on its specific terms and conditions.

Procedural issues and risks

Let me now examine the features and implications of the key international trade finance activities for bank management. In doing so, my objective is to highlight the risks that banks assume when they undertake any of the activities on behalf of their customers. While the banks may bear the risks in the normal course of business, there should be a foolproof means of mitigating the probability of their occurrence.

Opening of letter of credit

The initial request to open a letter of credit comes from the buyer. Usually the request is subsequent to an agreement between the buyer and the seller on the underlying purchase or sale contract. The agreement and contract are often contained in a pro forma invoice or final invoice that clearly states the mode of payment agreed to by the parties. Documentation requirements and steps in opening a letter of credit vary among countries. In Nigeria, for example, an importer would complete Form "M" (obtained from the bank), which is returned upon completion to the bank for registration, approval, or endorsement.

A typical Form "M" contains certain basic information about the under-lying transaction and the parties to it. It shows the following, amongst others:

- Names and addresses of the applicant and beneficiary of the letter of credit
- Full description or details of particulars of the goods to be imported with the letter of credit
- Details of cost of the goods to be imported, mainly the FOB (i.e., excluding freight) and CIF (i.e., including insurance and freight) costs. The freight reflects cost incurred for transportation of the consignment up to the port of discharge and is usually prepaid by the exporter
- Indication of the applicable tariff (represented as HS CODE in Nigeria), which the Customs Service requires to determine duty payable on the imported goods
- Mode of payment for the goods (the various modes of payment are described in this chapter). In countries adopting regulated foreign exchange regime, further information would include whether the transaction is valid or nonvalid for foreign exchange.

The completed Form "M" is returned to the bank with supporting documents: pro forma invoice, insurance certificate, application to open the letter of credit, product certificate (issued by the Standards Organization of Nigeria (SON) in the case of regulated products), and NAFDAC certificate (in the case of certain foods and medical products). The bank submits the endorsed Form "M" to approved destination inspection agent. Thereafter, the issuing bank issues (i.e., sends) the letter of credit instructions to the advising bank abroad.

Advising a letter of credit

A letter of credit will not be effective if it is not communicated to the beneficiary. A letter of credit is said to have been advised when its terms and conditions are communicated to the beneficiary by the advising bank designated by the issuing bank. This implies that the advising bank, usually located in the same country as the beneficiary, communicates the letter of credit terms and conditions. The advising bank fulfills certain important roles, including the following:

- Checks that the credit received from the issuing bank is authentic and affords the beneficiary all the protection of the most current revision of the UCP.
- Checks that the documents called for are consistent with the terms of shipment.
- If conflicting terms are expressed, the advising bank would request for clarification from the issuing bank.
- Checks whether the credit is confirmed or unconfirmed.

Where the nominated bank is not willing to advise the credit, it must immediately inform the issuing bank.

Variants of advised letters of credit

There are various types, or variants, of advised letters of credit. For instance, a letter of credit can be advised to the beneficiary *with* or *without* commitment for payment (i.e., confirmed or unconfirmed). Also, a letter of credit could be *revocable* or *irrevocable*, *transferable* or *nontransferable*, and *revolving* or *nonrevolving*. Other types of letters of credit could be opened on terms and conditions of *back-to-back*, *standby*, or *red clause* arrangements. Each of these types of letter of credit is associated with different credit risks for the issuing and advising banks.

Unconfirmed letter of credit

A letter of credit that is advised without commitment is referred to as an unconfirmed letter of credit. However, the exclusion of commitment does not preclude the advising bank's duty of ensuring that the letter of credit is authentic. It is expected that the advising bank should take reasonable care to check the authenticity of the letter of credit. It would appear that the advising bank does not assume any credit risk on unconfirmed letters of credit. However, risk will arise if the unconfirmed letter of credit is available by time drafts accepted by the advising bank.

Upon acceptance of the time drafts, the advising bank would have assumed full responsibility for payment of the letter of credit. In order to mitigate this risk, it is imperative for the advising bank to assess the creditworthiness of the issuing bank before advising the letter of credit. The issuing bank, on its part, should also be satisfied with the capacity of its customer (letter of credit opener) to pay for the letter of credit on due dates of the drafts. In order words, there is always need for proper credit analysis when importers request banks to open unconfirmed letters of credit on their behalf.

Confirmed letter of credit

In the case of a *confirmed* letter of credit, the advising bank adds its commitment to effect payment on the letter of credit. A mere advice of letter of credit *without* commitment does not convey any liability on the advising bank. In most cases, the advising bank's commitment derives from a prior such commitment that the issuing bank should also make to pay the letter of credit. Both the issuing and advising banks are individually and collectively committed to making payment on confirmed letters of credit. However, their commitment to honor drawings on the letter of credit requires full compliance with the letter of credit terms, including presentation of the stipulated documents.

Once its commitment is indicated, the advising bank assumes the status of a confirming bank. Once the letter of credit is confirmed, the confirming bank becomes liable to pay. The main risk of confirmed letters of credit, which is the probable inability of the issuing bank to honor payment, is borne by the advising bank. This makes it mandatory for the advising bank to critically evaluate the credit standing of the issuing bank, as well as the risk of the country from where the letter of credit is issued. The issuing bank, in turn, will do full credit analysis of the customer on whose behalf the letter of credit is being opened. In this case, credit analysis serves two main purposes. Firstly, it identifies risks that are likely to impair the ability of the L/C opener to pay the letter of credit in accordance with its terms and conditions. Secondly, it suggests how to effectively mitigate the identified risks.

However, considering the volatile nature of business environment in many developing countries and the concomitant high default rates, advising (i.e., confirming) banks often require proof of the commitment of issuing banks to pay letters of credit. This is achieved when an issuing bank deposits the amount of the letter of credit with the advising bank as a condition for confirming the letter of credit. The confirming bank would normally block the money so deposited against withdrawal by the issuing bank. Once secured in this way, the confirming bank applies the blocked deposit to pay the L/C beneficiary (i.e., supplier of the goods) in accordance with the terms of the letter of credit.

Standby letter of credit

The issuing bank may open a standby letter of credit that serves as an endorsement of the obligation of the applicant to the beneficiary without necessarily making the usual letter of credit cash deposit. This implies that the importer (i.e., applicant) must have entered into an agreement with the supplier (i.e., beneficiary), which, though requiring the opening of a letter of credit, would necessitate waiver of cash deposit. In opening the letter of credit, the issuing bank is assuring the beneficiary of an alternative means of repayment of credit granted to the applicant in the event of default. Thus, the letter of credit must have the potency of restitution to the beneficiary in the event that the applicant fails to perform in accordance with a contract between them.

A standby letter of credit therefore refers to the endorsement of the obligation of the applicant to the beneficiary by the issuing bank, through the establishment of a nonfunded letter of credit, which must be honored if the applicant fails to perform under a contract with the beneficiary. With a standby letter of credit, the issuing bank commits itself to paying the beneficiary's financial claims from the applicant upon service of such claims to it. The claims would arise on grounds of several considerations, including the applicants' default on their loans payment, nonperformance on the contracts, and so on.

The risk of a standby letter of credit to the issuing bank becomes a key credit issue where its underlying contingent exposure is unsecured. It will be wrong to assume that the beneficiary will not draw on the letter of credit since there is no cash commitment to back it up. There is yet another erroneous assumption. It is a possible belief that the applicant will nevertheless perform under the contract, thus foreclosing the likelihood of recourse to the letter of credit by the beneficiary. Yet standby letters of credit expose the bank to the usual lending risks and must therefore be adequately secured.

Irrevocable letter of credit

A letter of credit may also be advised on irrevocable terms that the issuing bank must clearly state in the letter of credit instrument. When a letter of credit is advised as irrevocable, the issuing bank must make a definite commitment to pay the L/C. However, for the issuing bank to pay the L/C, the beneficiary must fulfill all required terms and conditions, including presentation of the stipulated documents. The agreement of all parties is required before the letter of credit may be amended or canceled for whatever reasons.

Revocable letter of credit

A letter of credit may also be advised on *revocable* terms. In this case, the issuing bank may effect amendment or cancellation at any time. The only exception to this rule would arise where another bank had effected negotiation before the amendment or cancellation of the letter of credit is advised. In that case, the issuing bank must reimburse the other bank that had made the letter of credit available for payment.

Red clause letter of credit

This is a type of letter of credit in which the confirming bank is authorized to make advance to the beneficiary prior to presentation of documents for negotiation. The advance, usually agreed between the importer and exporter, is intended to enable the latter to manufacture, procure, or assemble the goods to be supplied or shipped under the L/C. With this letter of credit arrangement, the issuing bank assumes the risk of granting unplanned unsecured credit facility to its customer (i.e., the importer). The risk occurs when the issuing bank must repay any advance extended to the supplier because the beneficiary failed to present shipping documents for negotiation. However, the risk may be assuaged if the repayment could be effected from documentary drawings under the letter of credit, which presupposes presentation of documents.

Transferable letter of credit

When a letter of credit is advised as transferable, its original beneficiary could request the bank authorized to negotiate the letter of credit to make it available to another beneficiary. In most cases, importers request for transfer of L/Cs for particular reasons—usually when their transaction is threatened. However, for the transfer, in whole or part, to the second beneficiary to be effective and applicable, it must be specifically stated in the body of the letter of credit that it is transferable. Besides, only once could the same amount be transferred. The letter of credit may also be nontransferable.

Nontransferable letter of credit

When a letter of credit is advised as nontransferable, the bank authorized to negotiate it cannot make it available to another beneficiary. In most cases, a nontransferable clause is inserted into a letter of credit instrument to satisfy particular needs of the parties. Thus, the parties must work within terms and conditions of the original letter of credit.

Back-to-back letter of credit

A back-to-back letter of credit requires issuing of a second letter of credit at the request of the beneficiary of the original letter of credit in favor of a second beneficiary. The arrangement becomes necessary in situations where the original letter of credit is nontransferable. The backing letter of credit affords the second beneficiary the right of direct drawing under its terms and conditions.

Modes of letter of credit payment and risks

There are various types and modes of payment applicable to letters of credit. A letter of credit may be payable at *sight*, or by *deferred* payment, *acceptance*, or *negotiation*.

Sight payment

When a letter of credit is expressed to be available by sight payment, it means that payment would be effected immediately upon presentation of the required documents to the issuing, or designated paying, bank. It is almost similar to payment of check across the counter (i.e., immediate payment).

Deferred payment

A deferred payment letter of credit affords the seller the benefit of the funds after a specified number of days either from the date of shipment as shown on the bill of lading/air waybill or from the date of presentation of documents to the nominated bank. The number of days usually forms part of the credit terms and conditions. With a deferred payment letter of credit, it is not mandatory to present a usance draft since this condition is already embodied in the letter of credit text.

Acceptance

A letter of credit, which is available by acceptance, calls for the presentation of a tenured draft drawn on the nominated bank for acceptance specifying the maturity date. Otherwise known as a time letter of credit, payment is made at a date after presentation of the letter of credit documents, in accordance with its terms. This is usually evidenced by a time draft that the beneficiary draws for acceptance or on a deferred payment basis. Funds become payable after maturity of the draft.

Negotiation

In technical terms, and for purposes of letter of credit payment, the word *negotiation* means simply *giving value*. Thus, a negotiating bank is a bank that gives value to financial or commercial documents. Negotiation could be general or restricted. It is general, on the one hand, if the letter of credit is freely negotiable—which makes it possible for any bank to negotiate. A restricted negotiation, on the other hand, would limit the giving of value to a nominated bank. The vetting of documents for compliance with letter of credit terms and conditions by a nominated bank without giving value does not denote negotiation.

RISKS OF LENDING AND MITIGATION

A bank that lends money to fund confirmation of a letter of credit assumes certain risks that may depend on the loan type and structure. However, banks usually grant such lending for a short term. In most cases, the loan tenor does not exceed 120 days per transaction cycle. The applicable loans are import and export finance facilities.

Import finance facility risks and control

Import finance facility (IFF) is a popular type of short-term credit product. Banks offer it to importers of industrial goods (particularly raw materials) and (especially, for the emerging markets) consumer products.

Causes of lending risks

With a very high profile of consumption imports in most of the emerging markets, lending risks occur as a result of the following:

Deficiency of demand or excess supply: As a result of unanticipated deficiency of demand, or excess market supply, the imported goods might face market glut. When this happens, the goods may be offered for sale at a price that is lower than its cost. Under the circumstances, the sale proceeds might be inadequate to offset the loan balance. This situation, which would have been worsened by accumulation of compounded interest on the loan, could result in default.

New or unforeseen regulatory maneuverings: New or unforeseen regulatory maneuverings such as sudden changes in tariffs, inspection procedures (i.e., whether preshipment or destination, for instance) and requirements, and so on contribute to credit risk. For example, a cumbersome procedure for clearing consignments might cause undue delay at the seaport. For this reason, the imported goods could be unnecessarily expensive because the importer will want to defray the additional costs. Thus, sale of the imported goods at exorbitant prices might be difficult.

Stifling competitive pressure: There is also the issue of stifling competitive pressures. This can cause an unbearable thinning down of net sale margins (even with good turnover). The importer might not be able or willing to sell the goods at prices or discounts dictated by the market forces. The alternative—sale at the ruling market prices—might leave a loan repayment gap due to a possible shortfall in expected sale proceeds.

Fluctuation in foreign exchange rates: Fluctuation in foreign exchange rates (i.e., frequent changes in exchange rates between the domestic and convertible currencies) is usually a remarkable cause of credit risk. Its main negative impact is increase in the *landing cost* of the imported goods. In some cases, prices of imported goods may far outstrip those of competition. This would happen where the exchange rate for the domestic currency appreciates sharply and substantially *after* the customer had confirmed a letter of credit. Thus, subsequent importers opening letters of credit would gain the advantage of lower cost of importation.

Mitigation of IFF risk

The common transaction dynamics and security requirements to mitigate the risks of import finance facilities include warehousing arrangement, equity contribution (i.e., counterpart funding, or part financing, of the import transaction) by the borrower, analysis of the market, and so on. Often, effective risk mitigating measures include the requirement for counterpart funding and the structuring of the loan to ensure that it is self-liquidating. Equity contribution ratio could be anything but less than 10:90, depending on the amount involved and nature of the goods to be imported. In fact, equity contribution should always be made a critical condition for granting the IFF for two main reasons.

Firstly, counterpart funding establishes commitment of the customer to the import transaction. It is highly unlikely that borrowers would gamble with more than 10% of their money (i.e., the counterpart funding requirement) by going into an unfamiliar line of business. Unless we think that they are irrational—and no astute businessman is—it would be absurd for them to want to lose money in avoidable circumstances. Thus, equity contribution helps to build the confidence of both the bank and borrower in the transaction.

Secondly, with equity contribution, the bank's credit facility is cushioned against probable loss due to adverse market forces. Consider a situation where a bank takes up to 30% counterpart funding deposit from the borrower. In this case, it would take a total loss of more than this level of the borrower's financial commitment to, and any anticipated profit on, the transaction before the loan would be at risk. Thus, in financing importation of goods, a bank assumes less risk the higher the counterpart funding provided by the borrower.

Export finance risks and control

This is one of the major credit products of banks from which foreign exchange earnings are gained upon sale of the related export proceeds. Export items may be agricultural produce or other commodities such as rubber, cashew nuts, cocoa, ginger, palm produce (kernel or oil), shrimps, and so on. Sale of these commodities overseas remains the primary business of exporters in developing countries. However, export products could be in semiprocessed state or completely manufactured (i.e., finished goods) such as those the LDCs import from developed countries. In all cases, the lending bank must be satisfied that the items are of exportable quality, i.e., they must satisfy international standards. There should also be a proven export market for the items and local sources of supply.

The major considerations in granting export credit are intended to establish the borrower's ability to articulate a realistic financing proposal. The company's export experience is a necessary, although not sufficient, condition for acceding to its request. But it is imperative that the management team (in the case of corporate borrowers) has a reasonable export experience. In addition to these considerations, lending officers should take cognizance of the following:

- The goods to be exported must be easily assessed for value and quality. It is advised that the services of such reputable export-testing and inspection services companies as Intertek, SGS, COTECNA, and Bureau Veritas be engaged.

- Arrangement must be made for bonded warehousing, with a reputable warehousing agent, in which the bank finances not more than 70% of the value of goods in the bonded warehouse at any given time. This is often achieved under terms of a tripartite warehousing agreement between the bank, exporter, and a warehousing agent. Under the agreement, the in-store stock of export goods is held on trust for the bank until full execution of the export order secured by the borrower.
- The bank should not disburse funds to finance an export order or contract unless the exporter has secured a confirmed irrevocable letter of credit, established by the overseas buyer or importer. The letter of credit must be routed through the local bank that will finance the export order or transaction. The overseas issuing bank for the letter of credit should also be acceptable to the local financing bank.

The loan should be self-liquidating through sale of the export proceeds. Of course, the bank that financed the export order or contract has the first option to purchase the export proceeds from the customer. But the exporter has the option to decline sale of the foreign exchange to the bank if the bank's offer price is not competitive. In practice, however, this rarely happens as the parties would often somehow reach a mutual agreement for the sale of the export proceeds.

QUESTIONS FOR DISCUSSION AND REVIEW

1. Critically examine the general principles on which international trade payments and documentation are based.
2. What are the common types and features of trade finance credit facilities?
3. In what essential ways should banks analyze and mitigate risks inherent in import and export finance facility?
4. What is the need for a thorough understanding of transaction dynamics in trade finance? Your answer should elucidate on critical financing requirements for trade finance transactions.
5. Why is a sound payment system essential for successful execution of international trade finance transaction?
6. Identify and discuss letters of credit that best secure the parties to an international trade transaction, showing why and how they should be preferred to the others.
7. Compare and contrast confirmed and unconfirmed letters of credit, highlighting, in doing so, their credit risk implications.

REFERENCE

International Chamber of Commerce, 1984. Uniform Customs and Practices for Documentary Credits. Publication 400.

Medium and Long-term Lending

Chapter 13

Term Loan Structuring and Risk Control in Emerging Economies

Chapter Outline

LEARNING FOCUS AND OUTCOMES

Loans granted for medium and long terms have original tenor of more than 1 year. While the tenor of medium-term credit would not exceed 3–5 years, long-term loans have tenor of more than 5 years. As risk increases with tenor, a bank that grants medium-and long-term credit must adopt an effective risk analysis methodology. While this may not be different from the traditional credit risk analysis, it demands a rigorous prognosis of future events that might affect the performance of the loan.

Two basic considerations favor the adoption of a rigorous methodology for risk analysis in long-term lending. Firstly, the usual source of repayment of term loans—one on which banks reluctantly rely—is *uncertain* future earnings or cash flows. This is unlike what exists in short-term lending where loan repayment is often expected from liquidation of particular trading or other short-term assets. Secondly, long-term funds are usually in short supply relative to short-term deposits. This situation makes it difficult for banks to maintain a pool of stable funds for long-term lending.

The borrowers that banks favor most in long-term lending are often the blue chips, largely because they tend to have enduring and stable operations.

Besides, blue chip companies show commitment to their borrowing causes and loan repayment plans. In fact, they rarely default—a major reason banks covet their banking transactions and relationships. On the contrary, most banks would not want to risk depositors' funds on long-term lending to other categories of borrowers. In addition to concern about uncertainty of future financial performance of such borrowers, banks also consider that their markets and operations might be volatile in future.

However, in some exceptional cases, banks grant long-term loans to non-blue chip borrowers. A rigorous credit analysis and proven track record of financial performance are necessary in such cases. Yet, these and similar risk-based requirements do not assure easy access to term loans. Banks lend to non-blue chip borrowers against security of perfected property or other tangible assets that have stable market value.

Banks in emerging economies must develop competences for long-term lending. One reason is that analysis of term loan requests demands technical skills and rigor—both of which, sadly, are in short supply in the industry. The reader will learn about:

- The implications of deposit liability structure of banks for their long-term lending
- Main causes of long-term borrowing and how banks should evaluate them
- Critical risk elements in long-term lending and borrowing
- Methodological framework for credit analysis in term lending
- Issues in how banks should analyze and mitigate the risks of long-term lending

LENDING VERSUS DEPOSIT STRUCTURE

Medium- to long-term tenors for credit facilities remain a worrying source of lending risks for banks in emerging economies. For this category of loans, the major cause of risk is the term structure of deposit liabilities of the banks. In this regard, banks operating in the emerging economies are mostly disadvantaged; they often rely on short-term funds or usually find it difficult to attract long-term deposits to fund term loans. In most cases, the inability of the banks to attract long-term deposits is due to recurring unfavorable macroeconomic vagaries that make long-term financial planning practically impossible for most economic units.

With prevailing market uncertainties, caused mainly by inconsistent monetary and public sector policies, unpredictable regulatory maneuverings, and galloping inflation rates, banks and customers cannot but orientate their deposits to short-term structure. Under the circumstances, lending to finance medium- and long-term borrowing causes becomes antithetical to market realities and highly risky. This is because the loans would not satisfy the principles of term lending in view of instability of the funding sources.

The risk of long-term lending manifests itself in mismatch between the structure of loan and deposit liability portfolios. Yet, to all intents and purposes, banks must offer medium- and long-term credit facilities to their deserving customers. Not only is this one of the normal functions of a bank but it is critical for the realization of national economic development aspirations of governments in the emerging economies. This will be especially so when the loans are channeled to, or utilized for, projects or transactions in the so-called *priority*, *preferred*, or *productive* sectors of the economy. In some countries, governments offer certain incentives to encourage banks to lend to such economic sectors as manufacturing and agriculture on medium- to long-term basis.

How should banks in the emerging economies mitigate risks in term lending? What are the critical risk elements and how should the risks be analyzed and mitigated? What are the main causes of term borrowing? These are some of the questions to which I provide answers in this chapter.

CAUSES OF LONG-TERM BORROWING

The grant of term loans by banks, mainly to their corporate customers, is underscored by the need to support the execution of critical and viable projects with adequate funding. The borrower could need the loan as venture (start-up business) capital or for the expansion of existing lines of business. Term loans are also often required to finance profitable diversification of business, including new product development. But requests for term loans could also be justified on grounds of other considerations, including the need to, among others, sustain permanent working capital (PWC)—also referred to as working investment capital (WIC)—at an appreciable level, fund management buyout (MBO), finance mergers and acquisitions, and so on.

Customers investing in business or other regenerative projects require term loans largely in response to compelling demands of the business. For instance, it would be irrational to ask short-term credit facilities to finance such projects that in most cases have long gestation periods. Besides, it is expected that repayment of the loans will come from future cash flows from the projects. This expectation is normal unless the borrower provides credible secondary source of repayment for the loans. Yet the need for a term loan by a company could be offset with a large pool of shareholders' funds and continuing profitable operations, without jeopardizing working capital. Customers may even need term loans to fund leasing of operating equipment, buy houses on certain mortgage terms, and so on.

In the final analysis, the probability of default increases when banks and borrowers fail to tie loan repayment ability of borrower to expected but realistic cash flows that the project funded would generate. Not only is it advisable to always do this but it is also imperative to sensitize cash flow projection as a means of enhancing its reliability.

RISK ANALYSIS AND MITIGATION

The overriding focus of risk appraisal in term lending is often on the cash flow of the borrower that provides the primary source for loan repayment. Most term loans, especially those utilized to finance capital projects, run into hitches that often cause unintended default as a result of cost overrun, changing government policies, delayed completion, difficulty in securing raw materials, and so on. However, the usual procedure for risk identification, analysis, and mitigation as reflected in the so-called five C's of lending must be adopted in the first place. The following discussions are devoted to analyzing some of the key credit issues in term loans.

Management evaluation

The loan officer should appreciate that management evaluation is an important factor for analysis. Thus, it is considered necessary for credit analysts to painstakingly evaluate the management team in determining the quality, orientation, and focus of the decision makers of the borrowing company. In management evaluation, when lending to a corporate borrower, the loan officer should be interested in the composition of the board of directors and the core values, including business objectives, mission, or vision of the company. Risk is generally minimized when a company has a balanced board—one in which various ownership and stakeholder interests are adequately represented. Also, there should be a clear succession plan to key management positions as opposed to the ignominious rancor that often follows the filling of executive vacancies in some companies.

One of the critical factors to consider is the average age of the key management staff. Credit risk increases when the average age of staff that constitute the management team approaches the retirement limit. A young, active, and dynamic management team is easily the toast of bankers. Besides, a company that records an unusually high level of labor turnover at the management cadre does not appeal to banks. High labor turnover at that level is a danger signpost for lending purposes. It is also important to analyze the innovativeness of management—its general business track record. This is especially necessary in order to know how management would act when faced with unusual decision tasks.

Typical unusual challenges that a management team may face include turnaround projects, organizational reengineering, business diversification, and reinventing of the company. A well-managed company, in most cases, adopts the known best work practices. Such practices would include good career plans, effective intracompany communication system, option for staff shares purchase, and performance-related compensation package. These measures help to attract, retain, and motivate quality manpower. Finally, the quality of management information system used by the company is a critical factor in the lending decision.

Financial risk analysis

Financial analysts do not generally agree on the usefulness of financial analysis in appraising credit requests. Some argue that since the source documents (i.e., a company's financial statement and annual reports) are amenable to distortions, only a limited value should be placed on their analysis for lending purposes. Others argue that since historical data are often used in most financial analysis, juxtaposing the past on expected future events in making lending decisions may after all be misleading.

Yet banks rely heavily on financial analysis of the borrower both as part of the overall credit appraisal package and in making lending decisions. For purposes of credit analysis memorandum, the analyst reviews and comments on the financial performance of the borrower for at least the immediate past 3 years (generally for a new borrower) or from the date of the last such review (for existing accounts), including management accounts for the current period. The borrower may also be required, depending on the type, magnitude, and other such considerations, to furnish information on its projected financial performance for the next 12 months. With such information, the analyst offers an opinion on the reasonableness of observed performance and the extent of reliance to be placed on the projected performance of the borrower. The analyst determines the borrower's *cash flow* strength, profitability and growth, sales turnover and efficiency (asset quality), financial condition (capital structure, with emphasis on long-term liquidity and leverage). The veritable instrument for achieving this is the widely acclaimed ratio analysis.

In analyzing financial risk, the loan officer, first and foremost, examines the borrower's *capital* adequacy—the paid-up capital of the business, shareholders' funds—to assess how much the borrower has contributed as equity toward the operation of the business or for the execution of the transaction. In fact, business ventures are often run on the buffer of promoter's funds (equity) and borrowed funds (debt). On the liability side of the balance sheet (for a corporate borrower), the mix of these funding sources determines the *financial risk* of the business. A high debt-to-equity ratio imparts risk of capital structure to the business. This is a volatile condition that also adversely affects the long-term viability of the company.

In order to mitigate financial risk, the company must achieve an optimal mix of debt and equity in its capital structure. How can the borrower cope with this task? In a nutshell, how would the analyst define borrowers' financing needs to appreciate their borrowing causes? In the final analysis, capital is seen as a buffer to creditors in the event of failure and liquidation of the company. It also cushions financial leverage of the business. In a typical *balance sheet lending*, a leverage of more than 2.0 may be unacceptable to a bank for weak companies. Thus, banks look for comfort in the size and composition of the borrower's net worth, or equity contribution.

Operating performance risk

The *performance risk* is associated with the probability that the borrower would not achieve good earnings and profitability from operations. Here the analyst specifically tries to gain insight into what may happen to earnings from operations—whether they would be sustained, increased, or adversely affected in any way. It therefore becomes imperative to analyze the asset side of the balance sheet (in the case of a corporate borrower), with a view to ascertaining the *quality* and *efficiency* of asset utilization. A particular analysis may reveal the need to optimize the performance of *trading assets* or to increase *net working assets* as a means of achieving target *sales growth* and *net operating cash flow*.

Overall, the credit analyst must make and sensitize projections on key financial records of the borrower. The sensitivity analysis anticipates certain scenarios or events the occurrence of which might frustrate attainment of the financial projections. In the case of project finance, the analyst must accurately determine total requirements for capital expenditure, working capital, debt servicing, and so on. Credit analysts should also advise on net present value, breakeven point, and internal rate of return of projects before initialing their recommendation for approval or decline of the related loan requests.

Other borrower-specific risks

There is credit risk that is associated with *capacity* of the borrower. In analyzing this risk, the credit officer will be interested to know whether or not the borrowers have the *expertise, know-how*, and necessary skills appropriate for their trades. If they are adjudged to be incompetent to execute the transaction, the loans will have high probabilities of loss.

Risks associated with the quality and adequacy of man and material resources available to the borrower (in the case of a company) are also common. It would be less risky to lend to a company that has a highly motivated workforce, good training programs and facilities, and less labor unrest. In terms of material resources, emphasis would be on *premises, plant*, and *machinery*—owned or leased, tenure, and age. It is also important to consider capacity utilization of the plant, suitability or adaptability of business premises to the company's requirements, and the general condition of the premises, plant, and machinery.

Risk is minimized where a company wields a dominant influence in its industry—controlling a major segment or share of the market, with well-focused costing and pricing strategies. But risk is indicated in products that are highly price sensitive or when a company has high fixed costs—this being a major influence in assessing its operating leverage. It would normally take such a company a longer period to breakeven because of the level of fixed cost content of its output. Price sensitivity affects the elasticity of market demand for products. Thus, a company that manufactures or sells price-sensitive products would obviously be a high-risk borrower.

Industry-related risks

In some emerging economies, the general business *conditions* are a haven for particular credit risk. Operations of a company, its industry, and the general macroeconomic environment in which it operates inform the risk. Industry and macroeconomic factors pose risks of a *systemic* nature—those that cannot easily be mitigated through deliberate management efforts. Such risks include the threat of inflation, industry-wide strikes, and demand deficiency. Generally, for credit analysis purposes, there is need to mirror the dynamics of the industry in which the borrower operates or into which a prospective borrower hopes to enter. Risk is indicated more or less depending on the nature of competition, existing legislation, growth prospects, and the relative strengths of buyers and suppliers in the industry.

Industry risk increases with wide-ranging substitute products, government competition or intervention, and barriers to entry reflected in monopolistic tendencies or registration of proprietary *know-how*. The rapidity of growth of the industry or its *life cycle* stage, as well as its sensitivity to business cycles, fashion and fad are no less important factors for consideration. Risk is minimized when an industry enjoys high sales margin, usually a function of growth and stability, while undue pressure on margins characterize decline.

Macroeconomic risk

Macro risks exist in economic, political, and sociocultural influences that determine the performance capacity of a business at any point in time. Generally, macroeconomic risks are of a *systemic* nature and beyond the control of both the borrower and lender. They are also not easily foreseeable accurately. However, the easily identifiable and frequently analyzed macroeconomic risks that affect lending decisions derive largely from general government policies, especially the fiscal and monetary policies. Such policies affect the purchasing power of the people as, for instance, when foreign exchange market is liberalized or controlled. Of course, judging from Nigeria's recent experience, we know that foreign exchange policy could render export and import business volatile.

Yet governments have been instrumental in encouraging savings and investment that impart resilience to business. Where such business incentives are easily accessible to industry operators, risk of lending would be mitigated. It is also always necessary to examine environmental issues that could affect the ability of borrowers to repay loans. This is why, through moral suasion, governments persuade banks to lower lending rates as a means of encouraging the productive sectors of the economy. With rising borrowing interest rates and, therefore the cost of doing business, banks would not easily escape high default rate on credit facilities.

Other safeguards and issues

In some cases, the purpose of analyzing *other safeguards and issues* is served when the analyst discusses the three major safety factors commonly considered by banks in any serious lending situation. The factors relate to concerns about *seniority*, *protection*, and *control* that a bank has over the transaction being financed by it as explained below.

Seniority: With *seniority*, the bank is assured of first legal claim over the assets of the borrower that secure the credit, including (in the case of asset-based credit, equipment lease, or project finance) the particular assets being financed by the bank.

Protection: The consideration of *protection* establishes assurance of prevention of, or security of cover over, loss conferred on the bank in the way the credit is structured and its dynamics are envisaged.

Control: On the issue of *control*, the analyst discloses how and why the bank should monitor the transaction to achieve good utilization and timely repayment of the credit.

In general, banks in emerging economies should seek to insulate themselves against risks of long-term lending by executing legally binding loan agreements with borrowers. Though such an agreement is also often executed to legalize a short-term credit facility, it is never as rigorous as in the case of a term loan. In most cases, a short-term loan agreement operates as simply documentation of letters of *offer* and *acceptance* of the credit facility, which are enforceable in the law courts.

QUESTIONS FOR DISCUSSION AND REVIEW

1. What are the main causes and consequences of term loan borrowing by companies and organizations?
2. What are the critical risk elements in medium- and long-term lending? How should the risks be analyzed and mitigated?
3. Relate the deposit liability structure of banks to the banks' disposition to medium- and long-term lending.
4. What is the implication of the requirement for technical skills and rigorous credit analysis in long-term lending?
5. Assess the issues that underlie the methodology for credit risk analysis and mitigation in medium- and long-term lending.
6. Evaluate the capacity of banks to grant long-term loans in the face of vagaries of the future.

Chapter 14

Mortgage Risks, Control, and Property Market in Emerging Economies

LEARNING FOCUS AND OUTCOMES

Real estate financing has had its ups and downs following occasional instability of the financial system. Yet it remains an all-time attractive credit product for banks and investors in emerging economies. Investors covet real estate and see it as a safe haven. The sector is traditionally stable and commands respectable rates of return. Upswings in demand for residential and commercial property, despite occasional lulls, are evidence of investor interest in real estate. This is not surprising, considering that real estate is adjudged to be a store of stable economic value.

Unfortunately, not many people can afford their own homes. Most people struggle to save money to rent residential apartments. In doing so, they give a boost to the property market. The capitalists, mainly property developers, strive to meet the burgeoning demand of existing and prospective tenants. This situation sustains the boom in the property market. But it also underscores the significance of mortgages. Banks now offer mortgages to individuals and property developers alike—without undermining the property market.

Like individuals, companies and organizations also do have effective demand for mortgages. With mortgages, they can own office houses, factory buildings, warehouses, premises, staff quarters, and so on. On occasion, companies finance such capital expenditures from operating cash flows or shareholders' funds. Otherwise, mortgages become a fallback option for them. But they must also make the buy or build and own decision based on a careful analysis of their finances. Banks, on the other hand, must brace themselves for the challenges in house financing. While tapping into mortgages, they must contend with applicable risks. Mortgages usually have long tenors and depend on uncertain future cash flows for repayment. Thus, banks must devise an appropriate lending methodology, one that effectively mitigates credit risk.

This setting renders mortgage financing attractive to banks. But it also raises a number of questions. In what ways should banks be on top of their exposure on mortgages? How should banks anticipate future dynamics of the property market? With what methodology should banks effectively analyze and mitigate mortgage risks? It is important to appreciate the credit risk of mortgages. A key issue is how to analyze and mitigate the risk. In this chapter, the reader will learn about:

- Openings in mortgage financing and how banks could tap into the opportunities
- How banks should correctly anticipate future dynamics of mortgages and the property market
- Methodology that banks should adopt to analyze and mitigate risks of mortgages
- Ways in which banks should control their exposure and, doing so, optimize earnings on mortgages

OPENINGS AND BOOM TO BUST IN MORTGAGE LENDING

Sustained growth in demand for mortgages opened up a window of profitable lending opportunity hitherto relegated by banks in emerging economies. Until recently, commercial banks had adjudged mortgages riskier than traditional credit facilities. Banks assessed the risk of mortgages in the context of their long tenor, low returns, and uncertainty of future cash flows of the obligors. Low capitalization of most of the banks at the time worsened the risk avoidance posture of the banks. Besides, banks rarely were able to attract long-tenor deposits. For these reasons, the banks tended to shun mortgage financing while preferring the so-called self-liquidating loans.

In Pakistan, consumer financing for house building decreased in both fiscal year 2012—13 and 2013—14. However a decrease of Rs 0.1 billion (0.3%) during fiscal year 2013—14 was nominal compared to a decrease of Rs 2.4 billion (5.7%) in the same period of 2012—13. Thus the actual increase was Rs 2.3 billion (5.4%) during fiscal year 2013—2014. Yet the sector was inadequately funded in fiscal year 2013—14 considering that target financing for the sector was not achieved.

Mortgage lending in the Mexican banking industry reflects scepticism of banks in emerging economies about the ability of obligors to service and repay their loans. In the first quarter 2014, the total outstanding in mortgage lending was $1,671,613.2 million. The figure increased marginally by 0.4%, to $1,677,934.9 million in the second quarter. The situation was basically the same at the end of the third quarter when total outstanding mortgage lending amounted to $1,718,982.9 million, representing an increase of $4,104.8 million (0.2%) over the second quarter figure.

Yet, there are positive aspects of mortgages that should assuage fears of the banks. Investment in real estate can be converted into cash (i.e., liquidated)—though, on occasion, with some delay—without loss of value. Property value appreciates over time, if anything. Rather than sell, a property owner could pledge it as collateral to secure a loan from a bank. Demand for housing by landlords and tenants responds directly to population explosion in urban areas. In response to the apathy of the banks, governments in emerging economies establish mortgage banks. Some set up finance and investment institutions to fill the gap in funding their housing programs. In Nigeria, for instance, Lagos State Development and Property Company Limited (LSDPC) procures land, builds housing estates, and leases landed property to members of the public.

The Pakistani scenario highlighted above contrasts with that of India where sectoral deployment of bank credit to housing and commercial real estate shows commitment of banks and government to the sector. Aggregate credit disbursed to housing (regarded as a priority sector) increased to Rs 6,015.0 billion in 2014, up from Rs 5,185.0 billion in 2013. In real terms, there was a decline in credit deployed to the sector in 2014. While an increase of 16.0% was achieved in 2014, a 17.7% increase was achieved in 2013. On the contrary, aggregate credit disbursed to commercial real estate in 2014 increased more than the increase in 2013. In 2014, a total of Rs 1,643.0 billion, representing 15.1% increase, was disbursed as against Rs 1,428 billion disbursed in 2013, representing a 14.6% increase. Thus, there was an increase in real terms in credit deployed to the commercial real estate sector.

With the mergers and acquisitions that swept Nigeria's banking industry in 2005, banks acquired financial muscle to play in the property market. Nowadays banks confidently offer competitive mortgages to their customers. Banks now make huge annual budgets for mortgage financing to strengthen their balance sheets, increase market share, and improve earnings. Yet, financing house ownership fulfills both economic goals and an implied social responsibility for the banks. This makes business sense that the banks should not ignore.

The Singaporean case is quite interesting in the sense that the supply of mortgages exceeded demand in both the third and fourth quarters of 2014. The total banking system approved credit limit for owner-occupied property loans was S$150,431.5 million in the fourth quarter of 2014, representing an increase of S$1,722.6 over the 2014 third-quarter figure of S$148,708.9 million. Of these amounts, actual utilization totalled S$131,134.2 million in the fourth quarter and S$128,681.0 in the third. Thus, there was a marginal percentage increase of 0.7 in utilization of the loans, from 86.5% in the third quarter to 87.2% in the fourth quarter. Similarly, total utilization of aggregate bank credit limits granted for investment in property increased by 0.7% in the fourth quarter of 2014, from 86.7% in the third quarter to 87.4%. Actual limits granted were S$56,445.3 million and S$56,905.5 million, while utilization was S$48,962.8 million and S$49,716.9 million in the third and fourth quarters, respectively.

Banks certainly contribute boom to bust in mortgage lending in emerging economies. They tend to be bullish about mortgage lending when there are prospects in the property market. Often the attendant increase in lending creates a property glut as property developers get stuck in a market lull—a situation that often leads to loan default in the sector. This situation then forces banks to adopt a bearish lending disposition. As banks cut back on mortgage lending, the lull soon gives way to a dearth of residential and commercial property—forcing mortgage costs and house rents to increase. This outcome is yet unfavorable to the property market as it is also propitious to default. In most cases, it is difficult for banks and the authorities to strike the right balance in mortgage lending. A balanced financing outcome is one that satisfies both residential and commercial needs.

As banks brace themselves for the challenges in mortgage lending, they must contend with associated risks and uncertainties. The major risk-creating features of mortgages remain immutable. Mortgages are usually of long tenor and rely on largely uncertain projected cash flows for repayment. Thus, banks must devise appropriate risk-mitigating measures that ensure minimal loan loss provision. How should banks analyze and mitigate the lending risks? It is answers to this question with which I am largely concerned in this chapter.

Case Study 14.1

Anticipating Fraud in Mortgage Financing

Umar Jones applied to Upbeat Bank Limited for $200 million credit facility that he needed to buy a house in South Africa.[1] Prior to sending his loan request to the bank, he had gone to discuss the application with his account officer, Ann.

"How are you doing this morning?" he asked Ann, who was already standing to welcome him to her office.

"You look cheerful—as usual," he teased before sitting down.

"Thank you, Sir. I feel flattered by your kind words," responded Ann smiling.

"As you're aware, I've never applied to your bank for a credit facility since I opened and have been running my account in this branch," Umar intimated.

"I hope your bank won't disappoint me now that I have an urgent credit request—one that holds the key to my happiness now and in the future," he continued.

"Please let's discuss your credit proposal. We're here to serve you—including your financing needs," said Ann.

"There's this property here on the Island that I'm eager to buy. I've negotiated with its owner for a sale price of $286 million. I've decided to apply for a $200 million mortgage from your bank and supplement the loan with credit in my account. I'm making a 30% equity contribution toward the purchase of the house," Umar explained.

"There's no problem. Send in a formal application for the loan and let me do an appraisal of it. Once I'm done, I will get back to you," Ann promised.

Ann analyzed and recommended the credit request for approval. The bank granted the customer's mortgage request, with the house to be purchased with the loan as collateral. Based on the approval, Ann assembled the required security documents, including photocopies of the title deeds to the property. She went to see her boss, Ken, who was the manager of Central Victoria Island branch of Upbeat Bank where Mr Jacob's account was domiciled.

"Ken I've now collected all the necessary security documents in respect of the mortgage facility to Mr Jacob," she told him.

"Here you go." She handed him the documents.

The manager examined the documents critically even as he didn't doubt their authenticity.

"Did you sight the original title deeds?" Ken asked calmly.

"No, I didn't. Mr Jacob said that the owner of the property would not release the original documents at this time. But our certified check in his favor would dispose him to release the original title deeds in exchange for the check," she explained.

The manager concurred. Subsequently, he forwarded the documents with a memo to the bank's legal office for further processing. In his memo, Ken succinctly stated the status of security for the loan as follows:

I forward herewith this memo photocopy of the title deeds to the house bought with, and securing, the $200 million mortgage facility granted to Umar Jacob by the bank. The original documents are not available yet for sighting. Please advise us of the status of the property based on your legal search on the property.

Meanwhile, Umar had given his consent for the bank to perfect its charge on the house after disbursement of the mortgage. The understanding, in doing so, was to strengthen the collateral securing the mortgage. He executed a memorandum of deposit of the title documents and equitable mortgage on the house in favor of the bank to enable the bank perfect the charge. Based on foregoing mutual agreement, he applied for full disbursement on the mortgage. The bank approved disbursement as requested. However, the condition for disbursement was that payment for the house should be made directly to its owner in exchange for the original title deeds.

Umar had no objection to the disbursement condition. He submitted his request for a $200 million certified check in favor of the owner of the house to the branch manager. While requesting the certified check, he had urged the manager to ensure that the bank checked out the title documents to the house besides requesting the certified check.

"Please make sure that documents to the property are genuine before we release the certified check," he pleaded with Ken.

"Of course, as a bank, we will do all the necessary legal checks before parting with the instrument," assured Ken.

The manager passed the buck to the legal office. He phoned the legal office to confirm legal status of the collateral.

"Has the legal office conducted a search on the property securing Umar Jacob's mortgage facility yet?" Ken asked Joyce, a legal officer.

"Yes, the legal office has done the search," answered Joyce.

"What's the outcome? Ken further asked anxiously.

"Our search findings are satisfactory," Joyce informed.

"I hope that you guys bore in mind the need for caution and due diligence while conducting the legal search. We're talking of a whopping $200 million here, you know," Ken said—apparently filled with apprehension.

"There's no problem—I assure you," Joyce said and hung up.

The branch issued the certified check based on the feedback its manager, Ken, obtained from the legal office.

Ken accompanied Umar and personally presented the certified check for $286 million to the owner of the house. In return, he collected original title documents to the house. Using an official internal memo, he forwarded the documents to the legal office.

A week later Umar spoke to Ken on the telephone about the mortgages transaction.

"I'm devastated, Ken. Your bank has messed with my mortgage facility and the house!" He bemoaned.

"What's the problem, Mr Jacob?" asked Ken, his voice betraying fear that had gripped him on hearing those words from him.

"There's a major problem with the transaction. In fact, I'm in the soup as I speak to you," Umar lamented.

"Please tell me what's amiss," Ken demanded. "I hate surprises or to be kept in suspense."

Umar then informed him that the original title documents that the owner of the house gave to them in exchange for the certified check were forged. In fraud parlance, the documents were "cloned." The foregoing fact dawned when Umar wanted to gain entry into the house in order to take possession.

The real owner of the house emerged and dissociated himself from the sale of the house. He showed Umar authentic title documents to the house that differed in subtle ways from the ones in the bank's possession. Ken was at a loss over the incident. The legal office showed equal surprise at the fraud. Efforts to contact the seller of the house proved futile. Apparently, he had gone underground. Umar's claim that he didn't know him personally worsened the prospect of either tracking him down, or knowing his hideout.

Hints for Analyzing This Case Study

This is a typical case of a complicated credit fraud, one that is compounded by lax risk management. It is not clear whether the borrower, Mr Jacob, perpetrated the fraud. One reason is that he submitted to the due credit process of the bank. Secondly, he warned against an incautious search on the property. Another reason yet is that he contributed $86 million as his equity toward purchase of the property. Besides, he agreed that the bank should pay the cost of the house directly to its owner. A possible explanation of the fraud would be one that associates it with collusion. It is possible that the borrower, fake owner of the property, and some staff of the bank's legal office colluded to perpetrate the fraud. The fraud would have been prevented had the legal office conducted a search on the property with painstaking attention to detail. But they bungled the exercise— by either some omission or commission!

Questions on the case study
1. (a) What would you consider to be the major credit risk management failings of the affected staff of Upbeat Bank Limited?
    (b) In what ways, other than those stated or implied in the hints on the case, could branch staff and the legal office of the bank have prevented the mortgage fraud?
2. (a) Assuming you are the CEO of Upbeat Bank, who would you hold responsible for the bungled credit transaction and why?
    (b) What punishment would you consider appropriate for the responsible staff?

1. The use of South Africa as the setting for this case study is for illustration purposes only to demonstrate how the case study plays itself out in a typical emerging market. The names used for the company, bank, and individuals in the illustration are imaginary and do not relate to any known or unknown company, bank, or persons in South Africa or elsewhere.

ASSESSING BORROWING CAUSES

Lending officers should appreciate borrowing causes to be able to present good credit analysis and mitigate lending risks. Borrowing causes should be analyzed at two levels. Firstly, the analyst should know the cause and extent of a gap in a borrower's cash flows that necessitates a borrowing request. Doing so, the objective is to assess loan repayment capacity of the borrower based on realistic sensitivity analysis of projected cash flows. Secondly, the borrowing cause could be assessed in terms of purpose for which a loan would be applied. In this case, the analyst should discuss the applicable types of mortgages with the borrower.

The applicable borrowing cause or type of mortgage which a customer requests for should be properly discussed, investigated, and analyzed as part of the overall lending process. There are different reasons for mortgages. Some of the reasons for which individuals, companies, and organizations need mortgages include:

- Purchase or acquisition of land
- Construction or building of a new house

- Purchase of a house
- Home or house renovation
- Refinance of existing mortgage

Some borrowers might need mortgages to buy undeveloped property with the intention of building their houses in the future. In deciding to build at later dates, this category of borrowers tends to take cognizance of their current cash flow constraint. There are other borrowers who already have undeveloped plots of land and need a mortgage to build their houses. In this case, the bank would have to closely monitor disbursement of the loans and supervision of work at every stage of the construction of the houses. Monitoring and supervision are more or less required in lending for house renovation. Perhaps the most common mortgage request is for the purchase of an already built house while refinancing of an existing mortgage is about the least common.

I discuss the main features of the various types of mortgages, with implications for credit risk analysis and mitigation in emerging economies. Doing so, my objective is to suggest a practical analytical framework on which loan officers could rely in assessing creditworthiness of mortgage applicants.

CHARACTERIZING MORTGAGES

Mortgage loans share some of the features of other credit facilities. Some of their distinguishing characteristics include:

- Equity contribution as in import or project finance
- Long tenor as in long-term loans
- Market-influenced pricing
- Asset protection with insurance
- Optimum loan amount

However, there are certain basic features that make mortgages unique as a credit product. The same unique features embody credit risk of mortgages; they also underscore choice of analytical framework for mortgage risk. The exceptional characteristics of mortgages relate mainly to:

- Requirement for a certain loan service income
- Allowance, or disapproval of, prepayment clause
- Modes of drawdown and repayment, especially in mortgages for construction purposes
- Risk-induced discrimination between employed and self-employed applicants
- Prescription of age limit for accessing mortgages

In the context of the foregoing, let me briefly discuss the main features of mortgages. I do so with special reference to the dynamics of mortgage financing in emerging economies.

Amount and counterpart funding

It is expected that a bank should finance only a certain percentage of the total cost of the property requiring a mortgage, while the borrower contributes equity to meet the funding requirement. The funding ratios may vary from one bank to another. However, a common practice is for a bank to lend not more than 80% of the total cost of a property, while the borrower makes a 20% equity contribution. The equity contribution certifies commitment of obligors to repaying their mortgages. However, the amounts of equity often vary among banks depending on their cost of funds, risk acceptance criteria, competing needs for funds, and so on. While some banks ask for 30% equity (i.e., counterpart funding), others accept a 20% equity contribution. In all cases, the percentages relate to predetermined maximum lending limits as assessed by the bank for their preferred geographical locations of the property financed.

Tenor of the loan

As a long-term credit facility, the tenor of mortgages could be up to 20 years or more, depending on the verifiable age of the borrower. Most banks would not grant mortgages to applicants who would be more than 60 years old prior to the expiry dates of the loans. This implies that banks tend to calculate acceptable loans tenor by relating current age of the borrowers to their expected sixtieth birthday anniversary. In this context, the loans would typically fall due at the expiration of a maximum tenor of 20 years or prior to the borrower's sixtieth birthday anniversary, whichever comes first. This is the typical emerging economy scene, ostensibly not applicable in advanced countries like the United States, Canada, and Western European nations.

Pricing of the loan

In general, mortgage pricing takes into account the possibility of fluctuation in property market conditions. It is inevitable to do so considering that the loans are usually granted for a long term during which the original conditions that influenced their pricing might alter. In order to hedge against this risk, banks in emerging economies tend to apply variable interest rates, which are also benchmarked on their prime lending rates plus a certain margin spread or risk premium. In most cases, the banks charge all-in rates to take care of interest, fees, and commission on mortgages.

Insurance of the property

The borrower should insure the property for which they have obtained the mortgage against destruction. The bank's interest should be noted in the insurance as the first loss payee beneficiary. In most cases, there would be the need for mortgage protection insurance that covers the bank's interest in mortgages. With such insurance, banks in emerging economies are assured of adequate protection against risk of default arising from loss of property prior to expiry and repayment of mortgages that financed it. Unfortunately, the insurance industry in emerging markets is still in its most rudimentary form. On occasion claims on insurance covers suffer setbacks due to avoidable technicalities and flawed legal systems.

Loan service income

It is expected that borrowers should be able to service their mortgages and all their other credit facilities with not more than 33.3% of their net income. This satisfies international labor law to which most of the emerging economies subscribe. Thus, it is only mortgage applicants who have room to borrow from the savings of 33.3% of their net incomes that may be considered for mortgages. Ironically, not many banks in emerging economies adhere strictly to this mortgage rule. This exacerbates unintended credit risk, which some banks in emerging economies assume in the property market.

Repayment of the loan

There are basically three credit issues involved in analyzing and mitigating risks associated with repayment of mortgages. What are the possible repayment terms that would be acceptable to both the bank and borrower—monthly, quarterly, biannual, annual, or other structured payments? Would the bank allow a prepayment clause in the loan agreement? How should the obligors pay interest and repay the principal in the case of a mortgage for house construction? In most cases, under the loan agreement, the bank would give the obligor the option to prepay the loan. Otherwise, a common repayment arrangement is for the obligor to repay the loan on a structured monthly or quarterly basis. In the case of a mortgage granted for house construction, the obligor pays only interest on the loan until completion of the house.

RISK ANALYSIS AND MITIGATION

There are a number of basic risk issues to analyze and mitigate in normal mortgages. The major considerations relate to:

- Borrower's cash flows
- Market value of the property
- Title deeds evidencing ownership of the property
- Sale agreement documentation
- Government policy and requirements
- Location of the property

Cash flow analysis

Borrowers should present convincing evidence of their financial capacity to repay mortgages that may be granted to them. This information is usually ascertained from their cash flow forecasts and analysis. In most cases, risk-mitigating measures applicable to borrowers who have formal jobs differ from those who are self-employed. In the case of the former, the analyst should ascertain their net income, terminal benefits, and other verifiable sources of income. With the information, the analyst decides whether or not to recommend particular mortgage requests for approval.

The self-employed borrowers tend to have higher risk and default probabilities. Thus, credit analysts should obtain strong evidence of ability of borrowers to repay mortgages from their cash flows. Besides net incomes, loan officers should obtain and analyze financial and bank statements of the borrowers. While financial statements should be analyzed for at least the immediate past three years, bank statements should cover at least the last 24 months. It might also be useful to require maintenance of reserve accounts. With this suggestion, the obligors should have balances in reserve accounts that should be adequate to pay at least three months of installments on their mortgages. Thus, reserve accounts serve to minimize the risk of default in mortgage repayments.

There are other measures that a bank could adopt to further minimize the risk of lending to self-employed borrowers. The tenor of the loans may be limited to not more than 10 years, while the age of the borrower should not exceed 50 years. In addition, the equity contribution of the borrower should be at least 30% of the amount of the loan.

Value of the property

There should be proper valuation of the property that the borrower intends to buy or acquire with a mortgage loan. In general, the bank should require an authentic valuation report on the property. The report is more likely to be acceptable to a bank if assessment and valuation of the property are carried out by the bank's authorized estate agent.

Title deeds

It is important that lending officers carefully investigate the title to the property to be financed with a mortgage. There should be clear evidence that the vendor of the property is its true owner. In other words, ownership of the property should not be in contention between individuals or groups. Acceptable evidence of ownership may be a certificate of occupancy, letter of allocation from the government, power of attorney, and so on. However, lending risk is minimized when evidence of title is a certificate of occupancy—one that the bank could easily perfect to further secure the loan. While the obligor might have a certificate of occupancy, it is also important for the bank to check whether the property is held on leasehold or freehold terms.

Sale agreement

The request for a mortgage should be supported with evidence of a sale agreement executed between the property vendor and the borrower. In all cases, the agreement should be a contract of sale, a letter of offer from the vendor (i.e., owner) of the property, or both.

Government policy and requirements

The property should have approved or registered survey and building plans. Obtaining these documents from the responsible government agency or department is one of the conditions for considering applications for mortgages. Without these important documents, it would be difficult to ascertain the extent to which aspects of the documentation of the property comply with government requirements for authenticity.

Location of the property

Locations of property that banks in Nigeria prefer include Lagos, Abuja, and Port Harcourt. These locations enjoy high and continuous appreciation of property value. It is also easy to sell property in these locations. Lending risks tend to increase for property in markets that are outside the preferred locations. This risk assessment criterion applies to other emerging economies.

OTHER CREDIT ISSUES

Banks should adopt other risk-mitigating measures in lending to finance house construction. There should be bills of quantities, construction milestones or timelines, and progressive drawdown on mortgage based on bank-approved quantity certificates. In the case of refinancing of an existing mortgage, the amount of the facility should not exceed the outstanding balance on the original mortgage. In all cases, the property financed should be taken as collateral to secure the loan.

QUESTIONS FOR DISCUSSION AND REVIEW

1. How should banks in emerging economies correctly anticipate future dynamics of mortgages and the property market?
2. Why and how are the features of mortgages unique? What are the main characteristic features of mortgages?
3. With what methodology should banks effectively analyze and mitigate credit risk in mortgages?

4. In what ways should banks control their exposure—and, doing so, optimize earnings—on mortgages?
5. What factors facilitated contemporary interest of banks in emerging economies in mortgages and the property market?
6. Explain how government intervention paved the way for the emergence of a vibrant property market in a named emerging economy.

FURTHER READING

Banco de Mexico, 2015. Financing and Financial Information of Financial Intermediaries: Banking and Alternative Financing Sources to Domestic Private Sector.

Monetary Authority of Singapore (MAS), 2015. Data on Housing and Bridging Loans. (Based on MAS' Survey of Housing Loans for Selected Financial Institutions, Which Account for over 90% of Total Outstanding Housing Loans Extended by the Industry).

Reserve Bank of India, 2015. Deployment of Gross Bank Credit by Major Sectors.

State Bank of Pakistan, 2014. Pakistan Economic Survey 2013−14.

Chapter 15

Lease Financing Risk and Control in Emerging Markets

LEARNING FOCUS AND OUTCOMES

Pressure on personal and corporate finances informs the decision of someone or organization to lease rather than buy a particular asset. As in real estate where the *buy or build* decision is common, leasing presents a similar task in the *buy or lease* decision—considered to be inevitable for lessees. However, it is pertinent to note the difference between the two cases. In the former, either of the decisions leads to ownership of a house. If someone or organization applies a mortgage to buy or build a house, they will ultimately own the house after paying back the mortgage that financed its acquisition. In the latter, this is not the case—the reason being that a lease does not necessarily have to end in ownership of the leased asset.

Whether or not a lessee or lessor owns the asset at the end of the lease depends on some considerations. Conditions that determine ownership of leased assets at the end of leases are often built into the structure, types, and terms of leases. This implies that leases operate largely as conditional transactions. Lessees fulfill specific obligations, including full payment of rentals on leased assets, in order to own the assets. Otherwise, they must return the assets to the lessors at the end of the leases. In most cases, lessees make the choice of types of leases that best satisfy their particular financing needs.

Bank lending connects with leasing in three respects. The first is where a bank acts directly as a lessor. In this case, the bank is the investor— committing funds to procure and own assets that a lessee needs. The second is where a bank lends money to a lessor to procure specific assets that a particular lessee needs. This reflects the role of a bank as a financier in asset acquisition through leasing. Thus, the bank is not the legal owner of the asset, but has a lien on it. A variant of these two is where an asset owner sells the asset to a bank and leases it back from the bank. This practice, known as *sale and leaseback*, follows the usual leasing principles, but its approach is more rigorous.

The three situations are treated differently in a bank's books of accounts—usually for tax and balance sheet management purposes. This is always the case, notwithstanding that banks recognize funds committed to leases as assets in their loan books. Considering its background, I review development of lease financing as a credit product. The review builds on analysis of types, features, and risks of leases. It also highlights implications thereof and underscores the focus of interest in this chapter. The reader will learn about:

- Evolution of leasing as a credit product that banks offer to their customers
- Structure and types of leases, noting their peculiar characteristics
- Dynamics of, and credit risk management for, alternative forms of leases
- Significance of the parties to, roles in, and conduct of lease transactions

---

Case Study 15.1

Neglect of Investigation of Borrower

International Middle Trade Limited (IMT) was engaged in long-distance haulage of goods to major northern cities of Nigeria[1] like Abuja, Kaduna, Kano, Sokoto, Yola, and so on. It also traded on imported tires, matches, and some consumable items, such as rice. With the success of its lines of businesses and services, there was need to expand that necessitated borrowing from Isle Bank Limited. Isle's banking relationship with IMT started in March 2000. In April 2000, Isle Bank granted it credit facilities totaling ₦50 million—structured into import finance facility (IFF) ₦25 million, lease ₦20 million, and overdraft ₦5 million. The lease facility was used to finance importation of 10 Iveco trailer heads and bodies, while the IFF was utilized for the importation of tires, rice, and matches. The O/D was meant to augment the company's working capital needs.

The lease was secured as follows:

1. Legal ownership of the 10 Iveco trailer heads and bodies financed by the bank.
2. Legal ownership of 5 additional trailer heads and bodies already in the company's fleet.

    The estimated value of (1) and (2) was ₦12 million, both of which were pledged to the bank and covered by a sale-and-lease-back agreement, thus giving the bank repossession rights over the 15 trailers.
3. Comprehensive insurance of the trailers, noting Isle Bank as the first loss payee beneficiary.
4. All assets debenture over fixed and floating assets of the company.

    The O/D and IFF were secured as follows:

1. Lien over stock of brand new Siam and Otani tires worth ₦75 million in the company's warehouse, under dual key locks between IMT and Isle Bank's agent, covered by warehousing agreement. The stocks were warranted in favor of Isle Bank.
2. Repayment of the IFF was as follows:
    a. 10% counterpart funding by IMT at the point of establishment of each letter of credit.
    b. 10% repayment of principal at the point of endorsement or release of shipping documents.
    c. 40% principal repayment within 30 days of release of shipping documents
    d. 40% full balance repayment (principal and accrued interest) within 30 days thereafter.
3. Full and unconditional personal guarantee of Atani, the company's managing director and chief executive officer.
4. Stock level was to be maintained at a minimum of ₦35 million at any point in time.

    Isle Bank fully disbursed the loans. However, IMT did not establish any letter of credit with the bank. Rather, it had an understanding with its foreign suppliers for goods to be shipped to it through Cotonou; payment for the goods would then be remitted by means of telegraphic transfer. The credit officers accepted this arrangement, which deviated from the offer of the facility on terms of L/C. In March 2001, following inability of the company to service and repay due portions of the loans, the bank collapsed accrued interest and outstanding principal of ₦30.24 million on the IFF into its current account. This was done to achieve effective monitoring of the loan.

    In September 2001, the account became delinquent. Interest was not being serviced, while principal repayments had stopped. The compounding balances on the loan worsened prospect of full repayment. In line with this and considering the fact that the facility had expired, a meeting was held between the company and bank, where it was agreed that the facilities should be renewed. The loans were renewed and restructured to a reduced ₦35 million overdraft, secured by:

- Lien over stock of brand new Siam, Otani tires and other imported products worth ₦50 million under existing warehousing arrangement; and,
- All assets debenture covering fixed and floating assets of the company

    In view of the irregular fulfillment of repayment plan, the bank decided that stock release from the warehouse should be strictly against cash lodgment. Thus, apart from the requirement of ₦35 million minimum stock level at any point in time, the warehouse agent should not release any item of the stocks to the customer unless otherwise instructed by the bank.

In June 2002, the account officer went to IMT to get a replacement check for its dishonored check of ₦3.5 million and was told on arrival that Atani had absconded from Nigeria. As the news filtered into the market, other bank lenders to the company started indicating interest in aspects of the company's assets, which they held as collateral for their loans. This situation created problems as the banks disputed claims of ownership of the stock of goods in the company's warehouse.

Isle and Turk banks, for instance, disputed each other's claim of ownership of some items of the stocks, such as tires and matches, as each bank claimed it financed importation of the products. With the confusion about ownership of the stocks, Isle bank asked the warehousing agent to remove its stocks from the customer's warehouse based on the last stock report, which the agent gave to it and showed that the value of stock financed by Isle Bank was ₦50 million. This was not achieved. It was later found out that the agent connived with Atani to also warrant the same stocks in favor of Turk Bank from which it had taken loans using a different company's name. However, Isle Bank's loan preceded that of Turk Bank. But there were goods in the warehouse that had never been reported in the agent's warrants to, and could possibly not have been financed by, Isle Bank.

The agent admitted through a letter written to Isle Bank that its tripartite warehousing agreement predated that of Turk Bank. It promised to unravel what went wrong and report back to the bank with an updated stock position as soon as possible. The promise of sending a verified and updated stock position to Isle Bank was not kept. Meanwhile, the agent's staff that had operated the warehouse also absconded as the matter was being investigated. This compounded and weakened efforts at resolving the problem.

Several failed meetings were held with the police, with a view to amicably resolving the conflicting claims of the banks over stocks in the warehouse, which was seen as the only available source of repayment of part of the outstanding balances on the loans. Each of the banks had furnished the meeting with relevant evidence to justify its claim. However, Isle Bank was not in a position to prove its ownership of the stocks with L/C evidence other than by reference to stock warrants. The contending banks not only received warrants but showed letters of credit that they established on behalf of IMT to import the goods.

When the meetings could not yield fruition, Isle Bank decided to appoint a receiver manager to formally liquidate the company. The other banks reacted by instituting a legal action to restrain the receiver manager from exercising its powers pending determination of the ownership of the stocks. In a different suit, one of the banks had contended that the goods in question were not owned by IMT but by Cezal Nigeria Limited and were financed by it. The bank further argued that IMT never operated from the address supplied by Isle Bank. It maintained that the address belonged to Cezal.

1. The setting of this case study in Nigeria does not imply that the lending transactions took place in Nigeria. The case study is purely for learning and illustration purposes. Thus, the names used for the borrowing company, banks, and individuals in the case study are imaginary and do not relate to any known or unknown companies, banks, or persons in Nigeria or elsewhere.

MEANING OF *LEASING* AND A *LEASE*

Certain concepts describe aspects of leasing as a mode of financing available to individuals, companies, and organizations. In this chapter, I discuss the major concepts and features of leases, with implications for bank lending decisions.

The term *leasing* refers to a mode of financing in which an individual or firm is allowed the use of equipment in return for agreed lease payments. The owner of the equipment is the lessor, while the user of it is the lessee. Thus, a lease is different from an equipment loan. In a lease—unlike equipment loan—the equipment is owned by the lessor, not the lessee.

A *lease* may therefore be defined as an agreement between a lessor and a lessee by which the former permits the latter the use of equipment for an agreed upon period of time. In return, the lessee pays agreed rentals to the lessor. This understanding, including the rights and obligations of the parties, is usually documented in a formal contractual agreement between them.

This implies that lease agreements contain certain terms and conditions. While there may be variations with each transaction, a typical lease will indicate the lease tenor, amount or value of the equipment on lease, timing of rental payments, equipment specifications, end-of-term conditions, and so on.

FORMS AND FEATURES OF LEASES

There are different forms of leases. Yet, in broad terms, all leases may be classified into two main categories: *finance leases* and *operating leases*. The other descriptions of leases are simply variations of these.

As a lessor, a bank acquires physical assets, and as a lender, it grants loan to lessors. Therefore, in accounting for its lease portfolio, a bank could choose to report some of its lease commitments on-balance sheet and others off-balance sheet, depending on the structure and types of the leases. However, choices that banks make must fit with regulatory criteria for lease reporting.

In this chapter, I discuss the meanings and features of finance and operating leases, as well as present aspects of the other derivative forms of leases.

FINANCE LEASE

A finance lease is the most popular type of leasing arrangement. It is defined by IAS 17 as a form of lease under which "the lessor transfers to the lessee substantially all the risks and rewards incident to ownership of an asset. Title may or may not eventually be transferred." Often finance lease is used to refer to *capital lease* or *nontax lease*. Finance leases share the features of a purchase agreement. This implies that such leases may be shown as assets of the lessees and capitalized on the lessees' balance sheets. Thus, this form of leasing envisages that the lessee will eventually become the owner of the equipment at the expiration of the agreed rental payments. It is for this reason that the lessee is entitled to all the risks and benefits of equipment ownership, especially the tax benefits.

OPERATING LEASE

In simple terms, one may define any lease other than a finance lease as an operating lease. Thus, it is the converse of a finance lease. This is in consonance with the broad categorization of leases into finance and operating leases. However, an operating lease is characteristically defined as a lease under which the lessor does not necessarily transfer all the risks and benefits of equipment ownership to the lessee. In most cases, operating leases share the characteristics of *usage* agreements. It is for this reason, unlike finance leases, that operating leases are not required, from an accounting perspective, to be shown on the balance sheet of the lessee. It is pertinent to note that operating leases tend to have short terms, and the lessor reserves the right to repossess the equipment and lease it to another lessee.

OTHER LEASE DERIVATIVES

There are several forms of leases that are derived from the two main categories of leases, *finance* and *operating*, discussed above. The main derivative forms of lease include, but are not limited to, the following.

Assigned or discounted lease

This is a lease in which the lessor collects upfront cash for the lease payments from a funding source and, in return, allows the funding source to collect the future lease rentals. In most cases, the lessor is a leasing company while the funding source could be a particular financier. The arrangement becomes an assigned lease because the leasing company assigns its rights to the future lease rentals to the financier in return for upfront cash. The amount of the loan from the funding source corresponds to the upfront cash and equals the present value of the future lease rentals. Thus, an assigned lease is also referred to as a *discounted* lease.

Leveraged lease

This is a type of lease that involves at least three parties—lessor, lessee, and funding source—to a leasing arrangement. On nonrecourse basis, the lessor borrows money from the funding source to finance much of the equipment cost. The amount borrowed represents upfront cash equivalent to the future lease payment stream. In return for the borrowing (upfront cash), the lessor assigns the future lease payments to the funding source. In most cases, the lessor's equity contribution is small relative to the amount of the borrowing. It usually equals the amount by which the equipment cost is more than the discounted value of the assigned lease payments. The lessor, in a leveraged lease, takes the full tax benefits of equipment ownership.

Full-payout lease

Lessors sometimes do not rely upon the future residual value of leased equipment to fully recover all the costs they incur in leases and to earn their expected rate of return. Instead, they recover all the costs plus expected rates of return on leases from lease payments. This approach informs the meaning of a full-payout lease. Thus, in general, a full-payout lease refers to a lease in which the lessor recovers all costs in, and gains expected rate of return on, a lease from the lease payments—without reliance on future residual value of the leased equipment.

Bundled or full-service lease

A lease is referred to as *bundled* if it includes several additional services for which the lessor pays. Such services include maintenance, insurance, property taxes, and so on. While the lessors are required to pay for these services, they are allowed to build the costs of the services into the lease payments. In this way, lessors easily recover the service costs from the lessees. Thus, a bundled lease is also known as a *full-service* lease.

Closed-end lease

Sometimes lease agreements preclude purchase or renewal options. Where this is the case, it becomes mandatory for the lessee to return the leased equipment to the lessor at the expiration of the initial lease term. The lease is a closed-end one because its underlying agreement does not contain clauses that make it possible for the lessee to purchase the equipment, or renew the lease, at the end of its initial term.

Master lease

A master lease is a lease in which the lessee secures a *lease line of credit* with the lessor. The line of credit allows the lessee to obtain additional leased equipment from the lessor under the same basic terms and conditions to which the parties had originally agreed. Thus, in a master lease arrangement, lessees will not have to negotiate new lease contracts with the lessors whenever they want to lease equipment.

Net lease

A lease is said to be of the net type where the lease agreement makes it obligatory for the lessee to pay for all the costs associated with the use of the leased equipment. Such costs include maintenance, insurance, property taxes, and so on. These service costs, which the lessee pays separately, are not included in the lease rentals paid to the lessor. Therefore, the notion of a net lease depicts the fact that the lessee not only pays the lease rentals but also the costs associated with the use of the equipment.

Single-investor lease

This is a type of lease in which the lessor assumes full responsibility for the funding of the lease transaction. The lessor bears the financing risk of the lease. The risk in question essentially relates to provision of equity and pooling of funds to procure the leased equipment. While the lessor raises the equity funds from personal sources, the pooled funds are borrowed on a recourse basis from various funding sources.

Skipped-payment lease

A skipped-payment lease refers to a lease that does not have a consistent payment stream over its term. For example, the lease rental might be paid only during particular business periods of the year when the lessee's cash flow can accommodate the lease payments. The pattern of rental payments does not fit with the common practice of monthly, quarterly, or other standard payment arrangement.

Step-payment lease

When a lease is structured in a way that allows for either *increasing* or *decreasing* lease rental payments over its term, it is called a step-payment lease. In general, step-payment leases contain payment streams that either increase (step-up lease) or decrease (step-down lease) in amount over the term of the lease. With step-up leases, the amounts of the lease payments increase while with step-down leases, the amounts of the lease payments decrease during the lease terms.

ELEMENTS OF A LEASE TRANSACTION

There are certain basic elements that are present in every lease arrangement. In all cases of leasing transactions there are always events that characterize the *inception, duration,* and *termination* of the lease. The activities that mark the *inception* of a lease include payment by the lessor for the equipment and any incidental transaction costs. Also, at this stage, the lessee is expected to pay any required upfront fees such as *security deposits* and any other advance payments.

The *duration* of a lease is usually associated with receipts by the lessor of stream of *payments,* also known as *rentals,* on the lease from the lessee. As a flexible financing tool, leasing is amenable to various payment arrangements that satisfy the needs of the lessees. For example, the lessee could pay the lease rentals on a monthly, quarterly, semiannual, or annual basis. Also, the lessee could make the payments in advance or arrears. When advance payment is required, the lessee is expected to pay the rental at the beginning of each of the lease periods. In the case of payments in arrears, rental payments fall due at the end of each of the lease periods. There are yet further flexible lease payment arrangements. For example, there could be *equal* or *level* payments in which the lessee pays the same rental amount on the lease during each period of the lease. However, there could also be *step-up*, *step-down*, and *skipped* payments. While the lessee makes the mandatory lease payments to the lessor, considerations of tax benefits, equipment maintenance, and insurance underscore expectations of the parties to the leasing transaction.

The critical issue at the *termination* stage is the residual value of the equipment. The term *residual value* refers to the income that the lessor expects to earn from disposal of the leased equipment at the end of the term of the lease. The lessor may elect to dispose of the equipment through sale. In some cases, the disposal of the equipment may be achieved through a new lease. Residual value may or may not be guaranteed. If the residual value is not guaranteed, the lessor becomes exposed to the risk of failure to realize expected market value of the equipment at the end of the lease term. To mitigate this risk, lessors can take one of two possible actions. They can obtain appropriate insurance cover or secure a guarantee of the residual value in the lease agreement.

The three options available to the lessee at the end of a lease are to *purchase* the equipment, *renew* the lease, or *return* the equipment to the lessor. The lessee may purchase the equipment at its fair market value or at a bargain price with the lessor. If the lease is to be renewed, the renewal terms will include the additional time period after the expiry of the initial lease term and the renewal payment amounts. It should be noted that the lessor receives both the residual value and lease rentals as cash inflows. This implies that if the perceived residual value is high, the lessor is likely to charge fewer lease rentals on the equipment.

RISK ANALYSIS AND MITIGATION

The analysis of a lease proposal, to a large extent, follows the usual pattern of risk identification, analysis, and mitigation discussed in detail elsewhere in this book. However, there could be some variations in information and documentation requirements. From the usual loan request interview, and credit appraisal perspective, lending officers should discuss and analyze the following risk elements.

Justification of request

The loan officer should establish why the lessee needs the particular equipment. Is it to free funds to meet working capital needs? Does the lessee want to expand scope of business operations? Will the equipment help the lessee to satisfy the needs and expectations of customers more effectively? The applicable reason should reflect possible positive impact on the business operations of the lessee.

Technical competence

It is imperative to assess the prospective lessee's technical competence in the use and handling of the equipment. This is necessary to ensure that the lessee puts the equipment to a proper use so as to realize and optimize its acknowledged and potential benefits. A misuse of the equipment might impair its performance and therefore cause default on lease payments.

Cash flow analysis

As in other types of credit facility, cash flow provides the most reliable source of loan repayment in leasing. The analyst should ascertain the capacity of the lessee to pay the lease rentals from cash flows generated from the use to which the equipment would be put. It would also be necessary to analyze financial statements to determine if the prospective lessee's *general* cash flow position is adequate to make the lease payments.

Equipment valuation

The credit analyst should discreetly investigate the cost of the equipment with reliable vendors. In most cases, there would be need to obtain current invoices to authenticate the cost of the equipment to be leased. Cost and risk must be related to certain considerations: Is the equipment movable or immovable? Is it new or used? Can the lessee maintain and service the equipment?

Features and specifications

It is always necessary to obtain detailed technical features and specifications of the equipment to be leased. Some of the required vital information would include the brand name and year of manufacture of the equipment. There would also be the need to document available information regarding the model, part, serial, engine, and chassis numbers of the equipment.

Delivery certification

The lessee must acknowledge receipt of the equipment from the lessor. The acknowledgment will include certification that the equipment was received in good and working condition at the time of delivery. These statements serve as evidence that the lessor supplied the specified equipment—one that is suitable to the needs of the lessee.

OPTIMIZING LEASE PORTFOLIO

A bank should always seek to optimize earnings from its risk assets portfolio. In the case of lease facilities, portfolio earnings could be optimized in certain ways, usually through maneuvering of *pricing, residual value, upfront payments* (such as *security deposits*), *tax incentives, penalty* charges, *fees,* and *commission.* In order to realize their expected earnings, banks should carefully plan their lease portfolios. Besides, the banks should especially strive to achieve efficient *portfolio mix,* comply with applicable *regulatory policies,* and strategically time the *booking of leases.*

In general, lease portfolio mix would be efficient—and helpful in lease planning—if it achieves a good balance between leases and other risk assets that a bank might have in its loan portfolio. However, consideration of tax incentives underscores the need for effective planning of the portfolio mix. For instance, the volume of leases in a loan portfolio impacts the extent to which profit levels could be maximized through the tax shelter of equipment leasing.

The timing of booking of leases is a critical issue from the earnings optimization and financial reporting perspectives. Lessors try to optimize tax incentives by ensuring that capital allowances that they enjoy on qualifying assets exceed the related depreciation charges. For tax purposes, the logic in this action is that depreciation is added back to profit while capital allowance is deducted as expense. Deducting higher and adding back lower figures ensure that the lessors optimize tax benefits.

QUESTIONS FOR DISCUSSION AND REVIEW

1. Identify and discuss the salient issues on which credit analysts should build structuring of asset lease facility.
2. Evaluate the dynamics of the two main types of leases and approaches to managing credit risk applicable to them.
3. Discuss the significance of the parties to, roles in, and conduct of transaction in a leveraged lease.
4. Critically examine the treatment of particular leases as assets or nonassets, and accounting for them on or off-balance sheet in a bank's books.
5. Assess possibilities open to a bank, and limitations it faces, in trying to optimize its lease portfolio.

Hybrid and Irregular Credit Facilities

Chapter 16

Off-balance Sheet Bank Lending, Exposure and Risk Control

LEARNING FOCUS AND OUTCOMES

A bank may grant some category of loans for short-, medium-, or (rarely) long-term utilization depending on financing needs of borrowers. Loans in this category may be referred to as *hybrid* or *irregular* credits. Not only could they be granted for short to long term but they create *contingent liabilities*. Banks report the loans *off-balance sheet* in their books. Common off-balance sheet, hybrid, or irregular credits include *banker's acceptance, commercial paper, bid bond, bank guarantee, advance payment guarantee,* and *performance*

Emerging Market Bank Lending and Credit Risk Control. http://dx.doi.org/10.1016/B978-0-12-803438-5.00016-7
Copyright © 2016 Elsevier Inc. All rights reserved.

bond. Other irregular, or special (though not off-balance sheet) risk assets are created when banks:

- finance *contracts* for the execution of projects or purchase orders
- *syndicate* particular, sometimes multiple, credit facilities for large borrowers
- grant asset acquisition loans to borrowers under terms of some *lease*.

On occasion banks apply off-balance sheet credits to manage their lending portfolio. They do so to check overlending or to avoid direct lending in cash crunch situations. The suspension of lending lasts until existing borrowers substantially pay up or there is a significant increase in deposit base. These are precautionary actions that banks take to ward off liquidity crisis. Notwithstanding its benefits, it is important that banks handle off-balance sheet lending with utmost care. A bank, its customers, and, in fact, the public could be in a mess as a result of mishandling of off-balance sheet exposure. A potential mess is when a bank decides to securitize some assets in its portfolio so as to report them off-balance sheet. It is believed that such practice, especially seen in reckless derivative deals, was the root of the 2007 to 2009 global financial meltdown.

The lessons of the meltdown were very instructive. In their drive to meet budget goals, banks should constantly keep their risk-taking appetite in check. They should also not throw caution to the wind when they want to dress up their loan books. The urge to dress up the loan book often arises when a bank is under pressure to satisfy particular regulatory criteria or guidelines for risk assets creation or reporting. Yet, in doing so, there has to be a trade-off between risk and portfolio earnings goals.

In this chapter, I investigate aspects of off-balance sheet credits. I underscore the significance of off-balance sheet lending and risk assets in loan portfolios of banks in emerging markets. The reader will learn about:

- salient features of special, hybrid, and irregular credit facilities
- intricacies and safeguards in appraising, booking, and managing off-balance sheet credit facilities
- off-balance sheet elements in a bank's lending portfolio and risks associated with them
- why and how banks covet off-balance sheet transactions, and the dangers they portend for the banks

OFF-BALANCE SHEET CREDITS AND RISK EXPOSURE

Off-balance sheet exposures of banks create contingent liabilities that crystallize when the underlying risks associated with them occur. Major off-balance sheet exposures of banks arise from guarantees that the banks issue on behalf of their customers in favor of third parties with whom the customers have business transactions. There are different forms of guarantee that banks grant to their customers. Besides the normal guarantee, there are *performance bonds, advance payment guarantee, bid (tender) bonds,* and so on. Banks also often become exposed to their customers that are engaged in international trade. The exposures are created on documentary credits, especially on *unconfirmed* letters of credits, as well as on bills acceptance, on behalf of the customers.

Making of hybrid credits

It is pertinent to distinguish between *ordinary* or *regular* and *hybrid* or *irregular* credit facilities as used in this book. I have used the terms *hybrid* and *irregular* credits to refer to all off-balance sheet exposures that banks take directly or indirectly on behalf of themselves, their customers, or other counterparties. Further characteristics of off-balance sheet exposures are instructive. Usually off-balance sheet exposures are, by regulatory requirements, treated and reported as contingent credit facilities *below the line.* Off-balance sheet credits have other unique features that distinguish them from ordinary or regular credit facilities. The main differences—besides reporting of ordinary credit facilities on-balance sheet—include the following:

- Unlike ordinary credit facilities, off-balance sheet credits do not entail disbursement of funds by a bank at the time of, or after, the bank's commitment to the underlying transactions.
- With off-balance sheet credit facilities, there would be outflow of funds from the bank to the transactions only if the underlying contingent exposures crystallize. In other words, there would not be outflow of funds from a bank to fund a transaction on which it has a contingent exposure or liability. However, the bank would be called upon to fund the transaction only if the contingent liability that the exposure underlies crystallizes.
- Most off-balance sheet credit facilities could be granted for short-, medium-, or long-term tenor, depending on the special needs of the customers.

There is yet another distinguishing feature of off-balance sheet exposures. In ordinary lending situations, a bank disburses loans once the credit facilities are duly approved, offered, and accepted, and security documentation completed or perfected. However, this is not what happens in the case of off-balance sheet exposures. Disbursement of funds by a bank to redeem its contingent financial obligation when the underlying risks crystallize follows a rigorous due diligence process.

In most cases, the applicable due diligence process involves the following steps, amongst others:

- Certifying the genuineness of claims. In doing so, the bank will also want to certify the rightful beneficiary of the claims.
- Determining the causes of failure of the bank's customer or other counterparty to perform on the underlying transaction.

- Review of the bank's contingent exposure that has crystallized in the debt that it should settle.
- Assessing the exact amount of the contingent liability, or financial obligation, that is payable to the beneficiary.

In some cases, on the basis of findings from investigations, the bank might want to repudiate or contest its obligation. This implies that payment on a contingent liability—or redemption of a bank's obligation on it—when the underlying exposure crystallizes is never automatic.

Cause of interest of banks in off-balance sheet lending

The interest of banks in off-balance sheet credits is primarily in the need of the banks for an alternative portfolio management scheme. Off-balance sheet exposures become even more appealing to a bank when the bank is either overlent, does not want to increase its current lending portfolio through creation of new loans, or wants to satisfy its internal lending benchmarks (such as loan-to-deposit ratio) or some regulatory requirements (such as liquidity ratio) and so on.

Some banks earn substantial fee income from off-balance sheet transactions. Some of the banks even set ambitious targets on off-balance sheet fee income. Once this is done, credit and marketing officers feel challenged to meet the targets. In the process, unfortunately, undue risk taking—as opposed to deliberate risk aversion or mitigation—may be inadvertently encouraged.

In the circumstances, growing of earnings through increasing fee-based income from off-balance sheet exposures becomes a retrogressive business strategy. This will be especially so if a bank creates and bears unworthy contingent liabilities. A bank will fall prey to this credit trap when it becomes obsessed with income generation. It will suffer a similar fate if it neglects proper credit analysis of off-balance sheet lending prior to making a commitment on it.

Need for analysis of off-balance sheet credit proposal

As in ordinary lending situations, off-balance sheet lending embodies credit risk. It would be naïve to wish away the risk aspect because of its seeming remoteness at the time of the transaction that underlies it. Another fallible reason—one that might lead inexperienced or overzealous loan officers to play down risk—is that there is no cash outflow at the outset.

Yet risk characterizes every decision to commit a bank on any form of exposure on lending, whether for current or future credit transactions, as well as on *forward* deals. This implies that there must always be analysis of off-balance sheet credit facilities prior to a bank's commitment. The analysis should be as rigorous as in ordinary, on-balance sheet, lending. As much as possible, all the credit analysis criteria should be employed as a means of hedging against possible future losses that are likely to arise from current off-balance sheet commitments.

This approach will not totally remove all the risks that could be associated with transactions embodying contingent liability. Nevertheless, it mitigates the attendant risks considerably. More importantly, it saves banks the embarrassment of being caught napping. This happens when unanticipated contingent liability crystallizes. A bank would be caught unawares under the circumstances. The embarrassment would be worse if the bank is not in a position to redeem its obligation when the risk crystallizes. The lesson here is that banks should always do proper risk analysis and anticipate and mitigate credit risk.

BANK GUARANTEE

I presented a cursory explanation of the nature of *off-balance sheet* credit exposure of which *bank guarantee* (BG) is an integral part in the preceding topics of this chapter. This category of credit products constitutes a chunk of the lending portfolio of banks. It is therefore pertinent that I expatiate on its characteristics, risks, and how to present it as credit package to mitigate chances of losses to the banks. In doing so, I focus on the major variants of bank guarantee on which banks often take credit risk. Besides *basic guarantee*, the other important forms of guarantee are *performance bond*, *advance payment guarantee* (APG), and *bid (tender) bond*.

It should be noted that bank guarantee facilities, like all the other credit products, must always fulfill particular lending criteria. Thus, approved bank guarantee instruments should:

- contain the specific *amount* of implied financial obligation (i.e., contingent liability) to which lending officers are predisposed to commit the bank in return for some target earnings.
- indicate the *purpose* of the guarantee that should have been established, or corroborated, during its packaging process. The purpose must, amongst other requirements, satisfy the bank's TMD and RAC for the bank to be interested in the request for the guarantee in the first place.
- include the *tenor* during which the guarantee will remain operative, and beyond which it must expire and be canceled. In most cases, bank guarantee is granted as a short-term credit facility, with tenor of not more than 12 calendar months.
- specify *structure* of the transaction that underlies the guarantee. The structure should inform the dynamics of the guarantee and its transaction path. The path envisaged for issuing, releasing, and enforcing the guarantee— as well as for executing its underlying transaction—should always be clearly stated, understood, and complied with by the parties to it.
- define agreed *criteria* for calling in the guarantee, which its beneficiary should follow. For example, in their capacity as guarantors, banks often

demand a certain minimum period of notice of their customers' actual default, breach of events of default, and intention of a beneficiary of guarantee to call in the instrument.

- state other *conditions* under which the bank may redeem its obligation in the event of default by its customer. For example, guarantee beneficiaries must duly establish the customer's default. On occasion, a bank would corroborate, through independent investigation of default claimed by the beneficiary. The bank could also take exception to the claims of the beneficiary based on independent opinion of the investigators.

Of course, bank guarantee could be more or less risky than several other on-balance sheet credit facilities. For this reason, analysis of bank guarantee requests must take cognizance of the usual risk elements encapsulated in the canons, otherwise referred to as the five C's, of lending. In the same vein, identified risks should be mitigated with equal concern for safety of the contingent or implied credit facility. In specific terms, as in every other credit product, bank guarantee should be appropriately secured with a tangible or other form of collateral acceptable to the bank.

Variants of bank guarantee

It is pertinent to appreciate aspects of different types of bank guarantee. How may one isolate situations under which a particular BG would be more suitable than the others? Are there typical illustrations of such situations for the various BG types? In the following discussions, I analyze the major features of variants of bank guarantee. In doing so, I highlight implications of BG features for credit risk analysis and mitigation.

Ordinary bank guarantee

Banks often issue a straightforward, or basic, guarantee on behalf of their customers in favor of particular third parties. This implies that there are always three parties to a bank guarantee transaction. The first party is the bank that issues the guarantee at the request of its customer. The customer on whose behalf the bank issues the guarantee is the second party, while the beneficiary of the guarantee—that is to say, the person to whom and in whose favor the guarantee is issued—is the third party. These parties exist in all classes of bank guarantee transaction, whether in basic BG, APG, performance bonds, or bid bonds. In most cases, the purpose of the guarantee is to assure some third party that a bank's customer will do a particular job or fulfill a particular obligation. Lending officers should analyze and appreciate the cause of every guarantee, as stated or envisaged in a particular business contract or other transaction. Depending on the value of the guarantee, approval might require the endorsement of CRESCO, executive management, or the Board Audit and Credit Committee (BACC).

Ordinary, or basic, guarantee is used mostly by individuals, businesses, and organizations such as government, nongovernmental organizations (NGOs), schools, institutions, and so on to secure transactions with third parties. One reason is that a bank guarantee instills confidence in contracts and transactions between individuals, companies, and organizations. Another reason is that the parties feel secured, willing, and able to confidently close deals. There may be several illustrations of transactions requiring ordinary bank guarantee security. The following two examples are typical.

Where goods are to be sold on credit terms: There are often instances where goods, usually of high value, meant for sale would be released to the buyers on total or part credit basis. The sellers (i.e., the creditors) might then ask the buyers (i.e., the debtors) to provide them with a bank guarantee to assure them that the debts will be settled on agreed due dates. Thus, bank guarantee serves as collateral for the sellers to secure the buyers' debts on the transactions. The bank and buyers are the first and second parties, respectively, while the sellers are the third parties.

Where completion of a job precedes payment: This happens in situations where full payment for jobs or contracts may be processed and made to the persons or firms that did the work *only* after completion of the jobs or contracts. In most cases, this practice is common in public sector contracts where some time is required before money is released to meet such and other payment obligations of government ministries, parastatals, and other government agencies. As an example, let us assume that Nigeria Police contracts a builder to renovate its barracks and is to pay for the job upon its completion. The builder may or may not be paid a so-called *mobilization* portion of the contract amount. However, the contractor (builder) might demand a bank guarantee as collateral to secure any unpaid balance of the work proceeds. If the second party (the Nigeria Police) passes the relevant credit criteria, the bank (first party/issuer) would grant the BG request in favor of the builder (third party/beneficiary).

Performance bond

The need for a performance bond is to hedge against chances of failure by second parties to execute jobs awarded them by third parties. Assume now that the Nigeria Police in the preceding illustration is concerned about the ability of the builder to successfully complete the job. Completion success is measured in terms of capacity (i.e., the technical competence), prudence (largely in the use of mobilization funds), and commitment of the builder to meeting the agreed deadline, quality of finishing, and other contract criteria.

The builder's failure on any of these factors can frustrate completion of the job and therefore poses risk of financial loss to the Nigeria Police. In order to mitigate this risk, the Nigeria Police (now the third party/beneficiary) can ask the builder (i.e., the second party) to provide it with a performance bond from a reputable bank (as usual, the first party). In this example, the bank will have to analyze the creditworthiness of the builder, especially in relation to the sources of concern expressed by the Nigeria Police. If the builder satisfies the applicable lending criteria, the bank may issue the performance bond in favor of the Nigeria Police.

Thus, a performance bond operates essentially as an attestation. In the previous illustration, the bank attests that a named second party who, in most cases, is its customer, is qualified to be awarded a particular job or contract. It further attests that the customer possesses necessary technical skill and competence to successfully execute the contract. The bank issues the performance bond for an amount it agrees upon with the other parties. While the amount may not be exactly equal to the contract value, it should be an approximate of it. Once the bank issues the bond, it assumes full liability for chances that the contractor might fail to do, complete, or satisfy conditions of the contract.

Advance payment guarantee

As the name advance payment guarantee (APG) implies, an APG is usually issued by banks on behalf of their customers who are contractors or second parties in particular contracts or transactions. The purpose of the guarantee is to secure upfront payments to the contractors or second parties by third parties. Thus, an APG secures payment that a third party makes upfront to a contractor for a job awarded to, but not yet executed by, the contractor. The guarantee serves to protect the third party against loss of the upfront payment in the event that the contractor fails to execute the job or satisfy other terms and conditions of the contract.

In general, APG furnishes confidence that third parties (individuals, companies, and organizations) need to make advance payments to contractors. This implies that APG is collateral that secures advance, or upfront, payments. The bank issuing the guarantee also needs to adequately secure itself against risk of probable loss of the advance payment to some cause or the contractor. In order to secure itself adequately, the bank should, in addition to full credit analysis of its customer's request for APG, require the parties to satisfy particular conditions, two of which are as follows:

- Execution of tripartite domiciliation of payments agreement by which the third party awarding the contract agrees to pay proceeds of the contract, including advance payments, to the contractor through the bank.
- Disbursement of funds, including advance payments, to the contractor for the execution of the contract in tranches that reflect certified progressive work milestones to avoid diversion of the contract proceeds.

The bank should still take appropriate collateral to secure its exposure on the guarantee. It is imperative to take collateral, especially if certain credit risks identified in a credit analysis memorandum may not be easily mitigated in the course of envisaged dynamics of the transaction.

Bid (tender) bond

It is a common practice in the award of contracts by government, NGOs, and corporations to require prospective contractors to provide tender bonds in respect of advertised jobs for which they are bidding. This requirement is necessary mainly in institutions that strictly follow due diligence process in the award of contracts. The bids fulfill a number of purposes for parties to a contract. In most cases, the bids do the following:

- represent expression of interest by prospective contractors in particular jobs advertised by the institutions
- indicate the costs that prospective contractors prefer to execute particular jobs if their bids are successful
- state the experience and work competences that prospective contractors possess that may qualify them to handle particular jobs
- specify resources at the disposal of prospective contractors for executing the jobs if their bids are successful
- stipulate the time frame during which prospective contractors might or hope to complete the work

Bids may also be necessary and required in noncontract awarding situations. For instance, tenders may be called for in the sale of particular assets of the government, NGOs, or corporations to interested members of the public. In that case, the bids would serve only two of the aforesaid purposes, namely, expression of interest by prospective buyers in the advertised assets for sale and indication of the prices that the buyers are willing to pay for the assets if their bids succeed.

The risk at issue, one that a bond issued by a bank can secure, is the probability that the individual, company, or organization making the bid might either withdraw midway to the bid or not perform the obligation that the bid entails. In most cases, there are nonrefundable deposits that accompany bid bonds. These requirements impart seriousness to the tender process, remove frivolous bids, and forestall maneuvering of the entire exercise.

There are two possible risks associated with bid bonds. The first risk is the chance that the individual, company, or organization making the bid would lose the nonrefundable deposit. There could also be a risk in possible penalty that might be imposed for failure to honor terms of the bid. It is particularly the second risk that a bid bond is often intended to secure. Thus, the bank will be liable in the event that the risk crystallizes. However, the first risk is borne by the individual, company, or organization making the bid.

In some cases, a customer might request a bank to provide funds to satisfy the nonrefundable deposit condition. If the bank accedes to the request, it assumes total liability on the bid bond. For this reason, it is essential for the bank to adequately secure its exposure on the transaction.

BANKER'S ACCEPTANCE

A banker's acceptance (BA) is a financial instrument or bill used in financing short-term trade obligations or asset-based, self-liquidating, credit transactions. It establishes the liability assumed by a bank that *accepts* a bill to pay the face value of the bill to a named investor. However, the bank's liability crystallizes only in the event that the issuer of the banker's acceptance is unable to redeem it on maturity. Thus, a BA is a *guarantee* by a bank that the drawer of the BA will honor its obligations on it. This implies that the bank commits itself to offset debt on the BA in the event that the drawer fails to do so. Thus, the company that issues the BA and the bank that accepts the BA somewhat share liabilities on it.

The Central Bank of Nigeria (1997) offers a working definition of a banker's acceptance. The bank holds that a banker's acceptance is "a draft drawn on and accepted by a bank, unconditionally ordering payment of a certain sum of money at a specified time in the future to the order of a designated party." In its opinion, "since the instrument is negotiable, title to it is transferred by endorsement." The bank characterizes BA as "a unique instrument in that it is marketable thereby allowing a bank to finance its customers without necessarily utilizing its loanable funds." Doing so, it clarifies the source of financing for the BA when it notes that "instead, funds are provided by investors who are willing to purchase these obligations on a discounted basis." A bank may choose to invest in the banker's acceptance—implying that it directly lends money to the drawer, and consequently assumes primary obligation on the instrument. Otherwise, a more conventional approach is for a bank to assume a contingent liability by adding its guarantee, i.e., acceptance, to the instrument. The guarantee or acceptance is frequently given effect by the goodwill of the bank, especially in terms of creditworthiness.

Nowadays banker's acceptance facility is popular among banks. Its appeal is underscored by applications of it in managing the lending portfolio. This is especially the case when a bank wants to shed credits and bring its loan portfolio within its target growth or size. It also informs the attractiveness of BA to banks, especially in terms of its use to dress the balance sheet.

However, there is a limit to which banks can play bankers' acceptances and, indeed, off-balance sheet risk assets-based contingent liability without attracting sanctions from the CBN. For instance, section 20(1)(a) of Nigeria's Banks and Other Financial Institutions (BOFI) Act 1991, as amended, stipulates that 33.33% of a bank's off-balance sheet bankers' acceptances and guaranteed commercial papers will be applied in determining the bank's statutory lending limit to a single obligor. The phrase *single obligor limit* is defined in Nigeria's BOFI Act, No. 25 of 1991 (as amended) as follows:

> *A bank shall not, without the prior approval in writing of the Bank (i.e. the CBN), grant to any person any advance, loan or credit facility or give any financial guarantee or incur any other liability on behalf of any person so that the total value of the advance, loan, credit facility, financial guarantee or any other liability in respect of the person is at any time more than twenty per cent of the shareholders fund unimpaired by losses … (Section 20 (1)).*

Also, the CBN requires banks to maintain a total exposure on bankers' acceptances and guaranteed commercial papers of not more than 150% of their shareholders' funds unimpaired by losses. There is yet another limiting factor on the appeal of bankers' acceptances. Banks might want to mislead the public, especially external auditors and financial analysts, through improper treatment and reporting of off-balance sheet transactions. The CBN had in 1997 expressed concern that "there had been no proper understanding of the use and reporting of Bankers' Acceptances (BAs) among most banks in the system." It should be noted, according to the bank, that "in many cases, the documentation and reporting of such transactions were not only inappropriate but also misleading." It therefore warned that "any improper reporting of these and similar transactions would be regarded as rendition of false returns and would attract appropriate sanctions" (ibid.). The CBN circular was intended to "ensure standardized and uniform practice and correct reporting … (*and*) engender transparency and accountability by banks on the subject" (ibid.).

Features and risks of banker's acceptance

In Nigeria, the use and reporting of bankers' acceptances transactions must satisfy certain essential requirements prescribed by the CBN (ibid.). The requirements, according to the bank, which also serve as features of BA, are as follows:

- Every banker's acceptance must have an underlying trade transaction for which the bank should hold the title documents to the merchandise as collateral for the acceptance. These documents should be available for examiners' scrutiny.
- An acceptance must be represented by a physical instrument in the form of a draft signed by the drawer and accepted by the bank. All bankers' acceptances must be properly executed by the bank by affixing its ACCEPTED stamp, signature, and date on the face of the bill. These should be made available for the examiners' scrutiny.
- The bank must have a signed agreement for each acceptance it creates.
- By accepting the draft, the bank formally undertakes an obligation to pay the stated sum on the due date. Since the draft is a negotiable instrument,

and may be transferred by endorsement, the bank is obligated to pay the holder of the instrument on, but not before, the maturity date. The bank is therefore the primary obligor.

- The bank may discount its acceptance or sell same to an investor at a discount.
- Funds collected from customers for investment in bankers' acceptances should be treated as deposits until such a time that they are actually invested in the desired instrument.
- Investors in bankers' acceptances should be made aware of the identity of the issuer of the instruments.
- Any bank that, after acceptance, discounts the bill by disbursing its own funds shall report the transaction on-balance sheet as a loan.
- The bank may charge an appropriate fee for accepting a bill.
- The tenor of bankers' acceptances should not exceed 180 days (including renewals if necessary) excluding days of grace beyond which the facility should transform to a loan (on-balance sheet).

COMMERCIAL PAPER

A bank may want to arrange for credit facilities that third parties provide for customers of the bank. This financing arrangement works under particular conditions. There must be a customer—usually a corporate borrower—that is in need of a credit facility that the bank is unable to grant due, perhaps, to *portfolio constraint*. The customer requests the bank to raise the funds it needs at market rate of interest from third-party investors who may be individuals, companies, or organizations. Based on prevailing money market conditions, the bank negotiates the terms of the borrowing with the borrower. Thereafter, and on behalf of the borrower, the bank tries to attract prospective investors that might be interested in providing the money to its customer. The bank fulfills this role with the facility of *commercial paper* offer.

Strictly speaking, and as is commonly understood among bankers, the bank in the foregoing illustration is simply *sourcing*, not lending, funds to its customer. The bank does not assume any credit risk in this process and financial intermediation service. The actual lenders are the third-party investors from whom the bank raises the required funds through sale of commercial paper (CP). Doing so, and in marketing the commercial paper, the bank will be emphasizing the borrower's integrity, cash flow strength, reputation, and creditworthiness, amongst other risk-mitigating factors. Once it has done this, prospective investors make the ultimate decision of whether or not to purchase (i.e., invest in) the commercial paper. The prospective investors solely assume the risk of their investment in the CP—relying, in so doing, on any established *goodwill* of the borrower. It is expected that as rational human beings and economic units, the prospective investors should make good lending decisions. Their purchase of the commercial paper should be based on their independent appraisal of the financial strength (especially, the short- and long-term liquidity and stability) of the borrower.

However, where a commercial paper offer is from a weak source (borrower), it may fail to attract the required funds from the market. In that case, since the bank is not in a position to lend the money directly to the customer, it may decide to add its name to the commercial paper. This implies that the bank is *guaranteeing* the commercial paper. Doing so, it now assumes a credit risk. The nature of the risk assumed by the bank is a contingent liability, in the sense that it's now exposed to an off-balance sheet risk asset. What this means is that in the event that the borrower is unable to redeem the commercial paper on its due date, the investors will have recourse not to the issuer (borrower) but to the bank. At that point, the commercial paper would have crystallized and become on-balance sheet exposure.

In view of the foregoing, banks should always subject requests for commercial paper facility to the rigor of normal credit analysis. In providing a working definition of commercial paper, the CBN underscores its key attributes as a debt instrument. It equates a CP to "an unconditional promise by a person to pay to or to the order of another person a certain sum at a future date." However, as I have pointed out, the CBN clarifies that "such an instrument may or may not carry the bank's guarantee." Therefore, the risk to the bank, according to the CBN, arises "where the bank guarantees the CP to make it more marketable in the money market." In such a situation, "the instrument acquires the force of a BA and the bank incurs a contingent liability."

Other features and risks of commercial paper

In order to have a standardized use and reporting of commercial papers, the CBN prescribes the following essential features of this financial instrument:

- As with bankers' acceptances, funds collected from customers for investment in commercial papers should be treated as deposits until such funds are invested in the instruments. Investors in commercial papers should also be made aware of the identity of the issuers of the instruments.
- Commercial papers should only be guaranteed and not accepted since the intermediating bank is only a secondary obligor.
- When a bank invests in a commercial paper, by disbursing its own funds, the transaction should be reported on-balance sheet and treated as a loan. However, if the bank merely guarantees the instrument, it should be shown off-balance sheet as a contingent liability.
- Where a commercial paper, which had been guaranteed by a bank crystallizes by virtue of the inability of the issuer to pay on maturity, the bank as the *secondary obligor* is bound to redeem its guarantee by disbursing funds to the beneficiary. The transaction should then be reported on-balance sheet as a loan.
- The bank may charge an appropriate commission in line with the bankers' tariff for providing the guarantee.

From the foregoing, it is apparent that a commercial paper could actually become a normal credit facility. But this depends on its treatment by the bank.

Does the bank want to directly invest in the commercial paper by disbursing the required funds to the borrower? Should it wait to see if the commercial paper, as offered by the borrower, would succeed or fail and invest when the latter happens? What will happen if a guaranteed commercial paper fails in the market and, as the secondary obligor, the bank redeems it? In the first two cases, the act of direct investment in a commercial paper exposes a bank to on-balance sheet credit risk. In the third instance, the nature of the bank's liability will change from contingent to direct exposure. In all cases, whether a bank takes credit risk or not underlies the caution it should exercise in marketing a CP on behalf of its customer.

CONTRACT FINANCE, RISKS, AND ANALYSIS

Frequently, banks get involved in complex contract financing—some of which requires huge capital outlay—without adequately analyzing and mitigating risks of the underlying projects. For some banks, it is simply fulfilling to be associated with the execution of certain key economic projects. This is particularly the posture often adopted by the big banks or those that want to be identified with the big industry players or operators. In this craving for ego gratification, the small banks are usually left out, largely because they lack the required financial muscle.

For some economic sectors, such as energy (oil and gas), telecommunications, and government (infrastructure/utilities), contract financing could indeed be a difficult task for banks. The funding requirement might be enormous and perhaps difficult to raise at the time it is needed. For this and several other reasons associated with vagaries of the business environment, there could be uncertainty about the possibility of successful execution of contracts.

Causes of lending risk

Many of the risks of contract financing in the emerging markets arise mainly from some entrenched and unhealthy business ethics and work attitudes of the people. The key sources of risk include the following:

- People's attitude to work: Do people see work as a central life interest? Are people convinced of dignity in labor?
- How business is done: Do people appreciate honest, or rebuff cheap, wealth? Are the people conscientious and show commitment to business agreements?
- Regulation of business: Are government/business relations propitious to, or stifling, individual enterprise? Is the performance reward system efficient, fair, and equitable?

The risk of lending to which banks are exposed in the affected countries is an increasing function of the magnitude of the problems reflected in these questions.

In particular, people's deteriorating value system is a critical consideration. Why should a contractor deliberately divert proceeds of a bank loan meant for the execution of a public sector job to some personal uses? In what context does the behavior of workers who abandon their work on some flimsy excuse find meaning? Bank management must understand and appreciate the risk of lending to contractors in this context to minimize loan losses, especially in the emerging markets. The risk may not be fully mitigated in view of its systemic nature, but it can be considerably minimized.

We can yet explain lending risk from the perspective of differences between public and private sector contracts. In general, government contracts are riskier than those of the private sector. The risk increases with historical records of political instability, bribery, and corruption. Coupled with numerous other sociocultural and economic problems of the emerging markets, the risk of contract financing could really scare banks.

Risk control mechanism

In the final analysis, the banking system remains, and must not shy away from being, the main source of funding for economic development contracts. This implies that instead of being scared by risk, every bank should strive to put in place a foolproof risk assessment and control mechanism to meet its contract financing criteria. One sure way to reduce risk is to subject every request for contract finance to the rigor of credit analysis prior to approval, commitment, documentation, and disbursement of funds.

Risk should be analyzed at two main levels, in addition to the traditional approach discussed elsewhere in this book. On the one hand, lending officers must rigorously analyze the capacity of a contractor to successfully execute the job for which a bank loan is required. The loan officers should, on the other hand, critically evaluate the ability of government, company, or organization awarding the contract to fully and timely pay the contract value. Once these risks are identified, analyzed, and mitigated, the loan officers should focus on monitoring loan disbursement and utilization to forestall diversion of its proceeds or other abuses. One of the effective ways devised by banks for monitoring contract finance is the tying of loan disbursements to progressive certification of work milestones achieved by the contractor.

In this regard, loan monitoring involves site visits by loan officers. The visits help them to determine the extent of the contract work done relative to funds disbursed on it to the contractor. Loan officers should always report their findings objectively to senior management. On the basis of their report, bank management may allow or decline further loan disbursements. In other words, continuing utilization of the loan facility by the contractor depends on whether or not a satisfactory performance is achieved on previous drawings on the loan. Unfavorable findings serve as a default warning sign to bank management for which it should take a precautionary action. Loan officers should follow the usual principles of bank lending and then they cannot go wrong. Evaluating the five C's of lending remains a key requirement for successful lending.

QUESTIONS FOR DISCUSSION AND REVIEW

1. What features of off-balance sheet credits mark them as hybrid or irregular lending?

2. Why and how should off-balance sheet lending be managed to mitigate its credit risk?

3. Write short notes on each of the following:
Performance bond
Advance payment guarantee
Bank guarantee
Bid bond

4. Compare and contrast banker's acceptance and commercial paper.

5. Under what circumstances is a banker's acceptance facility reported on-balance sheet or off-balance sheet?

6. Why do banks covet off-balance sheet transactions? What dangers does the practice portend for bank management?

REFERENCE

Central Bank of Nigeria, 1997. Policy circular BSD/PA/4/97 in Nigeria Deposit Insurance Corporation. Review of developments in banking and finance during the second half of 1997. NDIC Quarterly 7 (3/4).

FURTHER READING

Nigeria Deposit Insurance Corporation (NDIC), 1997. Review of developments in banking and finance during the second half of 1997. NDIC Quarterly 7 (3/4).

Chapter 17

Consumer and Credit Card Lending in Emerging Economies

Chapter Outline

Emerging Market Bank Lending and Credit Risk Control. http://dx.doi.org/10.1016/B978-0-12-803438-5.00017-9
305

LEARNING FOCUS AND OUTCOMES

Consumer lending was for a long time neglected by banks, ostensibly to minimize risk taking in loans to individuals. The neglect was evident in the feeble attention it received from bank management. Banks tended to be averse to inconsequential lending characteristics of many consumer credits. Little activity in accounts, untenable credit risk, low earnings, and multiplicity of unmanageable loan requests and borrowing causes worsened the case against consumer lending products and transactions.

The foregoing factors demanded an increase in loan processing and administration resources that banks could ill afford to provide. Ultimately, this reality degraded consumer lending. It also underlay its neglect and the lack of interest of banks in consumer lending. Few individuals could obtain bank loans, and those who did paid unusually high interest rates and charges.

The emergence of private banking as an up-and-coming market redressed the situation. Coveting and catering to high net worth individuals rubbed off on consumer banking. The Internet after all triggered the boost to consumer lending. This happened against a backdrop of the globalization of the financial system. Once the Internet became widely accepted and accessible, banks keyed their services to it. They started developing and offering Internet-enabled financial services, most of which appealed to individuals.

Most of the products functioned as self-serviced, online transactions that customers could conduct from their homes, offices, and elsewhere. With ATMs deployed at bank premises and important commercial centers, it was easy for individuals to conduct their transactions with ease. The foregoing provided the setting in which banks braced themselves for innovative consumer lending. The credit card is perhaps the most popular, innovative, and revolutionary consumer lending product ever devised by banks. Individuals now use credit cards to borrow money from banks, and they do so anywhere in the world where banking and Internet facilities are available.

Credit cards ease lending by simplifying how individuals can access loans. Unfortunately, this benefit is associated with new credit risk. Issues concerning this benefit—risk dichotomy inform learning outcomes of this chapter. My purpose is for the reader to appreciate contemporary challenges of consumer credit.

Apparently the eagerness of banks to issue credit cards to individuals tends to match the enthusiasm of the cardholders. In this way, credit cards are beneficial to both the banks and cardholders. The reader will learn about:

- major consumer credit products—and be able to compare and contrast them
- features of consumer credits, and lending criteria for them
- global challenges in identifying, assessing, and mitigating credit card risk

OVERVIEW OF CONSUMER LOANS

There are numerous consumer credit products that banks market to individuals. Each product is targeted at particular unfulfilled borrowing need of customers and prospects. In most cases, the products are applied to drive competition. Many banks strive to have strong competitive footing in offering value-added consumer credit products. That would help them to satisfy customers, increase market share, and improve earnings. The myriad identical consumer credit products that banks offer sometimes reflects their desperation in the pursuit of these business goals.

While the foregoing business objectives may be critical to the marketing plan of a bank, paying equal attention to the risks of the credit products is pertinent. There is often a tendency to think that the risks of consumer loans are inconsequential because of their small unit amounts. This thinking might make sense on consideration of a loan granted to one borrower. However, on aggregation of all consumer loans, the volume and pool of risks of lending could be devastating. In some banks, the loan portfolio resulting from consumer lending could sometimes be really enormous. It may not be feasible to analyze all the risks associated with all the consumer credit products that all the banks offer to the market. However, it is possible to identify and analyze risks of the major credit products. My focus is on credit card lending. I present aspects of its features and suggest risk analysis and mitigating measures.

CREDIT CARD RISKS, ANALYSIS AND CONTROL

The credit card is easily the most revolutionary, innovative, and popular consumer lending product that banks ever devised to satisfy the borrowing needs of individuals. It is a welcome innovation for banks and consumers alike. Hitherto, the credit card was a developed country preserve, largely because it functions well in financial markets where cash transactions are relegated to minor expenses. Lately, it has started gaining widespread acceptance in emerging economies. In some emerging economies, the credit card's introduction was mired in suspicion that it is too risky and not foolproof. Reluctantly, banks in emerging economies embraced it, and are now marketing it forcefully to consumers, most of whom are sceptical yet. The credit card represents people's consuming interest in societies characterized by mass consumption—the advanced economies. People fall into the credit card trap when they become incautiously addicted to it. Cardholders who throw caution to the wind easily get caught up in the trap, while spendthrifts are its worst victims. Credit cards are a trap for banks that issue them in reckless disregard of risk. Thus, reckless lending sets the trap into which the banks fall. The foregoing shows that the credit card trap is real but avoidable.

Credit cards were introduced and started gaining acceptance in Nigeria in the aftermath of the 2005 consolidation of the country's banking industry. With increasing competition in the consumer lending sector, some of the leading banks in Nigeria floated the idea of the product. Then Ecobank launched the first-ever *naira*-denominated credit card in Nigeria back in 2006. Now the credit card is coveted by all the banks in the country. Unfortunately, some of the banks that pioneered the credit card in Nigeria got badly burned—and, for this reason, tinkered with it.

It is doubtful that banks in emerging economies have imbibed in the risk management philosophy of credit card. Credit literature richly tells of global risk attendant on issuing and using credit cards. Practical experience of banks and cardholders in the international financial markets corroborates the literature. Both cases are instructive and raise three pertinent questions:

- Have banks in emerging economies learned the lessons of experience of their counterparts in developed nations and financial markets?
- How can banks in emerging economies develop an appropriate methodological framework for managing global credit card risks?
- What options do parties to credit card lending have in handling the global frustrations of credit cards arising from such factors as inefficient or failure of Internet service?

Banks in emerging economies should learn the lessons of experience of their counterparts in developed economies. This way they can develop appropriate methodology for managing the risks of credit cards.

DEFINING CREDIT CARD RISK

It is necessary to review possible risks of credit cards, the requirements for effective credit analysis, and management devices to minimize probable loan losses. Certain questions are pertinent and must be asked to define the scope of my inquiry. What are the likely risks of credit cards in emerging economies? How should the risks be effectively analyzed to articulate likely patterns of their incidence? Is it possible to entirely forestall the occurrence of credit card risks? In what pragmatic ways can the risks of credit cards be mitigated? These and similar questions are subsumed in certain key credit issues, including probable flawed documentation, maneuvering of security of cards by fraudsters, disputation of transactions, incidence of default, and loan remedial hitches.

Risk in credit card lending has three main connotations. The probability that cardholders will default—i.e., will be unable to service and repay drawings on their credit cards—establishes the first level of risk. At the second level of risk, there are chances that cardholders might dispute some transactions and charges as "spurious." When this happens, if there is strong evidence, the affected merchants might be compelled to "charge back" the related drawings. This risk arises mainly in cases of stolen and unauthorized use of credit cards. Phony cardholders could compromise themselves by disputing legitimate charges on their credit cards. The third connotation of risk is the danger that activated credit cards may fall into the wrong hands due to some acts of the cardholders. Several factors cause the risks of credit card lending. The common factors include flawed documentation, breach of security of the card, possible disputation of transactions, forged and lost cards, hidden or built-in costs, misapplication of credit card, and multiplicity of credit cards. I discuss aspects of each of these risk factors below.

Flawed documentation

Documentation of credit card lending in emerging economies is anything but foolproof. Usually it is avoidably scantily documented. Documentation at best consists in filling out a loan application form. In general, the usual rigor of credit analysis is left out. This is quite a flaw in credit card lending but one that can be easily rectified. The reduction of loan appraisal and records to perfunctory documentation leaves room for risk of insufficient data on which effective lending often depends. However, banks tend to mitigate this risk through the Know Your Customer (KYC) philosophy and its strict imple-mentation. Lending officers must document and be satisfied with information about the character of the borrowers, their loan repayment track record, and evidence of their residence and places of functioning business. Cardholders must in particular be current or savings account customers of the bank. The foregoing risk mitigation approach is considered satisfactory for the appraisal of credit cards requests. The method invariably approximates the normal credit analysis common to ordinary credit facilities and could mitigate the risk of deficient documentation.

Breach of security of card

It may be possible for fraudsters to maneuver security of credit cards and swindle banks and cardholders. This risk annually causes huge loan losses to banks in developed countries. In such countries, credit card culture has been effectively entrenched as a borrowing, payment, and exchange mechanism. Whenever it has occurred, it has always presented a puzzle to unravel how security features of credit card, such as holograms, were manipulated to perpetrate fraud in cardholders' accounts. In some cases, there would be a tendency to suspect collusion with bank staff—those who have responsibilities in the credit card scheme. Yet with the facility of advanced technology at the disposal of fraudsters, it might be possible for them to maneuver security features of credit cards. Banks and cardholders in emerging economies should mitigate the risk of infringement of security of credit cards by being cautious and adopting the following measures.

- The banks should fortify confidentiality of cardholders' personal identification number (PIN) and, in doing so, place accountability for lapses on designated officers who are assigned cards operations and management duties.
- Cardholders should promptly report loss of their credit cards to appropriate authorities and departments of the banks to forestall their use by fraudsters to swindle the banks.
- Cardholders should notify the responsible officers of the banks of their loss of memories of their PIN in good time. The notification is to enable the banks carry out necessary security checks and, if satisfied with findings, facilitate change of the *lost* PIN.
- Cardholders should always ensure, especially while in the banking halls to make cash withdrawals, that they preserve the confidentiality of their transactions.
- There should not be any circumstance or consideration on which cardholders can disclose their PIN to their spouses, relatives, and others.

The adoption of these measures will, to a large extent, help to effectively mitigate the risks of credit card lending. Above all, the banks should continually educate their customers on the identified risks and management requirements. Banks should devise an appropriate customer enlightenment program to achieve this objective.

Disputation of transactions

The tendency of some cardholders to dispute transactions on their credit cards underscores the sore nature of its risk. Disputes over purchases or other expenses charged on credit cards are a common occurrence. Financial instruments such as checks, or other serious official funds withdrawal documents, are not required to make drawings on credit card. Instead, a microchip for data storage is embedded in the electronic credit card to enable banks and merchant acquirers to retain information on transactions in cardholders' accounts. With an appropriate electronic card reader device, banks and acquirers could retrieve data stored in the memory chips for transaction review, analysis, or other official use.

As for cardholders, the only evidence of their drawings are improvised forms that they fill out, and miniature electronic withdrawal loose slips produced by a POS, card reader, or other decoding machine. Besides, the monthly account statement sent to cardholders, unlike in demand deposit accounts, contains sparse details. However, the customers' lodgments are evidenced by the usual deposit slips. These shortcomings cause confusion about credit card transactions. An otherwise genuine transaction can become unnecessarily controversial under the circumstances. Contentious issues, in most cases, reflect failings in effective tracking of transactions and charges on credit cards. Often lapses that trigger disputes originate in cardholders' ignorance of the mechanics of credit cards.

In order to mitigate the risks, banks should improve the quality of statements of accounts for credit card products. In this context, quality is defined by the comprehensiveness, regularity of dispatch, and predisposition to clarifying the contents of the statements of accounts whenever the need to do so arises. It is particularly necessary to have easily verifiable data in the statements of accounts. For instance, cardholders should be able to easily verify interest computation and charges to their accounts.

Forged and lost cards

Credit card fraud has become commonplace and manifests itself mainly in fraudulent use of stolen credit cards. Besides loss of credit cards, fraud is perpetrated through forgery. Armed with a stolen or counterfeit credit card, a fraudster can hack into a credit card database or a cardholder's computer. Sadly, while credit card lending is booming in emerging economies, answers have not been found to equally burgeoning credit card fraud.

Hidden, or built-in, costs

Banks in emerging economies inadvertently contribute to credit card risk—the chance that a cardholder will default—through insensitive pricing of the product. This risk originates in a craving of the banks for profit. Driven by budget goals, banks arbitrarily hike up interest rates, fees, and commissions on drawings on credit cards. An unethical dimension of this practice is that chunks of income that banks appropriate from credit card accounts are really undisclosed or hidden costs. This is tantamount to taking undue advantage of ignorant cardholders, who, in the excitement of obtaining credit cards, bother less about the accounts.

Indebtedness on credit cards escalates unnecessarily with intrinsic and built-in costs. Informed cardholders become irate when they notice built-in, or intrinsic, charges in their account statements. They will not only want to reject the charges, they may want to get back at the bank by defaulting deliberately. Without full disclosure on credit card costs, cardholders are likely to repudiate their indebtedness on it. The public may over time renounce their faith in credit cards.

Misapplication of credit card

Many people misuse their credit cards and, surprisingly, banks in emerging economies tend to encourage the abuse. On occasion, cardholders utilize credit cards as though they are an overdraft, or line of credit, facility. This mode of utilization, rather than strictly to pay for purchases or services, embodies credit risk attendant to misapplication of credit cards. Overdrafts and line of credit facilities never have common attributes as credit cards. Abuse of credit cards is preponderant in situations where this distinction is blurred. The possibility of default increases when credit cardholders are able to draw cash on their cards *over the counter* or through ATMs. Such manner of withdrawal is typical of an overdraft line. Champions of financial intelligence kick out against the consumption orientation of credit cards. A craving of cardholders for credit card spending informs the observed high rate of default.

Multiplicity of credit cards

The cutthroat world of consumer lending reflects in indiscriminate issuing of credit cards—on occasion to nondeserving individuals. Multiple credit cards, issued by different banks, in an individual's possession are a common sight in emerging economies and elsewhere. The tendency is for individuals to want to use all the credit cards at their disposal, even though they really need less money than the cards altogether afford them.

Role of the internet

The Internet is a revolutionary technological breakthrough, one that impacts all facets of human activities. It is to the credit of the Internet that all humanity now lives in a so-called global village. However, just as its benefits to mankind are innumerable, the Internet has also dislocated the natural tendencies of most people in profound ways. One of the unbeneficial side effects of the Internet is its use to defraud banks and credit cardholders. Hacking into computers and credit card databases to perpetrate fraud, which the Internet makes possible, remains a worrisome albatross for banks and credit cardholders alike. A related global problem is the ignominious role of technology in facilitating credit card fraud. Nowadays technology allows fraudsters to clone themselves (or create multiples of themselves) and perpetrate credit card fraud! This is one of the crucial challenges in credit card lending in emerging economies.

INCIDENCE OF DEFAULT

As banks do in other lending situations, it is proper for them to assume that some cardholders will default. Default arises when obligors are unable to service their credit cards and repay drawings on the cards in accordance with the terms and conditions of the cards. However, there is a global challenge in any attempt to check default in emerging economies. Poor or absence of consumer records encourages default in such economies. In emerging economies, individuals who default on credit cards can easily change addresses and may never be traced. Whereas in the developed world, this cannot so easily happen as official records of individuals—from the day they were born or entered a country—are properly documented.

How should banks in emerging economies mitigate incidence of loan default in credit card products? Are applicable risk-mitigating techniques foolproof in all lending situations? What alternative risk control devices can banks in emerging economies put in place to forestall loan losses?

In general, loan default arises when the obligor is unable to service their credit facility and repay principal amounts in accordance with the terms and conditions that the bank agrees on with them. It would seem that banks in emerging economies rely on KYC, customers' integrity, and demand deposit account (DDA) turnover to make credit card lending decisions. This implies that banks tend to place risk analysis and control emphasis on track records of borrowers in their banking transactions. They do so with a sense of responsibility.

As well, the banks may be adopting a stricter risk control measure when they decide to approve credit card facility for only, or mostly, those that have formal employments. The rationale behind this risk control posture is that loan default is likely to be minimized when the obligor is an individual that has an adequate, regular, and predictable source of income. For this reason, it would be riskier to grant credit card facility to self-employed individuals. But this is a fallible assumption as certain self-employed people may be more creditworthy than those engaged in formal employment. Self-employed people often have strong cash flows from operations and therefore are not likely to default on their credit card obligations.

Yet the security comfort offered by verifiable jobs in which cardholders are engaged may be negated by unexpected vicissitudes of employment. Loan default risk tends to increase when cardholders lose their jobs because the source of loan repayment invariably becomes uncertain. In much the same vein, if risk analysis was based on the credibility of cardholders' employers, incidences of labor turnover would probably invalidate otherwise plausible conclusions.

Perhaps the risk-taking anxiety of banks in emerging economies becomes more evident largely in the restriction of borrowing limits of cardholders to not more than certain maximum *low* amounts. For instance, based on analysis of particular customers' loan requests, a bank can set maximum borrowing limits at amounts ranging from, say 25,000 to 50,000 dollars per cardholder.

DEFAULT DYNAMICS

Some cardholders do not take cognizance of their cash flows while using credit cards. This smacks of an abuse of privilege. It is believed that cardholders who show this trait might have questionable character. In this category are some consumers who deliberately default on their credit cards. They can repay credit card debts but default, ostensibly for some personal or inexplicable reasons.

Many consumers use credit cards as though they are debit cards. It is bad enough that such consumers tend to forget that the money they spend on their credit card is not their capital and must be repaid with interest and commission. Ideally, banks should not issue credit cards to individuals who do not have the capacity to pay debts charged on their cards. Yet some default results from impaired financial capacity of cardholders. This happens when cardholders' cash inflows unexpectedly become deficient relative to their cash outflows. Often distortion of forecast cash flows underlies financial incapacity of cardholders.

There could also be some unforeseen conditions, or happenings, that adversely affect a cardholder's finances. The vagaries of business, employment issues, and the so-called *force majeure* are some of the critical conditions that cause loan default. Under the circumstances—and this is a commonplace in many emerging economies—cardholders might default on their credit cards through no fault of their own. A bank that issues unsecured credit cards exposes itself to risk of possible default and loan loss. The risk increases with the tendency of individuals to borrow clean. Ironically, the psyche of borrowers impels them to want to repay secured credits. Banks should tap into this disposition to secure credit cards that they issue. Taking appropriate collateral is always good comfort. However, the onus is on government to create dependable consumer databases, strengthen the legal system, and empower law enforcement agencies. These actions will check default and exploitation of consumers through credit cards. In general, banks in emerging economies make imprudent loans when they issue credit cards uncritically to consumers who are insensitive to credit card debt.

MITIGATING CREDIT CARD RISK

Like in other lending situations, banks must strive to mitigate risks of credit card lending. They should put an effective risk control framework in place if they must not be caught in the credit card trap. This requires a clear understanding of issues involved in mitigation of the risks. But it also demands proper analysis of the peculiarities and practicalities of credit cards as a credit product in emerging economies.

Defining risk mitigation

In principle, risk mitigation in credit card lending has largely the same import as in other forms of bank lending. The subtle difference between them lies in the monitoring mechanism for the credit card transaction cycle. The transaction path and dynamics of a credit card demand collaboration between a bank and external parties—the acquirer, merchants (also referred to as retailers in credit card lending parlance), and credit cardholders.

The acquirer, usually a financial institution, processes credit card transactions on behalf of the parties. It fulfills three critical roles in the credit card transaction cycle. The acquirer does the following:

- acknowledges and maintains records of transactions in a credit card's utilization cycle

- distributes and remits payments for purchases made by cardholders to related merchants
- updates and informs banks of their liability for purchases made by cardholders, and the resultant debts

This is not the case in other lending situations. In normal lending, banks deal with counterparties whose credit risk they try to mitigate. Thus, in credit card lending, risk mitigation involves a process of integrating a series of actions of a bank, acquirer, merchants, and cardholders to check acts that impart risk to the credit card and render it unhealthy as a payment system. Such acts taint and discredit credit cards. It remains a global challenge to check tainting of credit cards by discreditable acts of unscrupulous individuals.

Credit card risk will also be significantly mitigated when it is possible to trace elusive cardholders who are in default. Thus, consumers should provide referees to back their credit card applications. Fulfilling the requirement of references for credit card accounts—as in opening current accounts—will go a long way toward ameliorating credit card risks. Therefore, banks should insist on verified references on credit card applicants as a risk-mitigating measure.

Structuring loan facility in credit cards

Structuring a credit card facility could be a thorny issue sometimes. Do all banks in emerging economies structure credit card lending well? Observed problems attendant on granting credit card facility show that all is not well with consumer loan packages offered by banks in emerging economies. Often the problems at issue are laid at the door of credit structure. For credit card lending, I now address the question of appropriate structure.

Question of appropriate structure

Proper loan structuring is the starting point for effective risk mitigation in credit card lending. Appropriate structure reflects an arrangement that ensures that utilization and drawings on a credit card are in accordance with terms agreed between a bank and cardholder. The elements that define credit card structure include its purpose, tenor, utilization, dynamics, security, pricing, mode, and source of repayment.

Critical issues for banks in emerging economies border on risk aversion. Firstly, a bank must decide the limit on an approved credit card. The limit defines the value of a credit card (i.e., the maximum amount of credit that a bank grants to the cardholder). Secondly, a bank should clearly define and enforce limitations to drawings on a card (i.e., its mode of utilization). It can do this in collaboration with accredited merchants. The crux of structuring in credit card lending is really about how to understand and harmonize defining needs of applicants with those of a bank.

In order to structure a credit card well, lending officers must do all of the following:

- Obtain credit bureau report on credit card applicants. The report provides information on the applicants' credit history and ratings, both of which help to judge their creditworthiness. Unfortunately, credit ratings are as yet at a very rudimentary level, if actually available, in many emerging economies.
- Verify amount and sources of regular incomes of credit card applicants. Credit card must be issued based on the conviction that a cardholder is able to service and repay drawings on it.

Should banks in emerging economies standardize credit card structure? This question underlies the problem at issue. One of the lessons learned from the experience of banks in developed economies is that standards vary among different groups of cardholders. Differentiation of credit cardholders is informed by their varying risk characteristics. So, the challenge here is really about how banks in emerging economies can discriminate low- from high-risk cardholders and apply appropriate credit card structure to differing groups. Low-risk cardholders are usually individuals who have excellent consumer credit records. Such persons do have known and verifiable credit histories and ratings. Three features distinguish high-risk credit card applicants. They do not have good consumer credit records. Either they have insufficient credit histories, or they do not have credit records and ratings at all.

Collateralizing credit card facility

In most cases, credit card lending is unsecured. Incidentally, when banks lend clean, they take avoidable credit risk that could snowball into crisis of delinquent debts. For this reason unsecured lending should be a preserve of low-risk cardholders—those who meet the criteria of a bank's prime customers—and applicants who satisfy other credit criteria of the bank. Like the prime customers, such applicants are often in a different league.

Another lesson to be learnt from the experience of banks in developed economies is that collateral is necessary to secure credit cards issued to high-risk applicants. Typically, collateral is cash that the credit card applicant has in a time or fixed deposit with the bank. The cash must be evidenced by a certificate of deposit issued by the bank in favor of the credit card applicant. The bank lends a certain percentage of the cash collateral to the applicant, based on analysis of particular credit issues, including the bank's credit policy at the time. Doing so, the bank taps into the benefits of cash-collateralized credit card lending—liquid collateral, minimal risk, high yield, and self-liquidating and funded credit. These benefits are realistic provided that banks closely monitor cash-collateralized accounts. This ensures that cardholders do not draw more than their approved percentage of the cash collateral. Also, the bank must check the tendency of cardholders to "charge over" their credit card limits. Overall, the success of credit card lending borders on institution of effective controls at every level of its implementation. This has been a global challenge for banks and difficult for them to achieve.

Standing of cardholders that informs lending to them either clean or secured could change, depending on their current credit ratings and sustainability of their ratings. A bank may upgrade high-risk cardholders to the status of low-risk cardholders and substitute their secured with unsecured credit cards. This happens when such cardholders build up satisfactory but verifiable credit histories and achieve good credit ratings. In the same vein, low-risk cardholders may be downgraded to the status of high-risk cardholders and asked to secure their credit cards. This happens when their credit ratings drop significantly. Such cardholders will need to recover to their pre-downgrading standing before they can regain their low-risk status.

CONTROL OF CREDIT RISK

The mechanics of credit card lending must be transparent to the public, especially to credit card applicants. Bankers should not mystify credit cards. In fact, a road map to mitigation of credit card risk should not be mystifying. If it is, then success will be elusive. Rather than mystify the public, credit card lending must bear the hallmark of transparency. In this way, bank management will gain the confidence of the public in credit card lending over time. Transparency is achieved when a bank's offer of a credit card to an individual approximates to a loan agreement. The offer must spell out in detail pricing, fees, commission, and penalties (if applicable) on a credit card. Full disclosure of all elements of credit card lending should inform an individual's decision to accept or decline a credit card and enhance the integrity of the credit process. Doing so, banks must demonstrate an earnest desire to control credit card risks. In order to do so successfully, bank management should keep an eye on risk at all times. Besides, it must strengthen internal oversight of lending, to make it responsive to emerging threats.

Hoping for a foolproof device

Authorities of the banking system in emerging economies are ever looking to institutionalize a foolproof framework for credit card lending. Unfortunately, this goal remains elusive. While the authorities work on this project, banks should take expedient actions to deal with credit card risk. Specific measures that mitigate global credit card risk include default control, proper documentation of lending, and transparent reports. Also, detailed and self-explanatory information on credit card drawings and applicable charges is an essential step to mitigating credit card risk.

In order to mitigate the risk of disputation of transactions, banks should improve the quality of statements of accounts for credit cards. Quality should be defined by the comprehensiveness, regularity of dispatch, and predisposition to clarifying the contents of statements of accounts whenever the need to do so arises. It is particularly necessary to have easily verifiable data in the statements of accounts. For instance, cardholders should be able to easily verify interest computation and charges to their accounts.

Overall, three key resources are essential for the success of risk mitigation in credit card lending. In the first place, credit card operations must be efficient. Secondly, as a high-tech credit product, reliable and up-to-date IT functions must drive credit card lending and operations. Thirdly, effective internal control system must be in place to ensure regular conduct of inspection and audit of credit card operations.

INSTITUTIONALIZING THE CREDIT CARD PROCESS

There must be an ordered way for the conduct of credit card transactions. Risk tends to mitigate when the dynamics of credit cards are well ordered. A standard process for signature verification, card authorization, and assurance of safety of cardholders' PINs—including prompt notification of lost or stolen credit cards—must be institutionalized. Cardholders must always look at their credit card reports with a critical eye. Two of the stages of a credit card transaction—swiping of card on POS and signing of POS slip as evidence of transaction—demand a cardholder's attention to mitigate risk. Cardholders should witness swiping of their cards on a POS, and verify amounts charged on their cards before signing the POS slip. These actions corroborate credit card reports.

Perhaps the greatest challenge in credit card lending in emerging economies is how to ensure that someone who is in possession of, and can use, a particular credit card is its authentic owner. In paying a check, for instance, a teller relies on signature, picture, and confirmation of the accountholder to forestall fraud. A similar process is followed to pay a traveler's check (TC). In the case of the latter, the TC holder signs their signature—the same as on their account mandate with the bank that issued the TC to them—in the presence of the teller. The teller then follows this with telephone confirmation of the TC. Surprisingly, these steps that are usually followed strictly and have proven effective in mitigating fraud in some of the international payment systems are not enforced or considered in credit card lending.

Security of credit card

Banks should continually educate cardholders on credit card risks that border on breach of security in handling and at points of use of the cards. Appropriate cardholder enlightenment programs will go some way toward checking risk. A credit card should be well protected with immutable security features, such as holograms.

Credit card database

The most cogent reason for a reliable and credible credit card database in emerging economies is to establish the genuineness of credit cards that banks issue to consumers. Without a comprehensive and regularly updated database, it will be difficult to establish the authenticity of credit cards. As a risk-mitigating measure, an up-to-date database provides information on lost, stolen, or countermanded credit cards. Also, information on social security numbers, credit histories, and ratings of credit cardholders is stored on credit card databases. In emerging economies, unfortunately, lack of these data undermines risk management in credit card lending. Easy but secured access to credit card databases by authorized lending officers helps to mitigate credit risk.

GLOBAL CHALLENGES FOR BANKS IN EMERGING ECONOMIES

The "internationally active banks" must work on improving credit card risk management. This task is especially necessary and urgent in emerging and developing economies where credit card lending still face a myriad of teething problems. Let me now provide international perspective on the problem and discuss the relevant factors at issue.

International perspective

Our perspective on credit card lending largely builds on lessons of experience of its origin and operation in the United States and other developed countries. We cannot talk of credit cards as a bank lending device without acknowledging the pioneering role of the Bank of America in issuing Bank-Americard in 1958. Subsequently, between the mid-1960s and late 1970s, Bank of America permitted banks in the US to issue BankAmericard under franchise. But it was not until 1977 that the franchisees integrated their BankAmericards and formed the present-day VISA. In doing so, VISA emerged as the first internationally acknowledged credit card brand in the world.

Now, 38 years on, credit cards are yet facing some avoidable global challenges as a payment system. For instance, many cardholders complain about their inability to easily use their credit cards in some countries—or outside their countries. In fact, cardholders from countries regarded in the international financial markets as risky, many of which are in the class of emerging economies, suffer this setback most. In these circumstances, the fate of such cardholders hangs in the balance when they travel out of their countries of domicile. The problem is even worse for cardholders who try to charge their online purchases on their credit cards. Some online stores reject credit card transactions originating from particular countries. This negates the spirit of credit cards as an international payment system.

I review contemporary global challenges in credit card lending against a backdrop of the foregoing background. I believe issues raised in the review hold important lessons for banks in the emerging and developing economies.

Underwriting of credit cards

One of the critical success factors in credit card lending is the ability and willingness of banks to underwrite credit cards that they issue. This implies that banks must take the credit risk of, and therefore total financial responsibility for, credit cards that they issue to their customers. This success requirement is taken for granted in developed financial markets. However, underwriting of credit cards is not always appealing for banks in emerging economies.

A bank will not want to issue, or underwrite, credit cards for individuals who do not qualify for clean lending based on their credit histories and ratings. Banks get cold feet when they are unable to certify that particular credit card applicants have proven ability to service and repay drawings on their cards. A way out, one to which banks in developed countries now easily resort—and those in emerging economies should adopt—is to opt for secured credit card lending. Once low-credit-rated applicants provide liquid collateral, a bank becomes indifferent to the distinction between secured and unsecured credit cards in making underwriting decisions.

Secured credit cards leave an opening for the banks to tap into a new profitable market. Banks covet this market because of its low-risk profile—lending is cash collateralized and self-liquidating within the transaction cycle of a credit card. Another way of reducing risk on a first-time credit card applicant or someone with a poor or low credit rating is to tie the applicant's card to a good credit user account. Thus, the person with good credit record becomes a guarantor and is held accountable for the low-rated or high-risk account. It is also possible for a low-risk credit cardholder, or creditworthy first-time credit card applicant, to underwrite their credit risk. This is done when the cardholder or applicant pledges an amount equivalent to their credit card limit in a fixed or time deposit with the bank that issues their credit card. The bank then exercises lien over the deposit and holds it as security for the credit card.

Control of loss exposure

For consumers in developed countries, credit cards have become a way of life. This has led to an explosion of exposure of banks and default on credit cards, a situation that now impinges on its development as a payment system in emerging economies. But banks will not want to let the problem rest. The banks continue to look for, and devise, ways out. An intriguing aspect of the banking culture in America—one that is now seen as a phenomenon in the industry—is the willingness of banks to reschedule debt on a credit card. The banks do so with a sense of responsibility.

Exposure to loss on a credit card often results from arbitrary pricing, hike in costs (e.g., fee and commission), and escalation of debt, all of which are characteristic features in the nature of credit card lending. One of the ways the banks have achieved remediation of default and loss exposure is to grant regular loans to cardholders to pay off their delinquent credit card debts. This action serves three main beneficial purposes for cardholders:

- it reduces financial burden on credit cards for cardholders by substituting less expensive regular loans for their costly credit card debts
- it frees credit cards encumbered by unpaid drawings and charges from cost-induced default
- it makes it possible for cardholders to continue to enjoy the use of their credit cards while paying back debts on the regular loans piecemeal at their income pace

It is doubtful that banks in emerging economies can easily grant such reprieve to their credit card customers. This disparity between the developed and emerging economies hinders evolution of a global uniform methodology for credit card lending administration.

Risk-based pricing

Global best practices link credit histories and ratings of individuals to credit card lending risk. Thus, risk determines pricing of credit cards, such that different groups of individuals may incur varying credit card costs depending on risk-influenced pricing of their credit cards. Another way to demonstrate this price discrimination is that unsecured credit cards are priced lower than secured credit cards. This is because the former is usually issued to prime or riskless consumers. The latter, on the other hand, is issued to high-risk consumers.

In both cases, risk is defined in terms of historical credit track record of the consumer. The import of this practice is that banks must have easy access to reliable credit histories and ratings of consumers held on regularly updated databases. In this way, the banks can rightly price credit cards for various risk groups of consumers. Herein lies a problem for banks in emerging and developing economies. Most emerging economies do not have documented details of consumers. Even where consumer information exists, it is often not held on easily accessible databases. In such situations, it becomes difficult for banks in emerging economies to price credit cards well or optimize returns on its pricing.

It must be noted that documentation of consumer details is done by some public sector agency as a social responsibility. At the private sector level, consumer details are also independently documented by credit assessment institutions (i.e., the credit bureau). This is why it is possible for banks in the developed world to forestall credit card pricing that is insensitive to risk. Besides, banks in developed economies can promptly track consumers who have delinquent credit card debts, quite unlike the case of banks in emerging economies.

Credit scoring of applicants

Consumer details that help to establish credit attributes of individuals may be obtained from databases of external credit assessment institutions (ECAI). The requisite information may also come from a bank's internal credit risk data based on its historical and current consumer lending experience.

At a rudimentary level, the use of data from ECAI is common. But in pursuit of more accurate consumer credit scoring, some banks blend their internal credit risk data with those of ECAI. With increasing sophistication of consumer behavior leading to unanticipated credit risk and credit card losses, some banks now resort to adaptive algorithms as a fallback option. If regularly updated, models in the algorithms family keep banks abreast of changing characteristics of particular consumer credit market segments. However, there is a challenge in the use of algorithm models for consumer credit scoring.

The models rely mostly on historical data for established consumer markets. Banks tend to be at a loss when they have to apply the models to new consumer credit markets. It is unrealistic and difficult to model unknown characteristics of a real credit risk. In the circumstances, the likely financial performance of prospective credit card applicants in this category defies the risk-predictive ability of the algorithm models. The foregoing poses a two-pronged challenge. It is one thing for banks to have accurate credit data and scoring for credit card applicants; it is another thing for the banks to do so using algorithm models in new market segments.

Besides, many banks in emerging economies lack the ability to track and apply credit attributes of credit card applicants in functional algorithms. Yet the pro-models academics insist on the use of algorithm functions for consumer credit scoring. Here again we see the flaw in the use of models as analytical frameworks for credit decision making and risk management.

Statistical loss forecasting

The use of mathematical models to forecast losses in credit card lending is also common. As in credit scoring using adaptive algorithms, lenders used to rely on historical consumer credit data for loss forecasting. In order to make forecasts, the lenders needed information on delinquent debts and charge-offs. Analysis of delinquency rates and trends in charge-offs provided insights into probable provisions for loan losses.

With continual improvement on this analytical framework, the lenders now use delinquency flow models analysis. Segmented vintage analysis augments analysis of delinquency flow models to produce more reliable outcomes. Again, as in the algorithm models, this approach works where consumers have common characteristics that make it possible to pool and segment them for study and analysis. Where it is difficult to segment the market because consumer characteristics are not homogeneous, the approach becomes impracticable. Dealing with this setback has been a major challenge in credit card lending risk identification, analysis, and control. Otherwise, delinquency flow models and segmented vintage analyses are commonly used loss forecasting techniques. They can help bankers to recognize the dynamics and behavioral tendencies of various segments of credit card lending portfolios.

Optimizing risk return

The essence of the mathematical models is to help credit card issuers to optimize return on significantly risk-mitigated portfolios. However, the lenders' objective in credit card portfolio analysis and management is to have an efficient mix of debts and risk. It is possible for card issuers to blend current with historical credit records of consumers in different risk segments. When this happens, it becomes practicable to mitigate credit risk by setting risk benchmarks and limiting exposures to the benchmarks. In this way, a bank can effectively mitigate concentration risk in credit card lending.

Painstaking portfolio analysis helps to mitigate credit risk in two main ways. It renders loss exposures amenable to control and eases application of risk-based pricing to credit card debts. However, the problem with credit card portfolio analysis and management concerns divisions between theory and practice regarding choice between alternative analytical models. A further challenge is that some of the analytical models are very advanced and embody technicalities—forcing the majority of lenders not to want to test, let alone adopt or apply, them. Yet the objective of the models remains the same—to assist credit card issuers to appreciate portfolio dynamics that yield optimal risk return in credit card lending.

LESSONS FOR BANKS IN EMERGING ECONOMIES

The outcomes of this chapter hold several lessons for bankers in emerging economies. However, 10 critical lessons, which follow, stand out:

- A credit card is a trap for banks that issue it in reckless disregard of risk. Thus, reckless lending sets the trap into which the banks fall.
- Phony cardholders could compromise themselves by disputing legitimate charges on their credit cards.
- It is possible for fraudsters to maneuver security features of credit cards with the facility of advanced technology.

- Often lapses that trigger disputes of charges on or to credit cards originate in cardholders' ignorance of the mechanics of credit card lending.
- Without full disclosure on credit card cost, cardholders are likely to repudiate their indebtedness on it.
- The possibility of drawing cash on credit cards *over the counter*, rather than through ATMs, increases the tendency to default.
- Standing of cardholders that inform lending to them either clean or secured could change, depending on their current and continuing credit ratings.
- Banks may consider granting regular loans to cardholders to pay off their delinquent credit card debts in remediation of default and loss exposure.
- Risk determines pricing of credit card, such that different groups of individuals may incur varying credit card costs depending on risk-influenced pricing of their credit cards.
- Where it is difficult to segment the market because consumer characteristics are not homogeneous, mathematical credit models become impracticable.

IMPLICATIONS FOR BANKS IN EMERGING ECONOMIES

Banks in emerging economies must build, generate, or have access to reliable databases on consumers. They can do this in collaboration with government and external credit assessment institutions. Once this is achieved, credit bureau reports—that highlight credit histories and ratings of consumers—should back decisions of banks to issue credit cards to individuals. This implies that banks in emerging economies must have easy access to reliable credit histories and ratings of consumers held on regularly updated databases. In this way, the banks can rightly price credit cards for various risk groups of consumers. There is need to differentiate credit card applicants on the basis of their risk characteristics.

Banks should discriminate low- from high-risk consumers. Unsecured lending should be a preserve of low-risk cardholders—those who meet the criteria of a bank's prime customers—and applicants who satisfy other credit criteria of the bank. Collateral is necessary to secure credit cards issued to high-risk applicants. The success of credit card lending depends on institution of effective control at every level of its implementation. Three key resources are essential for the success of risk mitigation in credit card lending. In the first place, credit card operations must be efficient. Secondly, as a high-tech credit product, reliable and up-to-date IT functions must drive credit card lending and operations. Thirdly, an effective internal control system must be in place to ensure regular conduct of inspection and audit of credit card operations.

The mechanics of credit card lending must be transparent to the public, especially to credit card applicants. Full disclosure of all elements of credit card lending should inform an individual's decision to accept or decline a credit card and enhance the integrity of the credit process. Banks should continually educate cardholders on credit card risks that border on breach of security in handling and at points of use of the cards.

QUESTIONS FOR DISCUSSION AND REVIEW

1. In what sense and context is the contention that "consumer lending features a unique benefit–risk dichotomy" logical?
2. Would you agree or disagree that technological innovation acted as a catalyst for consumer lending?
3. Why would an individual be enthusiastic about using a credit card? Do banks really issue credit cards eagerly and with ease?
4. What factors underlie the interests and fears of banks and individuals in emerging economies in credit card?
5. What global challenges do banks in emerging economies face in identifying, assessing, and mitigating risks of credit card lending?

Chapter 18

Micro Sector Credit Risk Control in Emerging Economies

Chapter Outline

LEARNING FOCUS AND OUTCOMES

Microcredit institutions are set up in pursuit of some economic agenda—mainly in developing countries. In most cases, the overriding issue is how to support entrepreneurial development among low-income populations in the society. There is no standard name by which the institutions are known in every country. While they are typified by Grameen Bank in Bangladesh, microcredit institutions or microfinance banks—as adopted in Nigeria—are rather common. The Bank seeks to empower the poor in Bangladesh and improve their socioeconomic conditions.

There are cultural impediments to opportunities otherwise open to the poor to improve their income earning capacity. This fact accounts for the strategy that Grameen Bank adopted to implement its credit and social programs.

The development implications of Grameen Bank's experience with poverty alleviation schemes in Bangladesh are quite instructive. However, operations of the Bank had positive impact on the borrowing and income generating ability of women, which reflected in observed partial fulfillment of their life needs. The broader implication is that Grameen Bank development initiative could indeed impart resilience to the drive for social change.

In the recent past, the Nigerian government had tinkered with economic policies targeted at the informal economy and its operators, mainly the so-called urban poor. Government established the People's Bank of Nigeria (PBN) in the late 1980s. The dramatic failure of PBN paved the way for the licensing of community banks by the Central Bank of Nigeria (CBN) in the 1990s. The CBN was yet to proscribe community banking and supplant it with microfinance banking soon after the 2005 consolidation of the banking industry.

In this chapter, I discuss aspects of credit risk management in microfinance lending to operators in the informal economy in emerging markets. The reader will learn about:

- The financing needs, problems, and prospects of microeconomic institutions
- How microfinance banks can satisfy the borrowing needs of microeconomic institutions without taking undue credit risk or incurring avoidable loan losses
- Workable options and methodology for credit risk analysis and mitigation in lending to microeconomic institutions

SCOPE OF, AND NEED FOR, MICROFINANCE CREDITS

It was believed that microeconomic institutions existed only in traditional societies where agriculture was the mainstay of economic activities. It was thought, in line with this belief, that while urban dwellers pursued white collar jobs in formal organizations, the rural populations engaged in various productive activities in the informal economy. However, as societies advanced, more people started relocating from the rural communities to the cities. In time, the drift of the rural populations to urban areas became unsustainable. Most of the people failed to find suitable means of livelihood in the cities. The situation gave rise to a new economic challenge for government as most of the people made statistics of the urban poor. The observed multiplicity of different forms of microbusinesses in urban centers has foundation in the ensuing unemployment crisis. Obviously, government failed to effectively tackle the problem. Thus, microeconomic units are found not only in the rural communities but also in the urban centers. In most cases, they operate at subsistence level in the informal economy. Typical microbusinesses commonly found in both rural and urban areas include petty traders, technicians, craftsmen, artisans, and peasants. These business units operate as sole proprietors.

Lately, there has been increased government interest in the developing countries in the economic activities that take place in the informal economies. The authorities have in particular realized that the financing needs of the microbusinesses operating in the informal sector of the economies can no longer be ignored if the countries are to accelerate the pace of their economic growth and development. There should therefore be long-term policies and institutional frameworks to promote the survival of this category of economic units.

The intervention of government should be geared to encouraging the emergence of small-scale industries from the pool of the microeconomic institutions. In developed countries, governments recognize the importance of small-scale industries and ensure that they have unrestricted access to *external* business finance. The economic burst of the United States in the mid-nineteenth century into the twentieth century was made possible by small- and medium-scale industries. In Nigeria, one notices some tenuous attempts by government and the CBN to solve the financing problems of the microeconomic units.

The establishment of government-owned development and people-oriented banks is intended to achieve this objective. For instance, the failed People's Bank of Nigeria was set up in the late 1980s to cater to the banking and financing needs of the microeconomic units. Unfortunately, the specialized banks were usually overwhelmed by problems. Either they were inadequately capitalized, or they were saddled with large stocks of nonperforming risk assets, or both. There was also the problem of political interference in the operations of the banks. These problems impacted negatively on management of the banks.

Microfinance credits come in handy not only as business support facilities but a means of actualizing long-term economic plans of government. While these needs are recognized, satisfying them remains largely elusive. In practical terms, the need for finance should be satisfied either directly by operators of microbusinesses or through the facility of government intervention. However, satisfying the needs through personal efforts of the operators has never been effective as most of them do not have the capacity to raise business finance. For this reason, the operators must essentially borrow funds to start, continue, or grow their economic activities.

Government assistance usually comes in the form of an enabling environment through the establishment of appropriate policy and institutional framework. A practical illustration of government intervention in this regard is the emergence of microfinance banks in Nigeria's financial system. The CBN provided the regulatory framework, policy guidelines, operational procedures, and administrative structures for prospective investors wishing to set up microfinance banks. In doing so, the CBN is encouraging the extension of banking and credit facilities to microeconomic units as part of the overall plan of realizing long-term economic objectives of the government.

CULTURAL BACKGROUND

The need for credit facilities to finance economic activities in the informal economy has both historical and cultural foundations. It is pertinent to review enduring cultural methods by which microeconomic units raise business finance in the informal sector. The review is intended to underscore the origins of informal credit transactions among operators of microbusinesses in Nigeria. In doing so, I discuss challenges that activities of the operators pose to orthodox banking, with implications for credit, marketing, and competitive deposit mobilization in the banking sector. Thereafter, I examine the emergence of microfinance banks to fill the roles that particular cultural practices fulfill in the informal sector of the economy.

The major weaknesses of the *esusu* thrift—one of the cultural methods employed by individuals and micro economic units to raise business finance in Nigeria—include the following possible risks:

- Denial of some, most, or all of the contributors' deposits by the operators because of lack of documentation of the *transactions*
- Loss of some, most, or all of the accumulated savings to theft in the collectors' home or elsewhere
- Misappropriation of the funds by the collectors to meet personal financial needs or obligations

From the foregoing analysis, it is obvious that banks can capitalize on the damning disadvantages of *esusu* to dislodge the system and its operators. In so doing, the banks could effectively unlock the savings and credit potential in the informal economy.

Most banks have simplified savings account documentation. They have also substantially reduced—and, in some cases, even waived—the requirement for an initial deposit to open a savings account. Many of the banks have also introduced appreciable operational flexibility and incentives for savings accounts. Some of the innovative improvements of savings accounts include the following:

- Ability of account holders to deposit and withdraw money from their accounts from any branch of the bank. This is made possible by the implementation of WAN by the banks. Introduction of WAN in turn facilitates online-real-time banking transactions.
- Issuing of checkbooks (usually *not valid* for clearing) to savings account holders. With the checkbooks, savings account holders could make regular withdrawals through third parties.
- Reduction, or waiver of the ceiling on the number of withdrawals to be made from savings accounts.
- Issuing of quarterly statements of accounts to savings account holders.

However, notwithstanding the foregoing corrective and competitive measures, which the banks have adopted, *esusu* thrift still survives. In fact, it accounts for a large chunk of money outside the orthodox banking system. Why and how does this practice survive the onslaught of the banks? Perhaps not many people realize that *esusu* thrift remains a flourishing business in the informal savings and credit economy in Nigeria. The reasons for the enduring survival of the *esusu* thrift are quite instructive. That *esusu* thrift is a flourishing business in Nigeria may sound a bit far fetched, but banks are not relenting in their quest to attract deposits trapped in the informal economy. However, they have to contend with the advantages of the *esusu* scheme. The system is relatively *more* simple, flexible, and convenient for the contributors and collectors. It is particularly highly *informal*. With these advantages, people continue to patronize despite the promises of marketing and economic development theories. While banks should not relent in their campaign against such unworthy competition, they should face the reality of the problem. The ultimate solution is for the banks to open as many rural branches as possible. In this way, they would be in a better position to cater to the banking needs of microeconomic units—especially those that operate in the informal economy.

A variant of the esusu scheme—money *contribution and collection* group—is also common in Nigeria. The group makes regular financial contributions (savings) with understanding that participants (contributors) will take turns to collect the sum of contributions of all the members on given dates or periods in particular months. The practice engenders *forced savings* habit among the participants outside the orthodox banking system. In most cases, the saving is *target* driven, implying that the participants have particular financial obligations that they intend to solve in particular months. Thus, the members take turns that tally with the months in which they intend to solve their particular financial obligations. Besides, the arrangement offers *interest-free loans* to the participants, without the rigors of documentation and collateral requirement. There might be exchange of postdated checks among the participants, which essentially provides only collateral *comfort*. This is why the group is effective and has survived.

In view of the foregoing challenges, some of the banks have tried to serve the banking needs of microeconomic units under broad small and medium enterprises (SME) schemes, funded or otherwise supported by government. However, this arrangement has not been effective largely because of relatively more attractiveness of the main SMEs to the banks. The microeconomic units, existing at the lowest rung of the ladder, are perhaps seen as a disorganized group that will be difficult to handle. Banks might consider that dealing with so large a number of small volume customers—and their myriad transactions—will be more costly and less profitable for them. Yet, in adopting this attitude, the banks and government have to come to terms with the reality that the microeconomic units have unfulfilled banking and credit needs. It is perhaps in realization of this fact that the CBN facilitated the emergence of microfinance banks in Nigeria.

RISK IDENTIFICATION AND ANALYSIS

Microcredit facilities are usually short tenured, simple in structure, and of small amounts. In fact, their designation as *micro* derives from the fact that they characteristically have very small amounts of risk assets. The loans are also typically spread over numerous borrowers in the informal economic sector. In general, credit facilities that banks might want to grant to micro-economic units may be in the form of advance, overdraft, purchase order finance, invoice discounting, and so on. I discussed the features, risks, and analysis of these types of credit facility in detail in Chapters 9 and 11 of this book in the case of lending to businesses in the formal economy. Yet the risk analysis issues that I diagnosed and management techniques that I suggested also largely apply in the case of microfinance lending. However, differences would exist between loans granted to formal and informal business units in terms of scale, transactions dynamics, and risks involved. Nonetheless, we should admit that lending to microeconomic units would sometimes require an unusual structuring, disbursement, and management flexibility. Ordinary banks are not always in a position to serve this need efficiently because of factors of orientation, focus, size, and transactions processing costs. For this reason, institution of microfinance banks is a timely intervention by government to fill the observed gap in the banking and credit needs of microenterprises.

Microeconomic units are characterized by diverse business orientations. The operators are found in virtually all sectors of the economy. Unfortunately, their banking needs and financing problems reflect similar diversity. As microbusinesses exist in various forms, it will be futile to attempt any meaningful discussion of their various economic activities or the risks associated with all of their possible banking transactions.

However, one can at any time isolate the common credit risk factors for analysis and mitigation. In most cases, the major causes of risks in micro-finance lending include *character* of the operators, *management* deficiencies, irregular *mode of operations*, *poor documentation* of transactions and accounts, inefficient *funds handling*, *collateral* issues, and unforeseen adverse *conditions*. These risk factors reflect the key credit issues in the acclaimed five C's of lending. I discuss each of them briefly below.

Character

In Chapter 22, I extensively discussed the issues involved in analyzing *character* of borrowers. In doing so, I also discussed its general implications for appraising, recommending, and approving credit facilities. In view of this, while I note the importance of *character* in analyzing microcredit risks, I will not replicate the discussion here.

Management

One of the significant features of microenterprises is the fusion of ownership, management, and control. This perhaps presents the most difficult challenge for banks in considering credit requests of the operators. Indeed, banks are often scared to take the credit risks of microbusiness operators on account of this risk factor. In Chapters 6 and 7, I extensively discussed many of the issues that loan officers should analyze about management of SMEs and microeconomic units.

Operations

Unstructured or irregular mode of operations also characterizes micro-businesses. Proper organization of business activities—far from what one knows of it among formal organizations—seems practically unattainable and therefore elusive. Thus, their future business activities cannot, in most cases, be accurately predicted on the basis of past patterns of operations. In view of their inconsistent business goals and practices, microeconomic units do not easily obtain bank credits, especially for the purpose of meeting working capital needs.

Documentation

There is risk associated with non- or poor documentation of operational and financial transactions. In fact, documentation of business and accounting data is characterized by incomplete records. Since banks place a lot of emphasis on documentation of business transactions, especially accounting records, it has often not been easy to meet the financing needs of their microbusiness customers. In fact, many banks actually categorize microbusinesses as high-risk accounts on the grounds of documentation setbacks.

Funds handling

Another major risk associated with lending to microeconomic units is the fusion of family and personal responsibilities of the operators. This problem is common in the management of financial resources. Most of the operators of microenterprises are barely able to maintain financial discipline necessary for business success. In the absence of total separation of business from personal funds, financial prudence may not be achieved. Of course, this situation sends out a risk-warning signal—one that builds on suspicion that if a credit facility is granted, it could be misused.

Collateral

The flow of credit to microbusinesses is sometimes constrained by their inability to back up their loan requests with acceptable collateral. In most cases, the operators do not have tangible collateral that may be acceptable to banks. Where they do have personal assets, the items are usually things that will not command, or be worth, reasonable economic value. Thus, it could be assumed that a bank that lends money to microenterprises would in most cases be assuming an uncovered exposure.

Conditions

Certain environmental issues impart risk to operations of microeconomic units. The nature of the risk is not systemic as it does not affect all other businesses in the economy. Instead, the risk derives from the location of the enterprises in the informal economy where the operators more often than not infringe business and operational bylaws. For example, the issue of *street trading* has been a major cause of friction between the local authorities and petty traders in metropolitan centers. While enforcing the relevant bylaws, agents of local councils often clash with traders. Such incidents usually cause unexpected business losses to the traders. When this happens, the operators would not be in a position to repay bank loans.

MITIGATION OF RISKS OF MICROFINANCE LENDING

Mitigation of credit risks in microfinance lending presents somewhat more difficult challenges than are normally encountered in granting loans to customers in formal economic sectors. In analyzing risks when lending to customers that operate businesses in formal economic sectors, loan officers try to proffer matching remedies for identified credit risks. However, this approach might not be feasible in the case of microfinance lending. Indeed, it may not be appropriate to adopt the same approach for the two categories of borrowers.

The reasons for this risk mitigation disparity relate to the exceptional characteristics of microenterprises. For example, it will be futile to insist that such economic units should have a certain caliber of management when it is certain that the *owner-manager* cannot be changed. The other identified risks of lending to microenterprises have similar adjustment characteristics. Therefore, loan officers must find alternative security measures for loans extended to microbusiness operators.

Below, I discuss a number of peculiar risk-mitigating measures that are considered appropriate in lending to microeconomic units. While the suggested measures are not exhaustive, they are some of the most likely workable options, given the unusual business and operating circumstances in the informal economy.

Cooperative lending

A bank can decide to lend money to only organized and registered cooperative societies for on-lending to, and utilization by, their accredited members. This implies that the bank may disburse approved credit facilities only to the cooperative societies to which the borrowers belong. Under this arrangement, the cooperative societies will be the primary obligors for the credit facilities. This arrangement is considered effective for several reasons:

- The bank will deal with the leadership, rather than numerous potential borrowing members, of the cooperative societies. This reduces the number of small value credit applications that the banks will receive, analyze, and approve or decline.

- It would be the responsibility of the leadership of the cooperative societies to monitor proper utilization and timely repayment of the loans. This reduces incidences of funds diversion, which otherwise is a common feature of bank lending to microenterprises.
- The cooperative societies would try to protect their financial integrity and, in doing so, do their utmost to safeguard their banking relationships and risk assets of the banks.
- Banks are relieved of the task of analyzing *elusive* character of potential borrowing operators of microeconomic units. The underlying assignment in character risk analysis is transferred to the leadership of the cooperative societies. In doing so, it is believed that the leaders are in a better position to appreciate the character of their members.
- Cooperators are bound by agreement that they are obligated to observe or face punitive sanctions. This impels them to do anything but fail in their commitment to their societies.

I should, however, point out that banks are not, in view of the foregoing arrangement, entirely abdicating their risk analysis and management responsibility. However, risk analysis by banks is restricted to analysis of objectives, formation, registration, integrity, financial standing, and achievements of the cooperative societies. Where a cooperative society is adjudged sound on these criteria, a bank can work with it to serve the borrowing needs of its members. This arrangement is both effective and amenable to risk control.

References

Banks may choose to deal directly with microcredit applicants on their merit, without going through associations to which they belong. In that case, they will need to obtain suitable references on prospective borrowers from creditworthy individuals, companies, and organizations. Such references serve particular risk mitigating purposes for the lending banks, including the following:

- The banks will normally have *comfort* in the references while granting credit facilities to the borrowers.
- Strong references may be as compelling as to predispose the bank to granting the related microcredit requests. In this context, a typical strong reference would be one that comes from the church or mosque where the prospective borrower worships. The bank may be more swayed by the reference if it is endorsed by the leader of the church or mosque.
- The implied *references* often carry immutable commitment and may serve as guarantee on which banks can effectively rely to grant microcredit

requests. It is pertinent, from the foregoing, to mention at once that the required *references* are altogether totally different from those that banks normally demand, receive, and accept for purposes of opening certain categories of demand deposit accounts for their customers. Thus, references simply requiring the completion of forms will not satisfy the expected risk-mitigating measure for lending purposes.

Guarantee

A somewhat variant of *cooperative lending*, also considered an effective microcredit risk-mitigating measure, is the requirement for *group guarantee* of prospective borrowers in favor of a bank. In this case, like in cooperative lending, the bank deals with organized and duly registered societies, groups, or associations with legally permissible objectives. However, while the bank may directly disburse loans to individual borrowers, it should ask them to provide guarantee from their vocational association groups. A number of borrowers, under one umbrella association, may provide a common guarantee from the association. Once the association issues the guarantee, it becomes responsible to the bank for ensuring that credit facilities granted to the borrowers are serviced and fully liquidated on due dates.

OTHER RISK CONTROL MEASURES

The risks associated with lending to microeconomic units could be minimized by other means that involve *knowing* the customers, lending for specific *transactions*, and strictly *monitoring* loan utilization. In conjunction with the risk control techniques identified in the preceding discussion, these measures will assist in minimizing risks associated with lending to microeconomic units. Let me briefly discuss each of the measures.

KYC implementation

The acronym KYC means *know your customer* and, as used in this chapter, implies having full knowledge of persons, businesses, institutions, or other entities that make up prospective and existing customers of a bank at any point in time. It is now a universal banking practice for bankers to insist on truly *knowing* their prospective customers as a condition for acceding to their account opening requests. The regulatory authorities have even made it mandatory for every bank to secure evidence that it actually knows its customers very well. The sum total of regulatory directives about this banking principle is embodied in the KYC philosophy. The KYC could be said to be an evolving paradigm, really a response to growing concern within the financial system about worsening incidences of bank fraud, financial malpractices, and laundering of illicit money through the banking system. Alarmed by observed annual financial losses that individuals, businesses, and other institutions suffer because of avoidable financial swindles and activities of fraudsters, regulatory intervention became inevitable.

In accordance with the KYC philosophy, banks are enjoined to do anything but open demand deposit accounts without first painstakingly fulfilling the following requirements:

- Identify prospective account holders, i.e., persons, companies, and other entities, in whose favor the accounts would be opened. For individual account holders, this requirement is satisfied with the sighting and depositing of photocopies of an original driver's license, national identity card, or international passport. In the case of corporate bodies, banks usually demand sighting of an original certificate of incorporation, memorandum and articles of association, relevant board resolutions, and so on, and submission of photocopies of these documents.
- Establish the exact locations and office addresses of prospective account holders. This information must be confirmed by responsible officers of the bank in site visit reports. It should also be evidenced by utility bills (such as receipts for payments of electricity, water, or fixed line telephone bills).
- Ascertain the names and contact details of key officers of prospective account holders (in the case of corporate accounts), especially those that would be signatories to the accounts. Information such as permanent residential and office addresses, telephone numbers, and personal and office e-mail addresses are also important.
- Ensure that prospective account holders obtain and submit to the bank at least two reference reports from existing customers of the bank or any other current account holders from other banks. The references so obtained must be favorable for the bank to accept a prospect's application to open and operate a demand deposit account.
- Investigate the trust and creditworthiness, as well as suitability, of the persons, companies, or other entities to operate current accounts. This requires the cooperation of other banks and recourse to the credit risk bureau service of the Central Bank of Nigeria.

It would seem that KYC implementation is restricted only to investigation of prospective demand deposit account holders. Why are similar inquiries about customers that have time deposits (i.e., holders of call and fixed deposit accounts), or other banking relationships with a bank, not considered pertinent? The answer to this question lies in appreciating how banking transactions of customers could crystallize in financial risks.

The regulatory authorities and banks tend to target only demand deposit accounts because of current payment systems that rely heavily on the use of checks. Thus, financial instruments such as checks, bank drafts, dividend warrants, and so on can only be cleared for account holders through their demand deposit accounts. On the contrary, only cash deposits could be made into, or withdrawn from, savings accounts—unless a bank does due diligence, of the type that is normally done on current accounts, before opening particular savings accounts. In that case, while financial instruments could be lodged into the savings accounts, only withdrawal by cash is permissible. Where a check is allowed for withdrawal from such savings accounts, the instrument is usually made invalid for *clearing*. The transaction could technically be said to be of the nature of cash, not check, withdrawal under the circumstances. This procedure marks a major distinction between the usual current and savings accounts.

Transactions lending

Banks can minimize default risk by lending money to borrowers for transactions-based purposes. Such transactions should be short tenured, self-liquidating, and have an unambiguous execution path. In most cases, advances or overdrafts that banks grant to meet working capital requirements do not meet these criteria. The level of possible loan utilization lapses and abuses increases the more it is difficult to relate the credits to particular transactions of the borrowers. It is therefore advised that banks should manage risk by identifying and understanding the transactions for which their customers are making particular borrowing requests. When this is done, it becomes easy to analyze risks, prospect of successful execution, and probable cycles of particular transactions. If these measures are adopted, a microcredit loan would have a high probability of being effectively utilized and repaid on the due date.

Loan monitoring

As in other forms of lending, effective monitoring of loan utilization remains a critical means of ensuring that disbursed microcredit facilities are not abused. Close monitoring for this category of credit facilities is intended to achieve timely repayment in line with terms and conditions agreed upon between a bank and borrowers. Lack of, or poor, loan monitoring has implications for possible default by the borrowers and loss of the risk asset by the bank. It is therefore imperative that a bank devises efficient means of ensuring that borrowers abide by the terms and conditions of credit facilities. Banks and borrowers should stick with their loan agreement throughout the tenor of credits up to the time the credits are fully liquidated.

QUESTIONS FOR DISCUSSION AND REVIEW

1. Briefly discuss enduring cultural methods by which microeconomic units raise business finance in the informal economy.
2. Why has the *esusu* thrift remained a flourishing business in the informal savings and credit economy in Nigeria?

3. Have the orthodox banks been successful in attracting customers from the informal economy?
4. What are the risks of lending to microeconomic units?
5. Why are risk-mitigating measures in lending to microeconomic units considered peculiar?
6. Why would ordinary banks not be in a position to satisfy the financing needs of microeconomic units?

Chapter 19

Loan Syndication Risk and Control in Emerging Economies

Chapter Outline

LEARNING FOCUS AND OUTCOMES

The notion of loan syndication is founded on the need for two or more banks to jointly lend money to a large borrower. In most cases, the loan amount is beyond the funding capacity of one bank. The loan may be unusually risky or have multiple components. Since no bank may be willing or able to grant the loan, a syndicate of banks must handle it. But the borrower, usually a large corporation or organization, sends the loan request to the bank with which it has a cordial and, usually, mutually beneficial banking relationship.

It is the bank to which it sends the loan proposal that subsequently leads the syndicate. Usually, it is with the lead bank that the borrower has its main accounts. In some cases, the borrower nominates a syndicate of banks that it wants to provide the loan. Otherwise, the lead bank takes the initiative and chooses the participating banks. Criteria for choice of the banks include relationship with the lead bank, unity of operations, and liquidity and capacity to lend. A critical success factor is mutual trust between the lead and participating banks, and among the participating banks. It is unlikely that a bank will want to be a syndicate member with banks with which it does not have common features.

However, a particular consideration—credit risk, how to correctly anticipate, analyse, and mitigate it—holds sway. It remains constant and influences the disposition of both the lead and participating banks. The lead bank arranges the syndicate of banks, ostensibly to mitigate the credit risk. That each bank analyzes the credit independent of the other participating banks before signing up for it assures comfort from collective diligence. The banks do so with a sense of responsibility—to ensure that the credit risk of the large borrower fits with their internal lending criteria.

Thus, mitigation of credit risk is at issue in syndication lending. This fact necessitates my evaluation of the conduct and process of loan syndication to underscore the significance of risk control. In doing so, I review critical aspects of loan syndication. My review reflects and builds on widespread acceptance of syndication lending in the banking industry. I also pinpoint emerging trends and issues in loan syndication. My ultimate objective is to assess the efficacy and implications of current methodology for the conduct of loan syndication deals.

Loan syndication aims to meet the credit request of a large borrower, which no one bank can handle or satisfy due to some legal limitation or other reason. The reader will learn about:

- Critical aspects of loan syndication, taking cognizance of its widespread acceptance
- Ways for mitigating credit risk associated with loan syndication
- The cause, conduct, and process of loan syndication
- Current methodology for loan syndication and its efficacy
- Emerging trends and challenges at issue in loan syndication

CAUSES OF SYNDICATION LENDING

Loan syndication has evolved with increasing pressure on banks to minimize excessive risk taking in lending activities. As the banks respond to the pressure, it becomes imperative to consider the amounts of loans and credit risks that a bank can take per obligor or group of obligors. In Nigeria, the regulatory authorities prescribe a single obligor limit of 20% of a bank's shareholders' funds, unimpaired by losses. This implies that a bank in Nigeria cannot lend more than the prescribed limit to one borrower or a group of related borrowers.

What then should a bank that receives a credit request from a prime customer that meets all but the single obligor lending criterion do? Should it decline such otherwise attractive credit proposal from a highly valued customer? Would its inability to handle the loan request not weaken its competitive strength as the customer is likely to take the proposal to another, competing, bank? These are some of the questions that banks may have to deal with whenever they are incapacitated to lend because of constraints imposed by legal factors (as in the single obligor limit) and, in general, the amounts or risks involved.

Banks try to get around the problem through the facility of loan syndication. I have used the phrases *loan syndication, syndication lending, syndicated loan*, and *consortium lending* interchangeably to convey the same meaning. In simple terms, loan syndication is a *consortium* lending arrangement involving more than one bank to meet the credit need of a large borrower. In most cases, loan amount requiring syndication may comprise multiple credit facilities that the large borrower needs. A typical syndicated loan would have overdraft and term loan components. However, there could be other possible combinations, such as overdraft, term loan, equipment lease, and so on. In a more complex syndication, there could even be a foreign currency component in the loan request.

In the discussions presented below, aspects of this important lending practice that have gained acceptance in the industry as a means of handling large ticket credit deals are analysed—with implications for credit risk management.

MEANING AND BENEFITS OF SYNDICATION

The phrase *loan syndication* may be defined as a lending practice or arrangement in which one bank, unable to grant a loan to a large borrower because of legal or internal lending limits, invites other banks to participate in providing the required credit facility. Thus, a syndication or syndicated loan refers to a single credit facility granted to a large borrower by more than one bank. Banks go into loan syndication for several reasons, including the urge to gain the following benefits:

- Syndication offers the ability to spread lending risks across the participating banks. Thus, it minimizes the risk of concentration of loans in one large borrower or group of related borrowers.
- With loan syndication, it is easier for the participating banks to integrate the borrower's banking relationships. The large borrower can easily deal with a manageable number of banks with assurance of ability to satisfy its banking needs.
- It permits banks to lend to large borrowers without infringing regulatory or internal lending limits, especially when the size of the individual loan is larger than legally permissible.
- Syndication tends to encourage competitive compromises among the lending banks. Thus, it fosters business cooperation among the banks without upsetting their competitive strategies.

- The lending banks can meet a collective vision of financing key development projects and businesses, especially in the preferred sectors of the economy.

It is expected that as banks evolve more effective risk management strategies, they will get more involved in syndication lending. This will require further and continuing exposure of lending officers to the intricacies of large ticket loans in volatile operating banking environments.

PARTIES AND ROLES IN SYNDICATION

Syndication lending is differentiated from other forms of credit facilities mainly because it involves more than one bank in granting and disbursing a loan to a borrower. In general, there are always three parties in syndication lending: the large borrower, lead bank, and participating banks.

The lead bank, also sometimes referred to as the syndication manager, arranges for the loan for a large borrower. Later, it sells off portions of the credit to other lenders—the participating banks and other lending institutions. This implies that the lead bank, in most cases, originates the credit transaction. Participating lending institutions complement the capacity of the lead bank to meet the borrower's need for the loan amount. The lead bank services the loan and earns agreed agency fee.

The participating lending institutions, also known as the syndicate members, lend directly to the borrower. This is notwithstanding that the lead bank originates the credit transaction, manages the borrower's banking relationship with the consortium, and is responsible for servicing the loan. Thus, the lead bank is the primary interface between the borrower and syndicate members. Notwithstanding its enormous influence, the lead bank may not forestall other banking dealings that the borrower might want to have with any of the lenders.

In consortium lending, the lenders assume separate obligations to the extent of their financial commitments to the borrower. For example, let us assume that bank A contributes $500 million; this amount represents the limit of its obligation in the syndication and to the borrower. In addition, the import of the separateness of each lender's obligation is that one lender cannot be made to bear responsibility for the financial commitment of another lender in the syndication.

As each member of the lending consortium shares in the risk of the credit, it is expected that each should also make its own lending decisions independent of the others. The scope of credit decision, and therefore the required credit analysis, should cover appraisal of the transaction, borrower, syndicate manager, and prospective participating banks and other lenders.

CATEGORIES OF SYNDICATION DEALS

There are basically two categories of syndication lending arrangements. In one, the syndicate members undertake to raise the required funds on a *best efforts* basis, while in the other, they make *firm* or *underwritten* financial commitments.

In the case of *best efforts* syndication, the lead bank analyzes the loan request, agrees on its terms and conditions with the borrower, gives its internal approval for the request, and then markets the credit facility to prospective participating banks and other lenders. The syndicate manager will normally market the loan under the terms and conditions it agreed on with the borrower. In the event that the lead bank's marketing efforts fail to attract full subscription of prospective lenders to the syndication, the intended credit deal is canceled. As the syndication is on a *best efforts* basis, the syndicate manager will not have financial or other obligation to the borrower.

Syndication in which there is a firm or underwritten commitment carries certain financial or other obligations that the lead bank bears. In this case, while the syndicate manager may fail to market the credit deal, it must nevertheless grant and disburse the loan to the borrower. In other words, the fact that the lead bank does not get full subscription to the syndication is inconsequential to its underwritten commitment to the deal. This happens because the lead bank must agree to disburse the loan regardless that it may not fully syndicate it.

In view of the foregoing scenarios, how should a bank in an emerging economy determine whether to underwrite loan syndication to a prospective large borrower? If it opts to underwrite the syndication, it makes a firm commitment to grant and disburse the loan. Where it decides to offer a *best efforts* alternative, it assumes a noncommittal posture. The factors that should influence the likely decision will derive from facts contained in the credit analysis memorandum (CAM), relationship considerations, and the bank's cash flow position. In both cases, however, the lead bank must market the loan syndication to other prospective lenders.

Often how readily a loan syndication proposal can be marketed in emerging economies depends on the credibility, standing, and relationship of the lead bank with the other lenders, especially the prospective participating banks. However, besides the integrity of the syndicate manager, there are certain basic marketing approaches that tend to aid sale of the loan to other prospective lenders. In order to succeed in selling portions of the loan, the lead bank should do all of the following:

- Package the borrower's loan proposal, with a clear transaction path, risk mitigation measures, and sound repayment plan and sources
- Target potential participating banks amongst those that have identical characteristics. In terms of size, performance, credit rating, and operations standards, the prospective syndicate members should be, as much as possible, equally categorized
- Specify the roles of the syndicate manager and participating banks, as well as their individual and collective relationships with the borrower

- Enumerate expected gains from the deal—spread income, fees, commission, and so on. The expected net yield should be commensurate with the identified risks of the transaction
- Obtain adequate tangible collateral from the borrower to secure the exposures of the participating banks and other lenders.

These factors affect the response of potential lenders to particular loan syndication proposals. Positive or negative responses should be expected where the lead bank properly or poorly clarifies the above issues.

LEGAL AND OTHER DOCUMENTATION

Syndication lending in emerging economies is often characterized by meticulous and extensive documentation of the underlying transaction. Similarly, interactions between the lead and participating banks, on the one hand, and the lenders and borrower, on the other, also tend to be painstaking. A key aspect of the required documentation is the endorsement of an elaborate agreement that governs the rights and obligations of the syndicate manager, members, and the borrower. This document, referred to as syndicate loan agreement, is perhaps the single most important instrument for managing the lending relationships among the loan parties. It is not uncommon to find other terminologies, such as consortium loan agreement, that are used to describe the document. Irrespective of the term used, its meaning and purpose remain the same.

There is yet another important legal document that is often executed in the course of finalizing loan syndication. The document, called an interlender agreement, specifies the rights and duties of the syndicate members, including the manager or lead bank. It is essential to have such a legal agreement, which is often detailed, to serve as a guide to actions that the participating banks and lenders may or may not take as syndicate members. Thus, the major difference between a consortium loan agreement and interlender agreement is the exclusion of the rights and obligations of the borrower in the latter. The scope of an interlender agreement essentially covers relationships between the syndicate members.

In addition to the foregoing legal documentation, there could also sometimes be an initial documentation of the syndication in form of an offer letter from the lead bank to the borrower. In most cases, the offer letter gives a general indication of possible terms and conditions of the credit facility that the syndicate manager hopes to sell to potential participating banks and other lenders. As in other lending situations, the borrower would formally accept the offer letter to pave the way for the marketing of the credit by the lead bank.

COMMITMENT, FEES, AND SERVICING

Syndicated credit facilities attract certain fees and commissions that the borrower pays to the lead bank, participating banks, and other lenders. The charges are always a major consideration in syndication marketing. The reasons for the significance of charges are often associated with the need to adequately compensate the lenders for taking the lending risks. The risks arise mainly as a result of the following factors:

- The usual term structure of syndicated credit facility that often extends beyond medium term. In some cases, a particular or several components of the loan may have long terms.
- Complex transaction dynamics, especially where multiple lending is involved, that often characterize loan syndication deals.
- Relationship management challenges that could sometimes be intractable. Often relationship issues result from possible maneuvering of the borrower's patronage by the competing lenders, and so on.

In addition to the normal interest and fees charged on loans, syndicated credit facilities attract certain other fees and commissions. The common syndication charges include *commitment*, *management*, *participation*, and *agency* fees. Each fee is usually charged as a flat payment and could be any rate from 0.25% to 2% flat, depending on the pricing factors that are considered.

Commitment fee

A commitment fee is charged based on the amount and undrawn portion of the credit facility. It compensates the lending banks for apportioning specific amounts of money as credit facilities to the borrower regardless of other equally competing lending prospects and needs. Thus, the fee serves as recompense to the lenders for the opportunity cost of the funds that they earmark and are willing to disburse on the credit facility.

Management fee

A management fee is paid to the syndicate manager, or lead bank, in the loan syndication. Often referred to as an *arrangement fee*, its purpose is largely to recompense the syndicate manager for initiating the syndication, assembling its participants, and generally overseeing the syndicate. A major role of the syndicate manager—one that justifies the charge of a management fee—is to ensure that the loan is serviced in accordance with its terms and conditions. Otherwise, the whole syndicate arrangement would be fraught with avoidable conflicts.

Participation fee

As its designation implies, a participation fee is paid to the syndicate participants for their various commitment of funds to the syndication. The fee is based on the amount of financial commitment that each of the participating lending institutions makes to the syndicate. In general, however, the main purpose of the fee is to attract potential lending institutions to the syndicate and encourage them to make definite commitments.

Agency fee

The syndicate manager may be paid an agency fee in the sum of a flat *amount*, say, $500,000 per annum, in the case of a regular syndication. However, the fee can be increased up to $5,000,000 a year in the case of multifaceted loan syndication. While the actual amount of the fee varies, its purpose remains to compensate the syndicate manager for servicing the loan on behalf of the borrower and participating lending institutions.

RISK ANALYSIS AND MITIGATION

The risks often encountered in syndication lending in emerging economies arise mainly from the amount and nature of the loan, transaction path, capacity of the borrower, disposition of the manager, term structure of the loan, collateral, and economic conditions. The main elements of risk in these factors are as follows.

Amount and nature of loan

The amounts of the loans involved in syndications are usually large, giving rise to chances of huge loan loss provisions in the event of default by the borrower. Notwithstanding that a number of lenders share in this risk, the relative exposure of each lender is more often than not large. This risk is compounded by the intricate nature of syndication loans where, for instance, there could be overdraft, foreign currency, and term loan components of a single loan package. To mitigate this risk, each lender should take stake in the syndication that will not thwart its portfolio plans or distend its risk appetite. In particular, a bank may choose to participate in only one of the loan components, say the overdraft facility.

Disposition of the syndicate manager

The syndicate manager plays an important role in mitigating lending risks in loan syndication. For instance, it acts as the primary interface or go-between for the borrower and lending institutions. In this capacity, the manager bears the responsibility of monitoring the credit transaction, relationship management, and collection of agreed fees and loan repayments from the borrower on behalf of the participating institutions. It remits the amounts so collected to the participating banks and other lenders in accordance with the terms and conditions of the loan.

The extent to which the syndicate manager performs these roles well or badly would to some extent determine the magnitude of the risk that the lending institutions might be taking as participants in the syndication. Perhaps the most assuring risk-mitigating action of the lead bank is to take stakes in chunks of the components of the total credit package. In doing so, and disclosing it in the information memorandum for the marketing of the syndication, potential participants would be convinced about the seriousness of the borrower and the lead bank.

Transaction path

In most cases, loan syndications tend to have complex transactions dynamics, especially where multiple credit facilities are involved. This implies that the lending banks and other institutions must have teams of loan officers who have strong analytical skills and capabilities for appraising transactions risks in the various sectors of the economy. Without such in-house analytical competences and resources, a bank might make erroneous and costly credit decisions.

Mitigation of the risk would require painstaking study of the loan proposal, the lending requirements, and conditions for the loan's performance. In doing so, the bank determines whether, how, or to what extent the transaction path is amenable to incidence of risk. If the transaction path is simplified, understood, and effectively monitored, the level of perceived risks would reduce, while prospects of risk mitigation would increase.

Capacity of the borrower

The question as to *capacity* relates to the experience, competence, and performance track record that may qualify the borrower to be granted the credit facility. It is indeed the duty of the syndicate manager to investigate, rate, and show willingness to take the risks implied in these factors before packaging and selling portions of the loan to potential syndicate participants. Often the capacity of the borrower in loan syndication is taken for granted. This is because such large borrowers are usually found among the blue chip and conglomerate companies or public sector establishments.

In general, this category of borrowers meets most of the lending criteria of banks. For this reason, banks deliberately court and covet their banking relationships. Yet, it is imperative for the banks to investigate the borrower's experience and technical competence in handling the underlying project for which the loan would be spent.

Term structure of the loan

There are always uncertainties about the future and therefore risks associated with probable incidences of unfavorable events that can cause business losses.

The likelihood of incidence of the risks and magnitude of possible losses escalates with increasing term structure of the loan. Given the volatile nature of emerging markets business environment, loan tenor of more than three years may be considered long term.

One of the ways to mitigate the risk of likely inability of the borrower to service and repay the loan in the future is to realistically sensitize cash flow analysis on which the lending decision would be based. In most cases, sensitivity analysis would reveal the extent to which the borrower's failure to achieve the projected cash inflows can adversely affect their ability to meet loan service and repayment obligations.

Following outcomes of cash flow sensitivity analysis, the lending banks can recommend actions that the borrower should take to mitigate identified negative influences that may frustrate attainment of the projected cash inflows. Alternatively, there may be need to introduce certain shock absorbers to the sensitivity analysis to counter such negative influences. In addition to sensitized cash flows, the syndicate should also take adequate tangible collateral to further secure its exposure.

Collateral to secure the loan

Collateral is never seen as a panacea for the risks of bank lending. Yet the law permits, requires, and enjoins banks to take collateral to secure credit risk that the banks take in their various lending activities. This implies that collateral taking forms an important integral part of the lending function. In view of this, my concern here is to suggest collateral that may be considered appropriate to secure syndicated credit facilities.

Unfortunately, the large borrowers—especially the blue chips, conglomerates, or other large corporations—like to borrow *clean* because of their obvious financial strength and standing. Ironically, banks often oblige their *clean* borrowing indulgence. Perhaps, the banks do so under the dictates of competitive pressure, to meet budget targets, or in coveting particular banking relationships.

Yet, in doing so, the banks should appreciate the need to remain law abiding by taking collateral from the borrowers. For instance, the use of a *negative pledge* and *letter of comfort* as collateral tends to bestow a sense of security to the banks. However, there could be instances where a mutual agreement can be reached to secure a loan with charge on the assets of the borrower.

Economic conditions

The issues usually associated with *conditions* as one of the five C's of lending relate essentially to factors in the economy, business environment, and natural phenomena over which both the bank and borrowers do not have control.

In syndication lending, such factors also affect the risks that the banks take. The requirements for mitigating credit risk would include thorough analysis of historical trends, incidences, and applicable actions taken by the relevant authorities to anticipate and ameliorate the risks. The analysis should show likely effectiveness of measures to mitigate the risks and to what extent the bank can rely on the measures in making lending decisions.

QUESTIONS FOR DISCUSSION AND REVIEW

1. How does the phrase "on a best effort basis" explain tasks involved in loan syndication?
2. What is an interlender agreement? In what ways does it mitigate credit risk in loan syndication?
3. Why is a syndicate, or consortium, loan agreement such a necessary legal document?
4. Identify and discuss aspects of loan syndication that underlie its cause, conduct, and process?
5. Why would a lead bank occasionly underwrite loan syndication despite the credit risk involved?

Part III

Credit Risk Dynamics, Analysis, and Management

Approach to Credit Risk Management

Chapter 20

Evolving Control of Bank Lending and Credit Risk in Emerging Markets

Chapter Outline

LEARNING FOCUS AND OUTCOMES

The topic of this chapter is not a regular subject in the credit literature. Neither is it a familiar issue in discussions of risk management in bank lending. I delved into it to strengthen the cause and theme of this book. I also want to further underline the foundation of the problem that I highlighted in the preceding chapters.

I discuss aspects of the modernizing process and stages of credit risk management. I assess the observed trend in the context of the need for effective risk management in bank lending. Using Nigeria as an example, and material from credit practice and literature, I propound five evolutionary stages of credit risk management and discuss their implications for bank management.

In doing so, I accomplish the learning outcomes of this chapter. You will, after reading this chapter, be able to:

- Identify evolutionary changes in the mechanics of the process of credit risk management
- Pinpoint advances made in credit risk management in the course of its evolution and discuss prospects for the future
- Relate market risk and uncertainty to the evolutionary stages of credit risk management

Emerging Market Bank Lending and Credit Risk Control. http://dx.doi.org/10.1016/B978-0-12-803438-5.00020-9

- Show how specific events corroborated and impacted the evolution of credit risk management in banking
- Discuss lessons of experience and implications of the observed trend for credit risk and bank management

OVERVIEW

Despite the seemingly intractable problem of credit risk crisis in banking, the lending process has evolved through critical stages of development into a modern methodical framework. The credit process has been radically transformed in response to changing operating environment. Indeed, many changes have taken place in modernizing the process of lending and credit risk management. Of course, the changes became inevitable following dramatic shift in demands of contemporary risk management in bank lending. Most of the observed changes really happened in nonlending functions under the auspices of the technological revolution.

In the lending function, strictly speaking, some of the changes happened naturally, while others were induced by regulatory intervention and supervisory actions. Some of the changes yet occurred as a result of interaction between economic conditions and forces in the financial system. In each case, depending on the state of the industry and lending practices, the observed changes had more or less significant impact on credit risk management. The evolution of credit risk management process may be said to have started with *naive lending*. There were subsequently *awakening*, *regulatory intervention*, and *financial meltdown* stages before the contemporary *reawakening* stage. Lessons of credit management experience learned from preceding stages informed risk mitigating policies adopted in subsequent stages.

However, it is pertinent to note that the stages and changes that they engendered did not happen in discrete steps or manner. In practical terms, the stages were not mutually exclusive because their characterizing features overlapped in some cases. It is also imperative that I mention at once that different patterns of the transformation may be applicable to different emerging economies and nations. Yet it remains a fact that risk management in bank lending has passed through particular evolutionary stages in every country, whether developed, less developed, or an emerging market.

It may be difficult to generalize the Nigerian experience that I used to explain this topic. Yet this experience guides us to know how the revolution of credit risk management might have happened in other countries. In the final analysis, the actual differences between the stages may be simply a matter of nomenclature—and not that the stages were unfounded. In the following sections, I discuss elements of the stages and how they impacted the development of credit risk management process.

I must mention at once that there is yet evolving thinking on how to improve credit risk management in "internationally active banks." The Basel Committee is perhaps the most vocal international voice on contemporary demands of credit risk management on global banks. With the relevant amendments to it, Basel I advances this cause more decisively.

NAIVE LENDING ERA

At this stage, pre-1900, lending and credit risk management were rudimentary. Whether at an individual or corporate level, banks were preoccupied with appreciating customers, their banking relationships, needs, and borrowing causes. They were also tuned in to riskless lending in building portfolios of earning assets. But lenders had indeed always devised means to hedge against loan default since time immemorial. This implies that credit risk has always been a problem at issue in bank lending.

In the past, for example, borrowers willingly pawned personal belongings to secure loans they obtained from lenders. The essence, in doing so, was largely to assure comfort to the lenders about commitment, or ability, of the borrowers to pay back loans they obtained. Yet, the true reliance of lenders for loan repayment was on trust in the borrowers. In most cases, the character of the borrowers reinforced the trust. Pawning belongings was essentially symbolic to the extent that it could be and sometimes was actually bypassed or waived in the lending process. Incidentally, there were fewer cases of loan default than we experience nowadays. However, risks were also less sophisticated, largely foreseeable, and quite amenable to control. Thus risk identification, analysis, and mitigation never received serious attention—contrary to what exists in the contemporary bank lending function.

During the naive lending era, risk management in bank lending was at best anything but precise and rigorous. Lenders and borrowers deliberately courted each other's relationship in pursuit of mutually beneficial transactions. It was therefore not surprising that lending institutions never easily or suddenly became distressed, or failed, as was the case in the 1930s, 1990s, and early 2000s experience in Nigeria. This is probably as a result of the fact that good bank—customer relationship was emphasized, and banks tended to heed it.

Borrowers appreciated that banks had defensible cause in demanding collateral in the assets that they pawned. To some extent, this was the forerunner of the modern practice of taking or pledging real or financial assets as collateral for loan. It would seem, ironically, that present-day maneuvering of the lending process originated in how lenders and borrowers got around the collateral question and rules. While contemporary lenders try to check borrowers from dictating to them, the borrowers respond in kind—all in a bid to remain relevant to the credit process. On occasion, this situation introduces acrimony in the credit relationship.

AWAKENING STAGE

A positive change in attitude toward risk, risk taking, and risk management in lending gained importance as banks continued to evolve their own methodological framework for credit risk management. The awakening stage relates to the post-1900 era, ending, in the case of Nigeria, in the late 1980s. In Nigeria, the awakening stage gained momentum during the period between establishment of the Central Bank of Nigeria (CBN) and deregulation of the banking industry. The changes that took place from 1958 when the CBN was established to 1986 when the government introduced the structural adjustment program (SAP) to deregulate the economy marked the highlights of this stage. The period of the awakening stage could be longer or shorter in different countries, depending on their peculiar circumstances.

During the awakening stage, banks gained practical risk management experience, tailored to banking needs at the time. Banks granted loans to finance largely common, regular, and simple transactions that were mainly secured with tangible or other types of collateral. But this trend was to change as banks acquired enhanced lending capabilities. In time, credit risk increased with increasing loan amounts, complicated lending dynamics, and default rate. More rigor was introduced to credit risk management as banks became more aggressive and interested in practical analysis of borrowers, borrowing causes, and transaction dynamics.

The focus of risk analysis at this stage was to determine and mitigate forces in borrowers, their markets and industries, as well as the national economy that might frustrate the ability of the borrowers to repay loans. Lending officers realized that risk identification, analysis, and mitigation were the crux of their job. Thus, more risk control measures were adopted to secure the exposure of banks on lending activities. In addition, documentation of loans was accentuated in the wake of, and to check, unanticipated and emerging intrigues in the lending process.

It became imperative to continually reassess and improve risk management framework and methodologies. Banks responded to the situation with strengthened commitment to risk management on the premise of a three-pronged approach reflected in Figure 20.1. The hope in doing so was that risk would be mitigated when banks painstakingly analyzed loan proposals, institutionalized credit compliance, and aggressively managed nonperforming loans.

Incidentally, this approach remains a highly favored method for dealing with the question of risk in bank lending. It supplanted the methodology of the naive lending era and has evolved into a reliable mechanism for credit risk management beyond the awakening stage. Its features are highlighted throughout this book, especially where topics on credit risk management are discussed.

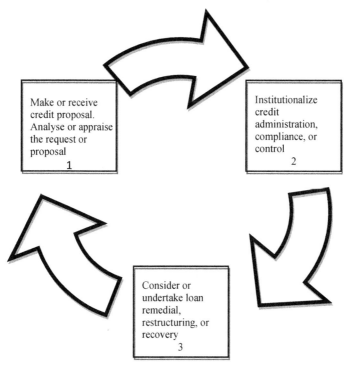

FIGURE 20.1   Modern credit risk management process.

REGULATORY INTERVENTION

From early 1987 to date, in the case of Nigeria, regulatory intervention has been a major feature in the management of credit risk in banks. Although measures taken at the awakening stage ameliorated credit risk management, loan default remained a critical issue and a worrying reminder that all was not well with the credit process. In many banks, and at aggregate level, the volume of nonperforming risk assets increased beyond projection. Recurring cases of distressed, failing, and failed banks during this period were traced to large and increasing stocks of nonperforming loans. Soon the poor quality of risk assets and diminution of earnings became more painful and disturbing. Loan loss provisions and write-offs on loan portfolios ravaged balance sheets and exacerbated distress of banks. This situation accounted, to a large extent, for the bank failures of the 1990s and 2000s in Nigeria.

In Nigeria, as was the case in many other countries, the Central Bank intervened with specific corrective measures to deal with worsening quality of earning assets of banks. It did so in order to reverse poor attitude to risk management, and the stifling provisions and write-offs on the lending portfolio. The remedial measures were encapsulated in regular credit and monetary policies that targeted recapitalization, single obligor limit, credit distribution, and specific compliance requirements. But the scope of the intervention varied from one country to another depending on the condition of banks. The banking industry surely needs such intervention to remain relevant, and the authorities are not relenting.

Unfortunately, pre-2005 regulatory intervention in Nigeria achieved less-than-expected results in addressing the problems of the banks. The authorities tried but all to no avail to reposition banks to always avoid reckless lending, and be prudent, more risk averse, and liquid. Several target regulatory policies barely tamed some of the excesses of the banks without completely resolving distress caused by poor lending practices. Yet, the rate and importance of regulatory intervention increased over time to reflect its need to stem credit-induced systemic distress in the banking industry. New controls were introduced as many banks started failing in the wake of credit-induced liquidity crisis. In time, more intervention became necessary and inevitable. Today, regulatory intervention has become an integral part of credit risk management in banking. It is likely to continue in the future, especially with increasing sophistication of the banking business and globalization of the financial system.

Forces underlying regulatory interventions

In Nigeria, increasing cases of distressed, failing, and failed banks have perhaps been the single most important reason for regulatory intervention in credit risk management. Bank failure has been a source of constant worry not only to bank customers but to bank owners and the regulatory authorities. It has indeed been a major cause of apathy toward banking in some countries. In many emerging markets, banking culture is anything but appreciable. There is widespread distrust in the banking system, caused by perceived risk of deposits in the banks. In most cases, past and recent experience of bank distress and failure inform lack of confidence in the banking system.

The problem has historically been evident in Nigeria. During the 1930s, distress tainted the banking industry, leaving all but one indigenous bank failed. Distress was yet to set in again in the early 1950s after the banking boom of the late 1940s. As in the 1930s experience, the indigenous banks were severely hit. Only four indigenous banks survived the scourge.

The adoption of SAP in 1986 led to deregulation of key industries and economic sectors, causing an explosion in the number of banks. However, by the mid-1990s, the boom had given way to distress and failure. In late 1995, out of the 120 private sector banks in Nigeria, at least 60 were considered distressed—up from 47 in 1994 and only 8 in 1991. As of December 1995, the problem had worsened, forcing the CBN to liquidate five banks, while it placed five others under interim management boards and took over 17.

In the recent past, especially prior to the experience of the global financial meltdown in 2007−2009, banks continued to be distressed and fail. In 2005, for instance, the CBN revoked the operating licenses of 14 banks while several others merged or were acquired, mainly to avoid failure or liquidation. The CBN announced further threat of distress in 2009 when it sacked the management boards of 8 of the 24 operating banks in the country at the time.

Ironically, while banks appreciate regulatory support and influences, they nonetheless tend to groan under the pressure with which the intervention comes. It is not uncommon that banks would sometimes want to blame Central Banks for some of the problems of the industry. This was often the case when particular regulatory policies produced a mix of positive and negative outcomes. Complaints usually became rife when envisaged positive results were more than offset by unintended negative outcomes. Yet, intervention has come to stay and will remain a veritable tool for fulfilling the supervisory roles of Central Banks as the public watchdog.

FINANCIAL MELTDOWN AND BAILOUT

Ideally, a combination of the analytical framework shown in Figure 20.1 and regulatory intervention should solve observed risk management lapses in bank lending. Unfortunately, this was farfetched. It would seem that particular risks defied corrective measures adopted by banks and regulatory authorities. Besides, risk management models became ineffectual in cases of insider abuse of the lending process. More often than not, reported cases of liquidity crisis and distress were traced to such insider abuse. Issues of bank distress and failures, traced largely to risky and reckless lending, also became recurring incidences. More than ever before, banks started facing complicated credit risks and management challenges.

A number of reasons accounted for the dilemma of the banks. Many banks ventured into highly risky and exotic credit products that the risk management framework in use at the time could not effectively support. The appeal of such lending was really doubtful or unfounded. Yet bankers committed incredible amounts of depositors' funds to doubtful credit products. Perhaps they did so with a sense of adventure and taste, or in pursuit of budget goals. Whatever the reasons, ignominious lending practices brought the banking industry into disrepute as the concomitant crunch embarrassed shareholders and customers. This was the experience in many financial centers around the world, which ultimately became a precursor to an impending global financial meltdown.

The meltdown experienced worldwide between 2007 and 2009 apparently overwhelmed government and regulatory authorities. Indeed, it marked the height of the ignominy of the banking system. The meltdown resulted mainly from failings in bank lending and credit risk management. Around the financial centers of the world, leading banks had taken huge and unmitigated exposures in financial derivatives, exotic, and other paper credit products.

It was found, when the crunch came, that collateral for most of the lending was unrealistic. Worse still, borrowers were not forthcoming with loan repayment. Liquidity squeeze pervaded the global financial system as had never been experienced in recent history. As though it was a contagion, the crisis spread and threatened national economies around the world. In Europe, the United States, and some other regions of the world, governments responded forcefully to the crisis. Large sums of taxpayers' money were doled out to bail out distressed and failing banks, as well as to rescue threatened key industries.

Some of the countries that pretended to be immune to the contagion soon paid dearly for it. Consider the case of Nigeria, for instance. The regulatory authorities gave a clean bill of health to all the banks in the country, only to reverse the decision a few months later. In the aftermath of the meltdown, the CBN clamped down on eight banks after declaring them terminally distressed. It sacked their management boards and appointed interim management boards to oversee the affairs of the banks. Its investigation of the banks revealed fraudulent lending that bordered mainly on insider abuse. Eventually, the CBN disbursed ₦620 billion of taxpayers' money in 2009 to bail out the eight banks in a rare intervention to avert crisis in the country's financial system.

Questions about financial meltdown border on the outlook for the future. Will it be experienced in the future? When again, or how often, may it be experienced? Can banks get bailout funds from government and regulatory authorities in the future? On what terms may bailout funds be advanced to ailing banks and industries? These questions cannot be answered with precision due to uncertainty of the future. Future incidence of financial meltdown is certainly unpredictable. Like bank failure, it might follow some indefinite cycle.

Incidentally, there is a striking difference in the way government and regulatory authorities responded to the meltdown and how they hitherto reacted to similar crisis. Prior to the meltdown, distressed banks were in most cases allowed to fail and be liquidated, or taken over. In the case of the meltdown, when the crunch came, the CBN quickly rallied funds to bail out distressed banks. This departure from its previous practice was a defining feature of the meltdown era.

There were other decisive measures that the regulatory authorities took to ameliorate the financial meltdown. For example, the CBN reengineered its liquidity support window for the banks. The window allows banks that have urgent short-term funding needs to overdraw their accounts with the CBN so as to meet the needs. The banks are expected to repay the overdrawn balance within a specified period of time. This window usually comes in handy and helps the banks to honor their interbank obligations, especially in periods of liquidity crunch.

Also, in Nigeria, Asset Management Corporation of Nigeria (AMCON) was established by legislation to recover liquidity for, and help in rescuing, distressed, failing, and failed banks. The immediate effect of the institution of

AMCON was direct and, to a large extent, satisfied the need to protect depositors' funds in the banks. The remedial role of AMCON kick-started with its takeover of three nationalized failed banks: Afribank, Bank BHB, and Spring Bank. The banks were christened "bridge banks" and were represented by Main Street Bank, Keystone Bank, and Enterprise Bank, respectively. This regulatory action was both expedient and innovative in the history of banking and rescue of banks in Nigeria.

Sometimes, banks avail themselves of the opportunity that bailout opens to them through mergers and acquisitions. Quite a few banks either merged or were acquired in the aftermath of major financial crisis. For example, the present United Bank for Africa (UBA) is the product of merger between the old UBA and Standard Trust Bank Limited. In the same vein, Fidelity Bank emerged from merger between Fidelity Bank, FSB International Bank, and Manny Bank. Other banks that followed suit included Stanbic IBTC Bank, Access Bank, Ecobank, First City Monument Bank, Sterling Bank, and Unity Bank formed from the merger of nine banks.

REAWAKENING STAGE

It is obvious that the recent financial meltdown greatly humbled regulators, bankers, and bank management. More than anything else, it opened their eyes to unimaginable risk management lapses right under their nose. Soon they realized that more ingenuity was needed in their approach to risk management and appreciating market discipline. Perhaps this was one of the credible means to free banks from punitive repercussions. This new thinking started to gain ground soon after the debilitating financial meltdown from which the global financial system emerged in 2009. But it gained global acceptance toward the end of 2010. At this time, most banks had seen the need to moderate their risk-taking appetite, strengthen risk identification, and adopt an effective risk mitigating policy framework.

Ideally the reawakening era should be considered to be now, and a response to anticipation of the future. In this context, I can say that it comprises two major aspects. It is a stage when:

- Banks are developing a more critical attitude toward risk taking and risk management in lending activities.
- Central Banks and deposit insurance corporations are firming up regulatory maneuvering and their oversight functions.

Banks, on the one hand, are propelled by a will to remain strongly going despite concerns about the financial meltdown, its cost, and other market shocks. The regulatory authorities, on the other hand, have statutory responsibilities to the banks, customers of banks, and the entire society. In both cases, existing risk management framework is subjected to intense scrutiny and questioned for efficacy.

It is instructive that the financial meltdown that I discussed earlier in this chapter triggered these changes. With increasing urgency to improve credit risk management, it becomes necessary to make securitization of loans more rigorous. Also, more emphasis is being given to rating of credits and borrowers, especially in emerging economies. All but one of the evolutionary stages—the naive lending era—benefited from the dawn of technological revolutions in the banking industry. However, the reawakening stage stands to benefit most from the advancing technological revolution in the banking industry.

QUESTIONS FOR DISCUSSION AND REVIEW

1. What factors contributed significantly to the evolution of contemporary credit risk management methodologies?
2. Given the volatile nature of the international financial market, how may "internationally active banks" effectively anticipate credit risk in the reawakening era?
3. To what extent does the Nigerian experience illustrate the evolutionary stages of credit risk management and its implications for bank management?
4. Critically examine how the contention that "the reawakening era should be considered to be now, and a response to anticipation of the future" attest to the influence of risk and uncertainty in bank lending.
5. Identify and discuss a named major incident in the development of Nigeria's financial system that significantly impacted any of the evolutionary stages of credit risk management in Nigeria.

Chapter 21

Emerging Markets and Debate on Framework for Credit Risk Control

Chapter Outline

LEARNING FOCUS AND OUTCOMES

There have been attempts dating back to the 1990s to supplant qualitative principles with mathematical models as a framework for credit risk management. The unfortunate outcome has been a raging debate between protagonists of a quantitative approach and qualitative principles regarding the views that each holds on the matter. However, in both cases, the objective of the two schools of thought remains the same and incontrovertible—how to improve the efficiency of credit risk control in bank lending. Disagreement exists only in terms of methodology to attain the goal.

In this chapter, I examine the factors at issue in the debate about whether mathematical models should supplant qualitative principles as methodology for credit risk management. You will, after reading this chapter, be able to:

- Appreciate the "qualitative principles versus mathematical models" debate in the context of evolving methodological swings
- Critically evaluate arguments in favor for and against mathematical models and assess the loopholes that they seek to address

Emerging Market Bank Lending and Credit Risk Control. http://dx.doi.org/10.1016/B978-0-12-803438-5.00021-0

- Review the age-old qualitative approach and determine whether it is still efficacious
- Compare and contrast qualitative principles and mathematical models and show how they reinforce or are opposed to each other
- Draw conclusions and make recommends based on the practicalities of credit risk management

CREDIT RISK FRAMEWORK DEBATE

Internal credit process, administered by bank management, remains in the melting pot. In this chapter, I am primarily concerned with discussing the analytical framework that explains foundation of the problem. My goal is to relate the identified problem to flawed bank lending and credit risk management practices and methodologies. In doing so, I highlight lessons and findings that impinge on the lending function.

The question of credit risk is about the hottest issue in banking today, and the trend is unlikely to change in the near future. I hold this view without prejudice to other contending banking issues bordering on market risk, operational risk, liquidity risk, and so on—some of which have attracted significant attention from the Basel Committee. It would be interesting to investigate the reason a lot of attention is directed to credit risk management in contemporary banking. A plausible explanation, on the face of it, is the need to protect depositors' and shareholders' funds. Without an ordered procedure for risk management in bank lending, stakeholders in banks would be exposed to the avoidable danger of possible loss of some or all of their investments in the banks. Often the loss is incurred when a bank becomes distressed, is failing, or actually fails. The real culprits in these cases are loan loss provisions and their ultimate write-off.

The credit literature is replete with topical issues and debate on risk management in bank lending, especially in the aftermath of the embarrassing 2007–2009 financial meltdown. Numerous scholarly articles have focused on the problem—albeit from different, often conflicting, perspectives. A number of books, critical of credit risk management in global banks, have been written, are perhaps being written, and, indeed, will be written in the future. A cursory search of the credit literature, credible Internet bookstores, and reputable online libraries—as well as brick-and-mortar bookshops and libraries—corroborates this view. An observable feature of some recent books in the credit literature is the use of technical models to measure and advise on credit risk. In the recent past, some banking and financial researchers have developed mathematical models that build on quantitative financial information and are expressed in functions, ostensibly to help bankers make, as well as predict, credit decisions. This move has triggered controversy about whether or not credit models should supplant qualitative principles as a credit risk management technique.

QUALITATIVE PRINCIPLES VERSUS MATHEMATICAL MODELS

The intellectual debate provoked by the formulation of mathematical models to supplant the qualitative approach is desirable. It shows that bank lending—nay, credit risk management—is tricky and deserves special attention. In the end, not only the banking industry but the entire financial system will be all the better for it. The debate should improve lending decisions and practice. But there cannot be a foolproof risk management technique in bank lending. The reason is that the variables that trigger, or precipitate, credit risk sometimes emanate from unexpected sources, such as force majeure, over which regulators and bank management do not have control.

Consider that even cash collateralized credit facility can become delinquent if the borrower does not service the credit. Under the circumstances, accrued interest and charges, which might have been unanticipated, create a hole in the collateral arrangement. One of my aims in this chapter is to take a critical look at issues underlying the credit risk framework debate and take an informed position on the debate.

The problem with mathematical modeling of credit risk is that it easily becomes unnecessarily too complex for the audience, especially the practitioners in emerging markets, at whom it is targeted. Secondly, we sometimes find authors writing on the subject in question from "outside" the credit industry, often relying more on their intellectual prowess than firsthand experience of the intricacies of credit risk. Thirdly, quantitative models and books embodying them are usually designed to fit the needs of practitioners in highly developed economies and financial markets. Hardly are they as useful to the situation of emerging markets and developing countries as they may be to the developed nations.

Besides, most of the practitioners in emerging markets and developing economies will find it difficult to adapt mathematical models to their professional and practical requirements for dealing with unpredictable and fickle borrowers. Incidentally, such borrowers account for most of the delinquent assets in the lending portfolios of the banks in those markets. On the other hand, the qualitative approach is easily applicable to developed, emerging, and developing financial markets.

Methodological swings

The pursuit of change, an alternative methodology for credit risk management, would be a feat if accomplished, but it remains elusive. So the question is can credit models—functions that seek to predict the behavior of lending variables and officers in relation to perceived credit risk—effectively supplant qualitative principles? Opposing answers and views are possible and will reflect the dichotomy between the proponents and opponents of credit models.

Paradoxically, a so-called "qualitative approach" is laden with, and not entirely devoid of, quantitative measures. Bank management sometimes makes lending decisions based on analysis of ratios between data obtained from financial statements, mainly balance sheet and profit and loss account. This practice is seen, and is especially relevant, in lending to corporate borrowers. Often, in a very real sense, some quantifiable measures are subsumed under the qualitative approach. Of course, it is common knowledge that risk can be statistically calculated and applied in the framework of the qualitative approach. Yet, statistical quantification of risk or accounting calculation of financial ratios—both of which every so often make input into the qualitative approach—contrasts with mathematical modeling of risk for lending purposes. This contrast informs the lingering debate, within academic circles mainly, about modeling credit risk.

Notwithstanding any setbacks, some academics in the forefront of the push for a change from qualitative approach to mathematical models are not relenting. In recent years, the academics have shown marked commitment to the cause and defense of their finely honed works. Methodological swings occasioned by their works have gained momentum of late as is evident in Bielecki and Rutkowski (2004) and Duffie and Singleton (2003). Other works in the mold of these include Lando (2004) and two of the more recent titles, Saunders and Allen (2010) and Gregory (2010). A major factor in the drive for a change of emphasis from qualitative approach to mathematical modeling of credit risk appears to be tracing of recurrent financial crisis of global banks to failings in credit risk management. My take on the debate is as follows:

- An ideal approach would be for credit risk to be analyzed, in some cases, using the framework of the five C's of lending (i.e., the qualitative approach) and, in others, through application of mathematical models (i.e., the quantitative approach).
- The character of a particular lending should dictate choice of appropriate methodology to use for its risk analysis and mitigation.
- Credit analysts should be looking, in both cases, to establish loan repayment ability of borrowers. An individual to whom a bank is considering lending money must demonstrate a strong capacity to repay the loan.

REVISITING THE QUALITATIVE APPROACH

A number of modern banking researchers, analysts, and authors lean toward the qualitative approach, just as we have some of their counterparts, such as the aforementioned, in the opposing school of thought. The works of Shimko (2004), Caouette et al. (2008), and Glantz and Mun (2010) are somewhat a departure from the hard line of proponents of mathematical models. This category of scholars has effectively tackled the crux of credit risk management, without necessarily delving into intricate mathematical modeling of the variables that make input into lending decisions. I cite them as typical examples to illustrate the continuing inclination toward the qualitative approach.

Incidentally, practitioners and regulators remain faithful to the time-honored qualitative approach. The age-old qualitative principles continue to appeal to them. The appeal is in the practical relevance of the principles to their work and to the cause and mechanism of credit risk management. The qualitative approach, for all intents and purposes, holds most of the aces and will continue to hold sway for as long as bankers continue to deal with capricious human nature and situations in lending. This fact, perhaps more than any other single consideration, explains why the principles come in handy. In a word, they are more expedient than mathematical models in making intricate lending decisions.

Observed shortcomings

There are basically three levels at which one can analyze the shortcomings of credit risk management methodologies, whether qualitative or mathematical models. Often credit risk problems arise from faltering management and staff commitment, doubtful inputs from weak boards, and weak and indecisive regulatory authorities.

Faltering management and staff commitment

It is imperative for a bank to have a crack team of analytical, operational, and field credit risk management officers, managers, and supervisors whose integrity and commitment are beyond question. Incidentally, while personnel of great resource are ever coveted, having them in critical lending positions is not a panacea for credit risk. Neither is a preponderance of such staff the most sought-after success factor. Realistically, a well-groomed and dedicated management that is tuned in to the need to build and sustain a functional credit risk culture bank-wide is the scarcest and most valuable asset. While I hold this view, I also take cognizance of the fact that bank management drives the credit process and has a profound influence on its outcomes. A strong bank management makes all the difference in the quest for an optimum credit risk framework.

Unfortunately, manipulation of the credit process for unprofessional ends sometimes happens under the auspices of bank management—and, often, right under its nose. This was usually a stunning finding in most cases of distressed and failed banks in Nigeria from the early 1990s to the late 2000s. An invaluable lesson learned from the fate that befell the banks is instructive. The rank-and-file staff took their cue from management that wallowed in insider abuse of the credit process. They engaged in various unprofessional conduct—pursuing, in so doing, some personal goals—to the detriment of the banks.

The maneuvering of diligent credit officers into working in tune with unprofessional dictates of their bosses was also common. Strangely, too, it was not uncommon for even officers of great resource to be swayed by budget goals to compromise their principles. Not infrequently, aberrations in the credit process like the foregoing only go to show deficiencies in a bank's credit risk management framework. If a credit risk framework is flawed, a management team that is bereft of scruples and lacking in commitment may exploit any loopholes in it. That is how, in such a situation, bank management fails to steer the credit process away from culpable maneuverings by lending officers and borrowers.

Yet, of all the important resources of a bank, *management* is perhaps about the most crucial for success. Frequently, a bank's success or failure is associated with the quality of its managers. In banking, strictly speaking, managers' roles are not only important but also precarious. Yet, bank management is accountable to the board of directors for efficiency and profitability of operations. However, the critical issue here is not necessarily *attaining* these ends. The *means*—coping with all sorts of conflicts—has been the salient consideration in assessing the effectiveness of management.

In banking, where most managers frequently come into direct contact with other people's money, managing assumes a dicey dimension. Besides the usual attributes required for a manager's success, bank managers must display a very high level of integrity, probity, and ingenuity. Above all, they must be persons in whom both the bank and customers can confide. Thus, integrity and trust are the hallmarks of managing in banking. Because of the need to win and retain the confidence of customers, fickle individuals must not be appointed bank managers.

A bank, like many other high-risk businesses, requires good management to succeed. The alternative—poor management—is perhaps the surest way to bank distress and failure. However, the variables that make up "good" management may not be easily identified and generalized for all banks in all situations. Bank management would be considered bad or poor if it fails to meaningfully scan its environment to determine and appropriately respond to contingencies that impart instability to the bank's operations. In such a situation, a manager might erroneously adopt a wrong leadership style. The result, in most cases, is poor morale, unsustainable labor turnover, and sabotage. In some extreme cases, the bank becomes insensitive to customers' needs and thus begins to lose market share and earnings.

The ineptitude of managers, especially those who flout bank policies and perpetrate insider abuse of sorts, has been a major cause of bank distress. With such managers, a bank will easily be afflicted with boardroom squabbles, fraud, and forgeries—the more serious of which frequently threaten and sometimes destroy the business foundation. Where such infraction of the operating rules was the reason for distress or failure, it usually would have dealt an irreparable ruin to the fortunes of the bank. Where management is adjudged weak and inefficient, the bank scores low in the ratings on risk assets quality, control of operational costs, and earnings capacity. Banks that are poorly managed tend to experience occasional liquidity problems because of mismatch of assets and liabilities. Poor management in this context is seen in the financing of highly risky transactions, high risk-taking appetite, and disregard for credit policy and controls.

Doubtful inputs from weak boards

As in manufacturing or other industries in the real sector of the economy, bank directors play crucial roles in shaping the outlook for success. The board of directors performs specific unique functions, one of which is policy formulation. But it also has oversight of executive management and plays a crucial role in organizational development. These roles should ordinarily contribute to efficiency of bank lending. Shareholders rely on the ingenuity of the board for safety of their investment. With well-constituted boards, directors are easily the most influential members of a bank.

Unfortunately, this influence is often misused through the pursuit of selfish gains at the expense of the bank. It is instructive that in almost all the cases of the 1990s bank failures in Nigeria, most of the bank directors were found culpable and liable to prosecution. Many of the directors infringed the credit process through insider abuse and were indicted for impropriety of conduct. Only a few maintained impeccable records of integrity and official conduct. Meanwhile, the board of directors has oversight of credit risk management. In this capacity, and through its audit and credit committee, it should forestall abuse of the credit process.

In broad terms, policy formulation is the primary objective of the board of directors. Critical issues requiring policy formulations in a bank include, but are not limited to, credit process, budget authorization, employment or key staff matters, and general corporate governance. In some banks, the board gets involved in several less important functions otherwise meant for the management team. This has frequently arisen where the board perceives the potency of such trivial matters in precipitating crisis that could threaten the existence of the bank if mismanaged. Yet, board usurpation of direct management functions is merely a reflection of crisis of confidence that may be detrimental to the corporate objective of the bank.

In such banks, the board is often personified in the managing director who not only functions as the chief executive officer but, in some cases, as the board chairperson. This situation has occasionally attracted criticism from the regulatory authorities, which, nevertheless, appear to be in abeyance as to evolving a means of dealing with negative roles of such *dictatorial* chief executives in banks. Organization development is perhaps the most tasking and dicey of all the objectives of bank directors and management. It involves anticipation of future challenges that impel *change* and the design of appropriate prognosis. A bank has to move along with changing times—increasing customer sophistication, for instance. In the process, old or current objectives and strategies are rendered ineffectual and moribund. The urge and need to evolve new *attainable* and *visionary* objectives become accentuated.

The manner and precision with which this challenge is handled determines how well the task of organizational development is accomplished.

In banking, the task of organizational development becomes more arduous given the rapidity of changes in the key variables that determine market patronage and loyalty in recent times. The observed changes occurred mostly in such areas as communication, data processing, information technology, and relationship management. It is the responsibility of the board and management to continuously scan the environment and harness available resources toward meeting the challenges and demands of the future business of the bank. On lending matters, success in fulfilling this role is necessary in managing the lending function well.

Weak and indecisive regulatory authority

With their supervisory oversight of credit and other bank functions, the regulatory authorities—mainly, in the case of Nigeria, the Central Bank of Nigeria and Nigerian Deposit Insurance Corporation—are well placed to check the excesses of lending officers. Through bank examination and banking supervision, the authorities can wield the big stick and whip up bank management when they stray from rectitude. But not a few financial experts believe that the authorities have not acted this role very well. In the past, prior to 2009, even in extreme cases when the authorities did wield the big stick, banks did not budge on the threat. The banks continued to circumvent critical credit policies, including even their internal lending guidelines, if anything. Surprisingly, they got off scot-free.

One pertinent question, nevertheless, agitates financial system observers and analysts. How are banks able to indulge in sharp and detrimental lending practices when the regulatory authorities have oversight of their activities? Investigation of failed banks in Nigeria by the authorities between 2005 and 2009 provided a revealing insight into the audacity of bank management. Executive and principal lending officers of failed banks flouted the credit process with impunity. Ironically, the authorities could not forestall flagrant violations of established lending criteria in the banks. Curiously still, the same authorities that exposed the credit process breaches in the banks in 2009 had hitherto given them a tacit clean bill of health. The authorities had condoned and ignored obvious infractions of the credit process. Thus, they neither built up to, nor braced themselves for, the fate that befell the banks, which, in most cases, was distress or failure.

QUESTIONS FOR DISCUSSION AND REVIEW

1. Of what relevance is the credit risk framework debate to the credit process? Your answer should show the pros and cons of the debate.
2. In what ways can the qualitative approach be improved and its loopholes addressed in the context of the principles on which it builds?

3. Do you think that mathematical models should supplant qualitative principles as the methodological framework for risk management in bank lending? Argue your answer with concrete illustrations.

4. **(a)** What are the main arguments of the proponents of mathematical modeling of credit risk?

    (b) To what extent are their arguments tenable in emerging markets' contemporary bank lending situations?

    (c) "Neither the qualitative principles nor mathematical models that seek to supplant them are foolproof." Discuss.

REFERENCES

Bielecki, T.R., Rutkowski, M., 2004. Credit Risk: Modeling, Valuation and Hedging. Springer Finance.

Caouette, J.B., Altman, E.I., Narayanan, P., Nimmo, R., 2008. Managing Credit Risk: The Great Challenge for Global Financial Markets, second ed. Wiley.

Duffie, D., Singleton, K., 2003. Credit Risk: Pricing, Measurement, and Management. Princeton University Press.

Glantz, M., Mun, J., 2010. Credit Engineering for Bankers: A Practical Guide for Bank Lending, second ed. Academy Press.

Gregory, J., 2010. Counterparty Credit Risk: The New Challenge for Global Financial Markets. The Wiley Finance Series.

Lando, D., 2004. Credit Risk Modeling: Theory and Applications. Princeton University Press.

Saunders, A., Allen, L., 2010. Credit Risk Management in and out of the Financial Crisis: New Approaches to Value at Risk and Other Paradigms, third ed. Wiley Finance.

Shimko, D., 2004. Credit Risk: Models and Management, second ed. Risk Books.

Chapter 22

Fine-tuning Principles of Bank Lending for Emerging Markets

LEARNING FOCUS AND OUTCOMES

In this chapter, I review the making of an effective framework for risk management in bank lending. I postulate that the credit risk management framework that the five C's of lending—and their underlying principles—furnish is dependable. I take this position bearing in mind that a number of academics have postulated alternative approaches that seek to model credit risk.

My main focus in this chapter is to look at the significance of the five C's from a different perspective. I establish a fit between the C's, their underlying principles, and the goal of contemporary risk management in bank lending. This discussion shows why and how the goal of risk management should be defined in the context of the underlying principles of the five C's such that the two ends are mutually reinforcing.

Taking the foregoing facts into account, after reading this chapter you will achieve the following learning outcomes:

- Understand the making of credit risk management framework in global banks
- Know the cardinal principles of bank lending and their impact on credit risk management

Emerging Market Bank Lending and Credit Risk Control. http://dx.doi.org/10.1016/B978-0-12-803438-5.00022-2

- Appreciate the fit between principles of lending and the goal of credit risk management in banking
- Be able to relate observed risk management methodologies to the cardinal principles of lending
- Know how the goal of credit risk management is best defined in the context of, and attained through a rigorous adherence to, the cardinal principles of lending

TINKERING WITH QUALITATIVE PRINCIPLES

In the preceding chapter I reviewed the debate about whether mathematical models should supplant qualitative principles as a framework for credit risk management. In the present chapter, I extend the discussion to showing improvements needed to strengthen the qualitative approach. It is obvious judging by the review and discussions that neither the qualitative principles nor mathematical models that seek to supplant them are foolproof. This may sound a bit far-fetched to the proponents of the mathematical models. But contrary to their thinking and view, the qualitative approach remains efficacious and immensely relevant to the credit process. All that matters, far from supplanting it, is to fine-tune it so that it is amenable to review and internal control. Fine-tuning should also improve and make it fit the vagaries of credit risk. I suggest aspects of the necessary fine-tuning as I discuss elements of the qualitative principles in this chapter.

One of my objectives—one that runs through the whole book—is to show how a critical analysis of qualitative variables is eminently suitable for risk management in bank lending. I need not belabor the point that the problems at issue in lending and credit risk management do not lend themselves to being formulated into standardized credit models. Most lending variables are capricious, in flux, and largely qualitative in nature. Since lending is fraught with contingencies, its vagaries deepen with differing obligors, borrowing causes, and risk management need. In view of this, it would be untenable to match borrowers correctly and apply a standardized mathematical model to managing the risk of lending to them. This fact underscores the relevance of a qualitative approach as a bulwark against credit risk and default. But there is need to tinker with the common qualitative framework so as to optimize its application and benefits.

If qualitative principles are ineffectual, it is because of the aforementioned shortcomings. In that case, mathematical models should not fare better, if anything. They are bound to suffer the same fate as qualitative principles. Thus, the solution lies in fine-tuning the qualitative approach rather than supplanting it. I hold and defend the foregoing view without fear of contradiction. I also do so with a sense of value for the achievement of the protagonists of mathematical approach to risk management in bank lending.

BULWARK AGAINST CREDIT RISK

Deposit money banks (DMBs) function essentially in a lending capacity in order to optimize the liability side of their balance sheets. In general, lending remains a basic bank function. It generates the single most important earning assets of a bank. However, it is also about the riskiest of all normal banking activities. It is therefore necessary to examine how this important banking function should be executed to mitigate risks, minimize or avoid losses, and fulfill the expectations of bank shareholders, customers, regulatory authorities, and the public.

Bankers have relied on basic qualitative lending principles to conduct credit risk management over time. Encapsulated in the so-called five C's of lending, those time-honored principles resonate with growing global concern about credit risk. At whatever level the question of credit risk is looked at, the principles hold sway. The reason is simple—the principles form the method-ological core of contemporary credit risk management in banking. To that extent, they are of cardinal importance. It could even be argued that the principles are omnipotent.

Ironically, credit risk remains a nightmare for bank management despite the concerted efforts of banking regulators and supervisors to strengthen the credit process and make it more responsive to modern banking challenges and risks. Usually, reckless lending was the main culprit in reports of regulatory authorities on investigation of distressed or failed banks. Besides the perceived recklessness of principal lending officers, bank lending had on occasion been found to be avoidably inefficient—a flaw that is often laid at the door of bank management. In each case, a common finding was that some bank officers either compromised their positions of trust or were obsessed by budget goals. Ostensibly, maneuvering of the credit process and regulation, the root of the catastrophic 2007–2009 global financial meltdown, arguably originated in the obsession of bankers with meeting financial budgets.

Bankers, on the other hand, compromise themselves when they engage in fraudulent lending. Observed cases of credit fraud manifested themselves mainly in insider abuse, manipulation of the credit process, and reporting of fictitious assets in the lending portfolio. Incidentally, in the case of Nigeria, the Central Bank of Nigeria found all eight banks that it declared terminally distressed and bailed out in 2009 guilty of these offenses. To underscore the seriousness of their crimes, the apex bank sacked the directors of the banks, appointed interim management boards to oversee the banks' affairs, and re-ported indicted directors of the banks to the Economic and Financial Crimes Commission for prosecution.

CRITERIA OF CONTEMPORARY BANK LENDING

I have elsewhere in this book discussed extensively the factors that are usually analyzed by loan officers in making lending decisions. In general, bank management is primarily concerned with, and makes policies that ensure, security and safety of credit facilities granted to customers. Several factors, including those that define the credit structure, underpin this *safety* consideration. The concern for protection of credit facilities reflects in the rigor of risk analysis—an integral part of credit analysis memorandum—that precedes credit approval in most banks. It is also essential that the credit is *suitable* for its purpose and returns adequate *profit* to the bank. Thus, without the assurance of safety, suitability, and profitability, a credit proposal may not be attractive to a bank. I briefly discuss these major constituents, or basic elements, of contemporary lending principles.

Safety of lending

It is of paramount importance to a bank that any credit it grants to a borrower is secured and protected against loss or diminution in value. Bankers generally implement the concept of credit analysis as a lending framework designed to identify and mitigate risks likely to adversely affect borrowers' ability to repay loans. Assurance of safety is accentuated when a bank takes collateral to secure loans. This is intended to further commit borrowers to doing their utmost to ensure that they repay their loans on due date. In general, collateral serves as an alternative source of repayment — a sort of fallback for a bank — in the event of default by a borrower. Its usefulness becomes apparent when the expected or primary source of repayment fails.

Appropriateness of loan

Consideration for appropriateness, or *suitability*, derives from the fact that granting a loan, defining its purpose, or ascertaining the borrowing cause must not conflict with economic policies, or regulatory guidelines, of the monetary authorities. Thus, a loan proposal should be declined if it fails the test of suitability, even if its risks are fully mitigated and there is assurance of repayment or safety. Examples of business activities to which a bank is not expected to grant credit facilities include gambling, betting or speculative transactions. On occasion a bank may have cause to consider some forms of credit proposal unsuitable. It would in such situations not be favorably disposed to grant the affected credit requests.

Earnings potential

A bank is expected to generate and sustain adequate earnings. It should be able to increase *revenue* and *profit* from operations to meet its operating expenses. It would be disturbing for a bank to produce a loss in any financial year. The reason is simple. A loss position might imply that the bank is distressed or experiencing cash flow deficiency, either of which could lead to a run on the bank. Loss on operations could result from huge provisions against loan loss. This is usually the case when a bank has a large stock of nonperforming loans and is compelled by regulation to write off the *lost* credits. In Nigeria, it is expected that a bank should not produce a loss in three consecutive financial years. The regulatory authorities will want to investigate a bank that falls foul of this rule. For these reasons, the profitability of loan proposals should be taken for granted in any consideration of principles of lending.

CARDINAL PRINCIPLES OF BANK LENDING

Bankers rely on five traditional, ostensibly omnipotent, principles for the analysis of loan requests. Before they make a decision to lend or not, they investigate, analyze, ask questions, and draw conclusions about the borrower's character, capacity, capital, faring in prevailing conditions, and ability to furnish collateral required to secure a loan. While the lending principles of safety, suitability, and profitability hold sway, these traditional principles remain omnipotent in every lending calculation. Perhaps bankers devised the best way to underscore their omnipotence when they tagged them the five C's of lending. In modern lending practice, every bank emphasizes them in making critical lending decisions.

Borrowers' loan requests may be granted or declined depending on their standings on the five Cs tests. Incidentally, both prospective and existing borrowers must pass critical tests that the bankers fashion to corroborate the time-honored five C's principles. Prospective borrowers, on the one hand, must satisfy them to be able to obtain credit facilities from a bank in the first place. Existing borrowers, on the other hand, must sustain good standing on them in order to continue to enjoy their extant credit facilities. Having identified the five C's of lending, my concern here is to discuss what bankers in emerging markets should look for when they analyze the C's for lending purposes. I am of course also concerned about how they go about analyzing the five C's in a way that mitigates lending risks.

Thus, there is no question as to whether the C's should be analyzed, and lending decision based on them, or not because they are taken for granted. Rather, the question is really about why and how the analysis should be done to achieve particular effects required or defined by the bank's lending criteria. In the following sections, I discuss these traditional principles of lending, popularly referred to as the five C's of lending.

Character of the borrower

Loan officers are required to investigate the character of borrowers before recommending credit requests to management for approval. It is generally believed that borrowers' creditworthiness and, in fact, the likelihood of loan repayment, make a derived function of their honesty and integrity. Yet character has ironically been the most poorly investigated risk factor in lending. Generally, the character of a borrower is associated not only with honesty and integrity, but attitudes, beliefs, and preferences. For corporate borrowers, the elements of character will usually include ownership structure, board composition, and management background.

Specifically, to analyze borrowers' character, lending officers should obtain vital information on their previous transactions with other banks and their business associates. In addition to this externally generated information, the borrowers should be interviewed firsthand on aspects of their business plans. Thus, through such credit inquiry and interviews, lending officers could gain insight into the lifestyles, attitudes, and beliefs of the borrowers and form opinions about their character. However, this is usually a difficult task, largely because character is a psychological trait and, as such, does not lend to quantitative analysis. At best, the analyst can draw inferences based on the observable behavioral tendencies of the borrower. But these inferences would largely relate to information elicited from the borrower by means of projective techniques. Therefore, they can be more or less accurate depending on the soundness of the opinions of the analyst. Over the years, banks have remained helpless by the failings in character investigation while, unofficially, the problem continues to account for a large proportion of annual reported loan losses of the banking system. Failings in character encourages a propensity to borrow and without the zeal to pay back—a problem that may persist for a long time unless banks take steps to redress certain weaknesses in their current procedure for interbank credit inquiry.

In some cases of loan default, banks painfully realize that the borrowers deliberately refused to comply with the terms and conditions of the credit facilities. However, in most cases of proven deliberate intentions to default on loans, banks are known to have declined the loan requests. In the late 1990s, a certain distressed bank in Nigeria, for example, threatened to publish the names of its loan defaulters who, in most cases, were in positions to or would be able to repay the loans. This kind of threat remained wishful thinking for several years until 2009 when the Central Bank of Nigeria actually did publish names of major loan defaulters in some national newspapers.

It is also not uncommon to find borrowers who habitually shop banks for credit facilities, obtain loans from one bank after another, and default on the loans in all the banks. Yet credit inquiries on such borrowers may actually fail to reveal the real creditworthiness and character of the racketeers! Unless banks have dependable reference points for credit inquiries and stop the infamous practice of simply stamping "considered suitable for normal banking transactions" as a response to credit inquiry, the risk associated with character in lending will even be exacerbated and continue to be a nightmare for the industry.

Capacity of the borrower

It is unlikely that a bank will want to lend money to borrowers that do not have a track record of success in their lines of business, pursuit, or other endeavor. Success in question here relates to the borrowers' continuing ability to attain personal or business goals as a result of possessing and diligently applying particular appropriate skills. Thus, borrowers must be competent in their businesses, or in projects and causes they engage in, to be able to obtain bank loans. Often incompetence of borrowers to execute projects for which they have obtained some credit facility is at the root of some loan defaults. This is not strange considering that awarding contracts on the basis of some dubious criteria has become commonplace. One notices this practice mainly in public sector contracts where on occasion government cancels contracts that it had previously awarded due to incompetence of the contractor.

The requirement for proof of borrowers' competence becomes more critical in particular lending situations, such as when borrowers apply for loans to:

- execute special, innovative, or one-off projects—those that differ from their regular or traditional transactions
- expand, modernize, or venture into completely new lines of business, often in response to changing markets
- start or fund operations of small-scale start-up enterprises, especially those that have a key person or owner-manager

In all of the above cases, banks should require the borrowers to demonstrate ability to successfully do the businesses, execute the projects, or carry out the plans. Although these three examples are not common borrowing causes, the need to appraise borrowers' capacity remains relevant in most lending situations.

What exactly does the term *capacity* mean? I have so far explained it without necessarily proffering a working definition. Yet we could infer the need to articulate the cause of capacity analysis for lending purposes. This cause borders on gaining insights into particular skills, experience, and track records of the borrower and raises some questions. How and in what capacity did the borrower acquire the skill and experience? Are the skill and experience relevant to the present borrowing request? To what extent may the bank rely on the skill and experience for efficient utilization and repayment of loan? Do the skill and experience adequately inform the observed track record? In most cases, these questions reveal attributes that constitute key success factors for the borrowing cause. The sum of issues in, findings and conclusions from investigation of the attributes underlines the crux of capacity analysis for bank lending purposes.

Through investigation of capacity, lending officers are able to make decisions about ability of borrowers to do and succeed in particular businesses, projects, or plans that require bank financing. This has more to do with assessing the level of ordinary and technical competences that the borrowers possess. Knowledge of borrowers' capacity gives confidence that they truly appreciate and have the ability to actualize their borrowing causes.

Capital available to the borrower

A business should be adequately capitalized so that it will be strong and capable of pursuing and fulfilling its objects. This is true for start-up and established companies. For a start-up, the possibility of failure and therefore loan default is high when it is undercapitalized. We often come across the phrase *adequately capitalized* and the word *undercapitalized* in literature on business and in financial analysis of companies. In most cases, finance writers and analysts use such concepts to show levels of funding for a company's operations. Often seekers and users of corporate financial data will want to know how much equity, debt, or both (i.e., a mix of them that defines the financial risk of a company) is in the funding of the company's operations. Concerns about this are usually informed by the need for a company to have good or stable capital structure.

Companies that employ more equity than borrowed funds tend to have less volatile operations and risk, and vice versa. In this sense, capitalization refers to the amount of money or resources—whether in cash, equipment, or other assets—that the promoters and other shareholders raise, bring, or invest to start, operate, or continue with a business. In finance parlance, such investment is termed *capital, equity* or *shareholders'* (i.e., owners') *equity.* It is entirely different, and connotes a different meaning, from *net worth* or *shareholders' fund*, which accounts for capitalization and retained earnings (i.e., accumulated profits not paid out as dividends to shareholders). While the former, on the one hand, depicts the company's capital structure, the latter, on the other hand, explains its financial structure.

The distinction between capital and net worth is often explained in terms of capital structure and financial structure, both of which reflect in the makeup of the liabilities side of the balance sheet. Analysis of capital structure will normally show amounts or combination of equity and debt in a company's balance sheet, while financial structure will tell of the content or mix of equity and retained earnings. A company may be adjudged risky for lending purposes if its operations are largely funded with debts. Banks especially tend to check owners' commitment in the amount of equity (i.e., investment) and profits (i.e., earnings) that they have or retain in the business when they analyze capital of a company. Yet, for lending purposes, they also analyze level of borrowing to determine the company's gearing. Thus, it is imperative to analyze both capital structure and financial structure to have an accurate indication of the financial risk of the borrowing company.

It is obvious from my discussion of the content and context of a company's capital that three variables—capitalization, commitment, and investment—are all related and critical in any analysis of a lending decision. Lending officers make and look out for standing of borrowers on these factors. Whether the borrowers are individuals or companies, good ratings help to predispose lending officers to their loan requests.

Conditions (current and anticipated)

I have emphasized in this book the point that the prevailing conditions in a particular country, community, or other location exert significant influence on the lending decision. In most cases, when we talk of conditions, what readily come to the mind are questions bordering on the political economy of a country. It is believed that favorable political and economic conditions are omnipotent in accounting for stability required for the success of business or other human endeavors. Let us admit that political upheaval and volatile economic situation are not propitious to fulfilling human and business enterprises. But they are in the same boat as other serious issues that constrain lending decisions. Concerns about the environment, culture, and markets also nowadays significantly condition thinking on how best to deal with the lending question and credit risk question. So also is the question of the legal system. Is the legal system efficacious? Does it guarantee or frustrate free enterprise? Do businesses and citizens have absolute faith in the courts?

Lending officers analyze these and other macro issues to understand how they impinge upon human and business performance in a particular country or location. They do so as a study, analysis, or evaluation of prevailing *conditions* in that country or location. Using their findings as basis, they make lending decisions. Whether a bank lends money or not may depend on opinions of the lending officers on perceived conditions in the operating base of the borrower. There is need for a good operating environment for human and business enterprises to flourish. Here emphasis is on stable sociopolitical organization, as well as prospects for economic growth, development, and rewards. Above all, there should be assurance of appropriate legal backing for life-fulfilling and environmentally friendly endeavors. Lending to borrowers is likely to be hampered in countries or places where these needs are unfulfilled.

Unfortunately, conditions that lending officers analyze and influence lending decisions are beyond control by borrowers. They can neither prevent nor change incidence of elements in the "conditions." However, bankers expect borrowers to correctly anticipate the elements, their occurrence and negative impact, and make provisions against them. It is the ability of borrowers to correctly act in this way that makes the difference between how a banker will see the impact of conditions on one borrower relative to another in the same business and location.

Collateral to secure the loan

Banks take collateral as a rule, and to complete documentation and security of approved credit facilities. In principle, it is never as such given prominence among factors in the lending decision. Yet banks do not take collateral just for the sake of it. Rather they demand collateral, in practice, as one of the important *conditions precedent* to drawdown on approved loans. In doing so it is informed by the fact that the relevance of collateral consists, first and foremost, in establishing the commitment of the borrower to the purpose or cause of the loan. It somehow instills discipline in the use of credit facility and protects a bank's assets financed with depositors' funds against willful loss or wastage by borrowers.

It is necessary, prior to suggesting the ways out, for credit analysts to provide information on the primary collateral for credits. They should explain the type, location, *how* to exercise control over, and—in the event of default—ultimately realize the collateral pledged by the borrower. A statement of the nature of the bank's lien over the collateral forms part of security analysis, as well as an inspection report, including the date of last inspection, current valuation of the collateral, and the basis of its valuation. Most banks accept only valuation reports from credible estate firms. Credit analysts should always offer personal opinions on any other observations about the collateral.

Qualities of good collateral

I should mention here that collateral that is not *perfected* might not provide the desired security in the event of default. It is paramount to take only good collateral. Collateral is adjudged good for lending purposes when it satisfies the following conditions:

1. It enjoys a stable or increasing long-term market value (i.e., its economic or monetary value may not be easily diminished by inflation or other wealth-ravaging forces).
2. On forced sale basis, it is easily realizable (implying availability of ready buyers or existence of *effective* demand for the asset at any point in time).
3. The asset used as collateral has a low or negligible cost of realization in the event of default by the borrower.
4. It is not outlawed (i.e., the asset must not have been forbidden by law or acquired illegally by the borrower).
5. There is no foreseeable future event that would prohibit its use as collateral for borrowing purposes.

Particular collateral may not have all of these qualities in equal degree at the same time. However, their relative importance reflects in the order in which they are listed above.

THE FINE-TUNING REQUIRED

Now the question is how can the ignominious trend be reversed and credible lending practices dawn in the banking industry? One major factor holds all the aces. That factor is the unalloyed commitment of management and principal lending officers of a bank to institutionalizing a functional, but practical, risk management framework powered by a robust credit culture. As critical resources for success, bank management and lending officers must have a dogged determination to work diligently, shun reckless lending, and generally keep an eye on the risk assets portfolio.

Ideally, a practical credit risk framework should derive from this success factor. But it is a factor that evolves out of deliberate management action to build a quality loan portfolio and takes root in banks where a sound credit culture exists. Then a pool of requisite in-house credit skills nourishes the framework that builds on this success factor. Over time, the evolved framework becomes institutionalized and founded on three long-term lending objectives that inspire bank management and the principal lending officers. The required in-house skills should also include staff that work in the credit policy and control unit.

The three overriding objectives of lending that inform the content and context of institutionalized credit risk management framework should be aptly defined to:

- enhance asset quality—evident in pursuit of no or small and sustainable amounts of delinquent loans, loan loss provisions, and charge-offs
- satisfy prudential standards and guidelines, with a policy of zero tolerance in lending, which a clean record in credit irregularities and sanctions should corroborate
- optimize returns at moderate risk level (i.e., to increase lending-based and related earnings without taking undue credit risk)

These three objectives inform the making and cause of credit risk management framework in a practical sense. A bank that adopts them as internal criteria for appraising the performance of its lending officers and risk assets portfolio cannot go wrong. This point is pertinent and is underscored by the structure and functioning of the framework, one that:

- specifies roles and responsibilities for the regulatory authorities, board of directors, and bank management
- codifies specific lending criteria in a book, such as a credit manual, that is accessible to all members of a bank
- makes it possible for bank members to be constantly apprised of the bank's credit policy, process, and control
- tames credit risk appetite of lending officers and predisposes bank management to realistic credit budget
- ensures that punitive measures are taken against bank staff and people or organizations who infringe the credit process

The regulatory authorities, boards of directors of banks, and bank staff and management should be the driving force behind effective credit risk management in banking. In a broad sense, these three bodies should constitute the real credit risk managers in the banking industry. On occasion, the regulatory authorities in emerging economies intervened in an effort to curb a canker of a sickening mess. Such interventions, unfortunately, came rather too late—sometimes when the banks that needed them were on the verge of failure or had actually failed.

A bank's credit risk management strategy must derive from the bank's overall vision, which for its members is really about defining, agreeing, internalizing, and practicing a certain collectively agreed and shared *core ideology*. This is germane to evolving a corporate culture, one by which the bank, its members, businesses and customers or products markets can easily be identified. With a clearly defined ideology, the members will be indoctrinated about the cause of the bank and its values. Understanding of the *cause of being* (i.e., core purpose) and upholding the agreed *standards*, *morals*, or *ethics* (i.e., core values) of the bank is important in evolving a workable long-range strategy. This is because it tunes the members to the challenges of competition in the bank's products markets.

Besides, strategy for the business has a strong significance for its financial analysis. A bank must first build capacity, define its strategic intent, and then start pursuing its goals with proven commitment. In Nigeria, as in several other emerging markets, there is keen competition in the banking industry. Banks that survived the distress crisis of the mid-to-late 1990s, on the one hand, learnt their lessons in a hard way and are determined to forge ahead. The public, on the other hand, are yet to fully restore confidence in the banking system. With dwindling, cautious patronage, and thinning margins, banks are more than ever before challenged by fierce competition that may nail the coffin of the weak ones. It is in this context that the business acumen of bank management should be exploited to ensure survival. Playing the hopeless challenger for too long can barely guarantee modest existence that will not impress the board and shareholders of the banks. It is expected that bank management must incorporate determination of the competition complexion of the bank's business into the framework of its regular business objectives. Doing so, it becomes set to tackle the more intricate contemporary challenges in competitive banking.

QUESTIONS FOR DISCUSSION AND REVIEW

1. How would you critique the notion that the five C's of lending are all omnipotent? Your answer should support, or be opposed to, reliance on qualitative principles for credit risk management.
2. Do you think that the goal of risk management in bank lending can be realistically attained through mathematical modeling of credit variables and risk?

3. In what ways can a fit be established between the five C's, their underlying principles, and the goal of credit risk management?
4. Why and how should the goal of credit risk management be defined in the context of the principles of the five C's such that the two ends are mutually reinforcing?
5. Do you think that the goal of credit risk management is best defined in the context of, and attained through a rigorous adherence to, the cardinal principles of lending?

Analytical Framework for Credit Risk Control

Chapter 23

Cash Flow Analysis and Lending to Corporate Borrowers

Chapter Outline

LEARNING FOCUS AND OUTCOMES

Banks have over time institutionalized the practice of making lending decisions based on cash flow strength of borrowers. The sense in doing so builds on realizing that most borrowing causes originate from *cash flow timing differences*. This is especially the case in lending to corporate borrowers. But it is also equally relevant to other forms of lending.

Let me briefly explain what I mean by cash flow timing differences. There are three ways in which I will define this phrase now so that readers can easily understand its import. It refers to changes that individuals or companies experience in the sources and application of cash available to them. Such changes affect patterns of cash receipts, expenditures, and reserves. The changes are informed by changing cycles of business seasons or other causes. A cash flow problem implied in the foregoing meaning can also manifest itself when there is alteration in the sources of cash available to an individual or business as a result of changes in periods when they receive, spend, or reserve cash from their operations. The third definition, a derivative of the second, is variation in the periods, sources, and amounts of cash that individuals or businesses may receive, spend, or reserve in the conduct of their operations. My leading objective is to demonstrate how to calculate and interpret cash flow for lending purposes.

The appeal of cash flow is in its ability to provide a dependable source of loan repayment. When borrowers—whether they are individuals or companies—are deficient of cash, they tend to default on loans and vice versa. It is therefore essential that credit analysts accurately determine cash flow strength of prospective borrowers as part of their credit analysis reports. It is not always easy to calculate cash flows, but credit analysts will not go wrong if they follow a proven methodological framework for cash flow analysis and interpretation. It is usually helpful to do so. The approaches that I set out in this chapter are reliable.

Against a backdrop of the foregoing, I present and discuss some of the practical and effective analytical procedures that credit analysts have at their disposal for cash flow calculation. In doing so, I examine critical aspects of cash flow analysis and lending. My objective is to provide knowledge that readers need to be able to handle the "questions for discussion and review" section of this chapter. This way, the learning focus and outcomes for this chapter will be realistic.

CONCEPT AND VALUE OF CASH FLOW

One financial element that facilitates effective running of business enterprises is *cash*. It is generally believed that cash is the lifeblood of a company. This implies that continuous generation of cash is an essential, though not sufficient, reason for a firm's continuing in business as a strongly going concern. In practical terms, receipts (inflows) and payments (outflows) of cash make it possible for economic units to effectively conduct business transactions.

The notion of cash flow depicts the necessity of cash in promptly meeting financial obligations that arise from normal transactional exchanges in business. Therefore, cash flow is instrumental in satisfying such critical financial obligations as settlement of creditors, repayment of debt, payment of employees' salaries, and so on. From lending perspective, the flow of cash is perhaps the single most important element on which banks hinge hope for prompt loan repayment. When cash flows of borrowers are weak, banks that lend money to them become exposed to a high risk of default. The converse is also true—loan repayment ability of borrowers tends to be enhanced with strong cash flows. In most cases, this explains why banks rely heavily, if not entirely, on cash flows in making critical lending decisions. The obsession of banks with cash flows has given rise to what is now termed *cash flow lending*. This phrase denotes the practical reliance of banks on cash flows of borrowers in making critical lending decisions.

Cash flow contrasts from, and is for a bank more important than, *profit* in any consideration of financial capacity of borrowers to repay loans. Profit might be declining whereas cash flows remain strong. For example, a company can sustain a good cash flow position in a given financial year by selling off certain equipment, or other assets, even though sales are insufficient. Cash realized from disposal of the assets offsets the impact of insufficient cash sales during the period. There could also be another scenario in which a company always replaces or increases stock levels. In this case, the company might not be in a position to preserve sufficient cash. On the contrary, a company that does not replenish stocks as fast as it uses them up will conserve cash. There is yet another important consideration that establishes the preeminence of cash flow over profit in making lending decisions. Whereas a company can easily manipulate its profit figures, it cannot maneuver the true cash it generates from operations. There are other critical distinguishing features of cash flow that I present in the following discussion.

IDENTIFYING CASH FLOW SOURCES

It is important for loan officers to appreciate the various sources from which prospective borrowers would generate cash flows required to meet their expected loan repayment obligations to a bank. Perhaps the most easily identifiable source of cash for a firm is its balance sheet. In subsequent discussions in this chapter, I establish how the balance sheet incubates cash and how to isolate the cash for credit analysis and lending purposes. However, the cash often available from the balance sheet is insufficient to meet a firm's operational needs. Therefore, there is need to explore other sources of cash available to the firm.

Cash flow drives liquidity and a company must remain liquid to be able to meet its obligations, especially the matured debts. To achieve this, the company must sustain cash generation and maintain its cash flows position at the desired level. Finance managers are often tasked to do anything but allow their companies to become cash deficient at any point in time. In doing so, they have three options on which they could rely. The options, which are not necessarily mutually exclusive, are as follows:

- Cash flows generated from normal business *operations*, which depend on market share and sales turnover. Cash flow *from operations* is often referred to as *net operating cash flows* (NOCF). It denotes the *net* amount of cash that a company generates from sales. The import of *net* in this definition is that the NOCF is arrived at only after deducting *cost of goods sold*, other *operating costs*, and *movements* in working capital.
- Some financial planning that may involve certain *refinancing* packages that could be accomplished through equity issue, increased liability, or debt. A company would be adjudged to have the financial flexibility required to service its debt if it can readily raise more equity or refinance its debt through banks or other financial institutions.

- Disposal of fixed, current, or trading assets. A company that demonstrates *operational flexibility* would be able to easily liquidate particular assets to repay its debt. In fact, there might even be the need to sell part of the company to raise the required cash.

Lending officers should analyze the loan repayment ability of prospective borrowers in the context of the above cash flow sources. In most cases, banks must rely on one or more of the identified cash flow sources for loan repayment. It is unlikely that bank management would grant loans to prospective borrowers that fail to demonstrate convincing capacity to generate adequate cash from any of the above sources on an ongoing basis. Otherwise, if granted, the obligors might not be able to repay the loans.

OBTAINING CASH FLOW INFORMATION

The importance and sources of cash flow might not be in doubt. However, it could be doubtful that a credit analyst would obtain accurate information on a prospective borrower's cash flow position. Yet, the analyst must obtain the right information to be able to make accurate judgment and recommendation. In what ways may credit analysts be assured that they get accurate cash flow information? In addition to audited financial statements, there are two pragmatic methods by which desired cash flow information could be obtained.

The analyst could examine either *sales records* or *bank statements* of prospective borrowers. In general, analysis of audited accounts is the most preferred method. Banks favor audited financial statements and annual reports of corporate borrowers for particular reasons, including:

- furnishing of detailed information on various accounting entries
- facilitating establishment of relationships between particular items of the accounts
- helping to explore observed performance trends over given periods

Thus, lending officers stick to audited financial statements of prospective corporate borrowers for cash flow analysis.

However, preliminary cash flow investigation could start from examining sales records and bank statements of prospective borrowers. Yet, in comparison with audited financial statements, these two cash flow investigation methods often provide only perfunctory information. Sales records could be inaccurate or falsified. Thus, while the analyst can request daily sales records to get evidence of cash that a business generates, the information may not be relied upon to make a critical lending decision.

Information provided in bank statements suffers similar setback as that obtained from sales records. Firstly, credit analysts might not have access to all of a borrower's clearing checks to be able to determine their account turnover

over particular periods. It is only a company's clearing bank that will have access to daily, weekly, or monthly information on its cash inflows and outflows. Secondly, unscrupulous borrowers might boost their account turnover through *check flying*. It becomes difficult to know true sales turnover or cash position under the circumstances.

In view of these considerations, analysis of audited financial statements and annual reports remains the most credible method of obtaining cash flow information for lending purposes. Sales records and bank statements should be used with caution as cursory alternatives to complement full reliance on audited accounts.

UNIQUE ATTRIBUTES OF CASH FLOW

In bank lending, cash flow is credited with unique attributes. It is generally regarded as a credible source of loan repayment. Its unique features are widely acknowledged in three main considerations, presented below.

Cash flow as an analytical tool

Cash flow serves as an analytical tool for bank officers responsible for credit appraisal. In this context, cash flow analysis can be relied upon to predict current and future capacity of borrowers to pay debts. The analysis can foretell the likelihood of business failure. This happens when NOCF is poor, indicating possible financial incapacitation of a business as a result of worsening deficiency of cash. Where analysis reveals a strong cash flow position, it could be taken for granted that the company has the financial capacity to pay its maturing debts. Thus, credit analysts must review records of ongoing generation of cash by prospective borrowers. Often such records help to predict the capacity of borrowers to meet future debt obligations.

Superiority over funds flow statement

On consideration of analytical precision, cash flow enjoys preeminence over funds flow statements. The latter is also referred to as statement of sources and applications of funds. The drawbacks of funds flow reflect the strengths of cash flow. The major strength of cash flow hinges on calculation and application of net operating cash flows (NOCF) in financial analysis. Of course, banks depend on it for loan repayment.

Cash flow has other notable advantages. For example, credit analysts can justify or decline particular loan requests based on cash flows' standing of the prospective borrowers. This is possible because cash flow can reveal a company's net financing surplus or deficit. Depending on the loan amount, a surplus position would imply that the firm might not really have a purported financing need. Financing requirements, perhaps in the amount that a borrower requests, would be justified if financing deficit is indicated. Thus, cash flow analysis determines if a bank would decline, grant a new, or increase an existing loan.

In the case of funds flow, some of the entries would be adjusted to arrive at a true cash position of the company. For example, funds flow does not isolate interest expense from interest income. It does not also separate ordinary activities, incomes, and expenses from supplementary activities. There is yet another disadvantage of funds flow in the adoption of accruals principle, rather than true cash position, in determining profit figure.

Funds flow is also criticized on the ground that it does not provide complete information on some of the accounting items such as cash balances and debts. This shortcoming arises because of a tendency of companies to net off some items of accounts. In the circumstances, it becomes difficult to ascertain the true cash position of the company. These limitations define the preeminence of cash flow over funds flow in appraising loan requests.

Informs integrity of credit report

Lending officers can rely on the integrity of properly analyzed cash flow statements to recommend approval or decline of particular loan proposals. In practical terms, it is difficult to manipulate cash flows the way companies often do with other accounting records. While companies can, and often do, window-dress their accounts to achieve particular financial reporting objectives, cash flow does not easily lend itself to such maneuvering. Depending on what is at stake, companies can fix their balance sheets, income statements, and funds flow statements. For instance, this can be done to get good results in ratio analysis of their accounts. It would be difficult, in the case of cash flow, to tinker with factual cash position. Thus, in comparison to other financial records, cash flow is, to a large extent, inviolate.

ELEMENTS OF CASH FLOW ANALYSIS

The basic profit and loss account equations provide the foundation for cash flow analysis. Credit analysts should appreciate how each of the items of the profit and loss account is derived. Such knowledge is critical, as we shall see below. It helps the analysts identify related balance sheet accounts that impart sources and uses of funds in analyzing a company's cash flow position. I am not concerned with the underlying accounting principles in constructing funds flow statement (i.e., statement of sources and applications of funds). Yet, I must mention the basic funds flow principles that underpin the following balance sheet equation:

$$\text{Assets} = \text{liabilities} + \text{capital}$$

This equation establishes the relation between assets and liabilities in a balance sheet statement. When an assets figure is increasing or decreasing, the liabilities figure must also be increasing or decreasing to maintain balance in the equation. However, for purposes of funds flow and cash flow analysis, increases and decreases in assets and liabilities have different implications.

In general, net decreases in assets and net increases in liabilities values represent sources of funds. In the converse, net increases in assets and net decreases in liabilities values indicate uses of funds. Thus, the net change in a company's cash position is derived by netting off uses from sources of funds. This information usually comes in handy in determining a company's true cash flow position. Acquainting credit analysts with the major equations of profit and loss account is pertinent at this point[1] (Table 23.1).

TABLE 23.1 Major Equations of Profit and Loss Account

Net Sales

   − Cost of goods sold

= **Gross profit (loss)**

   − Selling, general, & administrative expense (SG & A)

= **Operating income (loss)**

   + Non-operating income

   − Non-operating expense

   − Interest expense

= **Net profit (loss) before taxes**

   − Income tax expense

= **Net profit (loss) after taxes**

   + Extraordinary gains

   − Extraordinary losses

= **Net profit (loss) after taxes and extraordinary items**

A company can generate funds from sources other than its ongoing, normal business operations. This could happen, for example, when a company disposes of assets. Sale of assets might be one-off or irregular and therefore cannot be relied upon as a continuing source of cash. Thus, credit analysts should apply knowledge of the above equations in cash flow analysis with caution. They should emphasize and focus on determining a company's operating sources of funds, not just sources of funds. This is because only the operating sources of funds may be sustained (Tables 23.3−23.6).

---

1. Reprinted with permission from the Omega Performance Corporation; may not be copied or reproduced without the express written consent of Omega Performance Corporation.

TABLE 23.2 Cash Flow Summary Form

Cashflow for Year Ending		2002	2003	2004	2005
	Sales revenue				
+ (−)	*Changes* in				
	Accounts receivable				
	= Cash from sales (a)				
	Cost of goods sold expense (less depreciation)				
+ (−)	*Changes* in				
	Inventory (stock)				
	Accounts payable				
	= Cash production costs (b)				
a − b	**= cash from trading** (c)				
	SG & A expenses (less non-cash SG & A expenses).				
+ (−)	*Changes* in				
	Prepaid expenses				
	Accrued expenses				
	Sundry current asset/liability accounts				
	= Cash operating costs (d)				
c − d	**= cash after operations** (e)				
	Other income (expense)				
	Income tax expense				
+ (−)	*Changes* in				
	Deferred income taxes				
	Income taxes payable				
	= Taxes paid and other income (expense) (f)				
e − f	**= Net cash after operations** (g)				
	Dividends or owners' withdrawals.				

TABLE 23.2 Cash Flow Summary Form—cont'd

Cashflow for Year Ending			2002	2003	2004	2005
+ (−)	Change in					
	Dividends payable					
	Interest expense					
+ (−)	Change in					
	Interest payable					
	= Cash financing costs	(h)				
g − h	= **cash after financing costs**	(i)				
	Current portion long-term debt	(j)				
i − j	= **cash after debt amortization**	(k)				
+ (−)	Changes in					
	Fixed assets					
	Investments					
	Intangibles					
	Other non-current assets					
	= Cash used in plant and investments	(l)				
k − l	= **FINANCING SURPLUS (REQUIREMENTS)**	(m)				
+ (−)	Changes in					
	Short-term debt (notes payable).					
	Long-term debt					
	Preferred stock					
	Common stock					
	= **Total external financing**	(n)				
m − n	= **Financing surplus (requirements) + Total external financing**					
Proof: Change in cash and marketable securities						

Omega Performance Corporation proffers a robust cash flow analytical framework that credit analysts can rely on to do a good job. I adapted its Cash Flow Summary Form[2] (Table 23.2) to analyze Nigerian Breweries PLC financials (Table 23.8) for illustration purposes. The crux of assignment in cash flow analysis is to convert income statement from accrual basis to cash basis. This is achieved by adjusting income statement figures to reflect changes in their related balance sheet accounts. In doing so, differences between accrual accounting and cash flow approaches become more apparent. This unique difference between accrual and cash flow methods is demonstrated as shown below[3].

TABLE 23.3 Difference between Accrual Accounting and Cash Flow Approaches

Accrual Accounting Approach	Cash Flow Approach
Sales	Cash from sales
Cost of goods sold	Cash production costs
Gross profit	Cash from trading
Selling, general, and administrative expense	Cash operating costs
Operating profit	Cash after operations

Adjustments to income statement are usually the starting point in all analyses of sources and applications of funds. There are two logical steps to follow in analyzing sources and uses of funds for purposes of cash flow calculations. The steps may be summarized as follows:

Step 1

Compute funds generated from normal, ongoing operations of the company. This is achieved by adding noncash expenses to net income and adjusting the net income figure for nonoperating gains and losses as illustrated below.

Step 2

Establish how much sources and uses of funds relate to the various balance sheet accounts. Apply the figures to the adjustments made to the income statement in the computation of funds from operations. This procedure can be

---

2. Adapted with permission from the Omega Performance Corporation Cashflow Summary Form; may not be copied or reproduced without the express written consent of Omega Performance Corporation.
3. Reprinted with permission from the Omega Performance Corporation; may not be copied or reproduced without the express written consent of Omega Performance Corporation.

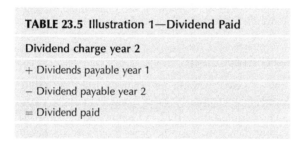

TABLE 23.4 Computation of Funds Generated from Operations

Net income (i.e., profit after tax)

+ Depreciation

+ Provision for bad debts

+ Amortization of intangibles

− Gain on sale of assets, say marketable securities

= Funds provided by operations

illustrated in the computations of dividends paid and net fixed assets as shown in Tables 23.5 and 23.6 below.

TABLE 23.5 Illustration 1—Dividend Paid

Dividend charge year 2

+ Dividends payable year 1

− Dividend payable year 2

= Dividend paid

TABLE 23.6 Illustration 2—Net Fixed Assets

Beginning balance (net)

− Depreciation expense

− Ending balance (net)

= Net fixed assets

Similar calculations should be done for all the other related balance sheet accounts. The adjusted final figures on each of the accounts should be added to, or subtracted from, their related income statement items depending on whether the figures represent sources or uses of funds.

With the foregoing information, credit analysts can proceed to fill out the cash flow computation form (often referred to as cash flow summary sheet). If carefully completed, based on the procedures outlined above, the form will yield an accurate figure of the exact cash flow position of the company. On the basis of the cash flow position, credit analysts can recommend probable amount to lend, or not to lend, to a company.

CASH FLOW ANALYSIS FORMULAE

In most cases, the figures that credit analysts need to complete cash flow summary sheets are found in financial statements and annual reports of the borrowing companies. The relevant accounts are profit and loss account, balance sheet, and funds flow statement. Often, the required figures are taken straight from these financial accounts without adjustments. However, there would be need for some calculations on, or adjustments to, the relevant accounts. Such arithmetic is necessary to establish the true cash position on particular items of the relevant accounts.

Credit analysts should be conversant with the simple arithmetic that goes with computation of cash flow figures. Depending on the complexity of the accounts, the adjustments to determine the true cash inflow or outflow may require certain computation and analysis of relevant data. The items of accounts often analyzed include net fixed assets expenditure, dividend paid, change in minority interest, taxes paid, and change in long-term debt. The usual formulae are as follows.

Net fixed assets expenditure

Depreciation charge year 2 should be obtained from the profit and loss account, while net fixed assets figures years 2 and 1 should be extracted from the balance sheet. The formula in Eqn (23.1) below underscores the need to discount the amount of disposals from the gross fixed assets acquisitions to arrive at cash expended on fixed assets during the year. However, further adjustments should be made to reflect revaluations and profit or loss on the assets disposed. Thus, the true cash outflow is achieved only after all of the necessary adjustments have been made to the fixed assets account.

$$
\begin{aligned}
\text{Net fixed assets expenditure} = \text{Depreciation charge year 2} \\
\textit{plus} \text{ net fixed assets year 2} \quad (23.1) \\
\textit{minus} \text{ net fixed assets year 1}
\end{aligned}
$$

Dividend paid

From the balance sheet, the figures for dividend payable years 1 and 2 are extracted while dividend charge year 2 is obtained from the profit and loss account. The adjustment required for computing dividend paid relates to script dividends, which is a noncash item. Depending on the timing of dividend payments, dividend payable at the end of year 1 will be the cash outflow in year 2.

$$
\begin{aligned}
\text{Dividend paid} = \text{Dividend charge year 2} \\
\textit{plus} \text{ dividend payable year 1} \quad (23.2) \\
\textit{minus} \text{ dividend payable year 2}
\end{aligned}
$$

Change in minority interests

For purposes of the computation, minority interest charge year 2 is shown in the profit and loss account, while minority interest years 2 and 1 should be extracted from the balance sheet.

$$
\begin{aligned}
\text{Change in minority interests} = {} & \text{Minority charge year 2} \\
& \textit{plus} \text{ minority interests year 1} \qquad (23.3) \\
& \textit{minus} \text{ minority interests year 2}
\end{aligned}
$$

Taxes paid

The formula in Eqn (23.4) relates to *current*, in contrast to *deferred*, taxes. Adjustments to reflect changes in deferred taxes should be separated from those of the current taxes paid. The amount of current taxes paid year 2 should be extracted from the profit and loss account, while current taxes payable years 1 and 2 should be obtained from the balance sheet.

$$
\begin{aligned}
\text{Taxes paid} = {} & \text{Tax charge year 2} \\
& \textit{plus} \text{ taxes payable year 1} \qquad (23.4) \\
& \textit{minus} \text{ taxes payable year 2}
\end{aligned}
$$

Long-term debt

All the figures for the computation of long-term debt—long-term debt year 2, current portion long-term debt year 2, and long-term debt year 1—should be obtained from the balance sheet. Current portion long-term debt is equivalent to current portion long-term debt year 1 found in the balance sheet.

$$
\begin{aligned}
\text{Long} - \text{term debt} = {} & \text{Long} - \text{term debt year 2} \\
& \textit{plus} \text{ current portion long} - \text{term debt year 2} \\
& \textit{minus} \text{ long} - \text{term debt year 1}
\end{aligned}
$$

CASH FLOW DEBT SERVICE RATIOS

The ability of borrowing companies to service their bank loans can be assessed using cash flow analysis data. As I pointed out earlier, this approach is justified on grounds that companies require cash to pay debts and other financial commitments. The major cash flow ratios with which credit analysts can predict debt service capability of borrowers include interest cover ratio, cash flow interest cover, financing payments cover, long-term debt payout, total debt payout, and debt service ratio. Using the formulae in Table 23.7, credit analysts should practice computing these ratios with data from cash flow

TABLE 23.7 Formulae for Computation of Cash Flow Debt Service Ratios

Interest cover	$= \dfrac{\text{Operating profit}}{\text{Interest expense (including lease payments)}}$
Cash flow interest cover	$= \dfrac{\text{Net operating cash flow}}{\text{Interest expense (including lease payments)}}$
Financing payments cover ratio	$= \dfrac{\text{Net operating cash flow}}{\text{Interest expense (including lease payments) + current portion long-term debt + dividends}}$
Long-term debt payout	$= \dfrac{\text{Total interest-bearing long-term debt}}{\text{Net operating cash flow}}$ (years)
Total debt payout	$= \dfrac{\text{Total interest bearing debt}}{\text{Net operating cash flow}}$ (years)
Debt service ratio	$= \dfrac{\text{Net operating cash flow}}{\text{Short-term, long-term debt repayable in one year and interest expense (including lease payments)}}$

analysis of audited financial statement and annual reports of Nigerian Breweries PLC as presented in Tables 23.8–23.12 below.

ILLUSTRATIONS AND ANALYSIS OF NIGERIAN BREWERIES PLC

In the following discussions, I illustrate the calculations in cash flow analysis of Nigerian Breweries PLC. I take the necessary adjustments to the income and balance sheet items into consideration. In some cases, I extracted the required data from cash flow statements prepared by the company (see Table 23.11). The results achieved, summarized in Table 23.8 below, follow the usual logical steps in cash flow analysis.

Cash from sales

In 2003, Nigerian Breweries PLC generated a total cash sum of ₦56.52 trillion from sales. The figure is derived as follows:

Sales revenue	56,508,797
Decrease in accounts receivable (Source of cash)	10,687
Cash from sales	56,519,484

The decrease in accounts receivable is a source of cash and therefore should be added to the revenue figure to get the actual cash from sales. Had the accounts receivable figure increased (a case of use of cash), it would have been subtracted from the sales revenue figure to get the actual cash from sales.

Cash production costs

The first step in calculating cash production cost is to determine the true cost of sales. This is achieved by deducting any depreciation that could have been charged to the cost of sales. In the case of Nigerian Breweries PLC, the depreciation charge for the year included in cost of sales amounted to ₦1.76 trillion. This figure should be deducted from the cost of sales figure to arrive at the true cost of sales. The relevant calculations are as follows:

Cost of goods sold	(25, 288, 194)
Depreciation included in cost of sales	1, 761, 047
Adjusted cost of sales	(23, 527, 147)

In order to obtain the cash production costs, there will be further adjustments to the adjusted cost of sales figure. The increase (use of cash) or decrease (source of cash) in inventory should be reflected. In the same vein, increase (source of cash) or decrease (use of cash) in accounts payable should also be reflected. These adjustments are shown, in the case of Nigerian Breweries PLC, as follows:

Adjusted cost of sales	(23, 527, 147)
Increase in inventory (use of cash)	(4, 832, 709)
Decrease in accounts payable (use of cash)	(734, 646)
Cash production costs	(29, 094, 502)

Cash production costs should be subtracted from cash from the sales figure to obtain the figure for cash from trading.

Cash from sales	56, 519, 484
Cash production costs	(29, 094, 502)
Cash from trading	27, 424, 982

Using knowledge of cash flow analysis formulae, the illustrations above, and the fundamental principles of sources and uses of funds in accounting as bases, the remaining cash flow analysis elements could be computed and presented in the required format as I have done in Table 23.8 below. The end product of cash flow analysis is in determining the sum of a company's financing surplus (or requirement) and its total external financing. If the computations are correct, the figure of the sum should be equal to change in cash and marketable securities of the company as of the accounting date.

TABLE 23.8 Nigerian Breweries PLC—*Cash Flow Analysis, December 31, 2003*

	Sales turnover		56,508,797
+ (−)	*Change* in		
	Accounts receivable (debtors)		10,687
=	Cash from sales	(a)	56,519,484
	Cost of goods sold (less depreciation)		(23,527,147)
+ (−)	*Changes* in		
	Inventory (stock)		(4,832,709)
	Accounts payable (creditors)		(734,646)
=	Cash production costs	(b)	(29,094,502)
(a)−(b)	= Cash from trading	(c)	27,424,982
	SG & A expense (less noncash SG & A expenses)		(17,211,469)
+ (−)	*Changes* in		
	Prepaid expenses		105,375
	Accrued expenses		—
	Sundry current asset accounts		(1,368,512)
	Sundry current liability accounts		2,923,436
=	Cash operating costs	(d)	(15,551,170)
(c)−(d)	= Cash after operations	(e)	11,873,812
	Other income (expense)		58,958
	Income tax expense		(2,794,366)
+ (−)	*Changes* in		
	Deferred income taxes		2,170,028
	Income taxes payable		(1,324,634)
=	Taxes paid and other income (expense)	(f)	(1,890,014)
(e)−(f)	= Net cash after operations	(g)	9,983,798
	Dividends		(7,371,526)

TABLE 23.8 Nigerian Breweries PLC—*Cash Flow Analysis, December 31, 2003*—cont'd

+ (−)	Change in		
	Dividends payable		3,268,425
	Interest expense		(2,326,603)
+ (−)	Change in		
	Interest payable		−
=	Cash financing costs	(h)	(6,429,704)
(g)−(h)	= Cash after financing costs	(i)	3,554,094
	Current portion long-term debt	(j)	−
(i)−(j)	= Cash after debt amortization	(k)	3,554,094
+ (−)	Changes in		
	Fixed assets		(13,019,178)
	Investments		−
	Intangibles		−
	Other noncurrent assets		−
=	Cash used in plant and investments	(l)	(13,019,178)
(k)−(l)	= Financing surplus (requirements)	(m)	(9,465,084)
+ (−)	Changes in		
	Short-term debt (notes payable)		14,522,774
	Long-term debt		−
	Preferred stock		−
	Common stock		−
=	Total external financing	(n)	14,522,774
(m) −(n)	= Financing surplus (requirements) plus total external financing		5,057,690
Proof: Change in cash and marketable securities			5,057,690

TABLE 23.9 Nigerian Breweries PLC—*Balance Sheet as of December 31*

	Notes	2003 ₦'000	2002 ₦'000
FIXED ASSETS	1	**50,041,941**	**37,022,763**
CURRENT ASSETS			
Stocks	2	18,407,866	13,575,157
Debtors	3	2,767,099	5,641,152
Foreign currencies purchased for imports		7,465,334	8,396,521
Bank and cash balances	4	6,415,268	1,357,578
TOTAL CURRENT ASSETS		**35,055,567**	**28,970,408**
CREDITORS			
Amount falling due within one year	5	(51,807,834)	(39,689,329)
NET CURRENT ASSETS		**(16,752,267)**	**(10,718,921)**
TOTAL ASSETS LESS CURRENT LIABILITIES		**33,289,674**	**26,303,842**
CREDITORS			
Amount falling due after one year			
Unsecured convertible loan stock	6	—	(5280)
PROVISION FOR LIABILITIES AND CHARGES			
Deferred taxation	7	(3,233,180)	(1,063,152)
Gratuity and pension	8	(3,869,748)	(2,300,000)
NET ASSETS		**26,186,746**	**22,935,410**
CAPITAL AND RESERVES			
Share capital	9	1,890,641	1,890,602
Bonus issue reserve	10	1,890,641	—
Capital reserve	11	8,636,577	8,645,627
Share premium	12	4,640,154	6,528,684
General reserve	13	9,128,733	5,870,497
SHAREHOLDERS' FUNDS		**26,186,746**	**22,935,410**

TABLE 23.10 Nigerian Breweries PLC—Profit and Loss Account for the Period Ended December 31

	Notes	2003 ₦'000	2002 ₦'000
Turnover	14	56,508,797	42,855,103
Cost of sales		(25,288,194)	(17,448,268)
Gross profit		31,220,603	25,406,835
Selling and distribution expenses		(8,752,651)	(8,895,054)
Administrative expenses		(9,407,075)	(6,958,536)
Operating profit		13,060,877	12,553,245
Net interest	15	(2,068,830)	(2,170,816)
Profit before taxation	16	10,992,047	10,382,429
Taxation	17	(3,639,760)	(3,085,983)
Profit after taxation		7,352,287	7,296,446
Appropriations:			
Proposed dividend	18	4,159,409	7,940,528
Transfer to general reserve	13	3,192,878	(644,082)
		7,352,287	7,296,446

TABLE 23.11 Nigerian Breweries PLC—Cash Flow Statement for the Period Ended December 31 (as published in the company's 2003 Annual Report)

	2003	2002
CASH FLOW FROM OPERATING ACTIVITIES	₦'000	₦'000
Profit before taxation	10,992,047	10,382,429
Adjustments:		
(Profit)/Loss on assets disposed	(13,144)	293,976
Depreciation	2,709,304	1,622,711
Interest income	(257,773)	(158,704)
Interest paid	2,326,603	2,329,520
Provision for gratuity	1,668,328	687,933

Continued

TABLE 23.11 Nigerian Breweries PLC—Cash Flow Statement for the Period Ended December 31 (as published in the company's 2003 Annual Report)—cont'd

Operating profit before working capital changes	17,425,365	15,157,865
Increase in stocks	(4,832,709)	(3,660,195)
Decrease/(increase) in debtors	2,874,053	(4,467,404)
Decrease/(increase) in forex purchases	931,187	(132,805)
Decrease in creditors and accruals	(734,646)	(514,712)
Increase in amount due to group company	2,923,436	3,047,236
Cash generated/used for operations	**1,161,321**	**(5,727,880)**
Income taxes paid	(2,794,366)	(1,735,142)
Gratuity paid	(98,580)	(69,869)
Net cash used in operating activities	**(1,731,625)**	**(7,532,891)**
CASH FLOW FROM OPERATING ACTIVITIES		
Purchase of fixed assets	(15,730,511)	(23,719,842)
Proceeds from sale of fixed assets	15,173	67,395
Interest received	257,773	158,704
Net cash used in investing activities	**(15,457,565)**	**(23,493,743)**
CASH FLOW FROM FINANCING ACTIVITIES		
Repayment of unconverted loan stock	(3130)	—
Dividend paid	(7,371,526)	(4,253,827)
Interest paid	(2,326,603)	(2,329,520)
Loan stock expense	—	(99,967)
Net cash used in financing activities	**(9,701,259)**	**(6,683,314)**
Net decrease in cash and cash equivalent	(9,465,084)	(22,552,083)
Cash and cash equivalent at January 1	(17,692,591)	4,859,492
Cash and cash equivalent at December 31	**(27,157,675)**	**(17,692,591)**
CASH AND CASH EQUIVALENT AT DECEMBER 31		
Cash and bank balances	6,415,268	1,357,578
Bank overdraft	(15,639,661)	(2,111,240)
Commercial papers	(17,933,282)	(16,938,929)
	(27,157,675)	**(17,692,591)**

TABLE 23.12 Nigerian Breweries PLC—Notes to the Accounts for the Period Ended December 31, 2003

1 FIXED ASSETS	Land and Buildings	Plant and Machinery	Vehicles, Furniture & Eqpmt	Capital Work in Progress	Total
	₦'000	₦'000	₦'000	₦'000	₦'000
Cost or valuation:					
At 1 January	4,509,992	17,772,515	3,041,449	24,963,014	50,286,970
Additions	1,186,123	3,825,803	145,613	10,572,972	15,730,511
Disposals	-	(28,052)	(156,057)	-	(184,109)
Transfers	9,643,274	24,565,571	663,791	(34,872,636)	-
At 31 December	**15,339,389**	**46,135,837**	**3,694,796**	**663,350**	**65,833,372**
Depreciation and amortization:					
At 1 January	1,564,359	9,607,912	2,091,936	-	13,264,207
Charge for the year	278,411	1,855,544	575,349	-	2,709,304
Disposals	-	(27,542)	(154,538)	-	(182,080)
Transfers	6,554	(21,111)	14,557	-	-
At 31 December	**1,849,324**	**11,414,803**	**2,527,304**	-	**15,791,431**
Net Book Value:					
For the period ended December 31, 2003	13,490,065	34,721,034	1,167,492	663,350	50,041,941
For the period ended December 31, 2002	2,945,633	8,164,603	949,513	24,963,014	37,022,763
Revaluation surplus included in Net Book Value	5,869,853	2,766,724	-	-	8,636,577

Plant, machinery and buildings were professionally revalued as at 30 June, 1995 by Knight Frank (Nigeria) – Chartered Surveyors. The values were incorporated in the books at that date. The surplus arising on the revaluation over the written down values is treated in these accounts as capital reserve. All subsequent additions are stated at cost.

	2003 ₦'000	2002 ₦'000
Depreciation charge for the year included in:		
Cost of sales	1,761,047	784,351
Administrative expenses	948,257	838,360
	2,709,304	1,622,711
2 STOCKS		
Raw materials	1,203,248	1,791,136
Finished products and products in process at production cost	1,537,635	867,710
Bottles and cartons at deposit value	5,115,231	4,785,558
Spare parts at cost	5,946,721	3,296,135
Non-returnable packaging materials	656,281	940,174
Sundry materials	558,631	428,587
Goods in transit at invoiced price and estimated clearing charges	3,390,119	1,465,857
	18,407,866	13,575,157
3 DEBTORS		
Trade debtors	661,625	672,312
Other debtors	1,812,767	4,570,758
Prepayments	292,707	398,082
	2,767,099	5,641,152

	Notes	2003 ₦'000	2002 ₦'000
4 BANK AND CASH BALANCES			
Cash at bank		5,873,435	372,909
Cash in hand		17,875	24,669
Short term deposit		523,958	960,000
		6,415,268	1,357,578
5 CREDITORS			
Amounts falling due within one year:			
Bank overdraft		15,639,661	2,111,240
Commercial papers and bankers acceptances		17,933,282	16,938,929
Creditors and accruals		4,155,390	4,890,036
Dividend	18	5,544,101	8,812,526
Due to group company		6,712,861	3,789,425
Taxation	17	1,822,539	3,147,173
		51,807,834	39,689,329

Borrowings
Borrowings are in the form of unsecured short term facilities, which are negotiated during the course of the year at market related interest rates.

Continued

TABLE 23.12 Nigerian Breweries PLC—Notes to the Accounts for the Period Ended December 31, 2003—cont'd

6 UNSECURED CONVERTIBLE LOAN STOCK			
At January 1		5,280	5,950
Converted to shares during the year	9	(39)	(12)
Transfer to share premium account	12	(2,111)	(658)
Unconverted loan stock liquidated		(3,130)	-
Balance not yet converted at 31 December 2003		0	5,280

In year 2000, the company raised ₦7 billion loan capital to finance the offshore element of its major program of investment by way of rights offer. The loan was unsecured and convertible at the option of the stakeholder. A total of 77,246 shares have been acquired during the year at prices which were dependent on the stock market price at the time of conversion.

7 DEFERRED TAXATION			
1. At January 1		1,063,152	798,055
Amortization		779,308	779,308
Movement		1,390,720	(514,211)
Charges to profit and loss account	17	2,170,028	265,097
At December 31		3,233,180	1,063,152

2. Deferred taxation had been shown by way of a note in the accounts for all years up to and including year ended December 31, 2000. The potential liability to deferred tax of ₦3,117,234,000 at December 2000 is being amortized over a period of four years in accordance with the statement of Accounting Standards No. 19 from the year ended December 31, 2001. One quarter of this amount being ₦779,308,500 has been charged in each year of the accounts for 3 years up to December 31, 2003, while the outstanding balance of ₦779,308,500 will be amortized in 2004.

8 GRATUITY AND PENSION			
At January 1		2,300,000	1,681,936
Charge for the year		1,668,328	687,933
		3,968,328	2,369,869
Payments during the year		(98,580)	(69,869)
At December 31, 2003		3,869,748	2,300,000

1. The liability for gratuity and pension represents the present value of the estimated future cash outflows resulting from employees' services provided to the balance sheet date. In determining consideration has been given to future increases in wage and salary rates, and the company's experience with staff turnover. Liabilities for employee benefits which are not expected to be settled within 12 months are discounted using appropriate discount rates. Actuarial gains and losses in respect of the employee benefits are recognized as income or expenses if the net cumulative unrecognized actuarial gains and losses at the end of the previous reporting period exceeded 10% of the present value of the defined benefit obligation at that date. The amount recognized is the excess determined above, divided by the expected average remaining working lives of the employees participating in that plan. The liability is determined by an independent actuarial valuation every year.

	Notes	2003 ₦'000	2002 ₦'000
9 SHARE CAPITAL			
1. Authorized			
At January 1		2,000,000	1,500,000
Increase during the year		-	500,000
At December			
4,000,000,000 ordinary shares of 50k each		2,000,000	2,000,000
2. Issued and fully paid			
Ordinary shares of 50k each			
At January 1		1,890,602	945,295
Rights issues	6	39	12
Bonus issue	10	-	945,295
At December 31			
3,781,281,170 ordinary shares of 50k each		1,890,641	1,890,602
10 BONUS ISSUE RESERVE			
At January 1		-	945,295
Transfer from share premium	12	1,890,641	-
Allotted		-	(945,295)
At December 31		1,890,641	-
11 CAPITAL RESERVE			
As at 1 January		8,645,627	10,372,873
Transfer to general reserve in respect of disposals in prior periods	19	-	(787,389)
Deferred taxation on revaluation reserve transferred to general reserve	19	-	(804,950)
Balance restated		8,645,627	8,780,534
Transfer to general reserve in respect of disposals for the year		(9,050)	(134,907)
Balance as at 31 December		8,636,577	8,645,627

TABLE 23.12 Nigerian Breweries PLC—Notes to the Accounts for the Period Ended December 31, 2003—cont'd

12 SHARE PREMIUM

At January 1		6,528,684	6,627,993
Transfer from unsecured loan stock	6	2,111	658
Loan stock expenses		-	(99,967)
Transfer to bonus issue reserve	10	(1,890,641)	-
At December 31		4,640,154	6,528,684

13 GENERAL RESERVE

At January 1		5,870,497	6,305,669
Prior year items adjusted	19	-	24,274
Balance restated		5,870,497	6,329,943
Transfer from profit and loss account		3,192,878	(644,082)
Transfer from unclaimed dividend	18	56,308	49,729
Transfer from revaluation reserve		9,050	134,907
At 31 December		9,128,733	5,870,497

14 ANALYSIS OF TURNOVER

1. Turnover represents the total of the amount invoiced to customers for goods supplied, net of Excise Duty and VAT. All sales were made from brewing activities.
2. The analysis of turnover and profit by geographical areas is as follows:

	Turnover		Operating Profit	
	2003	2002	2003	2002
	N'000	N'000	N'000	N'000
Local	56,508,797	42,855,103	13,060,877	12,553,245

15 NET INTEREST

Total interest expense		2,326,603	2,329,520
Less Interest income		(257,773)	(158,704)
Net interest costs		2,068,830	2,170,816

16 PROFIT BEFORE TAXATION

This is stated after charging/ (crediting):

Depreciation and amortization		2,709,304	1,622,711
Auditor's remuneration		12,188	8,155
Directors' emoluments:		63,188	50,692
Royalty and technical service charge		857,874	966,616
(Profit / Loss on assets disposed		(13,144)	293,976
Gains in foreign exchange transactions		522,703	(1,016,500)

17 TAXATION

1. Per profit and loss account:

Income tax based on the profit for the year		1,191,079	2,542,631
Education tax		278,653	278,255
Deferred tax	7	2,170,028	265,097
		3,639,760	3,085,983

2. Per balance sheet:

Income tax based on the profit for the year		1,191,079	2,542,631
Outstanding re prior years		352,807	326,287
Education tax		278,653	278,255
At 31 December	5	1,822,539	3,147,173

18 DIVIDEND

Unclaimed in prior years		1,441,000	921,727
Transfer to general reserve	13	(56,308)	(49,729)
		1,384,692	871,998
Proposed for the year		4,159,409	7,940,528
	5	5,544,101	8,812,526

19 PRIOR YEAR ADJUSTMENT

Revaluation Surplus on Disposals

Where assets have been disposed, the revaluation reserve initially recognized relating to the particular asset has been transferred from the revaluation reserve to the general reserve. No adjustment relating to this transfer had previously been made. The effect of this adjustment has been recognized in the accounting period when the as set has been disposed.

Non Recurrent Write-offs

During the year, the company carried out a review of its reporting systems. As a result of this review, certain balances reported in earlier periods were adjusted. These balances referred mainly to spare parts utilized in previous periods. Deferred taxation has also been adjusted accordingly.

Adjustments relating to 2002 have been restated in the 2002 income statement to the extent possible. Adjustment relating to before 2002 have been adjusted in the opening retained reserves as at 1st January, 2002. The impact on the opening retained reserves of the adjustments for surplus on disposals, write-off in non-recurring items and change in deferred taxation are as follows:

	Period before 2002
	N'000
Revaluation surplus on disposals	(1,124,842)
Less tax effects	337,452
	(787,390)
Non-recurring write-offs	2,240,094
Less tax effect	(672,028)

Continued

TABLE 23.12 Nigerian Breweries PLC—Notes to the Accounts for the Period Ended December 31, 2003—cont'd

	1,568,066
Deferred tax on revaluation reserve	(804,950)
Prior year adjustment	(24,274)

The impact on the 2002 income statement for write-off of non-recurring items and charges in deferred taxation are as follows:

Non-recurring write-offs	1,596,511
Less tax effect	(478,953)
	1,117,558
Increase in deferred tax charge	804,950
Total for year	**1,922,508**

20 CHAIRMAN'S AND DIRECTORS' EMOLUMENTS INCLUDING PENSIONS

21 EMPLOYEES
The staff costs including the provision for pension liabilities were ₦7,823,794,917 (2002 ₦5,096,969,855).

22 PROVIDENT FUND
The company and employees contribute to the provident fund. The funds are held in a separate Trust. The cost of ₦116,131,389 (2002 ₦106,246,639) is charged to profit and loss account of the year. The assets of the scheme are revalued by qualified actuarial valuers every year with the latest valuation as at 31 December, 2003. As at the latest actuarial valuation, the fund's assets exceeded liabilities.

23 COMPARATIVE FIGURES

24 GUARANTEES AND OTHER FINANCIAL COMMITMENTS
1. Contingent Liabilities
   Contingent liabilities in respect of guarantees given for staff car loans amounted to ₦236,657,192 (2002 ₦66,470,841).
2. Capital Expenditure
   Capital expenditure contracted but not provided in the accounts was ₦736,401,160 (2002 ₦204,087,040).
   Capital expenditure authorized by the directors but not contracted was ₦2,406,050,171 (2002 ₦602,797,826).
3. Pending Litigations
4. Financial Commitments

25 POST BALANCE SHEET EVENTS
26 RELATED PARTIES
The company sources certain raw materials and fixed asset additions from companies related to its majority shareholder Heineken NV. All transactions are made on arms-length commercial terms. Additionally, the company pays certain charges to companies within the Heineken group. These include:

	2003	2002
	₦'000	₦'000
Technical services fees	812,892	633,023
Royalties	44,982	333,593

27 APPROVAL OF FINANCIAL STATEMENTS

QUESTIONS FOR DISCUSSION AND REVIEW

1. (a) What are the functions and significance of cash flow in a business?
   (b) Distinguish between cash flow and funds flow. Which of them best fits the need for credit analysis?
2. (a) How does the balance sheet incubate, and is a source of, cash for a firm?
   (b) How can a loan officer isolate cash in the balance sheet for credit analysis?
3. On which specific cash flow sources should lending officers rely for analysis of loan repayment ability?

4. **(a)** What factors taint cash flow as a source of loan repayment?
   (b) How may lending officers assure that they get accurate cash flow information?
5. **(a)** Why is cash flow credited with unique attributes as a credible source of loan repayment?
   (b) Are the attributes foolproof in checking possible loan default?

Chapter 24

Analyzing and Interpreting Financial Statement for Corporate Lending

Chapter Outline

LEARNING FOCUS AND OUTCOMES

I have discussed most of the general issues on which credit analysis is usually focused elsewhere in this book. In this chapter, I focus on financial analysis of corporate borrowers. I do so against a backdrop of growing importance of balance sheet lending, which is easily the most critical credit approach in analyzing large corporations, conglomerates, and other organizations that have formal organizational structure for lending purposes.

This approach is mandatory and popular in lending to blue-chip companies whose loans are often unsecured. The *symbolic* collateral that banks take to secure loans to this category of borrowers is *negative pledge*. This explains the reliance of banks on financial analysis of the companies to corroborate their financial strength and ability to meet loan service and repayment obligations. It should also be noted that it is mostly for this market segment that negative pledge is considered at all, let alone accepted, by banks as collateral for loans. The value placed on negative pledge derives from the goodwill that such companies have built over several years of distinguished service to society, especially to consumers and the business communities in which they operate. But it more appropriately depicts the high success levels attained by the companies in terms of business, economic, and financial performance.

Emerging Market Bank Lending and Credit Risk Control. http://dx.doi.org/10.1016/B978-0-12-803438-5.00024-6
    419

Yet loan requests from large corporate borrowers should be appraised on their merit. Using financial ratios as tool of analysis, I demonstrate how loan officers should evaluate business, financial, and performance risks of corporate borrowers. In doing so, I assess tasks and challenges in analyzing corporate borrowers for bank lending purposes. I explain the basic concepts that the reader should know in order to understand the topics that I discuss in this chapter. The concepts in question are balance sheet lending, balance sheet analysis, financial analysis, and ratio analysis—all of which have a bearing to this chapter.

Cash flow analysis and lending, discussed extensively in Chapter 23, forms an integral part of financial analysis of corporate borrowers. Therefore, it should be studied together with this chapter. I separated cash flow lending from balance sheet lending in order to underscore the ever-growing significance of cash flow lending. This chapter teaches corporate lending based on balance sheet strength. It discusses the use of ratio analysis in making lending decisions. The reader will learn how:

- Financial ratios are a critical issue in appraising corporate borrowers
- Ratio analysis makes a significant input into balance sheet lending
- Banks use ratio analysis to evaluate the credit risk of corporate borrowers
- Interpretation of ratios is more critical than their calculation in corporate lending decisions
- Success in corporate lending depends on accurate financial analysis of the borrowers

ASSESSING BUSINESS, FINANCIAL, AND PERFORMANCE RISKS

Financial analysts—and lending officers are not exceptions—use ratio analysis to evaluate a company's business, financial, and performance risks. The pros and cons of ratio analysis in credit appraisal are worth mentioning to guide the reliance of bank management on them for lending purposes. It is not easy to accurately compare the financial circumstances of two different companies or one company over different accounting periods. Worse still, distortions are often introduced in financial statement analysis by changes in price level over time. Of course, different companies may adopt different accounting or reporting systems. This makes it difficult to accurately interpret ratios of the companies on a comparative basis. The difficulty is informed by possible differences in definitions of balance sheet and income statement items.

Financial ratios are yet criticized on some other grounds. There is widespread interest among different stakeholders in financial analysis. Ratio analysis has long been accepted as a reliable means of assessing a company's performance. When a bank lends short, on the one hand, it will be interested in the ability of the borrower to meet its claims for principal and interest payment at short notice. The basic focus of financial analysis will therefore be on *liquidity* strength of the borrower. The bank will, on the other hand, be more interested in *long-term solvency* and *survivability* of the borrower when it provides long-term capital. The critical issues for analysis immediately become *profitability* level over time, *cash flow* stream (to be assured that the borrower has the capacity to pay interest and principal over the long run), and capital structure (i.e., the mix of the various sources of funds available to the borrower).

In the case of long-term lending, the bank will further analyze projected financial statement of the borrower to confirm that observed historical good performance of the borrower would likely be sustained in the future. When observed financial performance is poor, analysis may indicate why and how expectation could be held for improved financial performance in the future. In other words, where historical analysis reveals poor performance, pro forma or projected financial statement analysis may indicate remedial measures for future profitability and cash flow generation that may be of interest to the bank.

In order to demonstrate applications of ratio analysis in credit evaluation, I present and analyze a comprehensive annual (audited) financial statement of Paterson Zochonis Industries PLC, a multinational, holding, conglomerate company, with headquarters in Lagos, Nigeria. I present the annual report and company accounts that form the basis of the analysis in Tables 24.1 and 24.2 below.

SPREAD SHEET

The first step in financial analysis of a corporate borrower for lending purposes is to prepare a spreadsheet of its audited financial statement and management accounts. In doing so, the analyst should also, where necessary, use information usually given in notes on the accounts. A spreadsheet highlights the key financial information on the basis of which desired relationships between income statement and balance sheet items are established. From raw financial statements and annual reports, it distills relevant statistical data with which credit analysts may measure or appraise a company's financial performance (historical and projected). The spreadsheets of PZ Industries PLC are presented in Tables 24.4–24.9 to demonstrate the use of financial statements in making corporate lending decisions. Table 24.10 shows *notes on the accounts* that provide additional information that I used in preparing the spreadsheets. One will begin to appreciate the potency of spreadsheets in analyzing corporate borrowers by relating Tables 24.1, 24.2 and 24.10 to those of Tables 24.4–24.9. The latter set was derived from the former after *spreading* the financial statement of the company. In this context, one will also appreciate the importance of *notes on the accounts* in preparing spreadsheets. Thus, Tables 24.4–24.9 will not make enough sense unless they are related to Tables 24.1, 24.2 and 24.10.

TABLE 24.1 Paterson Zochonis Industries PLC—Group Profit & Loss Account for the Year Ended May 31

	Notes	2000 (₦'000)	2001 (₦'000)
Turnover	1	15,362,258	16,089,203
Cost of sales		(12,112,536)	(12,521,074)
Gross profit		3,249,722	3,568,129
Selling & distr. expenses		(801,070)	(1,070,052)
Administration expenses		(758,793)	(718,595)
Operating profit		1,689,859	1,779,482
Net interest receivable/(payable)		(337,173)	7601
Profit before taxation	2	1,352,686	1,787,083
Taxation	3	(420,398)	(516,926)
Profit after taxation (out of which ₦1,111,210,931 [2000: ₦919,032,733] is dealt with in the company's account)		932,288	1,270,157
Appropriations:			
Dividend proposed		580,824	653,427
Sinking fund reserve	13	10,000	10,000
		(590,824)	(663,427)
Retained profit transferred to general reserve	13	341,464	606,730

Typical Spreadsheet

Some banks adopt a standard format of the spreadsheet. In such cases, the *spreadsheet form* is preprinted, kept, and used by credit analysts whenever they appraise corporate loan proposals for approval or decline by senior management. Some banks make changes to the original format to obtain additional information that they may require on the accounts. Variations in the formats of spreadsheets used by banks are an indication of risk-taking disposition of the banks. This is because, for each of the varied formats, emphasis is placed on some aspects of the financial statement in addition to the standard information.

In order to facilitate its use, some banks have computerized the mathematics of the spreadsheet. This is essentially about feeding the computer with

TABLE 24.2 Paterson Zochonis Industries PLC—Balance Sheet as of May 31

	Notes	2000 (₦'000)	2001 (₦'000)
Fixed assets	4	5,362,163	5,231,687
LT investments: shares in subsidiaries		7261	7261
Current Assets:			
Stocks	5	7,355,932	7,317,112
Debtors	6	419,944	388,406
Deposits for letters of credit		1,993,213	3,631,160
Investment in treasury bills		0	1,500,000
Cash at bank and in hand		242,350	216,512
		10,011,439	13,053,190
Creditors (due within One Year):			
Borrowings	7.1	557,966	786,511
Other creditors	7.2	4,019,024	4,113,873
		4,576,990	4,900,384
Net current assets		5,434,449	8,152,806
Total assets less current liabilities		10,803,873	13,391,754
Creditors (due after one year)	8	85,000	65,000
Prov. for liabilities and charges	9	1,133,158	1,324,118
Net assets		9,585,715	12,002,636
Capital and Reserves:			
Called-up share capital	10	558,485	726,030
Share premium	11	0	1,791,592
Revaluation reserve	12	3,948,572	3,948,572
Other reserves	13	5,078,658	5,536,442
		9,585,715	12,002,636

necessary formulae for deriving the required ratios. With this approach, the work of credit analysts is reduced to simply supplying the raw information from financial statements and notes on the accounts. Interpretation of the ratios, and deducing relationships between relevant balance sheet and income statement items, remain the main assignment of the analyst.

TABLE 24.3 Spread Sheet (Income Statement)

Income Statement for the Year Ended May 31

	2000	2001
Net sales	15,362,258	16,089,203
Cost of goods sold	12,112,536	12,521,074
Selling, gen & admin expenses	807,179	1,351,324
Depreciation	425,217	456,045
Other noncash excluding indemnity	0	0
Other operating expenses	0	0
Operating profit/(loss)	2,017,326	1,760,760
Fixed assets disposal G/(L)	0	0
Government subsidy	0	0
Other operating income	9,706	11,121
Nonoperating expenditure/(increase)	0	0
Profit before interest & tax	2,027,032	1,771,881
Interest charges	436,769	173,495
Other financing charges	26,965	18,478
Profit before tax	1,563,298	1,579,908
Income tax	420,398	516,926
Special income/(charges)	(337,173)	7601
Interest income	126,561	199,574
FX translation G/(L)	0	0
Profit b/f extra items	932,288	1,270,157
Extra ordinary including/(expenditure)	0	0
Net income	932,288	1,270,157

Once completed, analyzed, and interpreted, the spreadsheet is secured in a credit file with other documents relating to a particular credit facility. Indeed, credit analysis memorandum and documentation of loans to corporate borrowers will be incomplete without a spreadsheet. Almost always, in strictly balance sheet or cash flow lending, the decision to lend is made entirely on the basis of standings of borrowers in ratio analysis derived from spreadsheets of their financial statements.

TABLE 24.4 Spread Sheet (Financial Summary)

	Company:	Paterson Zochonis Industries PLC	
	Auditors:	KPMG Audit (Chartered Accountants)	
	Amounts:	in naira (NGN) ₦	
Date:	December 31	2000	2001
Key figures:	Sales	15,362,258	16,089,203
	Operating profit	2,017,326	1,760,760
	PAT/net income	932,288	1,270,157
	Net worth	9,585,715	12,002,636
	Total assets	15,380,863	18,292,138
	Working capital	5,434,449	8,152,806
Annual growth (%):	Sales		4.73
	Operating profit		−12.72
	Net income		36.24
	Total assets		18.93
Cash flow:	Gross operating funds		1,909,561
	Internal funds generation		1,909,561
	Net financing needs		(5,532,564)
	Net borrowings		228,545
	Net equity		(644,828)
Key ratios (%):	Net income/sales	6.07	7.89
	Net income/total sales	6.06	6.94
	Net income/net worth	9.73	10.58
	Operating profit/sales	13.13	10.94
	Op profit/assets xcl inv	13.12	9.63
	Tax/EBIT	26.89	32.72

Continued

TABLE 24.4 Spread Sheet (Financial Summary)—cont'd

	Company:	Paterson Zochonis Industries PLC	
	Auditors:	KPMG Audit (Chartered Accountants)	
	Amounts:	in naira (NGN) ₦	
Turnover efficiency:	Sales/total assets	1.00	0.88
	Sales/net fixed assets	2.86	3.08
	Days receivables	7	6
	Days inventories	219	210
	Days payables	84	70
	Cash cycle	141	146
	Current ratio	2.19	2.66
	Quick ratio	0.12	0.41
Leverage:	Total liabilities/ net worth	0.60	0.52
	LT liabilities/net worth	0.13	0.12
	Interest coverage	4.64	10.21
Investment indicators:	Net income/net worth	9.73	10.58
	Dividends/net income	0.00	0.00

Unfortunately, this practice has a negative effect or tendency that defeats the purpose of spreadsheet. As a result of undue reliance of banks on financial performance in making corporate lending decisions, the less credible borrowers may deliberately manipulate the source documents for financial analysis (i.e., the balance sheet, income statement, funds flow and cash flow statements) to achieve favorable ratings. This increases the risk of loans granted to such borrowers.

In order to mitigate the risk of forged, distorted, or manipulated financial statements, it is strongly advised that loan officers should as a matter of lending policy do comprehensive risk analyses for major loans being recommended to senior management for approval. Perhaps the only exception to this rule arises when analyzing blue chips, multinationals, or "A"-rated conglomerates.

TABLE 24.5 Spreadsheet (Balance Sheet Items)

The Highlights of the Key Balance Sheet Items of PZ Industries are as Follows:

	Bal. sheet items as of December 31	2000	2001
Assets:	Cash	242,350	216,512
	Investment in T-bills	0	1,500,000
	Trade debtors	296,865	279,685
	Inventory/stock	7,355,932	7,317,112
	Other debtors	92,688	99,302
	Deposit for L/Cs	1,993,213	3,631,160
	Prepaid expenses	30,391	9419
	Total current assets	10,011,43	13,053,190
	Net fixed assets	5,362,163	5,231,687
	Equity investments	7261	7261
	Total long-term assets	5,369,424	5,238,948
	Total assets	15,380,863	18,292,138
Liabilities:	Bank overdraft	537,966	766,511
	Trade payable	2,833,885	2,451,682
	Others	184,195	388,436
	Taxes currently due	385,641	524,837
	Dividend	581,061	653,664
	Intercompany account	34,242	95,254
	Current portion of LT loan	20,000	20,000
	Total current liabilities	4,576,990	4,900,384
	LT senior debt	85,000	65,000
	LT subordinate debt	0	0
	Total LT debt	85,000	65,000
	General provisions	1,133,158	1,324,118
	Total deferred liabilities	1,133,158	1,324,118
	Total liabilities	5,795,148	6,289,502

Continued

TABLE 24.5 Spreadsheet (Balance Sheet Items)—cont'd

The Highlights of the Key Balance Sheet Items of PZ Industries are as Follows:

Equity:			
	Paid-up share capital	558,485	726,030
	Retained earnings	4,993,658	5,461,442
	Share premium	0	1,791,592
	Revaluation surplus	3,948,572	3,948,572
	Other reserves	85,000	75,000
	Total net worth	9,585,715	12,002,636
	Liabilities & net worth	15,380,863	18,292,138

TABLE 24.6 Fixed Assets Reconciliation

		2000	2001
Opening net fixed assets		0.00	5,362,163
Add:	Assets acquired	1,838,808	(3,623,003)
	Assets revaluation	3,948,572	3,948,572
	Total additions	5,787,380	325,569
Less:	Depreciation	(425,217)	(456,045)
	Cash proceeds from disposals	0.00	0.00
	Fixed assets disposal loss	0.00	0.00
	Total deductions	(425,217)	(456,045)
Ending net fixed assets		5,362,163	5,231,687
Land & buildings		4,335,961	4,312,230
Office equipt. & motor vehicles		1,833,479	2,032,969
Others		0.00	0.00
Capitalized leases		0.00	0.00
Less: accumulated depreciation		(1,096,079)	(1,459,553)
Net fixed assets		5,362,163	5,231,687

TABLE 24.7 Net Worth Reconciliation

Opening net worth	0		0
Add:	Net income	932,288	0
	Sale of equity	(847,288)	(644,828)
	Other reserves	3,948,572	0
	Assets revaluation	3,948,572	3,948,572
	FNI (share premium)	0	1,791,592
	Total additions	7,982,144	5,095,336
Less:	Dividends	0	0
	Special (noncash)	0	0
	Total deductions	0	0
	Ending net worth	7,982,144	5,095,336

LIQUIDITY OF THE BORROWER

Neither lack, nor too much, of liquidity is propitious to a company's financial health. Illiquidity or insolvency is a dangerous signal that a company's ability to meet its obligation is impaired. A company in such a situation will easily lose the confidence of banks as a result of its poor credit rating. Ultimately, banks will not ordinarily lend money to such a company. However, excess liquidity is also inimical to a company's financial rating as a preponderance of huge idle trading assets signifies bad financial management. As idle current assets do not earn income, it is imperative that a company works out an optimum level of its need for liquidity at any point in time.

TABLE 24.8 Income Statement (% Sales)

Cost of goods sold	78.85	77.82
Selling, gen & admin expenses	5.25	8.40
Depreciation	2.77	2.83
Operating profit	13.13	10.94
Profit before interest & tax	13.19	11.01
Earnings before interest & tax	10.18	9.82
Profit before extraordinary items	6.07	7.89
Net income	6.07	7.89

TABLE 24.9 Paterson Zochonis Industries PLC

Spread Sheet (Source & Application of Funds for the Year Ended May 31)

		2001
Internal sources:	Operating profit	1,760,760
	Add noncash charges:	
	Depreciation	456,045
	Other noncash	0
	Indemnities	190,960
	Other income/(expenditure)	210,695
	Subtotal	2,618,460
	Deductions:	
	Taxes	(516,926)
	Interest	(191,973)
	Dividends	0
	Gross operating funds	1,909,561
	Nonoperating sources:	
	Sale of fixed assets	0
	Sale of investments	0
	Internal funds generation	1,909,561
Application of funds:	Increase/(decrease) current assets	
	Inventory	(38,820)
	Receivables	(17,180)
	Prepayments	(20,972)
	Sundry debtors	1,644,561
	Increase/(decrease) current liabilities	
	Trade payables	(382,203)
	Accruals	204,241
	Sundry creditors	133,615
	Taxes payable	139,196
	Change in working capital	
	Purchase of fixed assets	(3,623,003)

TABLE 24.9 Paterson Zochonis Industries PLC—cont'd

Spread Sheet (Source & Application of Funds for the Year Ended May 31)

		2001
	Investments	0
	Increase other LT assets	0
	Extraordinary items	0
	Indemnities	0
	Funds needed	(3,623,003)
	Net financing needs	(5,532,564)
Funding:	FNI plus sale of equity	1,146,764
	LT borrowings	0
	ST borrowings	228,545
Investment:	Less: ST debt repayment	0
	LT debt repayment	(20,000)
	Cash & liquid assets	(1,474,162)
	Net financing	(18,853)

How liquid is Paterson Zochonis Industries PLC? How strong is its short-term solvency and liquidity—that is to say, its ability to meet its current financial obligations or liabilities as and when they fall due? Liquidity ratios are employed in providing answers to these questions. Banks use two different ratios to measure a company's liquidity level. The first is *current ratio* while the second is *quick* or *acid test ratio*—both of which are calculated using a formula. Illustrating with the 2001 figures from Table 24.2, the two ratios are computed as follows:

$$\text{Current ratio} = \frac{\text{Current assets}}{\text{Current liabilities}} = \frac{13,053,190}{4,900,384} = 2.66 : 1$$

$$\text{Quick ratio} = \frac{\text{Quick (liquid) assets}}{\text{Current liabilities}} = \frac{1,996,197}{4,900,384} = 0.41 : 1$$

Current assets are *cash, marketable securities* (i.e., near cash items—those that can easily be converted into cash within a year or in the short run), *debtors* (i.e., accounts receivable), *stock* (or inventory), and *prepaid expenses*. The *liquid* current assets exclude *stock* and *prepaid expenses*. Liquid assets are characterized by the ease with which they can be converted into cash without

TABLE 24.10 PZ Industries PLC—Notes on the Accounts

		The Group 2001 (N'000)	The Company 2000 (N'000)
1) Turnover	Analysis by product category:		
	Consumer goods	16,089,203	15,362,258
	Analysis by location:		
	Nigeria	15,934,326	15,280,431
	Exports	154,877	81,827
		16,089,203	15,362,258
2) Profit	This is stated after charging or (crediting)		
before	profit on disposal of fixed assets	(11,121)	(9,706)
taxation	Depreciation	456,045	425,217
	Directors' emoluments:		
	Fees	142	200
	Others	9,905	7,510
	Debenture interest	18,478	26,965
	Interest on loans and overdrafts	173,495	436,769
	Interest receivable	(199,574)	(126,561)
	Auditors' remuneration	7,630	7,000

3) Taxation

	The Group 2001 N'000	2000 N'000	The Company 2001 N'000	2000 N'000
.1 Per profit and loss account				
Income tax:				
Based on the profit of the year	492,131	373,747	440,000	325,600
Under / (Overprovision) in prior year	9,051	(10,355)	10,047	(6,148)
Education tax:				
Based on the profit of the year	41,841	34,357	36,190	30,200
Under/overprovision in prior year	6,065	(38)	5,212	(28)
	549,088	397,711	491,449	349,624
Deferred tax (note 9)	(32,162)	22,687	(29,498)	17,393
	516,926	420,398	461,951	367,017
.2 Per balance sheet (note 7.2)				
Income tax:				
Based on the profit of the year	492,131	373,747	440,000	325,600
In respect of prior years	58,058	38,002	48,647	29,841
Education tax:				
Based on the profit of the year	41,841	34,357	36,190	30,200
In respect of prior years	500	-	-	-
	592,530	446,106	524,837	85,641

.3 The charge for taxation in these financial statements is based on the provisions of the Companies Income Tax Act (LFN Cap 60) as amended to date and the Education Tax Decree, 1993.

4) Fixed assets

	Freehold land and buildings N'000	Leasehold land and buildings N'000	Office equipment Plant & machinery N'000	& motor vehicles N'000	Total N'000
.1 The Group					
Cost/valuation:					
At 1 June, 2000	33,862	5,544,743	2,035,204	317,555	7,931,364
Additions	-	5,026	199,890	86,903	291,819
Disposals	-	(28,757)	-	(26,981)	(55,738)
At 31 May '01	33,862	5,521,012	2,235,094	377,477	8,167,445
Depreciation:					
At 1 June, 2000	217	144,875	805,277	248,507	1,198,876
Charge for the year	217	144,975	252,984	57,869	456,045
Eliminated on disposals	-	-	-	(24,560)	(24,560)
At 31 May '01	434	289,850	1,058,261	281,816	1,630,361
Net book value:					
At 31 May '01	33,428	5,231,162	1,176,833	95,661	6,537,084
At 31 May 2000	33,645	5,399,868	1,229,927	69,048	6,732,488

TABLE 24.10 PZ Industries PLC—Notes on the Accounts—cont'd

.2 The Company
Cost/valuation:

At 1st Jun, 2000	4,335,961	1,833,479	288,802	6,458,242
Additions	5,026	199,490	83,241	287,757
Disposals	(28,757)	-	(26,002)	(54,759)
At 31 May 2001	4,312,230	2,032,969	346,041	6,691,240
Depreciation:				
At 1 Jun, 2000	105,507	767,089	225,483	1,096,079
Charge for the year	103,608	228,933	54,514	387,055
Eliminated on disposals	-	-	(23,581)	(23,581)
At 31 May, 2001	207,115	996,022	256,416	1,459,553
Net book value:				
At 31 May, 2001	4,105,115	1,036,947	89,625	5,231,687
At 31 May 2000	4,232,454	1,066,390	63,319	5,362,163

.3 Land and buildings were revalued at 31st May, 1999 by Messrs Knight Frank, estate surveyors and valuers, chartered surveyors, on the following bases:
- Factory land and buildings
  Existing use basis, being the depreciated replacement cost plus site value
- Commercial land and building
  Open market value on the basis of existing use
  Subsequent additions to land and buildings and other fixed assets are stated at cost.

.4 Commitments for capital expenditure not provided for in these accounts amounted to:

	The Group		The Company	
	2001	2000	2001	2000
	N'000	N'000	N'000	N'000
Authorised and contracted	23,934	149,188	23,934	149,188
Authorised but not contracted	539,053	313,234	539,053	309,327

.5 Included in the value of leasehold land and buildings are revalued properties as follows:
Land held under statutory right

of occupancy	23,016	23,016	-	-
Existing leasehold interests:				
-50 years and above	3,770,706	3,770,706	3,130,619	3,130,619
-Under 50 years	1,748,911	1,748,911	1,170,420	1,170,420
	5,542,633	5,542,633	4,301,039	4,301,039

.6 The depreciation charge
for the year is derived from:

Historical cost	313,789	282,961	284,227	252,710
Revaluation	142,256	142,256	102,828	102,828
	456,045	425,217	387,055	355,538

.7 Depreciation charge for the
year is included in:

Cost of sales	347,047	329,153	322,997	305,062
Admin and distribution				
expenses	108,998	96,064	64,058	50,476
	456,045	425,217	387,055	355,538

.8 There is no asset for which there is no record of cost or production.

5) Stocks					
	Raw materials	4,360,736	4,545,943	4,148,533	4,304,870
	Work-in-progress	407,264	448,554	395,577	444,189
	Finished goods	2,227,334	2,041,669	2,213,124	1,965,573
	Spare parts and tools	559,878	641,300	559,878	641,300
		7,555,212	7,677,466	7,317,112	7,355,932

6) Debtors:					
	Trade debtors	283,359	299,119	279,685	296,865
	Prepayments	9,449	30,421	9,419	30,391
	Other debtors	351,242	332,849	99,302	92,688
		644,050	662,389	388,406	419,944

7) Creditors (due within one year)
.1 Borrowings (unsecured)

Bank loans and overdrafts	766,511	883,353	766,511	537,966
Floating rate redeemable				
debenture stock 1997/2004	7,500	7,500	7,500	7,500
Floating rate redeemable				
loan stock 1999/2006	12,500	12,500	12,500	12,500
	786,511	903,353	786,511	557,966

.2 Other creditors
Dividend

- Proposed	653,427	580,824	653,427	580,824
- Unpaid	237	237	237	237
Tax payable (note 3.2)	592,530	446,106	524,837	385,641
Trade creditors and				
accruals	2,576,213	2,991,660	2,451,682	2,833,885
Group companies	-	-	95,254	34,242
Deferred income	11,206	10,939	-	-

Continued

TABLE 24.10 PZ Industries PLC—Notes on the Accounts—cont'd

	Others	388,436	89,422	388,436	184,195
		4,222,049	4,219,188	4,113,873	4,019,024
		5,008,560	5,122,541	900,384	4,576,990

.3 The proposed dividend of ₦653,427,080 (2000 ₦580,824,071) is subject to deduction of withholding tax at the appropriate rate at the time of payment.

		The Group		The Company	
		2001	2000	2001	2000
		₦'000	₦'000	₦'000	₦'000
8) Creditors (due after one year)	.1 Borrowings (unsecured) Floating rate redeemable debentures stock 1997/2004	15,000	22,500	15,000	22,500
	Floating rate redeemable loan stock 1999/2006	50,000	60,500	50,000	62,500
		65,000	85,000	65,000	85,000
	.2 Other creditors Deferred income	8,053	24,338	-	-
		83,053	109,338	65,000	85,000

.3 The floating rate redeemable debenture stock 1997/2004 is unsecured and carries an interest rate of 3.25% above the Central Bank of Nigeria minimum rediscount rate subject to a maximum coupon of 19% per annum and minimum coupon of 12.5%. It is constituted under a Trust Deed dated 25th March, 1989 and is redeemable at par in eight equal annual instalments, commencing from 1997 with an option to redeem all or a part of the stock at any time before 31st March, 2004 at a premium calculated at the rate of 0.4% for each year or part of a year by which the redemption date precedes 31st March, 2004.

.4 The floating rate redeemable loan stock 1999/2006 is unsecured and carries an interest rate of 3.5% above the Central Bank of Nigeria minimum rediscount rate, subject to a maximum coupon of 23% per annum and minimum coupon of 12.5%. It is constituted under a Trust Deed dated 24th May, 1991 and is redeemable at par in eight equal annual instalments, commencing from 31st May, 1999 with an option to redeem all or a part of the stock at any time before 31st May, 2006 at a premium calculated at the rate of 0.25% for each year or part of a year by which the redemption date precedes 31st May, 2006.

		The Group		The Company	
		2001	2000	2001	2000
		₦'000	₦'000	₦'000	₦'000
9) Provisions for liabilities and charges	.1 Deferred taxation At 1st June, 2000	877,151	854,464	730,165	712,772
	P & L a/c (note 3)	(32,162)	22,687	(29,498)	17,393
	At 31st May, 2001	844,989	877,151	700,667	730,165
	.2 Gratuity and past service benefits	797,391	556,204	623,451	402,993
		1,642,380	1,433,355	1,324,118	1,133,158

		The Group		The Company	
		2001	2000	2001	2000
		₦'000	₦'000	₦'000	₦'000
10) Share capital	.1 Authorised: 2,000,000,000 (2000: 1,700,000,000) ordinary shares of 50k each	1,000,000	850,000	1,000,000	850,000
	.2 Issued and full paid 1,452,060,177 (2000: 1,116,969,367)				
	At 1st June, 2000	558,485	558,485	558,485	558,485
	Rights issue	167,545	-	167,545	-
	At 31st May, 2001	726,030	558,485	726,030	558,485

.3 At the annual general meeting held on 16th November 2000, the authorized share capital was increased to N1 billion by the creation of additional 300 million ordinary shares of 50 kobo each ranking pari passu with the existing shares of the company.

.4 At the extra-ordinary general meeting held on 21st March 2000, it was resolved that 335,090,810 ordinary shares of 50 kobo each ranking pari passu with the existing shares of the company be issued to the existing shareholders by way of rights. The issue was fully taken up.

	The Group		The Company	
	2001	2000	2001	2000
	₦'000	₦'000	₦'000	₦'000

TABLE 24.10 PZ Industries PLC—Notes on the Accounts—cont'd

11) Share premium	Arising on rights issue net of expenses of issue	1,791,592	-	1,791,592	-
12) Revaluation reserve	At 1st June, 2000	5,090,811	5,093,361	3,948,572	3,948,572
	Eliminated on disposal	-	(2,550)	-	-
	At 31st May, 2001	5,090,811	5,090,811	3,948,572	3,948,572
13) Other reserves	.1 Arising on consolidation	21,689	21,689	-	-
	.2 Sinking fund reserve				
	At 1st June, 2000	85,000	95,000	85,000	95,000
	Transfer from P&L a/c	10,000	10,000	10,000	10,000
	Trfer to general reserve	(20,000)	(20,000)	(20,000)	(20,000)
	At 31st May, 2001	75,000	85,000	75,000	85,000
	.3 General reserve				
	At 1st June, 2000	5,121,902	4,760,438	4,993,658	4,645,449
	Transfer from P & L a/c	606,730	341,464	447,784	328,209
	Transfer from sinking fund reserve	20,000	20,000	20,000	20,000
	At 31st May, 2001	5,748,632	5,121,902	5,461,442	4,993,658
		5,845,330	5,228,600	5,536,442	5,078,658
14) Directors and staff remuneration	.1 Chairman and directors' emoluments -	₦'000		₦'000	
	Chairman	142		850	
	Other directors	9,905		6,860	
		10,047		7,710	
	2 As fees	142		200	
	Other emoluments	9,905		7,510	
		10,047		7,710	
15) Technical services agreements	Amounts payable under the technical services and licensing agreements are based on applicable turnover.				
16) Guarantees and financial commitments	.1.Contingent liabilities				
	There were contingent liabilities at the balance sheet date arising in the ordinary course of business out of guarantees amounting to ₦16 million. In the opinion of the directors, no loss is expected to arise from these guarantees. There are legal actions against the company pending in various courts of law. According to lawyers acting on behalf of the company, the liabilities arising, if any, are not likely to be significant.				
	.2 Financial commitments				
	The directors are of the opinion that all known liabilities and commitments, which are relevant in assessing the company's state of affairs, have been taken into account in the preparation of these financial statements.				
17) Contingent	There are no material contingent liabilities as at the end of the year liabilities which have not been provided for in the liabilities financial.				
18) Post balance sheet events	There are no significant post balance sheet events for which provisions have not been made.				
19) Approval of financial statements	These financial statements were approved by the board of directors of the company on 5th of September 2001.				

losing value. In general, an asset is said to be liquid if it can be easily sold or converted into cash at little or no risk of loss in value.

Stock or inventory does not have the quality of a liquid asset. Inventory may not be immediately converted into cash, and even where it is possible to do so within a reasonable time, it may not be without the experience of fluctuation in or loss of value. Indeed, some time is almost always required to liquidate stock and this is also true in converting raw materials and work in process into finished goods. Also, for the obvious reason that a prepaid expense cannot be converted into cash, it is excluded from the quick or liquid assets category for purposes of quick ratio analysis. Current liabilities generally include *all debts that mature within a year*, as well as *creditors* (i.e., accounts payable), *bills payable, accrued expenses, current line* (or overdraft) facilities with banks, *current portion of long-term debt* (i.e., that part of long-term debt that matures during the current year), and *income tax* liability.

Once positive, a current ratio is ideally considered acceptable. It is particularly good or excellent if it is 2:1 or higher. In the case of quick (acid test) ratio, the acceptance standard is at least 1:1. These *rules of thumb* are justified, for the former, on the grounds that a company should be able to meet its short-term obligations as they fall due even when the value of its current assets is halved and, for the latter, to do so even with the exclusion of the nonliquid assets. Yet there are reservations in adopting these criteria. One setback is that such a ratio does not take cognizance of the fact that a company's current assets may comprise a high value of doubtful debts and slow-moving or unsalable stock. The company will face threat of short-term insolvency under the circumstances, as it cannot immediately settle its bills.

In the case of quick ratio, 1:1 is the minimum acceptable value. Yet, like current ratio, it should be adopted with caution since it suffers a setback in terms of quality of book debt, especially as not all of it may be easily liquidated. Of course, cash is seen as a fleeting asset that may be spent at any time to meet immediate expenditure needs of a company. The current ratio of PZ industries PLC satisfies the acceptance criterion. This implies that the company will be in a position to meet its short-term borrowing obligations. The comfort that PZ will not default in its short-term loan repayment is reinforced by the fact that it will take more than 150% loss of current assets for liquidity stress to begin to manifest. Then current assets and current liabilities would even out. It is obvious—given that it is a blue-chip company, with formal organization structure and excellent management—that such a situation would scarcely crystallize.

The quick ratio of 0.41:1 will be acceptable for PZ's standing. The ratio can also be justified on the grounds that a characteristic feature of large manufacturing cum trading conglomerates like PZ is the accumulation of high levels of inventories that are discounted in computing the quick ratio. For other, less strong companies, the ratio would be adjudged low and unacceptable. But in the case of PZ, the credit analyst will most probably conclude that a loan granted to the company will have a high probability of being repaid on due date. With such a conclusion, the analyst can recommend the loan for approval.

However, there are other ratios, as I show in the following discussions, which should also be considered before making the final decision to lend or not. Some of the important ratios relate to leverage, activity, profitability, and cash flow of the company.

BORROWER'S LEVERAGE

To what extent are the long-term solvency and liquidity, as well as long-term stability and survivability, of PZ Industries PLC assured? In order to answer the question, I compute and analyze its leverage ratio—a measure of the relationship between equity (i.e., owners' funds) and debt (borrowed funds) in the capital structure of a company. The ratio is employed in measuring financial risk involved in the application of debt to generate earnings for the stakeholders of a company. Thus, leverage ratios give indication of the relative claims over the company's assets by those who have invested in ordinary shares and debt instruments. I may not easily recommend that either of the two financing sources is all that a company needs. Yet a good mix must be worked out to achieve optimum returns on investment. In making the "either" "or" decision at all, the company must come to grips with the implications of the available choices or alternatives. In so doing, I will also answer pertinent questions: To what extent does PZ rely on debt in financing its assets? What is the ratio of debt in the company's total financing structure?

Banks (indeed, most investors and lenders alike) are generally skeptical about the financial health of a highly geared company—one in which the component of the owners' equity in the capital base is very little compared with debt. This reflects in the difficulty often experienced by such a company in trying to raise funds from its existing owners, let alone from the capital market or other categories of creditors or lenders. The main issue here is the increasing risk of lending to the company as the *buffer* (sometimes called *margin of safety*) provided by the owners' equity, which otherwise cushions the financial risk, thins out. In terms of risk, the bank seeks to know the extent of the risk it is about to take on a company that has employed more debt than equity in financing its assets. This is important for the reason that debt imparts more risk than equity to the capital structure as the company must service and repay the debt from or without profits or earnings. The common alternative is for the company to yield to litigation by its creditors and, in some situations, be liquidated if it has become bankrupt.

I should now calculate and analyze the leverage ratios of PZ Industries PLC using data from its annual reports and accounts as follows:

$$\text{Debt : equity} = \frac{\text{Total liabilities}}{\text{Shareholders equity}} = \frac{6,289,502}{12,002,636} = 0.52 : 1$$

$$\text{Leverage/gearing} = \frac{\text{Total liabilities}}{\text{Tangible networth}} = \frac{6,289,502}{6,187,492} = 1.02 : 1$$

It is pertinent to mention here that, from the point of view of stakeholders, certain circumstances favor the use of debt more than equity in financing a company's assets. In the first place, the risk of borrowing must be inconsequential—that is to say, it does not threaten the stakeholders' control of the company. Secondly, the borrowing should enhance earnings and ensure a higher return on equity. This will happen, in most cases, where the company borrows at a rate lower than it earns from its investments.

For PZ Industries PLC, a debt-to-equity ratio of 0.52:1 is excellent. Similarly, leverage and gearing ratios are 1.02:1 apiece and good. But it could be that the company is cautious about the use of more borrowed funds than owners' equity as a means of sustaining investor confidence. However, the observed ratios may not imply efficient capital, or financial, structure since a disproportionately high ratio of shareholders' funds to debt can limit expansion of scope of business in a growth market. This would translate to lost growth opportunity where, as a result of low or unfavorable conditions to increase borrowing, the company is unable to exploit available market potential in its lines of business.

The lending bank will most likely assume that PZ deliberately maintains the good ratios as a reflection of the commitment of its shareholders to the company. Then there would be a tendency to conclude that net worth will be retained at the desired level through plowing substantial portions of its annual net incomes to the business. Thus, for as long as the rates of increase of such retained earnings and other reserves are more than incremental debts, the leverage ratios will remain good.

A company that is consciously working to be low geared will go to the extent of directly increasing its share capital if increasing earnings, and therefore retention and capitalization of profits, is difficult. It can do this either through rights issue, private placement, or by public offer of its shares through the stock exchange. The use of bonus shares to boost the capital base is also popular, but it does not in real terms provide liquidity that can substitute the need for bank borrowing or other debt.

Interest coverage

Some analysts may also want to evaluate interest coverage ratio to determine the capacity of a borrower to service debts. In practice, the ratio indicates the cost or financial burden of debts on a company's earnings and profitability. It measures the number of times interest on debts is covered by net income in a given financial year. A high or low ratio implies a strong or weak capacity to service debt obligations from net earnings. For PZ Industries PLC, I calculate interest coverage ratio for 2001 using the formula as follows:

$$\text{Interest coverage ratio} = \frac{\text{Net profit before interest and taxes}}{\text{Total interest and lease charges}} = \frac{1,971,455}{191,973}$$

$$= 10.27 \text{ times}$$

This ratio implies that PZ covered its total interest expenses in pretax and financial charges profits more than 10 times in 2001. But it indicates a strong capacity to meet interest obligations to banks and other creditors. Given this result, a credit analyst would most likely recommend that a bank should grant a loan to the company.

ASSETS UTILIZATION

Measurement of efficiency of asset utilization is achieved through computation of activity ratios for the borrower. It is important to emphasize the level of efficiency attained in utilizing assets to meet the cause of a company. In most cases, corporate causes relate to the research, production, and sale of wants-satisfying, or market-determined, goods and services at affordable prices and profit. What is actually being measured is the rate of conversion of trading assets into sales, receivables, and cash. For this reason, the measures of a company's activity are otherwise known as *turnover ratios*. I calculate the key activity measures or ratios for PZ Industries PLC as follows:

$$\text{Inventory turnover} = \frac{\text{Cost of goods sold}}{\text{Average inventory}} = 1.7$$

where cost of goods sold is determined by subtracting *closing stock* from the sum of *opening stock*, *cost of purchases*, and *manufacturing costs*. I determine average inventory by calculating the average of *opening* and *closing* stocks for the trading period.

This ratio is low, indicating that the company should improve on the rapidity of conversion of inventory into accounts receivable and cash through sales. A related ratio—days inventory on hand (a measure of how long it takes a company to sell or dispose of inventory)—also showed slow-moving stock at 219 and 210 days in 2000 and 2001, respectively. There is a usual tendency to interpret a low inventory turnover as a reflection of inefficient inventory management. However, this is not always true. Thus, credit analysts should interview the customer to find out the exact cause of its slow-moving stocks.

However, the actual implications of a low inventory turnover is that the company accumulates a high level of slow-moving stocks, incurs increased stock carrying costs, may lose on profitability, and forgoes liquidity on funds tied up in the stocks. But it could be that such buildup of sluggish inventory derives from overtrading, obsolescence of the stocks, or deficiency of market demand. In order to make the lending decision, loan officers should find out the real state of the inventory, especially in terms of obsolescence and market acceptability. The importance of the finding is underscored by the fact that a company's liquidity, especially its working capital position, will plunge if provision is made against the stale, or obsolete, inventory.

The foregoing explanations do not suggest that *a too high inventory turnover* is always good for lending purposes. For instance, inventory turnover could be high because inventory level is very low in the first instance. Such a situation causes frequent stock-out and replacements, with concomitant costs to the company. In the final analysis, there are other activity ratios that have to be considered alongside inventory turnover ratio before a meaningful decision can be made regarding the efficiency of assets utilization.

I present some of the complementary ratios and the values that I calculate for PZ Industries PLC, as follows:

$$\text{Assets turnover} = \frac{\text{Total sales}}{\text{Total assets}} = 0.88$$

Assets turnover of 0.88, derived by dividing total sales by total assets, is low, although this could mean that the company had a relatively large stock of assets in 2001. It is expected, nevertheless, that with such a large asset base the company should generate compensating or proportionate sales. But the net fixed assets turnover of 3.08 is good. The two ratios show that in 2001, PZ generated sales that equaled to 88% of total assets and 308% of net fixed assets.

Credit analysts may also want to evaluate the quality of the company's debtors. In so doing, their interest will be in determining the liquidity of accounts receivable that ordinarily forms a major source of repayment of short-term loan that a bank may grant to a company. The relevant ratio in this case is debtors or receivables turnover, which I calculate as follows:

$$\text{Debtors turnover} = \frac{\text{Credit sales}}{\text{Average debtors}} = \quad (a)$$

$$\frac{\text{Total sales}}{\text{Debtors}} = \quad (b)$$

This ratio determines the average annual turnover rate of debtors or receivables. It is a measure of the average number of times per annum that debtors or accounts receivables are turned over. An efficient management of this trading (debtors) asset is indicated when the ratio is high. Otherwise, a company is not doing well on debtors' management when the ratio is low. The formula in (b) is employed when information or data on credit sales, opening and closing balances of debtors are not available in annual reports and accounts.

$$\text{Average collection period} = \frac{\text{Days in year}}{\text{Debtors turnover}} = \frac{\text{Debtors} \times \text{Days in year}}{\text{Sales}}$$

Average collection period, otherwise known as days receivables on hand, is a measure of the time lag between when credit sales are made and when cash is received from debtor customers. For PZ Industries PLC, the period averaged 7 and 6 days in 2000 and 2001, respectively. This implies that PZ's customers required only one-week credits. Depending on the credit policy of the company, it could be concluded that the quality or profile of its debtors is high and commendable since, on average, they are able to promptly pay their debts within a week.

The shorter the days receivables on hand, the more unlikely it will be for a company to fail in meeting its short-term financial obligations. The company, as in the case of PZ, would be a good candidate to grant bank credit facility. The company's liquidity is further enhanced by its ability to collect or recover credit sales within 7 days, while maintaining average debt payment period (i.e., days payables on hand) of 84 and 70 days in 2000 and 2001, respectively. Although sales and profitability might be low, cash flow—the more important consideration—is enhanced. This is mainly as a result of quick realization of credits and zero provision for bad debt losses.

OPERATING EFFICIENCY

Credit analysts should also review operating efficiency of a company in terms of profitability, as well as returns on equity and sales. Many people would rather argue that the ultimate goal of business is to remain profitable as a going concern. Accumulation of retained earnings or revenue reserves from annual profits from operations boosts the financial strength, growth, and resilience of a company. It follows therefore that a company that operates at a loss or low profit level will ordinarily experience difficulties in getting bank loans. Observed and possible streak of future losses will impair its ability to generate sufficient cash flows to repay loans. Loan granted to such a company would have a high probability of default and outright loss. The key ratios in which credit analysts would be interested are summarized in Table 24.4. In the case of PZ Industries PLC, the following indicators of operating efficiency were observed in 2000 and 2001, respectively: return on equity (9.73% and 10.58%), net profit margin (6.07% and 7.89%). These ratios should be related to the industry average to know if they are good or not.

CASH FLOW POSITION

Cash flow analysis is an essential part of any serious appraisal of the financial strength of a borrowing company. It establishes the volume of cash that a company generates from its normal operations from which it will service and ultimately repay loans that banks grant to it. The logic of cash flow analysis is about determining if, and how much, cash is available to service and repay a bank loan. Its knowledge builds on an understanding of a borrower's cash flow timing differences. A company that has a long asset conversion cycle may experience cash flow problems and be unable to repay its loan. Since, for such company, it takes a long time before assets are converted into cash, it would need to borrow to bridge any financing gap. In doing so, it would hope to repay the loan from liquidation of trading assets. The converse would also be true for a company that has a short asset conversion cycle. The company may not need to borrow, and even when it borrows it can repay the loan over a short term. Thus, the crux of the work of credit analysts is to follow logical steps to determine a borrower's net cash financing needs and net cash borrowings. These ratios help them in recommending how much money to lend to a company and in assessing its ability to repay the loan.

QUESTIONS FOR DISCUSSION AND REVIEW

1. What is a "spreadsheet"? Of what significance is a spreadsheet in corporate lending? Which accounting reports furnish spreadsheet data and why?
2. Critically examine the functions of ratios in financial analysis of a corporate borrower.
3. Why is too much, or lack of, liquidity inimical to a firm's financial health? How do loan officers determine optimum liquidity of a company?
4. What purposes do equity and debt serve in analysis of a firm's capital structure for lending purposes?
5. How do banks measure the level of efficiency attained by a company in the utilization of its assets?

Chapter 25

Bank Credit Structuring, Analysis and Approval in Emerging Markets

Chapter Outline

LEARNING FOCUS AND OUTCOMES

The structure of a loan is a critical element in the overall lending decision and credit administration. At the outset when a credit request is being appraised or granted, a bank often contends with the task of devising an arrangement that will ensure that utilization and repayment of the loan will be in accordance with terms agreed with the borrower. In so doing, the bank recognizes that appropriate structure for credits granted to borrowers is an imperative. Inappropriate credit structure portends risk of default because of possible conflict with borrowing cause. A particular credit facility should be tailored to satisfy a specific need of a borrower. If this is not done, there may be a mismatch between the needs of the borrower and bank for the credit. In such a situation, the borrower may default.

Unfortunately, borrowers tend to concern themselves with fulfilling conditions for and obtaining loans from banks. They seem to bother less about

Emerging Market Bank Lending and Credit Risk Control. http://dx.doi.org/10.1016/B978-0-12-803438-5.00025-8
443

loan structure. Yet the structure of loan granted to a borrower is as important as conditions of the loans in mitigating default risk. Often this fact begs for recognition by borrowers and lending officers alike. Incidentally, it behooves credit analysts to educate borrowers on appropriate and applicable structure for the loans they need. This should be done at the outset of a credit relationship and prior to loan approval and disbursement.

A clear understanding of loan structure is critical for successful loan utilization and repayment by borrowers. In most cases, delinquent loans have structural problems. Thus, loan workout should start with reviewing how the credit was packaged in the first place. While the reviewer may be critical of the credit package, it is always pertinent to bear in mind that remediation of observed or proven default is of the essence.

My primary task in this chapter is to examine credit structuring possibilities in contemporary bank lending. Thereafter, I identify and analyze factors affecting loan structure. My ultimate objective is to investigate if a tie-up exists between the factors and risks of elements of loan structure. I conclude with implications of findings for credit risk and its management.

It is important that a credit facility is structured in a way that meets the needs of the bank and borrower. This defines the focus of this chapter. You will learn how to:

- Structure credit facilities to meet the lending need of banks and financing needs of borrowers
- Identify and analyze factors that affect credit structure and on which lending officers build transaction dynamics
- Evaluate factors and risks inherent in loan structure and mitigate their negative impacts
- Assess implications of loan structure for credit risk analysis and management

MARKETING AND RELATIONSHIP ISSUES

The real challenge in granting a credit facility is to understand and harmonize the borrower's needs for *purpose, tenor, utilization, dynamics, collateral, pricing, mode,* and *source of repayment* of the credit with those of the bank. These issues, which essentially define the credit structure, must be clearly reflected in a formal loan agreement or contract (as is common with term loans) between the parties. In other lending situations, it may suffice for the borrower to simply accept (or execute) the bank's *offer letter* that embodies the terms and conditions of the credit.

Bankers may be persuaded by marketing concept philosophy to emphasize orientation of their business to *identifying* and *satisfying* unfilled needs of their customers at all times. However, this undoubtedly time-honored marketing philosophy should be adopted with caution in a lending situation. The reason is simply that a bank deals in financial products—involving, largely, taking deposits from, and granting credit facilities to, customers. For this reason a bank cannot afford to lose depositors' funds in pursuit of customer service. Thus, structuring a credit is not necessarily about doing what the customer wants or granting all the customer's requests about the loan. It is indeed about setting and agreeing on arrangements with the customer that will ensure effective utilization and timely repayment of the loan.

The need for an appropriate structure is to facilitate easy monitoring and general administration of the loan. It also helps to forestall default or loss of the credit to the borrower. In order to appreciate the constraints often encountered in devising appropriate structure for a credit facility, it is necessary to understand factors that affect a bank's lending decisions and practices. Thereafter, I consider taxonomy and qualities of good credit facilities. Let me first review the basic criteria of bank lending.

FACTORS AFFECTING LOAN STRUCTURE

Influences on a bank's loan policies do have a bearing on how the bank structures credit facilities to borrowers. What are the major influences on loan policy? Do they affect all banks equally? Why and how do they affect the structure of credit facilities? I identify the factors that influence a bank's loan policies and structure to include the following:

- Size of *capital* funds (the *paid-up* share capital, or shareholders' *equity*, plus accumulated revenue and reserves)
- The inescapable *risk—return* trade-off, which is intrinsic to business (*risk* and *earnings* associated with various loan types)
- Structure of a bank's *deposit* liabilities base (i.e., stability or volatility of deposits that make up its liabilities portfolio)
- Regulatory measures, especially *monetary* and *foreign exchange policies* that may limit or enhance lending programs
- Macroeconomic conditions, often reflected in *time value of money* calculations and projections
- Measurable *credit needs* (market demand) of borrowers that indicate the pattern and direction of economic activities and growth
- Adequacy of credit *experience*, *capability*, and *orientation* of lending officers. Officers in question are those who package and disburse loans, and manage banking relationships between their bank and borrowers.

The aforementioned questions are significant. Their significance is underscored by the fact that factors that influence loan policies and structure have varying degrees of importance in different banks. Yet a bank must face the challenges in structuring credit facilities well. In this way, banks will come to grips with the tasks of achieving a high quality risk assets portfolio. In the following discussions, I examine implications of the foregoing factors for bank management in lending situations.

Size of capital funds

A bank requires a minimum quantum of capital funds to be able to function effectively. I adapt the postulate of the big push theory as an industrialization strategy to inform this view. There is a critical level of equity capital or shareholders' funds that a bank requires for business takeoff and success. In Nigeria, for instance, prospective promoters of banks are expected to deposit a minimum paid-up capital of ₦25 billion with the Central Bank of Nigeria.

Capital adequacy is a critical measure of a bank's health. It not only cushions depositors' funds against loss but influences the value and types of risk that a bank can take. A bank in which the size of capital is large relative to deposit liabilities can afford to take more risks than one with a small capital base. In the former case, the bank can grant long-term credit facilities and offer large volumes of credit to borrowers at a time.

Where banking regulation stipulates that a bank should not lend more than a specified amount of its shareholders' funds (unimpaired by losses) to a single obligor and/or its subsidiaries (20% in the case of Nigeria), the significance and influence of capital on credit structure becomes apparent. It is obvious that small banks, which are poorly capitalized, cannot offer certain categories of credit facilities or take certain types of lending risk. In the final analysis, the worth of capital for a bank and its customers is seen in the buffer or protection it offers against loss of depositors' funds.

Risk–return trade-off

The nature of risk envisaged and return expected from particular lending activities sometimes influence loan policies and structure. Banks have varying appetites for risk taking. For example, banks that are risk averse do emphasize short-term, self-liquidating, and asset-based lending—with revolving tenors of not more than 90 or 120 days per transaction cycle. Such banks shun complicated, long-term loan proposals. But they also like to lend to well-structured, formal business organizations that generate adequate and predictable cash flows. Such riskless borrowers are found mainly among the blue chips and top-tier segment of the mass banking market.

The risk preference banks display aggressive lending tendencies. Their business goals are driven, in most cases, by profit-making considerations. Risk taking by this category of banks often reflects in the choice of target markets and ambitious lending types, amounts, tenors, and purposes. Typically, such banks would settle for small business and middle-tier accounts—especially, the wholesale traders in the import business—whose high-risk profile is more than offset by return on investment. Of course, customers realize that it is expensive to borrow money from such banks because of their inclination to profit making and risk taking.

Deposit base

The deposit liabilities base of a bank is perhaps the single most important determinant of its loan policies. Deposits are the lifeblood of a bank and directly affect its general business capacity. A bank would be distressed if its deposits or general liabilities are not adequately represented by tangible assets. Indeed, a bank would fail without deposits.

It is crucial for a bank to not only have a large pool of deposit liability but a stable deposit portfolio. Bank management should achieve optimal distribution of maturities in deposits portfolio to be able to formulate profitable loan policies. Yet, the types and structure of loan granted by a bank would ordinarily mirror the content and characteristics of its deposit base. With a small or highly volatile deposit portfolio, a bank may adopt restrictive loan policies to be able to maintain liquidity for its day-to-day operations. Large volume or term lending would not appeal to such a bank.

Nowadays, deposit base is the driving force behind competitive strength of banks. Prior to the 2005 banking system consolidation, the then three big banks in Nigeria (First Bank of Nigeria PLC, Union Bank of Nigeria PLC, and United Bank for Africa PLC) collectively controlled over 80% of liquidity in the banking system. Guided by monetary policy rate and other money market indices, they dictated pricing, especially lending rates, in the industry. This was one of the ways the big banks flexed their deposit muscles in addition to their preference for big-ticket transactions.

Monetary policy

The banking system is easily jolted by monetary and fiscal policies in emerging economies where regulations often distort the mechanism of market forces. Money market is rarely left to dictate the behavior of operators and financial exchanges in the industry. What is common is a jolting of banks into attempting to respond appropriately to one regulatory maneuvering or the other.

Some of the monetary policy elements that the authorities manipulate in a bid to influence lending policies and behavior of banks include monetary policy rate (MPR), cash reserve ratio (CRR), liquidity ratio (LR), and so on. For example, section 15(1) of Nigeria's Banks and Other Financial Institutions Act No. 25 of 1991 (as amended) requires banks to maintain certain holdings in cash reserves, specified liquid assets, special deposits, and so on with the Central Bank. The Act also restricts bank lending to a single obligor limit of 20% of shareholders' funds, unimpaired by losses (section 20(1)(a)). In section 13(1), the Act prescribes capital adequacy ratio for all licensed banks in the country.

The regulatory authorities tinker with the MPR, CRR, and LR depending on dictates of a country's monetary management. Variations in the ratios indirectly affect the capacity of banks to expand the loan portfolio. With cash reserve and liquidity ratios, a bank surrenders a certain percentage of its total deposit liabilities to statutory reserve requirement. Also, this implies loss of income that a bank would otherwise have earned on the deposits if it were to invest them in earning assets. In the case of changes in MPR, banks respond somewhat in kind—with the result that loan policy may be affected adversely or favorably. In Nigeria, for example, the lending capacity of banks is yet affected by the provision of BOFI Act No. 25 of 1991 (section 16), which requires every licensed bank to maintain a reserve fund to which it should transfer at least 30% of its annual net profit before dividend where the reserve fund is less than its paid-up share capital. If the reserve fund is equal to, or more than the paid-up capital, 15% of the net profit should be transferred to the fund.

In emerging economies, these restrictions are worsened by public policy inconsistencies in monetary and fiscal policies formulation and implementation. Restrictive monetary policies, on the one hand, create liquidity squeeze that ultimately limits the ability of banks to grant certain types of credit facility. With expansionary policies, on the other hand, funds are readily available at reasonable rates to finance lending activities. Thus, loan policies could be more or less liberal depending on the money supply situation. However, since liquidity or dearth of it may be a temporary incidence while their concomitant or underlying monetary policies settle with other interacting market forces, a bank should not rely solely on the prevailing situation in making long-term lending policy decisions.

Economic conditions

The prevailing economic conditions in a country affect lending activities of banks. Influence of economic conditions is particularly evident in decisions about types and terms of credits that banks grant to different sectors of the economy. It is pertinent to determine whether the economy is growing, stagnant, or declining. If it is a growth economy, lending officers should be interested in knowing the direction of growing economic activities. In particular, determining what might be the future leading sectors of the economy would also be of immense interest to them. Even where growth is indicated, it is yet important to be wary of lending activities in case the economy is subject to seasonal or cyclical movements.

In a stagnant or declining economy, there would be a general lull in business activities and banking will be no less affected. The salient issue for a bank in such a situation is to remain liquid and meet operating costs and customers' funds withdrawal needs. Lending would not be emphasized because of possible high incidence of loan default that characterizes periods of business decline. Loans granted to borrowers—if any should be granted at all—must essentially be of short-term, self-liquidating type. Thus, borrowers would have limited choice of loan structure because of the dictates of an unstable economy.

Needs of the public

Banks should ideally serve the credit needs of the public within their local communities. Each locality of a bank may present unique borrowing requirements that should compel bank management's attention. Therefore, a bank should take cognizance of the needs of the local markets—its customers and prospects—while formulating lending policies and structure. It should do this even as part of its overall social responsibility to the communities in which it operates.

In an attempt to enforce lending to certain sectors or businesses that appear less attractive to banks, the Central Bank of Nigeria sometimes prescribes and enforces sectoral distribution of credit facilities. At some point, the Central Bank of Nigeria started enforcing a policy that required banks to invest up to 10% of their profit before tax (PBT) in equity shares of small-and medium-scale enterprises (SMEs). The policy, known as Small and Medium Enterprises Investment Equity Scheme, soon became popular in business circles. It was intended to drive economic growth through the SMEs. The premise that SMEs are the superstructure of economic activities in most of the developed economies informs the policy. Thus, banks should not only lend to SMEs but invest in their equity stocks as well. Similar policy exists in other emerging economies, even as they might be christened differently.

Orientation of loan officers

Human elements involved in the lending function exert enormous influence and, indeed, do shape loan policies and structure. Relying on experience, abilities, and general credit orientation, bank personnel ultimately determine what, why, and how to lend to a particular customer or group. Indeed, a bank's loan policies and the structure of credit facilities it grants to borrowers reflect the pool of experience and orientation of the bank and its officers.

Consider, for example, that the now-defunct Investment Banking and Trust Company (Nigeria) Limited specialized in capital market activities for several years before its merger with Stanbic Bank (Nigeria) Limited. It did not—and of course did so by choice—offer some of the regular commercial banking services. With such business focus, the bank's target market comprised blue-chip companies and some category of high-volume, structured local corporates in the middle-tier market segment. Another bank, Standard Trust Bank Limited, which later merged with United Bank for Africa Limited and adopted UBA as the name of the new bank, decided to site at least one branch of the bank in each of the 36 state capitals and Abuja (Federal Capital Territory). It made this decision for the obvious reason that it targeted government or public sector patronage. For this reason, it concentrated its lending activities in this market segment. Doing so, it also derived the most deposit liabilities from the public sector.

The structure of credit facilities sourced from the capital market or granted to the public sector will normally differ from the traditional loans. Lending policies to guide activities in the two market segments also show marked differences from credit facilities granted to ordinary business concerns.

ELEMENTS OF LOAN STRUCTURE

The structure of a loan is characterized by agreement reached between a bank and borrower regarding amount, purpose, tenor, pricing, utilization, repayment, and collateral for the loan. But some constituents of loan structure are reflected in special terms, conditions, or covenants as may be embodied in a loan agreement, contract, or offer letter. Among banks, there may be varying levels of emphasis on documentation and implementation of the loan terms, conditions, or covenants.

Yet a common feature of loan structure is the strict documentation of all agreements reached between the bank and borrower prior to, and after, disbursement of a loan. Verbal agreement poses a risk to enforcement of terms and conditions of a loan. The risk crystallizes when the counterparty decides to repudiate particular obligations on the loan. This will happen, for example, when the counterparty wants to satisfy some selfish objectives at the expense of the other. Indeed, it is not uncommon for banks and borrowers to trade blame for poor loan performance or default—leading, in some cases, to mutual denial of any unwritten agreement that seems unfavorable to their interest, especially when the borrower defaults. For this reason, banks and borrowers must fulfill the following:

- Agree on a clear understanding of loan package and structure prior to approval and disbursement of the credit facility
- Endorse all necessary documents that establish or inform the loan agreement, especially security documents, to avoid unnecessary controversy
- Abide by agreed terms and conditions of a loan until its expiry date and liquidation

The loan structure should not be ambiguous or technical so that either of the parties to the loan will easily understand it. An ambiguous or technical loan structure creates room for avoidable maneuverings. The borrower, bank, or other party may claim ignorance of aspects of some agreement, expected roles, or other requirements for effective loan utilization and performance. Under the circumstances, a liable party who is sly may want to renounce responsibility for a failed credit transaction. The offended party would be helpless. Financial loss attendant on the transaction becomes a sad lesson of the avoidable cost of negligence in business.

Loan amount or limit

Lending officers should decide whether the amount of a loan request is both adequate and appropriate. In this way, they help to check overtrading observed among some categories of borrowers. Often businesses engaged in general commerce fall victim to overtrading. It is a commonplace that on occasion the amount of loan that a borrower requests is inappropriate. Critical appraisal of loan proposals sometimes shows that loan amounts requested would be inadequate for the related borrowing causes. In such situations, lending officers should recommend appropriate loan amounts for approval. But they should discuss and agree upon possible changes in loan amounts with the affected borrowers.

Loan amount should be stated in permissible, usually local, currency. Even when a loan is to be utilized to finance international trade (such as the establishment of letters of credit), the local currency equivalent of the credit should be determined at the outset. This approach will assist borrowers to better appreciate the magnitude of financial obligation into which they are about to enter when they accept particular credit facilities. But it will also help the bank to underline the exposure it plans to take on with the borrower or obligor. While foreign currency credit might be a small amount, its local currency equivalent will often be big.

One of the strange findings that scrupulous lending officers sometimes make in trying to establish an appropriate loan amount is that a borrower may be influenced to include a *float* in the loan amount. Often the inclusion of *float* is to facilitate or take care of some business interests that are not related to execution of the borrowing cause. For all intents and purposes, this is *fraud*. Surprisingly, some regard it as a necessary evil with which business must live. But it is abhorrent and introduces dilemma to the lending decision process. Should a bank lose a good lending transaction because the borrower is opposed to the practice? If one bank refuses the transaction, will all the other banks also reject it?

In most cases, the expediency of business and competitive pressure impels banks to ignore the moral issues that the practice raises. But it is wrong to do so. If the float accounts for a sizeable portion of the total loan, it might reduce earnings to a level where the borrower becomes incapacitated to fully repay the loan. This will happen where the transaction is affected by unanticipated adverse conditions that wipe off much of the loan's projected earnings.

Purpose of borrowing

Lending officers should discreetly ascertain the purpose of a loan. The purpose should be stated in unambiguous terms while appraising the loan proposal. Usually the purpose of a loan must fit with a dictate of genuine business pursuit or transaction that may interest a bank to finance. Credit facilities should not be granted to finance outlawed business activity or to subvert government monetary or economic policies. Borrowers are expected to properly articulate causes of their borrowing requests. They should do so in a manner that a bank is convinced, not confused, about the need for the loans.

It is imperative in complex lending situations for account officers and relationship managers to pay attention to the *actual* borrowing cause after the credit facility has been disbursed. One of the observed major causes of loan default is deliberate diversion of proceeds of a loan to unauthorized uses by the borrower. This happens more frequently where the integrity of borrowers is questionable and there is no, poor, or superficial loan monitoring. Borrowers become evasive and difficult to manage on usual relationship schemes under the circumstances. As much as possible, the purpose of a loan should be succinctly defined to avoid ambiguity and leave no room for manipulation by either the bank or borrower.

Sometimes, borrowers might have a genuine need to increase amounts of their loan. The purpose of the increase could be to provide finance for a related business transaction in which they are interested. In such a situation, it would be wrong for the borrowers to start transferring resources from proceeds of their existing loan to the new business transaction or venture. They should first discuss their intention with the bank and obtain the bank's consent, if anything. Thereafter, they should send a formal letter of request to the bank in which they clarify aspects of their proposal. The bank might wish to do either of two things:

- Package a new or additional credit facility for the borrower, provided that the request satisfies the bank's internal lending criteria
- Amend the original purpose and amount of the existing loan to accommodate the new request.

Often a bank will want to do something along the lines of the foregoing. This ensures harmony in the banking relationship between the bank and borrower.

Tenor or expiry date

For how long does a borrower intend to use a credit facility before repaying it? Is the bank willing to grant the loan for the tenor requested by the borrower? The tenor or maturity of a loan is as important as its purpose to the lender and borrower. Neither the borrower nor bank should decide the tenor of loan arbitrarily. Rather, it is the *transaction cycle* for the loan that should influence tenor. A loan's transaction cycle represents the period during which a borrower is expected to have utilized and repaid the loan. It specifically depicts the cumulative time spent on all activities undertaken by a borrower at every stage of the tenor of a loan up to the date of its repayment.

In all lending cases, the tenor of loan should be correctly foreseen. Lending officers should anticipate the probable tenor of an intended credit facility.

They should do so at the initial stage when borrowers negotiate credit facilities. Credit analysts may also anticipate appropriate tenor when they appraise proposed credit facilities and they cannot go wrong. In any case, doing so, lending officers should rely on their experience in similar prior lending situations. Otherwise, due to inappropriate tenor, a borrower might not be fairly tasked to repay the loan on due date or according to agreed terms and conditions. A bank, on the other hand, may *call in* a loan prematurely, while the borrower might yet need or not be prepared to liquidate the loan. This is why agreement on the tenor and maturity date forms an integral part of a loan package.

It is also important for agreement on the tenor of a loan to contain a clause on whether or not the credit facility would be subject to rollover after its initial and subsequent expiry dates. With such a clause, a bank will be guided on when to initiate loan recovery action if the loan is not fully repaid on its due date. However, it also defines appropriate prudential action to be taken at the point in time when it is obvious that agreed loan tenor might not be realistic after all.

Pricing of credit

Elsewhere in this book I thoroughly discussed the concept and dynamics of *pricing* as a competitive tool for bank management. For the purpose of lending, pricing refers to determining *interest rate, fees,* and *commission* that a bank might charge on particular credit facilities that it extends to particular borrowers. A credit facility might have implicit price elements that invariably increase its net yield to the bank. The price of a loan would have *other* elements where, for instance, there is a *penalty clause* in the loan agreement, contract, or offer letter to deter the borrower from defaulting on certain terms and conditions of the credit facility. Yet, it is possible to determine and appreciate the expected price of a loan facility at the outset of the borrowing relationship between the bank and borrower.

Determinants of price

In pricing a credit facility, bank management considers several factors. What are the major factors that are generally considered by banks in pricing of credit facilities? Most banks take cognizance of *cost of funds, risk, tenor, competition, yield, administering cost,* and *value of relationship.* Let me briefly discuss each of these pricing variables. The reader will appreciate why a *culture* of price discrimination subsists in banking.

Cost of funds

Perhaps the most critical determinant of loan price is *cost of funds* to a bank. Forces in the money market that influence prices of financial products and services are usually beyond the control of bank management. Thus, like in commodities trading, banks simply pass on their cost of funds *plus* a spread to borrowers. One of the ways that bank management could check cost of funds is to build capacity around savings deposits and DD accounts floats.

Degree of risk

The nature and degree of risk inherent in a particular credit proposal will obviously affect the price at which a bank will be disposed to grant the loan or take its risk. In general, there is always a premium for risk taking—however little—in business. But such a premium should be sufficient to compensate the risk bearer in the event that the risk occurs or crystallizes. Of course, we realize that banks trade off between *risk* and *return*—the riskier a loan proposal is, the higher the expected return from it to the bank and vice versa.

Loan tenor

The risk of lending increases the longer the tenor or maturity of credit facilities. Price of short-term loans should therefore be lower than that of long-term credits. This is because increasing tenor introduces uncertainties about possible unforeseeable future events that may undermine a borrower's ability to repay a loan. In addition, lending money for a long term with predominantly short-term funds available to banks would be an uncritical decision. The implied *mismatch* of deposit and loan tenors could adversely affect a bank's liquidity position and plunge it into financial crisis.

Competitive forces

Borrowers may have access to other sources of funds—perhaps, from other banks, or the capital market. Depending on the amount involved, they may choose to borrow from friends or relations. Banks will want to operate as though they are a cartel. Nevertheless, they are not and will never be allowed to operate as monopolies. Competition will always be the hallmark of their intermediary role in the financial services industry. Thus, at any point in time, borrowers have choices that banks cannot afford to ignore or trivialize. Since no bank will want to price itself out of the market, it is important to closely monitor pricing activities of the competition. This should be pursued and achieved within the overall strategy and budget for *marketing intelligence.*

Expected return or yield

Lending involves some *opportunity cost* to a bank in terms of foregone investment alternatives. There are always competing needs for funds available to a bank. Therefore, a bank would make optimal use of its financial resources if it applies them to financing *earning* assets that promise the most return. A bank may not want to invest funds in credit facilities if the related risk assets do not attract good pricing. In that case, the bank may channel its funds into other financial assets. For example, the bank could invest in securities that are safer, more liquid, and profitable. Where a loan must be granted, its price has to be right to justify the cost of forgone alternative investments.

Administering costs

Originating and administering particular types of credit proposals may involve unavoidable high costs. Examples will include such loans that require extensive initial investigation, close monitoring, regular performance review, and a high cost of collateral acquisition, maintenance, and control. Once the cost of administering the credit (as a percentage of the amount disbursed) appears high, the price of the loan tends to be high. On the other hand, credits with simple documentation and monitoring requirements are normally not cumbersome to administer. However, banks recover expenses that they incur in administering credit facilities from borrowers. Standard loan agreements, contracts, or offer letters of banks add a caveat that enables the banks to recover credit admin-istration costs. The caveat is that all expenses incurred in administering, monitoring, and enforcing the terms and conditions of a credit, including re-covery expenses in the event of default, are for the account of the borrower.

Value of the relationship

How valuable are customers' accounts to a bank? The answer to this question sheds light on the salient points of price determination and discrimination in bank lending. The concept of *prime lending rate* (PLR) evolved out of a desire to reward highly valued customers with the lowest possible loan prices. Banks treat such customers that merit PLR as not only prime customers but role models. In this capacity, prime customers often dictate the price that they are willing to pay on particular credit facilities. Pricing of credit facilities granted to other categories of customers is then benchmarked on the prime rate plus a *premium*. The premium reflects the value differential between the two sets of customers, prime and nonprime.

Loan utilization

After deciding on an appropriate overall structure, the first step toward ensuring repayment of a loan is to devise a proper mode for its utilization. In practice, the *transaction dynamics* determine the utilization mode. The need for a foolproof mode of utilization is to forestall *diversion* of proceeds of a loan to other, sometimes personal, needs of the borrower.

One of the ways to guard against misuse of a loan is to minimize, as much as possible, direct access of the borrower to proceeds of the loan. Banks must uphold this practice, unless a loan is of *personal* nature or a *direct advance* that they grant to individuals. Otherwise, the use for a credit facility should be restricted to funding only the agreed, and approved, borrowing cause. Credit facilities may have regular or irregular modes of disbursement. On occasion the nature of the transaction for which a bank grants the loan informs which of the disbursement modes would be appropriate. For example, there could be partial, full, or staggered disbursements of credit facilities.

The transaction dynamics of some credit facilities may dictate direct disbursement to the borrowers' suppliers of materials or equipment (as in finance of contracts or purchase orders). But this approach will not be practicable or appropriate for the disbursement of an overdraft facility. It is therefore important for lending officers to determine the most effective disbursement mode that guarantees envisaged proper utilization of a loan.

Repayment or liquidation

Often how to achieve full repayment or liquidation of a credit facility without a hitch is of paramount importance to bank management. In fact, it is seen as the *bottom line* in the overall consideration of credit structure. The *modes* and *sources* of repayment are crucial determinants of management disposition toward loan proposals. Will the loan be repaid from *cash flow* generated from normal business operations of the borrower? Are there alternative sources of repayment, sometimes referred to as *ways out* or *fallbacks*? Can particular borrowers make a simple bullet repayment, or will they prefer to repay in some agreed installments during the tenor of the loans? These are some of the questions that demand answers in deciding credit structure. Answers to the questions will help bank management determine suitable options for the repayment of particular loans.

However, lending officers should analyze each repayment option critically to be assured of its veracity. For example, a borrower might propose *sales* or *earnings* from operations as the source of repayment. In that case, it would be imperative to analyze the borrower's cash flow positions—both historical and projected. If the borrower pledges receivables, or fixed deposits, the bank should take effective charge or lien over such assets. In most balance sheet lending, banks should use financial or ratio analysis to determine the borrower's ability to repay a loan, whether in the short or long term.

Collateral to secure loan

A credit package is concluded with agreement between the bank and borrower on appropriate collateral to secure the loan. Usually borrowers propose collateral that they offer to banks as security for loans that they obtain from the banks. However, it is not uncommon for a bank to demand specific collateral for a particular type of credit facility. In Chapter 27, I extensively discussed issues involved in *collateral evaluation* and why banks take collateral to secure loans. I need only to mention here that every loan must somehow be secured to avoid the offense or charge (in Nigeria) of abuse of office. Often lending officers face charges of unsecured lending. This happens more frequently when particular loans turn bad and are provided for against earnings or written off from profits.

QUESTIONS FOR DISCUSSION AND REVIEW

1. Identify and discuss the contexts in which lending and borrowing needs are defined in a credit structure.
2. Why should the marketing concept philosophy be adopted with caution in a lending situation?
3. Why and how do influences on banks' loan policies have a bearing on how credit facilities are structured?
4. What does *pricing* connote in lending? Discuss the elements of a loan's price and the purposes they serve.
5. What is the relevance of *safety*, *suitability*, and *profitability* as basic elements of lending principles?

Chapter 26

Emerging Market Issues in Structuring Bank Credit Facilities

Chapter Outline

LEARNING FOCUS AND OUTCOMES

Loan agreement assumes a crucial role in defining credit structure, especially in term loans, syndication lending, and mortgages. In these categories of lending, explicitly defining the terms and conditions of a credit facility consolidates the loan agreement. A critical aspect of loan agreement is the inclusion of operating covenants. Covenants establish acts that the bank and borrower should, or should not, perform. This ensures that neither the bank nor borrower can willfully truncate a loan. In effect, covenants strengthen loan agreements.

Besides covenants, a typical loan agreement contains specific conditions precedent to drawdown, representations and warranties, and events of default. It is in the context of these slippery clauses of a loan agreement that occasional relationship friction is experienced between a bank and borrower. This happens frequently where the bank tries to enforce the clauses, sometimes in defiance of the borrower's plea for forgiveness or leniency in situations of avoidable default. In most cases, these planks of a loan agreement also form

Emerging Market Bank Lending and Credit Risk Control. http://dx.doi.org/10.1016/B978-0-12-803438-5.00026-X

the basis of ligation by an aggrieved party when there is a default or act that breaches good faith.

A major consideration that underlies the making of slippery clauses of a loan agreement is the need to build quality risk assets. Asset quality is considered good and assured when, in addition to mitigating the usual credit risk, arrangement for its operation and continuing performance is well documented in a loan agreement.

In this chapter, I critically examine how banks in emerging markets enforce the slippery issues of corporate loan structure. The corollary, which I also examine, is equally important. How do borrowers in emerging markets tackle banks on the slippery issues of corporate loan structure? Analysis and discussion shed light on the basis of lending and borrowing money on those slippery terms. I also draw practical lessons from my personal corporate banking experience. In conclusion, I highlight implications of findings for strengthening the bank—customer credit relationship. You will understand why:

- Certain structural credit issues are considered "slippery"
- Banks codify the slippery credit issues in a loan agreement
- You must comprehend every clause of the slippery credit issues before appending your signature on a loan agreement
- On occasion banks go out of their way to make a commitment to lend money
- You should be apprised of the qualities of a good credit facility

BANK'S COMMITMENT TO LEND

In its credit and indeed overall financial planning, a bank makes projections, among other needs, as to the type and volumes of credit facilities that it intends to grant during a given period of time. Such loan forecasts are based on the bank's anticipation of particular levels and costs of funding derivable from various sources that it would try to match with possible loan demands from its customers. In order to balance these interests—the lending and funding needs—the bank would seek to obtain the *commitment* of borrowers to utilize their approved credit facilities.

Once this is done, the bank would reserve or plan for funds to lend to the borrowers at the points in time that they have loan disbursement needs. If the borrowers, for any reason, fail to utilize funds purchased and set aside for particular loans, the bank would not be able to *match* asset and liability. I have used the term *purchased funds* to describe *funds sourced* by a bank that involve interest rate commitment for a fixed term or tenor. Thus, deposits mobilized through current or collection accounts are never treated as purchased funds. Therefore, the term relates to only *time* (including *call*) deposits. The point being made here assumes a theoretical perspective in which it is possible to *purchase* particular funds that could be tied to specific loan requests. In practice, however, it is difficult to *match* particular assets with specific funding sources at *unit* or *transactional* level in a bank's operating cash flows. What really happens is that banks *pool* all funds from various sources and finance assets acquisition from the pool. This implies that *cost of funds* to the bank might not be *fully* recovered. In other words, the bank might not realize its projected gain from investment of the *reserved* funds without lending it out to borrowers. This scenario tends to justify banks charging a *commitment fee*.

It is in a bid to forestall financial planning conflicts that banks often experience when borrowers fail to, or partially, utilize their approved credit facilities that a commitment fee on loans is charged. In this sense, a *commitment fee* is a *penal* financial charge that banks impose on borrowers that fail to, or do not fully utilize, approved, offered, and accepted credit facilities. Ideally, the charge is calculated on the portion of the *committed* amount of the global credit facility that the borrower did not utilize.

CONDITIONS PRECEDENT

It is conventional, as part of the overall loan agreement, for a bank to state the conditions that a borrower must fulfill prior to its disbursement or funding of a loan. If all of the conditions are not satisfied, the bank will not have a legal obligation to fund its commitment on the loan. In most cases, conditions precedent may deal with myriad issues such as the following:

- return of accepted offer letter, or executed loan agreement, to the bank by the borrower
- execution, and return to the bank, of all security documents in respect of the assets financed or pledged by the borrower to the bank as collateral to secure the loan facility
- perfection of the bank's legal charge over the security or title documents to the assets, including landed property, pledged to it by the borrower to secure the loan
- submission to the bank of the borrower's board resolution that authorizes the borrowing on the stated terms and conditions, as well as naming the principal officers that should operate the loan account
- payment of all upfront fees and commission on the loan facility, including processing, arrangement, management, or legal fees as might be applicable

Indeed, these conditions establish both the prima facie and the envisaged legally binding evidence of the contract between the lender (bank) and borrower (customer) in the lending relationship. For instance, there will be no basis for the bank to fund its commitment to lend if the customer does not accept its offer of the loan or execute the loan agreement.

The requirements for the execution of security or collateral title documents by the borrower and return of the executed documents to the bank are intended to ensure that the bank has a recovery fallback in the event of default. These requirements are meant to redress the ignoble tendency of some borrowers to become elusive or uncooperative with the bank in putting loan documentation in place after disbursement of funds. It is also for the same reason that some banks even insist on *perfection* of all legal charges over pledged collateral assets, including landed property, prior to loan disbursement.

However, in view of delay experienced in registering and perfecting collateral, there could be agreement to put the bank *in a position to perfect.* When this happens, the borrower is allowed to start utilizing the loan after endorsing and returning all the required security documents to the bank. There are obvious advantages to the bank in being put in a position to perfect. It is necessary, on the one hand, to meet the timing of the borrower's loan utilization without which the bank might lose the account to competition. The bank can, on the other hand, move to and actually perfect the executed security documents in its possession without reference to the borrower. This would happen if the borrower is experiencing persisting difficulty in servicing the loan or default appears imminent. But such action may lead to mistrust between the bank and customer, which can affect their banking relationship.

It is pertinent for the bank to request board resolution of the borrowing company authorizing the loan as a condition precedent to drawdown. In addition to establishing the general borrowing powers of the company at the analysis stage, the bank must ascertain the specific borrowing rights of the management. Otherwise, a loan granted to the company in contravention of this rule stands the risk of being repudiated by the directors or shareholders in the future.

REPRESENTATIONS AND WARRANTIES

As explained in Chapter 4, the credit process begins with loan application, acknowledgment, and interview. During this preliminary process, the loan officer tries to obtain vital information on which the lending decision will be premised. It is expected that the *prospective* borrower should furnish accurate information to the bank. The information so generated would complement information that the lending officer should obtain from other sources, including searches at the Corporate Affairs Commission, credit checks, and enquiries.

Thus, the bank usually requires, seeks, and obtains information on several issues about and affecting the borrower. The bank may—and this is often the case—want to know about the corporate status of the borrower, its creditworthiness, obligations to other lenders, and so on. It will rely on information so elicited from the borrower to make assumptions about suitability of the loan request (in terms of its purpose), ability of the borrower to fulfill its loan obligations (i.e., its financial strength), the borrower's previous experience with other lenders (i.e., its borrowing and relationship track record), and so on.

Based on these assumptions, the bank makes the decision to lend money to the borrower. In order to underline the seriousness of its reliance on the information and assumptions in making the lending decision, the bank documents them in the *representations and warranties* section of the loan agreement. As borrowers execute the loan agreement, they are confirming the accuracy of their information to the bank as of the date they sign the agreement.

Some of the representations and warranties commonly found in most loan agreements include the following:

- Financial statements (i.e., balance sheet, profit and loss account, cash flow statement, and statement of value added and so on) are correct as presented.
- There has not been any material adverse change in the financial condition of the borrower *after* the dates of the reported financial statements.
- The borrower's business is not subject to any litigation, whether pending or threatened, in the courts of law.
- Collateral offered to the bank to secure the loan belongs to the borrower and is not in any way encumbered.
- The borrower does not require superior approval or consent for the loan that is not yet in place.

Several other issues may be included in the representations and warranties section of the loan agreement, depending on the needs of the bank, type of loan, and the envisaged risks.

COVENANTS OF THE BORROWER

The bank and borrower negotiate covenants that are usually binding on the latter. Covenants generally represent the borrower's ongoing commitment to satisfying certain set minimum standards of future conduct and performance throughout the duration of the loan. With the covenants, the bank tries to minimize the risk of a borrower's possible default in loan repayment. But covenants also serve another useful purpose. They give early warning of likely default on a loan that could happen as a result of unmitigated deterioration in the financial condition of a borrower. There are basically two types of covenants that are common to most loan agreements: *affirmative* and *negative* covenants.

Affirmative covenants

Affirmative covenants are designed to emphasize actions that a bank expects a borrower to take to maintain or attain a good credit rating at all times. Most conscientious borrowers will ordinarily take similar actions in the interest of their businesses, not as a consequence of bank loans. There are numerous issues that are likely to be included among affirmative covenants. For some banks, two of the key covenants relate to *financial* and account *turnover* issues.

Financial covenant

A bank might want to know the financial health of a borrower at any point in time. It will therefore regularly review management accounts as well as audited financial statements of the company. As mentioned in Chapter 24, the purpose of such financial review is to reconfirm short-term liquidity, long-term solvency, efficiency of assets utilization, and profitability of operations of a company. The review is carried out on income statement, balance sheet, and cash flow statement of the company by means of ratio analysis (extensively discussed in Chapter 24). Favorable ratios would reassure the bank that a loan stands a good chance of being repaid on the due date.

Financial covenants would probably require the borrower to make its audited or management accounts available to the bank for review at least once every quarter. But this clause does not apply to companies with unstructured businesses, i.e., those that do not have formal organization, in which ownership is not clearly separated from management. This category of borrowers maintains incomplete financial records and, therefore, is not amenable to financial (ratio) analysis.

Financial covenants could provide early warning of an impending loan default. This is quite instructive. Account officers and managers can take the cue and reposition their relationship management strategies to forestall default on the loan. This might entail increased loan monitoring activities, such as tracking of the borrower's banking transactions and survey of the borrower's products markets.

Turnover covenant

A bank may want to forestall sharing or diversion of transactions generated from utilization of its credit facility with other banks from which the borrower has not received such financial support. In that case, the bank might include a turnover covenant in the loan agreement to compel the borrower to transact *most* of its banking business with the bank.

As distinguished from sales, *account turnover* is a measure of transactions volume—a sort of velocity or level of activities that a current account achieves in a given period of time, say one month. It depicts how active a current account is or is likely to be in future. Account turnover is usually associated with borrowing (overdraft) and nonborrowing accounts. Active current and overdraft accounts show marked swings in daily opening and closing balances. In Nigeria, banks relish the prospect of having turnover-driven demand deposit accounts. The banks are always favorably disposed to courting banking relationships with such accounts. The reason is simple. Accounts in this category have a strong earnings implication for the banks.

The Central Bank of Nigeria permits banks to charge a monthly processing fee, popularly known in Nigeria as *commission on turnover* (COT). The maximum COT that a bank can debit from a customer's current or DD account is ₦5 per mille on the total volume of withdrawals (debits turnover) from the account. However, banks also strive to increase the level of credits turnover, i.e., total monthly lodgments or inflows into current or DD accounts that their customers attain. The drive to do so derives from understanding that credit inflows ultimately beget debit turnover. In other words, customers must constantly be lodging money into their current accounts in order to meet expected debit turnover.

In view of the foregoing, an account turnover covenant in a loan agreement is intended to ensure retention of a customer's patronage and loyalty. This is given impetus when the clause states—as it always does—that in the event that the borrower fails to meet the agreed upon monthly turnover level, the bank reserves the right to charge COT to the account corresponding to the observed shortfall in debit turnover during the month. Thus, the choice is the borrower's—whether or not to divert transactions and pay or avoid the related penal COT charge. On its part, the bank would be indifferent to the choice that the borrower makes.

Other affirmative covenants

There could be several other important affirmative covenants, including the following:

- Utilization of the loan for its intended purpose, without diversion of portions of its proceeds to other, especially initially undisclosed, uses
- Maintenance of proper and accurate records of business, especially financial, transactions
- Concession to the bank of right of inspection of the borrower's premises, factories, assets, or general business operations at any time during the tenor of the loan
- Preservation of corporate existence of the borrower as a going concern during the tenor or duration of the loan
- Maintenance of the borrower's property, insurance, and other facilities with a view to ensuring their functionality

Negative covenants

Negative covenants essentially place certain restrictions on management decisions that could impair the borrower's ability to repay a loan on its due date. Doing so, the bank will be interested in ensuring that borrowers maintain acceptable levels of liquidity or solvency at all times for the duration of their loans. In particular, the covenants should include restrictions aimed at preventing any action that might jeopardize the bank's recourse to the earnings and assets of the borrower in the event of default. Restriction on asset depletion is perhaps the most important of the negative covenants. This is largely because of the heavy reliance of banks on assets of the borrower in making nontransactional lending decisions. This is especially the case with most of the so-called balance sheet or cash flow lending. Following is a discussion of asset depletion and other important negative covenants.

Asset depletion

In typical balance sheet lending—for working capital purposes—a bank relies greatly on the strength of the borrower's asset base in making a decision to lend money to a corporate borrower. There is always concern that continuing good performance of a loan hinges on preservation of existing and new assets, as well as acquisition of new assets. Banks tend to believe that with a strong and serviceable asset base, corporate borrowers would achieve their projected earnings and repay loans the banks grant to them. This would be especially possible when the companies market and produce need-satisfying goods and services. In fact, this should inform their need for a bank loan in the first place.

This implies that the capacity of a company to repay a loan would be impaired if, for any reason, there is avoidable depletion of its assets. A company's asset base would deplete as a result of the following:

- Prolonged neglect of maintenance resulting in substantial damage that renders some of the assets unserviceable
- Willful obliteration of assets by staff, owners, or other members of the company. This could happen, for instance, as a result of some bitter disagreement between certain key stakeholders of the company
- Outright sale or disposal of some of the assets to augment the company's cash flow position
- Bartering of any of the company's assets, which may be the consequence of cash flow deficiency, to acquire other assets.

A bank might include an *asset depletion clause* in a loan agreement to forestall occurrence of any of these events. In view of this clause, directors of the company would be restrained from taking any steps to—as well as committing actions that might—deplete the asset base without prior consent of the bank. As I stated earlier, this clause is common in loans granted to finance working capital requirements. But it is also often encountered in certain categories of term loans.

Negative pledge

A bank may require borrowers to commit themselves to restriction in the use of company assets as collateral to secure other creditors. This implies restriction on any form of *mortgages*, *pledge*, or *lien* over the present and future assets of the borrower during the duration of the loan. Thus, a negative pledge covenant serves to prevent possible encumbrance of the borrower's assets or earnings in favor of other lenders.

It is commonplace for banks that grant unsecured loans to insist on execution of a negative pledge by borrowers. The pledge only provides collateral comfort to the lender, as it is not tangible or effective collateral. Yet it is popular among banks, especially those that have good banking relationships with blue-chip companies or large local corporations. For such customers, a negative pledge easily substitutes for tangible collateral requirements because of the strong asset base of the companies.

In the final analysis, a negative pledge covenant seeks to pool assets and earnings of a borrower that should be available in the event of default, with a view to paying claims of unsecured creditors on equal basis. The pledge therefore removes the possibility of any creditor having a superior claim over others on the assets and earnings of the borrower in the event of default.

Other negative covenants

There could be several other issues that might be included among negative covenants that represent specific restrictions (in the interest of the bank) on exercise of certain managerial decisions by the borrower. A typical list of negative covenants will include restriction on mergers, sale of assets or subsidiaries, payment of cash dividends, repurchase of shares, voluntary prepayment of other indebtedness, and engaging in other businesses. Other important negative covenants include limitation on total indebtedness, capital expenditure, investment of funds, loans and advances, and so on. These covenants almost always form part of loan agreements in loan syndication and term loans.

EVENTS OF DEFAULT

Events of default are perhaps the most crucial, as well as controversial, issues with which bank management and borrowers must contend in loan agreements. If a borrower executes a loan agreement with stipulated events of default, the bank gets the right to terminate the loan, as well as the customer's borrowing relationship with it. Thus, the events of default section of a loan agreement must be carefully negotiated, precisely communicated, and properly understood by the borrower to avoid any future disclaimer of its provisions. Standard events that empower a bank to terminate a lending relationship include, but are not limited to, the following:

- Bankruptcy or insolvency, liquidation, or appointment of receiver-manager to realize the assets of the borrower
- Continuing failure or neglect of the borrower to service the loan as when due, reflected in accumulation of past due interest or principal repayments
- Impairment or destruction of collateral taken by the bank to secure the loan, annulment of guarantee or security agreement
- Change of ownership or management, which might affect the chances of maintaining an effective lending relationship with the borrower
- Breach of any of the provisions of the loan covenants or detection of any inaccurate representations and warranties

Inclusion of events of default in a loan agreement is one of the powerful instruments of control that a bank can invoke to accelerate loan repayment or terminate a lending relationship.

QUALITIES OF GOOD AND WELL-STRUCTURED CREDIT

It should be easy to recognize the attributes of a good credit facility. I must mention what good credit connotes at the outset. The phrase *good credit facility* does not just mean a well-packaged or structured credit facility. Indeed, the elements that constitute a good credit facility transcend considerations of structure alone but include a lot of other loan aspects in relation to which its structuring might even be of no or less significance. Yet without an appropriate structure, a credit facility can hardly be said to be altogether good.

Besides consideration of issues apposite to structure—for all practical purposes, especially from a banker's point of view—a credit facility is said to be good if its package, among other requirements, does the following:

- lends itself to easy, close, and effective monitoring by an account officer, relationship manager, and other loan officers of the bank
- engenders high volume of activities (turnover) in its operative current account from which the bank earns considerable transaction processing fee income, such as COT, applicable in Nigeria.
- triggers sales of other bank products to the borrower, such as foreign exchange, time or fixed deposits, funds transfer, and so on—all of which produce an income multiplier effect for the credit facility
- subsumes an unambiguous transaction path or dynamics that ensure that disbursements, utilizations, and repayments are conducted as envisaged at the time of granting the credit facility without a hitch
- conforms with tenets of the so-called self-liquidating credit facilities, which are common among asset-based loans
- offers loan loss remedial options—usually in terms of adequate, easily realizable, collateral to secure the credit facility—as well as other *ways-out* strategies
- save as a result of unforeseen contingencies or force majeure—the so-called *acts of God*—has a negligible probability of default. Typical examples of force majeure, occurrences beyond the control of the borrower, include war, fire, natural disaster, and so on.
- returns a reasonable value on investment as measured by relative net yield on the credit facility. Net yield on a credit facility is calculated as a ratio (usually percentage) obtained by dividing the sum of all incomes that the bank earned from the credit facility over a given period of time by the customer's average borrowings (i.e., utilization) on that credit facility over the same period. The ratio serves to compare the profitability of various borrowing accounts. However, banks also use it in appraising customers'

requests for concessions on certain banking transactions. A bank will likely grant a rebate (if requested) on interest charges or commissions to accounts that have high net yield.

Not many credit facilities satisfy all of the aforesaid attributes. Nevertheless, I can say that a credit facility that meets at least five of the required qualities (including, particularly the last four above) can be said to be good. Such a credit facility will obviously be among the most sought after by banks.

QUESTIONS FOR DISCUSSION AND REVIEW

1. What lending instrument defines the structure of a credit? Of what significance is the instrument?
2. What factors necessitate a bank's commitment to lend money to a borrower? How do banks enforce commitment on loans?
3. Is the inclusion of *representations* and *warranties* clauses in a loan agreement justified?
4. Discuss the basis, functions, and limitations of *covenants of the borrower* in a loan agreement.
5. Why are *events of default* regarded as the most crucial as well as controversial issues in a loan agreement?

Chapter 27

Credit Analysis Memorandum Fitted for Banks in Emerging Markets

Chapter Outline

Emerging Market Bank Lending and Credit Risk Control. http://dx.doi.org/10.1016/B978-0-12-803438-5.00027-1
471

LEARNING FOCUS AND OUTCOMES

Credit analysis memorandum (CAM) is really the starting point of an organized appraisal of a loan proposal. It kick-starts a formal process of packaging a loan request for approval. The preliminary work on an intended credit provides most of the raw materials that a credit analyst needs to prepare the CAM. But some useful information could be obtained from other—sometimes obscure—sources during the intervening period between exploratory information search and writing of the credit report. Note that writing a CAM is one of the major assignments of a credit analyst.

Without a CAM, it would be difficult to make any meaningful decision on major credit requests. This raises a number of questions that seek to clarify general aspects of a CAM: What do bankers mean by the phrase *credit analysis memorandum*? Why is a CAM such a critical document for bank lending? What are the components of a typical CAM? How should loan officers go about preparing a CAM to sustain its significance as the basis of lending decisions? What qualities should loan officers who prepare CAMs possess?

This chapter discusses and provides answers—both from the literature on bank lending and practice—to the foregoing and other important questions about CAM. My approach to the relevant topics, for all intents and purposes, reflects current practice in contemporary bank lending. The approach also underscores the unique place of CAM in bank lending. The examples that I use to illustrate the topics are based on true experiences of banks and corporate borrowers.

My intent in this chapter is to provide readers with the framework of a typical credit analysis memorandum. I do so against a backdrop of challenges that credit analysts face in packaging loan requests for approval. You will understand:

- The meaning, components, and import of a credit analysis memorandum (CAM)
- Why CAM is such a critical document for making and securing bank lending decisions
- The qualities that loan officers who prepare a CAM should possess in order to do a good job
- How loan officers prepare a CAM to sustain its significance as the basis of lending decisions

APTITUDE OF THE ANALYST

In order to prepare a dependable report, the credit analyst must be competent, of sound mind, unbiased, and trustworthy. Thus, apart from acquiring the requisite competences and technical skills, the analyst must have a high rating on integrity. We may assume that loan officers display a high level of integrity, competence, and professionalism. Yet these qualitative variables have a profound impact on a loan officer's job. Let us assume that banks employ competent loan officers or train them to acquire competence. Assume further that lending officers are oriented to and actually display a high level of integrity. These assumptions are necessary to avoid a situation in which a critique of the credit process would be unfair to loan officers. For example, critics will want to conclude that loan officers point accusing fingers to unfounded culprits in cases of loan default. Whether loan officers actually display high integrity, competence, and professionalism or not may be a subject of specific research in a different setting.

MEANING AND IMPORTANCE OF A CAM

A CAM is a loan report that details a credit officer's analysis and recommendations to senior management. The senior management to whom the report is usually made would most likely be the approving authority for the loan. But it could also be designated members of senior management who, for some considerations, could also approve the credit. A common practice, however, is to constitute the approving authority into a credit strategy committee whose endorsement is often required before the credit is sent to the chief executive officer, executive management committee, and board audit and credit committee for approval. The approval sequence is followed when the amount of the loan is beyond the authority of the prior level officers or committee. Unlike a credit approval form (CAF), which is one or two summary sheets, a CAM is a more serious document—rigorous, yet concise. It presents a detailed appraisal of every conceivable issue on which good utilization and timely repayment of a loan would depend. In banking parlance, when it is said that a loan is being packaged, what is implied is that a CAM for it is being prepared. Frequently, learning how to write the CAM is the starting point for the training of loan officers. Indeed, it is believed that acquisition of technical competence and ability to package good credits by staff of the lending units is an asset that bank management eagerly covets. In some banks, a relatively higher level of annual, nonsalary expenditure on staff is accounted for by outlay on training or courses in basic credit analysis and reporting.

A CAM assumes importance in initiating a formal process of assessing the worth of a credit proposal for purposes of approval by senior management. No matter how a lending decision is ultimately made, there should be a CAM to justify the loan, especially for future reference. It is a particularly important document to credit policy and control staff—those who independently administer a loan once it is approved, booked, and disbursed. Also known as credit admin function in some banks, its staffs ensure that a loan is not operated in a manner that violates the bank's credit policy. In carrying out this function, credit admin relies a great deal on the facts and recommendations upon which approval of the credit was predicated. Such facts are first and foremost usually established and documented in the CAM, but they are also highlighted in the CAF.

Bank management insists on a CAM—a thorough analysis of a credit proposal for which approval is being sought—because it formalizes the credit process. Amongst other functions of a CAM, it formalizes identification, appreciation, and suggestion of resolution of, as well as management requirements for, the so-called key credit issues. How do lending officers go about the task of producing this important report that forms the basis of lending decisions? The style of presentation of a credit proposal for approval varies among banks. Differences are informed by dictates of business expediency, risk appetite, and orientation of lending authorities of the banks. Yet a common feature of good credit reports is always the emphasis placed on risk analysis and mitigation. Otherwise, for similar credit proposals, differences in approach to credit appraisal may be dictated by the premium placed on the borrowing cause, transaction dynamics, allowable tenor, pricing or income expectation, and collateral taken to secure the loan.

ELEMENTS OF A CAM

A typical CAM focuses on analysis of specific critical issues. Among the important issues are the borrower's *background*, *proposed credit* facility, *management* evaluation, *risks* of the credit, and *collateral*. Now, I should demonstrate practical applications of the principles of credit analysis that I outline and discuss throughout this book. In order to do so, I present below a credit request and its analysis on the basis of which a loan is granted, utilized, and fully repaid by the borrower. For purposes of confidentiality, I have not used real names for the borrower, its shareholders, and the lending bank, as well as the borrowing cause. Note that the practical demonstration that follows will not satisfy all credit analysis requirements in all lending situations. More often than not, each loan request presents characteristics that may not be found in any other or even in another one from a borrower in the same line of business. For this reason, the demonstration should be regarded merely as a practical guide to issues that are usually and should be covered in a good credit analysis memorandum.

In this demonstration of a CAM, the petroleum marketing firm Energy Group Limited (EGL) had applied to Trans Border Bank Limited (TBB) for a loan of ₦100 million to meet working capital requirements, as well as for importation and local purchase of its stock-in-trade. I present the credit analyst's appraisal of the loan proposal and various components of the CAM as follows.

INTRODUCTION: THE STARTING POINT

As a rule, the CAM should be marked as an *internal memorandum* and start with identification of the credit analyst—by name, position or status, and lending unit to which they belong—who packaged the loan (see Table 27.1 below). It is this same officer who, at the end of the report, should sign the CAM with their boss, usually the relationship manager for the credit after disbursement of the loan.

TABLE 27.1 Internal Memorandum

From:	Ken Water – Mgr., Credit Department
To:	Credit Strategy Committee (CRESCO)
Date:	October 28, 2012
Subject:	Energy Group Limited
	₦100.0 million multiple credit facility

Initiating and starting point of the CAM

It is also pertinent to indicate the approving authority—in this case, the Credit Strategy Committee (CRESCO)—to which the CAM is addressed. However, choice of *senior management* as opposed to the CRESCO as the approving authority is common and often preferred. The reason is sensible and serves practical purposes. Addressing the CAM to senior management accommodates situations where approval of low amounts of credit would not require prior presentation to the CRESCO. In such cases, one or more designated loan approving officers would endorse the credit for approval. Otherwise, the CAM should be addressed to the CRESCO—even when the credit will require subsequent approval of the chief executive officer, executive management, and board credit committee.

The starting point of the credit will be incomplete without mention of the intended borrower, amount, and type of credit being proposed. Of course, in initiating the credit proposal, the credit analyst should indicate the date when the CAM was written.

SUMMARY OF LOAN TERMS

In this section of the CAM, the credit analyst outlines envisaged terms and conditions of the proposed credit. It begins with recapitulation of the identity of the counterparty or intended obligor. The name of the loan applicant must be disclosed. In doing so, the credit analyst should indicate the applicant's location, business, and ownership structure (in the case of a corporate borrower). As Table 27.2 shows, it is also useful to mention whether the banking relationship between the bank and loan applicant is new or existing. If it is an existing relationship, the credit analyst should evaluate the value of the relationship to the bank—showing, in so doing, whether it has been mutually beneficial or not—in an appropriate section of the CAM.

TABLE 27.2 Summary of Loan Parties, Terms, and Conditions

Lender	Trans Border Bank Limited (TBB)
Borrower	Energy Group Limited (EGL) — also the obligor
	Location: PC19, Brown Crescent, Ikeja, Lagos State, Nigeria
Business	Importation, local purchase, distribution, and sale of petroleum products in Nigeria
	Ownership: Owned 100% by indigenous investors
	Relationship: New
Amount	₦100,000,000.00 (one hundred million naira only)
Facility	Multiple, short-term, credit facility—comprising the following: 1. Overdraft (O/D) facility, for local purchase of stock-in-trade 2. Import finance facility (IFF) for establishment of letters of credit (L/C) 3. Bank guarantee in favor of local suppliers of products to Energy Group Limited
	The facilities expire 365 days from the date of initial drawdown or after acceptance of offer letter for the loan, whichever is earlier.
Purpose	To finance importation of, and/or local purchase and payment for, petroleum products, as well as for issuing bank guarantee to local suppliers of petroleum products to Energy Group Limited.
Tenor	365 days, however, each tranche of utilization of the letter of credit facility shall have a transaction cycle of not more than 120 days, barring any unforeseen contingencies.
Pricing	2.5% per annum above TBB's prime lending rate, currently 20% per annum, giving an initial gross lending rate of 22.5% per annum to the borrower.
	Processing fee: 1% flat, payable upfront
	COT: ₦1.50 per mille
	Commission: 0.75% flat on each letter of credit
Collateral	Lien over stock of petroleum products financed by the bank, administered under terms of a tripartite warehousing agreement between TBB, EGL, and a reputable warehousing agent acceptable to the bank.[a]

TABLE 27.2 Summary of Loan Parties, Terms, and Conditions—cont'd

	1. Counterpart funding, or equity contribution, of 20% of each letter of credit established, payment to local suppliers, or bank guarantee issued using or based on the credit facilities. 2. Comprehensive insurance cover over the imports, as well as storage tanks, products and facilities at the borrower's petroleum depot where the products are stored, noting TBB as the first loss payee beneficiary. Insurance covers for assets of borrowers provided by subsidiaries of the lending banks have become commonplace.
Repayment	The loans shall be repaid from proceeds of the sale of petroleum products financed by the bank.
Availability	Upon fulfillment of the following *conditions precedent* to drawdown: 1. Receipt of duly accepted copy of the bank's letter of offer of the credit facility to EGL on the stated terms and conditions. 2. Submission of a resolution of the board of directors of EGL authorizing the credit facility, as well as stating officers of the company who are authorized to accept the offer letter and operate the loan account on behalf of EGL. 3. Execution of a tripartite collateral and warehouse management agreement between EGL, TBB, and a reputable warehousing agent acceptable to the bank.
Other conditions	1. All expenses incurred in the arrangement, documentation, and enforcement of this credit facility, as well as all legal and monitoring fees, taxes, and commission, if any, will be borne by EGL. 2. The minimum turnover expected from utilization of the facility is ₦125 million per month. In the event that the minimum turnover is not achieved, EGL's account would be debited with a COT charge related to the amount of the shortfall in turnover at the agreed rate. 3. EGL shall provide TBB with its audited financial statement and annual reports not later than six months after its financial year end and interim or management accounts on a quarterly basis or whenever requested as long as the facility remains outstanding. 4. Utilization of the facility or any part thereof shall be at the sole discretion of TBB and is subject to satisfactory documentation and regulation of the Central Bank of Nigeria as may be prescribed from time to time. 5. The facility shall terminate and all sums due to TBB shall become immediately due and payable if EGL commits any breach or defaults under the terms of the credit or any other credit facilities granted to it by TBB or any other bank. 6. The facility shall become due and payable if in the opinion of TBB there is any material adverse change whatsoever in the business, assets, financial condition, and operations of EGL.

[a]The collateral arrangement for this credit facility is suitable for asset-based credits that are usually self-liquidating within the transaction cycle. However, some banks do not grant loans that offer collateral arrangement in warehousing of the stock financed. Such banks would prefer other forms of tangible collateral such as landed property, fixed assets, or floating debenture.

BORROWER'S BACKGROUND

Credit analysts must identify borrowers by name and address of business location. In the case of a corporate borrower, they should describe the company's management profile and ownership structure. This normally requires assessment of management stability and expertise in the company's line of business. It also involves, in most cases, a critical analysis of issues regarding the borrower's character, capacity, and capital.

The borrower's notable profile that is often highlighted in this section of the CAM includes business activities, market share, and competitive strength. In doing so, the credit analyst should briefly discuss features of the industry in which the borrower operates. It would be useful to mention the date of commencement of the banking relationship between the bank and borrower. It is equally important to determine long-term type and value of the envisaged account relationship.

In the case of existing customers, credit analysts should review the bank's experience with the borrower. For the existing customers, this implies a review of the historical performance of the account, especially in terms of earnings to the bank. Credit approving authorities would also be interested in knowing the quality of the account as reflected in its historical or current performance with other banks. For practical purposes, such details as outstanding credit facilities, their pricing, and how they are secured should be given. This is necessary to guide judgment on terms and conditions for the intended credit.

OWNERSHIP, BUSINESS, AND MANAGEMENT

EGL was incorporated in Nigeria on September 30, 1972 as a privately owned, limited liability company. The company is engaged in importation, local purchase, distribution, and sale of petroleum products. It is an indigenous company owned by members of the Mark Yusuf family, reputed for their long-standing experience in the oil services industry in Nigeria.

In order to take full advantage of the deregulation of importation and marketing of petroleum products in the country, the company recently acquired land and built a 25,000 M/T capacity petroleum depot in Apapa, Lagos. Its decision to make the investment also derived from pressure of demand from several independent and major petroleum marketers that do not have storage facilities to use its newly constructed tanks for storage of automotive gas oil (diesel), premium motor spirit (PMS), and kerosene (DPK). From its depot, EGL supplies the products directly to the local marketers and large industrial users.

The company's management has a thorough grasp of the market in which it operates. It intends to fully exploit the opportunities and its strength over the competition by buying products that are in high demand—and *on order* basis.

Unlike the competition, EGL enjoys a low operating cost profile. Thus, EGL does not suffer the disadvantage of high operational cost of the industry. This affords it the opportunity of dictating market prices of the products in view of its established low cost structure.

It is, of course, assumed that the analyst conducted credit checks or inquiries to ascertain the credibility and creditworthiness of the borrower prior to preparing the CAM. The results of such checks with the other banks where the borrower has a subsisting account relationship or had banked in the past, as well as any favorable references obtained in support of the credit proposal, should be mentioned to strengthen the credit. Where irredeemably unfavorable responses are received, the credit request should be promptly declined.

PROPOSED CREDIT

It is expected that credit analysts should painstakingly define the customer's credit request in this section of the CAM. In doing so, they may be confronted with multiple, syndicated, or other specialized credit requests. Yet it is the responsibility of credit analysts to study, understand, and explain the borrowing cause or purpose, tenor, structure, dynamics, mode of utilization, and source of repayment of the credit. The profitability of the proposed credit is also analyzed, as a bank may not be keen to grant a credit from which it would have a loss. An exception to this rule may be where a bank deliberately—perhaps, after careful consideration of other intrinsic factors in a proposed credit or future benefits—decides to grant the loan as a *loss leader*. The definition of credit facility in the summary of terms and conditions for the EGL's credit proposal above suffices for a proper explanation of the proposed credit required in this section of the CAM.

TRANSACTION DYNAMICS

Perhaps the most critical issue in discussing the proposed credit are the *transaction dynamics*, sometimes referred to as *transaction path*. The transaction dynamics are a vivid description of the mode of disbursement, utilization, and repayment of a credit facility, including fallback for the bank in the event that the borrower defaults. In a nutshell, it is really about *how a credit facility would operate* to ensure that it is fully repaid or recovered when its tenor expires. Thus, the transaction dynamics clearly establish the potency and burden of loan monitoring in credit management. Everything else might be right, but the credit would easily turn into a lost asset statistic if its transaction path is flawed. In the case of EGL's loan proposal, there is some complexity in its transaction path. For example, the transaction dynamics envisage three possible options for loan utilization. This is not strange as most multiple credit facilities often have a similar feature. In fact, what is unusual is to expect that all loan requests should have similar transaction dynamics. In terms of loan utilization, the dynamics of the EGL credit facility are as follows:

Utilization for letters of credit

- EGL submits completed Form M, L/C application form, pro forma invoice, and other supporting documents for the establishment of documentary credit to TBB.
- TBB opens dollar-denominated L/C in favor of EGL's overseas supplier (Mobil, Shell, or any other reputable company that has the products at the time of establishment of the L/C).
- From its origin (usually West Africa or Europe), the consignment arrives at the Apapa depot within 2—4 weeks, depending on the port of loading, and is discharged directly into EGL's tanks. Clearing formalities would have been concluded prior to the arrival of the vessel. This implies—unlike in an ordinary import finance facility—that shipping documents do not really offer security to the bank in this transaction.
- Acting for and on behalf of TBB, the warehousing agent ensures that the exact quantity of petroleum products financed by the bank is discharged into the tanks at the depot. It issues warrants conferring ownership of the products to the bank.
- Warehousing agent countersigns and retains a copy of every buyer's *authority to load* and deposit slip, certified check, or bank draft for products lifted. In other words, the warehousing agent will not allow loading of trucks without evidence of authority to load issued by EGL and payment evidence or instrument. TBB should in due course consider establishing a collection center at the depot that will make verification of documents for products loading easy and prompt.
- Warehousing agent submits daily report on stock position, showing quantity and proceeds of stock sold, to TBB.

Local payment for products

EGL may decide to buy the products locally rather than import them. In this case, it could place an order with a local major importer of the products. Each transaction cycle will be consummated as follows:

- Local suppliers sell a certain quantity of the products to EGL. Warehousing agent tests the products for quality prior to discharge into EGL's tanks and certifies the exact quantity supplied.
- Supplier of the product raises sale invoice showing the quantity, quality specifications, and price of products supplied. EGL accepts the supplier's invoice. The supplier presents the accepted invoice to TBB for payment and is paid full value of the products by the bank.

- The last three steps in respect of the dynamics for L/C transactions will also be followed in payments for local purchase of the products.

Issuing of bank guarantee

EGL may yet reach an agreement with a local major supplier that on the basis of a bank guarantee from TBB, it could be supplied petroleum products on certain credit terms. In this case, the bank will issue the guarantee prior to supply of the products to EGL. However, the guarantee will be effective only after the required quantity and quality of the products, as certified by the warehousing agent, is discharged into EGL's tanks. Documentation and control requirements as outlined in the aforementioned transaction dynamics also apply.

MARKET AND INDUSTRY ANALYSIS

Energy (oil and gas) sector

The Nigerian economy has over the years been monolithic, one that completely depends on proceeds of crude oil sales for foreign exchange earnings. Indeed oil accounted for over 90% of the country's export earnings more than 20 years after independence. Dependence on oil revenue is worsened by the fact that production and volume of sales are a function of quota allocation by OPEC and the vagaries of the highly volatile international oil price mechanism.

Though there are several refineries in Nigeria, most of them are operating at below installed capacity. Thus, more petroleum products are imported than locally refined. Thus, it is apparent that all is not well with operations of the refineries. This fact becomes glaring when the four major refineries owned by the federal government often shut down operations due to breakdown in the fluid catalytic cracking units, reforming units and there is poor turnaround maintenance.

In order to alleviate the problem, government sometimes imports and sells petroleum products at subsidized prices to the public. In order to make economic sense, government reviews prices of the products upwards. Realizing the strain on its purse and the continuous budget deficits over the years, the government started partial deregulation of the downstream oil industry effective January 1999. Licensed marketers are now allowed to import and sell the products, especially AGO, at market-determined prices. The principal products are as follows:

- *Premium motor spirit (PMS)*: This is popularly known as *petrol* for running petrol-driven engines.
- *Automotive gas oil (AGO)*: Known more widely as *diesel* for running heavy-duty engines like trucks, trailers, generators, and so on.
- *Kerosene (DPK)*: This is the most popular petroleum product among the ordinary people. Known simply as *kerosene*, it is used for domestic chores like cooking and for lamps.

- *Aviation turbine kerosene (ATK)*: Also known as *aviation fuel*, it is used in the aviation industry for running turbine engines.
- *Straight run gasoline (ARG)*: This is used in the petroleum industry as a solvent for extraction and exploration.
- *Low/high pour point fuel oil (LPFO/HPFO)*: Both are industrial fuels for running boilers and steamers. Hospitals and dry cleaning businesses mostly use these products.

Products survey and market

Automotive gas oil

Demand for AGO is approximately 300–500 million metric tons per annum. Consumers of this product range from households to industries. In homes, it is used for running diesel engines such as generators and cars. Its industrial uses are diverse, including trucks, forklifts, generators, and other heavy-duty engines. Lately, the need for this product has become more acute because of the incessant load shedding of the electricity power supply and incessant power outages for which PHCN does not yet have solution. Thus, reliance on privately owned sources of electricity power supply has been high.

A chronic shortage of this product in the past was propitious for the emergence of a black market that operated parallel to the formal market. With recent increases in prices of petroleum products, the pump price of AGO shot up to between ₦150 and ₦185 per liter in some retail filling stations. Notwithstanding deregulation and price increases, the product was not readily available at some gas stations.

The situation started changing with complete removal of the government subsidy on AGO. Occasionally, though, the product still becomes scarce. This usually happens when the National Union of Petroleum and Natural Gas workers or the Petroleum and Natural Gas Senior Staff Association of Nigeria calls a strike to protest government policy.

Kerosene

Kerosene is used mostly in homes for stoves and lamps. It is a substitute for stanched liquefied petroleum gas (butane), also called domestic cooking gas. Most Nigerian homes cannot afford gas cookers, as their prices are high. Coal and kerosene stoves are good substitutes. Though coal stoves do compete with kerosene stoves as well as gas cookers, their use in the metropolis is not popular and kerosene stoves are preferred.

There is perhaps no family in Nigeria—whether of the high, middle, or low income class—that does not have a kerosene stove as an alternative to a gas cooker as the case may be. The average demand for kerosene is between 500 million and 1 billion metric tons per annum. As in the case of AGO, nonavailability despite a pump price increase has also caused the running of black market alongside surface tank and gas station dealers.

FINANCIAL ANALYSIS

Auditor: FJK & Co. Financial year-end: 31 December
Opinion: Unqualified.

Sales and profitability

As Table 27.3 shows, sales improved by 143% in FYE 2002, from
₦32.5 million in 2001 to ₦78.9 million in 2002. The increase in sales resulted
from increases in quantity demanded and price of the products. The increase in
demand was reflected in increases in contracts awarded by PTF for road
construction and tarring. With the closure of some refineries and nonavailability of the product locally, most companies had to import the products,
giving rise to the observed increase in prices. This also impacted cost of goods
sold (COGS), which increased by 220.32%, from ₦18.7 million in 2001 to
₦59.9 million in 2002.

TABLE 27.3 Sales and Profitability

	2001 ₦'000	% Change	2002 ₦'000
SALES	32,541	142.71	78,981
COGS/Sales%	57.42	31.97	75.78
SGA/Sales%	25.98	(53.66)	12.04
NPAT	3337	70.81	5700

However, EGL was able to pass on part of the cost to buyers for the
products. Despite the general increase in cost of production, the company's
policy of ensuring efficient rationalization of resources and cost control
translated into a fall in SGA/sales ratio, from 25.98% to 12.04%. NPAT
increased by 71%, from ₦3.3 million to ₦5.7 million in 2001 and 2002,
respectively. This could have been more impressive but for the tax expense
that increased astronomically by 203%, from ₦806,000 to ₦2,440,000 in
2002.

Efficiency of asset utilization

Company's asset utilization efficiency is satisfactory. Despite increased sales,
WI dropped. The drop in WI is attributable to a significant increase in accounts
payable. As against that of 2001 when sales were ₦32.5 million, accounts
payable increased 100%, from ₦4.013 million to ₦8.040 million, while sales

increased by 143% (see Table 27.4). Though the increase in accounts payable impacted negatively on WI, APDOH improved from 78 days to 49 days. This could be because the company's adoption of sales on a *cash-and-carry* basis yielded more cash for settling debts.

TABLE 27.4 Efficiency of Asset Utilization

	2001 ₦'000	% Change	2002 ₦'000
WI	1193	(44.76)	659
WI/Sales%	0.040	(80.00)	0.008
AR	2250	67.20	3762
INV	2956	67.02	4937
AP	4013	100.35	8040
ARDOH	25	(32.00)	17
APDOH	78	(37.18)	49
INVDOH	58	(48.28)	30

However, the company's collection policy improved in FYE 2002, from 25 days to 17 days, showing a tightening of credit terms of trade with its buyers from 3 weeks to 2 weeks. This was achieved through a planned shift of the company's trading relationship to a few names in the construction business. The figures in 2003 would probably have been better with prompt payments from the company's major customers. INVDOH also improved from 58 days to 30 days showing a quicker turnaround time. This was basically due to increased demand for the products.

Liquidity and capital structure

EGL's liquidity position is satisfactory. Its ability to service its debt obligations from cash flows it generates from current operations is reasonable and largely assured. This is likely to improve in FYE 2003 with the *cash-and-carry* arrangement that the company entered into with most of its tested trading partners.

Table 27.5 shows that EGL's working capital worsened in FYE 2002 with a negative position, from ₦1.913 million to −₦697 million in 2002. This reveals a need for the company to inject more capital into the business, as short-term funds cannot reasonably be utilized for funding long-term assets.

TABLE 27.5 Liquidity and Capital Structure

	2001	% Change	2002
Current ratio%	1.15	(24.35)	0.87
Quick ratio%	0.72	(31.94)	0.49
Working capital (₦'000)	1913	(136.43)	(697)
Leverage	1.10	(1.82)	1.08
Asset leverage	2.10	(0.95)	2.08

RISK ANALYSIS AND MITIGATION

As I reflect throughout this book, for all intents and purposes, bank management is all about risk control. Indeed, risk analysis is the crux of CAM, largely because it draws inferences from all the aforementioned subjects of credit analysis. For this reason, if the preceding reports (background of the borrower, information about the proposed credit, and financial analysis) were suspect, the risk analysis report would itself be flawed. CAM would be a mere hollow and unreliable report if it is not rooted in a rigorous analysis of actual, perceived, and potential risks and suggestions for risks mitigation. I give recognition to the preeminence of risk analysis in bank lending. Thus, I discuss various ramifications of credit risk and its management requirements in several chapters of this book. In the demonstration with EGL's loan request and appraisal, I present the possible risks of the transaction and how to mitigate them as follows.

Product quality and storage

Credit risk is indicated in any situation where loan officers are unable to vouch for the quality of products received by EGL. In the same vein, the type, state, and suitability of EGL's storage tanks can introduce risk where products are contaminated as a result of a poor storage system or facility. Storage risk could also crystallize in terms of theft of the products.

EGL's suppliers (local and foreign) are experienced and major players in the oil industry. Currently, they supply the products to some of the major oil-marketing companies such as AP, Unipetrol, and so on. It is unlikely that inferior products will be purchased for sale to such renowned major marketers. Yet, EGL, like the major oil marketers, has quality testing facilities in its depot. The facilities are certified by both the Nigerian Ports Authority and Department of Petroleum Resources prior to issuing of marketing licenses to the company. Of course, the involvement of warehousing agent in quality testing further mitigates the risk of purchase of inferior products by EGL.

The risk of product contamination will not arise for the reason that EGL has various sizes of tanks specifically dedicated for each of the products—AGO, PMS, DPK, and so on. The company is committed to maintaining this arrangement. Above all, the management of EGL comprises highly experienced and professionally minded experts. There is an adequate 24-h security arrangement at EGL's depot. The depot itself is completely fenced off from possible trespassers, and it is guarded by a professional security company.

Insurance of depot and products

Without adequate insurance cover, provided by a reputable insurance company, risk of loss on the credit becomes accentuated. EGL's depot and in-storage products are insured for up to a total sum of about ₦397 million. However, the insurance covers only 70% of in-storage products in the tanks at the depot. To secure TBB's credit exposure, the company has caused the insurance company to note the bank as loss payee beneficiary in the event that the insured risks occur.

Change in price

There is the possibility of changes in the prices of petroleum products by the government after the marketing companies have placed or received orders, thus putting them in loss positions. As a sequel to the agreement reached between government and labor, there would be no price review until the completion of turnaround maintenance of the refineries and their commencement of production. It is expected that this would take not less than one year to realize. Yet, at the total average landing and storage cost of about ₦34.60 per liter, the products will remain profitable if sold at labor's offer prices per liter.

Foreign exchange risk

Activities of the company could easily be predominantly import dependent, which translates to large foreign exchange dependency. The uncertainty that pervades the oil market could lead to either unfavorable or favorable circumstances. However, the recent merging of the dual exchange rates is intended to ensure effective and efficient allocation of foreign exchange. Thus, availability of foreign exchange is assured.

Business risk

Apart from the known players in the petroleum industry, it is likely that there would be an increase in the number of importers and marketers of the products. This situation will accentuate competition with which EGL will have to contend. However, the location of the company puts it in an advantageous position over most of the other competitors in the industry. The company will enjoy economies of scale since it has the capacity to store large quantities of products. This capacity advantage will ultimately minimize cost per unit to the company.

Management evaluation

Often credit risk is associated with management's capability and continuity. The company's management is strong, focused, and stable. There is also the advantage of the usual business astuteness associated with the commonality of ownership and management. The company's chief executive officer had managed challenging tasks and operations in a leading petroleum exploration and drilling company. That was before he was engaged as the managing director of yet a major oil-marketing company, a position he held until 2000 when he retired from the company. The other directors of the company are no less experienced in their chosen endeavors.

Repayment risk

This risk will arise if a company's sales fall due to low demand, which would ultimately affect loan repayment. The items of trade are in high demand. They are necessities that do not have affordable substitutes. The issue really is the level of permissible margin for the marketers of petroleum products—not if profits would be made at all on the importation and sale of the products. Thus, the risk of deficiency of demand will not arise in the first place.

Other risks

There are sundry risks that could arise as a result of adverse change in government policy, reactivation of local refineries, profitability problems with increased competition, uncertainty concerning continuity of the boom in the industry, and so on. EGL went into dealership of petroleum products because of deregulation of the sector. Of course, the action was a calculated move to benefit from the attendant boom. Once it is no longer profitable for the company to market petroleum products, it can do one or all of the following:

- Exit from the sector and concentrate on its traditional line of production of petroleum-related products
- Lease out its depot to any government agency or authorized dealers that may be responsible for production, importation, distribution, or local supply of the products

In a democratic setting, any drastic action of the government that could cause such a change in the company's strategy will be foreseeable and its anticipated negative impact avoided by discerning business minds.

COLLATERAL EVALUATION

Banks take collateral as a rule, and to complete documentation and security of approved credit facilities. In principle, collateral is never given prominence among factors in the lending decision. Yet banks do take collateral for the sake of security of lending. They demand collateral, in practice, as one of the important *conditions precedent* to drawdown on approved loans. Doing so is informed by a fact of paramount importance. Collateral is relevant in the credit process. Its relevance consists, first and foremost, in establishing the commitment of borrowers to the purpose or cause of their loans. Collateral somehow instills discipline in the use of credit facilities and protects risk assets of banks financed with depositors' funds against willful loss or wastage by borrowers. Otherwise, it is unimaginable that a bank will grant loans solely on the consideration of collateral that borrowers might offer.

It is necessary, prior to suggesting *ways-out*, for credit analysts to provide information on primary *collateral* for the credits. They should explain the type, location, *how* to exercise control over and, in the event of default, ultimately realize the collateral pledged by borrowers. A statement of the nature of the bank's lien over the collateral forms part of security analysis, as well as an inspection report, including the date of last inspection, current valuation of the collateral, and the basis of its valuation. Most banks accept only valuation reports from credible estate firms. Credit analysts should always offer personal opinions on any other observations about the collateral.

Qualities of good collateral

I should mention at once that collateral that is not *perfected* might not provide the desired security in the event of default. It is paramount to take only good collateral. Collateral is adjudged good for lending purposes when it satisfies the following criteria or conditions:

- It enjoys a stable or increasing long-term market value (i.e., its economic or monetary value should not be easily diminished by inflation or other wealth-ravaging forces).
- On forced sale basis, it is easily realizable (implying availability of ready buyers or existence of *effective* demand for the asset at any point in time).
- The asset used as collateral has a low or negligible cost of realization in the event of default by the borrower.
- It is not outlawed (i.e., the asset must not have been forbidden by law or acquired illegally by the borrower).
- There is no foreseeable future event that would prohibit its use as collateral for borrowing purposes.

Particular collateral may not have all of these qualities in equal degree at the same time. However, their relative importance reflects in the order in which they are listed above.

The following is an analysis of collateral, which also shows security value and adequacy, for EGL's loan proposal.

Collateral adequacy analysis

The proposed collateral gives a comfortable security cushion of 165% for all values of products costs (see Table 27.6). It is unlikely that price of the products will be adjusted downward in the foreseeable future. In fact, marketers have been agitating for increased prices, if anything. In the worst case scenario, where price shrinkage can potentially cause loss to the importers or dealers, EGL will simply exit from the business and perhaps go back to its traditional business of production of petroleum-related products. Thus, the issue of borrowing from the bank will not arise in the first place.

TABLE 27.6 Collateral Adequacy Analysis

Loan amount:	₦100,000,000 (100 million naira only)
Security:	Tripartite warehousing agreement between EGL, TBB, and warehousing agent appointed by the bank
Security value:	₦165,000,000 (165 million naira only). This represents the average realizable value of a consignment of petroleum products worth ₦100 million
Adequacy:	165%

Yet, in the equally unlikely event of price slash after loan disbursement by TBB, the cut in price will scarcely be as high as to completely wipe off profit and erode principal. Such an adverse occurrence will only arise if the price is reduced to as low as ₦26 per liter. But for this to even happen, government will be heavily subsidizing local production or importation policy. It also runs counter to prescriptions of international financial monitors, donors, and agencies for a sound economy. They emphasize resource allocation in the public sector as a deliberate strategy of economic development.

Personal guarantee

In almost all lending situations, a bank will require the personal guarantee of the chairman, managing director, or chief executive officer of the borrowing company as part of the collateral arrangement. In certain lending situations, where the sole collateral for a loan is the personal guarantee of a third party, it is always useful to ask for collateralization of such personal guarantee to fortify security of the credit facility. However, as I have noted in other chapters, this is not yet popular among Nigerian banks and borrowers.

LENDING RATIONALE

The products have ready buyers that will take them on a *cash-and-carry* basis. It is expected that the products will be sold within two weeks, if purchased locally, with lodgment of proceeds from sales into the company's account with TBB. In the case of imported products, each drawdown shall be fully repaid two weeks after berthing of the ship and discharge of the products into EGL's tanks. Specific issues in the lending rationale are as follows:

Seniority

If products are to be imported, L/C will be opened through TBB and consignment shipped to the order of the bank through its lien on the products and title document. Although strictly speaking shipping documents do not constitute effective security (because the vessel berths and discharges products at EGL's depot), they legitimize any claim with the involvement of the warehousing agent to monitor loading and sales. The warehousing agent will warrant the products in favor of TBB.

In the case of local purchase of the products (which is the predominant mode of procurement of the products), the supplier's invoice will have to be accepted by EGL and certified by the warehousing agent for quantity and quality before TBB will pay the supplier. Of course, the products will have been discharged into EGL's tanks prior to the warehousing agent's certification.

Control

The warehousing agent will ensure adequate control over the facility. The transaction dynamics, discussed earlier, give details of the controls envisaged. Presently, and without direct bank financing, EGL has been lodging its sales proceeds in its account with the bank. During the past three months, the company maintained an average current account credit balance of over ₦8.2 million. Currently, it has a credit balance of ₦30 million in its account. Thus, lodging sales proceeds (cash flows) with the bank is already an established practice that we intend to secure or fortify with the warehousing agent's involvement.

Protection

The protection of the bank against loss of the credit is guaranteed by the transaction dynamics and risk mitigation measures to be adopted (see also, risk analysis and comments on security analysis and adequacy). The bank will require additional comfort in a negative pledge over the company's assets (depot) worth over ₦350 million. The components of the assets are as follows:

- Land (leasehold for 25 years effective November 2002)
- Storage tanks (1 no. 6000 tons; 2 nos. 2000 tons; 1 no. 1000 tons; 2 nos. 100 tons; 4 nos. 33,000 L)
- 2 nos. hot oil heaters; 5 nos. electric driven bitumen pumps
- Weigh bridge control room; service shade; workshop
- 1 no. 100 KVA generator; 1 no. 72 KVA generator

PROFITABILITY ANALYSIS

In view of the high volume of transactions expected from this account, the bank should grant various concessions to the company. Yet, the transactions remain profitable as shown in Table 27.7 (using assumptions as follows: interest rate at 22.5% per annum; L/C commission at 0.75% flat; processing fee at 1% flat; COT at ₦1.50/mille).

TABLE 27.7 Profitability Analysis

		(₦)	(₦)
Interest on ₦100 million for 120 days @ 22.5% per annum			7,397,260.27
Add:	L/C Commission	1,000,000	
	Processing/management fee	750,000	
	COT	150,000	
			1,900,000.00
Gross income per cycle			9,297,260.27
Gross yield (annualised)			27.89%

Gross yield is a measure of the true or actual rate of earnings on a credit facility. This is why it is sometimes referred to as *effective* charge or yield on the loan. It takes into account all quantifiable incomes derivable from a credit facility over its tenor.

Annualized yield is calculated by dividing the sum of all incomes earned on the loan (and its related transactions) during the interest computation period (usually twelve calendar months) by the total amounts disbursed on a loan. Sometimes lending officers find it is difficult to ascertain the exact amount of loan disbursed to or utilized by the borrower during the loan tenor. This is especially observed in the case of an overdraft facility utilized over a long period of time. Therefore, they tend to ignore computation of yield on the loan when they analyze or review the performance of the loan account.

In order to solve this problem, lending officers should first determine *average borrowing* on the overdraft account during the review period. Then they divide the total incomes earned on the loan during the interest computation period—in this case, 1 year—by the average borrowing. The phrase "average borrowing" refers to the actual proportion of the total amount of a loan that a borrower uses during its tenor or a given period of time. Using the formula below, the average borrowing is calculated as follows:

Average Borrowing = Sum of (Daily Closing Balances on the Loan Account × Number of Days before Each Closing Balance Changed)/Total Number of Days in the Related Period

Unfortunately, credit analysts tend to be confused about how to calculate the average borrowing—just as computation of average daily balances could also be confusing. In Tables 27.8 and 27.9, I demonstrate how these two important analytical results can be determined as an input into the appraisal of the profitability of a loan. Besides manual calculation, lending officers can also use a computer system facility to calculate yields on credit facilities.

WAYS-OUT ANALYSIS

On the issue of loan repayment, it almost every bank requires that credit analysts should suggest at least two *ways-out* strategies for a credit facility. This entails statement of the primary and secondary sources of repayment for the credit. The usefulness or application of two *ways-out* strategies is contingent on a borrower's default. It provides comfort to the bank under the circumstances. The secondary *way-out* offers an alternative recovery plan in the event that the expected primary source of repayment fails. It also comes in handy when collateral taken to secure the credit is inadequate or unrealizable. In the case of EGL's loan proposal, the primary source of repayment for the facility is upfront lodgments into the company's account by buyers of the products. The second way-out is liquidation of the stock-in-trade (i.e., petroleum products financed by the bank that are stored in EGL's tanks under the warehousing agent's control on behalf of the bank).

OTHER CONSIDERATIONS

- The bank stands to earn a minimum of about ₦768,236.31 from each cycle of the transactions. This gives an average yield of 37.39% per transaction cycle.

TABLE 27.8 Account Statement, 01-April-08 to 30-April-08, Illustrating Calculation of Average Borrowing

Date	Transaction	Credit ($)	Debit ($)	Balance ($)	Daily Closing Balance ($)	No. of Days	Average Borrowing ($)
a	b	c	d	e	f	g	(f × g/30)
01-April-08	Balance B/F	—	—	(255,678.98)	—	—	—
01-April-08	Deposit	125,000.00	—	(130,678.98)	—	—	—
01-April-08	Withdrawal	—	(54,000.00)	(184,678.98)	(184,678.98)	1	(6155.97)
02-April-08	Deposit	112,000.00	—	(72,678.98)	(72,678.98)	2	(4845.27)
04-April-08	Withdrawal	—	(342,500.00)	(415,178.98)	—	—	—
09-April-08		—	—	(415,178.98)	—	—	—
15-April-08		—	—	(415,178.98)	(415,178.98)	12	(166,071.59)
19-April-08	Deposit	110,000.00	—	(305,178.98)	—	—	—
19-April-08	Withdrawal	—	(55,000.00)	(360,178.98)		—	—
19-April-08		—	—	(360,178.98)	—	—	—
19-April-08		—	—	(360,178.98)	—	—	—
21-April-08		—	—	(360,178.98)	—	—	—
21-April-08		—	—	(360,178.98)	(360,178.98)	6	(72,035.80)
22-April-08	Withdrawal	—	(355,000.00)	(715,178.98)	—	—	—

Continued

TABLE 27.8 Account Statement, 01-April-08 to 30-April-08, Illustrating Calculation of Average Borrowing—cont'd

Date	Transaction	Credit ($)	Debit ($)	Balance ($)	Daily Closing Balance ($)	No. of Days	Average Borrowing ($)
a	b	c	d	e	f	g	(f × g)/30
22-April-08		–	–	(715,178.98)	–	–	–
22-April-08		–	–	(715,178.98)	(715,178.98)	1	(23,839.30)
23-April-08		–	–	(715,178.98)	–	–	–
23-April-08	Withdrawal	–	(218,700.00)	(933,878.98)	(933,878.98)	1	(31,129.30)
24-April-08	Deposit	400,000.00	–	(533,878.98)	–	–	–
24-April-08		–	–	(533,878.98)	–	–	–
24-April-08		–	–	(533,878.98)	–	–	–
24-April-08	Withdrawal	–	(800,000.00)	(1,333,878.98)	–	–	–
24-April-08		–	–	(1,333,878.98)	–	–	–
26-April-08		–	–	(1,333,878.98)	(1,333,878.98)	3	(133,387.90)
27-April-08	Deposit	500,000.00	–	(833,878.98)	–	–	–
28-April-08		–	–	(833,878.98)	–	–	–
28-April-08		–	–	(833,878.98)	(833,878.98)	2	(55,591.93)

Date	Type					
29-April-08	Withdrawal	—	(322,500.00)	(1,156,378.98)	(1,156,378.98)	1	(38,545.97)
30-April-08	Deposit	108,643.69	—	(1,047,735.29)	—	—	—
30-April-08	Interest charges	—	(8368.01)	(1,056,103.30)	—	—	—
30-April-08	COT	—	(10,738.50)	(1,066,841.80)	—	—	—
30-April-08	VAT	—	(536.93)	(1,067,378.72)	(1,067,378.72)	1	(35,579.29)
		1,355,643.69	(2,167,343.43)			30	(567,182.30)
	Average borrowing						(567,182.30)

A hypothetical illustration of manual computation of average borrowing.

TABLE 27.9 Account Statement, 01-March-10 to 31-March-10, Illustrating Calculation of Average Daily Balance

Date	Transaction	Credit ($)	Debit ($)	Balance ($)	Daily Closing Balance ($)	No. of Days	Average Daily Balance
a	b	c	d	e	f	g	$(f \times g)/31$
01-March-10	Balance B/F	–	–	255,678.98	–	–	–
01-March-10	Deposit	225,000.00	–	480,678.98	–	–	–
01-March-10	Withdrawal	154,000.00	–	634,678.98	634,678.98	1	20,473.52
02-March-10	Deposit	2,012,000.00	–	2,646,678.98	2,646,678.98	2	170,753.48
04-March-10	Withdrawal	–	(1,342,500.00)	1,304,178.98	–	–	–
09-March-10		–	–	1,304,178.98	–	–	–
15-March-10		–	–	1,304,178.98	1,304,178.98	12	504,843.48
19-March-10	Deposit	210,000.00	–	1,514,178.98	–	–	–
19-March-10	Withdrawal	–	(255,000.00)	1,259,178.98	–	–	–
19-March-10		–	–	1,259,178.98	–	–	–
19-March-10		–	–	1,259,178.98	–	–	–
21-March-10		–	–	1,259,178.98	–	–	–
21-March-10		–	–	1,259,178.98	1,259,178.98	6	243,712.06
22-March-10	Withdrawal	–	(355,000.00)	904,178.98	–	–	–
22-March-10		–	–	904,178.98	–	–	–
22-March-10		–	–	904,178.98	904,178.98	1	29,167.06
23-March-10		–	–	904,178.98	–	–	–

Date		Deposit	Withdrawal	Balance	Balance	Days	Product
23-March-10	Withdrawal	—	(718,700.00)	185,478.98	185,478.98	1	5983.19
24-March-10	Deposit	750,000.00	—	935,478.98	—	—	—
24-March-10		—	—	935,478.98	—	—	—
24-March-10		—	—	935,478.98	—	—	—
24-March-10	Withdrawal	—	(780,000.00)	155,478.98	—	—	—
24-March-10		—	—	155,478.98	—	—	—
26-March-10		—	—	155,478.98	155,478.98	3	15,046.35
27-March-10	Deposit	350,000.00	—	505,478.98	—	—	—
28-March-10		—	—	505,478.98	—	—	—
28-March-10		—	—	505,478.98	505,478.98	2	32,611.55
29-March-10	Withdrawal	—	(322,500.00)	505,478.98	505,478.98	1	5902.55
30-March-10	Deposit	182,000.00	—	182,978.98	182,978.98	1	11,773.52
31-March-10	COT	—	(18,198.50)	364,978.98	364,978.98	—	—
31-March-10	VAT	—	(909.93)	346,780.48	—	—	—
				345,870.56	345,870.56	1	11,157.11
		3,729,000.00	(3,638,808.43)			31	1,051,423.87
Average daily balance							1,051,423.87

A hypothetical illustration of manual computation of average daily balance.

- EGL is an account with a lot of earnings potential. It is one of the biggest names in the petroleum industry. Unlike most of the other players in the industry, it is not overbanked. This gives TBB an opportunity to attract most of its banking transactions with effective relationship management and efficient services.
- The company is regarded as a credit worthy and highly profitable concern. There are also attendant benefits of attracting other profitable accounts through its relationship to the bank.
- The marketing arrangement facilitates ease of monitoring and makes collection of sales proceeds hitch-free.
- The facility will be adequately secured with a warehousing agreement between EGL, the warehousing agent, and TBB, and a comprehensive insurance cover over the imports, with TBB noted as the loss payee beneficiary.

RECOMMENDATION

We recommend approval of the customer's request for a ₦100 million multiple trade finance facility based on the following considerations:

- EGL is a good industry name, with a high-powered ownership and management profile.
- With a huge equity investment of about ₦150 million, the owners of the company have shown adequate commitment to its success.
- The company's transactions that require bank financing usually have short cycles (maximum of 45 days), are self-liquidating, highly profitable, and thus justify man-hours invested in relationship management.
- EGL will in the future remain a source of income for the bank especially as its chosen line of business presents an entry barrier in terms of the huge capital requirement.
- It is envisaged that after a few cycles of the transactions, the company's need for external financing would have been served. Thus, TBB will enjoy substantial current account float and fee income from the account.

TABLE 27.10 Endorsement of CAM

Signed_____	Signed_____
Ken Water	Cliff Brown
Account officer/credit analyst	*Branch/relationship manager*

QUESTIONS FOR DISCUSSION AND REVIEW

1. Discuss the procedure that loan officers adopt to package a credit proposal for approval.

2. Enumerate the advantages of a credit analysis memorandum and its significance for the credit process.

3. What critical bank lending and borrowing questions does the CAM specifically answer?

4. How should borrowers apply for bank loans? What should they do in order to satisfy lending criteria of banks?

5. What must borrowers know about how banks appraise, decline or approve, and manage their borrowing requests?

Loan Documentation, Review and Compliance

Chapter 28

Authorization and Responsibility for Bank Credit in Emerging Markets

Chapter Outline

LEARNING FOCUS AND OUTCOMES

The decision of a bank to lend money to a borrower is made when authorized officers of a bank endorse the credit. This is a major event in the lending process as it triggers subsequent actions leading to disbursement of funds. Flawed credit approval imparts risk to a loan. Depending on the gravity of the flaw, the chance that the loan would add to lost credit statistics increases. For this reason, it is imperative that lending officers exercise caution in authorizing credit facilities.

Consider that banks grant loans primarily to generate earnings and, over time, achieve target growth. Initially, each new loan granted offers the prospect of increasing operating income and realizing planned growth through asset creation. In time, when some of the prior loans begin to expire unpaid or become delinquent, the euphoria of lending soon gives way to a gloomy reality of its negative consequences. In the circumstances, it becomes doubtful to still accord lending serious recognition as a reliable means to increase operating income, let alone achieve long-term growth!

The alternative—growing the liabilities side of the balance sheet—starts to become attractive. But in most cases, the business capacity of the bank would have been seriously hurt or impaired by huge loan loss provisions before the

Emerging Market Bank Lending and Credit Risk Control. http://dx.doi.org/10.1016/B978-0-12-803438-5.00028-3
503

need for such change of strategic focus is given any serious consideration or implemented. Some banks do, if not repeatedly, go through this unhealthy but avoidable learning curve or circle. It is also an expensive experience that could cause—and indeed had given rise to—if not effectively managed, bank distress and failure. That was what happened in the case of Nigeria during the banking system crisis of the mid-1990s.

In view of the fact that loans are financed largely with depositors' funds, a bank cannot afford to carelessly lose a credit facility. Thus, the decision to lend must be made by responsible bank officers who should be held accountable for the loans. I review the literature on the subject of this chapter in order to define and put the problem in the right perspective. Using the framework of my findings, I investigate due diligence that banks should introduce to ensure that credit authorization is foolproof and contributes to strengthening of risk management in bank lending.

This chapter focuses on loan approval issues and options, underscoring them as sore challenges in checking abuse of the credit process. From the topics discussed, you will learn about:

- Critical issues and options that tend to dominate the credit approval process
- Why and ways in which irrational tendencies are introduced to the credit approval process
- Making and mechanics of "insider abuse" in bank lending
- How bank management can handle infringement of credit policy and process

CREDIT STRATEGY COMMITTEE

When credit approval is flawed, for whatever reasons, loans and the lending decision process become exposed to risk. When this situation happens, the bank and borrowers often experience avoidable hitches in their banking relationship. Thus, lending officers must be diligent at all times in processing, approving, documenting, and disbursing credit facilities. As a response to the need for foolproof lending criteria, banks introduce checks and balances to the credit approval process. The checks and balances are intended to enforce due diligence among lending officers who have credit approval authority. A credit strategy committee (CRESCO) is one of the effective devices to achieve this goal.

The institution of a CRESCO in banks has been one of the important devices to strengthen the credit process. In most banks, the committee functions as a high-ranking credit review and approval authority. The structure and composition of CRESCO membership varies with size and risk management disposition of banks. Ideally, the committee should draw membership from the bank's senior management staff, including the chief executive officer, members of the executive committee who have lending and credit approval responsibility, heads of lending divisions (who are not EXCO members), head of credit risk management (i.e., chief risk officer), and a legal officer or adviser of the bank.

Once constituted in this manner, the committee's decisions would require ratification *only* by the board audit and credit committee (BACC). However, some banks try to minimize or check the authority and influence of the CRESCO by excluding the CEO and EXCO members from the CRESCO. In so doing, two additional credit approval authorities—CEO and EXCO—are introduced above the CRESCO. Thus, depending on the amount involved and other special considerations, proposed credit facilities would have to be approved by the CRESCO, the CEO, EXCO, and board—in that order.

However, it is at the CRESCO level that the rigor of credit review and approval may be best appreciated. At CRESCO's sessions, most of the thorny issues in loan proposals are tackled firsthand. Specifically, the committee's role in the credit process consists mainly in fulfilling the following functions:

- Review of the credit analysis memorandum (CAM) and credit approval form (CAF) and, in the process, detect any flaws that could forestall approval of credit facilities presented to it
- Determine appropriateness of proposed credit facilities, especially in terms of structure, transactions dynamics, risk mitigation, probable earnings, fit with target market definition, risk acceptance criteria, and so on
- Recommend amendments (if considered necessary) to the CAM and CAF, which should be effected to correct any observed weaknesses of proposed credit facilities
- Endorse on, or without, specific conditions—or decline support for—all the credit facilities that the lending units package for approval by senior management
- Invite credit analysts, loan officers, and relationship managers from whose lending units proposed credit facilities originate to appear before the committee to clarify any confusing issues and defend the CAM and CAF

In banks that have a properly structured and effective CRESCO, the quality and rigor of debate at its sessions keep loan officers ever prepared to defend any lurid claims in the CAM and CAF. For loan officers, especially those who defend credit proposals, it could rightly be said that *the fear of CRESCO is the beginning of credit wisdom.*

CREDIT APPROVAL FORM

As mentioned earlier, there should be a credit approval form on which the lending authorities append signatures for credit approval. It is a document that summarizes important information required to make the lending decision (see Figure 28.1). Information usually provided in the CAF includes: the lending unit; date of appraisal of the credit; and name, address, business, management,

Unit:	Date:	Page: 1 of 2	Preliminary ( ) Final ( )
Obligor(s): **City, State:**			
Ownership Structure:			
Business			
Management			
Facility			
Interest Rate	Claim ( ) or Debit A/C (x)		
Fees			
Purpose			
Repayment			
Expected Usage			
Amortization			
Collateral			
Guarantee			
Comments			

Aggregate Commitment	Officer's loan class:	Date:	Director related Yes ( ) No ( )
	Loan review classification:	Date:	Subordinated debt Yes ( ) No ( )

APPROVED/RECOMMENDED BY

NAME	INITIALS	DATE	NAME	INITIALS	DATE
CREDIT COMMITTEE					

This final commitment package consists of: CAF ( )   Spread Sheets ( )   Deal memo ( )
CAM ( ) Industry Analysis ( )   CAS ( )

FIGURE 28.1   Credit approval form.

and ownership structure of the borrower (in the case of a company). The amount, purpose, tenor, dynamics, and pricing of the credit are also clearly stated. Of course, the form would describe the collateral and any personal guarantee offered to secure the loan.

AGGREGATE COMMITMENTS AND OUTSTANDING AS @ _____

Amount (₦'000)	Loan class	Type of facility	Obligor	Outstanding
Related commitments				
Subordinated Debt				
Contingent Liabilities				

Relationship summary (₦'000)	Loan Spread Income	Balance Income	Fee Income	Other Income	Total Income	ROA %
Last Year ( )						
Year to date ( )						

Relationship comments: **Relationship commenced:** _____

FIGURE 28.1   cont'd

Detailed information on these items, together with the more rigorous *key credit issues*, would have been presented in the CAM (discussed in Chapter 27). The rating of credits, in terms of quality, by both credit *analysts* and *audit* or *loan review* unit in the CAF has become a commonplace. Provisions are also made on the form for the signatures of each of the recommending and approving authorities for the credit, beginning from the credit analyst up to board audit and credit committee as appropriate.

In order to be a complete package, and while presenting the proposed final loan commitment to senior management for approval, credit analysts support the CAF with relevant documents. The most important documents are the CAM, spreadsheets, deal memo, industry analysis, and credit analysis summary (CAS). The deal memo serves particular objectives in the booking of lending transactions. A deal memo sometimes represents a confidential agreement between a bank and borrower regarding certain aspects of the loan package that should not be discussed in the credit analysis memorandum. In some cases, it could simply be documentation of any special or extraordinary gain that a bank expects from a credit transaction of which the borrower might sometimes be unaware. A CAS substitutes for a CAM when the credit analyst is proposing renewal of a credit that is about to expire. Since a full CAM would have been written at the initial time when the loan was first granted, it would be unnecessary to repeat it at the time of credit renewal. The credit analyst would instead be required to present a CAS that summarizes important developments that might have affected the credit, positively or negatively, during its expiring tenor.

The CAS will yet suffice for a CAM when a loan request comes from a blue-chip company, or other triple "A" rated firm. In most cases, banks court banking relationships with such companies. In fact, banks offer credits to them on some unusual concessional terms as a marketing strategy. In the final analysis, it is consideration of a good risk rating that determines use of a CAS in place of a CAM for particular credit requests.

Significance of CAF

When properly signed-off by appropriate loan approval authorities, the credit approval form establishes the mandate to extend a particular credit facility to a particular borrower on specific terms and conditions, which the loan officers (especially, the account officer and relationship manager) must observe. It is the most important instrument on which evidence is anchored about the authenticity of a credit granted by a bank. Indeed, the CAF serves to protect loan officers whenever the regulatory authorities or credit auditors investigate impropriety of conduct or discretionary lending practices by bank officials. However, the protection is effective only if the loan officers complied with all the terms on which credit facilities are granted. However, it is also essentially a summarized record of the terms and conditions of a credit facility as approved by the management of a bank and to be communicated to the borrower.

CREDIT APPROVAL ISSUES AND OPTIONS

A common practice among banks is the unwritten adoption of group liability for loan losses. Depending on the type and amount of loan involved or other considerations, the group is comprised of a credit analyst or account officer, relationship manager, and group head (lending function), as well as members of the credit strategy committee, executive management (usually represented by the chief executive officer), and board audit and credit committee. In principle, depending on the type and amount of loan involved, at least two or more officers and members from the group will endorse a loan to signify its approval.

With this loan approval procedure, it becomes difficult to trace loan loss liability to, and therefore inappropriate to sanction, any one of the responsible officers. Of course, it would be absurd to simultaneously sanction all signatories to a bad loan. Thus, the group liability practice is upheld for want of a credible alternative. However, it accentuates the tendency and cloak under which lending officers might hide to book bad loans, classify, and ultimately write off nonperforming loans. This cloak is rationalized on a simple consideration. Each next higher-level approving officer ought to be satisfied with most, if not all, aspects of an intended credit before appending their signature to the CAF. But this has been a debilitating factor in checking the incidence of bad loans. A further justification of group liability for loans derives from the assumption that each of the approving officers could indeed exercise an option to decline a loan. Therefore, when all of them sign or endorse the CAF, they become collectively responsible for the loan.

However, as most experienced bankers know or would attest to, there are always some dominant officers among the approving authorities for every loan. The other signatories simply sign the loan because the decision to lend had apparently been made by the boss—even before it is packaged and presented in a CAF and CAM for formal approval. In other extreme situations, the loan might have actually been disbursed before a credit analyst is asked to package it for formal approval. A somewhat reverse situation is where an account officer or credit analyst willfully presents a lurid account of an otherwise bad credit request and supports it with illusory market information just to obtain approval for the loan. The other unsuspecting approving authorities might sign the credit based on the officer's fallible recommendations. The analyst could do this out of ignorance or deliberately to gain some selfish advantage at the expense of the bank.

In view of possible conflict of interest in the lending function, it would be appropriate for credit approval liability to be personalized in whomever is the dominant recommending or approving authority. It should be noted that any of the recommending and approving authorities for a loan—account officer, relationship manager, group head (lending function), and so on—could exercise a dominant influence in approving a loan. However, the chief executive officer is in the best position to know whom to hold accountable or liable for particular loans. Otherwise, the regulatory authorities should of necessity hold the CEO responsible for every loan that a bank grants. This appears to be an effective way of counteracting the outrageous incidence of bad debts in banks.

Integrity in loan approval

Many would argue that discredited banking practices are a reflection of questionable standing of bank management on integrity. Indeed, some believe that a low rating of bankers on integrity is significant in accounting for unethical banking practices. In almost all cases of failed banks in Nigeria, bank management was found culpable on several counts of abuse of office and unprofessional conduct. Let me now define a framework for analyzing the problem of integrity and assessing its implications for bank management. The distinction between integrity and corruption is instructive. In order to be rated high on integrity, those entrusted with bank management should not cheat the bank, customers, and even the larger society by virtue of their advantageous or privileged position of trust, whether in the bank or elsewhere. This implies that a manager must always uphold the values of honesty, transparency, and openness in all dealings, not only with customers and members of the society but his or her bank and its stakeholders.

It is ironic that integrity on which most banks would ordinarily seek to build a business foundation because of its profound appeal to the need of the public is nowadays perhaps about the most elusive marketing ingredient for bankers. Indeed, many bank analysts would see paradoxes in the inverse relationship between the principles of integrity and the practical demands of business in modern societies. For example, strictly upholding integrity implies that a manager should have impeccable character—meaning that he or she will be consistent, above board, principled, uncompromising, and truthful on all issues at all times. It also means that he or she should not renege on promises or agreements with other parties, especially customers, notwithstanding the turn of events. Of utmost importance is his or her ability to always overcome, and not be swayed by, monetary enticements.

Unfortunately, most of these determinants of integrity are scarcely realistic in a practical sense. The trappings of office inevitably become a snare with which most managers must contend in a bid to uphold integrity. Thus, it would be wrong to censure bank managers for lack of integrity in the absence of an institutional framework to deal with the snares. It is therefore right that the score of an individual on integrity or ethics should be a reflection of the value system of the society to which he or she belongs. A society that is bereft of scruples will hardly produce people with integrity. Also, societies character-ized by corruption as a way of life will thrive in fraud, and managers in such environments will obviously be lacking in integrity. The problem seems to affect all societies, albeit, in varying degrees. Lack of integrity could be a major cause of bank distress and failure. Without appreciation of the values of integrity, bank management loses focus of the professional and legitimate cause of the bank, as it tends to build up an irrational propensity for unethical practices. Such propensity may benefit a bank in the short run on some considerations. However, it ultimately sets the stage for distress and failure when, as perpetrators of unethical acts, managers begin to personally gain at the expense of the bank in more than proportionate terms. In time, it becomes obvious that the managers are working more for their personal gains than for the interest of the bank. This is what occurs where managers who are lacking in integrity occupy high positions and are generously empowered and given very sensitive responsibilities. This situation breeds inefficiency as a result of distraction and indulgence of the managers. One of the ways to stem bank distress and failure is to cleanse the larger society of corruption and, in so doing, install an efficient reward system in all aspects of national life. In this way, as members of a cleansed society, bank managers will be in a position to resist the temptation of corruption on which inefficiency feeds and integrity is disabled as a way of life.

Insider abuse

Incidents of bank distress and failure in Nigeria in the 1990s revealed incredible levels of contributory factors in unethical practices. Many banks ran into trouble as a result of *insider* abuse, especially taking uncovered exposures in loans to directors and major shareholders, which after all turned bad. Such loans were usually of large volumes and, in most cases, granted without proper documentation or collateral. In time, when the crunch came, the net fair value of assets had irretrievably depleted to levels that could not sustain liquidity required for normal banking transactions and operations. Some believe that the unsavory fate of the failed banks derived mainly from avoidable unprofessional or unethical practices by bank members. Such discredited acts are observed mainly in insider-related credits. Perhaps the reasons for the observed discredited practices, many of which I have also discussed above and elsewhere in this book among the causes of bank distress, are rooted in the growing tendency of banks to unprofessional business conduct.

QUESTIONS FOR DISCUSSION AND REVIEW

1. What critical issues and options dominate the credit approval process?
2. In what ways are irrational tendencies introduced to the credit approval process? Suggest effective methods for dealing with the problem.
3. What do you understand from the expression "insider abuse" in bank lending? Mention and discuss the mechanics of insider abuse.
4. Why must loan officers exercise adequate care and diligence in approving and disbursing credit facilities?

5. Critically examine the tendency of banks to rely on lending to sustain long-term operating income and growth.
6. Discuss five ways in which bank management and lending officers perpetrate insider abuse. Which of the methods do you consider to be credit fraud?
7. **(a)** How may bank management be able to uphold the spirit of best practice in the lending function?
   (b) In what ways can it successfully handle possible challenges that it might face in the process?

Chapter 29

Security and Documentation of Credits in Emerging Economies

Chapter Outline

Emerging Market Bank Lending and Credit Risk Control. http://dx.doi.org/10.1016/B978-0-12-803438-5.00029-5
513

LEARNING FOCUS AND OUTCOMES

Banks would more readily lend money to borrowers if there is collateral for the loans. Security in bank lending has a fundamental basis. It ensures that borrowers fulfill their primary obligation of repaying loans granted to them. With adequate collateral, a bank is put in a preferred position in case of insolvency of the borrower.

Security provides banks with an alternative source of loan repayment. The importance of this is that a bank could recover a loan if a borrower either cannot or will not voluntarily pay back the loan. Thus, security reduces risk of investment in risk assets. A bank may be optimistic about a borrower's ability and willingness to pay back a loan. Yet, as a matter of prudence, the bank should still seek additional protection over and above mere promise of the borrower to perform. A loan is secured when it is backed up by collateral and right of recourse over and above the personal promise of the borrower.

Good collateral has particular qualities, the most critical of are discussed in Chapter 27. It is only when collateral is characterized by the identified qualities that it can offer dependable security for a credit facility. This implies that choice of collateral type for particular credit facilities should not be made arbitrarily. It should be based on carefully thought out and workable criteria. Perhaps the best way to choose collateral for a particular credit facility is to relate the structure of the loan to its security need. Chances are, in doing so, that a bank will find an appropriate match between features of the credit and its collateral. For example, it would be inappropriate to secure temporary overdraft with legal mortgage. It would be too costly to do so, largely because of documentation requirements to perfect a legal mortgage for such a short-term credit.

Based on the foregoing perspective, my focus in this chapter is on a critical assessment of types of security for bank lending. I explore contemporary challenges in taking and documenting collateral to secure loans in emerging markets. I also examine the intricacies of perfecting loan security and documentation.

It is settled that banks should secure lending with collateral. However, defining collateral for particular types of lending is not settled. If anything, it is in a state of flux—and, on occasion, controversial. Some authors − Sykes (1972), Goode (1988), Smith (2001) and Smith (2007) − have made positive impacts on the subject of this chapter through their works. Theirs and others in the mold of them have contributed significantly in advancing the cause of security and legal documentation of credits in contemporary lending functions of banks and other lending financial institutions − especially in emerging markets. Their views are taken into consideration and reflected in discussions of some of the topics of this chapter. After reading this chapter, you will understand:

- Why it is necessary for banks to secure loans with good collateral
- Classifications, types, and benefits of security in bank lending

- Concept of "perfection of mortgage," procedure for perfection of mortgage in Nigeria, and why perfection of mortgage is a thorny issue
- Problems of security creation and realization in emerging economies

BASIS AND BENEFITS OF SECURITY

The provider of advance would more readily make funds available if there is an appropriate mechanism to ensure repayment of the advance. The search for a means to ensure that the primary obligation of repayment of debt or fulfillment of obligation under an agreement is achieved is the basis for the concept of security. A creditor may be optimistic about a debtor's ability and willingness to fulfill particular financial obligations. Yet the creditor will often, as a matter of prudence, seek additional protection over and above mere promise of the debtor to perform. Security, in the sense discussed in this chapter, relates to credit facilities that are backed up by right of recourse over and above personal promise of the debtor.

My interest here is to examine the different but practical types of security that banks and other lending financial institutions can apply to secure credit facilities they grant to borrowers. Security serves specific purposes and offers certain commercial benefits to banks. Some of the important benefits of security are as follows.

Fallback for banks

Security places a bank in a preferred position in case of insolvency or liquidation of a borrower. Liquidation value is hardly enough to meet the claims of creditors. Thus, security protects a bank loan from the consequences of corporate insolvency. It provides banks with an alternative source of recouping their funds if borrowers either cannot or will not pay their debts voluntarily.

Mitigation of credit risk

Incidents of risk with respect to a bank's investment in credit facilities are reduced. Banks take a great risk when they rely only on the promise of borrowers to pay their debts. With security, the risk that may be involved where borrowers fail or are unable to fulfill their promise is reduced. This is possible because security provides some other means of ensuring repayment.

Enforcement of obligation

The primary purpose of security is to render the performance of secured obligation more certain. Thus, security compels borrowers to ensure that they take necessary steps toward performance of their secured obligation. Often borrowers feel obligated to comply with this requirement because their property or interest is at stake if they fail to fulfill their obligation. Security therefore creates a sense of commitment in borrowers.

Boost to the economy

Provision of security helps to achieve economic growth and development. This is possible because security makes granting of credit more readily available. Thus, security is a major means by which free movement of capital is enhanced. Provision of security for advance remains the most potent vehicle for advancing financial transactions. This is seen mainly in granting of credit facilities by banks.

Facilitation of loan recovery

The right of a bank to proceed against security after a borrower defaults is at the heart of security. Security enables a bank to bypass the difficult and slow procedure that an unsecured creditor will have to go through to enforce mere promise to pay in court. There is a snag though. Loan defaulters tend to frustrate the judicial process when secured creditors institute legal actions to realize their security. It is a known fact that debtors are in the habit of exploiting lax in the legal system. The laxity in our judicial system makes it possible for them to frustrate the right of a secured creditor to realize security. This fact tends to make nonsense of the advantages of security.

Taming insider credits and abuses

Security has been identified as a means of ensuring that insider-related credits are repaid. This explains the rationale for provisions in BOFI Act, No. 25 of 1991 (as amended) and many CBN circulars prescribing adequate security for credit facilities extended to directors and major shareholders of banks, as well as their companies and relations. Security therefore provides a means of curtailing the excesses of influential members of banks in treating credit facilities extended to them as ex gratia.

Comfort to banks

Security—in one form or another—gives banks a psychological sense of comfort. It encourages lending and boosts availability of more funds to borrowers to fund their business transactions.

CLASSIFICATIONS OF SECURITY

There are various ways of classifying security depending on the purpose or basis of the classification. For example, in the case of Halliday v. Holgate,[1] Wiles classified security into three as follows:

---

1. (1868) LR 3 Exch. p. 299 at 302.

Proprietary security

In proprietary security, the title in the subject matter of security is passed from the debtor to the creditor. An example is seen in the case of legal mortgage where the title in a landed property is passed to the mortgagee by the mortgagor.

Possessory security

With possessory security, there is transfer of possession in the subject matter of security from the debtor to the creditor. A typical example to illustrate this type of security is where a pledge or pawn is taken as security.

Appropriation of interest

There is yet a third type of security—one which has neither proprietary nor possessory transfer, but a mere appropriation of interest in the subject matter of security. Examples of this type of security include a charge or hypothecation.

The foregoing classification has its origin in the grant theory on security. It is seen in the definition of security interest propounded by Goode (1988). Security interest, according to him, is a right given to one party on the assets of another party to secure the performance of an obligation. This definition is suggestive of the fact that a security interest is the result of a grant to creditors rather than a reservation by them. The grant theory therefore does not recognize any other form of security where there is no right granted to creditors on assets of debtors. Hence, four conventional forms of security (mortgage, pledge, charge, and lien) are recognized under the theory as reflected in the aforesaid classification. Goode (1988) also agreed that these four types of consensual security are the only ones known to English law.

A rigid classification of security as stated above may not be useful. This is because security under the same heads of classification may exhibit different features. On the other hand, security under different heads of classification may exhibit similar features. For example, a mortgage is a proprietary security, but a mortgagee can enter into possession to collect rents and profit on the mortgaged property.[2] In the same vein, though English pledge is a possessory security it gives the pledgee a right of sale—a remedy that is peculiar to proprietary type of security.

As shown in the discussion of new trends in security, some other means of making money more assured in its payment have developed. The new trends do not recognize the basis of foregoing classification. However, the classification provides the requisite insight that a creditor should have when thinking of what security to take or create. The classification thus affords

---

2. See Four – Maids Ltd V. Dudley Marshal (properties) Limited (1957), Chapter 317 at 320 of All E. R. 32 at 36.

creditors information about remedies available under each head of classification to enable them to adapt the relevant ones to transactions peculiar or appropriate to them.

TYPES OF SECURITY

I will examine here well-known, different traditional forms of security and also review new forms of security that are currently in use in the banking industry. Under each of the types, I consider the requirements of the law for taking valid security, as well as the requisite documents for their perfection.

Mortgage

A mortgage can be created over land or chattel, but mortgage of land or landed property is by far the most commonly used form of security for advance all over the world. This is also true of security that banks and financial institutions in Nigeria take for credit facilities. Financial institutions, including banks, find mortgage of land more suitable as security because it provides a reliable and invaluable security for credit facilities.

Mortgage of land gives the following benefits that are not obtainable in other forms of security:

- Fixity of land
  The immovable nature of land makes it impossible for a debtor to physically hide the security.
- Control
  Physical control of the property is hardly necessary as the transfer of title to creditors through the mortgage deed adequately protects their interest. However, a mortgagee has the option to enter possession if need be.
- Appreciation
  Unlike other forms of security that can depreciate in value, land appreciates in value. In view of this, creditors are compensated for possible fall in the value of money during inflation.
- Reliability
  Availability of land registries where title of mortgagors can be ascertained and previous transactions on particular land investigated makes mortgage of the land more reliable. Such registries are not available for other forms of property.

Creation of mortgage

Capacity

Like any other contract, parties to a mortgage transaction must have legal capacity to make or take a mortgage. Banks must ensure that mortgagors are not infants, persons of unsound mind, or trustees. Where a mortgagor is a statutory corporation (i.e., registered company), it is necessary to ensure that the mortgage transaction is allowed under the statute creating the company, as well as the company's memorandum of association. This is a critical requirement in bank lending. In fact, banks should demand and study memoranda and articles of association of all companies wishing to open accounts with them. The import of this practice is informed by a fundamental legal rule. A contract into which a company enters, or a transaction it does, which its memorandum of association does not authorize may be declared ultra vires.

Investigation of title

The reliability of a mortgage transaction depends on valid title in the property residing in the mortgagor. For this reason, it is important to conduct proper investigation of the mortgagor's title.

The bank should obtain a valuation report on the property from a reliable estate valuer. In addition to the valuation report, the account officer should make a site visit to the property. The purpose of the visit is to carry out physical inspection of the property. The visit affords the account officer an opportunity to ascertain the location of the property, assess its structural state, and so on. It is also important to conduct a search on the property. Usually a legal search is conducted at the land registry of the state where the land is located. The search serves two main purposes. It helps to ascertain the authenticity of the mortgagor's title and previous transactions on the land. In doing so, the bank wants to ensure that there are no subsisting encumbrances on the property.

It must be noted that the following documents are the appropriate evidence of title on land since the advent in Nigeria of Land Use Act in 1978:

- Original copy of certificate of occupancy (C of O) duly registered at the land registry of the state where the land is situated and executed by the governor of that state.
- Original copy of deed of assignment on a property covered by a certificate of occupancy duly stamped and registered with the consent of the governor or his delegate duly affixed.
- Original copy of deed of conveyance duly stamped and registered conveying the title in the property to the titleholder before 1978 (in the case of Nigeria).

Due to problems often encountered in ascertaining title and authenticating the rightful owner of property in family land, it is not advisable to accept family land not registered for mortgage purposes. Apart from the fact that such land is not recognized at the lands registry until certificate of occupancy is issued on them, there is no file on which the mortgage can be registered. Land covered by local government certificate of occupancy should also be treated with caution. The Court of Appeal decision that held that municipal council under the Federal Capital Territory has no power to issue certificate of occupancy on any land within the FCT[3] informs the need for caution.

Banks should verify and ensure that the property is not under acquisition. This should form part of the investigation of title to land. It is in this regard that compensation payable on the property upon acquisition is made payable to the mortgagee if the property is acquired after creation of the mortgage by a clause in the mortgage deed.

Legal and equitable mortgage

Legal mortgage

A legal mortgage is created by the transfer or conveyance of the whole interest of the mortgagor in real estate to the mortgagee by a deed of mortgage. The mortgage must be duly stamped and registered. In order to be complete and effective, the bank must obtain consent of the governor (of the state where the real estate is located) to the transaction.

Equitable mortgage

An equitable mortgage may be created in a number of ways, including the following:

- Equitable interest
  Where the interest the mortgagors have in the property is an equitable interest, they can only give an equitable mortgage.
- Suing in equity
  Where there is agreement to create a legal mortgage wherein the equitable mortgagee can enforce the execution of a legal mortgage by suing in equity for specific performance.
- Deposit of title deed
  An equitable mortgage is also created when borrowers deliver title documents relating to their land or building to the bank with intention to use the documents as security for a credit facility.
- Operation of law
  Equitable mortgage can also be created by operation of law, for example, where there is a defect in a legal mortgage as it happened in the case of Savannah Bank of Nigeria Limited v. Ajilo (1989). In this case, the effective mortgage in law does not preclude the existence of a valid mortgage in equity.

---

3. Joseph Ona & Another V. Alh. Ramoni Atanda Suit No. CA/A/5A/97 delivered in March 2000.

Simple and third-party mortgage

It is important to note also that there are two types of mortgage: simple mortgage and third-party legal mortgage. The latter is also known as tripartite legal mortgage.

Simple mortgage

A simple mortgage is created when account holders, who are also the borrowers, mortgage their property directly to the bank as security for credit facilities that the bank grants to them. A simple mortgage can also be created where a company or corporate body mortgages its property directly to the bank as security for a credit facility. In this case, two parties are involved: the mortgagor (the borrower) and the mortgagee (the bank). This is a common type of mortgage, and it is popular among banks and borrowers alike.

Third-party legal mortgage

A third-party legal mortgage is created where property that is in the name of a third party is mortgaged to secure a credit facility that a bank grants to a borrower. In this case, the mortgagors who are the titleholders on property used to secure loans are not the borrowers. However, the mortgagors release their property to the borrowers or bank for use as security for credit facilities that the bank grants to the borrowers. Thus, three parties are involved in a third-party legal mortgage: mortgagor, borrower, and bank. This type of mortgage is common in corporate lending where directors of a company may secure a loan that a bank grants to the company with their personal property.

Perfection of mortgage

Perfection of security has to do with ensuring that the various legal requirements for valid documentation upon which reliance can be placed for security realization are complied with. For mortgage on property to be effective, the bank must obtain the following documents:

- Original title documents on the property.
- Duly executed deed of legal mortgage.
- Current tax clearance certificate of the mortgagor (where the mortgagor is a company). Current tax clearance certificate of two directors of the company are also required.
- Receipts evidencing payment of ground rent, tenement rate, development levy, PAYE, and so on.
- In Lagos State of Nigeria, the mortgagor should be made to execute the land Form 1C that stands as application for the governor's consent for the mortgage.

It is noteworthy that documentation requirements for mortgage vary from one state to another. For a mortgage to be an effective security for a credit facility, it must be perfected. A mortgage is duly perfected when the following actions have been carried out with respect to the mortgage:

- Governor's consent sought and obtained. This is in fulfillment of the requirement of section 22 of the Land Use Act 1978.
- The mortgage must be duly stamped. It attracts ad valorem duty.[4] An unstamped mortgage is inadmissible as evidence but may be stamped at any time upon payment of penalty for late stamping.[5]
- The mortgage must be registered. A mortgage is a registerable instrument.[6] Failure to register a mortgage makes it subject to priority of subsequent instruments created after it. A registered instrument has priority over other competing instruments that are not registered.
- The mortgage must also be registered at the Corporate Affairs Commission apart from the registration required at the land registry. This procedure is applicable in Nigeria—where the mortgagor is a corporate body.

Enforcement of mortgage security

Smith (2007) recognizes five methods by which mortgage can be realized as security. The methods are cumulative and not exclusive so that where one method does not satisfy the debt, the mortgagee can adopt another method. However, where the method of foreclosure is embarked upon, the mortgagee cannot utilize any of the other methods. The five methods are:

Enforcement of covenant to repay
Entering into possession
Sale of mortgaged property
Appointment of a receiver
Foreclosure of the equity of redemption

It is imperative to note that chattel mortgage also falls under this category. In this case, chattels (i.e., personal property other than land) are mortgaged as security for the liabilities of the mortgagor. The bill of sale laws of respective states govern chattel mortgages, which deal with charges created over specific movable property, usually machinery.

Debenture

A debenture deed is a document of acknowledgment issued by a company as evidence of its corporate indebtedness. The security usually creates a charge

---

4. See S.22. Stamp Duties Act Cap 411 LFN 1990.
5. See S. 80(3) Supra.
6. See S. 2 Land registration act 1924.

on a company's stock or property. Debenture issued by a company will therefore be secured by a charge over the company's assets. The following are the advantages of obtaining a charge through debenture on the assets of a debtor company:

- In the event of insolvency of a company, a secured creditor will have priority over unsecured creditors.
- Secured creditors will also have the right of pursuit where the chargee disposes of the property subject to the charge.
- The charge gives its holder the right of enforcement without hindrance.
- It affords a chargee a measure of control over the business of the debtor company.
- In general, debenture is simple to execute and enforce.

Types of debenture

There are three different types of debenture deed that a company can issue or execute on its assets. However, the types of assets that a company has determine the type of debenture that the company can issue.

Floating debenture

A floating debenture is created when a company charges its floating assets and uncalled capital. A floating charge is an equitable charge over the whole or specified part of the undertaking or assets of a company, including cash and uncalled capital, both present and future.

Mortgage debenture

In this type of debenture, a company charges its fixed assets (especially, landed property) in favor of a creditor. In practice, fixed assets and the landed property that belong to a debtor company are charged together with the company's floating assets under a mortgage debenture.

All-assets debenture

In all-assets debenture, both the fixed and floating assets of a company are charged. In this regard, an all-assets debenture is used where fixed assets owned by the company are other forms of fixed assets other than landed property (e.g., machinery).

Debenture applies only to companies. It can be created pursuant to the powers contained in the memorandum and articles of association of a company and a resolution of the board of directors authorizing it. Section 173 (2) of the Companies and Allied Matters Decree 1990 provides that debenture may be secured by a fixed charge on certain of the company's property in a floating charge over the whole or a specified part of the company's undertaking and assets, or by both a fixed charge on certain property and a floating charge.

The perfection of debenture on the assets of a company involves ensuring that the following are in place:

- Duly executed debenture deed by the company (two directors of the company must sign the document, or a director and company secretary to sign with the company seal duly affixed).
- Resolution of board of directors of the company to create the charge on the company's assets.
- Registration of the debenture deed at the Corporate Affairs Commission within 90 days after the date of the creation of the deed.[7] The Commission, upon conclusion of the registration, normally issues a certificate as an evidence of the registration.
- It must be pointed out here that where a mortgage debenture is to be perfected, the governor's consent is required and it must be obtained since alienation of property is involved. After the governor's consent has been obtained, the mortgage debenture should also be registered at the lands registry of the state where the land is situated.
- Stamping of the debenture deed is a necessary condition for its registration at the lands registry and at the Corporate Affairs Commission. In addition, the requirement of stamping must be satisfied in order to make the deed admissible in evidence.

Enforcement of debenture holder's security

The security of a debenture holder can be enforced on the occurrence of any of the following:[8]

- Where the debtor company fails to pay any installment of interest or the whole or part of the principal owing under the debenture within one month after it becomes due.
- Where the company fails to fulfill any of the obligations imposed on it by the debenture.
- Where any circumstances occur that by the terms of the debenture deed entitle the debenture holder to realize security.
- Where the company is wound up.
- Where the assets charged are in jeopardy.[9] Where the company ceases to carry on business or the assets covered by the debenture suffer diminutions in value.

---

7. See S. 197, Companies and Allied Matters Act 1990.
8. See S. 208 (1) Supra.
9. See S. 389(1) (b) Supra.

The following remedies are available for debenture holders to realize security:

- Enforcement of covenant to pay. A debenture holder (i.e., the bank) may sue for the recovery of such principal sum and interest and may, upon judgment being obtained, levy execution on the property of the company.
- A debenture holder may commence a winding up proceeding by presenting a petition for winding up as a creditor to the company on grounds of the latter's inability to pay its debt. To justify an order for winding up, there must be negligence in paying the debt or demand or omission to pay without reasonable excuse. Thus, a mere omission to pay does not amount to negligence; the petitioner must show inability or unwillingness on the part of the debtor company to pay.
- A power of sale may be exercised by the debenture holder where such a power is contained in the debenture deed or pursuant to a court order.
- A debenture holder may bring a foreclosure action, the effect of which is the same with the one of mortgage.
- A debenture holder may also appoint a receiver manager to receive and manage the business of the company that issued the debenture toward liquidation of its indebtedness.

Stocks and shares as security

In general, creditors prefer shares quoted on the stock exchange as security. This is because quotation makes it easy to determine the value of the shares. Besides, it is easier to find buyers for quoted shares in the event of enforcement of the security. There are basically three methods for creating security over shares and stocks:

- Creation of a mortgage over the interest in shares and stocks
- Causing a court of law to make a charging order on the shares and stocks
- Creation of lien over documents related to the shares or stocks

The following rights are available to the creditor in whose favor the shares or stocks are mortgaged:

- Right to dividends on the shares
- Right to bonus shares
- Right to vote at company meetings
- Right to transfer the shares

The procedure normally adopted to create a mortgage on shares has changed with the establishment of the Central Security Clearing System (CSCS). Information obtainable from the depository of the CSCS now helps to ascertain shares of companies quoted on the stock exchange. This is unlike what happened in the past when share certificates obtained from the debtor evidenced shares quoted on the stock exchange. The share certificates are now retained for cancellation (i.e., immobilized).

In order to have effective security on shares or stocks, the following procedure under the CSCS should be followed:

- The debtor will make available to the creditor or bank the stock position slip issued by CSCS showing the extent of the interest of the debtor in the particular company.
- The creditor or bank confirms the content of the stock position slip with the CSCS.
- A joint memorandum (the format of which is presented in Exhibit 29.1) should be executed jointly by the creditor and the debtor. The effect of the memorandum is to jointly instruct the CSCS to place a lien on the shares of

The Managing Director
Central Securities Clearing System Ltd
Stock Exchange House
2/4, Custom Street,
Lagos

Dear Sir,

Use of shares in CSCS depository as collateral for credit facility

JOINT MEMORANDUM

THIS AGREEMENT is dated _____ day of _____ 2000
between_____ of
_____ (hereinafter referred to as "the
borrower") and _____ a bank/company incorporated in Nigeria and having its registered
office at _____ (hereinafter referred to as "the lender") in
consideration of the sum of ₦_____ (_____ in words _____) granted to the
borrower by the lender, we hereby jointly agree as follows:

a) That CSCS Limited should place a lien on the following stock(s)/securities in CSCS depository until it receives a
   letter of discharge from the lender:

Security	Units
_____	_____
_____	_____
_____	_____
_____	_____
_____	_____
_____	_____

For further details see the attached

b)(i) That the lien shall be in place for (duration) _____ months,
   (ii) That the effective drawdown date is _____

c) That the borrower undertakes to fully redeem his/her financial obligation to
   _____ (the lender)

d) That the lender undertakes to inform the borrower in case of his/her default and inform CSCS with such evidence

e) That the lender reserves the right to sell the stock(s)/securities in the event of default in payment by the borrower
   at the expiration of the loan due date, without recourse to the borrower

f) That CSCS is not obliged to obey/recognize any instruction/agreement/ arrangement which is not part of this
   memorandum

g) That this joint memorandum is in fulfilment of CSCS requirements for the use of shares as collateral for loan
   facility

h) That the CSCS is hereby indemnified and remain indemnified by the parties from any breach of this agreement

Dated this _____ day of _____ 2000

_____   _____
   Signed (borrower)   Signed (lender)

_____
Commissioner for stamp duties/commissioner for oaths

EXHIBIT 29.1   Illustration of joint memorandum.

the debtor in their depository until the creditor informs it in writing that the debtor has settled the related indebtedness.

- After execution, the joint memorandum should be stamped. Thereafter, it should be forwarded to the CSCS after payment of the prescribed fee. Also, the bank must obtain an undated letter signed by the borrower authorizing the bank to sell the shares in the event of default at the expiration of the due date of the loan.
- The CSCS thereafter will issue a letter confirming that the shareholding has been moved into a CSCS reserved account with the interest of the creditor noted.

With the introduction of the procedure stated above, it has become easy to place a lien on shares as security for lending. The enforcement of security under this arrangement has also been simplified. Where there is default in liquidation of indebtedness, the CSCS is instructed via a letter from the creditor to remove the lien to enable a sale to be effected.

The creditor has an obligation to show that the debtor has defaulted after the expiration of the due date of the loan and that a demand notice has been served on the debtor in this regard. The creditor can thereafter give a copy of the undated letter written by the borrower to a stock broker firm listed with the Nigerian Stock Exchange for the purpose of sale of the shares. CSCS always advises that funds should not be disbursed to the debtor until the letter that places a lien on the shares is received from the CSCS.

OTHER FORMS OF SECURITY

Life insurance policy

A life insurance policy is a contract whereby the insurer, in consideration of a premium paid by the insured, undertakes to pay in the event of death of a named person, a certain sum of money to a person named by the insured. A right under life policy insurance is a choice in action that may be assigned.[10] The assignment here is not of the policy per se but an assignment of the right to receive the proceeds of the policy. A mortgage can therefore be created on life policies as security for credit facilities by way of assignment of interest in the policy to the lender. The mortgage may be legal or equitable. Notice of the assignment must be given to the insurance company at its principal place of business as required by law stating the date and purport of the assignment.

Lien over account deposit

A lien over fixed deposit also offers effective security for bank lending. The procedure for the use of a fixed or other deposit as security for a credit facility

---

10. S. 64 (1), Insurance decree, No. 2, 1977.

is simple. The owner of the deposit must authorize the bank to block the deposit against withdrawal until the loan is fully liquidated. Having done this, the bank will be at liberty, in the event that the borrower defaults on the loan, to utilize the deposit or balance in the deposit account to offset outstanding debts of the borrower to the bank.

The recourse of the bank to the deposit may be in full or partial settlement of the borrower's liabilities on the loan. Apart from a letter of authority that may be obtained in this regard, it is banking practice to require customers to execute a letter of setoff when they open an account. The letter authorizes the bank to set off any indebtedness of the customer against any balance in any of its accounts or related accounts. A bank does not need the customer's consent to apply the letter of setoff once the customer executes it.

This form of security arrangement is reliable and without problem. However, the snag is that it is not easy to come across customers with deposits in their accounts that will still need credit facilities. This can, however, be the case where the deposit of a customer has not matured and he is in need of funds for an urgent project or business.

Guarantee and bonds

The use of a guarantee or bond usually involves a tripartite relationship. In this case, a person known as the guarantor undertakes to indemnify the bank against any loss arising from exposure of the bank to another person who is a customer of the bank. Guarantee is often used in addition to other types of security and the liability of the guarantor under a guarantee is secondary. This is because the guarantor is only to discharge the principal debtor's obligation if the latter fails to do so.

A contract of guarantee is not the same as a contract of indemnity. A contract of indemnity in contrast to a contract of guarantee is one in which the indemnitor agrees with the creditor to make good all or an agreed measure of any loss the creditor may suffer. The person giving the indemnity assumes primary liability for the debt. There are two kinds of guarantee that are used to secure bank lending: personal and corporate.

Personal guarantee

Banks demand a personal guarantee when they grant credit facility to a corporate borrower. A company is seen in law as an artificial person and therefore has distinct legal capacity from its members. As a result, where there is no personal guarantee of one or more of the directors or members, an individual cannot be held responsible for the corporate liability of the company. Personal guarantee therefore makes it possible to hold the personal guarantor personally liable for the debt of the company. The worth of the person giving the guarantee needs to be ascertained to ensure that the guarantee being given has reasonable value.

Corporate guarantee

This is a guarantee issued by a corporate body to secure credit that a bank grants to an individual or another corporate body. Corporate guarantee of related sister companies are normally obtained where one of the companies in a group is taking a credit facility. It is important that a director and secretary of the company giving the guarantee duly execute the guarantee—with the company seal duly affixed to it. It is in this regard that bank guarantee can be issued as security for credit facility given by another bank to a customer.

A letter of comfort also falls under this category. A letter of comfort is usually given by a parent company on behalf of its subsidiary. The effect of a letter of comfort is that the lender can have recourse to the issuer of the letter should the lender feel uncomfortable during the course of the underlying credit transaction. Therefore the purpose of letter of comfort is to assure the lender that there will be due performance on the credit facility.

Equipment lease agreement

A security in equipment lease agreement is useful for lease facilities. In this case, a bank grants a loan to a borrower (i.e., its customer) who is in need of equipment for business purposes to purchase the equipment. Usually the agreement is made under seal. Under the agreement, title in the equipment purchased for the use of the customer is vested in the bank. Thus, the bank leases the equipment to the customer. In doing so, it prescribes rentals that the customer should pay to it for the use of the equipment during the tenor of the lease.

The usual and reliable practice is to put a sale-and-leaseback agreement in place. There are usually two parts to a sale-and-leaseback agreement. The equipment is sold to the bank by one leg of the agreement, while the second leg of the agreement leases the equipment to the customer as the lessee. There is often a clause in the lease agreement permitting the lessee to purchase the equipment at the end of the lease.

The bank must ensure that the following steps are taken with regard to the lease. The lease agreement must be duly executed by the parties, especially the lessee.

- The agreement should be duly stamped.
- There should be an insurance policy that names the bank as the first loss payee beneficiary on the equipment. This must be in place as part of documentation of the lease agreement.
- The bank should obtain title deeds and other documents on the leased equipment.

Hypothecation of stocks

This form of security arrangement is used mostly for import finance facility whereby the imported goods are kept in the warehouse of the bank's agent.

Usually, a *warehousing agreement* strengthens stock hypothecation as security for bank lending. Under the arrangement, goods in the warehouse are released piecemeal for sale by the borrower. The proceeds of sale are credited to the borrower's loan account toward liquidation of the loan.

Further approval is granted, following the foregoing procedure, for the release of more goods until the loan is fully liquidated. The warehousing agent renders a report from time to time on the amount of goods in its custody to the bank. The report enables the bank to compare the value of goods in the warehouse with the outstanding balance in the loan account.

The bank may want to realize the security if there is default in settlement of the borrower's indebtedness. It can exercise its right of lien on the goods by way of sale. The bank can also take a lien on shipping documents where the customer is expected to settle his indebtedness upon importation of the goods. The shipping documents endorsed to the bank are therefore not released until the customer settles its indebtedness.

Also connected with import finance facility is the practice of insisting on equity contribution by the borrower toward importation of the goods. The essence of equity contribution is to create a sense of commitment in the borrower to the transaction. It is also intended to ensure that borrowers perform their due obligations on credit facilities that banks grant to them.

Trust receipts

The use of a trust receipt is also closely related to import finance facility whereby the goods imported are the subject of security. A trust receipt is used where borrowers need to sell the goods imported to enable them to settle their indebtedness to the bank. In this case, the borrowers sign a document called a trust receipt whereby they undertake to pay the proceeds of sale of the goods to the bank. In doing so, the borrowers acknowledge that they are mere agents or trustees for the bank in the sale of the goods. Upon execution of the trust receipt, the goods that should be in the custody of the bank are released to the borrower for sale. It must be pointed out that this type of security arrangement can only be put in place when dealing with an honest borrower whose integrity is not in doubt. This is because a fraudulent borrower can sell the goods and divert the funds. Yet account officers and relationship managers should closely monitor sale of the goods to ensure that the proceeds liquidate the loan.

Domiciliation of payment

This is yet another form of security, one that is largely applicable to contract financing. There are usually three parties to this security arrangement: employer, borrower, and bank. The *employer*, under a contract awarded to the *borrower*, undertakes to make payment for the contract directly into the borrower's account with the *bank* upon due completion of the contract. In most cases, this arrangement works by way of domiciliation of payment agreement executed by the employer, the borrower, and the bank. It could also be achieved through a letter of undertaking issued in favor of the bank by the employer to effect payment directly to the bank. Usually, banks are more willing to accept domiciliation of payment from reputable companies or government parastatals with a track record of prompt payments on executed contracts. Typically, for example, banks are more inclined to accept domiciliation of payment as security if the employer is a well-known oil or blue-chip company.

Letter of comfort

A letter of comfort is a letter that a blue chip or other reputable company writes to a bank in support of a loan that the bank has granted or intends to grant to its subsidiary. The letter merely states that the writer of the letter knows the borrower and that the writer has no reason to believe that the borrower will default in payment. Thus, the letter essentially stands as some assurance of good performance that a parent company gives on behalf of its subsidiary. It must be noted that the letter carries no legal commitment and cannot be acted upon unless the letter states otherwise.

Assignment of debts

A borrower can assign debt to a bank as security for a credit facility. This is done where there is indebtedness outstanding in favor of the borrower from a third party. Thus, the borrower can assign the debt to the bank to secure a credit facility or other financial obligation. Therefore, the borrower's debtor is expected to settle the debt by paying the amount of the debt to the bank to which the debt is assigned. The use of this type of security is not common. A bank might not be willing to rely on debt owed to someone (i.e., a loan applicant) as security to grant the applicant's loan request. The fact that payment of the debt is not certain further reduces the worth of assignment of debts as security for bank lending.

Negative pledge

The importance of negative pledge in collateral considerations for bank lending purposes is discussed in Chapter 26. I presented the term *negative pledge* as part of the discussion of the *covenants of the borrower*, which are found in standard loan agreements. The reader should also consult the index to find more sources of information about negative pledge as security for lending.

PROBLEMS OF SECURITY

It is important to appreciate and note the problems that are peculiar to some forms of security in terms of creation and realization.

Governor's consent requirement for mortgage of land

This requirement, prescribed in section 22 of the Land Use Act 1978, is a problem. Documentation requirements in some states for seeking and obtaining the consent of the governor are excessive. This is especially the case in Lagos State where all manner of things are demanded for the purposes of obtaining the governor's consent. Also, the long period of time it takes to obtain the governor's consent and the excessive charges that the consent attracts are not in the best interest of business. With many controversial cases[11] following promulgation of the land use act, it is obvious that the requirement for governor's consent serves no useful purpose. Multiple opinions hold that this consent requirement for mortgages should be removed from our statute books to pave way for a simple process in creating mortgages. Where it is confirmed that the actual owner of the property is the mortgagor, there should be no form of delay in registering the mortgage. Our law ought to enable quick, cheap, and simple creation of security rights.

Delay in administration of justice

Delay associated with dispensation of justice in Nigeria has a telling consequence on enforcement of security. Unscrupulous borrowers owing banks tend to develop an attitude of running to court to obtain spurious orders to restrain the banks from exercising their rights over subject matters of security. Delay associated with adjudication in Nigeria makes it possible for this category of borrowers to abuse the court process for realization of security. They somehow succeed in frustrating banks when the banks attempt to realize security. It is in this regard that the demand of banks and the Chartered Institute of Bankers of Nigeria for the establishment of commercial court to handle bank-related matters is in the right direction. It is good that courts are now divided into divisions in Lagos State with specific areas as focus. One of the newly created divisions is the commercial division where bank-related matters should be handled. It is expected that this will result in expeditious handling of cases, thereby enhancing speedy resolution of disputes on security matters.

---

11. Savannah Bank V. Ajilo; Ugochukwu v. Co-operative and Commerce Bank Limited; Ogunleye v. Oni.

Undue technicalities and requirements for taking security

There is the need to remove undue and unnecessary technicalities associated with security for bank lending. For example, where a bill of sale does not conform strictly to the requirement of the bill of sale law, it cannot be enforced. Many unnecessary documents that are required for perfection of mortgage, especially in Lagos State, need to be reconsidered. It is understandable that the request for various tax papers is to ensure that taxes are paid and to generate revenue for government. However, a situation where taxes payable are based on the amount of loan is unjustifiable. This is also not in the best interest of the borrower who bears the cost of perfection. Government has a responsibility to make enforcement procedures for security realization at market value prompt and the cost of taking, maintaining, and enforcing security minimal. Security should reduce the risk of granting credit facilities, leading to increased availability of loans to individuals, companies, and organizations.

QUESTIONS FOR DISCUSSION AND REVIEW

1. **(a)** Why is it necessary (or not) for banks to take collateral for loans?
   (b) What are the qualities of good collateral?
2. **(a)** Explain the term *mortgage* as applied in security of a loan.
   (b) What benefits does mortgage of land have over charge on goods and chattel?
3. How should banks create effective mortgage? Your answer should highlight challenges in doing so.
4. **(a)** Explain "perfection of mortgage."
   (b) Discuss the required procedure for perfection of mortgage in Nigeria.
   (c) Why is perfection of mortgage a thorny issue in Nigeria?
5. **(a)** What is a debenture deed?
6. **(b)** What benefits does charge on the assets of a company confer on a bank?

REFERENCES

Goode, R.M., 1988. Legal Problems of Credit and Security, second ed. Sweet & Maxwell, Centre for Commercial Law Studies, London.

Smith, I.O., 2007. Practical Approach to Law of Real Property in Nigeria, second ed. Ecowatch Publications (Nigeria) Limited, Lagos.

FURTHER READING

Smith, I.O., 2001. Nigerian Law of Secured Credit. Ecowatch Publications (Nigeria) Limited, Lagos.

Sykes, E.I., 1978. The Law of Securities, third ed. Law Book Company Limited, Australia.

Chapter 30

Administering Credit and Portfolio Risk in Emerging Markets

Chapter Outline

LEARNING FOCUS AND OUTCOMES

In some banks, the unit or department responsible for administration of the lending portfolio is referred to as *credit compliance, credit control*, or *credit admin*. I have used these phrases interchangeably in this chapter. In doing so, the overriding consideration is to underscore the commonality of the import of the concepts in terms of the postmortem thrust of the functions of credit admin.

The tasks involved in administering the lending portfolio could be far more daunting than in its creation. However, this depends—first and foremost—on the quality of the risk assets. Where the lending portfolio comprises a large stock of

Emerging Market Bank Lending and Credit Risk Control. http://dx.doi.org/10.1016/B978-0-12-803438-5.00030-1

nonperforming loans, or a bank operates in an environment where default rate is high, credit admin becomes even more excruciating. In banks that have quality risk assets portfolios, managing the loan portfolio, in most cases, is less arduous.

Nonetheless, it is the responsibility of credit admin to create, review, and update the risk assets database. It maintains credit files, manages regulatory returns, and enforces classification of risk assets. My interest in this chapter is to critique issues and conflicts among bank officials involved in credit policy, approval, and control functions. In doing so, I discuss ways to strengthen postloan disbursement functions in global banks. I do this within the framework of roles fulfilled by lending officers and roles in administering the lending portfolio.

The crux of bank lending is usually three pronged. I depict this as the three pillars of credit risk management: credit analysis (pillar 1), credit adminis- tration (pillar 2), and loan recovery (pillar 3). Credit analysis institutionalizes a process for assessing credit risk well. Credit admin enforces credit control and compliance. Loan recovery follows failure of workout and remedial actions on delinquent loans. The approach to, and methodology for, dealing with issues implied in the pillars have witnessed dramatic changes over time. Yet, the goal of credit risk management remains immutable.

My focus in this chapter is on the second pillar. In doing so, I review its mechanics and functions. I also examine contemporary challenges of credit admin and measures to cope with them. Credit admin performs largely postloan disbursement functions. In addition to the functions, you will learn about:

- Prudential classifications of, and provisioning on, the lending portfolio
- How credit admin institutionalizes review of risk assets database as an integral part of its functions
- Making, functions, and limitations of credit strategy committee
- Why banks set up and institutionalize a watch-list committee
- How credit admin fulfills its role as a bulwark against credit risk and inefficient lending

OVERVIEW OF CREDIT ADMIN

I have so far in this book discussed issues involved in the appraisal and approval of credit facilities. With that background, I now discuss roles fulfilled in the administration of the lending portfolio as an integral part of the credit process. In doing so, I use the terms *loans*, *credits*, and *risk assets* interchangeably.

Credit admin creates, reviews, and updates the risk assets database of a bank. It maintains credit files, manages returns on risk assets to the regulatory authorities, and enforces classifications of risk assets. Overall, it fulfills specific roles toward credit risk management. In general, credit admin is expected to carry out the following functions:

- Maintain custody of copies of loans documentation, including collateral, credit approval form (CAF), credit analysis memorandum (CAM), credit

analysis summary (CAS), temporary overdraft (TOD), drawing against uncleared effects (DAUE), and so on
- Ensure that all waivers and deferrals on loans are approved prior to drawdown on credit facilities
- Maintain proper records of the bank's credit exposures to all the borrowing customers
- Keep records of maturity profiles of the lending portfolio and advise lending units of impending maturity of loans
- Ensure complete documentation of credit facilities as specified in the CAF and offer letter prior to disbursement
- Ensure proper booking of loans after approval and fulfillment of all conditions precedent to drawdown, including changes in rates, maturity dates, approved limits, loan amounts, and so on
- Ensure that it receives and reviews relevant loan reports from IT department and advises senior management of any exceptions

The following discussions present details of the foregoing and other important functions of the credit admin unit.

NEED FOR CREDIT ADMINISTRATION

Credit admin is one of the most critical functions in managing a bank's lending portfolio. It is the second of the three-part schemes of credit risk management—the first being credit *analysis*, while the third is loan *recovery*. Credit admin fulfills *postmortem* lending roles that ensure that loan officers do anything but neglect credit facilities *after* approval and disbursement. In this role, credit admin checks the tendency of account officers and relationship managers to abandon loan monitoring after its disbursement. This is especially the case when initial income applicable to a credit facility has been recognized for the lending unit. In doing so, the goal of credit admin is to prevent a situation in which disbursed credit facilities *avoidably* go bad, are classified, and become potential or actual additions to *charged-off* statistics.

Bank management covets the functions of credit admin and is ever disposed to deploying necessary resources to enable it to fulfill its roles. In coveting their roles, as in all control functions, management shields credit compliance officers against direct business influences. Such influences may be experienced in appraising loan applications, marketing, and managing lending relationships. This standing justifies the confidence into which credit admin officers are taken in carrying out their functions. For example, they are expected to and do closely monitor the condition and performance of credit facilities. They do so with a view to alerting senior management of—and possibly forestalling—deterioration of risk assets quality. In most cases, risk assets quality deteriorates with flawed implementation of their terms and conditions to which banks and borrowers agreed. Often, risk assets quality worsens where relationship management is either weak or neglected. Thus, credit admin must be able to decipher and warn against probable lapses in loan monitoring responsibilities.

Credit admin must continuously make concrete contributions toward stemming incidence of nonperforming risk assets. It must at all times strive to check the upsetting waste of earnings through needless loan loss provisions. Otherwise, the profit that banks would make from normal operational activities will continue to be depleted because of provisions against loan losses on nonperforming risk assets. In this chapter, I discuss dimensions of risk assets protection that credit admin offers in the bank credit process. Using the discussion and banks' institutional support framework as underpinning, I examine some of the practical challenges in administering the lending portfolio. Based on analysis of the relevant factors, I recommend that all responsible lending parties should show more concern for the success of credit admin functions and the overall credit process.

BULWARK AGAINST INEFFICIENT LENDING

The functions of credit admin may be divided into five broad categories. In general, the credit admin *confirms documentation* of credit facilities; *maintains database* of risk assets portfolio; *enforces compliance* with credit policies; *preserves reports* of credit and marketing; and *renders returns* on risk assets portfolio. In the context of these work roles, credit admin assumes importance as a key element of the credit process.

Loan documentation

Credit analysts and relationship managers assess, recommend, and obtain legal documents to secure credit facilities granted to borrowing customers. Not only should they assemble, they must also get confirmation of appropriateness of security documents before any loan may be disbursed. The credit admin unit furnishes the necessary confirmation. In so doing, *it prescribes certain conditions that the lending units must fulfill*, including the following:

- Submission of duly executed *original* copies of offer letters, loan agreements, and collateral-securing credit facilities
- Satisfaction of all terms and conditions, especially those that are *precedent* to drawdown or disbursement of loans
- Proof of *waiver* or *deferral*, by senior management, of any conditions precedent to drawdown on, or disbursement of, loans
- Evidence, corroborated by the legal unit's endorsement, that relevant *security* documents are in place and *duly* perfected or that the bank is in a position to perfect security in due course

Every credit policy manual upholds the principle that loans should not be disbursed until perfection of necessary security documentation is concluded.

In practice, however, it is difficult to actualize security perfection due to delays often experienced in the process. In order to solve the problem of delays, without overstretching the patience of borrowers, most banks accept assemblage of all the necessary security documents, which puts them *in a position to perfect* as fulfilling the security perfection requirement.

Credit admin must ensure that these and other relevant loan documentation such as original copies of the *credit analysis memorandum, credit analysis summary, credit approval form, temporary overdraft, excess over limit* (EOL), *drawing against uncleared effects,* and so on are properly secured in *standard credit files.* In liaison with the legal unit, it should make sure that all original security documents are lodged in the bank's *vault* for safekeeping.

A credit file characteristically contains eight important sections: loan commitment, security documentation, operations memoranda, internal memoranda, call memoranda, correspondence, market information, and financial statements.

Loan commitment

Critical loan documents—CAF, CAM, and CAS—are filed in this section. It also contains renewals, rollovers, enhancements, and any other modifications of the original loan commitment. The current commitment is usually filed on top of the other documents in this section of the credit file.

Security documents

Photocopies of all the collateral, pledges, guarantees, liens, and so on that borrowers give to the bank as security for their credit facilities are filed in this section. All other legal documents and agreements between the bank and borrower, such as accepted loan offer letters, domiciliation of payments or receivables agreements, loan covenants, and so on should also be filed in this section of the credit file.

Operations memoranda

This section of the credit file contains photocopies of important transactions in the account, including monthly statements of the account. Typically, transactions documented in this section include loan disbursements, letters of credits established, shipping documents released, travellers' checks issued, and so on.

Internal memoranda

Often, in the course of their day-to-day internal transactions, the various units and departments of a bank involved in attracting, appraising, packaging, approving, and managing credit facilities give and receive memos to and from one another. Such memos, filed in this section, deal with a myriad of issues affecting credit facilities, borrowers, and banking relationships.

Call memoranda

It is expected that account officers, relationship managers, and some senior management staff will or do occasionally visit borrowers. The purpose of such visits could be to maintain business warmth with the borrowers, understand functioning of their businesses, assess utilization of their loans, monitor their transactions with other banks, and so on. The outcome of each visit is often documented as a call memo that is filed in this section of the credit file.

Correspondence

The correspondence section of the credit file contains letters and correspondence between the borrower and bank regarding loans that the bank grants to the borrower. The issues dealt with through correspondence vary, depending on the type, depth, and complexity of the loan. However, only serious and nontrivial matters should be communicated in writing. Closeness and warmth of a banking relationship would reduce the resort to letter writing between a bank and borrower.

Market information

In this section of the credit file, information (such as publications, news reports, and so on) about the industry, competition, opportunities, and threats, and so on are filed. There are perhaps innumerable sources of relevant marketing information, but it is advised that credit and marketing officers should do all of the following as a means of obtaining market information:

- Peruse available magazines, journals, articles, and so on that relate to the banking industry, products, services, and practices. From these information sources, they could gain or update their vocational knowledge.
- Read useful and related books, especially those that focus on the banking industry, products, services, and practices.
- Read in-house magazines and other publications of banks, Central Bank of Nigeria (CBN), Nigeria Deposit Insurance Corporation (NDIC), Nigerian Stock Exchange (NSE), Securities and Exchange Commission (SEC), and so on. Marketing personnel should, as much as possible, also read in-house magazines and publications of competing banks.
- Get information from the press, including, in particular, newspapers, radios, televisions.
- Solicit, and obtain relevant marketing information from banking prospects, especially those that are currently banking with the competing banks.
- Visit and obtain information from factories, marketplaces, warehouses, business offices, and so on.

Perhaps unusual sources of pertinent marketing information are customers and prospects. As much as possible, credit and marketing officers should interact freely with them in a bid to understand their needs and wants and get useful marketing information. It is strongly advised that marketing officers should seek and get information from those with whom the bank has enduring business relationships. Useful information could be obtained from both satisfied and dissatisfied customers. This has proven to be one of the most veritable sources of marketing information.

Annual report and accounts

At any point in time, a credit file should contain audited financial statements of the borrower for at least the immediate past three years. Also, the accounts and their analyses in spreadsheets, together with computed relevant financial ratios, should be filed in this section of the credit file.

Risk assets database

The credit admin unit should keep accurate data on the bank's lending portfolio, including specific information on each credit facility and borrowing account. This entails *further security of documentation* as contained, and approved by senior management, in the CAF. The unit should create and regularly review the risk assets database of the bank, including ratings of individual credit facilities in line with the prudential guidelines for risk assets classifications. There are two types of risk assets database report. A typical risk assets database contains summarized—sometimes tabulated—information relating to each of the borrowing accounts. Another useful risk assets database report comprises summarized information on *performing, nonperforming*, and *charged-off* risks assets.

Performing risk assets

As the CBN (1997) advises, "a credit facility is deemed to be performing if payments of both principal and interest are up-to-date in accordance with the agreed terms." The performing risk assets database report should be a regular monthly report that the credit admin unit prepares and distributes to members of the credit strategy committee (CRESCO). The report must provide the following information, amongst others:

- Maturity profiles of the performing risk assets
- Values and state of perfection of collateral securing the risk assets
- Gross yields of individual risk assets and the total portfolio
- Sectoral distribution of the loan portfolio

Nonperforming risk assets

The CBN (1997) holds that "a credit facility should be deemed as nonperforming when any of the following conditions exists:

- interest or principal is due and unpaid for 90 days or more;
- interest payments equal to 90 days interest or more have been capitalized, rescheduled or rolled over into a new loan (except where facilities have been reclassified…)"

The nonperforming risk assets are also known as *loans of doubtful value*. Credit admin should prepare and distribute a report on this category of risk assets to CRESCO members on a weekly basis. The report must show, amongst other items:

- Cash value balance—also known as *cash basis balance*—for each of the affected nonperforming risk assets. Cash basis balance is the net outstanding balance on a loan at the point in time when it was classified as a lost credit, earmarked for recovery actions, and provision for its charge-off took effect.
- Update on and prospect of recovery of each of the risk assets earmarked for recovery
- Data on improvement on previous classifications of loans that constitute the lending portfolio
- Status of collateral (i.e., perfection) and performance of lawyers and agents engaged in recovery of particular risk assets
- Specific provision on particular credit facilities, as well as general provision on the total portfolio of nonperforming risk assets

Nonperforming risk assets are a drain on a bank's earnings. They neutralize the performance of an otherwise profitable bank through loan loss provisions. Ideally, nonperforming credits, according to the CBN (1997), should be grouped into three categories as follows:

Substandard credits

This category of nonperforming risk assets encompasses credit facilities for which unpaid principal and or interest remain outstanding for more than 90 days but less than 180 days. With appropriate remedial measures, substandard credits may regain lost favorable ratings.

Doubtful credits

Risk assets classified as *doubtful* represent credit facilities for which unpaid principal and or interest remain outstanding for at least 180 days but less than 360 days. Another feature of doubtful credits is that they are not secured by legal title to leased assets or perfected realizable collateral in the process of collection or realization.

Lost credits

Classifying particular risk assets as *lost* credit facilities implies that unpaid principal and or interest on the credits remains outstanding for 360 or more days. Also, such credit facilities are not secured by legal title to leased assets or perfected realizable collateral in the course of collection or realization.

Charged-off loans

Reports on charged-off loans may be presented on a monthly basis to provide data showing:

- Cash basis balance for each of the charged-off risk assets
- Current outstanding balances on each of the loans
- Update on and prospects of recovery of the charged-off loans
- Status of collateral (i.e., perfection) securing the loans
- Performance of lawyers and agents engaged to recover the loans

Enforcement of compliance

The next crucial duties and responsibilities of the credit admin unit begin to demand attention soon after completion of loan documentation and disbursement. An important aspect of its functions is its oversight of activities of lending units and officers. Its primary assignment is to ensure strict compliance with internal credit policies and applicable regulatory guidelines. The scope of this responsibility includes close monitoring and enforcement of compliance with approved terms and conditions of credit facilities and reporting observed exceptions to senior management.

The aspects of credit policies on which lending officers frequently infringe are worthy of note. On occasion they forget to charge the necessary interest, fees, and commission in accordance with agreed terms and conditions of credit facilities. Credit admin verifies that income related to these and other charges are correctly debited from loan accounts. It also ensures that all credit facilities operate within their approved limits. This is an important function that saves banks the risk of carrying large amounts of *excess over limit* balances on approved credit facilities. Of course, available collateral might not cover such EOL balances.

There is yet another important role of credit admin. It guards against risk of allowing current accounts to be *overdrawn* without proper authorization. Often this is caused by unauthorized DAUE, which is tantamount to granting unsecured loans. Such unauthorized loans have a high probability of loss if the underlying banking instruments are dishonored at clearing. Perhaps the most critical function of the credit admin unit is to detect, report, and enforce regularization of all such unauthorized overdrafts. This kind of overdraft is created when, without the express endorsement of the relevant lending officers,

- customers, probably in collusion with some bank staff, overdraw their current accounts as utilization of temporary overdrafts
- ordinarily nonborrowing current accounts are allowed to be in the red, or have debit balances, caused by buildup of in-house charges to the accounts

- the debit balances in otherwise properly approved overdraft facilities exceed their borrowing limits
- customers are allowed to withdraw money against checks or other banking instruments that are yet in the process of clearing

In carrying out a compliance check on unauthorized overdraft, credit admin offers an effective control over negative and wasteful practices of the lending units.

There are several other important compliance functions of credit admin, including reminding lending units of impending loans' maturity—usually one month before the due dates. Ideally, the lending unit should in turn give at least three weeks' loan maturity notice to the borrowers. The bank may set targets for sectoral distribution of its loan portfolio, target markets for its risk assets, and general credit risk acceptance criteria. In such a situation, the credit admin will regularly report to senior management on the extent of compliance with, or deviations from, such targets.

RENDITION OF CREDIT RETURNS

The credit admin unit prepares, documents, and submits regular returns on the risk assets portfolio to the regulatory authorities. As a statutory requirement, failure to render the returns, especially to the CBN, could attract specific sanctions. In most cases, credit admin works with the chief compliance officer in defending and answering any regulatory queries about specific loans or the whole risk assets portfolio. In carrying out its rendition of returns function, the unit also plays an advisory role when it counsels senior management on the implications of infraction of any of the lending regulations. Whenever necessary, credit admin draws from the experience of sanctions meted out to erring banks to strengthen its advice to senior management of the bank.

The credit admin unit works to keep the marketing and relationship management officers on their toes. This is one of the means of ensuring timely repayment of loans, minimizing loan default, and reducing loan loss provisions. Its effectiveness is enhanced by the fact that it operates as an independent unit. In most cases, credit admin is staffed by personnel different from those involved in marketing, credit analysis, and relationship management. Ideally, the credit control's work should complement that of the internal control department of the bank that reports directly to the chief executive officer. Credit admin is shielded from customers' influences and inducements. This is done to ensure that its officers are and remain unbiased in carrying out their assignments. A further justification of the independence of credit admin is in limiting interaction of its staff to only its internal customers. Usually the main internal customers of credit admin staff are credit and marketing officers who attract, manage, and seek to retain borrowing accounts and relationships.

Rendition of returns on the risks assets portfolio to the regulatory authorities is nowadays about the most sensitive function of the credit admin unit. As the

CBN relies on the returns in formulating macroeconomic policies, it must be satisfied that data that banks provide in the returns are authentic—not falsified, or misleading. This is why the CBN insists that returns on risk assets portfolios must be endorsed by chief executive officers of the banks. In doing so, the returns would be credible, dependable, and acceptable for use in macroeconomic planning. In addition to the normal specific sanctions for failure to render the returns, the CBN threatens to severely sanction chief executives of banks that render misleading, falsified, or flawed credit returns.

With the new disposition of the CBN on returns on risk assets portfolio, a new challenge has been introduced to the functions of credit admin. In the past, statutory returns of banks to the regulatory authorities could be endorsed and furnished by heads of the responsible units and departments. Now, while credit admin staff furnish data and prepare credit returns, their chief executive officers are accountable for authenticity of the returns. Therefore, the stakes in credit administration's traditional function of preparing, documenting, and submitting regular returns on risk assets portfolios to the regulatory authorities have been significantly raised. Another factor that has heightened the stakes is the CBN's posture of *zero tolerance* of infraction of any of its banking regulation and supervision rules.

Thus, there is a new challenge in credit admin functions—one that requires its commitment to saving chief executives of banks from embarrassment that would arise if returns to the regulatory authorities were found to be erroneous. To meet this challenge, credit compliance officers need unusual thoroughness in the discharge of their duties. They must also be firmer in checking the unfortunate tendency of lending units and officers to feel less bothered about the performance of credit facilities after the credits have been appraised, approved, disbursed—and income on them booked. This is a necessary, though not sufficient, condition to ensure that credit facilities are timely repaid, loans default mitigated, and loss provisions reduced.

CREDIT AND MARKET REPORTS

Credit admin staff must be involved in maintenance of information about markets and developments in the sectors of the economy to which their banks grant substantial credit facilities. In doing so, their aim should be to keep abreast with evolving opportunities and threats in the markets, which might have a bearing on the present and future performance of risk assets portfolios of banks. Pertinent data could be obtained from various sources about products-markets, macroeconomic trends and projections, competitive strategies, and so on. However, credit information gathering is not the sole responsibility of credit admin staff. Any bank staff can get useful credit information. However, for purposes of proper documentation and necessary actions, such information should always be passed on to the credit admin office. Much of the desired information is often obtained and secured through marketing intelligence or espionage.

In general, frontline staff—usually lending officers, account officers, relationship managers, and marketing officers—lead in information search, gathering, and reporting for documentation purposes. They do so in the course of their day-to-day interaction with customers, market operators, and competitors. But they are expected to, first and foremost, use knowledge of such information to strengthen their assignments and enhance the performance of credit facilities.

ADMINISTRATIVE FRAMEWORK

Every bank must set up a standing administrative framework to support credit admin functions. This suggestion envisages a growing need for institutional schemes or arrangements for senior management's involvement in administering the lending portfolio. A particular scheme could be in the form of devising a regular forum for the interaction of senior management with lending officers, account officers, relationship managers, and credit control staff. Such an arrangement will help to bridge avoidable communication gaps in establishing, managing, and controlling credit relationships. While it is evident that bank management acknowledges this need, the effectiveness of its implementation in some banks is doubtful. The most popular administrative frameworks for supporting credit admin functions in banks are the institutions of the credit strategy committee and the watch-list committee.

Credit strategy committee

The CRESCO is one of the management devices to strengthen the credit process. Banks have a specific aim in instituting the CRESCO. They look to fulfilling the need for credit approval authorities to stay focused. Thus, the institution of CRESCO is a means to harmonize, unify, and adopt common credit review, decision making, approval process, and strategy at the senior management level. The CRESCO functions as a high-ranking credit review and approval authority. In general, it deals with decisive and thorny issues in credit proposals as packaged in the CAM and CAF. It fulfills critical roles for the bank in the area of credit risk management. The CRESCO supports effective discharge of credit admin functions by providing a medium for interaction between senior management, lending officers, and credit admin staff. At CRESCO's sessions, the representative of credit admin (if any, or on invitation) would report observed lapses in extant credit facilities. He or she could also suggest certain risk-mitigating measures for the CRESCO's consideration. Such recommendations, usually for intended credit facilities, are based on the practical experience of credit compliance staff in administering individual credit facilities and the total lending portfolio.

Watch-list committee

A watch-list committee is set up to meet regularly to review the status of nonperforming risk assets. It also gets reports on efforts and achievements of responsible officers of the lending and loans remedial units toward recovery of bad loans. The committee works closely with credit admin to ensure that loan loss provisions are minimized. However, it also pursues a specific agenda for possible remedial of *classified* or *criticized* credit facilities, as well as recovery of *lost*, but not let off, credit facilities. The committee recommends necessary actions to revive particular loan accounts, strengthen ailing credit relationships, and maintain surveillance over the performance of particular loan accounts and credit facilities. It supports credit admin functions in practical terms. In addition to having a representative on the watch-list committee, credit admin makes useful input to such decisions.

CONTEMPORARY CHALLENGES

The triggers of contemporary challenges in credit admin could be sifted out from its role as a bulwark against credit risk. The challenges are embedded in certain corrective lending actions that credit admin officers do take in routine and occasional discharge of their credit compliance responsibilities. Such actions include, but are not limited to the following:

- Security documentation
  Credit admin staff should and do strictly enforce security documentation of credit facilities, particularly the perfection of legal title deeds. This factor is in consonance with commitment to checking deterioration of quality of risk assets. On occasion, insisting on perfection of collateral causes a rift in the day-to-day interface and working relationship between marketing and credit control staff. Role conflicts may also be triggered where credit admin officers assert their authority on credit policy and control matters regardless of equally important marketing responsibilities.
- Rendition of returns on risk assets
  Credit admin has the unenviable task of convincing senior management on the need to render accurate returns on risk assets portfolios to the regulatory authorities. There might be internal pressure to falsify, or misrepresent, some aspects of the returns. Often this happens when the returns conflict with budget goals. Resolving the pressure, on the one hand, and the conflicts between risk management (i.e., attaining *risk-free* lending portfolio) and marketing (i.e., meeting overall profit) goals, on the other, require compromise and mutual tolerance of the parties.
- Check on credit concentration
  One of the duties of credit admin is to warn against a tendency to concentrate much of the lending portfolio in particular economic or market sectors. If account officers, relationship managers, and bank management

heed such warning, it would be easy to forestall increasing rate of default on credit facilities. In some cases, business development officers might have reasons to disregard credit control's advice. Thus, credit admin would have to contend with opposing forces in recommending realistic criteria for target markets definition and risk acceptance criteria for purposes of risk assets creation.

- Building quality loan portfolio
  Credit admin also seeks to enhance the quality of the lending portfolio through effective check on negative attitudes of borrowers and lending officers. This is a particularly demanding responsibility. One reason is that it often results in confrontation with people who have deep-seated negative behavior that exacerbates loan default. Another reason is that credit admin must somehow forestall the negative tendencies of the individuals—mainly its internal customers. Here, credit control officers must be bold and assertive in order to succeed.

Some would argue that the creation of loans (i.e., appraisal, documentation, and disbursement of credit facilities) and managing lending relationships are challenging. In most cases, these roles are indeed quite challenging. Yet, relative to credit appraisal and relationship management, the postloan disbursement functions of credit admin are daunting.

Consider, for example, that credit analysts and approving authorities sometimes do shoddy jobs in packaging and granting loan facilities. They might not have asked the right questions. Perhaps they might not have obtained certain necessary data. They might yet not have put measures that would mitigate identified lending risks in place. Nevertheless, the lending units would somehow appraise, recommend, and obtain approval for the loans. Often, when this happens, the credit admin staff would be saddled with mitigating risks arising from failings in such otherwise complementary lending roles.

As I mentioned earlier, it is given that in fulfilling their role, credit admin officers sometimes confront entrenched negative lending and borrowing practices. As a bulwark against credit risk, credit admin staff must overcome this problem—one that has become the most debilitating contemporary challenge of their functions. Indeed, the success of credit admin depends mostly on ingenuity with which its officers discharge such responsibilities. Another success requirement is ability of credit admin officers to be neutral but assertive at all times, especially on controversial lending matters—no matter whose ox is gored.

In practical terms, credit admin is challenged by certain tasks that tend to diminish its roles in some banks. Its contemporary challenges derive mainly from attitudes of the parties to credit relationships. There are yet challenges that result from regulatory maneuverings, legal difficulties, and role conflicts between marketing and credit control staff. In the same vein, the quality of the lending portfolio, socioeconomic environment of business, and characterizing morals and values of the people shape the challenges of credit admin functions. I present these issues in the following discussions.

Attitude of loan parties

Banks that have foolproof lending criteria tend to have authoritative credit administration units. Such banks have clear target markets definition, risk acceptance criteria, and unambiguous delineation of lending responsibilities. In terms of attitude, credit admin staff would most likely discharge their duties with ease in banks that are characterized by the following attributes:

- Strong and responsible management, as well as disciplined, honest, and dedicated lending officers
- Zero tolerance for extant or prospective borrowing accounts that show a tendency to fraudulent activities
- Passion for quality risk assets portfolio that strictly align with prudential guidelines for risk assets classifications
- Unwavering lending focus in less volatile sectors of the economy and, especially, on riskless transactions

The foregoing implies that the effectiveness of credit admin can be more or less enhanced depending on values that banks uphold. Credit admin would be effective in banks that strive to conduct lending activities in strict observance of credit policy guidelines. On the other hand, credit admin would be ineffective in banks that pay lip service to credit policy.

It is doubtful that banks that have weak lending disposition will or do prescribe appropriate sanctions against officers who flout credit policy. From the customers' perspective, credit admin functions would be less daunting in banks that have few or no fraudulent borrowers than in banks that have a large number of dubious borrowing accounts. Thus, administering the lending portfolio would pose an intractable challenge where borrowers deliberately cheat banks or default on the terms and conditions of their credit facilities.

In dealing with negative attitude of borrowers, credit admin has a two-pronged contemporary challenge. Firstly, it should be capable of evolving and sustaining devices for a comprehensive tracking of loans performance. Secondly, it should be able to detect early warning signs of loan default. With proven data gathering capability, it should effectively furnish senior management with up-to-date reports on both individual credit facilities and the total lending portfolio. Of these two challenges, detecting early signs of loan default is more challenging. This is due to obvious problems of understanding and dealing with unpredictable human behavior. Yet, there are basic indicators of impending loan default.

Most bad loans would have exhibited certain traits as default warning signs before they eventually became bad debts. Discerning credit admin officers will detect such early default warning signs. Once detected, appropriate remedial actions should be devised and enforced to remedy the affected loans. Often loan default follows a decisive pattern. The loan deteriorates to substandard performance, degenerates to a doubtful asset, and ultimately makes a lost asset statistic.

How can credit admin officers identify early warning signs of loan default? When identified, what appropriate steps could they take to reverse the trend? These questions add to the challenges of administering the lending portfolio. The early warning signs of loan default that show consistent pattern of incidence in most banks relate to unusual customer actions, changing loan attributes, and informal third-party inquiries.

Environment of business

The task of administering the lending portfolio can indeed be really challenging. This is especially the case where many borrowing customers operate in highly volatile business environments. Difficulty also arises where most of the borrowers engage in speculative or other risky transactions. An unstable business environment creates risk management tension bank-wide. Given this situation, the challenge of credit admin is to ensure that all safety measures are put in place to safeguard risk assets against adverse effects of turbulent business environment.

Some of the causes of business volatility, and the related risks of lending, might not be correctly foreseen at the time of packaging credit facilities. Therefore, credit admin officers must provide a prognosis of the future risks of credit facilities that a bank is considering granting to borrowers. They should be able to anticipate and proffer measures that will mitigate the impact of the risks if they eventually occur. Thus, credit admin functions would be adjudged to fail where avoidable risks cause actual or potential loss of credit facilities. This is notwithstanding that such risks might not have been anticipated at the time of granting the loans.

Some would argue that credit compliance officers should not be held accountable for incidence of credit risks and losses associated with them. After all, they do not package credit facilities in the first place. They also do not interact with borrowers and their businesses. It is possible to glean information about current and anticipated business trends and risks through these avenues. This school of thought posits that credit and marketing staff—credit analysts, account officers, relationship managers, and, indeed, members of the lending units—rather than credit control officers, should be accountable for lapses in anticipating, analyzing, and updating risk-mitigating measures. In its opinion, these issues form part of marketing intelligence to which credit admin is not orientated.

The counter arguments, nonetheless, are also worth mentioning. The opposing school of thought contends that credit and marketing staff are driven more by business (budget or profit) than risk management goals. Thus, they are less likely than credit control staff to show interest in, or appreciate, future risks of extant and intended credit facilities. Therefore, someone that would not be distracted by income and profit considerations—most preferably, credit compliance staff—must do the work.

The appropriate thing is for credit control staff to account for losses arising from unmitigated risks of unpredictable business environment. Management must of necessity clarify this position to all members of the bank. Once it does so, credit admin staff should assume primary responsibility for credit risk management advocacy bank-wide. This also becomes a challenge that they must face up to. Otherwise, there would be unnecessary buck passing between credit admin, credit appraisal, marketing, and relationship management staff. In such a situation, the bank will be the real loser.

Ameliorating quality of loans

One of the important contemporary challenges of credit administration functions is determination of how, what means, and with what resources, to ameliorate the quality of risk assets. Most banks seek to achieve planned reduction in amount of delinquent loans. Thus, they work to check the rates of deterioration of risk assets quality and therefore default on credit facilities. In order to achieve these goals, the bank management continually reinforces credit admin functions and activities as a deliberate risk management strategy.

A remarkable finding about the low quality of risk assets portfolio in most banks is undue concentration of lending in particular, often highly risky, sectors of the economy. Such undiversified lending might be driven by profit motive, but it does more harm than good to the bank's bottom line in the end. Why, for instance, should more than 25% of a bank's risk assets portfolio comprise loans granted to, say, commerce or trading enterprises? In some banks loan concentrations in such risky economic sectors are yet as high as more than 75%!

Credit admin should seek to reverse this unhealthy lending trend with a view to spreading risk of lending and ensuring that the bank is ever resilient. It should always uphold this principle—notwithstanding the turn of events in times of unexpected market shocks. One of the ways of attaining this goal is to work out modalities for sectoral distribution of credit facilities. This should be done without jeopardizing or distorting budget targets of the lending units. Indeed, marketing, lending, and income targets should be defined in the context of risk management programs. Once this is done, it becomes the responsibility of credit admin to provide monitoring support to attain the expectations of bank management on risk mitigation.

Maneuvering returns on risk assets

Most banks are nowadays under immense pressure to render certain statutory returns to the regulatory authorities in ways that suit their special circumstances. This is particularly the case with returns on risk assets portfolios that form part of the functions of credit admin. The immediate question to ponder is how credit admin would deal with the dual tasks of meeting the special circumstances of the bank without infringing on regulatory requirements and incurring avoidable sanctions. In extreme situations, the pressure could culminate in falsification of the returns data.

Perhaps misrepresentation of credit returns data is more glaring in the specific areas of reporting insider credits, ratings, and classification of credit facilities according to the prudential guidelines. Ordinarily, credit admin will want to render accurate returns based on observed facts of credit facilities that make up the lending portfolio. However, its disposition to doing so might be constrained by certain entrenched (internal) negative interests. Often, the negative interests exist at directorate and executive management levels and are oiled by greed and selfishness. Sometimes, the internal interests could be positive for the bank but detrimental to the interests of society or the public. This happens, for example, when returns on particular credit facilities or the entire lending portfolio are manipulated to obviate sanctions against obvious cases of breach of regulatory policies. A typical example to illustrate this practice is seen in the flouting of rules for the Small and Medium Enterprises Investment Equity Scheme.

In these conflicts of interest, credit admin would come under fire if it misreads the mood of bank management. Credit admin might appreciate and not want to disregard the special circumstances of the bank. However, such circumstances might be in conflict with regulatory requirements and guidelines. While satisfying the interests of the bank, it is yet expected not to infringe upon the rules of returns to the regulatory authorities. This is one of the critical contemporary challenges that credit admin faces in the exercise of its functions.

MAKING CREDIT ADMIN WORK

One of the difficult decisions that bank management must make is how—not whether—to empower credit admin officers to be able to discharge their duties without fear or favor. Yet, a more intractable decision is whether or not to uphold that credit admin should always render accurate returns to the regulatory authorities—no matter whose interest is at stake. Credit admin officers will discharge their responsibilities more or less effectively depending on the direction in which these important decisions tilt. In the absence of support, understanding, and cooperation of bank management and the lending units, credit admin staff would be frustrated. They would lose the zeal with which they should discharge their oversight responsibilities under the circumstances.

QUESTIONS FOR DISCUSSION AND REVIEW

1. What is the significance of prudential classifications of, and provisioning on, the lending portfolio?

2. Why should credit administration institutionalize review of the risk assets database as an integral part of its functions?
3. **(a)** What are the functions of the credit strategy committee (CRESCO)?
   (b) How can the performance of CRESCO be optimized in the cutthroat world of banking?
4. **(a)** Why would a bank set up and institutionalize a watch-list committee?
   (b) What are the limitations of the committee?
5. How does credit admin fulfill its role as a bulwark against credit risk?

REFERENCE

Central Bank of Nigeria, 1997. Policy circular BSD/PA/4/97 – Prudential guidelines for licensed banks. In: Nigeria Deposit Insurance Corporation. (1997). Review of developments in banking and finance during the second half of 1997. NDIC Quarterly, 7(3/4)

Managing Non-Performing
Credit Facilities

Chapter 31

Incidence and Crisis of Delinquent Loans in Emerging Markets

LEARNING FOCUS AND OUTCOMES

The lending portfolio of a bank typically comprises both performing and delinquent credit facilities. In most cases, performing loans dominate the portfolio—contributing quality income to the bottom line. Nonperforming credits, on the other hand, trigger troubles for a bank. Often they plunge a bank into crisis when they impair the ability of a bank to meet its liquidity needs. It is imperative for this reason that banks work out an effective credit risk management methodology, one that anticipates delinquent loans and offers remedial options for them.

Unfortunately, the exact reasons behind the worrying incidence of delinquent loans in banks in emerging markets are by no means fully understood. That the banks have methodological frameworks for managing lending risks may not be disputed. Rather, what may be disputed is the quality of lending decisions. Certainly, banks in emerging markets adopt standard credit analysis techniques that focus on variables related to the borrower, industry (in the case of corporate borrowers), and prevailing economic conditions. Yet, bad debt

Emerging Market Bank Lending and Credit Risk Control. http://dx.doi.org/10.1016/B978-0-12-803438-5.00031-3
557

remains one of the most disturbing problems of the banks and has on occasion threatened the survival of the industry.

Perhaps in addition to the traditional credit risk factors, there is an interplay of hidden elements that crystallizes loan default. What are these elements? How should they be anticipated and controlled? I set out in this chapter to provide answers to these questions. In doing so, my objective is to contribute knowledge about how to mitigate the incidence of nonperforming risk assets. Under the assumption that risk correlates positively with bad debt, I postulate that the real problem lies in the approach to risk identification, analysis, and control. This postulation builds on my investigation of factors that lending officers overlook in credit analysis. My assessment of the extent to which these factors contribute to the problem of bad debts in bank lending strengthens the postulation.

Against the backdrop of the foregoing background, I examine risks inherent in the lending function, review the approach to credit risk management, and identify lapses in current practice and the credit policy implications of the observed lapses. My conclusions shed light on the evolving global trend and crisis of bad loans in banks. A way forward, to my mind, lies in the methodology.

The crisis of credit risk has assumed immense dimensions of late. Banks are grappling with the problem with little success. After studying the topics discussed in this chapter, you will have learned:

- The major causes and consequences of credit default and crisis in banks
- Why credit analysis has not been totally effective in solving loan defaults
- The implications of bad debts and credit risk crisis for bank management
- About issues in the contemporary crisis of delinquent loans in banks
- The import and dynamics of "fulfillment illusion" in analyzing the causes of bad debts in banks

MEANING OF "BAD DEBT" IN BANKING

In general business, the usual meaning of the phrase *bad debt* is often associated with credit sales that have low probability of being recovered from debtors. It depicts, strictly speaking, debtors from whom a seller, supplier, or contractor of goods or services has little or no hope of recovering any or all receivables or credit sales. In other words, the loss of the debt could as well be regarded as a foregone conclusion—and therefore should be provided for and written off in the annual financial statements of the company.

In banking, however, the term *bad debt* assumes a somewhat more rigorous meaning. It denotes the climax in the progressive deterioration of the condition of a credit facility (i.e., a risk asset) that a bank grants to a borrower, such that the probability of recovery of the loan tends to zero. For the bank to face this level of credit risk, the loan must first and foremost be *classified* in the bank's books as nonperforming. The classification may be made by the bank, its auditors, or the regulatory authorities—which in Nigeria are represented by the Central Bank of Nigeria and the Nigeria Deposit Insurance Corporation. The nonperforming loans—otherwise referred to as *loans of doubtful value* (LDV)—are then categorized according to prudential guidelines into substandard, doubtful, and lost credit facilities—depending on the degree of deterioration in their quality.

Following the categorization, lost credits represent the terminal risk of lending for banks. Ideally, it is this category of nonperforming loans (i.e., those classified as *lost* credit facilities) that should ordinarily be regarded as the real bad debts. This is notwithstanding that provisions are required against possible losses on the substandard and doubtful loans. Indeed, the substandard and doubtful credits represent intermediate risks, as they often still have high probabilities of being repaid, even on their due dates. This implies that in the banking parlance, the phrase *nonperforming loan* is broader in meaning than *bad debt*.

SUMMARY OF GENERAL OBSERVATIONS

Banks adopt a standard risk management approach involving analysis of the borrower's character, capacity, capital, and collateral, as well as the general conditions of the economy. These risk factors subsume a wide range of elements usually analyzed as *key credit issues*, including financial statements and ratios, feasibility reports, and transaction dynamics, as well as the borrower's company, product markets, and industry. It would appear that this approach has generally not been totally effective, judging by the high rate of increase in the incidence of nonperforming loans in banks.

Credit officers suggest appropriate *ways out* for risks that they identify with the loans they recommend for approval. The suggestions should have the potency to cushion the effects of a risk or prevent a loan loss if properly administered. In principle, where a *way out* cannot be found for a risk, the bank should decline the credit request. However, surprisingly, loans may yet be granted based on a relationship or other considerations, even though the risks have not been mitigated.

Loan default can be minimized by properly structuring credit facilities and requiring loan guarantors to collateralize their guarantees. Presently, most banks do not ask for collateral against personal guarantees securing loans to third parties. As a result, the requirement for a personal guarantee has been a mere procedural issue in the lending process. Borrowers will be more committed to their transactions and repayment of credit facilities if their guarantors collateralize their pledges.

It would appear that the greatest threat to a bank's competitive strength is the observed high rate of bad and doubtful loans. If a bank has a quality risk assets portfolio, it will have improved competitive strength. Indeed, bad debts should be minimized to a level that ensures that a bank's competitive position is not undermined. This provides a feasible way to insulate the bank against liquidity crisis, distress, and failure.

How then should banks identify and manage the unusual credit risk factors that sometimes crystallize bad debts—risks that are not usually identified and analyzed as part of the general credit process? It is to this question that I now turn my attention as I discuss the critical causes of loan default.

CRITICAL CAUSES OF LOAN DEFAULT

Credit risks arise when a bank lends money with the expectation that the borrower will service and repay the loan in accordance with its terms and conditions. This expectation usually hinges on pertinent considerations, particularly the lending officer's favorable judgment about the:

- Borrower's creditworthiness
- Capacity of the borrower to execute the transaction for which the bank grants the loan
- Collateral the borrower offers to secure the loan
- Borrower's stake or capital in the business
- Anticipated impact of extraneous conditions on the credit

Credit risk crystallizes when the borrower defaults on the loan as a result of adverse alteration in the lending officer's expectations of one or more of foregoing variables. The default may be a result of nonpayment or delayed payment.

In the process of financing a diverse group of borrowers in the economy, this becomes worrying in view of the fact that banks are often constrained to borrow short and lend long. This raises the question as to why borrowers default on loans. The traditional credit analysis technique, by itself, has not been effective in solving all loan-related risk and default problems. The *hidden* or sometimes *overlooked* factors that create risk management difficulties for lending officers include but are not limited to the following:

- Inability to *monitor* loan utilization and the performance that the borrower achieves on the loan
- Lack of credit analysis capability in several lending areas in which banks venture
- Use of *distorted* financial statements and business information as a credit analysis base
- Relying on *uncertain* operational cash flows, projected on assumptions or from historical data, for loan repayment
- Failure of lending officers—including top management staff with credit approval authority, and board members (especially those with majority equity investments in banks)—to observe significant internal credit approval and disbursement rules

- Unanticipated adverse changes in the original terms and conditions of a credit facility
- Insider abuse perpetrated by bank officials through fraudulent lending and transactions

In managing the lending portfolio to attain desired results, a bank should pay adequate attention to the foregoing factors. The considerations at issue might not be applicable in all lending situations, or they could be of less consequence in some loan proposals. But it is important that whenever risk is indicated on account of poor analysis of any or all of the factors, the lending decision should be suspended, declined, or made with satisfactory mitigating conditions. In the following discussions, I try to analyze the incidence and possible effects of risk-contributory elements to the crisis of bad debts in banks.

Poor monitoring of loan

It is a regrettable fact that many credit facilities granted by banks do easily go bad nowadays. Yet one of the critical responsibilities of lending officers is to do anything but carelessly allow a credit facility to degenerate to a nonperforming or lost credit statistic. Consider that the practice of ensuring that borrowers repay their credit facilities follows guided processes of packaging, approval, documentation, and disbursement of loans. Assuming that each of these loan commitment stages has been painstakingly carried out—as should ordinarily be the practice—why would the borrower after all default on the loan?

As I pointed out earlier, several reasons could be adduced for loan default, but lack of or poor monitoring of credit facilities *after* disbursement is curious, as it leaves a lot to be desired. Huge annual loan losses due to nonmonitoring or poor monitoring of credit facilities remain one of the most worrisome risks of lending for banks. Failings in loan monitoring inexplicably continue to exacerbate the risk of bank lending. One reason is that as a risk-mitigating device, the monitoring of a loan is within the control of a bank. So if a bank cannot effectively manage credit risk with in-house resources—such as the use of lending officers to monitor credit facilities—how on earth can it cope with other, more tasking, risks of lending that are outside its control? This question underscores concerns of banking experts and analysts about the incidence and crisis of delinquent loans.

However, some would argue that loan officers do not deliberately neglect to carry out the monitoring assignment. Rather, it's often argued that the *inability* of lending officers to monitor certain credit transactions is the matter at issue. This argument tends to absolve lending officers from blame. There could be merit in this viewpoint. There could be situations in which modes of loan utilization might be complex. Also, the dynamics of some credit transactions might dictate reliance on the borrowers' integrity for good utilization and satisfactory performance on the credit facilities. Such transactions might not lend themselves to any predetermined monitoring schemes by the lending officers. Even where reasonable control over funds utilization can be achieved, lending officers would probably still find it difficult to monitor borrowers' *continuing* good performance with regard to the terms and conditions of credit facilities. A loan that faces this risk will have a high probability of being lost to the borrower. This problem is common in granting an overdraft facility to finance working capital needs. In that case, the bank depends mainly on the borrower's financial performance to achieve satisfactory loan repayment.

Those opposed to the foregoing thinking would argue that many lending officers are simply lazy. Lending officers, according to this school of thought, tend to feel fulfilled once income on a loan is booked and the asset portfolio increases as a result of the incremental lending—and management recognizes these *positive* performance criteria as the officer's contributions. This fulfillment *illusion* does not abate until the performance of the credit facility begins to relapse. Then the need for close monitoring of the loan and the borrower's actions becomes accentuated—but it would have been too late. The illusory good performance of the loan at the early stages of the banking relationship with the borrower is perhaps the *culprit* which bank management should deal with.

There are certain controls that bank management could put in place that could forestall the *lazy* or *laidback* attitude of some credit officers that results in the observed loan monitoring failings. I mention three such controls as follows:

- Once identified—in terms of prolonged poor loan performance warning signs—the tendency of lending (or account) officers to rest on their oars *after* disbursement of credit facilities should be promptly sanctioned with formal *queries, caution,* or *warning* letters.
- Documentation of important *call memos*—copied to responsible senior management staff of the bank—with respect to occasional visits to major borrowers (including periodic reviews of their businesses and financial performance) should be mandatory for all account officers and relationship managers.
- Lending or account officers and relationship managers who manage loans that go bad as a result of proven negligence, nonchalance, or dereliction of duty reflected in loan monitoring failings should be appropriately punished. Punishment could be to defer their promotion or withhold their performance bonus or other perquisites.

The incidence of loan default as a result of nonmonitoring or poor monitoring would be minimized, if not entirely eliminated, if these measures were introduced and effectively implemented. The recommended sanctions against negligent officers are intended to underlie the importance of loan monitoring to the survival or continuing success of a bank. However, in a competitive work environment, the corollary should not be ignored. Lending or account officers and relationship managers who achieve superior performance with respect to loan monitoring should be rewarded with promotions, bonuses, or other perquisites.

Lack of credit analysis capability

There could be instances where banks poorly define their critical target markets, risk acceptance criteria, and resource requirements for lending purposes. In some cases, strictly speaking, these business criteria might not have been given serious consideration in making lending decisions. Besides, banks tend to jump on the bandwagon when they choose particular lines of lending or play in certain target markets. By doing so, they tend to sacrifice credit risk to the following fallible considerations:

- Perceived probable *profitability* of lending transactions
- *Prestige* of transacting business in particular coveted target markets
- Insatiable urge to keep expanding the *growth* of the bank

Blurred by these flawed business goals, the bank could be plunged into avoidable credit crisis in the future when some or most of the loans become delinquent and make the lost credits statistics.

In the Nigerian setting, consider the flourishing banking business of lending to the energy (oil and gas) sector of the economy. The *boom* was dictated by the consideration that energy was easily one of the vibrant sectors of the Nigerian economy at the turn of the twenty-first century. One reason is that it attracts the largest foreign direct private investment and returns the most foreign exchange earnings to the country. Indeed, crude oil exports account for over 80 percent of Nigeria's foreign exchange earnings. Unfortunately, these fallible considerations seem to blur the risks inherent in lending to the energy sector. The ideal response, which is the filling of any in-house skills gaps, is inexplicably neglected. This has resulted in huge loan losses for banks.

Some banks that uncritically delved into energy-sector lending without the requisite in-house technical expertise ended up counting their losses. Soon they become susceptible to bank distress syndrome as a result of the accumulation of large stocks of nonperforming risk assets. Some of Nigeria's new-generation banks in the country's pre-banking-system-consolidation era that had recurring or lingering liquidity crises had huge nonperforming loans to the oil and gas sector.

In general, loan difficulties might originate from or be triggered by several factors, including the following:

- Poor *structuring* of credit facilities
- Conflicts caused by unanticipated *indistinct* transaction dynamics
- The bank's superficial knowledge of or *inexperience* in the lines of business it finances

These lending problems become acute where credit analysts don't have the required technical proficiency to produce thorough and rigorous appraisals of particular loan requests. Perhaps driven by competitive pressure, some banks tend to engage in or undertake certain lending activities for which they do not possess the necessary credit analysis capabilities. This could arise when the purpose of lending is to finance a *technical* transaction for which a certain level of expertise, which the bank does not have in-house, can be relied on for *quality* risk analysis.

There might be the need to engage some external assistance to understand the details of the credit proposal and to prepare a realistic credit report on the transaction. However, banks rarely refer such unique credit analysis jobs to *external* experts for their professional advice. This reluctance by banks might be a result of their inclination to maintain the confidentiality of customers' transactions. The concomitant credit reports—under the circumstances—would be flawed, lead to wrong credit decision, and increase the probability of loan loss.

Distorted financial statements

Lending decisions are sometimes based on an assessment of financial performance derived from analysis of the *distorted* financial statements of the borrower. Most companies prepare audited accounts to suit their external financing needs and tax liability expectations. This category of financial reports generally yields *good* performance indicators from liquidity and leverage analyses. The incidence of loan default tends to be high, however, when bank management relies on the analysis of such financial reports to make lending decisions. In a bid to mitigate the risk associated with the use of distorted financial statements in making lending decisions, banks started stipulating standards for acceptance of financial statements for credit analysis.

Banks nowadays demand that financial statements of borrowers must be audited and certified by reputable chartered accounting firms. This is now a prerequisite for the use of financial statements as source documents for credit analysis and in making lending decisions. There is no doubt that the use of certified audited financial statements has helped to mitigate credit risk. Yet it has proven incapable of completely *preventing* misleading accounting data, and reports, that influence lending decisions. The implied risk of lending is also prevalent in analyzing start-up projects for lending purposes based on misleading feasibility reports. Overall credit risk increases with incomplete or inaccurate information relating to the loan request—after all, some would argue, *people's judgments cannot be better than their information.*

The failure of traditional credit analysis methodology derives from its inherent weaknesses. One of the weaknesses is that bank management relies heavily on financial statement analysis in making lending decisions. As I pointed out above, this approach is fraught with inadequacies. For this reason and practical purposes, it is advised that bankers place only limited reliance on audited financial statements in making lending decisions.

Notwithstanding this contention, financial statement analysis remains invaluable to bank management in lending functions. In order to be more useful to lending decisions, historical and projected financial statement analysis should be subjected to critical sensitivity tests. The tests should be based on realistic assumptions about probable future trends in economic, business, and financial performance. Credit analysts can deduce conclusions from possible scenarios of anticipated future events that might alter forecasts and observed historical financial data.

The view that I uphold in this book is that quality corporate lending decisions are made when lending officers painstakingly analyze financial statements of borrowers in relation to the types and amounts of loans they request. I demonstrated this with analysis of the financial statements of Nigerian Breweries PLC and PZ Industries PLC in Chapters 23 and 24 of this book. Yet it would be inappropriate to rely *solely* on such historical financial reports and analyses to ultimately make lending decisions. Other factors that might have an impact on a bank's decision to lend should be equally considered. I demonstrated how credit analysts can analyze a medley of credit risk factors in Chapter 27 of this book.

Uncertain cash flow projections

There is also need to examine the influence of cash flow statements and analysis in bank lending. Let me state at the outset that the consideration of cash flows exerts an enormous influence on the decision whether to lend money to loan applicants. Indeed, lending officers generally have unwavering confidence in the strength of cash flow analysis and projections for loan repayment. With adequate controls, the efficacy of cash flows in meeting loan service and repayment obligations can be taken for granted—especially in self-liquidating asset-based transactions. This is because the transaction dynamics of such credit facilities are usually simple—consisting mainly of fulfilling the following:

- Identifying the asset to be financed
- Determining how the asset would be liquidated—and by whom
- Ascertaining the possible value to be realized
- Making the lending decision

In balance sheet lending, there is usually an assumption that observed cash flow performance is a good basis for future cash flow forecasts. Thus, supported with general business assumptions, lending officers often inadvertently recommend financing of otherwise risky transactions—especially long-term projects—on the strength of uncertain future cash flows. This approach might not be justifiably criticized. The prominence accorded to cash flow in credit analysis is technically defensible on the grounds that it relates to the flow of cash without which borrowers cannot repay their debts, pay wages and salaries, and meet other financial obligations. But the risk of this approach crystallizes when borrowers fail to realize projected cash inflows.

This implies that there should not be total dependence on cash flow projections in making lending decisions. Perhaps, except for start-up projects (in which case there will be no past financial records), it would be useful to compare the actual (historical) and projected (future) cash flows before recommending the credit proposal to senior management for approval. Also, as in analyzing distorted financial statements, projected cash flows should be sensitized to indicate or gauge the possible effects of certain adverse events on the projections.

Perversion of credit process

Risks are also often introduced in the lending process when lending officers fail to observe credit approval and disbursement rules. In most cases, unfortunately, perversion of the credit process happens in furtherance of lending fraud. A standard lending procedure commonly adopted by banks is as follows:

- Credit officer prepares a loan report detailing analysis and recommendations to senior management. The report becomes the basis of a further consideration of the loan request by the credit strategy committee—and depending on the amount involved, by the board audit and credit committee.
- If the credit facility is granted, the borrower is issued an offer letter, a copy of which the borrower executes to indicate acceptance of the credit facility on its particular terms and conditions. In some lending situations, an elaborate loan agreement would be required in addition to the offer letter.
- Borrower submits and executes all security documents required by the bank as collateral for the loan. The legal unit vets and perfects the bank's charge on the collateral.
- Credit policy and control unit reviews the credit process to ensure that it meets the bank's lending criteria. It also manages documentation of the credit and confirms satisfaction of conditions precedent to drawdown by the borrower.
- The credit facility is disbursed according to the agreement between the bank and the borrower.

Most of these requirements would be satisfied before a bank disburses the credit facility. However, on occasion banks find it expedient to disburse certain credit facilities without putting proper documentation in place or perfecting the necessary legal charges. This avoidable situation creates most of the lending risks that cause loan default. Indeed, banks often make hasty lending decisions. This frequently results in loan losses as a result of poor structuring and perhaps nonmonitoring of the utilization of approved credit facilities. This avoidable practice deviates from professional lending practices.

An uncritical disposition to the lending function would portend grave future liquidity consequences for the bank. But it is absurd to contemplate, let alone really observe, that bank management often makes unnecessary hasty lending decisions. One reason is that the careless loss of a credit facility has a general income depletion multiplier effect on the bank. In other words, the income expected from a hastily granted credit facility might be infinitesimal compared with the impact of the loan loss on the bank's earnings. It is important for bank management to follow due process in granting credit facilities. By doing so, the bank's interests should be placed above the individual interests or self-interests of the loan-approving authorities.

Unanticipated adverse conditions

Lending officers often make erroneous judgments about loan defaulters when they believe that the inability or failure of a borrower to pay back a loan is deliberate. It is now common knowledge that most of the factors that cause loan default are exogenously induced, especially in less-developed countries. Often in less-developed countries, the inability or failure of borrowers to honor their loan repayment obligations arises mainly from distortions in the business environment or malfunctions of the economy. The effects of a dismal economy become more debilitating to businesses when they are, for all practical purposes, unanticipated or unpredictable.

Consider, for example, the situation in Nigeria when in 2002 it took an average of three months to clear a container of consignment from Apapa Wharf. The delay was caused by a sudden change in inspection policy that introduced 100 percent destination inspection as against the previously adopted preshipment inspection. The change had far-reaching effects on transactions that benefited from bank lending:

- Business calculations were dashed—perishable goods (such as fruit juice drinks) financed with bank loans were damaged.
- The amount of unpaid accrued and compounding interest on credit facilities soared.
- Allegations were rife about brazen corruption of officials at the seaports that exacerbated the problems of bank-funded credit transactions.

One importer actually took photographs of his rotten and stale juice drinks at the seaport to his bank to prove the reason for his failure to repay his import finance facility with the bank. His account officer, who visited the seaport at the time, corroborated the incident and thereafter recommended classification of the loan with a view to writing it off in due course. Such unfortunate mishaps, whenever they occurred, were borne largely by the borrowers, many of whom defaulted on their bank loans. The lending banks eventually also share in the losses.

There was also an instance where traders who borrowed funds from banks to import goods that were levied duty at not more than 40% woke up to the stark reality of an unanticipated hike of custom duty on the goods to 100%. The upward revision of the duty rate in some cases took retroactive effect and caught the traders napping. But they must meet their obligations to the banks that financed the import transactions.

Insider abuse

The incidence of problems associated with flagrant abuse of office by bank officials with lending responsibilities has been a major cause of loan defaults in banks in Nigeria. It would seem that the problem defies solution, given that it reverberates around most analyses of bank distress and failure. Some would probably argue that insider abuse in bank lending functions has degenerated to a systemic crisis level. Those who hold this view believe that the problem should be confronted with the arsenal of banking regulation and supervision, for the survival of the industry.

Why are these acts perpetrated in banks? Who are indeed the parties responsible for these enduring but discredited lending practices? In what ways have these acts retarded the growth of the banking system? What legal framework exists to deal with the problem of insider abuse in bank lending? It would be interesting to investigate the issues implied in these questions, but they are beyond the scope of this book.

QUESTIONS FOR DISCUSSION AND REVIEW

1. What are the major causes and consequences of loan default?
2. In what sense is the term "bad debt" used and understood in banking?
3. How can you account for the contemporary crisis of delinquent loans in banks?
4. Do you agree that there is a bandwagon effect in the making of credit crises in banks?
5. What are the dynamics and import of "fulfillment illusion" in the analysis of the causes of bad debts in banks?
6. Why has credit analysis not been effective in solving loan default?

Chapter 32

Demystifying Loan Default Warning Signs in Emerging Markets

Chapter Outline

LEARNING FOCUS AND OUTCOMES

It is instructive that most risk assets that have high default probabilities show early warning signs. First they deteriorate to substandard performance. Then the loans degenerate to doubtful accounts before ultimately becoming lost credits statistics. In Chapter 30, I discussed substandard, doubtful, and lost credits in the context of prudential provisioning as approved by Nigeria's banking system regulatory authorities. In the present chapter, I focus on the early warning signs of loan default. How can lending officers identify early warning signs of loan default? When identified, what appropriate steps could they take to reverse observed threats to a credit facility?

When a loan is performing in accordance with the agreement between the bank and borrower, servicing of interest is up to date, turnover of transactions in the account are appreciable, principal and the agreed mode of repayment are observed. Also, the borrower is disposed to visit and meet with bank officials in a bid to strengthen the banking relationship for their mutual benefit. The yield on the loan would depict a consistent, sometimes increasing, and positive contribution to earnings. Incidentally, a loan that tends to default would be associated not only with the reverse of these attributes, but certain preemptive signs. Some of the obvious early warning signs of loan default could be inferred from actions of the borrower, changing attributes of the loan, and

Emerging Market Bank Lending and Credit Risk Control. http://dx.doi.org/10.1016/B978-0-12-803438-5.00032-5

sometimes curious inquiries from third parties. I must mention at once that there is no uniform pattern of early warning signs applicable to all credit facilities and borrowers.

How can lending officers in emerging markets effectively anticipate the early warning signs of loan default? When identified, what appropriate steps could account officers and relationship managers take to check possible threats to the loan? While answering these questions, I proffer remote causes of loan default and the implications of the early warning signs for credit risk management in bank lending—based on true lessons of experience.

In emerging markets, a loan that is destined to go bad exhibits observable traits that discerning loan officers could detect. Once detected, follow-up becomes necessary and informs the appropriate management response. You will learn how:

- Banks in emerging markets may guide their management and lending officers to appreciate their credit risk appetite
- Lending officers in emerging markets can anticipate and possibly address early warning signs of loan default
- Appropriate steps taken by lending officers can check possible threats to a bank's risk assets
- Direct liability for poor credit decisions can improve the quality of a bank's risk assets portfolio
- Banks in emerging markets can strengthen their credit risk management techniques and capabilities

UNUSUAL CUSTOMER ACTIONS

It is frequently observed that in most cases where loans tend to default, the borrowers become elusive. They not only subtly flout the loan agreement, but also deliberately avoid the bank and its loan officers. Without regrets, the borrowers in this situation begin to act in strange ways. Typically, they:

- snub invitations to meetings with lending and other bank officers
- rebuff telephone calls from their account officers and relationship managers
- feign to be inaccessible even when they are in their offices

A careful review of the loan accounts of borrowers in this category at this point would reveal a tendency to default. Perhaps, interest is not being serviced, principal repayment might be past due, scheduled rental payments might be in arrears (in the case of lease facilities), and transaction turnover may have shrunk to a dismal low level.

There are several other borrower actions that show obvious signs of impending loan default that, unfortunately, lending officers often overlook. Often, once borrowers are convinced that they are not able to repay their loans, they begin to make hollow excuses. In most cases, the excuses border on lies about the deteriorating state of their businesses. The borrowers would not be remorseful about their failed promises, such as to make specified lodgments to their loan accounts. But the lies that they tell are meant to camouflage imminent default on their loans. At this point, borrowers generally parry questions and inquiries by their account officers or loan officers. Crafty borrowers pretend to be sorry—and might indeed gain the sympathy of the bank—about the *adverse* turn of events affecting their businesses and accounts. Particular references to verifiable or specific business feats on which loan repayment is anchored might after all be flukes. Unknown to the bank, in most cases, the borrowers could be merely buying time before actual default on their loans becomes apparent and unavoidable.

Under the circumstances, there would be a spate of miscellaneous complaints and threats by the borrowers to repudiate one or more of their loan covenants. With such complaints, it would be apparent that all might not be well with the loan account. This would be especially so if the complaints are unusual and expressed in difficult requests. Such problematic complaints are commonly observed in borrowers' requests for the following:

- An interest rebate that does not take account of the cost of funds to the bank or prevailing money market conditions
- Concession on or waiver of fees and commissions, as well as resistance to any form of charges to the account
- Rescheduling of loan repayment terms—extensions of due dates, rollovers, or renewals of loans with unsatisfactory performance

In most cases, borrowers try to rationalize these requests on the grounds of poor business that has adversely affected their cash flow projections. But the complaints are often preceded by recurrent periods of sluggish activity levels reflected in dwindling transaction turnover and low gross yields on loans.

Soon the loans begin to experience partial abandonment as the accounts become somewhat dormant. Lending officers should seek to preempt this risk by investigating and mitigating the declining fortunes of loan accounts. They should start by asking the following pertinent questions:

- Could it be that the borrowers have switched patronage to other banks where, perhaps as nonborrowing customers with high turnover potential, they enjoy some preferential treatment?
- Is there any real link between observed waning performance of the loans and the prevailing business climate?
- Have the borrowers put up any positive checks or responses against any threats to their businesses?

These questions must be answered if lending officers will successfully determine whether the borrowers deliberately want to default. But the situation clearly represents an early warning sign that the loans in question could go bad.

CHANGING LOAN ATTRIBUTES

Identification of loans destined to default, from the perspective of their attributes, is perhaps the easiest for lending officers, bank auditors, and regulatory authorities. Actions of borrowers who default could be illusory on account of the subjective nature of human behavior. However, adverse changes in largely objective characteristics of loans can scarcely be misrepresented. For example, recurring incidents of returned checks for a borrowing account that never had such a history would be a sign that the loan could be facing a risk of default.

A similar inference could be drawn from observing a sustained declining volume of transactions and profitability of a loan account to the bank. From regular daily lodging of cash and checks, inflow of deposits into the account becomes rather occasional. In some cases, inflows into the account might even stop for days, weeks, or months—depending on the real condition of the loan. The observed decline of the loan may be the result of a lull in business, or deliberate diversion of transactions to another bank from which the borrower might have also obtained a loan. Ordinarily, it is expected that when borrowers are experiencing losses in their businesses, their loan accounts may not be performing. Thus, the resilience that the businesses impart to the loan accounts would be lost.

Perhaps the clearest indications of early warning signs of imminent loan default are provided in the prudential guidelines that strictly characterize nonperforming loans in both objective and subjective terms. Among the subjective criteria, prudential guidelines for risk assets classification depict nonperforming loans as credit facilities that display well-defined weaknesses that could affect the ability of borrowers to repay, such as inadequate cash flow to service debt, undercapitalization or insufficient working capital, absence of adequate financial information or collateral documentation, irregular payment of principal and/or interest, and inactive accounts where withdrawals exceed repayments or where repayments can hardly cover interest charges.

The objective criteria suggest that "a credit facility should be deemed as nonperforming when any of the following conditions exists:

- Interest or principal is due and unpaid for 90 days or more
- Interest payments equal to 90 days interest or more have been capitalized, rescheduled or rolled over into a new loan."

Thus, a credit facility that shows the foregoing attributes should be earmarked for close monitoring, and remedial or recovery actions, as soon as possible.

THIRD-PARTY INQUIRIES

In some cases, hints about impending loan default are gleaned from the market, where competing banks could be making frantic efforts to win the borrower's account. In the process, marketing officers of banks chasing the account might make curious inquiries that inadvertently insinuate to a possible continuing performance risk of the loan. The initial loan risk warning, in this context, would be felt when another bank makes a credit inquiry or check about the borrower, the credit facility, or the underlying transaction.

Credit inquiries usually seek information about the character, integrity, and creditworthiness of borrowers, as well as credit facilities granted to them, and the status of their loans. Ideally, inquiries of competing banks should not jolt the borrower's present bank. However, the repulsion implied in borrowers' actions is that they are perhaps switching to other banks without first settling their obligations to their present banks. The borrowers might not have even discussed the frustration that might be responsible for their planned change of bank with their account officers or other officers of their present bank(s). For this reason, it would be appropriate for their account officers to suspect that something phony is in the offing. In most cases, it turns out that subsequent events vindicate the doubts of the account officers about the genuineness of the intention of the borrowers. Such borrowers are phonies, to say the least.

At an informal level, such third-party inquiries have also proven quite useful in detecting the intention of borrowers to default on their loans. The likelihood of default on a loan could be inferred from casual inquiries at clubs or other social gatherings, where people who know particular borrowers intimately might be asking revealing questions about their personality, or the conduct of their accounts or banking transactions. Some useful information could be divulged about negative borrowing habits of the individuals. Account or lending officers who receive the privileged information should subsequently work on it with a view to reestablishing the borrowers' real standing on any worrying aspects of their credit facilities.

OTHER VIEWS ON LOAN DEFAULT

It is often assumed—on occasion erroneously—that loan officers display high levels of integrity, competence, and professionalism. These qualitative variables have a profound impact on the loan officer's job. We may agree with the view that associates bad debts with failings in the integrity and competence of loan officers. The regulatory authorities, especially in diagnosing failed banks, tend to take this position. They use phrases such as *insider abuse* to qualify situations where lending officers and certain members of bank management grant credit facilities not in accordance with approved procedure. Such lending, they argue, is usually intended to gratify the *fraudulent* desires of the lending officers or approving authorities.

On the other hand, we can take it for granted that banks employ competent lending officers or train them to acquire competence. Let us also assume that lending officers are oriented to and actually display a high level of integrity. This distinction—between the opposing views of the role of lending officers—is pertinent. If we don't make the distinction, we may have a situation in which an analysis of the problem will conclude a priori that loan officers point accusing fingers to unfounded culprits in cases of loan default. What is important, however, is realizing that the quality of credit decisions is more or less affected, positively or negatively, by the integrity and competence of lending officers.

IMPLICATIONS FOR BANK MANAGEMENT

The nature of credit risk assumed by a bank conditions its long-run liquidity and profitability. One reason is that bad debts result from poor risk management or taking uncovered exposures in lending. Banks should therefore continually identify and effectively manage the risks that crystallize in bad debts, cause distress, and threaten the survival of the banking industry. But they should also aim at creating balanced portfolios of risk assets in line with the economic outlook of the country. This requires knowledge of the business environment, anticipated and existing lending regulations, and shareholders' expectations.

It is the responsibility of bank management to position the bank to make good lending decisions. Thus, credit officers should be guided to know the bank's risk appetite in the provision of credit facilities. Bank management should define the bank's risk acceptance criteria as a positioning strategy. What is needed to minimize the high and growing incidence of nonperforming assets in banks is a realistic prognosis of the future of credit risk management strategy. Such a strategy will incorporate the principles of prudential guidelines adapted to credit analysis, control, and reporting.

Most of the factors that cause loan default are indeed beyond the loan officer's control. In particular, risks that arise from market, economic, and political uncertainties are beyond the control of lending officers. I make the following recommendations to help strengthen procedures currently adopted by banks in managing credit relationships:

- Quality customer service
  Banks should maintain high-quality customer service without compromising credit standards. The service culture should be clearly defined and applied bank-wide to ensure that it permeates every aspect of the bank's operations.
- Proper structuring of credits
  Credit facilities should be structured to simultaneously meet the borrowing needs of the customer and the lending needs of the bank. Poor structuring or a mismatch of the needs of the parties may result in loan default.
- Monitoring of loan utilization
  Banks should adopt a cost-effective means of monitoring loan utilization and the performance achieved by the borrower. They should, where necessary, engage the services of external consultants who specialize in

risk asset management. The consultants in question are not debt recovery agents. The mode of operation of debt recovery agents flouts democratic norms.

- Credit competence
  Loan requests that cannot be meaningfully analyzed within the bank's level of credit competence and capabilities should be declined. But if the loan must be considered at all, the request should be referred to someone, such as a consultant, with the necessary expertise to critically review the borrower's application.
- Audited financial statements
  Banks should insist on obtaining financial statements and annual reports from prospective borrowers that are audited by reputable firms of chartered accountants.
- Cash flow projections
  Reliance on cash flow projections for loan repayment should continue to be emphasized, especially in self-liquidating asset-based transactions. But it should be minimized in term and project loans where macroeconomic uncertainties usually distort forecast cash flows. In this case, the emphasis should be on the credit judgment of lending officers, which should reflect their analysis of *conditions* using the Cs of lending.
- Collateralization of guarantee
  Banks should require loan guarantors to collateralize their personal guarantees and be willing to indemnify the bank against default by the borrowers.
- Documentation of loans
  Lending officers should ensure that credit facilities are not disbursed without putting proper documentation in place or perfecting the legal charge over security documents.

Overall, the task of bank management in the lending function should be to minimize bad debts to a level at which the bank's competitive strength is not undermined by huge provisions on the portfolio.

EFFECT ON MARKET COMPETITION

Good credit management has a direct relationship to competitive strategy formulation. The relationship is seen mainly in terms of the safeguards it provides against loan loss, its enhancement of profitable operations, and its strengthening of revenue reserves and shareholders' funds. This is more important for older banks that require sustainable campaigns in order to retain market position. At maturity, a bank may likely experience a declining rate of growth in customer patronage. There might be a tendency to be complacent about current performance without discerning emerging threats to the business. Yet there may be no organizational situation that tasks management as much as being faced with market maturity. The tasks are driven by the need to develop and manage an effective competitive strategy capable of sustaining customer loyalty and increasing or retaining market share.

The greatest threat to a bank's competitive strength is a high rate of doubtful and bad accounts. Ordinarily, a bank would be rated high on competitive strength if it satisfies the following performance criteria:

- A good capital base that satisfies the Basel Capital Accord criteria
- High cash reserve and liquidity ratios
- A good asset base funded by a large and increasing deposit liability portfolio
- Professional and quality customer service
- Highly skilled, trained, and motivated staff
- Good marketing and operations strategies

Scarcely is a quality risk assets portfolio given any prominence in the competitive strength rating. Yet huge provisions against doubtful and bad accounts usually affect the easily considered factors. It follows therefore that if a bank has a quality risk assets portfolio, achieved through the adoption of effective credit analysis techniques, it will have an improved competitive advantage.

BANKING RELATIONSHIP CONCERNS

Several cases of bad debts occur in an attempt to maintain some banking relationships. This is illustrated in a review of certain banking cases exemplifying practical lending experiences of selected American banks with customers that both suddenly came to the verge of collapse and needing financing support for survival. Some of the companies occasionally needed additional credits (above approved limits) to sustain business growth or to finance certain unusual projects. The banks realized that the financial predicaments of the companies and the new loan requests arose mainly from the initial poor structuring and monitoring of utilization of the credit facilities. There was also the factor of the predominant desire of the customers to use more of *other people's money* (bank loans) than internally generated funds in the running of their businesses.

In some cases, the banks elected to restructure the credit facilities with a view to inculcating some financial discipline in the management of the companies. They did so by means of the following actions:

- Imposition of realistic financial loan covenants
- Requiring loan guarantors to collateralize their guarantees
- Demanding additional security

A finding that might surprise a Nigerian or other emerging market banker in these cases is that additional loan requests could still be and were in fact granted by the American banks, even to some accounts that had already been relegated to a "D" classification. The major consideration for doing so was often driven by a felt responsibility of the banks to sustain friendly, cordial relationships even in the face of adversity. But the banks didn't foresee that some of the companies were still to fail a few years later.

The nature of companies' financial problems revealed by the cases is also common in emerging markets. However, the relationship issues that the procedure for resolving the problems raises may not be readily adapted to the emerging market banking environment. It would appear that emerging market banks are more risk averse than the banks studied in the cases. It would arguably be only in very special cases that (rather than calling in a loan on which the borrower has defaulted) officers of an emerging market bank would be deeply concerned for many months, with meetings and financial counseling to the borrower aimed at fostering an understanding of the default. But to encourage former profitable accounts that found themselves in distress, the pro-American cases favored doing so.

Lending against security of *inventory* and *accounts receivable* was common in the cases analyzed. While emerging market banks take security on inventory in *asset-based* transactions, the use of accounts receivable as a borrowing base is not popular. But the cases revealed the need for efficient monitoring and management of these *trading assets* to be able to ascertain the *eligible* components that can be acceptable to the banks as part of the borrowing base. However, security commonly taken by emerging market banks accommodates these assets under fixed- and floating-assets debentures that the banks often take to secure loans.

The following lessons from the pro-American case studies are worthy of note:

- Banks have a responsibility to understand the financial needs of their customers in a setting of a friendly, cordial credit relationship.
- Undue favor for a good bank—customer relationship in credit transactions can be costly to a bank. This will especially be the case where recognition is given to past profitable transactions while making current lending decisions for exposures that carry high risks.
- Banks pay a high price for hasty credit decisions, poor structuring of credit facilities, and the nonmonitoring of utilization of approved credits. Paying proper attention to these credit flaws will improve the quality of the lending portfolio of banks.

It would be useful if emerging market banks began to require collateralization of personal guarantees for high-risk credits. They should also try using eligible *trading assets* as a borrowing base to determine lending limits to customers applying for revolving short-term credit facilities. In order to qualify for this consideration, the customer must have few but large accounts receivable and fast-moving inventory. This arrangement would appeal to banks that take collateral in tripartite warehousing agreements for short-term asset-based financing—where the goods financed or other stocks provide security for the loan.

QUESTIONS FOR DISCUSSION AND REVIEW

1. In what ways can a bank guide its lending officers to appreciate its credit risk appetite?
2. How can lending officers anticipate early warning signs of loan default?
3. What appropriate steps could account officers take to check possible threats to a risk asset?
4. Critically examine the recommendation of direct liability of lending officers for poor credit decisions.
5. What measures can a bank take to strengthen its credit risk management techniques?

Chapter 33

Loan Workout and Remedial Actions for Banks in Emerging Markets

Chapter Outline

LEARNING FOCUS AND OUTCOMES

It is possible to imagine a world of banking in which there will be no bad loans in the risk assets portfolio of a bank. This could easily be the wish of bank management and staff involved in loan workout and recovery actions. On occasion, the majority of such staff feel bad about the drudgery of remediating delinquent risk assets. Unfortunately, it is unrealistic to hope for a world in which bank lending would be devoid of bad loans. To assume that it is possible to have such a world is just wishful thinking. The sad reality is that there will always be bad debts in a bank's lending portfolio!

In Chapters 31 and 32 of this book, I explained some of the curious causes and early warning signs of loan default. With that background, in this chapter I examine the approaches that banks should adopt in managing nonperforming credit facilities. In discussing the relevant topics, I am guided by pertinent questions: What approaches should banks adopt in dealing with the problems of nonperforming loans? What issues and options does the management of a bank face in dealing with the problems of nonperforming loans? In what forms have the loan remediation strategies and actions of banks evolved over time?

Altogether, Chapters 31 to 34 cover the incidence, causes, and management of nonperforming loans in banks. It should be noted that banks adopt various

Emerging Market Bank Lending and Credit Risk Control. http://dx.doi.org/10.1016/B978-0-12-803438-5.00033-7

approaches in managing nonperforming loans. There is no uniform approach or strategy used by all banks for particular types of nonperforming loans. However, some of the effective options that I discuss in this chapter are in common use among banks in Nigeria. Yet there remains a need for innovative approaches to strengthen the framework of loan workout and remediation actions. My suggestion for innovation is informed by the need to check remedial loan frictions.

Drawing from lessons of my personal experience in practical credit risk management in bank lending and a review of related literature, I evaluate options available to bank management for tackling or remedying nonperforming loans. Based on analysis of findings, I assess the effectiveness of the loan remediation tactics in current use, with suggestions for improvement.

Banks look to loan workout and remediation to revitalize their risk assets portfolios. Some categories of delinquent loans especially demand loan workout and remediation actions—in line with prudential guidelines. You will learn how:

- Lending officers deal with remedial loans in practical ways
- Loan remediation tactics and actions work in credit risk management
- Loan workout functions as a remedial measure for delinquent loans.
- Banks often resort to primary and secondary loan remediation actions
- A watch list committee fulfills the loan remediation needs of a bank

WATCH LIST COMMITTEE

Perhaps, the setting up and sustaining of a watch list committee is the first conscious effort that banks in emerging markets should make toward managing the problems of nonperforming loans. Indeed, the regulatory authorities require every bank to have a standing watch list committee that should meet regularly to review the status of nonperforming risk assets as well as efforts and achievements toward their recovery. The overall objective of the committee is to ensure that loan loss provisions are minimized as much as possible to avoid depletion of returns to shareholders.

In some banks, the watch list committee meets once a month to deliberate on all aspects of the problems of, and recovery strategies for, nonperforming risk assets, or loans of doubtful value. The term *watch list* refers to the grouping of all borrowing accounts or loans that a bank, its external auditors, or the regulatory authorities classify as substandard, doubtful, or lost in line with *prudential guidelines*. Ideally, the watch list should include loans that, though not yet classified, show potential default warning signs. Such loans equally require close monitoring and firming up of recovery plans to forestall their degeneration to nonperforming status.

The watch list committee members are usually drawn from credit strategy committee (CRESCO) members and heads of lending units in the bank.

But branch managers who have watch list credits may be invited to the watch list committee meetings. Ordinarily, the watch list committee exists and functions as a subcommittee of CRESCO. At the end of its meetings, decisions are taken—subject in some banks to ratification by CRESCO and executive management—on actions necessary to revive particular accounts, strengthen certain credit relationships, or maintain surveillance over the performance of specific nonperforming credit facilities.

The committee could make tough decisions on nonperforming loans. Such decisions often culminate in *workout* and outright *recovery* actions. In such situations, if ratified by CRESCO and executive management, the bank would be constrained to *call back* the affected loans.

LOAN REMEDIATION ACTIONS

It has nowadays become practically inevitable for banks in emerging markets to embark on loan workout operations to stem the increasing volumes of annual loan loss provisions. The *loan workout* actions that are appropriate to the situations of banks in emerging markets could be primary or secondary in terms of the orientation and methods employed.

PRIMARY ACTIONS

Primary actions represent the schemes—often *disguised*—that a bank adopts to wind down a nonperforming credit facility. How the schemes and their momentum are commenced, driven, and sustained also make for primary loan remediation actions. The bank could take the following underlying actions at this stage to initiate the planned loan workout.

Repudiation of renewal offer

The bank may subtly repudiate any offer to renew or roll over the credit on maturity. Lending officers might tell borrowers that the renewal is temporarily deferred. They should give some cogent reasons, such as a fleeting *portfolio constraint*, for the decline of the loan renewal request. On their part, account officers should provide more relationship warmth and improved quality of service to strengthen this position. They should make regular visits to borrowers to monitor activities and assess the performance of their businesses. This approach reinforces the reasons the bank gives for repudiating borrowers' loan renewal requests.

Borrowers in this situation might not tolerate undue delay in the renewal of their credit facilities—especially if, for instance, the outstanding loans are tied up in projects with long gestation periods and require more funding to generate their expected cash flows. This would be really problematic if the bank's winding-down posture is predicated on a contrary view about the prospects of realizing expected cash flows, and it would therefore want to cut its possible losses on the loans.

The bank should under the circumstances maintain its position of "no further lending to the projects or borrowers." However, the bank should do a lot of relationship management and try to suggest acceptable alternatives to borrowers.

Perfection of collateral

The holding of documents of legal title to a collateral property on terms of *equitable mortgage* is fast losing its relevance in managing lending portfolios. In the event of loan default and foreclosure on the property, when the crunch comes, the bank will have to first obtain a court order against the borrower before it can dispose of the property. In the alternative, the bank must first *perfect* the collateral before it can sell it. Unfortunately, these legal requirements are onerous to satisfy, usually resulting in a grinding delay when urgent action is needed. This is the regrettable implication of acceptance of an equitable mortgage in the security documentation of loans.

Yet, there could be instances where, at the time a loan is being granted, the bank *only* asks the customer to execute all legal title documents to the property that the borrower has pledged to it as collateral to secure the loan. For some reasons, the bank and borrower may enter into an unwritten agreement that the former should not *perfect* the legal title documents (i.e., legally registering its charge over the property), but hold them on terms of a simple deposit or equitable mortgage. Thus, the borrower would only execute a memorandum of deposit of the title documents signifying the pledge of the property to the bank. In effect, this arrangement often betrays the true essence of taking collateral in the first place—which is to provide an effective alternative means of recovering a loan in the event of default.

However, at the primary loan workout stage, it would be imperative to commence effective perfection of all such security documents hitherto held by the bank on an *equitable* basis. This should be done as soon as it becomes expedient to put the bank in a position to dispose of the collateral, even if on forced sale terms, to recover the loan. It may be uncritical to debit the borrower's loan or other account with perfection expenses at this stage. Doing so will betray and possibly frustrate the bank's plan to foreclose on the collateral. Thus, the bank may initially charge the expenses to a suspense account to be reimbursed in time from recoveries on the loan.

Overall, it is not advisable to leave collateral unperfected until a crisis ensues. At that point, especially if the *discreet* perfection scheme fails, the bank might not receive the necessary cooperation from the borrower. If borrowers who are in default decide to be phony, they could effectively stop the bank from either perfecting or disposing of their loan collateral. Therefore, all documentation requirements and processes should be put in place at the initial stage when borrowers are enthusiastic about obtaining credit facilities from the bank.

Urging continuing paydown

A bank may request continuing *paydowns* on particular loans while repudiating further disbursements on the credit facilities. This implies that borrowers might not withdraw lodgments from their loan accounts, or they could withdraw only part of the lodgments. A bank should be tactful in making the request, as it might sound nonsensical to borrowers. A discreet disposition is imperative, because borrowers whose loans are current or awaiting renewal should expect that they should be able to operate their accounts without restriction or any form of avoidable hitch.

In most cases, borrowers resist this implied *clogging* of their business by the bank. The unfortunate fact is that if borrowers fail to stop the bank's action, they start diverting their cash inflows to their accounts with other banks. It would indeed be dicey to ignore the feelings of borrowers under these circumstances. It is therefore advised—and this has proven effective in resolving such a dilemma—that some concession be granted the borrowers. The bank should allow them to withdraw certain proportions of their total daily, weekly, or monthly lodgments into their accounts. In this way, the bank could retain some portion of the lodgments and apply it to reducing the outstanding balances in their loan accounts.

Enforcement of primary loan workout actions commences once the bank is convinced that any previously observed *default warning signs* now pose real risks of partial or total loss of the loans.

SECONDARY ACTIONS

Depending on the level of success attained, a bank may move forward with the aforementioned *disguised* recovery actions to the secondary stage. In general, this stage involves the following four critical actions:

- Opening up to the borrower
- Restructuring, working out, and agreeing to new terms for loan repayments
- Enforcement of the loan agreement
- Encouraging sustained loan repayments

Opening up to the borrower

At this stage, it is expedient for the bank to *open up* to the borrower about its exact intention to enforce full liquidation of the loan. Ordinarily, the position of the bank should not be surprising to the borrower for at least the following two reasons:

- Reading of the primary discreet actions
  The primary discreet workout actions should have sensitized the borrower to the direction of the bank's thinking regarding continuing availability of

the loan after its due date. Only borrowers in helpless situations would ignore the bank's insinuations about its possible demand for repayment of the loan after its due date or even prior to the expiration of its tenor. Otherwise, the borrower is expected to make efforts aimed at returning activity to the account. Striving to settle as many obligations due on the loan as possible should complement efforts to return activity to the loan account. The combined efforts might cause the bank to reconsider its position on the loan.

- Appreciating that the loan is not performing
  It would have been obvious to the borrower that the loan has not been performing, even if it has not been formally classified as such in line with prudential guidelines. The account officer must have been advising the borrower of the bank's unfulfilled performance expectations for the credit facility. Not infrequently, waning performance starts with declining activity level (i.e., dwindling transaction turnover). The situation evolves over time to the inability to service interest charges and repay principal when due. It is also not uncommon for other loan officers and CRESCO members who know the borrower and about the nonperforming credit facility, to advise the borrower, usually informally, of the need to regularize the loan account.

It is essential for the bank to open up to the borrower about the loan remediation actions it intends to take. The bank should do so with a view to allowing the borrower the benefit of self-initiative toward liquidation of the loan. The workout plans could fail if the bank abruptly carries out formal recovery actions without first making the borrower see the reasons behind them. This should be done in recognition that the bank, after all, needs the borrower's cooperation to avoid a rancorous loan recovery exercise.

Restructuring of the loan

A common finding about most loan defaulters is a tendency to ask for more time or the restructuring of their loans on more favorable terms as a means of facilitating repayments. However, borrowers who are in default might request the deferment or rescheduling of loan repayments. Their intention in doing so might be to initiate a holding action on the bank. It could also be that they want to buy time during which they can foresee and devise appropriate responses to any actions that the bank might take to recover the loans. In most cases, the bank would feel able to oblige the request when it considers the borrowers' intention genuine.

The bank and borrower would then discuss and, if possible, agree on mutually acceptable *restructured* terms for loan repayments. When doing so, the parties would seek to renegotiate critical aspects of the loan. This implies that secondary loan remediation actions often entail outright alteration of the original tenor, pricing, mode, and sometimes source of repayment. Loan repayment emphasis then shifts from the ideal to the pragmatic—focusing on what is practicable or plausible under the prevailing circumstances of the borrower. It is pertinent for bank management to get to grips with this reality of loan remediation actions.

The beneficial result of restructuring the nonperforming loan to the borrower is perhaps the facility for various concessions that the bank could grant to ease repayment of the loan. The common concessions that banks make on nonperforming loans that are restructured for remedial purposes include the following:

- Rebate on accrued interest
- Reduction or outright waiver of future interest, fees, and commissions on the loan
- Acceptance of a hybrid mode of loan repayment
- Rebooking the loan for a new (extended) tenor

In the exercise of loan restructuring, the bank loses earnings—more as a relationship sacrifice than as the only feasible option to recovering much of the outstanding loan balance. In anticipation of the depletion of *recognized* loan earnings, the bank (if proactive) would start in time to make regular provisions against the expected loan loss. Otherwise, it could charge but suspend interest until the loan is fully repaid or charged off—usually upon the failure of remediation and recovery actions.

Enforcement of agreement

The bank should, after restructuring the loan on mutually agreed *new* terms and conditions between it and the borrower, ensure that the parties fulfill the agreement. There should be more and effective monitoring of the borrower's business, transactions, and social activities so as to detect and, if possible, prevent any avoidable abuses that could result in another default on the loan. Also, the act of close monitoring of the loan is emphasized at this stage. Effective monitoring will help the bank identify forces in the borrower's personality, its business, and the environment that might impinge on successful implementation of the agreement on the restructured credit facility.

It is pertinent to realize that borrowers who, unknown to the bank, *deliberately* default on their original loans would most probably also renege on the restructured loan agreement. This behavioral tendency is often expressed or rooted in the *character* of the borrower. Unfortunately, most banks inadvertently fail to thoroughly investigate this main source of credit risk before granting credit facilities. Most practicing and professional bankers would attest to the intractable nature of managing banking relationships with borrowing customers who are lacking in integrity, dishonest, or untrustworthy. However, where default is caused by objectively ascertainable failings of the business, the likelihood that the loan account will regain performance with the restructured loan terms and agreement will be high. The bank should watch out for these possibilities prior to, during, and after initiation of secondary loan remediation actions.

Account officers or relationship managers might want to be strict with borrowers while enforcing a new loan agreement. But rarely do they succeed in cases where the defaulting borrowers are among those to whom the bank has granted substantial credit facilities. Ironically, this category of borrowers displays incredible deftness in dealing with senior management. Often they easily plead with senior bank officials to intercede on their behalf. Unfortunately, such intercession often dilutes the effectiveness of loan remediation actions. Some would argue that this happens frequently in situations where such borrowers are *benefactors* of, or have *personal* relationships with, certain key management staff of the bank. In most cases, the *benevolent* management staff may have played a major role in approving the loans in the first place. Usually, this situation poses a difficult credit risk management problem.

The foregoing insinuation of abuse of office might not be substantiated. Yet it casts aspersion on the will of senior management in dealing with the problems of nonperforming loans in banks. I have elsewhere in this book dealt with problems associated with the integrity of bank members. So, it will be futile if I start discussing any aspects of discredited banking practices. I must mention nonetheless that informal relationships between loan defaulters and bank officials are a setback for the effective enforcement of the agreement on restructured repayments for nonperforming credit facilities.

Encouraging repayment efforts

It is not enough that the loan is restructured and the agreement enforced in remedial situations. It is also crucial to encourage the borrower to repay the loan. The bank could offer specific incentives to the borrower. Effective incentives include *additional* lending—where this is inevitable—to rescue the borrower's business. Also, additional lending may be granted to ensure that operations of the borrower are sustained so as to generate earnings to repay the loan. This might seem an uncritical suggestion, considering the debilitating intrigues with which some loan defaulters are often associated. Yet, it is imperative for a bank to always be favorably disposed to additional lending in pursuit of its overall loan remediation agenda. The incremental lending may be appropriately tagged *lending to workout*—to distinguish it from the normal credit facilities that the bank grants to first-time and existing borrowers.

The bank could also encourage loan repayment by creating conditions that are propitious for fulfillment of the restructured loan agreement by the borrower. This could be achieved in several ways. One possible way is to build up the borrower's rational sense of the value that the bank places on its banking relationship despite temporary business setbacks. The propitious condition will also entail *patiently listening* and *proffering possible solutions* to the borrower's complaints and problems while trying to satisfy the terms and conditions of the loans. Unfortunately—perhaps because of the high stakes of, and *concerns* about, the loan—patience becomes a scarce resource for most banks whenever a loan is classified as *nonperforming*. Yet, the lesson that most lending officers often fail to learn is that the loan remediation agenda suffers once the bank becomes impatient with the borrower or is not disposed to helping solve the genuine problems of nonperforming credit facilities.

As most bankers involved in loan remediation assignments know—a fact to which they would easily attest—it is counterproductive to antagonize loan defaulters. Rather than antagonize them, they should be made to feel invaluable and wanted—without compromising the remediation agenda. Such a disposition will most likely make borrowers more determined and committed to repaying their nonperforming loans. Borrowers will, under the circumstances, strive to fulfill the terms and conditions of their restructured loans. They will want to do so as a means of consolidating their banking relationships that now hold out promises of great future benefits. Indeed, some loan remediation cases turn into fruitful relationships after the reversal of their deprecation through the resuscitation of sustained activities and repayment of the loans.

The end toward which account officers, relationship managers, and indeed bank management should work is to redress the loan-defaulting stigma. The stigma should be transformed into a positive outlook that the future is promising and holds mutual benefits for the bank and borrowers. This is by no means an easy assignment. On occasion, it craves unusual ingenuity from lending officers. Its accomplishment—in the final analysis and to a large extent—determines the level of success that loan remediation actions can attain.

QUESTIONS FOR DISCUSSION AND REVIEW

1. How should loan officers deal with the task of loan remediation in a practical way?
2. What loan remediation tactics and actions are at the disposal of bank management?
3. Explain the concept of "loan workout" as a remedial measure for delinquent risk assets.
4. Compare primary and secondary loan remediation actions that banks often adopt.
5. What is the relevance of the watch list committee in the loan remediation scheme?

Chapter 34

Proofed Strategies for Recovery of Bad Loans of Banks in Emerging Markets

Chapter Outline

LEARNING FOCUS AND OUTCOMES

Loan recovery is usually the terminal action that a bank may want to take in a failed credit relationship. It starts when remedial measures taken to revive a delinquent account prove unsuccessful. Banks in emerging markets should constantly seek to improve the quality of their lending portfolios. They could achieve improved loan portfolios in three ways. A bank should first and foremost strive to grant loans that satisfy its internal and regulatory criteria for acceptance of credit risk. Secondly, it should have a program for appropriate prudential provisioning on its criticized and classified risk assets. Thirdly, it must regularly charge off terminally bad loans from its risk assets portfolio. When taken, the second and third measures unavoidably deplete earnings and shareholders' funds. In order to recoup income lost to charge-offs and loan loss provisions, the bank must embark on aggressive loan recovery operations.

Thus, the basis of loan recovery is that a bank cannot afford to carelessly lose a risk asset. In other words, bank management is accountable to its supervising board and shareholders for avoidable loan losses. Unfortunately,

Emerging Market Bank Lending and Credit Risk Control. http://dx.doi.org/10.1016/B978-0-12-803438-5.00034-9
589

borrowers who default on their loans don't seem to appreciate this fact when they face the prospect of loan recovery actions such as foreclosure. This explains why unscrupulous defaulters would want to thwart reasonable loan recovery actions. A typical example to illustrate this infamous attitude is a frivolous court order obtained by a borrower who is in default on a loan to stop a bank from enforcing its rights to recover the loan.

Yet the pursuit of the recovery of bad loans is both a legitimate cause and course of action for a bank to sustain quality risk assets portfolio. While holding this view, I should at once give bankers a piece of advice. Loan recovery actions should have a human face. Contrary to popular belief in banking circles, it's possible to conduct loan recovery with a human face. One reason is that it helps to check intrigues that characterize loan recovery actions. Also, even in default, borrowers expect that loan recovery personnel should have the milk of human kindness. In the absence of this attribute, loan recovery might prove an arduous task—mainly because of avoidable frustration with its cause.

I focus on the foregoing issues in this chapter. In doing so, I assess the effectiveness and implications of alternative loan recovery strategies and actions. Loan recovery is often regarded as a necessary evil. Banks engage in it as a last resort when efforts to remedy bad loans fail. For borrowers who default, it's usually a bitter pill to swallow. You will learn:

- Steps that a bank may take to recover bad loans
- Some of the effective loan recovery options and strategies
- How a bank can ensure that its loan recovery operations are effective and without hitches
- Problems often associated with the recovery of bad loans and how to minimize them

STAKES IN LOAN RECOVERY

The classification of a loan as a nonperforming, and especially *lost*, credit facility, as well as the subsequent pursuit of its recovery, is undoubtedly the most excruciating task in managing the lending portfolio. Not infrequently, a bank's decision to embark on full-scale *overt* recovery operations is reached after its efforts to remedy particular bad loans, accounts, or banking relationships have failed. Three issues would be at stake for the bank and borrowers under the circumstances:

- Possible loss of the credit facility
  The bank confronts the probability of the loss of an *earning asset* in the nonperforming or *lost* credit facility. If the loss occurs, the bank will write off the total amount of the loan plus accrued interest, which will come from current earnings or reserves (if any). Either of these actions will deplete earnings and returns to shareholders.

- Fate of borrowers in default
  Borrowers, for their part, face up to the reality that they have *called-back* credit facilities that they must settle *now* by some compulsion. Without planning for this, they are likely to become restive and resigned to their fates. The concomitant frustration, largely of a psychological sort, could indeed undermine self-confidence in their lives and businesses.
- Breakdown of the relationship
  In most cases, enforcement of recovery operations evidences the breakdown of amicable loan repayment negotiations between a bank and borrowers that often leaves both parties worse off. At this time, the banking relationship between the bank and borrower would turn sour.

In view of these stakes, everything possible must be done to prevent deterioration of a loan to nonperforming status, especially to the lost credit category. Banks and borrowers should always be committed to this cause. Otherwise, they might unwittingly be insensitive to the very essence of courting, starting, and establishing their banking relationship in the first place. Besides, it would cause self-inflicted injuries to borrowers if their default were willful. But the bank would suffer negative publicity and perhaps incur the wrath of the public if it tries to forcibly recover bad loans. In the Nigerian context, this could be especially so if loan recovery operations involve the sale of landed property such as the borrower's residential house.

What steps should a bank take to recover a bad loan without undue loss of value? What would be the effective loan recovery options and strategies? How may loan recovery operations be enforced without hitches? What are the problems often associated with loan recovery? How and why should bank management resolve such problems? I provide answers to these questions in the following discussions.

APPROACHES, OPTIONS, AND STRATEGIES

A bank typically takes certain cautious actions—besides the aforementioned *workout* activities—aimed at recovering its nonperforming or classified loans. Most banks as a matter of necessity set up special loan recovery units or task forces that deal with the day-to-day problems of *nonperforming* credit facilities. Obviously, this is the first and most fundamental step that a bank could take in pursuit of its *overt* loan recovery agenda. In some banks, the loan recovery unit forms part of the *risk management* group and is charged with specific responsibilities, including the following:

- Maintaining an internal *database* of all loans earmarked, after approval by management, for recovery operations
- Identifying and implementing the bank's plans for *overt* loan recovery operations as advised by CRESCO

- Coordinating activities of external debt collection agents assigned by the bank to recover specific bad loans
- Reporting regularly, and making recommendations, to CRESCO on the progress of loan recovery operations

In carrying out its assignments, the unit obtains legal advice from the bank's in-house lawyers. In some cases, the unit is staffed by trained credit and legal officers with special expertise in problem loans and laws relating to contract, debt, or borrowing relationships. But it also works closely with and obtains assistance from certain *specialized* external solicitors. Once it is set up and its assignments clearly specified, the watch list committee and risk management group assume interdependent supervisory roles over the operations of the loan recovery unit to ensure success. The focus of performance assessments of the unit would be on the specified assignments that I discuss below.

Internal (recovery) database

The recovery unit should maintain a database that contains up-to-date general information about all credit facilities approved and earmarked for recovery. This is a critical requirement as it facilitates assignment of loan recovery responsibilities based on the intricacies and peculiar circumstances of each loan.

A typical loan recovery database contains—for each borrower—summarized and sometimes tabulated information relating to the following:

- Names and *current* addresses of accounts or borrowers—sometimes referred to as the obligors
- Identification and addresses of the promoters, principal officers, and directors—necessary where borrowers are corporate entities
- Statement of guarantors' net worth, and whether any or all of the persons specified above in the case of corporate borrowers guaranteed the loans
- Status of security documentation—are the loans secured or unsecured? What types of collateral secure the loans? Are legal title deeds and security charges on the loans perfected or not?
- Outstanding balances on the loans as of certain dates—broken down into principal, interest, charges, and so on
- Cash basis balances and value of the loans, as well as *recommended* and *actual* loan loss provisions made on the loans up to the date of report. The phrase *cash basis balance* denotes the net outstanding balance on a loan at the point when it was classified as nonperforming, earmarked for full recovery operations, and the provision for its charge-off took effect. However, these three conditions do not necessarily need to be satisfied in determining the cash value balance for the loan. Rather, what is important is to establish when the bank *lost* hope of normal repayment of the loan and started making a *provision* against its ultimate charge-off after its *classification* as a lost credit facility.

- Tenor, value, and expiry dates of the loans, as well as dates of their classification as a substandard, doubtful, or lost credit facility—including dates when the loans became dormant and last had lodgments or cash inflows
- List of all charge-offs (i.e., lost credit facilities against which full loan loss provisions have been made, or the amounts have been written off or charged to income, but not forgiven or let off by the bank)
- Names of account officers, relationship managers, or other loan officers to whom inquiries may be directed regarding the credit facilities
- Names and current addresses of external agents or solicitors to whom the credit facilities have been assigned for recovery on behalf of the bank
- Details and updates of daily, weekly, or monthly recovery achieved and by whom—loan recovery unit, agents, solicitors, and so on

Information in the database, generally considered confidential, should be stored in an electronic retrieval system and be primarily accessible to officers of the loan recovery unit. The unit's report is usually prepared on a regular basis for the watch list committee and CRESCO meetings. But specific aspects of the report may be made available, on demand, to external agents and solicitors engaged by the bank for loan recovery assignments.

Implementation of strategies

The bank must decide on specific, realistic, and workable action plans to recover bad loans. This essentially involves devising strategies that are appropriate and will achieve the desired result for each loan. As most loans do not share similar characteristics, each presents unique recovery challenges when it goes bad. This is where lending officers, especially loan recovery strategists, must pay attention if they are to succeed.

But no generally accepted loan recovery strategies have been found that are effective for all types of credit facilities and workable in all situations. Yet, some strategies—e.g., litigation, sale or liquidation of collateral assets, engagement of debt-recovery agents—appear to be in common use even as they have mixed effectiveness and results. Once the decision has been taken to use any or all of these or other strategies, the loan recovery unit should devise ingenious means to ensure the successful implementation of the strategies.

Moral suasion and appeal

Loan recovery staff of banks might begin to appeal to the conscience of borrowers—pointing out, in so doing, the bank's consideration in granting credit facilities to them at the time they desperately needed the loans. Although such recourse to moral suasion seldom achieves significant results, it still is somewhat effective to the extent that it tends to put loan defaulters in a position of acknowledged guilt. The appeal to morality should be continuous, with indications that the bank is still disposed to providing financial assistance to the borrowers in the future. Borrowers should be constantly reminded that their inability to redeem their present financial obligations to the bank would taint their business integrity and creditworthiness—both of which are inimical to accessing bank loans in the future. The appeal to conscience can be extended to close relations and associates of the borrowers for whom the borrowers have high respect. The bank can complain to such people about the default of the borrowers, especially their indifference (if exhibited) about repayment of their loans.

Formal letter of demand

If moral suasion fails, the loan recovery unit could advise the legal unit of the bank to make a formal written demand for full repayment of the loan. The letter, ideally strongly worded, often gives a maximum grace period of four weeks from its date. It also indicates the possible actions that the bank might take in the event of failure by the borrower to repay the loan within the grace period. The demand letter carries the implication that relationship management overtures either have failed or will no longer be tolerated by the bank. It also signals possible resolve of the bank to pressure the borrower to repay the loan *unconditionally*. This is lent credence and given impetus by the origin and execution of the letter of demand in the legal unit. The unusual distancing of account officers, relationship managers, or other loan officers—those with whom borrowers have had relationship interactions prior to default on their loans—is no less a warning sign that the recovery threat is real. In order to be more effective, the actions threatened in the letter, or equivalent measures, should be carried out if the borrower fails to repay the loan on expiration of the four-week ultimatum. Otherwise, recovery plans might begin to lose momentum, as the borrower is likely to begin to rebuff subsequent loan repayment demands from the bank.

Foreclosure on collateral

In the most severe cases of loan default, borrowers would probably not be in a position to comply with a *formal demand letter* to repay their loans. The bank may at this point assume ownership and proceed to sell any *perfected* collateral that the borrowers had pledged to it to secure their loans. In view of the perfection of its charge over the assets, there might not be the need for recourse to the court for an order to sell. The affected assets could be land, buildings, hypothecated stocks-in-trade, shares of quoted companies, and so on. The loan recovery office could dispose of the assets through agents as follows:

- Shares of quoted companies
  Quoted shares could be sold through a stockbroker registered with the Nigerian stock exchange (NSE). The sales price of the shares would largely reflect prevailing market conditions at the point when the shares are sold.

- Hypothecated inventories
  The bank may dispose of stocks-in-trade hypothecated in its favor by using the services of a professional debt collector or recovery agent. The suitability of such agents is dictated by the fact that the sale would in most cases require the forcible removal of stocks from the debtor's shops or warehouses to a convenient bank-favored location. This is intended to ensure that the sale is hitch-free and especially to avoid interruption by the debtor during the sale exercise.
- Forced sale of trading assets
  The disposal of collateral stocks is usually conducted on a *forced sale* basis. Ideally, the sale should be preceded by and backed up with an executed and perfected bill of sale or court order. In that case, the court bailiff would be responsible for the removal and forced sale, or auctioning, of the goods.
- Sale of landed property
  Landed property may be sold through professional estate agents and appraisers. Here, the first step in exercising the option to sell is to ask the agent to provide a valuation of the property—showing the current market value and the value in a forced sale. Next, the bank should advise the owners of the property—who may be the borrowers, their relations, or guarantors—of the valuation report. This is useful to avoid rejection of the sale value by the owners for reasons of possible undervaluation and sale. However, it must be pointed out that the need for the consent of the owners to sell is not a condition or prerequisite for the sale, since the bank has a perfected charge over the property.

Referral to external solicitors

Often the outstanding balance in a loan account would not be fully liquidated after selling and applying the proceeds of collateral assets on which the bank has foreclosed. When this happens and such residual balance is substantial, the loan recovery office will under normal circumstances seek and obtain management's approval to officially transfer the credit facility and its file to the legal office for further and sustained recovery actions. Where collateral assets are not perfected, loan default cases may, with management's approval, be transferred from the recovery unit to the legal office of the bank at the expiration of a four-week *demand notice*.

The transfer of the credit file to the legal office presupposes that the chosen recovery strategy is to institute legal action against the borrower. In that case, in-house lawyers will do all of the following:

- Summarize the terms and conditions of the offer and acceptance of the credit facility by the bank and borrower, respectively
- Indicate the terms and conditions of the loan that the borrower has breached and that necessitated callback of the loan by the bank

- Instruct external solicitors, approved by the bank, to take specific legal actions to recover the loan on behalf of the bank—for a fee—as soon as possible

Once it receives the brief from the bank, the solicitors take full responsibility for the recovery of the loan. In carrying out their assignments, they regularly consult with and report to the legal unit of the bank, through which they in turn receive advice, guidance, and feedback from bank management. Based on such consultations, the solicitors decide on the appropriate legal actions to take at each stage of the recovery operations.

There could be diverse objects in the recourse to loan recovery litigation. However, the most favored expected major outcomes include court orders granting the bank leave to do any or all of the following:

- Sale of collateral assets
  In this case, the bank is empowered to dispose of specific assets such as landed property (land, buildings, factories, premises, and so on) that the borrower had pledged to it on an *equitable basis* as collateral to secure the loan.
- Sale of noncollateral assets
  With an appropriate court order, the bank can sell any identifiable assets of the borrowers, including those of their relations or other third parties who *guaranteed* the loan in favor of the bank. However, this order could be obtained against these persons *only* if they duly acknowledged but could not settle the debt, perhaps on the grounds of business failure or insolvency.
- Windup of corporate debtor
  The bank may appoint a receiver manager to wind up the business of the borrower—in the case of a debtor company. But this is possible only if the bank has a previously registered (i.e., perfected) debenture over the fixed and floating assets (i.e., an all-assets debenture) of the company.
- Exercise of setoff over deposits
  One of the actions that a bank can easily take in pursuit of loan recovery is to appropriate any net credit balances, in identified deposit or other accounts of the borrower, to the bank itself, other banks, or elsewhere. Although a bank has an inherent right of setoff over accounts maintained with it by its customers, it is often still useful to get a court order in order to avoid unnecessary litigation after the exercise of its right of setoff. Thus it is mandatory for the bank to apply to the court to obtain a *garnishee* order to any identified other banks where the borrower has accounts with net credit balances. A garnishee order refers to an order of a court by which a debtor is restrained from paying money to its creditor because the creditor is in turn indebted to the person, firm, or institution that obtained the court order. In the context of litigation to recover bank loans, it denotes a court order obtained by a bank (garnisher) that compels another bank (garnishee) to freeze any net credit balances in identified accounts of the garnisher's

debtor maintained with the garnishee. This has proven quite effective in loan recovery operations in some emerging markets, especially where the borrower is proving unnecessarily difficult or the bank has totally lost patience with the borrower for sundry reasons.

Appointment of loan recovery agents

Where the decision is to employ an *extrajudicial* recovery strategy, the recovery office would most likely engage the services of debt collectors or recovery agents that have proven track records of performance. These agents are firms or individuals registered to carry on the business of professional recovery of bad debts on behalf of individuals and corporate bodies. They often employ unorthodox means to achieve desired results—including *calculated continuous embarrassment* of the borrower, especially at very sensitive places. But they also sometimes adopt orthodox strategies such as litigation.

Perhaps the use of debt-recovery agents proves most useful when they successfully act as a go-between. In this role, agents create room for compromise and the amicable resolution of any problems frustrating the repayment of bad loans. This outcome is especially possible in situations where borrowers, as a result of anger or some perceived or apparent misdeeds of the bank or its officials, rebuff entreaties to dialogue with the bank. If the agents can make borrowers feel that they are neutral in the matter, the borrowers might open up about their resistance and grouse against the bank. After hearing both parties, the agents could bring them together to discuss the way forward in the matter.

I should point out at once that resolution of a face-off between a bank and loan-defaulting borrowers against whom the bank has appointed debt-recovery agents is not usually an easy task. In most cases, the bank would not want to interfere with the recovery operations once it gives out the brief to the agents. The bank is likely to reason that meeting with the borrowers at this stage under the auspices of the agents might be detrimental to its desired recovery momentum. Banks reward loan recovery agents with payment of up to 15 percent of the amounts of loans recovered, depending on the nature of the underlying assignments.

Coordination of loan recovery efforts

It is the responsibility of the loan recovery office to coordinate the activities of the bank's in-house legal office, external solicitors, and debt-recovery agents. It's essential to fulfill this duty to ensure that there are no conflicts of roles in loan recovery assignments. Besides, it helps in achieving maximum results in the general loan recovery exercise. It also ensures that those involved in loan recovery assignments do not work at cross-purposes. The recovery office should therefore maintain close contact with all those, and external offices, involved in loan recovery operations. When doing so, it should serve as a liaison for the external solicitors and agents—answering questions on their assignments; supplying them with data, documents, and other materials that they require to carry out their assignments; and giving them feedback from the bank's management, especially on performance expectations.

QUESTIONS FOR DISCUSSION AND REVIEW

1. What steps should a bank take to recover a bad loan without undue loss of value?
2. What would you consider effective loan recovery options and strategies?
3. How can a bank ensure that its loan recovery operations are effective and hitch-free?
4. (a) What are the problems often associated with loan recovery?
   (b) How should bank management resolve such problems?
   (c) Why is resolution of the problems critical to the success of credit risk management?
5. (a) What is "moral suasion?"
   (b) Assess the effectiveness of moral suasion as a loan recovery strategy.

Chapter 35

Obstacles to Recovery of Bad Loans in Emerging Economies

Chapter Outline

LEARNING FOCUS AND OUTCOMES

Issues that influence and are informed by loan recovery actions of banks in emerging economies have witnessed dramatic changes of late. The observed changes are due mainly to the responses of banks and borrowers to the continually modernizing banking system. From the legal perspective of human rights of loan defaulters to implications for marketing and relationship management, recovery of bad loans is facing grave challenges. Banks have responded forcefully to some of the defining challenges through the adoption and strict implementation of KYC philosophy.

The KYC theory is based on the assumption that frauds in banking will be significantly checked if accurate data on customers are painstakingly documented. Banks eagerly embraced the theory, worked hard to enforce it, and are still doing so. Bank management had hoped that the era when borrowers defaulted and disappeared into thin air was all over. But the lessons of their experience have proven them wrong. Obstacles to recovery of bad loans have persisted and have continued to task the wills of banks and regulators.

The myriad causes and intricate nature of the obstacles underscore the grave challenges that banks face in loan recovery. On occasion, borrowers who are in default work hard to sabotage loan recovery actions. Unscrupulous bank employees and agents surprisingly compromise themselves and aid the nefarious activities of some loan defaulters. The situation is worsened by the

Emerging Market Bank Lending and Credit Risk Control. http://dx.doi.org/10.1016/B978-0-12-803438-5.00035-0
599

frustrating attitudes of influential loan defaulters. Unfortunately, the hope that banks should ordinarily pin on the legal system for justice sometimes also suffers avoidable setbacks. Protracted legal proceedings render resort to law courts for settlement of loan defaults unappealing.

Dealing with the obstacles requires innovative approaches that regrettably are in painfully short supply in the banking industry in emerging economies. It is therefore not surprising that obstacles to recovery of bad loans have festered over time. However, bankers should not lose heart in the face of this seemingly hopeless situation. There are still effective ways to get around the obstacles without infringing the rights of the borrowers that are in default. I highlight some of these ways as I discuss the topics of this chapter. Bank management must be determined to face up to the obstacles to the recovery of bad loans. It should devise new and unusual strategies to deal with the problem if it is to succeed. This will not be easy, but a start is now necessary. In this chapter, you will learn how:

- To identify and evaluate the critical obstacles to loan recovery actions in emerging markets
- To analyze the problems of loan recovery in order to underscore the lessons of experience for bank management
- To sensitize bank management and lending officers to the evolving demands of loan recovery

STATEMENT OF THE PROBLEM

Bank loan recovery assignments are rarely conducted without hitches in emerging economies. In fact, a common feature in the nature of loan recovery actions is often resistance to such actions by the defaulters. This situation raises a pertinent question: In what context can the problems of loan recovery be discussed so that they highlight the lessons of experience for bank management? Answering this question—with a view to sensitizing lending officers to the need for thoroughness while committing their banks to particular loans—is my main objective in this chapter.

In most cases, the banking relationship between a bank and borrower breaks down when the bank decides to forcibly recover a loan. In response, borrowers often resort to plotting the failure of the actions. The plot manifests in various ways—in order to frustrate or create obstacles to recovery actions. The frustration becomes more debilitating in the following situations:

- The amount of the loan to be recovered is large
- Bad loans are either unsecured or not secured with tangible collateral
- Bank officials—especially lending officers—compromise themselves
- Borrowers who are in loan default are influential persons in society
- The loan agreement contains legal loopholes that borrowers can exploit

These issues offer perspectives that underlie the framework that I adopt to analyze problems of loan recovery in this chapter. In doing so, my overriding goal is to propound proactive strategies that can forestall or neutralize the problems. Let me now discuss the elements of my framework of analysis.

LARGE-LOAN EXPOSURES

Large-unit bad loans are, more often than not, difficult to recover. Such loans might be of hybrid nature with a complicated structure. When the loans are secured, the collateral value will also be large. This makes it more difficult to dispose of the collateral, as there may not be many who can afford and are willing to buy the collateral assets.

Consider that as a result of large loan size, a bank takes security in the borrower's factory (in the case of a manufacturing corporate borrower). When the loan goes bad and the bank decides to sell the factory, it might not be easy to dispose of it. The high factory cost, the anticipated additional costs of its revival, and the expense of relaunching its products could be real disincentives. In most cases, the bank would invoke its legal charge over the factory—often secured in an all-assets debenture—to appoint a receiver-manager to liquidate the factory. The actual winding up of the factory will likely be—and in most cases is—a nasty experience for both the bank and borrower. In the exercise of their windup duties, liquidators sometimes have to contend with employee sabotage, frustration by loan defaulters, and legal technicalities—all of which could indeed be debilitating. The problem is not abated when the loan is secured with real estate or even stock-in-trade. In both cases, the bank will have to engage an *auctioneer* to dispose of the collateral assets on a *forced sale* basis. In most cases, this might involve the following actions:

- Several advertisements in various communications media to create awareness of the intended sale
- Dealing with several small-lot buyers (in the case of disposal of large quantities of stock-in-trade)
- Recognizing certain *cultural* values (when the recovery action involves the sale of landed property in the borrower's hometown or other *sensitive* localities)

Frequently—and most practicing bankers would readily cite several instances to illustrate this—in a bid to frustrate the sale of collateral assets, loan defaulters will contest offer prices that the bank or auctioneer advertises. Often, the bank will make efforts—but all to no avail—to set offer prices that are mutually agreed upon between it and the borrowers. But in rejecting any proposed offer prices for collateral assets, borrowers might be deliberately working toward the failure of the bank's recovery actions. Thus, when it becomes apparent that the bank would nevertheless sell the collateral assets at reasonable offer prices without their consent or despite their objection, borrowers might go to court to seek an order to stop the bank. Often, the court would give the order, sometimes ex parte. When this happens, loan recovery actions become temporarily clogged.

In most cases, the bank does not go through these hassling experiences when the amounts of bad loans are relatively small. Thus, the size and type of loan, as well as the nature of its collateral, limit the effectiveness of loan recovery actions.

UNSECURED LENDING

Many would argue—and I subscribe to the thinking of some banking pundits—that collateral is not and should not be the primary consideration in making lending decisions. This stand on collateral is often justified on the grounds of a pragmatic consideration. In the final analysis, repayment of loans comes from cash inflows that borrowers generate with the loans during the tenor of the credit facilities. There is also the issue of bad publicity associated with disposing of collateral, especially on a *forced sale* basis. Yet, it is as well pertinent to consider counterarguments that support the reliance of banks on collateral as a secondary source of loan repayment. The following arguments are pertinent:

- Commitment of borrowers
  Where a bank lends *clean*, borrowers may not be effectively committed to repayment of the loan, as nothing would be at stake for them. This view is without prejudice to the time-honored recognition of the capacity of *blue chips*, *multinationals*, and *conglomerates*—to which banks generally lend clean or on terms of a *negative pledge*—to timely satisfy their loan obligations.
- Fate of unsecured loans
  The fate of unsecured loans hangs in the balance. A bank that grants unsecured credit facilities does so based on the trust that borrowers will not default. But it would be absurd for a bank to rely solely on *trust* in the ability of borrowers to repay their loans—when in fact, lending decisions are based purely on expectations or projections of future or uncertain positive financial outcomes that may after all not happen. Thus, *trust* becomes really baseless and unrealistic—a sort of gamble to which bankers are not and should never be oriented.
- Justification of collateral
  The essence of collateral is that a bank cannot afford to expose depositors' or shareholders' funds to avoidable risk of depletion or loss. Unsecured lending is about the surest way to plunge a bank into avoidable financial crisis. Bank deposits and shareholders' funds are put at risk when unsecured credit facilities become bad debts and make the charge-off statistics.

- Legal requirement

   The BOFI Act, No. 25 of 1991 (as amended), requires banks to take collateral to secure loans that they grant to borrowers. The act stipulates punishment for bank managements and officers who infringe its provisions. Bank officers who grant unsecured loans would be liable on conviction to specified fines, sanctions, or jail terms. The courts demonstrated the efficacy of this law in the trial of the former chief executive officers of banks that the CBN had bailed out in 2009 after it intervened in their financial crisis.

In view of the foregoing, there is nothing pejorative about asking for collateral to secure credit facilities. The alternative (taking unsecured lending exposures) is worse for the bank, especially when borrowers default—thus accentuating the need to recover the loans granted to them.

Recovery of a *properly* secured bad loan may not be easy, but its collateral gives hope that the credit will after all be recovered. Yet it is better, for instance, that time is wasted and expenses incurred while *liquidating* collateral to recover a bad loan than having no collateral on which to fall back. Where a loan is unsecured, the bank may have to obtain court orders, employ debt-recovery agents, or adopt some unorthodox methods to recover the loan. Often these cumbersome loan recovery devices introduce irrational tendencies in resolving bank—borrower differences. In most cases, they lead to actual breakdown of the banking relationship between the bank and borrower. When this happens, it becomes particularly difficult to get the borrower's full cooperation with the bank in recovering the bad loan.

COMPROMISING LOAN OFFICERS

How would a bank go about pursuing the recovery of bad loans for which borrowers allege that they *settled* with certain officers of the bank before they were granted the credit facilities? In other words, the borrowers claim that they did not utilize the full amount of their credit facilities. Thus, the bank does not have the moral basis to compel them to repay the full amounts of their loans. Some borrowers who might have been victims of this type of *fraud* may not be disposed to divulging information that they consider sensitive. However, whether such sensitive information is divulged *after* the loan has gone bad and is being forcibly recovered by the bank is immaterial. What is critical is the fact that unknown to the bank, such an *unethical* practice could be and indeed often is committed surreptitiously by lending officers. The seriousness of the problem is indicated by the extent and nature of the task involved in unraveling incidents of loan default, and the burden of recovering bad debts when there is such *insider abuse*. For such bad loans, recovery actions will run into a hitch on the grounds of the discovery of a conflict of interest—perhaps in the packaging, approving, and disbursing of loans by certain key officers of the bank.

I should also consider a related issue in probing why the borrower might have defaulted on the loan. Could it be that the borrower deliberately defaulted on the loan because of the compromise of the loan officers? The uncritical answer might be a loud "yes!" The purist would argue that it would be irrational for borrowers to repay money they did not utilize for the business purposes of their loans. In a different context, some would question the basis for asking borrowers to repay the loans considering their subjection to gratifying the selfish interests of the lending officers. In fact, the loan default could be excused on account of the (large) amount of the graft. But it is not uncommon that mischievous loan defaulters might want to make excuses for failing to meet their obligations to the bank. To that extent, claiming that they bribed some officers of the bank to approve their loans would be inconsequential to the bank's recovery actions. Such a claim should be largely disregarded, as it could be a ploy to embarrass the officers for some obscure reasons. For this reason, the bank should not believe the claim of the borrowers. It should insist that the claim lacks substance and merit.

However, the bank should order a thorough investigation of the claim by its inspection staff on one condition. It should do so if there is demonstrable evidence that particular lending officers compromised themselves. If the claim is proven, the affected officers should be sanctioned in accordance with the prescriptions of the code of ethics and professionalism for bankers. Depending on the degree of the offense, the bank may terminate the appointments of the affected officers. This would serve as a deterrent to other staff of the bank who might engage in such unethical practices. Yet, notwithstanding actions that the bank might take against the offending officers, loan recovery actions should continue. In other words, the borrower must be made to repay the full value of the loan plus accrued interest. This action will deter borrowing customers from corrupting bank officers with bribes. While the bank has a duty to punish its staff for professional misconduct, it should not be liable for losses incurred by borrowers who lure lending officers to compromise their principles.

Meanwhile, the recovery of bad loans enmeshed in this sort of controversy will certainly be intractable. Some banks would place the indicted staff on indefinite suspension pending full recovery of the loans, after which they would be sacked. Others would hand the staff over to the police with clear instructions to recover the loans. This could sometimes be done with the assistance of the police and the debt-recovery agents appointed by the bank. These actions introduce more bitterness into the recovery of bad loans.

INFLUENTIAL BORROWERS

Banks ordinarily court relationships with influential members of society—especially so-called high net worth individuals. Also, the few banks that have financial muscle often long to attract multinationals, conglomerates, or other powerful large corporates for banking relationships. In the process, and in order to retain customers, banks strive to provide them with *error-free* transactions processing, *effective* relationship management, and easily *accessible* borrowing facilities. But the ease of lending to this category of corporate customers is often premised on consideration of their efficient *organization*, strong *cash flows*, and good *management*. In most cases, the loans would be large and unsecured, with a *negative pledge* as the only comfort.

However, there is another—perhaps remotely business-driven but nevertheless rational—consideration for the observed favorable disposition of banks to strive to satisfy the banking and especially borrowing needs of such customers. As I point out below, while fulfilling the business goals of banks, such a consideration could become an albatross for banks when relationships turn sour as a result of default or other reasons. With this assertion, certain questions must be asked: What is the *other* consideration for craving banking relationships with influential customers? Why do the relatively big banks cling to *that* consideration as one of the means of driving the business? How and why does *the* consideration after all pose loan recovery problems? What should bank management do to circumvent the tendency of influential customers to dictate the terms of repayment of their *nonperforming* loans? Answers to these questions would help bank management to appreciate how to anticipate, mitigate, and assume the risk of banking with influential customers.

Let me at once mention that hardly do multinationals, conglomerates, and other large corporates default on their loans. Indeed, their ability to generate sustained cash flows and high transaction volumes, and in so doing promptly repay large loan amounts, has been the primary incentive to lend to them. However, where default becomes inevitable and occurs, the loan recovery process in this case tends to pose a unique problem. The problem derives largely from the difficulty in coping with, or trying to reverse, the preferential treatment hitherto given to such customers. But the problem becomes daunting when influential individuals are involved. It is this category of influential loan defaulters—individuals and corporates—with which I am presently concerned.

In coveting influential accounts, banks sometimes look beyond expectations of transaction gains—such as current account float, time deposits, interest income, fees, and commissions. These are some of the benefits that accrue *directly* from the accounts. Yet another consideration is the *indirect* benefits that may be realized from the links provided by influential customers. For instance, with influential customers a bank can have *some* access to certain business, social, and governmental networks. Such networks can help banks to accomplish the following:

- Improve liquidity and cash flow stability with huge and cheap deposit inflows, and float from collection accounts
- Expand or improve the quality of customer bases and profiles. This is a necessary long-term growth requirement for most banks
- Gain critical favorable public perception as well as improved market ratings and acceptability—all of which are essential to competition

- Attract and sustain profitable banking deals and transactions that largely increase the earnings profile
- Penetrate and consolidate the share of certain target markets in which banks want to operate for reasons of acceptable risk profiles

While business and social contacts remain important, the craze and race for the accounts of influential customers, and hence the aforementioned benefits, are even more evident in the pursuit of public sector banking relationships. Comprising the three tiers of government—federal, state, and local councils— and their agencies—ministries, parastatals, institutions, and so on—banks continue to take stakes in the characters and banking habits of the public sector. They do this for obvious reasons. In Nigeria, as would be the case in other and most developing economies, the public sector drives the economy as government remains the single biggest spender and generator of funds. Therefore, a bank that garners a chunk of public sector transactions would be assured of substantial earnings, time deposits, and current account float, among other benefits.

Influential customers could also intercede for their bankers in disputes involving the latter and certain third parties. Incidents requiring such inter- cession may not be easily identified and generalized for all or most banks. However, very influential customers may become worried and seek to inter- vene when the *continuing* existence of their banks is threatened—by a liquidity crunch, litigation, or the unintended infringement of banking law by the banks. These are examples of situations in which banks sometimes find themselves, thus becoming vulnerable and needing the external help that may come from influential customers. Yet while such help is usually very much treasured, it is often scarcely received freely. The real cost of such help transcends token gifts or the mere deference usually ascribed to highly valued customers. But its *opportunity cost* is the loss in earnings arising from the *waiver* of certain transaction costs, granting of *rebates* on interest and COT charges, and so on. In other words, the underlying accounts in essence attain the status of *prime* customers, the most significant benefit of which is general pricing concessions on all banking transactions. Influential customers are sometimes metaphori- cally designated "friends" or "family members" of the bank to underscore appreciation of their support to the bank.

With the foregoing setting in mind, imagine the dilemma of a bank that must recover the *nonperforming* loans it granted to influential customers. In the first place, the bank might not want to take any drastic actions against customers who were once its benefactors. For the bank, it could be scary that the customers might employ their awesome networks to inflict business injury on it. Above all, the bank might see reason in the proverbial *a friend in need is a friend in deed* to somewhat tolerate default on the loans. Loan recovery actions under these circumstances will be ineffective. On several occasions until 2009, some Nigerian banks threatened, but all to no avail, to publish the names of their influential debtors who had defaulted on their loans. The loan defaulters were believed to have the capacity to repay their loans, but chose not to. Banks in such cases appreciate that forceful recovery actions would be countered. However, a bank in this situation should adopt *moral suasion* as the main approach to recovering the loans. Depending on the amounts involved—where large sums of money are at stake—the bank might request that its key board members talk to customers on its behalf. If such appeals to the conscience of customers—reinforced by the mediation of key directors—fail, the bank may decide to employ subtle but embarrassing loan recovery tactics. Perhaps, the most embarrassing actions that a bank could take against an influential loan defaulter would include but are not limited to employing a debt-recovery agent. The agent may adopt any or all of the following embarrassing tactics:

- Confront the loan defaulter at a major public gathering
- Disclose the customer's indebtedness to the leadership of their religious faith—church or mosque
- Publish the loan default, with the name of the borrower, in major national newspapers

These actions deal damage to the customer's *ego* and *self-concept*, and the public's *perception* of its *personality*.

The embarrassment option is favored as a fallback largely because, as influential members of society, these customers will do their utmost to avoid negative publicity. More often than not the tactic is effective, particularly in cases involving the following personalities:

- Politicians seeking elective positions in government
- High-ranking office holders in the public service
- Renowned industrialists or so-called "captains of industries" who lead private sector businesses

Certain factors or conditions contribute to the success of this loan recovery strategy. It should be obvious to influential borrowers that the bank really is determined to recover its loans. Evidence of the bank's determination could be shown by any or all of the following actions:

- Demonstration that the bank has a dire need to recover the loans
- Loss of patience with borrowers' delayed, unreliable, or neglected loan repayment plans
- Determination to embarrass customers for their loan defaults

Frequently, customers' indifference gradually begins to shift to concern for the amicable settlement of their indebtedness, once they come to grips with the foregoing actions.

It would not be unlikely that the customers would soon request a dialogue and negotiation with the bank. Dialogue and negotiation, under these circumstances, would aim to achieve particular results:

- Resolution of possible breakdowns in communication between the bank and borrower
- Investigation of claims of possible mismanagement of the borrower's loan accounts
- Review of disputed transactions, fees, and charges to loan accounts
- Reconciliation of the bank's statements on the loan accounts with the customer's records

These are some of the controversial issues on which the most influential loan defaulters might hinge delays or objections to the repayment of their credit facilities. Thus, commencement of dialogue between the bank and the customer signifies progress toward recovery of the loans.

FLAWED LEGAL SYSTEM

Loan recovery actions sometimes end, or may be ultimately resolved, in the law courts. The court should ideally be the vehicle for execution of the processes of loan recovery by banks. Unfortunately, in many emerging markets, the functioning of the legal system does not hold much hope for the speedy trial of lawsuits. For sneaky borrowing customers, the flawed legal system offers a safe haven to perpetrate loan default and sometimes end up scot-free. Such customers might take advantage of loopholes in the legal system, or in loan contracts, to dupe banks. The problem becomes exacerbated where loan agreements contain avoidable legal flaws. Often such flaws place banks in a disadvantageous position when they embark on loan recovery through court action against borrowers who are in default. Therefore, for most banks the settlement of loan disputes or defaults in court would be pursued as a last resort. The reasons for this assertion are quite instructive:

- The legal system is relatively inefficient and may have loopholes that crafty loan defaulters may exploit.
- The *direct* and *indirect* costs of lawsuits as a means of loan recovery— losses of time, money, and goodwill—could be quite substantial.
- A bank might lose an otherwise legitimate claim on a loan default through the application of technical considerations in court.

Thus, even where a bank institutes a court action to recover a loan, it sometimes after all would not be averse to settling the matter with the borrower out of court. Yet, settlement out of court is a weak loan recovery option because it ends up twisting the arm of bank management about making concessions on terms for repayment of the loan. Material concessions—usually expressed as rebates on or outright waivers of certain charges, fees, and commissions— deplete earnings on the loan. A concession could also be granted in terms of rescheduling the loan repayment tenor. This might depend on a substituted source of repayment that eases the strain on cash flows. However, the grant of such a concession sets a negative precedent on which other loan defaulters, who could have easily repaid their loans, might rely in order to negotiate settlements with the bank. Contrary to possible thinking in some quarters, the aforementioned weaknesses of out-of-court settlement are not mitigated by brandishing it nowadays as a *compromise* that the bank and borrower should accept in the interest of their future banking relationship.

Banks avoid litigation as a means of recovering loans. However, litigation tends to be unavoidable in a democratic culture where due process of the law should be followed to establish the case against loan defaulters. Banks always have recourse to court actions if the collateral securing nonperforming loans are not perfected. There is the argument that in upholding the modern principles of rule of law in society, the courts remain the most civilized medium for the settlement of disputes between citizens, governments, businesses, institutions, and other organizations. This per se is incontrovertible. However, it is the abuse of the judicial process by borrowing customers as a means to frustrate the loan recovery efforts of banks that is abhorrent and inimical to effective bank management. The usually sinister abuses are accomplished by various methods that sometimes hopelessly incapacitate loan recovery actions. The common abuses include the following:

- Court action
  Loan defaulters institute court action against a bank based on the *hint* that the bank could soon send a loan demand letter to or commence loan recovery actions against them. In this case, the bank has not yet decided to take court action against the borrower. The bank will therefore be responding to the borrower's claims—which in most cases would be spurious.
- Preemptive court action
  Sensing that the bank will ultimately sue them on account of their loan default, based on information they *glean* from informants, the borrowers decide to take preemptive court action against the bank. This represents a situation where the bank could have decided to go, but has not yet gone, to court to obtain judgment against the borrowers.
- Countersuit
  As a reaction to a court summons served on them, and to prevent the bank from obtaining an unexpected but timely judgment against them, the borrowers file a countersuit against the bank. With this development, both cases would run concurrently. Thus, even if judgment is delivered in one case, levying of execution might await determination of the other.

There could be several other examples of impediments to loan recovery actions resulting from a flawed legal system. Variations in the impediments relate mainly to the character of the loan defaulters involved.

The purposes that the observed legal loopholes serve for borrowers who want to dupe banks through loan default are quite revealing. Besides technical issues of law often raised to weaken the bank's case, loan defaulters seek to deliberately delay repayment of the loan. They succeed in achieving this objective when it takes up to two years or more to get court judgment on one case. While the case lingers, the bank would be constrained to start making provisions on the loan in line with prudential guidelines for risk assets classification. Assuming that the bank even wins the case, the court would most probably fix the rate of interest to be charged to the loan, and usually at far below the market rate. The exceptionally low interest rate usually takes effect retroactively—from the commencement of the lawsuit until the loan is fully repaid. While banks protest this implied income loss, the courts remain adamant.

In the framework of the legal ploy that crafty loan defaulters adopt are various claims in court of *unfair and unprofessional treatment of transactions* in their loan accounts. The following serve as specific examples to illustrate the claims:

- *Excessive* interest charges
- Wrong value dating of transactions, especially deposits to loan accounts
- *Spurious* fees and commissions
- *Hidden* or *intrinsic* charges on transactions

The process of investigating the issues in these claims would probably require the following, among other things:

- Evidence of the claims by the borrower of unfair treatment of transactions—which the bank might contest
- Reconciliation of the loan accounts to ascertain the most likely or accurate indebtedness of the borrower to the bank—which might not receive the desired cooperation from the bank
- Tendering of statements of the loan accounts by the bank—which the borrower would most likely dispute

All this tends to increase delays and the mutual resentment of the parties toward each other. Thus, settlement or recovery of loans enmeshed in this situation can be anything but hitch-free. Relating this outcome to the frequent adjournment of court cases, one begins to appreciate the dilemma of banks that might want to recover bad loans through the courts.

COLLUSION WITH BANK EMPLOYEES

Certain factors or conditions can easily frustrate loan recovery actions. One of the causes of frustration is where certain key or responsible officers of a bank collude with loan-defaulting customers or loan recovery agents appointed by the bank. Another cause is where loan recovery agents collude with loan-defaulting customers. These situations rarely happen, but when they do—and they sometimes do—loan recovery actions become messy. Also, the bank finds itself in a dilemma when the surreptitious activities of its own employees or agents incapacitate its loan recovery efforts.

It is believed that bank officers and agents that engage in this *fraud* are often led to the act by greed and the selfish desire to enrich themselves to the detriment of the bank. The officers and agents who engage in such acts give the impression that they are dissatisfied employees looking for opportunities to swindle the bank—perhaps as compensation for their apparent career failure. It is therefore instructive for bank management to constantly monitor the activities of its employees—especially those who hold sensitive positions or are given sensitive assignments. This will enable it to apply appropriate sanctions against any proven cases of official misconduct.

A variation of the problem of collusion is observed where ineffective agents are retained for key loan recovery assignments. This often happens in situations where the borrower successfully "settles" the agent—persuading him, in the process, to a compromise position against the interest of the bank. When this happens, the result of recovery actions will be poor while the loan-defaulting customer remains unperturbed. In order to avoid the undue waste of time resulting from such fraudulent compromises, it is advised that bank management should set achievement targets for agents—in terms of recovery amounts and the time frame over which their performance on loan recovery assignments must be evaluated.

Loan recovery briefs may be given for an initial, or probationary, period of 90 days. During this period, the bank expects the agent to demonstrate the ability to effectively execute its recovery assignments. Once it becomes obvious that particular agents are not serious or lack the capacity to perform, they should be debriefed—and this should form part of their contract with the bank. The bank should also avoid the uncritical practice of giving agents advance payments for loan recovery assignments. In some cases, agents will collect the money without either doing the job or doing it to the satisfaction of the bank.

As much as possible, banks should cut their losses on nonperforming loans. This is notwithstanding that a standard clause in their offer letters commits borrowers to paying expenses associated with loan recovery. In principle, borrowers must bear all expenses that the bank incurs on its loans, including the costs of loan recovery in the event of default. In practice, however, it is not always possible to recoup such expenses when a loan goes bad.

QUESTIONS FOR DISCUSSION AND REVIEW

1. What do you consider the most critical obstacle to loan recovery in emerging markets and why?

2. In what context can the problems of loan recovery be analyzed to underscore its lessons for bank management?
3. How should bank management effectively sensitize loan officers to the evolving demands of loan recovery?
4. In what ways do "large-loan exposure" and "influential borrowers" pose loan recovery challenges?
5. What are the arguments for and against unsecured bank lending?

Part IV

Asset Portfolio Quality, Risk and Control

Basel Accords and Credit Portfolio Issues in Emerging Economies

Chapter 36

Applications of Basel Accords in Emerging Economies

LEARNING FOCUS AND OUTCOMES

The credit risk crisis in global banks has continued to attract attention in international financial circles. The thinking is that "internationally active banks" should devise effective methodologies for risk management if they are to survive the scourge of the credit risk crisis. The Basel Committee has been at the forefront of international efforts to tame the crisis. Its Basel I and Basel II Accords are classic cases in point.

Unfortunately, banks in developing countries are finding it difficult to fully implement the Accords. Unlike their counterparts in developed countries that

Emerging Market Bank Lending and Credit Risk Control. http://dx.doi.org/10.1016/B978-0-12-803438-5.00036-2
Copyright © 2016 Elsevier Inc. All rights reserved.

have adopted the Accords, banks in emerging and developing economies simply cherry-pick and implement only some aspects of the Accords—especially those that meet their immediate needs. Taking cognizance of the foregoing, you will have accomplished the following in reading this chapter:

- Identify the founding basis and goals of the Basel Committee[1] and show how the goals inform the Basel I and Basel II Accords
- Evaluate ways in which the Basel Accords are useful in the management of the credit risk of banks in emerging economies
- Examine the credit risk management issues in emerging markets banks that the Basel I and Basel II Accords address
- Discuss practical difficulties in implementing the credit risk management goals of the Basel I and Basel II Accords in emerging economies
- Assess the extent to which the Basel I and Basel II Accords have achieved their set objectives

TOWARD BASEL I AND BASEL II ACCORDS

Global bank risk management has undergone meaningful transformation under the auspices of the Basel Accords. Starting from 1988 when Basel I was released, risk management in bank lending assumed unusual importance in countries around the world. In drawing up the Basel II Accord in 2004, the Basel I Accord was consolidated with significant changes in risk management policies, devices, and models. The Basel III Accord, published in 2010, further advanced the cause of Basel I while building on the provisions and strengths of Basel II. Nevertheless, Basel III is beyond the scope of this book. Besides, it is not significantly applicable to the situation in emerging economies.

Ironically, each of the Basel Accords followed a period of banking crisis and money panic that jolted financial system regulatory authorities around the world. While the financial crisis of the 1970s and 1980s gave birth to the Basel I Accord, the Basel II Accord was informed by a similar crisis in the 1990s. Of course, the financial meltdown that swept the global financial system between 2007 and 2009 gave rise to the Basel III Accord. The three Accords yet share a common feature. Their underlying objective is to strengthen the regulatory framework for the supervision of internationally active banks. But this objective is founded on the need to stem the liquidity crises, distress, and failures of global banks. In order to achieve this goal, the Basel Accords recommend that global banks adopt specific risk management criteria, policies, and models.

This chapter provides answers to questions bordering on the mechanics of the Basel I and Basel II Accords. However, emphasis is on identifying,

---

1. I have used the terms "Basel Committee" and "G-10" interchangeably to refer to the Group of Ten countries that established and constituted the initial members of the Basel Committee on Banking Supervision.

discussing, and drawing lessons from the impacts of the Accords on credit risk management in global banks. While situating the Basel Accords in this context, this chapter provides an overview of the Basel Committee—its founding, goals, and work. A critical evaluation of the purport and practicalities of the Basel Accords raises pertinent questions as presented below.

- What are the founding basis and goals of the Basel Committee, and how do the goals inform the Basel I and Basel II Accords?
- In what respects are the Basel Accords useful to the management of global banks?
- Are there practical difficulties in implementing the Basel I and Basel II Accords?
- What credit risk management issues for global banks do the Basel I and Basel II Accords specifically address?
- To what extent have the Basel I and Basel II Accords achieved their set objectives?

MAKING OF BASEL ACCORDS

The Basel Accords, easily the most influential blueprint for international banking reform, provide both an authoritative and a controversial framework for credit risk management in global banks. The Accords offer possibilities into which regulators and bank management can tap to temper and possibly forestall credit risk. In what ways do the Basel Accords provide guidance on how bankers could manage credit risk well? How effective are credit risk management methodologies under the auspices of the Basel Accords? These are the central questions that this chapter addresses.

The Basel Accords represent agreement of member countries of the Basel Committee on the need and method to strengthen regulation in order to achieve and sustain a sound international banking system. The Accords are designed to satisfy a yearning of industrialized countries for a common framework for the supervision of internationally active banks. Incidentally, the member states and several nonmembers will want to implement the Accords even as the Basel Committee lacks legal power to enforce its resolutions. Peculiarities in different countries inform the decision of the Committee to refrain from enacting law to enforce the Basel Accords. The decision to legislate on aspects of the Accords is rather left at the discretion of the Committee's member countries.

It is interesting that critical analyses dot the literature on the Basel Accords. While some scholars, authors, analysts, and other interested parties applaud the Accords, others are critical of their purport and practicalities. Yet the finance literature is replete with more views that underscore the significance of the Basel Accords. This is understandable considering the mounting risks in international banking and finance that the Basel Accords have tamed to a large extent. But we must also admit that the road to any degree of success of the Basel Accords is rough, laced with thorny issues concerning effective implementation. As I now discuss the Basel Accords, effort is made to weigh the credits of each Accord against its failings.

THE BASEL COMMITTEE

The Basel Accords resulted from the work of the Basel Committee that the Central Bank governors of the Group of 10 countries (i.e., the G-10) set up in late 1974 in response to recurring global banking crises. Initially, 11 industrialized nations, represented by senior representatives of their bank regulatory authorities and Central Banks, constituted the membership of the Basel Committee as referred to by the G-10. Ostensibly, their intention was to stem the bank distress and failure that had marked the evolution of the global banking system.

The founding countries had set up the Committee, which meets every quarter, in the wake of the preceding banking crises. The Committee seeks and fosters international cooperation in the quest for an effective regulatory framework for, and supervision of, global banks. It works and cooperates with Central Banks of its member countries "to enhance understanding of key supervisory issues and improve the quality of banking supervision worldwide" (Basel Committee, 1988). A more succinct statement of its role emphasizes that

The Committee does not possess any formal supranational supervisory authority, and its conclusions do not, and were never intended to, have legal force. Rather, it formulates broad supervisory standards and guidelines and recommends statements of best practice.

(Basel Committee, 1988)

It's obvious from the foregoing that the G-10 instituted the Basel Committee in an apparent move to check future financial shocks that might be similar to or of greater magnitude than those of the 1970s and 1980s.

An important aspect of the work of the Committee is to harmonize international banking standards as a means of advancing regulation and supervision of global banks. However, the notion, basis, and preoccupation of the Basel Committee originated in its founding goal. Since its founding, it subscribes to "extend regulatory coverage, promote adequate banking supervision, and ensure that no foreign banking establishment can escape supervision" (Basel Committee, 1988). In pursuit of these principles, the Committee aims "to close gaps in international supervisory coverage" (Basel Committee, 1988). The foregoing principles remain the overriding cause of the Basel Committee. In fact, the main thrusts of the Basel I, Basel II, and Basel III Accords are informed by these principles.

The underlying goal and principles of the Basel Committee are unlikely to change, or cease to dictate, the responsibility of its member countries in the future. Unfortunately, as noted above, the Committee functions only in an advisory capacity. While it could propose standards to advance the cause of international banking regulation and supervision, it does not have the legal power to enforce its recommendations. It becomes, in this sense, the proverbial "toothless bulldog." The responsibility to enforce its recommendations rests with the Central Banks of its member countries. This perhaps informs the free hand that the Central Bank governors of its member countries have to freely discuss issues on the Committee's agenda.

BASEL I ACCORD

In formal terms, and as expounded by the Basel Committee itself, the Basel I Accord is referred to as the *International Convergence of Capital Measurements and Capital Standards.* However, popular usage and literature references to the Accord document often refer to it as simply Basel I or the Basel Capital Accord. It was originally drafted and published in July 1988 following the agreement of the Central Bank governors of the G-10 countries.

Basel I essentially specifies a "framework for measuring capital adequacy and the minimum standard to be achieved" by internationally active banks (Basel Committee, 1988). Its application is restricted to the G-10 countries. Yet the Accord gained acceptance in non-G-10 countries, especially newly industrializing countries. Perhaps the non-G-10 countries welcomed Basel I as a panacea for their banking reform problems. This is notwithstanding that the Basel Committee had opined that the Basel I Accord should not be applied in emerging markets.

The Committee's stance was informed by glaring differences between the reform needs of industrialized nations and those of emerging markets. However, there is another possible reason for the adoption of Basel I in non–Basel Committee member countries. The view is held that "the adoption of Basel I standards was seen by large investment banks as a sign of regulatory strength and financial stability in emerging markets" (Basel Committee, 1988).

Basis of Basel I

The Basel I Accord originated in discontent with the state of international finance following the banking crisis of the 1970s and 1980s. Prior to the crisis, some global banks had been tainted by reckless lending, excessive risk-taking, and weak corporate governance. The boom that preceded the banking crisis of the early 1980s encouraged profligacy. Some banks had during the boom also ventured into offshore banking in quest of "regulatory arbitrage" in less developed, more liberal, and more profitable financial markets.

Thus the drafting and publishing of Basel I had its basis in four main considerations, namely—

- The banking crisis of the 1970s and 1980s, which posed an urgent threat to the fabric and functioning of the global financial system;
- The predisposition of banks to highly risky lending and OTC derivatives that contributed to the financial crisis;

- The practice of "regulatory arbitraging," which created distortions in evaluating the performance of global banks; and
- The need to evolve a unified regulatory framework to ease and strengthen the supervision of operations of global banks.

In the following sections, it will be apparent that these considerations are reflected in the contents and conduct of the Basel I Accord. This is especially seen in the formulation of objectives of Basel I.

Objectives of Basel I

The 11 industrialized nations that established the Basel Committee at the end of 1974 had a commanding interest that influenced the making of Basel I. The interest was to standardize and institutionalize an appropriate regulatory framework for the capitalization of global banks. With robust capital structures, the thinking of the Committee was that internationally active banks would have the resilience to withstand future financial crises and market shocks. Drawing from this thinking and subsequent actions taken by the Basel Committee, it is apparent that Basel I sought to achieve three main objectives, namely—

- To harmonize a framework for standardizing the regulation of capital adequacy of internationally active banks within the G-10 countries;
- To set uniform standards for the capitalization of internationally active banks in the member countries of the Basel Committee; and
- To use a methodical framework to determine quantitative standards for regulating and checking the credit risk of global banks.

While the Accord established "minimum" capital that global banks should attain, regulatory authorities in individual countries were free to set higher levels of required capital. The Basel Committee focused on and worked toward achieving these objectives until it became apparent that aspects of the Basel I Accord needed to be amended. The amendment was effected with revisions of the Accord in 1996 and enactment of Basel II in 2004.

Elements of Basel I

The body of Basel I comprised three main sections—the *constituents of capital*, the *risk-weighting system*, and a *target standard ratio*. The Accord identified two tiers of capital that constitute the total capital base of a bank (i.e., the constituents of capital). While tier 1 capital denotes a bank's core capital (i.e., its equity capital and disclosed reserves), tier 2 capital connotes noncore capital items (referred to in Basel I as "supplementary capital"). In isolating the two tiers of capital, the Accord clarified aspects of their components and qualifying attributes.

On the risk weighting of assets, Basel I assessed capital adequacy in the context of the credit risk that a bank assumes. It proffered a logical approach to assessing capital adequacy based on the relationship of capital to risk-weighted assets and off-balance sheet exposures. Thus, the Accord recommended a "weighted risk ratio" as a measure of capital adequacy. This ratio weights and relates the riskiness of a bank's assets and off-balance sheet exposures to its capital.

Each asset and off-balance sheet exposure was assigned a risk weight reflecting the perception and assessment of its riskiness. The risk weights ranged from 0% to 100%. Assets risk-weighted at 0% tend to be the riskless, risk-free, and safest investments on the balance sheet of a bank. Such assets include T-bills and sovereign (government) bonds. On the contrary, assets risk-weighted at 100% (usually unsecured credit facilities) are considered riskiest. The resultant risk ratio can then be used to assess capital adequacy. The structure comprises a framework of five risk weights, each of which can be assigned to particular categories of risk. Basel I offered broad definitions of risk categories to which specific risk weights applied. The weights reflected the riskiness of assets and off-balance sheet exposures of a bank. Thus, assets were assigned risk weights that showed that they were riskless or risk-free, low-risk, or highly risky.

In the third section, Basel I set a target standard risk ratio of 8% that every internationally active bank should satisfy. This ratio relates a bank's capital to its weighted risk assets. It implies that a bank's tier 1 and tier 2 capital should cover at least 8% of its risk-weighted assets. Of the 8% risk ratio, the Accord recommended that at least 4% must be covered by tier 1 capital. It is believed that the risk ratio mitigates credit risk and assures the safety of funds in deposit-insured global banks.

Usefulness of Basel I

There is no doubt that Basel I made a positive impact on the global financial system during the period of its implementation. The usefulness of Basel I is perhaps most evident in its adoption by all member countries of the Basel Committee, as well as some nonmembers. The non-G-10 countries that also adopted the Accord within 10 years of its enactment included leading emerging economies—China, Russia, and India. Several other emerging economies followed suit. Specifically, Basel I was an appropriate response to the financial crisis of the 1970s and 1980s. The crisis at the time was a wake-up call to bankers, banking regulators, and governments around the world. The situation demanded the urgent solution that Basel I effectively provided. The Basel I Accord especially helped to stabilize the global financial system and save it from a ruinous downward spiral in the wake of the crisis.

In the aftermath of the crisis, it dawned on authorities that an ordered framework for international banking system regulatory cooperation was needed. It is noteworthy that Basel I yet filled this need. This is not a mean achievement considering the time taken and level of work done by the Basel Committee to reach the Basel I Accord. The Committee spent several years deliberating on the banking supervisory problems threatening international financial system that had caused the distress and failure of some global banks. That the Basel Committee held regular meetings to arrive at the Basel I Accord should be taken for granted. However, that it held several brainstorming sessions as part of or in course of its meetings may not.

Shortcomings of Basel I

Criticisms of Basel I abound in the international finance literature. The main criticisms of the Accord, discussed below, stem from its shortcomings and the controversies that trailed it.

Narrow scope and focus

Basel I adopted a very narrow view of the challenges facing international banking and finance and how to solve them. Due to its limited scope, it failed to address some of the critical problems of the global financial system. For instance, the Accord focused on only credit risk, and by doing so targeted only the G-10 countries for its adoption. Yet, both G-10 and several non-G-10 countries adopted the Accord. Unfortunately, the Accord neither tamed banking excesses nor fulfilled the popular expectation that it would serve as a panacea for global financial crises. Omission of equally important banking issues—market, operational, and liquidity risks—in the Accord rendered it ineffectual. Besides, its exclusion of market discipline negatively impacted the strict observance of its guidelines. For these reasons, the global financial system remained unstable and prone to avoidable crises.

Nonsensitive to risk

One of the common criticisms of the Basel I Accord is that it was not sensitive to credit risk. This criticism stems mainly from the use of a uniform risk weight for a category of assets, when in reality the riskiness of individual assets within the category varies. Consider the case of a bank's corporate lending. Basel I recommended a standardized 100% risk weight on loans granted to private sector corporate borrowers. This uniform risk weight, which bears a charge to the bank's regulatory capital, was adopted irrespective of differences in size, credit rating, market share, and financial performance of corporate borrowers. It did not reckon with the fact that the loan repayment abilities and track records of corporate borrowers also reflect marked differences. On this count, the Basel I Accord was anything but foolproof in its guidelines for the calculation of capital adequacy.

Maneuvering of risk weights

Basel I left room for banks to manipulate its risk-weighting system in a bid to satisfy regulatory capital requirements. This was possible because Basel I provided for the use of absolute risk weights to calculate risks of assets, and therefore regulatory capital. In time, it was possible for banks to misrepresent their real risk levels. Banks maneuvered the risk-weighting process to have reduced risk-weighted assets on paper, while assuming more real risk. This implies that banks were exposed to risk that was not really accounted for or reflected in their regulatory capital. With this so-called "regulatory capital arbitrage," banks took more risk with less capital. While they took more risk, they avoided the concomitant increase in regulatory capital. In such a situation, bank capital would be inadequate to offset the increase in risk.

Verdict on Basel I

It may not be straightforward to say whether Basel I succeeded or failed. And to perfectly assess the extent to which the Accord achieved its mandate would boggle the mind. Yet it is pertinent to review the performance of the Accord in relation to its goals. I should do so by comparing milestones attained in its reform agenda with its observed failings. First, I have pinpointed specific achievements and drawbacks of Basel I. Now, I can say whether the Accord truly achieved its goals, and to what extent.

Basel I assumed that global banks could surmount liquidity crises and market shocks if they were well capitalized. Capital adequacy, which underlies the making of Basel I, was at center stage of the Accord's agenda. Thus, Basel I prescribed required minimum capitalization for global banks to meet its capital adequacy criterion. The required minimum capital was seen as a buffer against the credit risk that global banks assumed.

It could be argued that the Basel I Accord succeeded to a large extent with regard to its aforementioned objective. G-10 and several non-G-10 countries successfully put the standard risk ratio of 8% into practice, as well as requiring that 4% of the 8% risk capital be covered by tier 1 capital. This is a commendable achievement, one that provided a good foundation for subsequent work of the Basel Committee in enacting the Basel II and Basel III Accords. That the standard "risk-weighted assets ratio" of 8% was retained in both Basel II and Basel III shows that the effort put into formulating it yielded fruition. It is also noteworthy that Basel I engendered international cooperation in a bid to formulate a uniform regulatory framework for the supervision of global banks. By doing so, it pointed regulatory authorities to a new direction for the attainment of a sound and stable international banking order.

Unfortunately, the Basel I Accord did not proffer a foolproof way of mitigating credit risk. Credit-induced money panics, bank distress, and bank failures remained disturbing reminders that all was not well with Basel I. Perhaps this was most evident in the banking crisis of the 1990s that defied Basel I. Ostensibly, the capacity of Basel I to ensure a sound and stable international banking system needed to be tuned up. The Basel Committee addressed this and other shortcomings with Basel II.

BASEL II ACCORD

The need for the Basel II Accord, which originated in the shortcomings of Basel I, became apparent in the wake of the banking crisis of the 1990s. Like previous banking crises, that of the 1990s posed a serious threat to international banking and finance. It informed the decision of the Basel Committee in 1999 to urgently revise the 1988 Basel Capital Accord. The revision afforded the Committee the opportunity to plug observed loopholes in the Basel I Accord. The Basel Committee clearly stated its overriding purpose in revising the Basel I Accord. Besides consolidating important aspects of the Basel I Accord, the revision exercise aimed to regain stability of the international financial system.

The three fundamental objectives stated below, according to the Basel Committee (2004), informed its work to revise the Basel I Accord. The objectives that guided formulation of Basel II were based on the need to—

- develop a framework that would further strengthen the soundness and stability of the international banking system;
- maintain sufficient consistency that capital adequacy regulation will not be a significant source of competitive inequality among internationally active banks; and
- promote the adoption of stronger risk management practices by the banking industry.

As can be inferred from the foregoing, the Basel Committee recognized the need to improve on Basel I. In its thinking, such improvement should result in a sound and stable international financial system. Besides, the Committee intended to check the "regulatory capital arbitrage" through which banks maneuvered the Basel Capital Accord. I appraise the achievements of Basel II in the context of these objectives in the course of this discussion. How did Basel II improve on the Basel Capital Accord? Did Basel II achieve international convergence of the regulatory framework to ensure a level playing field for internationally active banks? Did it stabilize the international financial system? These questions define the focus of my analysis and discussion.

Structure of Basel II

Basel II is structured around three Pillars with the aim of correcting observed lapses in the Basel Capital Accord. Each of the three Pillars defines a key area of responsibility for the attainment of this goal. The issues that the Pillars address border on ways banks and regulatory authorities should—

- Determine minimum capital requirements that are informed by or are sensitive to credit, operational, and market risks.
- Put in place a supervisory review process that ensures effective oversight of all possible banking risks, and in doing so adjusts regulatory capital requirements to reflect risks that are omitted under Pillar 1.
- Instill appropriate market discipline that enhances transparency of a bank's risk profile, including improved disclosure of risk—concentration, distribution, management, and so on.

These responsibility areas correspond respectively to Pillar 1 (i.e., Minimum Capital Requirements), Pillar 2 (i.e., Supervisory Review Process), and Pillar 3 (i.e., Market Discipline).

The effect of these Pillars is that risk management assumes more importance under the Basel II Accord. Pillar 1 reflects obvious improvements to the Basel I Accord. It significantly expands the scope of Basel I and adopts a more risk-sensitive methodology for the calculation of capital adequacy. It also enlists bank management responsibility for effective implementation of the minimum regulatory capital requirements. Pillar 2 institutes a supervisory program that furthers the regulation of operations of internationally active banks. By doing so, it provides a framework that helps bank management to moderate credit risk-taking.

With Pillar 3, Basel II underlines the role and significance of markets in the conduct of the international financial system. The intent of Pillar 3 is that markets should be an effective check on the performance of bank management and banking system regulatory authorities. Success is attained when markets forestall reckless lending, excessive risk-taking, and insider abuses. Above all, it is the role of markets to ensure that bank management and regulators are made accountable for their actions.

In Pillar 1, Basel II clarifies procedures for the calculation of Minimum Capital Requirements. Under the Pillar 1 framework, input into the calculation of regulatory capital comes from the assessment of credit, operational, and market risks. Here Pillar 1 seeks to determine the regulatory capital that cushions the impact of these risks. In respect of the risks, it fulfills a particular risk assessment need as summarized below.

Credit risk	How to risk-weight, rate, and provide for risk inherent in bank assets, mainly the risk assets (i.e., loans and advances)
Operational risk	Devising means to hedge against the risk of abuse, infringement, or the failure of a bank's internal operating system
Market risk	How to reflect losses that a bank suffers as a result of fluctuations in asset prices

The credit risk aspect of Pillar 1 encompasses three methodologies that underlie the risk weighting and rating of bank assets to determine regulatory capital. These are the *standardized approach, internal ratings-based approach,* and *securitization framework.* These innovative approaches redress the criticisms of the methodology Basel I adopted for the assessment and rating of the riskiness of bank assets.

Strengths of Basel II

A critical issue in the revision of the Basel I Accord was how to get regulatory capital properly aligned with credit risk. In order to improve on Basel I along this line, Basel II was made more complex and rigorous than the original Basel Capital Accord. In this way, Basel II contrasts sharply with the simplicity of Basel I. Specifically, Basel II improved on Basel I in six significant credit risk management ways that are widely acknowledged. It is noteworthy and acknowledged that Basel II, among several other achievements—

- broadened the scope of risk factors used for the calculation of global bank minimum capital requirements
- improved the risk-weighting system, and in doing so ensures that appropriate risk weights are assigned to assets. Thus, Basel II is credited with being more sensitive to risk than Basel I.
- introduced the use of risk data provided by external credit rating agencies as input to the risk weighting of bank assets.
- recognizes credit risk data that banks generate from their internal risk models as complementary data for the calculation of their risk-weighted assets
- offers methodological options and informed choices to banks and regulatory authorities for the calculation of minimum capital requirements
- consolidates the assets of holding companies in their home and host countries in order to ascertain the true risk profiles of internationally active banks.

Let me now briefly explain aspects of these improvements.

Broadening of risk factors

Pillar 1 broadened the scope of the risk-determining factors of the regulatory capital requirement. In addition to credit risk, it recognizes market risk (i.e., the 1996 amendment to Basel I) and operational risk as inputs into the calculation of the minimum capital requirement (i.e., regulatory capital). In contrast, Basel I focused only on credit risk. The introduction of market risk and operational risk as additional determinants of regulatory capital lends credence to the cause of credit risk management.

Improved risk measurement

Pillar 1 introduced an improved approach to the measurement of capital adequacy that is more sensitive to credit risk than that of Basel I. Credit risk was poorly assessed under Basel I due to its assignment of mechanistic risk weights to the assets on which regulatory capital largely depended. Risk weighting of assets of banks under Pillar 1 of Basel II eliminates the loopholes that this situation created. By doing so, it plugged loopholes that banks had exploited under Basel I to manipulate regulatory capital to camouflage their high risk profiles.

Basel II was enacted, in contrast to Basel I, to institutionalize a more risk-sensitive disposition in the conduct of global bank credit transactions. The Basel Committee pursued and accomplished this goal. By doing so, it redressed the most criticized flaw of the Basel I Accord. Basel I had used an absolute risk weight for all categories of claims of banks on private sector counterparties. Yet marked differences in risk characterize the obligors (i.e., counterparties) in this sector and the claims on them. This flaw undermined any reliance on credit risk as a measure of or check on global bank regulatory capital. In redressing the flaw, Basel II introduced the use of realistic but relative risk weights to calculate regulatory capital. This approach ensures that regulatory capital is responsive to credit risk, unlike what was obtained under the Basel I Accord.

In this sense, global bank capital requirements will be informed, or influenced, by bank risk appetites. This outcome has three major implications for bank capital, bank management, and capital regulation:

- If a bank takes or wishes to take more or excessive credit risk, it should beef up its relative levels of regulatory capital.
- There is a need for banks to improve on credit risk management in order to operate efficiently and compete internationally. Under the Basel II Accord, improved risk management has a bearing on operating efficiencies.
- A bank that chooses to take less credit risk or to be risk-averse to lending will be able to allocate relatively less regulatory capital.

These implications underscore the intent of the Basel II Accord to institutionalize effective credit risk management in bank lending. It is either that a bank does well with risk management and avoids pressure to increase regulatory capital, or that it does badly and will be under pressure to allocate more capital to hedge against credit risk.

Introduction of credit rating

Assignment of risk weights based on credit ratings of obligors is a significant improvement on the Basel I Accord. The thinking is that credit ratings would help banks to determine the relative riskiness of their claims on counterparties. Basel II allowed banks to use risk data obtained from external credit rating agencies. It is assumed that broadening of risk data sources this way will impart credibility to the risk-weighting system. This will in turn improve the quality of the risk-weighted assets of banks. It will also help to achieve more accurate minimum regulatory capital requirements for them.

Use of internal credit risk data

In revising the Basel I Accord, the Basel Committee weighed, corroborated, and gave banks an option to conduct and use, risk data from banks' internal credit ratings for the calculation of capital requirements. However, there is a caveat to the freedom of banks to use such internally generated credit risk rating data. Thus, Basel II recognizes the credit risk data that banks generate in this way as complementary to those that external credit rating agencies provide. In both cases, provided there is compliance with prescribed criteria, risk data from the two sources may be used to assign risk weights and determine capital requirements.

Options for capital calculation

Basel I adopted a uniform single approach to measuring capital adequacy, one that related credit risk to regulatory capital. Basel II, on the other hand, offers four optional approaches, each of which a bank could use to calculate regulatory capital for credit risk. The four options are subsumed in the following two sets of approaches that Basel II recognizes:

- The "standardized" approaches (i.e., the first set) comprise the simplified standardized approach and the standardized approach, both of which use credit ratings and risk data supplied by accredited external credit rating agencies.
- The second set, comprising the "internal ratings-based" (IRB) approaches, is made up of the foundation internal ratings-based approach and the advanced internal ratings-based approach. As the name implies, the IRB approaches use internal ratings based on credit risk data that banks generate in-house.

Banks and regulators can use any of the options that constitute the two sets of approaches. The options are provided with adequate information to enable banks to make informed choices.

Basel II tasks banks with building technical competence, a broad base of risk databases, and a rigorous methodology for risk management. By doing so, they should be in a position to use the rigorous framework of the advanced approaches for capital adequacy measurement. Yet, the beauty of the options is that banks can choose those that best suit their risk management needs and the current level of their technical and quantitative capabilities. This is seen as a great innovation, one that was lacking in Basel I. It is also proof of more commitment by the Basel Committee to ensure that every asset of a bank is adequately sensitized to the credit risks that regulatory capital requirements should offset in a crisis situation.

Consolidation of assets

A financial crisis that an internationally active bank experiences in its home country can negatively affect the operations of its subsidiaries in their host countries and vice versa. With the Basel I Accord, this fact was not taken into account in the calculation of regulatory capital requirements. However, Basel II took decisive action to deal with this issue. It provides for the consolidation of assets of holding and subsidiary companies of internationally active banks.

Further clarification is required in order to appreciate the asset-consolidation strength of the Basel II Accord. The Basel Committee provided the necessary clarification. It did so while enunciating the philosophy behind the asset-consolidation criterion. The intention of Basel II is unequivocal. But it underscores the thinking of the Basel Committee that informed it.

> *The scope of application of the Framework will include, on a fully consolidated basis, any holding company that is the parent entity within a banking group to ensure that it captures the risk of the whole banking group. Banking groups are groups that engage predominantly in banking activities and, in some countries, a banking group may be registered as a bank*
>
> (Basel Committee, 2004).

In the opinion of the Basel Committee, "the Framework will also apply to all internationally active banks at every tier within a banking group, also on a fully consolidated basis." (Basel Committee, 2004) If properly applied, this recommendation will help to stem credit risk in global banks.

Weaknesses of Basel II

Basel II has some weaknesses despite its widely acclaimed improvements on the Basel Capital Accord. Basel II appears too technical and might be misconstrued at some levels of implementation. This unintended shortcoming informs the thinking that Basel II might not be effectively implemented in many non—Basel Committee member countries. Some critics like Balin (2008) point to this weakness as a factor in the failings of the Basel Accords in emerging markets.

The greatest weakness of the Basel II Accord came to the fore with the global financial crisis of 2007—2009 that triggered money panics in both industrialized nations and emerging markets. The crisis, popularly known as a "financial meltdown," dealt a severe blow to Basel II, roundly discrediting its Accord. It particularly humbled banking authorities around the world. Ostensibly, authorities could not prevent the meltdown from taking a toll on international banking and finance. In some countries like the United States and the UK, government provided bailout funds to key financial institutions and industries to assuage the distress resulting from the meltdown. It became obvious that the Basel II Accord was not foolproof after all. Were it to be, the crisis would have been prevented or preempted, or would not have arisen in the first place.

There is yet another important weakness of the Basel II Accord, one that derives from the foregoing. It would seem that Basel II anticipated that a liquidity crisis could be disastrous for a bank. Thus, it provides a check—albeit indirectly—against liquidity risk within its Pillar 1 framework. The check is embedded in the management of credit risk, operational risk, and market risk. Yet, credit risk has often been the trigger point for liquidity crisis, bank distress, and bank failure. Credit risk was also largely the root cause of the financial meltdown of 2007–2009. In most cases, the credit risk in question defies the odds by being able to crash the financial market. Unfortunately, Pillar 1 of Basel II omitted, and indeed never anticipated, such credit risk. Undue emphasis was rather put on identifiable traditional risks that are amenable to management control. This was done at the expense of risks that defy logic and, in the financial crisis of 2007–2009, for which the world paid dearly.

Implications of Basel II

It is evident from the foregoing discussion that Basel II made far-reaching improvements to the Basel Capital Accord. Some of the improvements considered significant are presented in the discussion of strengths of Basel II. However, the way in which Basel II altered the regulatory framework for global bank supervision has profound implications for the conduct of banking business. The implications of Basel II for credit risk management in banking are as follows.

Lending to emerging markets

Emerging economies are generally characterized as high-risk markets for lending purposes. This characterization is not helped by the highly risk-sensitive framework of the Basel II Accord. Banks that lend to such markets may be obliged to increase their regulatory capital requirements. The Basel Committee corroborates this possibility. It found, through its Quantitative Impact Study, that banks would have to allocate more regulatory capital to offset credit risk and operational risk in emerging markets. As banks bear the burden of higher risk-based capital charges, they may take one of three possible actions:

- Reduce lending to borrowers in high-risk economies
- Increase the cost of credit to them
- Reduce lending and increase credit cost to the borrowers

When this is done, the flow of critical capital to affected economies will be short of their growth and developmental needs. This is the unfortunate but perhaps unavoidable fallout of the increased risk sensitivity of the Basel II Accord.

Adjustment of asset portfolio

It is likely that banks will adjust their credit target markets, criteria, and asset portfolios to reflect the risk-based-capital-charge orientation of the Basel II Accord. Specifically, banks may want to shun certain credits, such as commercial mortgages, that attract higher capital charges, and reduce their portfolio of such assets. On the contrary, assets that bear low capital charges, such as residential mortgage loans, will be attractive to banks. Banks will want to increase their portfolios of low-risk assets.

Thus, there are concomitant portfolio adjustments on the asset side of a bank's balance sheet. Two factors, differences in risk weights and risk-based capital charges applicable to different borrowers and assets of a bank, engender the portfolio adjustments. In this case, changes in portfolio composition will likely increase holdings of low-risk assets due to their lower capital charges. The reverse is also true. There will be decreased holdings of high-risk assets because of their higher capital charges. Besides, there is a tendency for the flow of credit to different sectors to increase or reduce depending on the riskiness of loans in those sectors. While lending to high-risk sectors will be unattractive, banks are likely to be keen to lend to low-risk sectors. This pattern of shifts in the flow of credit to various economic sectors may have adverse effects on some macroeconomic aggregates.

Selective implementation

One of the strengths of Basel II—options for the calculation of capital adequacy—also poses a risk of flawed implementation of the Accord. Banks may take advantage of the wide array of options that Basel II offers. There is room, between the simple and technical approaches to measuring capital adequacy, in which banks could maneuver.

This will happen where, for instance, it is possible to reduce bank capital even as the risk profile is increasing. In order to circumvent Basel II in this way, a bank selectively builds its lending portfolio around riskless assets at the expense of relatively risky assets. The undue advantage is that the bank is able to satisfy regulatory capital requirements with lower capital charges (i.e., lower risk weights) while taking higher risks.

Exacerbation of business cycles

Basel II recognizes the impact of cyclical changes on the business and financial performance of banks. In anticipation of economic downturn, the Accord emphasizes higher loan loss provisions. Increased provisioning, coupled with higher required risk weights for certain categories of assets, puts pressure on bank capital and the capacity to lend. Banks will want to pass on such pressure to borrowers in the form of higher borrowing costs for loans. Difficulties may result from excessive costs of loans, constraints on capacity to lend, or both.

Promotion of credit rating

It is possible, with Basel II, for external rating agencies to make inputs into the credit processes of global banks. This is largely because the standardized approach under Pillar I of the Accord encourages banks to institutionalize credit ratings as part of their overall methodology for credit risk assessment. Thus, in addition to other credit risk assessment criteria, banks can use borrower ratings furnished by external rating agencies to determine risk weights for particular assets.

It would be difficult to implement the standardized approach under Pillar I of Basel II in the absence of credit risk ratings for major borrowers. In that case, banks would be left with no other option than to apply the standard risk weights of Basel I. However, Basel II provides criteria that regulators should adopt in assessing the quality of the rating agencies. The criteria are objectivity, independence, international access, transparency, disclosure, resources, and credibility. The rating agencies must satisfy these criteria in order for their ratings to qualify for use in credit risk assessment under Basel II.

QUESTIONS FOR DISCUSSION AND REVIEW

1. Given the volatile nature of international financial markets, how may "internationally active banks" effectively anticipate credit risk?
2. What are the founding basis and goals of the Basel Committee, and how do the goals inform the Basel I and Basel II Accords?
3. In what respects are the Basel Accords useful to the management of credit risk in global banks in emerging economies?
4. Identify and critically discuss the practical difficulties in implementing the Basel I and Basel II Accords.
5. What credit risk management issues for global banks do the Basel I and Basel II Accords specifically address?
6. To what extent have the Basel I and Basel II Accords achieved their set objectives?
7. In what specific ways did Basel II improve on the Basel Capital Accord? Identify and discuss any five such ways.
8. (a) How will adoption of the Basel II Accord benefit banks in emerging economies?
   (b) What practical difficulties do banks in emerging economies currently face—or likely face in the future—with implementing the Basel II Accord?

REFERENCES

Balin, B.J., 2008. Basel I, Basel II, and Emerging Markets: A Non- Technical Analysis. The Johns Hopkins University School of Advanced International Studies, Washington DC.

Basel Committee on Banking Supervision, 1988. International Convergence of Capital Measurement and Capital Standards, as Amended. Bank for International Settlements, Basel.

Basel Committee on Banking Supervision, 2004. International Convergence of Capital Measurement and Capital Standards: A Revised Framework, as Amended. Bank for International Settlements, Basel.

FURTHER READING

Basel Committee on Banking Supervision, 2002. Third Quantitative Impact Study. Bank for International Settlements, Basel.

Chapter 37

Bank Credit and Capital Regulation and Supervision in Emerging Economies

Chapter Outline

Emerging Market Bank Lending and Credit Risk Control. http://dx.doi.org/10.1016/B978-0-12-803438-5.00037-4

LEARNING FOCUS AND OUTCOMES

One unanswered question continues to agitate the minds of analysts and observers of happenings in the banking industry in emerging economies. The question borders on regulatory aberration. Why, despite regulation and supervision, has the condition of some banks deteriorated to levels where failure becomes inevitable? This has been a puzzling question over the years. It is usually too late to save ailing banks by the time regulators eventually intervene! Doing too little too late in this way compounds the problem for banks. In most cases, banks become terminally distressed such that they lose merger or acquisition appeal.

Certainly something is wrong with the regulatory oversight of deposit money banks in emerging economies. The public, especially banking experts and analysts, believes that the approach to banking regulation and supervision leaves a lot to be desired. Banking supervision and indeed regulatory authorities are tainted, once they are found wanting as the stakeholders' watchdog. There are more postmortem activities than anticipation and prognosis of the risks envisaged in the master contingency plans of banks. For example, in the aftermath of the 2007−2009 financial meltdown, the Central Bank of Nigeria (CBN) sacked the boards of eight banks—Afribank, Bank PHB, Equitorial Trust Bank, FinBank, Intercontinental Bank, Oceanic Bank, Union Bank, and Spring Bank—and appointed an interim management board for each. The CBN accused executives of the banks of professional misconduct. The misconduct was evident in abuse of office and insider abuse—especially in granting credit facilities. A typical insider abuse was the granting of unsecured loans to directors of the banks and their cronies. The lending not only contravened the law but made nonsense of the best practices and internal credit policies of banks.

Curiously, the same CBN had given all banks in the country a clean bill of health while the global financial crisis was well underway! Although banking supervision had earlier uncovered the rot in the banks, it was 2009 before the hammer fell on the affected distressed banks. Investigation of the banks revealed how their CEOs subverted lending policy and control—and especially the internal credit processes of the banks. Executives of the banks not only compromised themselves but also rendered banking supervision ineffectual. That was how, against the foregoing backdrop, this critical oversight function of the CBN started losing significance. It took courage—which Sanusi Lamido Sanusi, then the new CBN Governor, had in abundance—to restore confidence in the country's banking supervision. In 2009, the Governor took decisive steps toward reforming the banking sector. One of the major planks of the reforms was the prosecution of indicted executives of failed banks in Nigeria. The payoff was worth the trouble involved in carrying out the reforms.

Now the public has a significant measure of confidence in the banks that survived the onslaught of the difficult reforms. Besides, many see nationalization of failed banks, as opposed to liquidation of them—as was the practice in the past—as a welcome development. The immediate import of the creation of "bridge banks" (i.e., nationalized banks) is that customers of banks are assured of the safety of their deposits in the event that a bank fails or becomes distressed. The bridge banks—Enterprise Bank Limited, Keystone Bank Limited, and Main Street Bank Limited—represent the former Spring Bank PLC, Bank PHB PLC, and Afribank PLC, respectively.

The foregoing Nigerian example illustrates typical banking regulation flaws common to all emerging economies. My approach to this chapter is to first define the crux of the issues in banking regulation in emerging economies. Then I review prescriptions of the Basel Accords for bank capital and credit risk regulation. From the two discussions, I distill how the mode of regulation adopted in emerging economies diverges from the Basel Accords. The divergences are observed mainly in regulating capital, measuring capital adequacy, regulating liquidity, and responding to failing banks—all of which I discuss in detail in this chapter. The reader will learn about:

- The focus of banking regulation and factors constraining effective banking supervision in emerging economies
- The supervisory framework that banking regulators in emerging economies adopt, and how it relates to Basel Accords
- Why and how banking regulatory practices in emerging economies tend to diverge from the Basel Accords
- The basis and implications of regulatory divergence from the Basel Accords for credit risk control in emerging economies

---

Case Study 37.1

Savannah Bank of Nigeria PLC

The general public in Nigeria woke up to the shocking news of the unanticipated closure of Savannah Bank of Nigeria PLC[1] by regulatory authorities. The announcement of the CBN's revocation of the operating banking license of the 41-year old bank, with over 95 branches nationwide, came as a reminder to the people of the mass bank failures experienced in the late 1990s. The authorities did not waste time in justifying closure of the bank in the following press statement.[2]

Savannah Bank of Nigeria PLC (SBN) had been in financial crisis since its "rancorous Annual General Meeting of 1993, which plunged it into a boardroom crisis." Since the outbreak of this crisis, the CBN had adopted various measures to resolve the problems, including a takeover of the bank between 1995 and 1996, close monitoring, and holding a series of meetings with the board and management. The crisis was compounded in July 1999 when the International Resource Agency (IRA) of the United Kingdom acquired an initial 59.9 percent controlling interest in SBN through the Nigerian Stock Exchange for US$7 million. Instead of

IRA's equity contribution of $7 million being brought into Nigeria, the bank claimed that $6.8 million of the money was spent on computerization. A check by the CBN examiners showed that "not only did the IT equipment on the ground not justify the expenditure of $6.8 million; such expenditure was at the expense of addressing problems of liquidity and insolvency." Since the takeover by IRA, the CBN had been seriously concerned about "the state of health of the bank, the way it has been managed and the extent to which inaccurate and misleading information has been given to the regulatory authorities, notably the CBN and NDIC."

A series of meetings was held between the bank's management and CBN with the purpose of identifying the problems and proffering solutions. But the IRA, which sacked the Martin I. Ikediashi−led board on November 4, 1999 and replaced it with a new board at an emergency general meeting in Port Harcourt on April 3, 2000 has "remained largely inept and ineffective" in the management of its activities. Investigation into the bank under the board of IRA showed:

1. Negative shareholders' funds of ₦2.9 billion as of March 31, 2000;
2. The bulk of the management staff recruited by the new management had no documents in their files to indicate that they were interviewed, and also there were no references from their previous employers, such that the CBN was unable to approve the bank's nominees for top management appointments;
3. The bank's March 31, 1999 and 2000 draft accounts showed that the bank made losses of ₦694.9 million and ₦2.8 billion, respectively. Indeed, the draft 2000 accounts were qualified by the bank's external auditors, who expressed doubt about its ability to continue in business as a going concern.

The precarious financial situation of the bank caused the CBN to order a joint special examination of the bank with the support of the Nigeria Deposit Insurance Corporation (NDIC) on March 31, 2001. The report revealed the bank's:

1. continuing financial deterioration, as 74 percent of the bank's total credit exposure of ₦10 billion as of March 31, 2001 was found to be nonperforming;
2. total provision for loans and other known losses were determined to be ₦10.3 billion, as compared with the bank's figure of ₦8 billion;
3. the recapitalization requirement was determined to be ₦5.4 billion as of March 31, 2001, compared with ₦3.4 billion as of March 3, 2000;
4. unaudited profit of ₦50.8 million as of March 31, 2001 was a mere paper profit attained through the understatement of expenses that were warehoused with nonexisting assets of ₦1.7 billion;
5. the interbranch account was unreconciled such that it had a net interbranch debit of ₦4 billion as of March 31, 2001.

The management of the bank was also alleged to have spent ₦97.5 million for a 30-year leasehold on the bank's Onitsha branch; the owner had offered the property to the bank for ₦40 million as a freehold. The CBN and NDIC examiners also found that the bank's:

1. unaudited profit of ₦76 million as of December 12, 2001 was attained through the recognition of interest income of ₦760 million, the bulk of which came from nonperforming accounts;
2. plan to recapitalize through the issuance of ₦3 billion in debenture stock not only was considered impracticable given the realities of the Nigerian capital

markets, but even if successful would not change the bank's capital adequacy ratio;

3. the liquidity ratio of 44.6 percent from its November 2001 returns to regulatory authorities was not real for the following reasons:

   a. the liabilities for Treasury Bills of ₦2.1 billion, which were financed with borrowings from banks and discount houses, and which were held for only three days—November 30–December 3, 2001—were not fully disclosed;

   b. Its current account with CBN as of the end of the prior November was overstated by ₦975 million;

   c. Cash on hand of ₦2.2 billion could not be confirmed, as several rural branches were purported to be holding cash in excess of their deposit base.

Despite the appointment of a new board and management, the bank's financial condition has continued to deteriorate as the liquidity ratio had remained below the minimum requirement while its capital adequacy ratio had been consistently negative. The bank has resorted to distress borrowings from the interbank market and a worsening situation may cause systemic risk. With all the aforementioned revoking the bank's license was the most cost-effective means of resolving its distress.[3]

1. This illustration of indicators or causes of bank distress, depicting the case of Savannah Bank of Nigeria PLC (whose banking license was revoked by the Central Bank of Nigeria effective February 15, 2002), was taken from the "press briefing" by Alhaji Ahmed Aman Imala—Director, Banking Supervision, Central Bank of Nigeria—on the revocation of the operating banking license of Savannah Bank of Nigeria Plc. See *The Guardian*, Tuesday, February 19, 2002, p. 3.

2. The first paragraph of this case study and the rest of the statements following it represent the "press briefing" by Alhaji Ahmed Aman Imala—Director, Banking Supervision, Central Bank of Nigeria—on the revocation of the operating banking license of Savannah Bank of Nigeria PLC as reported by *The Guardian*, Tuesday, February 19, 2002, p. 3.

3. It should be noted that the shareholders and management of Savannah Bank of Nigeria PLC later instituted and won a legal action against the CBN over the revocation of its operating license in 2002.

DEFINING ISSUES IN BANKING REGULATION IN EMERGING ECONOMIES

Regulation of banking in emerging economies is an arduous task, no doubt about it. Unstructured regulatory frameworks and halfhearted enforcement informed by unnecessary bureaucracy compound the task. A feature of the approach to regulation seen in most emerging economies is a significant divergence from the Basel Accords. Regulatory authorities acknowledge this fact when they admit their inability to strictly adopt the Basel Accords. Authorities hold this view on aspects of Basel II and all of Basel III. Yet regulators have to exercise their oversight of banking one way or the other.

There are four main findings that shed light on disturbing issues in the regulation of banking in emerging economies. The findings relate to actions of regulatory authorities and the response of bank managements to those actions. While authorities are ever evolving and enforcing policies largely on a pragmatic basis, bank managements respond in kind—ever exploring expedient means of getting around the rules. I summarize the four findings as follows:

- The simple regulatory expedient of issuing occasional monetary policy circulars to deposit money banks
- Central Banks taking a more pragmatic approach to the regulation of banking practices that often diverge from Basel Accords
- Imposition of fines, sanctions, and penalties on erring banks to serve as deterrents to breaches of banking rules
- Bank management falling back on banking expediency to circumvent difficult regulations

The foregoing introduces conflict in the making and enforcement of banking regulations in emerging economies. Often it results in flawed banking supervision and truncated enforcement of banking rules. Regulators and banks go on doing their own things in this unhealthy way—ostensibly not wanting to rock the boat, but apparently risking systemic crisis in the financial system. Occasional roundtable discussions of the underlying issues by regulators and chief executives of banks under the auspices of Bankers' Committee meetings end in horse-trading.

Yet in order to prevent the financial system crises in emerging economies that are often caused by unchecked credit risk-taking, banking regulation and supervision must have teeth. Giving these oversight functions teeth would require an overhaul of the current approaches and mechanisms adopted by regulatory authorities. Ideally, banking supervision should anticipate and preempt criticized lending practices. One of the lessons of experience learned about banking regulation in emerging economies is that the rubber-stamping of banking supervision reports is inimical to a sound banking system. Regulatory authorities have a responsibility to the public to be diligent in the exercise of their oversight functions. In this way, the major outcome of banking supervision would be a strengthened banking system. Strengthening the banking system will serve the interests of banking stakeholders and the public.

The factors that define issues in banking regulation demand attention at the same time. I discuss the two most critical issues now. First I examine the question of autonomy for banking regulatory authorities, mainly the Central Banks. Then I explore the albatross of banking supervision in emerging economies. In doing so, I highlight implications for credit risk control in emerging economies.

AUTONOMY FOR BANKING REGULATORY AUTHORITIES

It is widely believed that banking regulatory institutions should be strengthened and empowered to be able to effectively deal with the problems of the industry. There is a need for Central Banks to have full autonomy so that they could deal decisively with any threat of financial distress in the system. This has been elusive in some emerging economies owing to bureaucratic encumbrance. Government freely interferes and often meddles with banking regulatory policies. In most cases, the functioning of the banking industry—nay, the financial system—is distorted as a result.

A related problem to the lack of autonomy for Central Banks in emerging economies is political interference in banking policy initiatives and implementation. Ordinarily, government should distance itself from banking regulation for the sake of industry and stakeholders. Friction often observed between governments and Central Banks in emerging economies arises where the former meddles in the regulatory roles of the latter. Friction arises especially where governments and Central Banks pursue conflicting policies borne out of contrasting perspectives on the financial economy of the country. In order to avoid national embarrassment bordering on recrimination, the two bodies should harmonize their perspectives on monetary and financial policy management. In most cases, recriminations follow from failures to account for conflicting policies.

In Nigeria, some success was achieved in 1998 when the CBN was granted instrument autonomy. The partial autonomy granted the CBN, according to Sanusi (2001), "insulates it from undue political interference in its conduct of monetary and financial policies and, thereby enables it to act more pro-actively and promptly in its policy responses to changes in economic conditions." The CBN was yet further empowered by legislation in 2007 when the country's National Assembly passed the CBN (amendment) Act that grants it full autonomy. This fits with best practices, the hallmark of efficiently functioning banking systems around the world. Autonomy should go hand in hand with a competitively composed board of directors (mostly experts in economics, banking, and finance). With the governor as chairperson of the board, the independence and accountability of Central Banks in monetary and financial policy management would be better assured.

ALBATROSS FOR BANKING SUPERVISION

Often the way that banks in emerging economies maneuver regulations completely confounds regulatory authorities and other banking stakeholders. Financial analysts are no less intrigued by the seeming inability of authorities to tame bank managements. Without disillusioning the reader, there are cracks in banking regulation and supervision in emerging economies. Ironically, supervised banks constitute an albatross for regulatory authorities. Banks discreetly cut corners, cook the books, and perfect counters to punitive regulatory policies. In most cases, the financial statements and accounts of banks are just window dressing.

Regulators tend to dish out monetary and credit policies while seemingly oblivious to banking rot. Banks circumvent key banking rules in several ways, including:

1. Cutting back the size of the outstanding portfolio of nonperforming loans and advances, often in collaboration with obligors
2. Rebooking nonperforming but not yet charged off credit facilities—usually with the cooperation of obligors
3. Generally dressing up the loan book to avoid huge specific loan loss provision on classified risk assets
4. Boosting deposit liability through the negotiated rollover of maturing fixed deposits and similar purchased funds
5. Taking interbank funds to satisfy critical evaluation indices—mainly cash reserve, loan-to-deposit, and liquidity ratios

The first three of the circumvention modes address issues on the assets side of the balance sheet, while the last two deal with liability concerns.

Overall, banks employ the five methods above to manipulate financial records in end-of-month returns to regulatory authorities. With any luck, banks are assured of lower risk-based charges to their regulatory capital on the asset side. Satisfying the regulatory liquidity ratios identified in (5) above addresses the liability concerns. There is no uniform approach that all banks in all emerging economies adopt in pursuit of the foregoing. Differences in methods may be observed among banks and economies, depending on the states of development of the financial system and the regulatory framework. For this reason it will be futile to attempt here to discuss details of the applicable approaches. Rather it suffices to appreciate that banks in emerging economies have ways of maneuvering regulations and supervision contrary to the spirit of the Basel Accords. Were banks to fully adopt the Basel Accords, many of them would go under even as enforcement of the Accords were underway. I revisit the question of insider abuse to corroborate this view.

REVISITING THE QUESTION OF INSIDER ABUSE

Incidents of bank distress and failure in Nigeria in the 1990s and first decade of the twenty-first century revealed incredible levels of contributory factors in unethical practices. Many banks ran into trouble as a result of insider abuse, especially taking uncovered exposures in loans to directors and major share-holders that became bad after all. Such loans were usually in large volume, and in most cases were granted without proper documentation or collateral. In time, when the crunch came, the net fair value of assets had depleted to levels that could not sustain the liquidity required for normal banking transactions and operations. Some believe that the unsavory fate of failed banks derived mainly from unprofessional and unethical practices by bank members. Such discredited acts, observed mainly in insider-related credits, were best enunciated in a late 2001 CBN circular, tagged *Exposure draft circular: Insider-related credit facilities*, to all banks in Nigeria.

In the circular, the CBN identifies "one of the major endogenous factors responsible for the last distress in the *Nigerian* financial system *as* the magnitude of non-performing *credit* facilities granted to key shareholders and directors of banks and their related interests." It observes that "the reports of routine examinations of the banks by both the Central Bank of Nigeria (CBN) and Nigeria Deposit Insurance Corporation (NDIC) have indicated that many banks have continued to record huge amounts of insider-related credits, many of which have been classified either as doubtful or lost." The CBN gives specific "examples to illustrate the seriousness of the situation." It cited the following observed insider abuses in lending:

- The examination report of a relatively small new-generation bank revealed that credit facilities totaling more than ₦3 billion were granted to a director and his related interests in wanton disregard of the relevant provision of the Banks and Other Financial Institutions Act (BOFIA) 1991, as amended. The same director and his related interest had credit facilities in excess of ₦2.8 billion at two other new-generation banks where he was also a board member.
- Also, the routine examination report of a big old-generation bank revealed the existence of huge nonperforming insider-related credits totaling over ₦690 million and granted to one of its directors and his related interests.
- In another small bank, a director had a total nonperforming facility of about ₦440 million, representing 89% of the bank's total nonperforming insider-related facilities.
- The quarterly returns on insider-related credit facilities received from another major old-generation bank indicated that out of a total of ₦347 million granted to a former director, ₦345 million had been classified as nonperforming.
- Out of over ₦351 million in insider-related credits reported by a medium-sized bank, nearly ₦324 million was granted to just two of its directors and their related interests.
- The quarterly returns as of June 30, 2001 from another medium-sized bank indicated that without regard to the relevant provisions of BOFI Act, it had granted credit facilities in excess of ₦1.3 billion to a director and his related interests.

According to the CBN, "in addition to the examination reports, the offsite monitoring of the banks compliance with the regulatory requirement for the banks to submit quarterly returns of insider related advances, loans, and credit facilities granted to their individual directors and key shareholders and their related interests reveal:

- a reluctance and, often times, outright failure on the part of many banks to comply with this reporting requirement. The Department has had cause to impose monetary penalties on some erring banks in this regard in the past.
- the rendering of inaccurate returns, whereby some banks deliberately understate the amount of their exposure to particular directors.
- most banks would appear to have been violating the provisions of Section 18(1) (b) of BOFIA No. 25 of 1991 as amended, which requires bank managers and other relevant officers of a bank to ensure that adequate security, *where required* is obtained prior to the granting of any credit facility."

Perhaps the reasons for the observed discredited practices are rooted in the growing tendency of banks toward unprofessional business conduct. This situation provoked the Nigeria Bankers' Committee to advise acceptable standards for professional banking practices. The committee identifies and classifies certain conduct as unprofessional or unethical for bankers. One of the frequently infringed areas of professional and ethical conduct identified by the Committee is insider abuse, the components of which are:

- Meeting recapitalization requirements by means other than the actual injection of fresh or genuine funds
- Improper granting of loans to directors, insiders, and political interests
- Insiders' conversion of bank resources for purposes other than business interests
- Granting of unsecured credit facilities to directors in contravention of the provisions of BOFIA
- Granting of interest waivers on nonperforming insider credits without the CBN's prior approval as required by BOFIA
- Diversion of bank earnings through the use of subsidiaries or "secret accounts" to deny the bank of legitimate earnings

There is no doubt that banking regulators in several other emerging economies face the same or similar challenges. There is a need for regulators to restructure their supervisory frameworks and generally reengineer their oversight functions. By doing so, regulators should reposition themselves as a responsive banking stakeholders' watchdog. Above all, regulators should be firm and fair in the discharge of their statutory oversight functions.

BASEL ACCORDS APPROACH—CAPITAL CHARGES FOR CREDIT RISK

Stakeholders, as owners, contribute equity capital to set up a bank. In this sense, the capitalization of a bank evidences commitment of the shareholders to the bank. Over time, and as the bank capitalizes profits or retained earnings and other reserves, its capital base broadens. The shareholders' funds then provide the net financial buffer on which the bank can confidently assume some of the risks of lending and other operating activities. The emphasis on a net financial buffer depicts the inclination of banks to apply equity capital to finance investments in buildings (or office accommodation), the acquisition of fixed assets (or fixtures and fittings), and the provision of work equipment (such as computers, vehicles, chairs, and tables).

Shareholders' funds are built over time as a bank's earnings and reserves increase with profitability. But this depends on the bank's dividend policy. A bank that favors growth and capital gains would emphasize earnings retention, while one that believes in maximizing shareholders' wealth in the short run would tend to adopt a high dividend payout policy. In the event that a bank is not profitable, its net worth declines. The decline results from the erosion of shareholders' funds by current and accumulated losses. In time, the bank may become distressed and fail. It is instructive that the choice of any capital financing option has cost implications for the bank. But what specifically constitutes the capital base of a bank? When can we say that a bank is adequately capitalized? Why should bank management necessarily be concerned about capital adequacy? To what extent do authorities regulate bank capital? These questions lead to the problem definition, with implications for the effective management of banks' capital resources.

One of the significant achievements of the Basel Accords with respect to credit risk management is the linking of capital adequacy to credit risk. Thus, risk weights assigned to particular bank assets bear on the adequacy of global bank capital. The import of this approach to determining capital adequacy is that the management of global banks should be wary of the credit risks they take. By doing so, they would be able to avoid unnecessary diminution of the capital base of their banks. It also implies that credit risk can make or break the operations of a bank.

BASEL CAPITAL ACCORD

Basel I demonstrated how the "capital measurement system" and "credit risk measurement framework" would work in practice. It did so in three sections, represented as the *constituents of capital*, the *risk-weighting system*, and the *target standard ratio*. I present summaries of these components of the Basel I Accord as follows.

Constituents of capital

The Basel I Accord identified two tiers of capital that it recommended should constitute the total capital base of a bank. While tier 1 capital denotes a bank's core capital (i.e., its equity capital and disclosed reserves), tier 2 capital represents noncore capital items (referred to in Basel I as supplementary capital).

In isolating the two tiers, the Accord clarified aspects of their components and qualifying attributes as follows:

Core capital (basic equity)

A bank's core capital, also referred to as basic equity, has three components (as shown below) that make it up and constitute tier 1 capital. But the two primary categories—namely, equity capital and disclosed reserves—that contain the three components are the defining constituents of core capital. Basel I underscored core capital in "requiring at least 50% of a bank's capital base to consist of a core element comprised of equity capital and published reserves from post-tax retained earnings." Specifically, core capital represents the sum of the monetary value of a bank's—

1. equity capital, comprising—
   a. issued and fully paid-up ordinary shares or common stock of a bank;
   b. noncumulative perpetual preferred stock, excluding cumulative preferred stock; and
2. disclosed reserves (i.e., reserves from profit after tax and published in a bank's audited accounts).

In view of its nature, noncumulative perpetual preferred stock is treated as an integral component of equity capital. Basel I recognized equity capital and disclosed reserves as the key to "securing a progressive enhancement in the quality, as well as the level, of the total capital resources maintained by major banks." Thus, a bank can work on core capital to meet or surpass the minimum capital standard without losing sight of the fact that quality of capital counts as well as its level.

Supplementary capital

A number of items subsumed in the total capital base of a bank do not count as part of the bank's core capital. Such items of capital other than equity capital and disclosed reserves, referred to in Basel I as supplementary capital, make up tier 2 capital. The Accord stipulated that this category of capital items "will be admitted into tier 2 up to an amount equal to that of the core capital." Basel I recognized five constituents of supplementary capital as summarized below.

Undisclosed reserves

This category of capital depicts "reserves which, though unpublished, have been passed through the profit and loss account and which are accepted by the bank's supervisory authorities." Two attributes of undisclosed reserves stem, or can be inferred, from this definition: firstly, they are accounted for in the profit and loss account even though they are not explicitly stated, reflected, or shown in the account; and secondly, the Central Bank or other banking regulatory authority approves them as a qualifying constituent of a bank's capital.

Revaluation reserves

Some banks include revaluation reserves as part of their total capital resources. These reserves are a sum of money calculated and recognized in a bank's books as the capital appreciation on specific assets. Thus, revaluation reserves are created when current market values of particular assets exceed their historical costs (i.e., book values). The objective of revaluation is to bring the historical book value up to the current value of assets. However, Basel I made a proviso that must be fulfilled before revaluation reserves would be admitted into the capital base of a bank. It recommended a discount of 55% on the amount by which the market value of assets exceeds historical book value.

General loan loss reserves

Banking regulatory authorities usually require banks to make general as well as specific provisions on loan portfolios. The prudential rate approved for the general provision differs from the rates for specific provisions. While the former is a uniform rate, rates for the latter depend on the state of the specific nonperforming loans to which they apply. Basel I, on the one hand, permits inclusion of general loan loss provisions in tier 2 capital as general loan loss reserves, while on the other it precludes the inclusion of specific provisions.

General loan loss reserves are considered an element of capital because they "are created against the possibility of losses not yet identified." Besides, such reserves "do not reflect a known deterioration in the valuation of particular assets." On the contrary, specific loan loss provisions are thought to lack admissible attributes of capital and should be discounted from the capital base of a bank. Two reasons, noted in Basel I, informed this thinking. Firstly, specific provisions "are created against identified losses or in respect of an identified deterioration in the value of any asset or group of subsets of assets. Secondly, such provisions "are not freely available to meet unidentified losses that may subsequently arise elsewhere in the portfolio."

The inclusion of general loan loss reserves in tier 2 capital is not absolute. Basel I specified "a limit of 1.25 percentage points of weighted risk assets" for the amount of general loan loss provisions that should be admitted into tier 2 capital.

Hybrid (debt/equity) capital instruments

The makeup of supplementary capital, according to Basel I, should include capital instruments that share some but not all of the attributes of equity and debt. However, it is believed that the quality of capital instruments tends to satisfy requirement for inclusion in tier 2 capital when those instruments "have close similarities to equity." Thus, Basel I recommended their inclusion in tier 2 capital, especially "when they are able to support losses on an on-going basis without triggering liquidation." This implies that a bank that holds such capital instruments does not necessarily have to liquidate them, but can apply them to offset a loss position.

Basel I noted that while "their precise specifications differ from country to country," hybrid capital instruments should satisfy the following set of criteria (Basel Committee, 1988).

- They are *unsecured, subordinated,* and *fully paid up*;
- They are *not redeemable* at the initiative of the holder or without prior consent of the supervisory authority;
- They are *available to participate in losses* without the bank being obliged to cease trading (unlike conventional subordinated debt);
- Although the capital instrument may carry an obligation to pay interest that cannot permanently be reduced or waived (unlike dividends on ordinary shareholders' equity), *it should allow service obligations to be deferred* (as with cumulative preference shares) where the profitability of the bank would not support payment.

Where cumulative preference shares have these characteristics, they would be eligible for inclusion in this category (ibid.).

Subordinated term debt

Basel I expressed reservation about inclusion of subordinated term debt instruments as a constituent of the capital base of a bank. Such debt instruments are criticized for capitalization purposes "in view of their fixed maturity and inability to absorb losses except in a liquidation." These attributes render them deficient and ineligible for inclusion in tier 2 capital. Nonetheless, Basel I allowed for the inclusion of "subordinated term debt instruments with a minimum original term to maturity of over five years (in) the supplementary elements of capital." However, it did so with a proviso that such instruments should account for "a maximum of 50% of the core capital element and subject to adequate amortization arrangements."

Subordinated term debt "includes conventional unsecured subordinated debt capital instruments with minimum original fixed term to maturity of over five years and limited life redeemable preference shares." It is pertinent to reflect that such "instruments are not normally available to participate in the losses of a bank which continues trading." It's for this reason that Basel I upheld that "during the last five years to maturity, a cumulative discount (or amortization) factor of 20% per year will be applied to reflect the diminishing value of these instruments as a continuing source of strength" (ibid.: 16).

Deductions from capital

It is imperative to adjust a bank's capital base to reflect its true quality and usefulness as buffer for its risk assets portfolio. The essence in doing so is to be able to calculate an accurate risk-weighted capital ratio for the bank. Thus, Basel I identified deductions that should be made from the capital base of a bank in order to calculate this ratio. The first—goodwill—is to be deducted from tier 1 capital. The second deduction is "investments in subsidiaries engaged in banking and financial activities which are not consolidated in national systems." These deductions enhance the quality of a bank's capital base and better reflect it in published accounts.

Risk-weighting system

Basel I assessed capital adequacy in the context of the credit risk that a bank assumes. It defended a logical approach to assessing capital adequacy based on the relationship of capital to risk-weighted asset categories and off–balance sheet exposures. It is against the backdrop of these considerations that it recommended the use of "a weighted risk ratio" as a measure of capital adequacy. This ratio[1] weights and relates the riskiness of assets and off–balance sheet exposures to capital.

In justifying this method, the Basel Committee insisted that "a weighted risk ratio in which capital is related to different categories of asset or off-balance-sheet exposure, weighted according to broad categories of relative riskiness, is the preferred method for assessing the capital adequacy of banks." A risk ratio (i.e., the risk weights method) is considered more rigorous and relevant than the gearing ratio approach. It has particular advantages over the gearing ratio, which Basel I identified, in assessing capital adequacy. Unlike a gearing ratio, a risk ratio:[2]

- provides a fairer basis for making international comparisons between banking systems whose structures may differ;
- allows off–balance sheet exposures to be incorporated more easily into the measure;
- does not deter banks from holding liquid or other assets that carry low risk.

The risk ratio approach, seen now as a reliable method for the calculation of capital adequacy, is justifiable. One reason is that asset quality has a direct bearing on capital. Thus, an increasing portfolio of nonperforming assets erodes a bank's capital base through loan loss provisions and write-offs. Another reason, one that derives from the first, is that capital adequacy would be dubious when asset quality deteriorates at a faster rate than increases in capital. Capital adequacy in that case would hardly be sustainable for the desired level of operations.

---

1. The terms *risk ratio*, *weighted risk ratio*, and *risk-weights method* refer to the same concept and are used interchangeably in this chapter.
2. See Basel Committee. 1988. *International convergence of capital measurements and capital standards*. Bank for International Settlements. Basel

Elements of the weighting structure

Basel I adopted a weighting structure that relates capital to specific asset and off–balance sheet risk weights. The resultant risk ratio can then be used to assess the adequacy of bank capital. The structure comprises a framework of five risk weights, each of which can be assigned to particular categories of risk. Basel I offered broad definitions of risk categories to which specific risk weights applied. The weights reflected the riskiness of assets and off–balance sheet exposures of a bank. Factors considered in identifying the risk categories and recommending risk weights are discussed below.

Risk categories

Global bank risk arises for the most part from "the risk of counterparty failure" (i.e., credit risk) and "country transfer risk." Over the years credit default has been a major cause of liquidity crises for banks. So it's not surprising that the risk-weighting framework that's an integral part of Basel I focused on this kind of risk. Yet there are several other kinds of risks to which global banks are exposed and should direct management attention. Investment risk, interest rate risk, exchange rate risk, and concentration risk were some of such risks identified in the Basel I Accord.

The risk weights

In its buildup to formulating a standard weighted risk ratio for global banks, the Basel Committee was mindful that the risks of assets and off––balance sheet exposures differ between countries. For this reason, Basel I categorized assets and off–balance sheet exposures using some definite criteria. For each category, it recommended an appropriate uniform risk weight. Thus, we have a comprehensive schedule of risk weights in Basel I that should be applied to specific categories of assets and off–balance sheet exposures. The schedule of categories of on and off-balance sheet exposures of global banks and risk-weights assigned to them are presented in Tables 37.1 and 37.2.

Implications for credit risk management in emerging economies

The intent of Basel I was to establish a common standard to measure the adequacy of capital of internationally active banks. It adopted a harmonized framework that regulators should adopt to ensure observance of the stipulated capital adequacy standard. The regulatory framework, on the one hand, was meant to aid supervision of global bank capital, lending activities, and portfolios. Standardized capital adequacy, on the other, sought to mitigate credit risk that such banks assume, especially in times of financial crisis. Thus, Basel I underscored worldwide the new and growing attention to how credit risk

TABLE 37.1 Risk Weights by Category of On-Balance-Sheet Assets[a]

0%	1. Cash[b] 2. Claims on central governments and central banks denominated in national currency and funded in that currency 3. Other claims on OECD[c] central governments[d] and central banks 4. Claims collateralised by cash of OECD central-government securities or guaranteed by OECD central governments[e]
0, 10, 20, or 50% (at national discretion)	Claims on domestic public-sector entities, excluding central government, and loans guaranteed by or collateralised by securities issued by such entities
20%	1. Claims on multilateral development banks (IBRD, IADB, AsDB, AfDB, EIB, EBRD)[f] and claims guaranteed by, or collateralised by securities issued by such banks 2. Claims on banks incorporated in the OECD and claims guaranteed by OECD incorporated banks 3. Claims on securities firms incorporated in the OECD subject to comparable supervisory and regulatory arrangements, including in particular risk-based capital requirements,[g] and claims guaranteed by these securities firms 4. Claims on banks incorporated in countries outside the OECD with a residual maturity of up to one year and claims with a residual maturity of up to one year guaranteed by banks incorporated in countries outside the OECD 5. Claims on non-domestic OECD public-sector entities, excluding central government, and claims guaranteed by or collateralised by securities issued by such entities 6. Cash items in process of collection
50%	1. Loans fully secured by mortgage on residential property that is or will be occupied by the borrower or that is rented
100%	1. Claims on the private sector 2. Claims on banks incorporated outside the OECD with a residual maturity of over one year 3. Claims on central governments outside the OECD (unless denominated in national currency—and funded in that currency—see above) 4. Claims on commercial companies owned by the public sector 5. Premises, plant and equipment, and other fixed assets 6. Real estate and other investments (including non-consolidated investment participations in other companies) 7. Capital instruments issued by other banks (unless deducted from capital) 8. All other assets

[a]Tables 37.1 and 37.2, including their footnotes, were extracted from the Basel Capital Accord. See Basel Committee (1988).
[b]Includes (at national discretion) gold bullion held in own vaults or on an allocated basis to the extent backed by bullion liabilities.
[c]For the purpose of this exercise, the OECD group comprises countries which are full members of the OECD (or which have concluded special lending arrangements with the IMF associated with the Fund's General Arrangements to Borrow), but excludes any country within this group which has rescheduled its external sovereign debt in the previous 5 years.
[d]Some member countries intend to apply weights to securities issued by OECD central governments to take account of investment risk. These weights would, for example, be 10% for all securities or 10% for those maturing in up to one year and 20% for those maturing in over one year.
[e]Commercial claims partially guaranteed by these bodies will attract equivalent low weights on that part of the loan which is fully covered. Similarly, claims partially collateralised by cash, or by securities issued by OECD central governments, OECD non-central government public-sector entities, or multilateral development banks will attract low weights on that part of the loan which is fully covered.
[f]Claims on other multilateral development banks in which G-10 countries are shareholding members may, at national discretion, also attract a 20% weight.
[g]i.e., capital requirements that are comparable to those applied to banks in this Accord and its Amendment to incorporate market risks. Implicit in the meaning of the word "comparable" is that the securities firm (but not necessarily its parent) is subject to consolidated regulation and supervision with respect to any downstream affiliates.

TABLE 37.2 Credit Conversion Factors for Off-Balance-Sheet Items

Credit Conversion Factors	Instruments
100%	Direct credit substitutes, e.g. general guarantees of indebtedness (including standby letters of credit serving as financial guarantees for loans and securities) and acceptances (including endorsements with the character of acceptances)
50%	Certain transaction-related contingent items (e.g. performance bonds, bid bonds, warranties and standby letters of credit related to particular transactions)
20%	Short-term self-liquidating trade-related contingencies (such as documentary credits collateralised by the underlying shipments)
100%	Sale and repurchase agreements and asset sales with recourse, where the credit risk remains with the bank
100%	Forward asset purchases, forward deposits and partly-paid shares and securities, which represent commitments with certain drawdown
50%	Note issuance facilities and revolving underwriting facilities
50%	Other commitments (e.g. formal standby facilities and credit lines) with an original maturity of over one year
0%	Similar commitments with an original maturity of up to one year, or which can be unconditionally cancelled at any time

could be effectively managed. The Basel Committee states the underlying purpose of the foregoing:

> As one of the principal objectives of supervision is the protection of depositors, it is essential to ensure that capital recognized in capital adequacy measures is readily available for those depositors. Accordingly, supervisors should test that individual banks are adequately capitalized on a stand-alone basis (Basel Committee, 2004).

The Basel Committee did not mince words and unambiguously stated the commanding focus of the Basel I Accord. It stated that its "framework is mainly directed toward assessing capital in relation to credit risk (the risk of counterparty failure)." However, it's noted in the Accord that "other risks, notably interest rate risk and the investment risk on securities, need to be taken into account by supervisors in assessing overall capital adequacy" (Basel Committee, 1988). The emphasis on credit risk was predicated on the fact that such risk accounted mostly for the troubles of distressed, failing, and failed banks in several countries. It's also assumed that credit risk was the root of the crisis into which the global financial system was thrown in the 1970s and 1980s. In time, it's hoped that implementation of the Accord would check reckless lending and its concomitant liquidity crisis in the internationally active banks.

Basel I also noted a possible loophole in credit risk management at the time that might impact the adequacy of capital of global banks. The probable loophole was in judging capital ratios independent of the quality of risk assets and the level of loan loss provision. As a caveat, the Basel Committee made the point that "capital ratios, judged in isolation, may provide a misleading guide to relative strength. Much also depends on the quality of a bank's assets and, importantly, the level of provisions a bank may be holding outside its capital against assets of doubtful value" (ibid.). While identifying the close relationship between loan loss provisions and capital, Basel I responded to the negative effect of provisions on capital. It did so by seeking "to promote convergence of policies" within the member countries of the Basel Committee. The high point of the impact of Basel I on credit risk management was its formulation of specific means to assess capital adequacy and risk assets quality. The Accord offered a "capital measurement system (*which*) provided for the implementation of a credit risk measurement framework with a minimum capital standard of 8%." Of the 8% "target standard ratio of capital to weighted risk assets," the Accord recommended that "at least 4% will be the core capital element" (ibid.).

REGULATION OF BANK CAPITAL IN EMERGING ECONOMIES

As I pointed out earlier, the Basel Accords' approach to bank capital and credit risk regulation diverges from what obtains in practice in emerging economies. The assessment of capital adequacy for banks is one of the critical elements in banking regulation in emerging economies, no doubt about it. A bank may have a numerically high value of shareholders' funds; however, it could indeed be undercapitalized relative to its portfolio of deposit liabilities or risk assets exposure. On the contrary, another bank may have a small amount of capital even though it is well capitalized in relation to the types and volume of business it undertakes. This is why it is necessary to devise a scientific approach to determining the adequacy of a bank's capital base.

A rule of thumb would be that capital adequacy is a function of the growth strategy, risk-taking appetite, and deposit drive of the bank. If a bank is pursuing an aggressive growth strategy—influenced by high-risk preference behavior in lending practices and a rising deposit liability profile—it will definitely require more capital resources. Here the problem still is how to measure what constitutes adequate capital resources for a bank. The concern about what constitutes the adequate capital base for a bank mirrors the anxiety caused by possible overtrading by some banks. It is perhaps more in banking than in any other business that investment in assets outstrips owners' equity or borrowed funds—in the form of deposit liabilities or other purchased funds. This certainly defines the risk of banking for most practical purposes.

It truly can be said that no amount of capital may be too much for a big bank or a growth-oriented small bank. Yet a benchmark should be set to take care of the minimum expectations of depositors and other stakeholders in the bank—especially in the sad event of bank failure.

Measuring a bank's capital adequacy

Determining appropriate capitalization for banks is usually a major issue in the regulation and supervision of banks in every country. In emerging economies, the matter assumed a disquieting dimension. The common measures of capital adequacy relate to ratio analysis of key bank balance sheet items. It is used as a standard of measurement geared to establishing quantitative relationships between capital funds and total deposits, total assets, or total risk assets. In so doing, credit analysts wish to determine the extent to which any losses incurred by a bank could impair the safety of customers' deposits. The overriding consideration is to gain insight into the adequacy of a bank's capital funds for absorbing business upsets without the loss of depositors' funds.

Most Central Banks in emerging economies adopt an official minimum required capital adequacy ratio of 10 percent. In practice, however, banks in some emerging economies achieve higher rates. For example, the State Bank of Pakistan reported achievement of "overall capital adequacy ratio at 14.8 percent as of end March 2014" (Pakistan Economic Survey 2013—2014: 71—72). Banks are encouraged to pursue the targets through improved asset quality. One of the ways to improve the ratio is through adequate provisioning against nonperforming risk assets. In the Pakistan case, the ratio of nonperforming loans to total loans was 13.3 percent in March 2014, down from 15.8 percent in March 2013. (ibid.)

The common measure of capital adequacy—which relates capital funds to risk assets—is as follows:

$$\text{Capital adequacy} = \frac{\text{Capital funds}}{\text{Total risk assets}} \times 100$$

In order to serve regulatory purposes, minimum and maximum capital adequacy levels should be set. However, ratio analysis has its limitations. It does not tell anything about the nature and magnitude or the quality of operations and risks of a bank relative to the size of its capital resources. Yet once assessed by regulatory authorities, the ratios become standards for determining a bank's capital adequacy. All banks are therefore expected to meet the recommended capital adequacy ratio or risk being classified as undercapitalized.

Regulation of capital base of banks

The monetary authorities in emerging economies tend to stipulate three approaches to regulating the capital adequacy of banks. They focus on the start-up or base capital, single-obligor limit, and weighted risk assets ratio.

Start-up or base capital

There is a minimum start-up capital (i.e., owners' equity) requirement that must be met by prospective investors or promoters of a new bank. Existing banks, by the same regulation, are also expected to have a certain minimum paid-up capital at any point in time. New and existing banks must satisfy these minimum standards as a condition for obtaining or retaining their banking licenses. Existing banks and promoters of new banks in Nigeria are respectively expected to maintain or raise minimum equity capital of ₦25 billion.

Single-obligor limit

The single-obligor limit on bank lending is intended to ensure that a bank's capital funds really do cushion depositors against losses inherent in risk assets. Such risks become more apparent when loans are either not performing, require provisioning from earnings against possible losses, or have to be charged off. The notion of the single-obligor limit suggests that a bank should not lend more than a certain percentage of its shareholders' funds (unimpaired by losses) to a single borrower or group that are subsidiaries or share common ownership. In Nigeria at the moment, the single-obligor limit for banks is 20% of shareholders' funds (unimpaired by losses).

Weighted risk assets ratio

The weighted risk assets ratio relates shareholders' funds to the total risk assets portfolio. This is essentially a typical measure of capital adequacy for banks in emerging economies. In Nigeria, and for regulatory purposes, capital adequacy is presently set at 10% of shareholders' funds. However, the CBN could vary the ratio depending on the prevailing macroeconomic situation.

REGULATING BANK LIQUIDITY RISK IN EMERGING ECONOMIES

A common observation among banks in emerging economies is that they rarely rely on or comply with liquidity ratios—even internally generated ratios. The reason is not far-fetched; bankers see the limits imposed on business generation by strict observance of the ratios as not only unnecessary but punitive. Thus, as long as their banks remain going concerns, they strive to find ways around a temporary liquidity crunch when it occurs or hits the market. This is a wrong disposition to the task of liquidity management. It is better to limit growth to sustain liquidity and ultimately the integrity or credibility of the bank. Using the balance sheet of First Bank of Nigeria PLC, presented in Table 37.3, I examine the three approaches to liquidity measurement commonly used by banks in emerging economies. A bank's liquidity position can be assessed using one, a combination, or all three methods: loan-to-deposit ratio, cash reserve ratio, and liquidity ratio.

TABLE 37.3 First Bank of Nigeria PLC—Balance Sheet as of 31 March

	2002 (₦'m)	2001 (₦'m)
ASSETS		
Cash and short term funds	132,800	108,875
Bills discounted	54,178	37,049
Investments	780	501
Loans and advances	61,918	46,111
Other assets	8664	12,855
Equipment on lease	190	202
Fixed assets	7826	7308
TOTAL ASSETS	266,356	212,901
LIABILITIES		
Deposits and current accounts	168,175	148,279
Taxation	1176	1740
Deferred taxation	694	453
Other liabilities	78,564	45,336
	248,609	195,808
CAPITAL AND RESERVES		
Called-up share capital	1016	813
Capital reserve	1893	1893
Statutory reserve	3252	2655
Exchange difference reserve	2055	2738
General reserve	5769	5792
Bonus issue reserve	254	203
Reserve for small and medium-scale industries	1129	620
Core capital	15,368	14,714
Fixed assets revaluation surplus	2379	2379
Shareholders' funds	17,747	17,093
TOTAL LIABILITIES	266,356	212,901
Contingent liabilities and other obligations on behalf of customers and customers' liabilities thereof	76,883	25,797

Loan-to-deposit ratio

This ratio compares the volume of loans outstanding in a bank's loan (risk assets) portfolio to its total deposit liabilities at a given point in time. A bank determines its liquidity position using this method by dividing the total of its outstanding portfolio of risk assets by the sum of its deposit liabilities, and comparing the quotient or ratio so obtained with the industry average or the target set for it by regulatory authorities. In other words, the ratio expresses a bank's total deposit liabilities as a percentage or fraction of its outstanding loan stock as shown below:

$$\text{Loan-To-Deposit Ratio} = \frac{\text{Total Outstanding Loans}}{\text{Total Deposit Liabilities}}$$

Most banks that emphasize liquidity will target a maximum loan-to-deposit ratio of 70%, implying that realistically up to one third of the bank's total deposit liabilities should not be loaned to customers at any point in time. Banks that are less driven by profit maximization will target lower ratios—say, 60%. In the First Bank of Nigeria example, the ratios were far lower at 36.82% and 31.10% in 2002 and 2001, respectively, depicting the high liquidity status of the bank. The ratio for each period is calculated as follows:

Balance sheet figures as of March 31		2002	2001
Total loans and advances (₦'m)		61,918	46,111
Deposits and current accounts (₦'m)		168,175	148,279
Loan-to-deposit ratio	=	61,918	46,111
		168,175	148,279
	=	36.82%	31.10%

Yet, the loan-to-deposit ratio could be as high as 100% or more for banks with high risk appetites. This category of banks sometimes relies on capital reserves and/or nondeposit float accounts or products to sustain liquidity, fund incremental lending activities, and meet profit targets. However, an extremely high loan-to-deposit ratio might be a warning sign of an impending liquidity crisis, which would scare discerning depositors from investing in such banks. Thus, the significance of the loan-to-deposit ratio is that it is inversely related to a bank's liquidity. This implies that a bank would be more or less liquid depending on the ratio. The bank would be more liquid, the lower its loan-to-deposit ratio, and vice versa.

When the ratio is considered high or more than the industry average, the bank may adopt a restrictive loan policy to check the likely negative impact on liquidity and the restriction of other profitable operations or activities. It would most likely also begin to discriminate among customers who make credit requests by being critical and selective on proposals to grant new credits. The bank may also increase its requirements for the accessing of loan facilities by some customers. Frequently, when the ratio is rising, lending rates tend to increase in kind as a bank hikes interest rates to reflect its tight liquidity position.

Unfortunately, many such loans frequently become delinquent, with concomitant loan loss provisions. When this happens, the expected income from the aggressive lending policy would not be realized. In fact, the bank may even make a net loss on balance in the performance of the total loan portfolio. It is indeed apparent that a bank would rarely make money or continually meet its net profit expectation through the irrational buildup of the loan portfolio.

Merits of loan-to-deposit ratio

Measuring a bank's liquidity position by means of the loan-to-deposit ratio is credited with the advantage of establishing an acceptable level of depositors' funds that could be invested in loans and advances without jeopardizing a bank's liquidity position. The ratio is rationalized on the premise that since loans rank among the least liquid earning assets of a bank, the proportion of deposits invested in loans and advances cannot be increased without regrettably sacrificing liquidity. The choice is therefore for bank management to decide its preferred loan-to-deposit ratio in line with its long-term business focus, orientation, and market demands.

Despite the fact that a bank can choose whatever loan-to-deposit ratio it considers reasonable, its real value consists in offering a warning signal on the state of its liquidity position, especially when the ratio starts rising to an unsustainable level. In such a situation, there might be a need for the bank to begin to reconsider its investment policies and growth strategies with a view to recovering liquidity. The ratio gives insight into the extent of a bank's risk aversion or preference tendency, from which one could discern those banks that emphasize liquidity more than profitability and vice versa.

Shortcomings of loan-to-deposit ratio

The shortcomings of this approach to liquidity measurement are also worth mentioning. It is criticized on the following grounds:

- Erratic and volatile deposit liabilities

  A bank with an erratic and volatile deposit base may have a higher risk of illiquidity than a bank that has a high loan-to-deposit ratio on a stable deposit base. It is also not uncommon to find situations where a few large deposits cause major swings in the ratio. In such cases, the ratio may give the wrong picture of the exact condition of the risk of the lending portfolio in relation to the deposit liabilities base.
- Attributes of a bank's loan portfolio

  It does not factor the key attributes of a bank's loan portfolio into the computation of the ratio. For instance, a loan portfolio might be composed of a large stock of short-term, self-liquidating, and performing risk assets that can be easily recovered if the need arises to do so. It is therefore important to determine the maturity profile of the loan portfolio, assess the borrowers' source(s) and modes of repayment, and review the bank's loan repayment experiences with its key borrowing customers.

- Degree of liquidity needs of banks

    The ratio fails to account for, or recognize, the fact that banks have varying degrees of liquidity needs. That a particular bank has a higher loan-to-deposit ratio than another does not necessarily mean that the latter is more liquid. Interpretation of the ratio should really be seen as reflecting conclusions on a composite set of variables, which reveal the practical relevance of the ratio itself. For instance, we cannot conclude that a bank with a higher loan-to-deposit ratio than another is less liquid. Such a conclusion does not tell anything about the stability or volatility of the deposit portfolio of the two banks.

- Risk assets versus deposit liabilities

    Relying solely on the relation between risk assets and deposit liabilities in measuring a bank's liquidity could be misleading for obvious reasons. Besides loans and advances, there are other assets on a bank's balance sheet. Yet the loan-to-deposit ratio ignores all but risk assets in the computation of liquidity. It is necessary that the composition and nature of a bank's assets be critically examined in assessing its liquidity position. This should be done for the reason that two or more banks may have the same loan-to-deposit ratio and yet not be equally liquid. Differences in the liquidity level between two banks could arise simply because the assets of one are more liquid than those of the other.

Cash reserve ratio

The cash reserve ratio, also known as the cash-to-deposit ratio, measures liquidity by relating the average volume of cash or liquid assets to the bank's total deposit liabilities or total assets. Sometimes, computations of the cash reserve ratio take into account the deposit liabilities or total assets of banks of similar size for all banks in that category. The ratio is calculated by regulatory authorities such as the Central Bank and enforced on banks. The following formula is applied in calculating the cash ratio:

$$\text{Cash Reserve Ratio} = \frac{\text{Total Volume of Cash Assets}}{\text{Volume of Deposit Liabilities}}$$

Merits of cash ratio

In dividing cash assets by total deposit liabilities of the bank at any point in time, this ratio offers insight into the proportion of depositors' funds held in liquid form. This would give an idea of a bank's ability to meet depositors' withdrawal demands based on the availability of cash or reserves.

Shortcomings of cash ratio

The disadvantages of the cash ratio, and therefore the reserve requirement, as an approach to liquidity measurement tend to take away from its merits. There are critical shortcomings of the ratio. For instance, the cash ratio does not take account of the fact that a large proportion of cash assets are not, in practice, available to a bank to meet its liquidity needs. The ratio excludes short-term funds and marketable securities in its computation; yet these are considered highly liquid assets—especially T-bills. It also fails to recognize the possibility and tendency of a bank to raise cash from alternative sources to meet liquidity needs.

Liquidity ratio

Calculation and application of the liquidity ratio has been a regular approach to assessing the liquidity of banks. Traditionally, regulatory authorities and deposit insurance corporations have highly favored the use of the liquidity ratio as a means for determining the liquidity position of a bank. The ratio is calculated by dividing a bank's portfolio of specified liquid assets by the bank's total current liabilities as shown below:

$$\text{Liquidity Ratio} = \frac{\text{Specified Liquid Assets}}{\text{Total Current Liabilities}}$$

The critical issue in the use of this ratio appears to be determining the composition of qualifying liquid assets. In Nigeria, the Central Bank specifies the following liquid assets and current liabilities for the purpose of computation of the liquidity ratio:

Liquid assets

- Cash
- Balance held with the Central Bank less cash reserve requirement (8% of the sum of demand deposits, purchased funds, and domiciliary account balance);
- Balance(s) held with domestic or internal banks (excluding uncleared effects) less balances held for domestic or internal banks (if net minus, add to current liabilities);
- Treasury Bills;
- Placement(s) with discount houses less takings from discount houses;
- Money at call held with other banks less money at call held for other banks;
- Fixed deposits placed with other banks less fixed deposits held for other banks;

Current liabilities

- Balances in demand and time deposit accounts;
- Negotiable Certificates of Deposits issued (with not more than 18 months to maturity);

- Excess balance(s) held for domestic or internal banks;
- Excess placement(s) held for discount houses;
- Excess money at call held for other banks;
- Excess deposits held for other banks;
- Balances held for external offices less balance(s) held with external offices (if net minus ignore).

The liquidity ratio computation for banks in emerging economies (specifically Nigeria) is illustrated in Table 37.4 below.

TABLE 37.4 Illustration of Liquidity Ratio Computation for Banks in Emerging Economies

	₦'000	₦'000
LIQUID ASSETS		
Cash		22,935
Balance held with CBN	(400,539)	
Less cash reserve requirement (12.5% of demand deposit and purchased funds)	267,913	
	(668,452)	(668,452)
Balances held with internal banks (excluding uncleared effects)	620,160	
Less Balances held for internal banks (if net minus, add to current liabilities	993,986	
	(373,826)	0
Nigeria Treasury Bills (NTBs)	0	0
Nigeria Treasury Certificates	0	0
Placements with discount houses	169,801	
Less Placements held for discount houses (if net minus, add to curr liabilities	158,000	
	11,801	11,801
Money at call held with other banks	0	
Less Money at call held for other banks (if net minus, add to current liabilities	0	
	0	0
Fixed deposits placed with other banks	0	
Less Fixed deposits held for other banks (if net minus, add to current liabilities	160,000	
	(160,000)	0

Continued

TABLE 37.4 Illustration of Liquidity Ratio Computation for Banks in Emerging Economies—cont'd

	₦'000	₦'000
Nigeria certificates of deposit held (of not more than 18 months to maturity)	0	
Government securities—eligible development stocks—(i.e., of not more than) 3 years to maturity	0	
Less Nigeria certificates of deposit (NCDs) issued	0	
	0	0
Bankers Unit fund		
Stabilization securities	0	
Less Foreign exchange market (FEM) deposit	0	0
TOTAL LIQUID ASSETS (A)		(633,717)
CURRENT LIABILITIES		
Current time/deposits accounts		2,143,307
NCDs issued (of not more than 18 months to maturity)		0
Excess balance held for internal banks		373,826
Excess placements held for discount houses		0
Excess money at call held for other banks		0
Excess deposits held for other banks		160,000
Balance held for external offices	0	
Less Balance held with external offices (if net minus, ignore)	0	
	0	0
Collateral deposit		0
Cash collected for financial services		0
Balance held for other external banks	0	
Less Balance held with other external banks (if net minus, ignore)	0	
	0	0
TOTAL CURRENT LIABILITIES (B)		2,677,133
LIQUIDITY RATIO A/B		−23.67%
Nigeria Treasury Bill (NTB) ratio NTB/B		0.00%

Justification of liquidity ratio

The ratio must be met on a monthly average basis—but could fluctuate during any days of the month. It provides a guide to banks in managing occasional swings in its stock of reserve assets, which could exceed or fall short of the statutory requirement at any point in time. In the case of the former, a bank could dispose of its surplus holdings of liquid assets or reserves to reduce the income loss associated with carrying such non- or low-earning assets. In the event of a shortfall, the bank will resort to increasing its deposit base, even if by taking call money in the interbank money market.

Weakness of liquidity ratio

The usual victim in all observed situations of a persisting shortage in the required liquidity level is lending activity. At first blush, management is averse to the curtailment of further lending activity in order to shore up liquidity. Yet this is acclaimed to be an effective liquidity management strategy, as excessive lending activities drain liquidity. If the rate of growth in lending is not matched by deposit mobilization, the bank may begin to experience cash flow distress resulting from illiquidity. But the alternative—one that implies the forgoing of earnings, growth, and profitability as a sacrifice to improve liquidity—is also not palatable or beneficial to the bank.

REGULATORY RESPONSE TO FAILING BANKS IN EMERGING ECONOMIES

It would be wishful thinking to believe that regulation is a panacea for bank failure. Even in highly developed economies such as those of the United States and Japan, it is ordinary that banks, like other enterprises, fail in the course of business. This may be why the CBN postures equal minds in allowing free entry as it enforces exit on distressed banks. The CBN Governor on January 30, 2001 announced that in continuation of distress resolution efforts, three banks had their licenses revoked and were transferred to the NDIC for eventual liquidation. He also stressed that efforts would be sustained in 2001 to address any symptom of distress in the system in a timely and decisive manner. It was not strange that the CBN was bluntly sounding that warning, considering the country's recent experiences with large-scale bank distress and failure that had brought untold hardships to the people.

The CBN and NDIC have control over and management responsibilities for distressed and failing banks. Sections 33 (2) and 34—36 of the Banks and Other Financial Institutions (BOFI) Act No. 25 of 1991, as amended, empower the CBN to deal with distressed and failing banks. I now discuss various approaches often adopted by regulatory authorities in emerging economies to resolve bank distress. My objective is to assess the effectiveness of the various measures in the Nigerian environment.

Moral suasion

Prior to and during distress, regulatory authorities adopt moral suasion as a means of sensitizing banks to the dangers of distress and how to avoid it. In most cases, moral suasion involves specific recommendations to, and counseling of, bank management on the need to maintain healthy operations. The CBN specifically urges banks to observe appropriate and approved operating guidelines, render accurate statutory returns, and strive to achieve the required health and performance ratios. The authorities hold regular interactive sessions with the chief executives of banks to discuss matters affecting banks in particular and the financial system in general. Under the auspices of the Chartered Institute of Bankers of Nigeria, the Bankers' Committee provides perhaps the most effective forum for such interactions. However, it does not seem that moral suasion has been effective in managing or preventing bank distress in Nigeria. The problem has obviously defied such a persuasive measure.

Option of holding actions

The more drastic measures, usually adopted whenever moral suasion fails, are prescribed in the BOFI Act 1991. Section 33 (2) empowers the Governor of the CBN to make an order restricting the activities of a distressed or failing bank. In line with the Act, the Governor may, by order in writing:

- prohibit the bank from further extending any credit facility; and
- require the bank to take any steps or any action, or to do or not to do any act or thing whatsoever, in relation to the bank or its business or its directors or officers, that may be considered necessary

Often the scope of such holding actions is sweeping and covers a broad spectrum of restrictions. For instance, a failing bank may not, without the consent of the CBN, continue to advertise for deposits, embark on new capital projects, or dispose of any fixed assets. Such a bank is expected to beef up internal controls, recapitalize the business, perfect loan security documentation, and emphasize debt recovery. There are numerous other miscellaneous requirements that failing banks must satisfy in their turnaround bids.

It is doubtful that holding actions are an effective means of resolving bank distress in Nigeria. Of over 50 banks on which the CBN has administered holding actions since the 1990s distress syndrome, less than a 5% success rate has been attained. The high failure rate of the actions derived mainly from the magnitude of the observed distress prior to intervention by regulatory authorities. For instance, the holding actions were most often imposed after the paid-up capital of distressed banks had been completely wiped out, while their stock of unsecured or undocumented nonperforming loans had become rather excessive. Thus, it becomes overwhelming for the owners and management of the bank to attain any measure of turnaround success, especially in terms of recapitalization. Some may argue that the delay in imposing "holding actions" is justified; authorities should be convinced beyond all doubts that such interference in the affairs of the bank is really the next resort in the plans to save the bank. This implies that the management of the bank has completely failed in restructuring or reengineering the bank for normal banking business in line with regulatory prescriptions.

Assumption of control

Once holding actions fail to yield fruit, the CBN invokes the law to assume control of the bank. The power to take over management of a failing bank is given in Sections 34 and 35 of the BOFI Act 1991. Meanwhile, Section 33 (2) (d) and (e) empower the CBN, as a prelude to assumption of full control of a distressed bank, to:

- remove from office any director of the bank;
- appoint any person or persons as a director or directors of the bank; and
- appoint any person to advise the bank in relation to the proper conduct of its business

In the event that the foregoing measures fail to rescue the bank, that is to say, "the state of affairs of the bank does not improve significantly," the BOFI Act 1991 provides that the CBN may assume control of the whole of the property and affairs of the bank, carry on the whole of its business and affairs, or assume control of such part of its property, business, and affairs as *it* considers necessary, or appoint persons to do so on its behalf (Section 34 (1)).

The assumption of control of a distressed bank by the authorities may be temporary, if the action succeeds, or lead to stiffer action if it fails. Success is attained when, and assumption of control by the authorities remains in force until such time as:

- the CBN is satisfied that adequate provision has been made for the repayment of deposits; and
- in the opinion of the CBN, it is no longer necessary for it to remain in control of the business of the bank (Section 35 (1)).

Regulatory authorities became innovative in the exercise of the foregoing power when they nationalized three failed banks in 2010 and christened them "bridge banks"—without assuming direct control of the banks.

Acquisition, revocation of license, or liquidation

The last resort of regulatory authorities in the process of distress management is to acquire, restructure, and sell the failing bank, or revoke the operating license of and wind up the bank. The power of the CBN to do this is given in

Section 36 (a) (b) of the BOFI Act 1991, where it stipulates that if the paid-up capital of the distressed bank is lost or unrepresented by available assets, the CBN may:

- apply to the Federal High Court for an order for it or its nominee to purchase or acquire the bank for a nominal fee for the purpose of restructuring and subsequent sale; and
- make an order revoking the bank's license and requiring its business to be wound up

In Nigeria, the need has been identified to fully empower the Central Bank and NDIC to deal with any threat of bank distress. The application of such empowerment climaxes when authorities, to pave the way for liquidation, withdraw the operating license of a bank. Yet, for practical purposes:

- it does not make good business sense to resolve distress through the liquidation of affected banks
- liquidation generally causes great financial pain to depositors, shareholders, and employees
- revocation of banking license further erodes the fragile confidence that citizens may have in the banking system.

Even when bank liquidation is unavoidable, there are still problems: Firstly, it could take up to three years before the NDIC begins paying depositors. Secondly, not only will depositors of a failed bank suffer such a prolonged delay, each of them gets no more than the insured portion of their deposits, irrespective of the amount of their deposit with the bank. For bank depositors, this practice negates the true essence of insurance. It is an aberration of the acknowledged principle of indemnity on which the business of insurance is founded.

If the monetary authorities really want to help build a long-term deposit banking culture and reinstill confidence in the banking system, the NDIC should pay appropriate compensation to depositors of failed banks. This will allay the fear of loss of deposits due to bank distress or failure, and help to attract movement of much of the huge amount of money in private vaults to banks. Over the long run, it would become less attractive to hold money outside the banking system. Also, projections of money stock in the system for regulatory purposes will be more accurate and reliable. In the same vein, the impact of monetary policies will to a large extent be predictable, while unintended monetary shocks will be minimized.

QUESTIONS FOR DISCUSSION AND REVIEW

1. **(a)** How will adoption of the Basel I and Basel II Accords benefit supervision of banks in emerging economies?
   (b) Why and how do modes of banking regulation in emerging economies diverge from Basel Accords tenets?

2. (a) Why has determination of appropriate amount of bank capital always been a thorny question for bank management and regulators in emerging economies?

(b) In what ways did the Basel Committee on Banking Supervision deal with the problem of global bank capital adequacy and quality?

3. Discuss the role of bank management and regulators in the implementation of the Basel Accords, taking cognizance of peculiar situation of banks in emerging economies.

4. How, notwithstanding supervision, would the condition of a bank deteriorate to a level where failure becomes imminent?

5. Do you think that recent banking reforms in some emerging economies will address the problem of vested interests in bank lending?

REFERENCES

Basel Committee on Banking Supervision, 1988. International Convergence of Capital Measurement and Capital Standards. as amended. Bank for International Settlements, Basel.

CBN (Central Bank of Nigeria), 2001. Exposure Draft Circular: Insider Related Credit Facilities.

Sanusi, J.O., 2001. 'Keynote Address' (Delivered as Governor, Central Bank of Nigeria) at the National Workshop on Monetary and Financial Policies Management, Lagos.

State Bank of Pakistan, 2014. Pakistan Economic Survey 2013−14.

Chapter 38

Bank Credit Portfolio Structure, Quality, and Returns in Emerging Economies

LEARNING FOCUS AND OUTCOMES

Bank lending in emerging economies should seek to correct variances between policy prescriptions and compliance. Banks should especially direct more lending to meet loan targets for preferred economic sectors. They may consider minimizing the current emphasis on credits to commerce and other nonreal sectors. Also, lending to enterprises whose activities produce linkages to the preferred sectors should be encouraged. Such loans can be classified as credits granted for purposes of economic development. Of course, this has implications for managing the lending portfolio. The main thrust of bank management in the lending function should be to create a balanced and profitable portfolio of risk assets in line with the economic outlook. This requires knowledge of the business environment, anticipated and existing lending regulations, and shareholders' expectations.

It is common that assets comprising the loan books of banks are classified into three broad categories, usually based on their terms to maturity. This classification recognizes short-term, medium-term, and long-term loans. However, there is no common understanding among banks about the exact periods to which these terms relate. For example, depending on their risk appetites,

Emerging Market Bank Lending and Credit Risk Control. http://dx.doi.org/10.1016/B978-0-12-803438-5.00038-6
671

what one bank might regard as medium-term may be seen as long-term by another bank. In most cases, nonetheless, banks typically regard a period of 12 months or less as short-term.

I assess the foregoing classification method, considering that an efficient, quality loan portfolio is best accounted for in the categories of risk assets that comprise a bank's loan book. In order to characterize the loan book's risk assets well, I make and defend a change in the popular method of classifying assets in the loan book. The change is about grouping medium-term and long-term loans together, but retaining the short-term category while isolating hybrid or irregular credit facilities.

Based on this approach, the loan portfolio of a bank comprises three main categories of risk assets—short-term loans, medium-to long-term loans, and hybrid or irregular credit facilities. My objective for this chapter is to highlight the features, dynamics, and management requirements for the loan book and for each of the risk asset categories that make it up. With respect to bank lending in emerging market economies, the reader will learn about:

- Constituents and dynamics of the credit, assets, and liabilities portfolios of the banking industry
- Issues in credit concentration and risk associated with deploying lending in particular sectors
- Distribution of the lending portfolios of the banking industry according to sectors and industries
- Maturity profiles of risk assets that constitute the lending portfolios of the banking system
- Risk characteristics and indicators of quality of the lending portfolios of the banking industry

ELEMENTS AND COMPOSITION OF ASSETS PORTFOLIO

Assets constitute a significant component of a bank's balance sheet—representing "uses" to which its capital, reserves, and liabilities are put to generate earnings, growth, and returns to shareholders. Thus, assets management must be efficient and ensure attainment of a reasonable level of profit in order to achieve the overall desired outcome, which is to increase shareholders' wealth. If assets are poorly managed, a bank may experience liquidity problems as a result of diminution of earnings. In such a situation, maturing obligations and liabilities may not be timely settled and at a reasonable cost. A bank in this situation might begin to experience distress that could ultimately lead to bankruptcy and failure. This is why it is imperative to understand and appreciate the dynamics and import of effective management of assets in banking.

The usual assets of a bank comprise cash, short-term funds, securities, loans, fixed assets, and others. The liquidity of these assets varies, with cash being the most liquid and fixed assets the least. Of course, the more liquid an asset, the less earnings or return it generates. I adopt a two-pronged approach to analyzing composition of assets portfolios of banks in emerging economies. In the first instance, I use the balance sheet of Zenith Bank (Nigeria) Limited, presented in Table 38.1, to illustrate typical items of assets and liabilities of a bank. Then I relate the analysis to entire banking system lending portfolios in select emerging economies. In doing so, I establish any observable pattern that sheds light on problems and prospects of bank lending portfolio management in emerging economies.

Cash items

Consisting of currency notes and coins, cash does not earn income for the bank. It is yet needed to satisfy the statutory regulation for required reserves kept with the Central Bank and to meet deposit withdrawals by customers and for general operating expenses. We can at any time isolate three distinct locations for a bank's cash balances. They are the Central Bank (cash reserves), strong rooms of branches and the head office (vault cash), and deposits with other, sometimes local or correspondent, banks (due from other banks). It is obvious that cash is important for its use in meeting statutory requirements, customers' withdrawal requests, and working capital needs.

Short-term funds

Cash assets may include short-term funds. On occasion cash and short-term funds may be separated to have a finer distinction between their meanings and applications. Clarity of their meanings adds value to a better understanding of their differences. The phrase "short-term funds" is used to describe checks or other instruments deposited by a bank's customers for clearing (i.e., outward clearing checks). As instruments in the process of collection, they are devoid of immediate value to depositors. With the introduction of check truncation in Nigeria, the check clearing cycle was reduced to two days—from $T + 2$ to $T + 1$—effective August 10, 2012. Thus, unless the instruments receive value after clearing, they cannot be correctly described as cash. They are at best regarded as "near" cash items.

Zenith Bank, whose balance sheet is presented in Table 38.1 for illustration purposes, boasted strong liquidity, as its cash and short-term funds accounted for a whopping 70.90 percent of the bank's total assets. Further evidence of the bank's strong liquidity showing is seen in its loan-to-deposit ratio of 40.90 percent. Other performance indicators of the bank are shown in the table under key accounting ratios. Most highly liquid banks in emerging economies will boast similar accounting ratios. On a consolidated basis for the entire banking system, the result is about the same across emerging market economies.

In Taiwan, as Table 38.6 shows, the loan-to-deposit ratio achieved by the entire banking system was satisfactory at 77.49 percent in 2014, even as the

TABLE 38.1 Zenith Bank (Nigeria) Limited—Balance Sheet as of June 30, 2002[a]

	(₦'000)	% of Total
Assets		
Cash and short-term funds	65,628,625.00	70.90
Placements	1,800,000.00	1.94
Loans and advances	20,144,168.00	21.76
Advances under finance lease	360,781.00	0.39
Investment securities	359,743.00	0.39
Other assets	1,285,878.00	1.39
Fixed assets	2,983,702.00	3.22
	92,562,897.00	
Liabilities		
Deposit liabilities	50,134,281.00	60.22
Other liabilities	32,759,311.00	39.35
Deferred taxation	363,337.00	0.44
	83,256,929.00	
Capital and reserves		
Called-up share capital	1,026,658.00	11.03
Reserve for SMEs	833,144.00	8.95
Share premium	300.00	0.00
Other reserves	7,445,866.00	80.01
Shareholders' funds	9,305,968.00	
	92,562,897.00	
Confirmed credits and other obligations on behalf of customers and the corresponding thereon	19,986,187.00	
Total assets plus contingent liabilities	112,549,084.00	
Key accounting ratios		
Loans and advances to deposits		40.90
Total assets to total liabilities		111.18
Contingent liabilities to total assets		21.59
Contingent liabilities to net worth		214.77
Total liabilities to net worth		894.66

[a]Published in Nigeria's ThisDay Newspaper, Vol. 8, No. 2654, Monday, July 29, 2002, p. 7.

TABLE 38.2 Pakistan Banking System—Key Variables of Balance Sheet and Profit and Loss Statement

	2013 (Rs. billion)	2014 (Rs. billion)	% of Assets (2013)	% of Assets (2014)
Total assets	10,537	10,752		
Investments (net)	4305	4662	40.86	43.36
Advances (net)	4047	4014	38.41	37.33
Deposits	8318	8151	78.94	75.81
Equity	939	956	8.91	8.89
Profit before tax (year to date)	165	51		
Profit after tax (year to date)	111	33		
Nonperforming loans	585	602	5.55	5.60
Nonperforming loans (net)[a]	126	134	1.20	1.25
Capital adequacy ratio (all banks)	14.9	14.8		
Loan-to-deposit ratio	48.65	49.25		

[a]Excluding specific provisions.
Extracted from State Bank of Pakistan, *Pakistan Economic Survey 2013–2014*. All ratios were computed based on data extracted from this source.

standard benchmark is 70 percent or less. Further evidence of the appreciable liquidity attained by banks in Taiwan was the record deposit to liability ratio of 82.89 percent that the industry posted during the review period. With such a strong showing in customer deposit accounts, the country's banking system operated from a position of liquidity strength.

The case of Pakistan, presented in Table 38.2, is not significantly different. The ratio of customer deposits to the banking system's total assets was quite high at 75.81 percent, resulting in a loan-to-deposit ratio of 49.25 percent in 2014. The capital adequacy ratio of 14.8 percent for all banks in the country during the period complemented the good standing on loan-to-deposit ratio.

Marketable securities

Investment in marketable or debt securities is almost always a significant element in a bank's assets portfolio. They are largely government IOUs that banks purchase in fulfillment of part of their statutory liquidity requirements, as well as to earn income and serve as collateral for specified deposit liabilities such as interbank takings. Mainly treasury bills, treasury certificates, debentures, commercial paper, federal government development stocks, and bonds, such government obligations are almost riskless and account for the largest proportion of a bank's security investments at any point in time.

However, this is not evident in the case of Zenith Bank. The bank managed a paltry 0.39% investment in marketable securities. This may not be surprising considering that financial markets in many emerging economies like Nigeria are as yet rudimentary. This may sound a bit far-fetched, but this departure underlies a major cause of the imbalances in the finances of banks. Notwithstanding lukewarm dispositions, banks crave particular marketable securities. The most popular debt securities among banks are T-bills and treasury certificates, negotiable certificates, and federal government development stocks, in which banks invest surplus funds largely on considerations of safety. The risk—return trade-off is eminently relevant here. From marketable securities, returns are generally low; but they provide a portfolio of highly liquid assets because of their tradability in the secondary money market. In other words, such debt securities can be sold to the Central Bank before their maturity dates with little or no loss of value—a process commonly referred to as rediscounting of the bill.

Thus banks in emerging economies should favor investments in debt securities. There are at least three reasons for them to do so. Firstly, such financial instruments get virtual riskless ratings. Secondly, they are amenable to rediscounting with the Central Bank prior to maturity. Thirdly, the ability to rediscount instruments helps banks meet urgent liquidity needs. There are other—and certainly not usually attractive—securities or commercial bills in which banks in emerging economies could also invest. They are nongovernment securities that bills of exchange and acceptances mainly represent.

Investments

Banks are sometimes availed other investment windows in certain products floated by the Central Bank or a group of banks. The Deposit Certificate, introduced in February 2001 by the Central Bank of Nigeria (CBN), is an example of such an investment opportunity. The Certificate has a minimum investment period of 180 days, but is also available for 360 days. It offers a competitive market-determined rate of interest. The Certificate is essentially a money market instrument aimed at mopping up excess liquidity in the banking system and the economy. In order to achieve this objective, the Certificate does not have a secondary market value; thus, investors must hold it for the period to maturity. It is also not discountable with the Central Bank. With such an appreciable rate of interest (often above the T-bill and monetary policy rate), the Certificate adequately compensates investors for its lack of a secondary market. Yet it was welcomed as a veritable liquidity management instrument.

There was once in Nigeria the Call Money scheme (called Federal Funds in the United States), floated by some banks to meet urgent liquidity needs. The Scheme was later taken over and directly administered by the CBN. The participating banks maintained a certain minimum statutory deposit balance with the CBN, where they had set up a Call Money Fund. Members that had surplus deposits above the agreed minimum balance lent the excess to the Fund. Conversely, borrowing on an overnight basis from the Fund covered deficit deposit positions. However, unlike the CBN Certificate, interest on Call Money was below the T-bill rate. The main advantage of the Scheme was the assurance of liquidity and income on excess overnight balances with the CBN for participating banks.

Investments with other banks, usually in the form of fixed deposits evidenced by certificates of deposits and negotiable certificates of deposits, sometimes account for a substantial proportion of short-term investments on a bank's balance sheet. The same goes for money at call and short notice held with the Central Bank. This could also be quite substantial. Of the total Rs.2,417.75 billion assets that banks in India held with the Reserve Bank of India as of January 23, 2015, for instance, money at call and short notice accounted for Rs.403.29 billion, representing 16.68 percent (see Table 38.3). Balances with other banks—amounting to Rs.1,506.36 billion—were held in current accounts (Rs.92.67 billion) and other accounts (Rs.1,413.69 billion), and accounted for 62.30 percent of the assets with the banking system.

Generally, the most significant and perhaps controversial element in a bank's nondebt or nonmarketable securities investments is equity securities. For instance, a bank in Nigeria may, according to Section 21 of the BOFI Act, No. 25, of 1991 (as amended), invest not more than 10 percent of its shareholders' funds, unimpaired by losses, in the equity stock of any medium-scale enterprises—including agricultural, venture capital, or any other business enterprise approved by the CBN. This is the concept espoused in the Small and Medium Industries Equity Investment Scheme through which government intended to accelerate the growth of the industrial sector of the economy. Under the scheme, such shareholding or equity investment should not exceed 40 percent of the company's paid-up capital. Also, the total of a bank's investments in such enterprises should not exceed 20 percent and 50 percent of its shareholders' funds unimpaired by losses, for commercial and merchant banks, respectively.

With the introduction of universal banking in Nigeria in January 2001, the CBN now requires all licensed banks to invest not less than 10 percent of their profit after tax at the end of each financial year in a small- or medium-scale manufacturing enterprise. Any bank that fails to comply with this directive within 18 months of its financial year-end shall forfeit the amount to the CBN.

The banking system in Pakistan has a strong commitment to asset investments as Table 38.2 reflects. Collectively the ratio of investments to the entire banking system assets portfolio amounted to 43.36 percent in 2014. This is high

TABLE 38.3 India—Scheduled Banks' Statement of Position in India, January 23, 2015

	Rs. billion	% of Total
Assets	98,382.66	
Cash	534.72	0.54
Balances with Reserve Bank of India	3587.02	3.65
Assets with banking system	2417.75	2.46
Balances with other banks	1506.36	62.30
Current accounts	92.67	6.15
Other accounts	1413.69	93.85
Money at call and short notice	403.29	16.68
Advances to banks (i.e., due from banks)	133.77	5.53
Other assets	374.33	15.48
Investments (at book value)	25,893.49	26.32
Central and state government securities	25,869.07	99.91
Other approved securities	24.38	0.09
Bank credit (excluding interbank advance)	65,949.68	67.03
Loans, cash credits, and overdraft	63,740.26	96.65
Foreign bills purchased	245.78	0.37
Foreign bills discounted	441.82	0.67
Inland bills purchased	350.76	0.53
Inland bills discounted	1171.02	1.78

Extracted from Reserve Bank of India, *Scheduled banks' statement of position in India, January 23, 2015*. All ratios were computed based on data extracted from this source.

compared with the industry's commitment of 37.33 percent of its assets in loans and advances during the period.

Fixed assets

Fixed assets are sterile in nature, as they do not directly generate earnings for a bank. They are employed to facilitate the performance of general banking activities. The funding of asset acquisitions should not come from deposit liabilities. Ideally, fixed assets are funded from shareholders' funds or paid-up capital of the bank. In fact, asset acquisition should be primary evidence of the owners' stake in the business. However, a common observation nowadays among banks in emerging economies is a tendency to make huge investments—perhaps unwisely—in fixed assets in the evolving culture of ambience in the banking industry. This is wrong and should be discouraged, as the huge funds so spent could be used more productively to finance the ever-growing borrowing needs of bank customers.

Loans and advances

Credit facilities extended to customers constitute the single most important earning asset of a bank. Lending portfolios serve the profit-making goal of the bank. Unfortunately, banks pursue this goal at the risk of possible diminution in value or outright loss of the assets. This happens when borrowers default on loan repayment and the resultant bad debts are charged off from earnings. This is why loans and advances are more appropriately described as risk assets. While the purpose of bank lending, in most cases, is to generate income or make profit, it also serves to meet the financing needs of the local or business communities where the banks are located. In the absence of a secondary market for such financial claims, loans are largely nonliquid assets. Credit facilities may not be easily liquidated through sale to third parties (individuals or institutions). Besides profit consideration, the lending objective is also driven by the need to have a balanced portfolio and meet prudential and other regulatory requirements for risk assets creation.

In general, superior lending decisions are achieved when a bank painstakingly defines its target markets and risk acceptance criteria. This becomes the guiding post for choosing types of risk assets in which to invest and the volumes to hold in the lending portfolio. Usually loans and advances, including financing under leases, account for a significant proportion of a bank's risk assets portfolio. In the case of Zenith Bank, the ratio of this critical asset to the entire asset portfolio of the bank was 21.76 percent. The picture is the same for the entire banking system.

As Table 38.6 shows, the ratio of total credit portfolio of domestic banks in Taiwan to the country's banking system's assets portfolio was 59.89 percent as of June 30, 2014. Also, loan loss provision of 1.23 percent evidenced a high-quality asset portfolio. The deposit-to-liability ratio of 82.89 percent for the industry during the period was also a comforting pointer to the liquidity of banks in Taiwan. However, the banks tended to take undue risk in off-balance sheet exposures. The ratios of off-balance sheet exposures to total loans, total liabilities, and total assets portfolios are quite high at 93.35 percent, 59.96 percent, and 55.91 percent, respectively. This should give serious cause for concern to regulatory authorities and other stakeholders. The reason is simple. Banks in emerging markets tend to have a fallback option in off-balance sheet lending when they are overlent on-balance sheet.

The huge commitment of funds to building risk assets portfolios is also evident among banks in Pakistan. In 2014, as Table 38.2 shows, total loans and advances (net of provisions) amounted to Rs.4,014.0 billion, representing 37.33 percent of the entire banking system's assets portfolio. With the volume of gross nonperforming loans at Rs.602 billion during the period—accounting for 5.60 percent and 15.0 percent of the industry's total assets and total loan portfolios, respectively—it can be said that the banks maintained quality risk assets portfolios. This is further evident in the industry's net loan loss provision of 1.25 percent during the period.

CREDIT CONCENTRATION AND RISK

The Central Bank may require banks to maintain balanced portfolios of risk assets. Such a policy is often influenced by credit expansion criteria designed to drive economic growth in a particular way. However, the purpose of a policy of balanced credit portfolios in the banking industry is often stated in broader terms. In most cases, it is to ensure that economic development is pursued along the lines of national planning and fits with monetary policy. In pursuit of this goal, the Central Bank sometimes prescribes limits of sectoral allocation of risk assets for banks. On occasion such credit expansion limits are waived for healthy banks. But regulatory guidelines for risk asset structures remain enforceable on all licensed banks.

A balanced loan portfolio is a critical success factor in a bank's strategy for credit risk management. The balance in question is achieved when a portfolio comprises a medley of risk assets spread across a potpourri of economic sectors. Thus, a bank should strive to spread its credit exposures with painstaking attention to risk mitigation. It can do so by planning its lending activities in a way that enables it to grant and secure risk-mitigated loans to borrowers in different sectors and industries. This credit distribution pursuit is informed by some risk-mitigation goal. Its import as a credit risk management strategy is that a bank should be able to avoid portfolio concentration risk.

Now, what do I mean by portfolio concentration risk? This question may be answered in three different but related ways. In bank lending, the term concentration risk refers to:

- The danger that a bank's operations might be impaired when it holds its risk assets portfolio in particular economic sectors
- The chance that a bank may experience a liquidity crisis, or be distressed, when a few large borrowers make up its loan portfolio
- The possibility that a bank might be plunged into crisis when its risk assets portfolio comprises few types of credit facilities

Concentration risk, in the foregoing sense, is completely different from risk diversification. In bank lending, the latter is both the alternative and solution to the former—and always desirable. A bank will diversify its credit portfolio risk when it grants different types and amounts of loans to various borrowers in different target markets, industries, or economic sectors.

Table 38.4 shows distribution of Brazil's financial system credit portfolio according to economic activities in which the borrowers were engaged. Distribution of the portfolio between public and private sectors indicates a risk-mitigation disposition. Only 6.49 percent of total credit exposure went to the public sector while a whopping 93.51 percent was deployed in the private sector. While these levels do not reflect a balanced portfolio, nevertheless bank lending in emerging economies is oriented toward the private sector. Banks tend to be wary of lending to government and its agencies and parastatals, if anything. Thus analysis of portfolio distribution should focus more on the private than public sector.

In the case of Brazil, the manner of deployment of the financial system's total credit portfolio reflects a near-even distribution. With 28.59 percent, households constitute the lion's share of the lending portfolio. Credits deployed to industry, real estate, and other services follow with 19.54 percent,

TABLE 38.4 Brazil—Financial System Credit: Balance by Economic Activity as of February 11, 2015

	2012 (R$ m)	2013 (R$ m)	2014 (R$ m)	% of 2014 Total
Public sector (a)	118,867.00	150,302.00	196,165.00	6.49
Federal government	63,298.00	70,562.00	85,946.00	43.81
State and municipal government	55,569.00	79,741.00	110,219.00	56.19
Private sector (b)	2,249,471.00	2,565,069.00	2,825,607.00	93.51
Industry	462,092.00	516,397.00	552,200.00	19.54
Real estate	298,314.00	395,241.00	502,434.00	17.78
Rural	167,528.00	218,045.00	257,748.00	9.12
Commerce	227,355.00	242,098.00	254,342.00	9.00
Households	708,855.00	767,539.00	807,935.00	28.59
Other services	385,327.00	425,749.00	450,948.00	15.96
Total (a + b)	2,368,338.00	2,715,371.00	3,021,772.00	

Extracted from Central Bank of Brazil (Banco Central Do Brasil), *Financial system credit: Balance by economic activity as at February 11, 2015*. All ratios were computed based on data extracted from this source.

17.78 percent, and 15.96 percent, respectively. We can say that concentration risk is not indicated in Brazil's case. However, it is curious that only 9 percent of the portfolio went to commerce—ordinarily a popular sector for bank lending in developing and emerging economies.

Concentration risk is not also reflected in the distribution of loans and advances of Singapore's domestic banking units (DBUs) to nonbank borrowers, as presented along industry lines in Table 38.5. Total lending to business accounted for 61.11 percent of the entire industry's credit portfolio,

TABLE 38.5 Singapore—Loans and Advances of Domestic Banking Units to Nonbank Customers by Industry

	S$ million	% (a, b)	% (a + b)
Total loans to business (a)	371,520.2		
Agriculture, mining, and quarrying	6245.6	1.68	1.03
Manufacturing	29,618.8	7.97	4.87
Building and construction	103,712.4	27.92	17.06
General commerce	78,084.2	21.02	12.84
Transport, storage, and communication	21,128.5	5.69	3.48
Business services	8586.9	2.31	1.41
Financial institutions	80,895.0	21.77	13.31
Professional and private individuals—business purposes	9746.0	2.62	1.60
Others	34,502.8	9.29	5.68
Total consumer loans (b)	236,439.9		
Housing and bridge loans	177,434.6	75.04	29.19
Car loans	8641.5	3.65	1.42
Credit cards	10,422.4	4.41	1.71
Share financing	989.6	0.42	0.16
Others	38,961.8	16.48	6.41
Total loan portfolio (a + b)	607,960.0		
Key financial ratios			
Business loans to total loans			61.11
Consumer loans to total loans			38.89

Extracted from Monetary Authority of Singapore, *Loans and advances of DBUs to non-bank customers by industry.* All ratios were computed based on data extracted from this source.

while the balance of 38.89 percent was deployed to the consumer sector. This is a fair portfolio distribution. As in Brazil's case, lending to households—in Singapore's case, housing and bridge loans—again got the lion's share at 29.19 percent of the total credit portfolio of the banking system. Credits to building and construction followed with 17.06 percent, while 13.31 percent and 12.84 percent of the industry's total credit portfolio were deployed to financial institutions and general commerce, respectively. In both Brazil and Singapore, the emphasis on lending to finance housing is unmistakable. There was also good showing for industry and households.

Central Banks in emerging economies should not relent in enforcing policies that define appropriate credit portfolio structure for money deposit banks. However, the efficacy of regulatory policies is sometimes undermined by the banking expediency of lending to less risky or even riskless but profitable accounts. This is why banks often flout the regulations. For instance, a bank in emerging market might find it more expedient to lend, say, $5 million to an enterprise engaged in trading than grant the same credit facility to a farm enterprise. The preference indicated in this illustration is dictated by differences in expected earnings and risk characteristics of the two businesses. Yet banks should play down such considerations and lend support to the broader national goal of developing preferred sectors of the economy.

PORTFOLIO DISTRIBUTION AND MATURITY PROFILES

Knowledge of patterns of portfolio distribution and risk assets maturity profiles across banking systems in emerging economies is pertinent to an understanding of the workings of credit risk control. Such knowledge also informs regulation of the structure and quality of the credit portfolios of banks for effective risk management. Ideally, banks will want to lend to borrowers with low risk. Banks will tend to scout around for such borrowers in their target markets. Playing it safe in this way, they crave so-called self-liquidating lending while shunning risky credits across economic sectors. That forms the basis for devising means to exploit the full banking potential of the sectors and borrowers that satisfy their risk acceptance criteria. Usually the expectation of maximum earnings at low to moderate risk is the driving force behind this lending strategy.

In practice, however, many banks tend to be adventurous. They commit huge lending to risky sectors and borrowers—usually in the expectation of earnings that meet their aggressive budget targets. Often reckless lending underlies excessive risk-taking in the pursuit of such budget goals. This unfortunate situation has been the bane of the banking industry in emerging economies. Curiously, this pattern of risk assets creation is not always evident in the returns that banks make to regulatory authorities. As Chapter 37 shows, banks have a way of circumventing or skirting around the infringements of regulatory policies and control. That way they escape a damning report on their lending activities. How else can recurrent distress in the industry—despite good credit portfolio returns made to regulatory authorities—be explained?

The foregoing implies that issues in credit portfolio distribution and maturity profiles for banks in emerging economies may not be apparent from statistical data that their Central Banks furnish based on returns they receive from banks. Yet looking at Tables 38.2−38.9 with a critical eye, one begins to gain insight into the problem of lending portfolios of banks in emerging economies. The problem tends to be structural in nature and evident in the mismatch between the need for deposits-driven liabilities and lending-based earnings. The need defines liquidity and profitability goals—both of which are critical for success in banking. If the issue is not mismatched portfolios, it is a misapplication of deposits in funding risk assets. In both cases, banks contend with a possible threat to smooth operations. Ideally, banking regulation, complemented by effective supervision, should address these conflicts. But a combination of intractable factors and forces, some of which I discussed in Chapter 37, constrain the effective supervision of banks in emerging economies.

Take a look at Table 38.6, for instance. Do you see a structural problem with the consolidated balance sheet of Taiwan's domestic banks? The first striking observation is that much of the funding for risk assets came from short-term deposits. A disproportionate volume of the deposits was utilized for funding medium- and long-term loans. These two categories of loans accounted for 73.82 percent of the entire industry's portfolio of risk assets. This finding—coupled with the fact that savings deposits accounted for 49.90 percent of the reported deposit portfolio—informs the seriousness of the problem. This mirror of the asset structure of the industry should be worrisome. There should have been more reliance on equities and time deposits than short-term deposits in funding the industry's asset portfolio.

The problem is also evident in the case of Singapore, and reflected in Table 38.7. Obligations falling due within 180 days accounted for 88.46 percent of the industry's liabilities portfolio. Compared with 46.01 percent of risk assets in medium- to long-term maturity categories, the structural defect of the mismatch between assets and liabilities portfolios becomes more apparent. A relatively low ratio of assets, at 49.02 percent, had the same maturity period. A clearer indication of the problem emerges when ratios of funds applicable to different asset and liability tenors are compared. For instance, while 46.01 percent of assets had medium to long terms, only 5.87 percent of liabilities fell within the same maturity categories.

Ironically, the distribution of Taiwan's banking system's loans was a departure from a common observation of short-term lending skewing the risk assets portfolio. Table 38.7, showing data on maturities of assets and liabilities of the banking system in Singapore, is typical of what obtains in a majority of emerging economies. Interestingly, comparing Tables 38.6 and 38.7 in terms of

TABLE 38.6 Taiwan—Consolidated Balance Sheet of Domestic Banks as of June 30, 2014

	NT$ Million	Ratio (%)
Total assets	41,032,662.00	
Loans and discounts	24,573,284.00	
Import bills purchased	3006.00	0.01
Export bills purchased	179,014.00	0.73
Discounts	18,073.00	0.07
Overdrafts	67,979.00	0.28
Short-term loans	6,104,550.00	24.84
Medium-term loans	8,110,565.00	33.01
Long-term loans	10,028,738.00	40.81
Nonaccrual loans	61,359.00	0.25
Allowance for doubtful accounts	302,057.00	
Total liabilities	38,258,247.00	
Deposits	31,710,418.00	
Check deposits	395,303.00	1.25
Demand deposits	3,463,017.00	10.92
Time deposits	5,228,205.00	16.49
Savings deposits	15,822,775.00	49.90
Foreign currencies deposits	6,215,517.00	19.60
Government deposits	585,601.00	1.85
Total equities	2,774,415.00	
Total liabilities and equities	41,032,662.00	
Off-balance sheet items	22,939,575.00	
Loan commitments	14,683,740.00	63.81
Guarantees	1,066,072.00	4.65
Letter of credit issued	354,736.00	1.55
Liabilities trusted	6,880,027.00	29.99
Key accounting ratios		
Equities to assets		6.76
Loans to deposits		77.49

Continued

TABLE 38.6 Taiwan—Consolidated Balance Sheet of Domestic Banks as of June 30, 2014—cont'd

	NT$ Million	Ratio (%)
Loans to assets		59.89
Off-balance sheet items to loans		93.35
Off-balance sheet items to liabilities		59.96
Off-balance sheet to assets		55.91
Deposits to liabilities		82.89
Loan loss provision		1.23

Extracted from Central Bank of Republic of China—Taiwan, *Consolidated balance sheet of domestic banks as at June 30, 2014*. All ratios were computed based on data extracted from this source.

assets portfolio distribution by maturities sheds light on Taiwan's departure from the common pattern. In Taiwan on the one hand, and Singapore on the other, short-term loans (or assets) accounted for 24.84 percent and 53.99 percent of the entire industry's assets portfolio, respectively.

On a sectoral basis and analysis, a significant volume of aggregate bank lending in India went to so-called priority sectors. Priority sectors distilled

TABLE 38.7 Singapore—Maturities of Assets and Liabilities of Domestic Banking Units

	Assets S$ Million	Liabilities S$ Million	Assets to Liabilities Ratio (%)	Ratio to Total Assets (%)	Ratio to Total Liabilities (%)
Up to 6 months	481,038.30	793,247.10	60.64	49.02	88.46
Over 6 months to 1 year	48,794.50	50,809.80	96.03	4.97	5.67
Over 1–3 years	121,981.90	32,640.90	373.71	12.43	3.64
Over 3 years	329,568.00	20,021.20	1646.10	33.58	2.23
	981,382.70	896,719.00	109.44		

Extracted from Monetary Authority of Singapore, *Maturities of assets and liabilities of Domestic Banking Units (DBUs)*. All ratios were computed based on data extracted from this source.

TABLE 38.8 India—Deployment of Gross Bank Credit by Major Sectors as of December 26, 2014

Economic Sector	Amount (Rs. billion)	% of Sector Total
Gross bank credit	59,330.00	
Food credit	1065.00	1.80
Agriculture and allied activities	7512.00	12.66
Industry (micro and small, medium, and large)	25,752.00	43.40
Micro and small	3684.00	14.31
Medium	1268.00	4.92
Large	20,800.00	80.77
Services	13,502.00	22.76
Transport operators	883	6.54
Computer software	171	1.27
Tourism, hotels, and restaurants	360	2.67
Shipping	96	0.71
Professional services	717	5.31
Trade	3313.00	24.54
Wholesale trade (other than food procurement)	1649.00	
Retail trade	1664.00	
Commercial real estate	1643.00	12.17
Nonbanking financial companies	3000.00	22.22
Other services	3320.00	24.59
Personal loans	11,499.00	19.38
Consumer durables	147	1.28
Housing (including priority sector housing)	6015.00	52.31
Advances against fixed deposits	600	5.22
Advances to individuals against share, bonds, etc.	41	0.36
Card outstanding	303	2.64
Education	630	5.48
Vehicle loans	1457.00	12.67
Other personal loans	2307.00	20.06

Reserve Bank of India, *Deployment of gross bank credit by major sectors*. Ratios were computed based on data extracted from this source.

TABLE 38.9 Singapore—Classified Exposures as a Percentage of Total Exposures

Pass	97.27
Special mention	1.98
Substandard	0.52
Doubtful	0.15
Lost	0.08
Classified exposures (net of specific provisions)	0.58

Extracted from Monetary Authority of Singapore (MAS), Classified exposures as a percentage of total exposures.

from Table 38.8 include agriculture and allied activities, micro and small enterprises, housing, microcredit, education loans, and export credit. Total volume of loans outstanding against the sectors was Rs.19,552 billion, representing 32.95 percent of the industry portfolio. Industry (excluding micro and small enterprises) accounted for Rs.22,068 billion, representing 37.20 percent of the total outstanding loan portfolio. Thus priority and nonpriority segments of industry accounted for 70.15 percent of the total outstanding loan portfolio.

On occasion, it is difficult to tell the quality of risk assets portfolios of banks in emerging economies due to the maneuvering of the returns made to regulatory authorities. While all banks make the mandatory general provision on their loan portfolios, it is often difficult to strictly enforce specific cases. The net effect is that reported portfolio quality is usually good on paper and satisfies regulatory requirements. Table 38.9 shows the standing of Singapore's banks on assets quality as mirrored in the Monetary Authority of Singapore's report on classified exposures. The ratios, as is always the case—except in full-blown distress situations—are good.

QUESTIONS FOR DISCUSSION AND REVIEW

1. Why should banks in emerging economies always strive to have a balanced and profitable portfolio of risk assets?
2. (a) What are the main components of the assets portfolio of banks in emerging economies?
   (b) How do loans and advances compare with investments in the assets portfolio?
3. (a) Define the terms *credit concentration* and *concentration risk* as understood in the context of credit portfolios in the banking industry.

(b) In what ways, using the consolidated balance sheet of banks in a named emerging economy as the basis for discussion, does concentration impart risk to loan portfolios?

4. How do banks in emerging economies tend to frustrate the banking regulation and supervision that affect credit portfolio distribution and maturity profiles?

5. (a) When would it be appropriate to christen some economic activity or group a priority sector?

(b) Why does credit portfolio regulation often favor strict adherence to target deployment of loans to so-called priority sectors?

6. Can the risk assets quality of bank portfolios in emerging economies be realistically measured on the basis of returns made to regulatory authorities? Your answer should show understanding of the dynamics of data maneuvering to circumvent regulation.

Index

Note: Page numbers followed by "f", "t" and "b" indicate figures, tables, and boxes.

Printed in the United States
By Bookmasters